Criminology

Reviewers

Jay Albanese *Virginia Commonwealth University*
Thomas E. Allen, Jr. *University of South Dakota*
Stephen Brodt *Ball State University*
Daniel Burgel *Vincennes University*
David A. Camp *Culver-Stockton College*
Daniel D. Cervi *University of New Hampshire*
Bernard Cohen *Queens College, New York*
Cavit Cooley *Truman State University*
Richard P. Davin *Riverside Community College*
Julius Debro *University of Hartford*
Albert Dichiara *Eastern Illinois University*
Sandra Emory *University of New Mexico*
Edna Erez *Kent State University*
The Late Franco Ferracuti *University of Rome, Italy*
Edith Flynn *Northeastern University*
Karen Gilbert *University of Georgia*
Ronald J. Graham *Fresno City College*
Clayton Hartjen *Rutgers University*
Marie Henry *Sullivan County Community College*
Matrice Hurrah *Southwest Tennessee Community College*
Joseph Jacoby *Bowling Green State University*
Deborah Kelly *Longwood College*

Dennis Kenney *John Jay College of Criminal Justice*
Nicholas Kittrie *American University*
Anna C. Leggett *Miami Dade Community College*
Linda Lengyel *The College of New Jersey*
Coramae Mann *Indiana University, Bloomington*
Harry L. Marsh *Indiana State University*
Robert McCormack *The College of New Jersey*
Lydia Rosner *John Jay College of Criminal Justice*
Lee E. Ross *University of Wisconsin*
Harjit Sandhu *Oklahoma State University*
Clayton Steenberg *Arkansas State University*
Austin T. Turk *University of California, Riverside*
Prabha Unnithan *Colorado State University*
James Vrettos *John Jay College of Criminal Justice*
Charles Wellford *University of Maryland at College Park*
Frank Williams *California State University, San Bernardino*
The late Marvin E. Wolfgang *University of Pennsylvania*

Criminology

Freda Adler
Rutgers University

Gerhard O. W. Mueller
Rutgers University

William S. Laufer
University of Pennsylvania

Fifth Edition

Boston   Burr Ridge, IL   Dubuque, IA   Madison, WI   New York
San Francisco   St. Louis   Bangkok   Bogotá   Caracas   Kuala Lumpur
Lisbon   London   Madrid   Mexico City   Milan   Montreal   New Delhi
Santiago   Seoul   Singapore   Sydney   Taipei   Toronto

CRIMINOLOGY

Published by McGraw-Hill, a business unit of The McGraw-Hill Companies, Inc. 1221 Avenue of the Americas, New York, NY, 10020. Copyright © 2004, 2001, 1998, 1995, 1991, by The McGraw-Hill Companies, Inc. All rights reserved. No part of this publication may be reproduced or distributed in any form or by any means, or stored in a database or retrieval system, without the prior written consent of The McGraw-Hill Companies, Inc., including, but not limited to, in any network or other electronic storage or transmission, or broadcast for distance learning.

Some ancillaries, including electronic and print components, may not be available to customers outside the United States.

This book is printed on acid-free paper.

2 3 4 5 6 7 8 9 0 VNH/VNH 0 9 8 7 6 5 4

ISBN 0-07-255951-9

Publisher: *Phillip A. Butcher*
Senior sponsoring editor: *Carolyn Henderson Meier*
Senior marketing manager: *Daniel M. Loch*
Media producer: *Shannon Gattens*
Senior project manager: *Christina Thornton-Villagomez*
Production supervisor: *Carol A. Bielski*
Design manager: *Laurie J. Entringer*
Supplement associate: *Kathleen Boylan*
Photo research coordinator: *Nora Agbayani*
Photo researcher: *Barbara Salz*
Art editor: *Jennifer DeVere*
Permissions: *Marty Granahan*
Cover design: *Heidi Baughman*
Cover image: *Tony Ourlser's "The Influence Machine," photo by Aaron Diskin*
Typeface: *10.5/12 Palatino*
Compositor: *Carlisle Communications, Ltd.*
Printer: *Von Hoffman Press, Inc.*

Library of Congress Cataloging-in-Publication Data

Adler, Freda.
   Criminology / Freda Adler, Gerhard O. W. Mueller, William S. Laufer.—5th ed.
     p. cm.
   Includes index.
   ISBN 0-07-255951-9 (softcover : alk. paper)
   1. Criminology.   I. Mueller, Gerhard O. W.   II. Laufer, William S.   III. Title.
HV6025.A35 2004
   364—dc21   2003052651

www.mhhe.com

To David S., Daniel A., Julia A., Noah A., Zoe A., Hannah M., Nicolai A., John J., Lauren E., Stephen W., Anna L., Erik D., Johann D., Sasha K., Misha K.

About the Authors

FREDA ADLER is Distinguished Professor of Criminal Justice at Rutgers University, School of Criminal Justice. She received her BA in sociology, her MA in criminology, and her PhD in sociology from the University of Pennsylvania. Dr. Adler began her career in criminal justice as an evaluator of drug and alcohol treatment programs for federal and state governments. Since 1968, she has taught such subjects as criminal justice, criminology, comparative criminal justice systems, statistics, and research methods. She has served as criminal justice advisor to the United Nations, as well as to federal, state, and foreign governments. Dr. Adler's published works include 17 books as author or coauthor, 9 books as editor or coeditor, and over 90 journal articles. She has served on the editorial boards of the *Journal of Criminal Justice, Criminology,* and the *Journal of Research on Crime and Delinquency.* Dr. Adler serves as editorial consultant to the *Journal of Criminal Law and Criminology* and coeditor of *Advances in Criminological Theory.* She also has served as president of the American Society of Criminology 1994–1995).

GERHARD O. W. MUELLER is Distinguished Professor of Criminal Justice at Rutgers University, School of Criminal Justice. After earning his JD degree from the University of Chicago, he went on to receive a master of laws degree from Columbia University. He was awarded the degree of DrJur (hc) by the University of Uppsala, Sweden. His career in criminal justice began in 1945, when he served as a chief petty officer in the British Military Government Water Police, where he commanded a Coast Guard cutter. His teaching in criminal justice, begun in 1953, was partially interrupted between 1974 and 1982, when, as Chief of the United Nations Crime Prevention and Criminal Justice Branch, he was responsible for all United Nations programs dealing with problems of crime and justice worldwide. He continues his service to the United Nations as Chairman ad interim of the Board of the International Scientific and Professional Advisory Council of the United Nations Crime Prevention and Criminal Justice Programme. Professor Mueller has been a member of the faculties of law at the University of Washington, West Virginia University, New York University, and the National Judicial College. He is the author or editor of some 50 books and close to 300 scholarly articles.

WILLIAM S. LAUFER is Associate Professor of Legal Studies Sociology at the Wharton School of the University of Pennsylvania and Director of the Carol and Lawrence Zicklin Center for Business Ethics Research. Dr. Laufer received his BA in social and behavioral sciences at the Johns Hopkins University, his JD at Northeastern University School of Law, and his PhD at Rutgers University, School of Criminal Justice. Since 1987, he has taught such subjects as corporate and white-collar crime, business ethics, criminal law and criminal procedure, and criminology. Dr. Laufer's research has appeared in law reviews and a wide range of criminal justice, legal, and psychology journals, such as the *Journal of Research in Crime and Delinquency, American Journal of Criminal Law, American Criminal Law Review, Law and Human Behavior, Journal of Personality and Social Psychology,* and *Business Ethics Quarterly.* He is coeditor of the *Handbook of Psychology and Law; Personality, Moral Development and Criminal Behavior;* and *Crime, Values and Religion.* Dr. Laufer is coeditor with Freda Adler of *Advances in Criminological Theory.*

Contents in Brief

List of Boxes xix
Preface xxi

PART I — Understanding Criminology 1
Chapter 1 The Reach of Criminology 2
Chapter 2 Counting Crime and Measuring Criminal Behavior 22
Chapter 3 Schools of Thought throughout History 58

PART II — Explanations of Crime and Criminal Behavior 81
Chapter 4 Psychological and Biological Perspectives 82
Chapter 5 Strain and Cultural Deviance Theories 114
Chapter 6 The Formation of Subcultures 142
Chapter 7 Social Control Theory 166
Chapter 8 Labeling, Conflict, and Radical Theories 188
Chapter 9 Environmental Theory 212

PART III — Types of Crimes 235
Chapter 10 Violent Crimes 236
Chapter 11 Crimes against Property 288
Chapter 12 White-Collar and Corporate Crime 316
Chapter 13 Public Order Crimes 352
Chapter 14 International and Comparative Criminology 382

Notes N-1
Glossary G-1
Photo Credits C-1
Indexes I-1

Contents

List of Boxes xix

Preface xxi

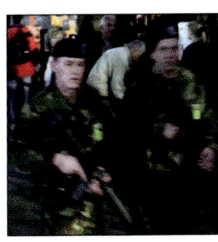

PART I
Understanding Criminology 1

■ CHAPTER 1
The Reach of Criminology 2

The Reach of Criminology 4
  Terrorism 4
  Illicit Drug Trafficking 4
  Money Laundering 5
  Infiltration of Legal Business 5
  Computer Crime 6
  From the Pages of *The New York Times:* Financing Terrorism through Legitimate Fronts 6
  Illicit Arms Trafficking 7
  Traffic in Persons 7
  Destruction of Cultural Property 7
What Is Criminology? 10
  Window to the World: *Russians and Americans Share a Crime Problem* 10
The Making of Laws 13
  Deviance 13
  The Concept of Crime 13
  The Consensus and Conflict Views of Law and Crime 14
The Breaking of Laws 15
  Of Immediate Concern: *Vipers in the Desert* 16
Society's Reaction to the Breaking of Laws 17
  Criminology and the Criminal Justice System 18
  The Global Approach to the Breaking of Laws 18
Research Informs Policy 19

Review 20
Criminology & Public Policy 20
You Be the Criminologist 21
Key Terms 21

■ CHAPTER 2
Counting Crime and Measuring Criminal Behavior 22

The Ingredients of Crime 24
  The Seven Basic Requirements 24
  The Act Requirement 24
  The Legality Requirement 25
  The Harm Requirement 25
  The Causation Requirement 25
  Mens Rea: The "Guilty Mind" Requirement 26
  The Concurrence Requirement 27
  The Punishment Requirement 27
The Defenses 27
Typologies of Crime 28
Measuring Crime 28
  Methods of Collecting Data 29
  Ethics and the Researcher 33
The Nature and Extent of Crime 33
  Police Statistics 34
  From the Pages of *The New York Times:* Can Politics Influence Crime Data? 35
  Victimization Surveys 36
  Self-Report Surveys 38
Measuring Characteristics of Crime 39
  Crime Trends 40
  Locations and Times of Criminal Acts 41
  Of Immediate Concern: *Why Does Crime Drop?* 42
  Severity of Crime 44
Measuring Characteristics of Criminals 44
  Age and Crime 45
  Window to the World: *Measuring World Crime* 47

ix

Gender and Crime 50
Social Class and Crime 53
Race and Crime 54
Review 55
Criminology & Public Policy 55
You Be the Criminologist 56
Key Terms 56

■ CHAPTER 3
Schools of Thought throughout History 58

Classical Criminology 60
  Window to the World: *Stone Age Crime and Social Control* 61
  The Historical Context 62
  Cesare Beccaria 62
  Of Immediate Concern: *Utilitarianism Gone Astray* 65
  Jeremy Bentham's Utilitarianism 66
  The Classical School: An Evaluation 66
Positivist Criminology 67
Biological Determinism: The Search for Criminal Traits 67
  Lombroso, Ferri, Garofalo: The Italian School 68
  A Return to Biological Determinism 72
Psychological Determinism 73
  Pioneers in Criminal Psychology 74
  From the Pages of *The New York Times*: *Who's Responsible?* 74
  Psychological Studies of Criminals 75
Sociological Determinism 75
  Adolphe Quételet and André Michel Guerry 75
  Gabriel Tarde 75
  Émile Durkheim 76
Historical and Contemporary Criminology: A Time Line 77
Review 78
Criminology & Public Policy 79
You Be the Criminologist 79
Key Terms 79

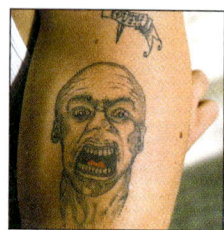

PART II
Explanations of Crime and Criminal Behavior 81

■ CHAPTER 4
Psychological and Biological Perspectives 82

Psychology and Criminality 85
  Psychological Development 85
  Moral Development 86
  Maternal Deprivation and Attachment Theory 87
  Learning Aggression and Violence 90
  From the Pages of *The New York Times:* *The Apple Doesn't Fall Far* 91
  Of Immediate Concern: *The Taboo Crime of Parricide* 92
  Window to the World: *Censoring TV Violence* 95
  Personality 96
Mental Disorders and Crime 98
  Psychological Causation 100
Biology and Criminality 101
  Modern Biocriminality 101
  Genetics and Criminality 102
  The Controversy over Violence and Genes 104
  The IQ Debate 105
  Biochemical Factors 106
  Neurophysiological Factors 109
Crime and Human Nature 110
  Criticisms of Biocriminology 110
  An Integrated Theory 111
Review 112
Criminology & Public Policy 112
You Be the Criminologist 113
Key Terms 113

CONTENTS

CHAPTER 5
Strain and Cultural Deviance Theories 114

The Interconnectedness of Sociological Theories 116
Anomie: Émile Durkheim 116
    The Structural-Functionalist Perspective 116
    Anomie and Suicide 117
Strain Theory 117
    Window to the World: A Social System Breaks Down 118
    Merton's Theory of Anomie 119
    Modes of Adaptation 120
    Tests of Merton's Theory 121
    Evaluation: Merton's Theory 123
    Institutional Imbalance and Crime 124
    From the Pages of The New York Times: A Head Start Really Does Help 125
    General Strain Theory 126
    Theory Informs Policy 126
Cultural Deviance Theories 127
    The Nature of Cultural Deviance 128
    Social Disorganization Theory 129
    Tests of Social Disorganization Theory 132
    Of Immediate Concern: Cults—Culture Conflict—Crime 133
    Evaluation: Social Disorganization Theory 134
    Theory Informs Policy 134
    Differential Association Theory 135
    Tests of Differential Association Theory 137
    Evaluation: Differential Association Theory 138
    Theory Informs Policy 138
    Culture Conflict Theory 139
Review 141
Criminology & Public Policy 141
You Be the Criminologist 141
Key Terms 141

CHAPTER 6
The Formation of Subcultures 142

The Function of Subcultures 144
Subcultural Theories of Delinquency and Crime 144
    The Middle-Class Measuring Rod 144
    Corner Boy, College Boy, Delinquent Boy 145
    Tests of Cohen's Theory 146
    Evaluation: Cohen's Theory 147
Delinquency and Opportunity 147
    Tests of Opportunity Theory 149
    Evaluation: Differential Opportunity Theory 151
The Subculture of Violence 151
    Tests of the Subculture of Violence 152
    Evaluation: The Subculture of Violence Theory 152
Focal Concerns: Miller's Theory 153
    Tests of Miller's Theory 155
    From the Pages of The New York Times: Street Gangs of New York: From the 1860s to the 1960s 155
    Evaluation: Miller's Theory 156
Gangs at the Turn of the 21st Century 156
    Guns and Gangs 157
Female Delinquent Subcultures 158
    Early Research 158
    Recent Studies 158
    Of Immediate Concern: The Girls in the Gang 160
Middle-Class Delinquency 161
    Explanations 162
Theory Informs Policy 162
    MOBY 162
    Other Programs 163
    Window to the World: America's Changing Ethnic Gangs 164
    Getting Out: Gang Banging or the Morgue 165
Review 165
Criminology & Public Policy 165
You Be the Criminologist 165
Key Terms 165

CHAPTER 7
Social Control Theory 166

What Is Social Control? 168
Theories of Social Control 169
    The Microsociological Perspective: Hirschi 169
    Social Bonds 170
    Empirical Tests of Hirschi's Theory 172
    Evaluation: Hirschi's Social Control Theory 173
Social Control and Drift 175
Personal and Social Control 175
    Failure of Control Mechanisms 175
    Stake in Conformity 175
    Of Immediate Concern: Defying Convention and Control: "In Your Face" 176
Containment Theory 177
    From the Pages of The New York Times: Social Control—Punishing the Cheat 178
    Empirical Tests of Containment Theory 179
    Evaluation: Containment Theory 180
Recent Theoretical Explanations 180
    Developmental/Life Course Theory 181
    Integrated Theory 182
    General Theories 182
Theory Informs Policy 183
    Family 183
    School 183
    Neighborhood 183
    Window to the World: Nations with Low Crime Rates 184
Review 186
Criminology & Public Policy 186
You Be the Criminologist 187
Key Terms 187

CHAPTER 8
Labeling, Conflict, and Radical Theories 188

Labeling Theory 190
    The Origins of Labeling Theory 191
    Basic Assumptions of Labeling Theory 191
    Labeling in the 1960s 192
    Empirical Evidence for Labeling Theory 193
    From the Pages of The New York Times: Racial Profiling: Labeling Before the Fact 195
    Evaluation: Labeling Theory 195
Conflict Theory 196
    The Consensus Model 197
    The Conflict Model 197
    Of Immediate Concern: The Rights of the Poorest 198
    Conflict Theory and Criminology 200
    Empirical Evidence for the Conflict Model 201
Radical Theory 202
    The Intellectual Heritage of Marxist Criminology 202
    Engels and Marx 202
    Willem Adriaan Bonger 203
    Georg Rusche and Otto Kirchheimer 203
    Radical Criminology since the 1970s 204
    Evaluation: Marxist Criminological Theory 205
    Window to the World: The Forgotten Criminology of Genocide 207
    Emerging Explanations 208
Review 210
Criminology & Public Policy 210
You Be the Criminologist 211
Key Terms 211

CHAPTER 9
Environmental Theory 212

Situational Theories of Crime 215
    Environmental Criminology 215
    Rational-Choice Perspective 215
    Routine-Activity Approach 217
    Window to the World: Decresting the Lovebug, Worldwide 218
    Practical Applications of Situational Theories of Crime 219
Theories of Victimization 222
    Lifestyle Theories 223
    Victim-Offender Interaction 224
    Repeat Victimization 224
    Hot Spots of Crime 224
    Geography of Crime 225
    Interrelatedness of Theories 225

CONTENTS

Preventing Crimes against Places, People, and Valuable Goods 226

From the Pages of The New York Times: *New York City Cracks Down on "Hot Spots"* 226

Situational Crime Prevention 227

Of Immediate Concern: Maximum-Security Schools 230

Displacement 232

Theory Informs Policy 232

Review 233

Criminology & Public Policy 233

You Be the Criminologist 234

Key Terms 234

PART III
Types of Crimes 235

CHAPTER 10
Violent Crimes 236

Homicide 238

Murder 238

Manslaughter 239

The Extent of Homicide 240

The Nature of Homicide 241

A Cross-National Comparison of Homicide Rates 246

Assault 247

Family-Related Crimes 248

Spouse Abuse 249

Child Abuse 251

Abuse of the Elderly 252

Rape and Sexual Assault 253

Characteristics of the Rape Event 254

Who Are the Rapists? 254

Rape and the Legal System 255

Community Response 256

Kidnapping 257

Robbery 257

Characteristics of Robbers 258

The Consequences of Robbery 258

Organized Crime 259

The History of Organized Crime 260

The Structure and Impact of Organized Crime 261

Window to the World: The Business of Organized Crime 262

The New Ethnic Diversity in Organized Crime 266

Emerging Problems 267

Terrorism 268

Hate Crimes 272

Militias 273

Of Immediate Concern: An Epidemic of Hate Crimes? 274

Violence in Schools 276

Violence and Gun Control 279

The Extent of Firearm-Related Offenses 279

Youth and Guns 280

Controlling Handgun Use 281

From the Pages of The New York Times: *Does the Brady Law Work?* 284

The Gun-Control Debate 284

Review 286

Criminology & Public Policy 286

You Be the Criminologist 286

Key Terms 286

CHAPTER 11
Crimes against Property 288

Larceny 290

The Elements of Larceny 290

The Extent of Larceny 291

Who Are the Thieves? 291

Shoplifting 292

Art Theft 293

Motor Vehicle Theft 295

Boat Theft 297

Window to the World: Crime on the Oceans: Whose Problem? 298

Fraud 298

Obtaining Property by False Pretenses 299

Confidence Games and Frauds 299

Check Forgery 300

Credit Card Crimes 300
Insurance Fraud 301

High-Tech Crimes: Concerns for Today and Tomorrow 302

Characteristics of High-Tech Crimes 302

Of Immediate Concern: Insurance Fraud on the Rise: New Jersey's Experience 303

Computers and the Internet: Types of Crime 304

From the Pages of The New York Times: Whose Identity Is It Anyway? 307

Characteristics of the High-Tech Criminal 309

The Criminal Justice Problem 310

Burglary 310

Fencing: Receiving Stolen Property 311

Arson 312

Comparative Crime Rates 313

Review 313
Criminology & Public Policy 313
You Be the Criminologist 314
Key Terms 314

CHAPTER 12
White-Collar and Corporate Crime 316

Defining White-Collar Crime 318

Crimes Committed by Individuals 319

Types of White-Collar Crimes 321

Window to the World: Tracking Progress in the Fight against Corruption: The Emergence of a National Integrity System 324

From the Pages of The New York Times: Rave Reviews or Questionable Quotes? Deceptive Advertising Goes to the Movies 328

Corporate Crime 331

Frequency and Problems of Definition 331

Phases of Corporate Criminal Law 332

Theories of Corporate Liability 336

Models of Corporate Culpability 337

Governmental Control of Corporations 338

Investigating Corporate Crime 339

Environmental Crimes 341

Curbing Corporate Crime 344

Of Immediate Concern: Dangerous Ground: The World of Hazardous Waste Crime 346

The Future of White Collar and Corporate Crime 347

Review 350
Criminology & Public Policy 350
You Be the Criminologist 351
Key Terms 351

CHAPTER 13
Public Order Crimes 352

Drug Abuse and Crime 354

The History of Drug Abuse 354

The Extent of Drug Abuse 357

Patterns of Drug Abuse 357

Crime-Related Activities 360

The International Drug Economy 360

Drug Control 364

From the Pages of The New York Times: One City Wonders: Can We Win the War on Drugs? 365

Alcohol and Crime 367

The History of Legalization 368

Crime-Related Activities 368

Sexual Morality Offenses 370

Deviate Sexual Intercourse by Force or Imposition 371

Prostitution 371

Pornography 373

Of Immediate Concern: Cyberporn: Problems and Controversies 374

Window to the World: Global Sexual Slavery: Women and Children 376

Review 379
Criminology & Public Policy 379
You Be the Criminologist 380
Key Terms 380

CHAPTER 14
International and Comparative Criminology 382

What Is Comparative Criminology? 384

The Definition of Comparative Criminology 384

The History of Comparative Criminology 385

The Goals of Comparative Research 386

CONTENTS

Engaging in Comparative Criminological Research 386
- Preparatory Work 386
- Comparative Research 390
- Comparative Research Tools and Resources 391
- The Special Problems of Empirical Research 392

Theory Testing 394
- **Of Immediate Concern:** *Cross-Cultural Research: Smoking One's Way into Cheyenne Culture* 393
- Validation of Major Theories 394
- The Socioeconomic Development Perspective 395

Practical Goals 395
- Learning from Others' Experiences 395
- **From the Pages of** *The New York Times:* *The Youngest Victims of International Crime* 396
- Developing International Strategies 395

Window to the World: *BCCI: International Fraud* 405
- Globalization versus Ethnic Fragmentation 406

Review 406
Criminology & Public Policy 406
You Be the Criminologist 407
Key Terms 407

Notes N-1
Glossary G-1
Did You Know? C-1
Photo Credits C-2
Text/Illustration Credits C-3
Index I-1

List of Boxes

 Window to the World

Russians and Americans Share a Crime Problem 10
Measuring World Crime 47
Stone Age Crime and Social Control 61
Censoring TV Violence 95
A Social System Breaks Down 118
America's Changing Ethnic Gangs 164
Nations with Low Crime Rates 184
The Forgotten Criminology of Genocide 207
Decresting the Lovebug, Worldwide 218
The Business of Organized Crime 262
Crime on the Oceans: Whose Problem? 298
Tracking Progress in the Fight against Corruption: The Emergence of a National Integrity System 324
Global Sexual Slavery: Women and Children 376
BCCI: International Fraud 405
Carlos the Jackal: No Place to Hide 417
Interpol: The International Criminal Police Organization 450
Judging at the World Level 503
Torture and Abuse in Prison: A Worldwide Problem 532

 The New York Times

Financing Terrorism through Legitimate Fronts 6
Can Politics Influence Crime Data? 35
Who's Responsible? 74
The Apple Doesn't Fall Far 91
A Head Start Really Does Help 125
Street Gangs of New York: From the 1860s to the 1960s 155
Social Control—Punishing the Cheat 178
Racial Profiling: Labeling Before the Fact 195
New York City Cracks Down on "Hot Spots" 226

Does the Brady Law Work? 284
Whose Identity Is It Anyway? 307
Rave Reviews or Questionable Quotes? Deceptive Advertising Goes to the Movies 328
One City Wonders: Can We Win the War on Drugs? 365
The Youngest Victims of International Crime 396
The Rules of the Games 440
One Police Officer's Dilemma 458
Reflections on the Matter of Life and Death Sentencing 518
Beyond the Conjugal Visit 541

 Of Immediate Concern

Vipers in the Desert 16
Why Does Crime Drop? 42
Utilitarianism Gone Astray 65
The Taboo Crime of Parricide 92
Cults—Culture Conflict—Crime 133
The Girls in the Gang 160
Defying Convention and Control: "In Your Face" 176
The Rights of the Poorest 198
Maximum-Security Schools 230
An Epidemic of Hate Crimes? 274
Insurance Fraud on the Rise: New Jersey's Experience 303
Dangerous Ground: The World of Hazardous Waste Crime 346
Cyberporn: Problems and Controversies 374
Cross-Cultural Research: Smoking One's Way into Cheyenne Culture 393
In re Gault: The Demise of Parens Patriae 428
Fear of Crime Decreases—Fear of Police Increases 475
A New Crime: Hate; A New Punishment: Sentence Enhancement 512
Boot Camp: A Military Option for Corrections 556

xvii

Preface

Criminology is a young discipline—in fact, the term "criminology" is only a little over a century old. But in this brief time, criminology has emerged as an important social and behavioral science devoted to the study of crime as a social phenomenon. Criminology fosters theoretical debates, contributes ideas, and suggests solutions to a crime problem that many consider intolerable. Problems as vital and urgent as those addressed in this book are challenging, exciting, and, at the same time, disturbing and tragic. Moreover, these problems are immediately relevant to students' lives. This is especially true today, where we see threats of additional terrorist attacks against the United States and daily revelations of new corporate scandals.

Our goal with this book has always been, and remains, to discuss these problems, their origins, and their possible solutions in a clear, practical, straightforward fashion that brings the material to life for students. We invite teachers and students alike to join us in traveling along criminology's path, exploring its domain and mapping out its future.

THE FIFTH EDITION

In the four preceding editions of this text, we have prepared students of criminology to understand the contemporary problems with which criminology is concerned and to anticipate those problems which society would have to face in the twenty-first century. We have now entered that century. It is time to face the new century's problems as we simultaneously continue to work on solutions to old problems. Because of the forward-looking orientation of previous editions of *Criminology* and the wide respect and acceptance that those editions have enjoyed, we have maintained the book's established structure and approach with only two substantive changes.

First, we give the crime of terrorism center stage in Chapter 1. No single crime has ever shaped and reshaped the field of criminology like the crime of terrorism. Although it has only recently exploded into criminological prominence, there can be no doubt that terrorism will continue to be studied intensely by criminologists around the globe, and that their research will result in practical, policy-relevant proposals.

The emergence of a new age of corporate malfeasance represents the second substantive change in this fifth edition. We have expanded our coverage of white-collar crimes, from Martha Stewart's questionable stock trades to the organizational deviance of Enron, Andersen, Tyco, Global Crossing, and a host of other Fortune 500 companies. Like the crime of terrorism, white-collar and corporate offenses have been on the periphery of the field of criminology—but not for much longer.

As in prior revisions, we have vigorously researched, refined, and updated every chapter of the text—not only to maintain the book's scholarly integrity, but also to ensure it's relevance for today's students. In addition to updating every chapter's research base and statistical information, we have expanded coverage of the most critical issues facing the field of criminology in the twenty-first century:

- As noted, Chapter 1, "The Reach of Criminology," has been rewritten to introduce students to the crime of terrorism and the crimes that support terrorism. Not only does this new chapter provide timely and complete coverage of one of the key issues in criminal justice today, it also reinforces our commitment to making criminology relevant for today's students. This commitment extends to integrating discussions of theory and policy in ways that allow students to understand the importance of theory in generating long-term, sustainable, criminal justice policies and programs.

- The text of Chapters 2 and 10 from previous editions now form a single chapter—a new Chapter 2, "Counting Crime and Measuring Criminal Behavior"—that focuses on what crime is *and* how we measure it. Our goal with this change is to make the material on crime measurement—which can sometimes be difficult for students to grasp—more meaningful, relevant, and understandable by presenting it alongside the more inherently concrete discussion of what crime is.

- Chapter 12, "White-Collar and Corporate Crime," is a new and important addition to the text. Students will find the definitional and theoretical problems of white collar and corporate crime to be a welcome change from a field (and a text) that has as its focus more traditional violent and property offenses.

Inasmuch as developments in criminology influence and are influenced by media reports of national significance, the student will find discussion and analysis of recent major current events such as:

- The suburban Washington, D.C., snipers
- The indictment and conviction of Arthur Andersen, Ltd.
- The "hockey dad's" deadly dispute
- The conviction of Andrea Yates for drowning her five children
- The arrest of *Baretta* star Robert Blake
- The conviction of Kennedy cousin Michael Skakel
- The conviction and sentencing of the killer of seven-year-old Danielle van Damme
- The murder conviction of long-time fugitive Ira Einhorn

As in previous editions, we have endeavored not only to reflect developments and changes, but to anticipate them on the basis of the latest criminological data. After all, those who study criminology with our text today must be ready to address and resolve new criminological problems tomorrow when they are decision makers, researchers, teachers, and planners.

The aim, however, remains constant: to reach a future as free from crime as possible.

ORGANIZATION

As with previous editions, there are two versions of this text. *Criminology* consists of three parts; *Criminology and the Criminal Justice System* has four parts. For schools that retain the traditional criminology course, which includes criminological coverage of criminal justice, *Criminology and the Criminal Justice System* would be the ideal text. For schools that offer both an Introduction to Criminology course and an Introduction to Criminal Justice course, *Criminology* is the more appropriate text for their course, since it omits Part IV, "A Criminological Approach to the Criminal Justice System."

Part I, "Understanding Criminology," presents an overview of criminology—now made more exciting via integrated coverage of terrorism and related crimes—and describes the vast horizon of this science. It explains what crime is and techniques for measuring the amount and characteristics of crime and criminals. It also traces the history of criminological thought through the era that witnessed the formation of the major schools of criminology, classicism and positivism (eighteenth and nineteenth centuries).

Part II, "Explanations of Crime and Criminal Behavior," includes explanations of crime and criminal behavior on the basis of the various theories developed in the twentieth century. Among the subjects covered are theories that offer biological, psychological, sociological, sociopolitical, and integrated explanations. Coverage of research by radical, socialist, and feminist criminologists has been updated. Theories that discuss why offenders choose to commit one offense rather than another at a given time and place are also covered in this part.

Part III, "Types of Crimes," covers the various types of crimes from a legal and sociological perspective. The familiar street crimes, such as homicide and robbery, are assessed, as are other criminal activities such as white-collar and corporate crime, which are so much in the spotlight these days, as well as other high-tech crimes that have been highlighted by re-

PREFACE

searchers only in recent years. The chapter on comparative criminology—an area with vastly increased practical and policy implications—has been expanded and updated in light of the growing research in the field.

Part IV, "A Criminological Approach to the Criminal Justice System" (only in *Criminology and the Criminal Justice System*), includes an explanation of the component parts and the functioning of the system. It explains contemporary criminological research on how the people who run the system operate it, the decision-making processes of all participants, and the interaction of all the system components.

PEDAGOGICAL AIDS

Working together, the authors and the editors have developed a format for the text that supports the goal of a readable, practical, and attractive text. In addition to all the changes already mentioned, we include plentiful, current photographs to make the book even more approachable. Redesigned and carefully updated tables and figures highlight and amplify the text coverage. Chapter outlines, lists of key terms, chapter review sections, and a comprehensive glossary all help students to master the material. Always striving to help students see the relevance of criminology in their lives, we also include a number of unique, innovative features in this edition:

- *Crime Surfing*. Particularly interesting Web addresses accompanied by mini-exercises that allow students to explore chapter topics further.
- *Did You Know?* Surprising factual realities which provide eye-opening information about chapter topics.
- *Research Informs Policy*. Brief sections at the end of theory chapters that demonstrate how problems identified by criminologists have led to practical solutions
- New *Theory Connects* marginal inserts. Notes in the text margins that correlate the intensely applied material in Part III of the text ("Types of Crimes") with the heavily theoretical material in Part II ("Explana-

tions of Crime"), giving the students much needed cross-reference material and posing critical-thinking questions that will help them truly process what they are reading
- New *Criminology & Public Policy*. exercises End-of-chapter activities that challenge students to explore policy issues related to criminology

We are particularly proud of our new "box" program. In these boxes, we highlight criminologically significant issues which deserve special discussion. Each chapter has three boxes: "Of Immediate Concern," "Window to the World," and the all new "From the Pages of *The New York Times*."

- *Of Immediate Concern* boxes highlight problems "of the moment," due to their technological nature or human implications, that challenge us to come up with specific effective responses right now. Thus, in the wake of school killings, should we create maximum security schools? In light of our experience with hate-motivated crimes, are harsher laws called for? Cyberporn is viewed as a major global problem; what can we do about it?
- *Window to the World* boxes examine developments abroad that affect America's crime situation. Since international terrorist threats plague nations around the globe, in countries as diverse as the United States and Russia, what can be done to deter terrorists? Now that ethnic gangs have emerged around the world and are, among other things, forcibly transporting women and young girls to be sex slaves, how can nations deal with the problem?
- *From the Pages of* The New York Times boxes discuss current issues and problems reported on in *The New York Times*. These boxes are doubly beneficial to students: not only do they relate chapter material to what students see every day on the news—Al Qaeda, the newly created Homeland Security Office, the film "Gangs of New York," racial profiling, and so much more—because they are pulled from the

pages of *The New York Times,* a policy-oriented media outlet, they provide yet another means of keeping students focused on all important policy issues in criminology.

SUPPLEMENTS PACKAGE

As a full-service publisher of quality educational products, McGraw-Hill does much more than just sell textbooks. The company creates and publishes an extensive array of print, video, and digital supplements for students and instructors. This edition of *Criminology* is accompanied by an extensive, comprehensive supplements package:

For the Student
- *Making the Grade CD-ROM.* This free electronic study guide packaged with every text includes chapter quizzes with feedback indicating why each answer is right or wrong, an Internet guide, a study skills primer, and much more.
- *Online Learning Center Website.* An innovative website features unique *Interactive Explorations* that allow students to explore some of the hottest topics in criminal justice today—terrorism, serial killers, gangs, and so on. The website also features PowerWeb, online access to articles from the popular and scholarly press, weekly updates, daily newsfeeds, a search engine, and more. All of this material—plus flashcards that can be used to master vocabulary and a wealth of other review materials—is organized by chapter for ease of use when studying for exams or writing papers.
- *CyberJustice Website.* This custom-crafted criminal justice supersite features a large library of URLs for help in writing papers, a unique assortment of supplementary readings on terrorism, and much, much more.

For the Instructor
- *Instructor's Manual/Testbank.* The manual includes detailed chapter outlines, key terms, overviews, lecture notes, and a complete testbank.
- *Computerized Testbank.* Easy-to-use computerized testing program is compatible with both Windows and Macintosh computers.
- *PowerPoint Slides.* Complete, chapter-by-chapter slide shows feature text, art, and tables.
- *Online Learning Center Website.* Password-protected access to supplements and other important instructor support materials and additional resources.
- *NBC News Lecture Launcher Videotape.* Available for the first time with this fifth edition, this unique video features several brief clips from *NBC News* that can be used to jump-start lectures in the most exciting, relevant ways.
- *Full-Length Videotapes.* A wide variety of videotapes from the *Films for the Humanities and Social Sciences* series is available to adopters of the text.
- *Course Management Systems.* Whether you use WebCT, Blackboard, e-College, or another course management system, McGraw-Hill will provide you with a *Criminology* cartridge that enables you either to conduct your course entirely online or to supplement your lectures with online material. And if your school does not yet have one of these course management systems, we can provide you with PageOut, an easy-to-use tool that allows you to create your own course Web page and access all material on the *Criminology* Online Learning Center.
- *Primis Online.* This unique database publishing system allows instructors to create their own custom text from material in *Criminology* or elsewhere and deliver that text to students electronically as an e-book or in print format via the bookstore.

All of the above supplements are provided free of charge to students and instructors. Orders of new (versus used) textbooks help us defray the cost of developing such supplements, which is substantial. Please contact your local McGraw-Hill representative for more information on any of the above supplements.

PREFACE

IN APPRECIATION

We greatly acknowledge the assistance and support of a number of dedicated professionals. At Rutgers University, the librarian of the N.C.C.D./Criminal Justice Collection, Phyllis Schultze, has been most helpful in patiently tracking and tracing sources. We thank Professor Sesha Kethineni, Illinois State University, for her tireless assistance on the first edition, Deborah Leiter-Walker for her help on the second, Kerry Dalip and Nhung Tran from the University of Pennsylvania for their assistance on the third, and Smita Jain from the University of Pennsylvania for her assistance on the fourth. Gratitude is also owed to the many former and current Rutgers University students who have valiantly contributed their labors to all editions. These include Susanna Cornett, Dory Dickman, Lisa Maher, Susan Plant, Mangai Natarajan, Dana Nurge, Sharon Chamard, Marina Myhre, Diane Cicchetti, Emmanuel Barthe, Illya Lichtenberg, Peter Heidt, Vanja Stenius, Christine Tartaro, Megan McNally, Danielle Gunther, Jennifer Lanterman, Smita Jain, and Jim Roberts.

Many academic reviewers (listed facing title page) offered invaluable help in planning and drafting chapters. We thank them for their time and thoughtfulness and for the experience they brought from their teaching and research.

We thank our colleagues overseas who have prepared translations of *Criminology* to help familiarize students of foreign cultures with criminological problems which are now global, with our theories, and with efforts to deal with the persistent problem of crime in the years to come:

The Arabic translation:
   Dr. Mohammed Zeid, Cairo, Egypt, and Rome, Italy
The Japanese translation:
   Dr. Toyoji Saito, Kobe, Japan, and his colleagues
The Hungarian translation:
   Dr. Miklos Levai, Miskolc, Hungary, and his colleagues
The Georgian translation:
   Dr. Georgi Glonti, Tbilisi, Georgia

Finally we owe a special debt to the team at McGraw-Hill: to editorial director Phil Butcher and senior editor Carolyn Henderson Meier for their encouragement and support; to Julie Abodeely, editorial coordinator, for her attention to the day-to-day details; to Barbara Salz, for her photo research; and to the production staff in Burr Ridge.

A combined total of over 100 years of teaching criminology and related subjects provides the basis for the writing of *Criminology*, Fifth Edition. We hope the result is a text that is intellectually provocative, factually rigorous, and scientifically sound and that offers a stimulating learning experience for the student.

Freda Adler
Gerhard O. W. Mueller
William S. Laufer

A Guided Tour

Up-to-the-Minute Coverage

Terrorism and the crimes that support it are now given center stage in Chapter 1, and corporate and white collar crime receive more extensive coverage.

New, Policy-Oriented *From the Pages of The New York Times* Boxes

Detailed discussion of the very issues and problems students hear about in the news helps them relate these issues to chapter and lecture material.

From the Pages of The New York Times

Street Gangs of New York: From the 1860s to the 1960s

In December of 2002, Martin Scorcese's long-awaited film, *Gangs of New York*, was released. It was based on a book by Herbert Asbury, written in 1928, about the gangs that existed in New York City in the late 1800s. These gangs caused major problems for law-abiding citizens, and were one of the precipitating factors behind the rise of a strong city-wide police force.

One of the most frightening times in New York City history (before September 11) occurred in 1863, when for three days gangs rioted and took over much of the city. Most of the members of the gangs were Irish workers who were angry at their plight in general (they lived in the most densely packed neighborhood in the world), and were specifically angry at the new National Conscription Act, which made virtually all able-bodied men eligible for the draft. The Act, however, allowed wealthy men to get out of service by paying a $300 fee—more than most lower-class workers made in a year. Historians report that 119 people were killed in the riots, and hundreds more were injured.

Gangs of ethnic origins continued to flourish in New York, brought to public attention again in the late 1950s and early 1960s with the musical *West Side Story*. In 1958, *The New York Times* wrote a seven-part, front-page series examining the antisocial behavior of adolescents in the "shook-up" generation. Some of these gang members attended a reunion of sorts in 1999. In the late 50s, photographer Bruce Davidson spent several months hanging out and photographing a street gang in Brooklyn. Forty years later, several gang members showed up to see an exhibit of these photos at the International Center of Photography.

The gang members recalled the violence of the time. They grew up in Brooklyn, and called themselves the Jokers and the Eighth Avenue Boys. Their fathers were factory workers who were frequently laid off, with no way to support their large families. Many came from homes with two alcoholic parents. It was a place, said one former gang member, where "a kid wished he was dead a million times." They didn't have guns then, but if they had, several former gang members said, they probably would have used them. They fought instead with chains and pipes, knives and baseball bats. Many of the gang members were long since dead. Some died in jail, some died from drugs, some from alcohol, and some from bullets that eventually became the weapon of choice.

There were, however, signs that gang life doesn't necessarily lead to death and destruction. Among the living gang members, who struggled long and hard to fight their way out of poverty and addiction, were two retired police officers, an electrician, a retired transit worker, a hospital administrator, a singer, and an addiction counselor. Most have children who grew up in New Jersey or on Long Island, and who knew nothing of gangs, except from the papers and dad's stories over dinner.

Source
Geoffrey C. Ward, "Gangs of New York," *The New York Times*, October 6, 2002. Blaine Harden, "With Brass-Knuckled Tales, 50's Street Gang Looks Back," *The New York Times*, February 15, 1999. Reprinted with permission.

Questions for Discussion
1. Obviously, gangs in New York (or anywhere else for that matter) are not a modern phenomenon. The gangs described in the story above—both in the 1860s and the 1960s—came from lower, working-class families. How does this support Albert Cohen's "delinquent boys" theory? How do the circumstances not support the part of the theory that says their delinquent acts serve no useful purpose?
2. What can we make of the fact that many of the gang members went on to get good jobs and raise middle-class families with middle-class lifestyles and values?

Window to the World

Russians and Americans Share a Crime Problem

Despite many differences, Americans and Russians had one thing in common: freedom from terrorism at home. This commonality was shattered for Americans on February 26, 1993, when a bomb tore a huge hole in the World Trade Center (WTC) in New York City, killing 6 people. Russians were awakened to the reality of terrorism on August 31, 1999, when a bomb exploded at Moscow's upscale Manezh shopping center near the Kremlin, killing 1 person and injuring 40. So, once again, Americans and Russians have something in common: domestic terrorism and the fear that goes with it. In America, the WTC terrorist attack was followed by the Oklahoma City bombing, on April 19, 1995, which killed 168 people, and the Olympic Park bomb explosion in Atlanta, Georgia, on July 30, 1996, which killed 1 person and injured many. And then came the shock of the 911 disaster that took almost 3,000 lives. Of course, Americans have been victimized by terrorist attacks outside the country, including, among many others:
- The destruction of Pan Am flight 103 over Lockerbie, Scotland, in 1988 (270 dead).
- The destruction of a U.S. military residence in Dhahran, Saudi Arabia, in 1996 (19 dead, many injured).
- The destruction of the U.S. embassies in Nairobi, Kenya, and Dar-es-Salaam, Tanzania, in 1998 (224 dead, 4,300 injured).

Russians suffered five brutal terrorist attacks within the span of 3 weeks:
1. August 31, 1999. Manezh Shopping Center, near the Kremlin, Moscow (1 killed, 40 injured).
2. September 4, 1999. Dagestan, Russia (64 killed).
3. September 9, 1999. Moscow apartment building (94 killed).
4. September 13, 1999. Moscow apartment building (118 killed).
5. September 16, 1999. Volgodansk, Russia, apartment building (18 killed).

There was a time when terrorism could be categorized in terms of political versus profit motive, foreign versus domestic, and so on. These lines have become blurred, and the profit motive seems to have disappeared. While there may still be a domestic form of terrorism, such as the terrorism perpetrated by fanatics and cultlike private militias who see the government as an enemy, most terrorism appears to have an international base and is directed against people and their governments. In particular, Islamic fanatic fundamentalist terrorists are increasingly identified with attacks against U.S. and Russian targets.

There also was a time when terrorists enjoyed the support, both

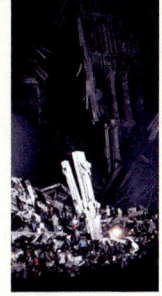
Rescue workers search for survivors at the collapsed towers of the World Trade Center after September 11, 2001.

of the twenty-first century, it is clear that these problems demand more of criminology than it is capable of delivering as yet. The principal crime problems are totally globalized. Criminology has to become equally globalized.

Seemingly we have neglected street crimes and delinquency in this survey of the reach of criminology. These topics are, and will remain, a major focus of criminologists—in competition with all the other forms of criminality to which we have alluded. Now that you are acquainted with the reach, or expanse, of criminology, we next introduce you to what this discipline is all about.

WHAT IS CRIMINOLOGY?

In the Middle Ages human learning was commonly divided into four areas: law, medicine, theology, and philosophy. Universities typically had four faculties, one for each of these fields. Imagine a young person in the year 1392—100 years before Columbus came ashore in America—knocking at the portal of a great university with the request: "I would like to study criminology. Where do I sign up?" A stare of disbelief would have greeted the student, because the word had not yet been coined. Cautiously the student

---

Classic *Window to the World* and *Of Immediate Concern* Boxes

Acclaimed thematic box program—one box devoted to highlighting the international dimensions of criminology, another to introduce criminological problems that are "of the moment."

Of Immediate Concern

An Epidemic of Hate Crimes?

The media, academics, advocacy groups, and politicians have created what has been described as a hate-crime epidemic. But is the problem really as great as we have been led to believe? Consider that the media can shape public opinion and reinforce the idea that there is an epidemic through the use of these types of headlines:
- "A Cancer of Hatred Afflicts America"[1]
- "Rise in Hate Crimes Signals Alarming Resurgence of Bigotry"[2]

Books and articles are often inflammatory, argue James Jacobs and Jessica Henry.[3] The authors suggest that some scholars simply assume a grave problem exists, in spite of an overwhelming lack of evidence. This can be a dangerous assumption, for the idea of hate crime divides the community and becomes a self-fulfilling prophecy. "Crime sells—so does racism, sexism, and homophobia. Garden-variety crime has become mundane." [3]

Advocacy groups representing blacks, Jews, gays and lesbians, women, and the disabled have embraced the idea of a hate-crime epidemic, much of which is based on dubious statistics. For example, the 1997 Uniform Crime Reports show only 8,049 reported hate crimes, less than .001 percent of all reported crimes. Is this an epidemic?

Jacobs and Henry point out that American history shows attacks on racial and ethnic groups started from the moment European settlers arrived and made Native Americans a target. Historically, blacks, Jews, Catholics, and recent immigrants have also been targeted. The 1990s brought a greater intolerance for this behavior, but, Jacobs and Henry say, there still is no epidemic.

Yet it matters little whether the spate of hate crimes is real or merely perceived; significant developments have taken place in consequence. Throughout the 1980s, media reports of increasing numbers of hate-motivated crimes (also know as *bias crimes*) pressured states to adopt statutes dealing with such crimes. These statutes prohibit acts of ethnically or religiously based intimidation, enhance penalties for these crimes, or raise the level of the crime from a misdemeanor to a felony. In addition, many criminal justice agencies have developed programs for dealing with bias crime, and at the federal level the Hate Crimes Statistics Act of 1990 mandates that local law enforcement agencies compile data on such crimes.

As defined by the federal Hate Crimes Statistics Act of 1990, hate crimes are crimes that show evidence of prejudice against certain group characteristics. The act mandates the collection of data that show evidence of prejudice based on race, sexual orientation, ethnicity, or religion. The Hate Crime Statistics Act was later amended by the Violent Crime and Law Enforcement Act of 1994 to include crimes motivated by bias against persons with disabilities.

Many bias crimes fall into the categories of simple assaults, vandalism, and harassment. Because these are relatively less serious crimes, they ordinarily get little attention. They can, however, have a major impact on the community by increasing the level of fear and hostility between groups. So extra attention to them is warranted.

In the twenty-first century, two trends are likely to continue, with increased challenges for legislators, judges, and criminal justice specialists. First, legislatures are adding sentence enhancements for crimes committed with the motive of hate. Such statues allow or require judges to add additional prison time for those convicted of crimes committed with a hate motive. Second, the reach of hate-crime legislation is likely to be expanded. For example, under existing federal law, hate crimes can be prosecuted only if the hate (bias) is directed at religion, sexual orientation, national origin, color, and disability. But under the Hate Crime Prevention Act of 1998 the reach has been expanded to any "violent act causing death or bodily injury "because of the actual or *perceived* race, color, religion, national origin, sexual orientation, *gender*, or disability" of the victim [emphasis supplied]." This act likely will become law and be followed by similar state legislation.

Sources
1. Spencer Rumsey, "A Cancer of Hatred Afflicts America," *Newsday*, May 27, 1993, p. 129.
2. Benjamin J. Hubbard, "Commentary on Tolerance," *Los Angeles Times*, Apr. 4, 1993, p. B9.
3. James B. Jacobs and Jessica S. Henry, "The Social Construction of a Hate Crime Epidemic," *Journal of Criminal Law and Criminology*, 86 (1996): 366–391.

Questions for Discussion
1. Wisconsin's sentence-enhancement law was challenged by a defendant who claimed that his First Amendment (freedom of speech) rights were violated because the statute punishes offenders' bigoted beliefs and not just their acts. Do you agree with the U.S. Supreme Court decision to uphold the Wisconsin statute?
2. An FBI study found that intimidation was the most common type of hate crime, followed by vandalism and assault. Do you think these crimes are serious enough to warrant the extra attention they receive?

XXV

Chapter-Opening Previews

Succinct chapter-opening outlines, key terms lists, and overviews help students focus on the chapter's critical theories, concepts, and terminology.

Fascinating Did You Know? Facts

Intriguing, little-known facts related to specific chapter topics engage students' natural curiosity about criminology.

Unique *Crime Surfing* Inserts

Brief Internet exercises integrated into every chapter enable students to explore the web in directed fashion.

xxvi

New *Theory Connects* Icons

Margin notes correlating the applied material in Part III of the text ("Types of Crimes") with the theoretical material in Part II ("Explanations of Crime") help students see how theory applies to and explains street and white-collar crime.

Unique *Criminology & Public Policy* Exercises

End-of-chapter activities that challenge students to explore and think critically about policy issues.

xxvii

Easy-to-Use End-of-Chapter Reviews

Clear, concise chapter summaries and key terms lists—tabbed along the side of the page for easy reference when studying for an exam—provide students with essential review materials.

Unique *You Be the Criminologist* Exercises

Chapter-ending exercises challenges students to use their critical thinking skills to apply what they have read about in the chapter.

Classic *Theory Informs Policy* Sections

Acclaimed coverage of the interrelated nature of theory, policy, and practice highlights the practical aspects of what criminologists do.

xxviii

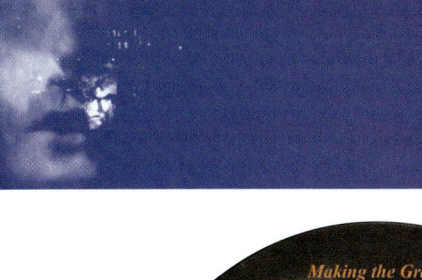

Free *Making the Grade* Electronic Study Guide

A CD-ROM packaged free with every text can help students study for and improve their grades on exams.

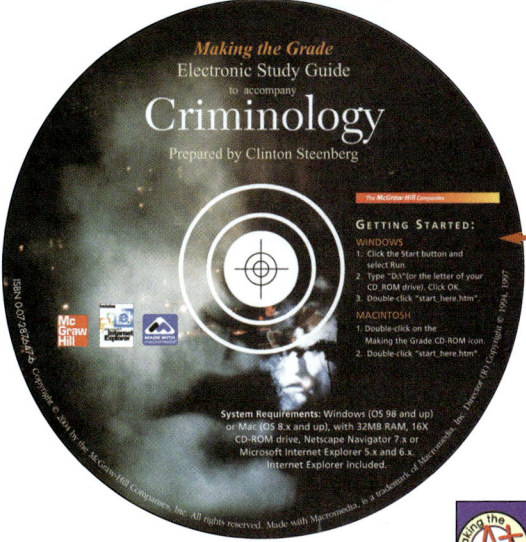

Chapter-by-Chapter Quizzes

Multiple-choice quizzes with feedback explaining why responses are right or wrong help students master material.

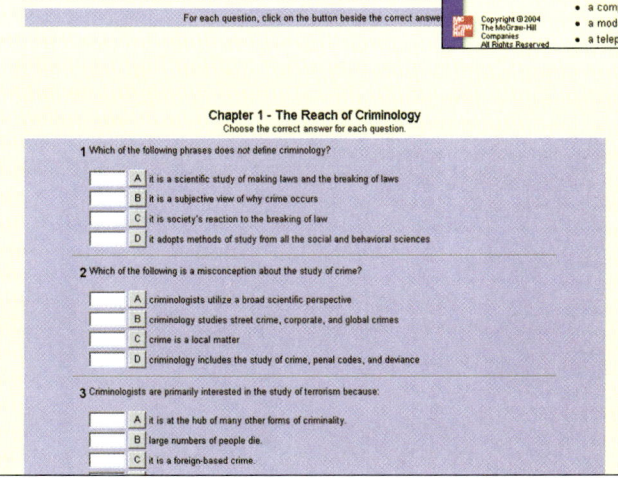

And More . . .

In addition to 18 separate quizzes, the electronic study guide includes such important resources as an Internet guide, a study skills primer, and more.

Online Learning Center Website

Unique, book-specific website features *Interactive Explorations* that enable students to think about and explore some of the latest issues in criminal justice today. The website also includes online access to scholarly articles, the media, flashcards that can be used to master vocabulary, and many other chapter review tools.

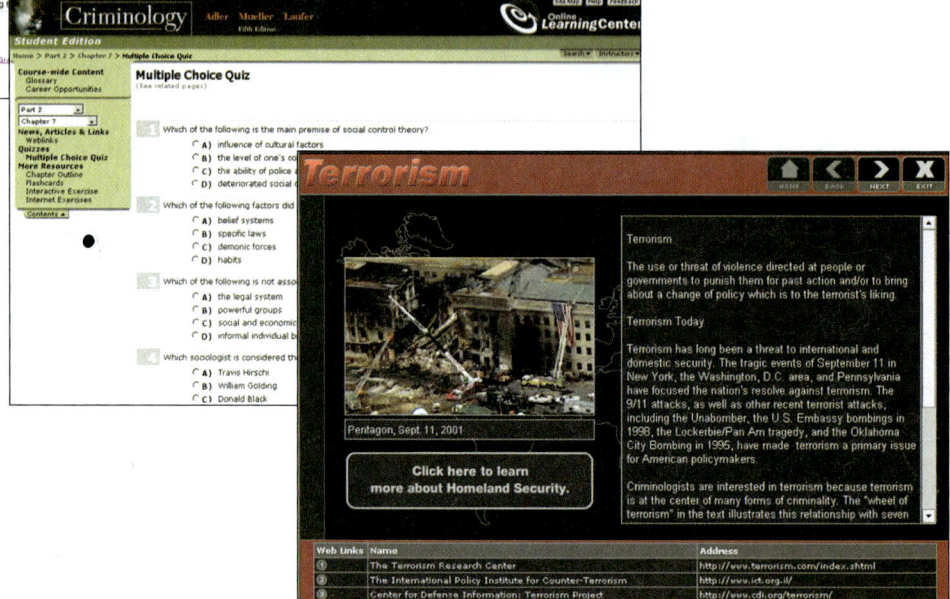

CyberJustice Website

This unique website features a large library of URLs for assistance in writing papers, a "Careers" corner, and much more.

Criminology

PART I

Understanding Criminology

Criminology is the scientific study of the making of laws, the breaking of laws, and society's reaction to the breaking of laws. Sometimes these laws are arrived at by the consensus of most members of a community; sometimes they are imposed by those in power. Communities have grown in size, from village to world, and the threats to communities have grown accordingly. World-level threats necessitated that criminological research and crime prevention strategies become globalized. Nationally and internationally, criminological research has become influential in policy making (Chapter 1).

Criminologists have adopted methods of study from all the social and behavioral sciences. Like all other scientists, criminologists measure. They assess crime over time and place, and they measure the characteristics of criminals and crimes (Chapter 2).

Throughout history, thinkers and rulers have written about crime and criminals and the control of crime. Yet the term "criminology" is little more than a century old, and the subject has been of scientific interest for only two centuries. Two schools of thought contributed to modern criminology: the classical school, associated predominantly with Cesare Beccaria (eighteenth century), which focused on crime, and the positivist school, associated with Cesare Lombroso, Enrico Ferri, and Raffaele Garofalo (nineteenth and early twentieth centuries), which focused on criminals (Chapter 3). Contemporary American criminology owes much to these European roots.

CHAPTER 1
The Reach of Criminology

The Reach of Criminology
 Terrorism
 Illicit Drug Trafficking
 Money Laundering
 Infiltration of Legal Business
 Computer Crime
 Illicit Arms Trafficking
 Traffic in Persons
 Destruction of Cultural Property

What Is Criminology?

The Making of Laws
 Deviance
 The Concept of Crime
 The Consensus and Conflict
  Views of Law and Crime

The Breaking of Laws

Society's Reaction to the Breaking of Laws
 Criminology and the Criminal
  Justice System
 The Global Approach to the
  Breaking of Laws

Research Informs Policy

REVIEW

CRIMINOLOGY & PUBLIC POLICY

YOU BE THE CRIMINOLOGIST

KEY TERMS

Boxes
 From the Pages of *The New York Times*: *Financing Terrorism through Legitimate Fronts*
 Window to the World: *Russians and Americans Share a Crime Problem*
 Of Immediate Concern: *Vipers in the Desert*

Special Features
 Crime Surfing
 Did You Know?

KEY TERMS
conflict model
consensus model
crime
criminal justice system
criminologist
criminology
deviance
social norms

Our world post–9/11: Members of the National Guard and other military personnel join federal, state, and local law enforcement in patroling bus stations, railway stations, and airports.

Criminologists study crime from a broad scientific perspective in an effort to understand its causes and, ultimately, its prevention. They are not, as some TV programs suggest, the scientists who engage in crime scene investigations. (The people who do that are called "criminalists" or "forensic scientists.")

Largely as a result of media portrayal, a second popular misunderstanding is that criminologists are only, or at least primarily, interested in street crime as it affects our lives and our fears. It is true that criminologists are very much concerned with murders, robberies, burglaries, and thefts. But consider for a moment that while all of America's thieves (excluding automobile thieves) cause us a loss of $4 billion annually, a single rogue Wall Street trader may cause that much of a loss all by himself. So criminologists must extend their focus beyond street crime and include other criminal activities that may be less visible but cause far greater harm to human beings all over the globe.

A third popular misconception is that crime is a local matter, to be handled by the local police force or the sheriff's department. That is far from correct. The most dangerous types of crime reach beyond local boundaries and may even be global, threatening all humans on earth (e.g., terrorism).

A fourth misconception is that criminologists examine only crimes, as defined in penal codes, and only criminals convicted of such crimes. This notion, held half a century ago by some notable criminologists, has given way to an expansionist view which includes in the criminologist's domain not only crime as defined in penal codes, but all other forms of deviance which once have been, or easily could become, or currently incorporate, parts of existing criminal definitions. Once again, terrorism is an example.[1]

THE REACH OF CRIMINOLOGY

911 is the number Americans call when they need police protection from a criminal attack or similar emergency. In a very real sense, then, 911 starts the process of criminal justice and its inquiry about perpetrators and victims, causes and motivations, offenses and defenses. 911, therefore, is a good symbol with which to start a course—or a book—dedicated to criminology. In 2001, 911 took on yet another meaning, not only to the worldwide public, in general, but to criminologists, in particular.

It was in the morning hours of September 11, 2001, that four airliners were diverted in flight, by perpetrators who had subdued or killed the crews. Two of the jumbo jets crashed into the New York World Trade Center. The third plane smashed into the Pentagon, in Washington, D.C. The fourth plane, apparently headed toward Washington, D.C., crashed into a field in Pennsylvania, as a result of passengers trying to overpower the hijackers.

The World Trade Center collapsed within the hour; the Pentagon was in flames; all passengers and crews of the airplanes died in fiery crashes. The death toll was nearly three thousand. It was the worst criminally caused catastrophe in American history. To this day neither the American economy nor the American psyche has recovered from this act of terrorism. Terrorism! Is it a crime?

Terrorism

In the federal and state penal codes there are a number of crimes referring to terrorism. The federal penal code has listed several new crimes regarding terrorism, including "acts of terrorism transcending national boundaries," "use of certain weapons of mass destruction," and "financial transactions" to finance terrorism. Several states have adopted similar legislation, many of which are based on global United Nations conventions.[2] Few of these laws define terrorism as such. Most incorporate crimes which terrorists are likely to commit in furtherance of their objective, such as murder, arson, kidnapping, and so on. The U.S. Department of State has defined "terrorism" as the "premeditated, politically motivated violence perpetrated against non-combatant targets by sub-national groups or clandestine agents, usually intended to influence an audience."[3] Most definitions imply the use of violence or other significant forms of criminality to achieve the perpetrators' purpose. We are proposing our own definition: "The use or threat of violence directed at people or governments to punish them for past action and/or to bring about a change of policy which is to the terrorist's liking." This concept incorporates many forms of criminal conduct and is therefore of prime significance to criminologists.

There is a second and equally important reason for criminologists to study terrorism: It is at the hub of many forms of criminality which feed or are fed by terrorism. This can best be demonstrated by a wheel, the hub of which is terrorism. The seven spokes of the wheel are the seven forms of transnational criminality (see Chapter 14) that are directly relevant to terrorism, either because they support it or because they are a consequence or by-product of it. Let us continue our search for the reach of criminology by examining these seven categories. (See Figure 1.1.)

Illicit Drug Trafficking

Terrorists need money for their operations. The drug trade provides easy access to large funds. The Taliban have financed their terrorist activities from the vast opium production of Afghanistan. Terrorists in Colombia derive their funds from the coca trade of Latin America. And that holds true for just about every other terrorist group around the world. Globally, there is about $500 billion in "dirty" drug money available for financing illegal activities, including terrorism. United Kingdom Prime Minister Tony Blair, in a speech at a party conference on February 10, 2001, bluntly declared: "the arms the Taliban are buying today are paid for with the lives of young British people buying their drugs on British streets. That is another part of their regime we should seek to destroy."[4] While the "war on drugs" had received widespread attention in the media and on the part of government officials and criminologists, the "war against terrorism" has virtually replaced the prior emphasis. This is particularly disturb-

PART I   Understanding Criminology

FIGURE 1.1 Wheel of terrorism.

ing when it is becoming ever more clear that the drug trade nurtures terrorism and fosters the growth of international criminal organizations.[5]

Money Laundering

"Dirty" (illegally obtained) money cannot be spent freely. While there is evidence that terrorist weapons have been obtained by direct exchange for drugs, or for "dirty" money, most expenditures by terrorists are for goods or services obtained on the free market, which demands clean cash. Hence, much of the dirty money must be laundered in a vast criminal enterprise called "money laundering." Of course, it is not just drug money that requires laundering. All illegally obtained funds, for example, bribery, black market activities, corruption, extortion, and embezzlement, require laundering. Thus, money laundering is an activity aimed at making illegally obtained and, therefore, untaxed funds appear legitimate. Usually this is done by depositing such funds in numbered but unnamed (secret) accounts in banks of a number of countries where that is still possible. From there the funds are rapidly transferred elsewhere, and yet again, until it becomes impossible to trace them to the criminal activity which created them.[6] Despite increased international cooperation to curb money laundering, it appears that terrorism has benefited greatly from this criminal activity.

Infiltration of Legal Business

Dirty money, once laundered, can be used freely, for example, to buy or establish a legitimate business. By way of example, police in Hamburg, Germany, discovered that the innocent-looking import-export firms Tatari Design and Tatex Trading G.m.b.H. were not so innocent at all. They had been established as fronts for Al Qaeda operatives to smuggle money, agents, and supplies.[7] Of

Money laundering allows crime to pay by permitting criminals to hide and legitimize proceeds derived from illegal activities. According to one recent estimate, worldwide money laundering activity amounts to roughly $1 trillion a year.

Source: U.S. State Department, "The Fight against Money Laundering," *Economic Perspectives* **6**(2), May 2001, http://usinfo.state.gov/journals/ites/0501/ijee/ijee0501.htm.

course, it is just as likely that laundered funds, rather than directly financing terrorist enterprises, will be invested in businesses controlled by organized crime, like trash hauling, construction, seafood, or investment banking.[8]

Computer Crime

Cyberspace is there for everyone to use—or to abuse, and these abuses are increasingly being discovered and, indeed, legislated as crime. Above all there is the abuse of cyberspace for money laundering, ultimately to support terrorist groups.[9] Beyond that, there is the potential of cyberattacks on the national security of the

---

FROM THE PAGES OF

The New York Times

Financing Terrorism through Legitimate Fronts

Since the attacks on September 11, the United States has been busy imposing new regulations to thwart money-laundering opportunities. But a report by the United Nations issued in September 2002 indicates that Al Qaeda and other terrorist groups still have access to between $30 million and $300 million—controlled by ostensibly legitimate businesses.

One of the primary goals of the United States and its allies is to disrupt the flow of money to Al Qaeda and its operatives around the world, but it's no easy task. Many suspected front companies are in countries with few regulations and can pack up and vanish overnight.

Take Maram, for example—a company set up in Istanbul as a travel agency and import-export business. One of its principal owners, Mamdouh Mahmud Salim, had a history of moving money and shopping for weapons for Al Qaeda. A few months after Salim created Maram, he transferred shares in the company to two men American authorities have identified as members of Al Qaeda. When Salim was arrested in connection with the 1998 bombings of the American Embassies in Kenya and Tanzania, the company cleaned out its offices overnight and disappeared.

Although the United Nations report said the terror network was "alive and well" and still had access to huge sums of money, many American officials disagreed, stating that arrests made worldwide—and the freezing of $112 million in suspected terrorist funds—had weakened the organization.

Some European banking officials, however, believe that Al Qaeda had prepared for the possibility of limited access to cash by shifting its assets into diamonds and gold before September 11. "The real problem for the Americans is not freezing bank accounts," a Swiss banking regulator stated. "The biggest challenge is stopping the unknown number of apparently legitimate businesses set up to move money around the globe to terrorists."

Source
Douglas Frantz, "Qaeda's Bankrolls; Front Companies Said to Keep Financing Terrorists," *The New York Times,* Sept. 19, 2002.

Questions for Discussion

1. What steps, if any, might be taken to stop the flow of money from legitimate businesses to terrorist or criminal organizations? And how can this be accomplished in our increasingly global economy?
2. At the time Mamdouh Mahmud Salim opened his Maram company, he was already suspected of having ties with Al Qaeda. Should he have been prevented from opening another business?

Internet cafes, like this one in Istanbul, Turkey, can be found in most cities of the world. Without them, transnational crime would be difficult to conduct.

United States. The security community generally expects terrorists to launch major strikes through computer networks in the immediate future.[10] Al Qaeda is deemed to possess the capacity for these major cyberattacks.[11]

Illicit Arms Trafficking

The wars of the past have provided terrorists of the past—and the present—with surplus and remnant arms and munitions to fight for their causes. The market in small arms is vast and mostly clandestine. The novelty, however, is the market for weapons of mass destruction: nuclear, bacteriological, and chemical. There is considerable evidence that nuclear materials have been diverted from now-defunct former Soviet installations. It is feared that rogue states which have traditionally supported terrorism are seeking these materials for the creation of weapons of mass destruction. In March 2003, the United States found itself at war with one of these states, Iraq, over the issue of United Nations inspections of suspected Iraqi nuclear arms facilities. Criminologists may now have to consult with weapons specialists in their efforts to help find solutions.

Traffic in Persons

Smuggling would-be illegal migrants from less-desirable homelands to more promising lands of opportunity has become a huge criminal enterprise, involving millions of human beings, billions in funds paid to smugglers, and the loss of a great number of innocent lives. Many of the countries of destination fear the growth of immigrant communities that might be a terrorist haven, like the refugee camps of Palestine. Even greater is the fear that terrorist organizations deliberately infiltrate their members into immigrant populations. To their dismay, for example, Italian law enforcement authorities have learned that among the waves of illegal immigrants washing ashore in Sicily, there are increasing numbers of persons linked to terrorist organizations.[12] There are also masses of illegal aliens who have moved from Iran, Iraq, and Turkey—across the Aegean Sea—into Northern Africa where they become vulnerable recruits for terrorist activities.

Destruction of Cultural Property

Lenin's terrorists became infamous for their effort to destroy the evidence of a culture past: Christian churches were destroyed. Hitler's terrorists

Sailors of a Spanish naval vessel—part of an international armada—boarding an unflagged ship, the *Sosan*, 600 miles off the coast of East Africa, after the captain refused to identify the vessel. Initially, the North Korean master of the vessel claimed she was carrying cement. The Spanish search revealed 15 missiles and other sophisticated weaponry.

burned down the synagogues of Germany and every other cultural symbol, especially literature, art, and music deemed inconsistent with the new "culture" they wanted to impose. The Taliban took delight in firing artillery shells into two ancient statues of Buddha, the largest in the world—reducing them to rubble. And when the 911 terrorists destroyed the World Trade Center, they not only eradicated a symbol of American trade leadership, but also a beautiful, unique structure of American architecture. Terrorists, especially those with millennial goals, or of religious or political extremism, seek to destroy past cultures and to impose their own vision of culture.

We have completed our examination of the hub and the seven spokes of our criminological wheel. These represent terrorism and 7 other forms of criminality which support or are the product of terrorism. These 8 forms of criminality are part of a group of 18 which the United Nations has defined as "transnational criminality." Not crimes by themselves, but rather a mixture of other crimes, they all have in common that they transcend national boundaries, affecting several nations, and therefore are hard to deal with by just one nation. (We shall return to transnational criminality in Chapter 14 where we will discuss the remaining 10 forms.)

Our effort to demonstrate the reach of criminology has not yet been completed. As any exposure to today's media will tell you, there is a competition for attention among those who deem terrorism to be the principal national problem and those pointing to our lagging economy. And why? Democrats and Republicans might give you differing answers, but all agree that the collapse of a whole series of world-leading financial institutions lies at the root of investors' lack of confidence in the market, thus accounting for the market's decline. And what explains this sudden, staggering series of collapses among enterprises? Corporate giants, like Enron, World Com, Adelphi, Chevron Texaco, Tyco, and many others, have become bankrupt or are in serious financial straits because management has criminally deceived their shareholders, business partners, the government, and the public. Billions of dollars have been embezzled, stolen, illegally transferred, and withheld from tax authorities.[13] You will find more on this topic in Chapter 12.

By this time, you may be asking: Is there no limit to the reach of criminological inquiry? There is not, since every human activity is capable of abusive action, thus requiring criminological scrutiny. Not even the ocean is the limit. It is the oceans, covering nearly three quarters of the world's surface, which make life on earth possible. Yet the oceans are being threatened by many types of criminality, of which the most deadly is pollution. In earlier editions of this book we had discussed the case of the supertanker *Exxon Valdez*, which negligently had ruptured her hull in Alaska waters, spilling eleven million gallons of crude oil. This caused the greatest environmental disaster North America had known. At the time we had expressed our hope that this criminally caused disaster would lead to greater efforts to prevent recurrences. But no. Oil spill disasters that should have been prevented have occurred with heightening regularity, off the coasts of China, South Africa, the Galapagos Islands, the United States, American Samoa, Denmark, Thailand, Brazil, Finland, Germany, the Netherlands, and Vietnam, among others.[14] This criminality, destroying the environment, is called "ecocide." There is yet another task for criminologists.

As far as the reach of criminology is concerned, do not be deceived by the media and their symbiotic relationship with legislatures. Today's focus of the media on a given crime problem is no indication of the extent of criminology's tasks. In the 1960s the emphasis was on juvenile delinquency; in the 1970s attention turned to street crime in general and drugs, in particular, which led, in the 1980s, to a focus on prison overcrowding, on the one hand, and target hardening, on the other. Then, in the 1990s, more attention was being paid to foreign influences on our crime rates, in the wake of globalization. Domestic (school shootings) and foreign violence along with terrorism dictated the market for ideas, along with the competing attention on computer, white collar, and corporate criminality. Today, well into the first decade

A gaping hole in the mountain is all that is left of Buddhism's most prized religious symbols: the colossal Buddhas of Afghanistan—purposefully destroyed by Taliban artillery.

Window to the World

Russians and Americans Share a Crime Problem

Despite many differences, Americans and Russians had one thing in common: freedom from terrorism at home. This commonality was shattered for Americans on February 26, 1993, when a bomb tore a huge hole in the World Trade Center (WTC) in New York City, killing 6 people. Russians were awakened to the reality of terrorism on August 31, 1999, when a bomb exploded at Moscow's upscale Manezh shopping center near the Kremlin, killing 1 person and injuring 40. So, once again, Americans and Russians have something in common: domestic terrorism and the fear that goes with it. In America, the WTC terrorist attack was followed by the Oklahoma City bombing, on April 19, 1995, which killed 168 people, and the Olympic Park bomb explosion in Atlanta, Georgia, on July 30, 1996, which killed 1 person and injured many. And then came the shock of the 911 disaster that took almost 3,000 lives. Of course, Americans have been victimized by terrorist attacks outside the country, including, among many others:

- The destruction of Pan Am flight 103 over Lockerbie, Scotland, in 1988 (270 dead).
- The destruction of a U.S. military residence in Dhahran, Saudi Arabia, in 1996 (19 dead, many injured).
- The destruction of the U.S. embassies in Nairobi, Kenya, and Dar-es-Salaam, Tanzania, in 1998 (224 dead, 4,300 injured).

Russians suffered five brutal terrorist attacks within the span of 3 weeks:

1. August 31, 1999. Manezh Shopping Center, near the Kremlin, Moscow (1 killed, 40 injured).
2. September 4, 1999. Dagestan, Russia (64 killed).
3. September 9, 1999. Moscow apartment building (94 killed).
4. September 13, 1999. Moscow apartment building (118 killed).
5. September 16, 1999. Volgodansk, Russia, apartment building (18 killed).

There was a time when terrorism could be categorized in terms of political versus profit motive, foreign versus domestic, and so on. These lines have become blurred, and the profit motive seems to have disappeared. While there may still be a domestic form of terrorism, such as the terrorism perpetrated by fanatics and cultlike private militias who see the government as an enemy, most terrorism appears to have an international base and is directed against people and their governments. In particular, Islamic fanatic fundamentalist terrorists are increasingly identified with attacks against U.S. and Russian targets.

There also was a time when terrorists enjoyed the support, both

Rescue workers search for survivors at the collapsed towers of the World Trade Center after September 11, 2001.

---

of the twenty-first century, it is clear that these problems demand more of criminology than it is capable of delivering as yet. The principal crime problems are totally globalized. Criminology has to become equally globalized.

Seemingly we have neglected street crimes and delinquency in this survey of the reach of criminology. These topics are, and will remain, a major focus of criminologists—in competition with all the other forms of criminality to which we have alluded. Now that you are acquainted with the reach, or expanse, of criminology, we next introduce you to what this discipline is all about.

WHAT IS CRIMINOLOGY?

In the Middle Ages human learning was commonly divided into four areas: law, medicine, theology, and philosophy. Universities typically had four faculties, one for each of these fields. Imagine a young person in the year 1392—100 years before Columbus came ashore in America—knocking at the portal of a great university with the request: "I would like to study criminology. Where do I sign up?" A stare of disbelief would have greeted the student, because the word had not yet been coined. Cautiously the student financial and material, of some foreign governments. That support no longer exists. Very few countries can be counted among the supporters of current terrorist groups.

In 1993—before most of the terrorist events discussed here took place—a meeting of over 200 counterterrorism experts and Pentagon officials concluded "that the proliferation of ethnic and regional conflicts will spawn new radical movements, leading inevitably to new terrorism." "We're going to see a global increase in anarchy," said one Defense Department analyst. Some at the meeting worried about what they term "mass terrorism," like that spawned by ethnic conflicts. Others were more concerned about what they are calling "single-issue" terrorism, attacks by radicals who share no ideology, only the hatred for a particular enemy.(1)

Americans have been very active in bringing terrorists to justice. The WTC and Oklahoma City terrorists have been convicted. One Pan Am 103 terrorist has been convicted in the Netherlands, and air-strike retaliation has taken place against the embassy terrorist groups in Africa. Russian law enforcement authorities have tentatively identified some Chechen terrorists, although no arrests have been made yet. But Russia has conducted retaliatory air strikes against Chechen targets.

Terrorism against Russians at home. Explosion destroys buildings in Moscow, September 9, 1999.

Source

Douglas Waller, "Counterterrorism: Victim of Success?" *Newsweek,* July 5, 1993, pp. 22–23.

Questions for Discussion

1. International terrorism is a criminal activity that can involve an almost limitless number of specific crimes, individuals, and countries. How would you devise a strategy to combat it at the national and international levels?

2. How would you go about studying trends in terrorism and the impact of terrorist attacks on society and the economy?

Window to the World

---

would explain: "Well, I'm interested in what crime is, and how the law deals with criminals." The university official might smile and say: "The right place for you to go is the law faculty. They will teach you everything there is to know about the law."

The student might feel discouraged. "That's a lot more than I want to know about the law. I really don't care about inheritance laws and the law of contracts. I just want to study all about crime and criminality. For example, why are certain actions considered wrong or evil in the first place, and. . . ." The official would interrupt: "Then you must go to the faculty of theology. They know all there is to know about good and evil, heaven and hell." The student might persist. "But could they teach me what it is about the human body and mind that could cause some people and not others to commit crime?" "Oh, I see," the official would say. "You really should study medicine." "But, sir, medicine probably is only part of what I need to know, and really only part of medicine seems relevant. I want to know all there is to know about. . . ." And then would come the official's last attempt to steer the student in the right direction: "Go and study philosophy. They'll teach you all there is to know!"

For centuries, all the knowledge the universities recognized continued to be taught in these four faculties. It was not until the eighteenth and nineteenth centuries that the natural and social sciences became full-fledged disciplines. In fact, the science of criminology has been known as such for only a little more than a century.

In 1885 the Italian law professor Raffaele Garofalo coined the term "criminology" (in Italian, *criminologia*).[15] The French anthropologist Paul Topinard used it for the first time in French (*criminologie*) in 1887.[16] "Criminology" aptly described and encompassed the scientific concern with the phenomenon of crime. The term immediately gained acceptance all over the world, and criminology became a subject taught at universities. Unlike their predecessors in 1392—or even in 1892—today's entering students will find that teaching and learning are distributed among 20 or 30 disciplines and departments. And criminology or criminal justice is likely to be one of them.

Criminology is a science, an empirical science. More particularly, it is one of the social, or behavioral, sciences. It has been defined in various ways by its scholars. The definition provided in 1934 by Edwin H. Sutherland, one of the founding scholars of American criminology, is widely accepted:

> Criminology is the body of knowledge regarding crime as a social phenomenon. It includes within its scope the process of making laws, of breaking laws, and of reacting toward the breaking of laws. . . . The objective of criminology is the development of a body of general and verified principles and of other types of knowledge regarding this process of law, crime, and treatment or prevention.[17]

This definition suggests that the field of criminology is narrowly focused on crime, yet broad in scope. By stating as the objective of criminology the "development of a body of general and verified principles," Sutherland mandates that criminologists, like all other scientists, collect information for study and analysis in accordance with the research methods of modern science. As we shall see in Chapter 3, it was in the eighteenth century that serious investigations into criminal behavior were first conducted. The investigators, however, were not engaged in empirical research, although they based their conclusions on factual information. It was only in the nineteenth century that criminologists began to systematically gather facts about crime and criminals and evaluate their data in a scientific manner.

Among the first researchers to analyze empirical data (facts, statistics, and other observable information) in a search for the causes of crime was Cesare Lombroso (1835–1909) of Italy (Chapter 3). His biologically oriented theories influenced American criminology at the turn of the twentieth century. At that time the causes of crime were thought to rest within the individual: Criminal behavior was attributed to feeblemindedness and "moral insanity." From then on, psychologists and psychiatrists played an important role in the study of crime and criminals.

By the 1920s other scholars attributed the cause of crime to the influx of immigrants and their alien behaviors. The search then moved on to cultural and social interpretations. Crime was explained not only in terms of the offender but also in terms of social, political, and economic problems.

In increasing numbers, sociologists, political scientists, legal scholars, and economists have entered the arena of criminology. Architects too have joined the ranks of criminologists in an effort to design housing units that will be relatively free from crime. Engineers are working to design cars that are virtually theft-proof. Pharmacologists play a role in alleviating the problem of drug addiction. Satellites put into space by astrophysicists can help control the drug trade. Specialists in public administration work to improve the functioning of the criminal justice system. Educators have been enlisted to

> **:// Crime Surfing**
>
> http://www.ussc.gov/money law/monisum.htm
>
> One of the components of Sutherland's definition of criminology focuses on the making of laws. For example, Congress created the offense of money laundering in 1986. How did Congress define this crime?

prepare children for a life as free from delinquency as possible. Economists and social workers are needed to help break the cycle of poverty and crime. Biologists and endocrinologists have expanded our understanding of the relationship between biology and deviant behavior. Clearly, criminology is a discipline composed of the accumulated knowledge of many other disciplines. Criminologists acknowledge their indebtedness to all contributing disciplines, but they consider theirs a separate science.

In explaining what is meant by Sutherland's definition—"making laws," "breaking laws," and "reacting toward the breaking of laws"— we will use a contemporary as well as a historical perspective on these processes, and a global as well as a local focus.

THE MAKING OF LAWS

Conjure up a picture of a crowded supermarket just after working hours when most people are eager to get home after a busy day. The checkout counters have long lines of carts overflowing with groceries. One counter—an express line—takes 10 items only. You have 15, but you get in line anyway. People behind you in the line stare. Your behavior is not acceptable. You are a nonconformist, a deviant.

Deviance

Criminologists use the term **deviance** to describe behavior that violates **social norms**, including laws. The customary ways of doing everyday things (like not exceeding the posted limit of items at supermarket express lines) are governed by norms other than laws. More serious deviant behavior, like taking someone else's property, is governed by laws. Criminologists are interested in all social norms and in how society reacts to success or failure of compliance.[18] They are interested in what society does when customary ways of doing things no longer prove effective in controlling conduct perceived as undesirable. New Yorkers concerned over the problem of dog droppings provide an example.

Disciplined city dwellers had always observed the custom of curbing their dogs. Street signs warned them to do this. But as more and more dog owners failed to comply, New Yorkers decided that the cleanliness of the sidewalks was an important issue. Laws were enacted making it an offense not to clean up after one's dog. In Beijing, China, and Reykjavik, Iceland, dogs have been severely restricted or banned from the city altogether.

The difference between crime and other forms of deviance is subject to constant change and may vary from one state or country to another and from one time to another. What yesterday was only distasteful or morally repugnant may today be illegal. Criminologists are therefore interested in all norms that regulate conduct. Making something that is distasteful into a crime may be counterproductive and detrimental to the social order. If everything deviant (inconsistent with the majority's norms) were to be made criminal, society would become very rigid. The more rigid a society, the more that behavior defined as violating social norms is prohibited by law.

Jack D. Douglas and Frances C. Waksler have presented the continuum of deviance as a funnel (Figure 1.2). This funnel consists of definitions ranging from the broadest (a "feeling that something is vaguely wrong, strange, peculiar") to the narrowest (a "judgment that something is absolutely evil"). Somewhere between these two extremes, deviant behavior becomes criminal behavior. The criminologist's interest in understanding the process begins at the earliest point—when a behavior is first labeled deviant.[19]

Although criminologists are interested in all deviant behavior—even that of no interest to the law—their primary interest is in criminal behavior, that which violates the law.

The Concept of Crime

A **crime** is any human conduct that violates a criminal law and is subject to punishment. What leads a society to designate some deviant behavior as a crime and leave other wrongs to be settled by private or civil remedies? For centuries, natural-law philosophers, believing in the universal rightness and wrongness of certain human behavior, held the view that some forms of behavior are innately criminal and that

FIGURE 1.2 The funnel of deviance.

Most inclusive

I. Feeling that something is vaguely wrong, strange, peculiar
II. Feelings of dislike, repugnance
III. Feeling that something violates values or rules
IV. Feeling that something violates moral values or moral rules
V. Judgment that something violates values or rules
VI. Judgment that something violates moral values or moral rules
VII. Judgment that something violates morally legitimate misdemeanor laws
VIII. Judgment that something violates morally legitimate felony laws
IX. Judgment that something violates moral human nature
X. Judgment that something is absolutely evil

Least inclusive

Source: Adapted from Jack D. Douglas and Francis C. Waksler, *The Sociology of Deviance* (Boston: Little, Brown, 1980), p. 11.

all societies condemn them equally. Homicide and theft were thought to be among these.

This notion is no longer supported. Raffaele Garofalo, who gave our discipline its name, defended the concept of natural crime, by which he meant behavior that offends basic moral sentiments, such as respect for the property of others and revulsion against infliction of suffering. Nevertheless, he admitted that although we might think such crimes as murder and robbery would be recognized by all existing legal systems, "a slight investigation seems to dispel this idea."[20]

Garofalo was right. The earliest codes, including the Babylonian Code of Hammurabi (about 1750 B.C.) and the Roman Law of the Twelve Tables (451–450 B.C.), do not list homicide or ordinary theft as crimes. Problems like these were settled without resorting to punishment. But all early societies imposed punishment for acts detrimental to their own existence: treason. Other crimes depended on socioeconomic needs (destroying a bridge was a crime among the Incas; stealing a beehive was a crime among the ancient Germanic tribes; stealing a horse or a blanket was a crime among American Plains Indians).

The question arises: Who in a society decides—and when and under what circumstances—which acts that are already considered deviant in that society should be elevated to the level of gross deviance or crime, subject to punishment?

The Consensus and Conflict Views of Law and Crime

In the traditional interpretation of the historical development of legal systems, and of criminal justice in particular, lawmaking is an accommodation of interests in a society, whether that society is composed of equals (as in a democracy) or of rulers and ruled (as in absolute monarchies), so as to produce a system of law and enforcement to which everybody basically subscribes. This is the **consensus model.** According to this view, certain acts are deemed so threatening to the society's survival that they are designated crimes. If the vast majority of a group shares this view, we can say the group has acted by consensus.

The model assumes that members of a society by and large agree on what is right and wrong, and that codification of social values be-

> **Did You Know?**
> . . . that in the early days of the common law, judges made the laws? Legislatures (parliament) took over lawmaking only about three centuries ago.

The Code of Hammurabi, king of ancient Babylonia, is the oldest complete legal code in existence (approximately 1750 B.C.). The 8.2-foot carving, found in Iraq in 1902, is now on display in the Louvre in Paris. The only exact replica is at the United Nations building in New York.

comes law, with a mechanism of control which settles disputes that arise when some individuals stray too far from what is considered acceptable behavior. In the words of the famous French sociologist Émile Durkheim, "We can . . . say that an act is criminal when it offends strong and defined states of the collective conscience."[21] Consensus theorists view society as a stable entity in which laws are created for the general good. Laws function to reconcile and to harmonize most of the interests that most of us accept, with the least amount of sacrifice.

Some criminologists view the making of laws in a society from a different theoretical perspective. In their interpretation, known as the **conflict model**, the criminal law expresses the values of the ruling class in a society, and the criminal justice system is a means of controlling the classes that have no power. Conflict theorists claim that a struggle for power is a far more basic feature of human existence than is consensus. It is through power struggles that various interest groups manage to control lawmaking and law enforcement. Accordingly, the appropriate object of criminological investigation is not the violation of laws but the conflicts within society.

Traditional historians of crime and criminal justice do not deny that throughout history there have been conflicts that needed resolution. Traditionalists claim that differences have been resolved by consensus, while conflict theorists claim that the dominant group has ended the conflicts by imposing its will. This difference in perspective marks one of the major criminological debates today, as we shall see in Chapter 8. It also permeates criminological discussion of who breaks the criminal laws and why.

THE BREAKING OF LAWS

Sutherland's definition of criminology includes within its scope investigating and explaining the process of breaking laws. This may seem simple if viewed from a purely legal perspective. A prosecutor is not interested in the fact that hundreds of people are walking on Main Street. But if one of those hundreds grabs a woman's purse and runs away with it, the prosecutor is interested, provided the police have brought the incident to the prosecutor's attention. What alerts the prosecutor is the fact that a law has been broken, that one of those hundreds of people on Main Street has turned from a law-abiding citizen into a lawbreaker. This event, if detected, sets in motion a legal process that ultimately will determine whether someone is indeed a lawbreaker.

Sutherland, in saying that criminologists have to study the process of law-breaking, had much more in mind than determining whether or not someone has violated the criminal law. He was referring to the process of breaking laws. That process encompasses a series of events, perhaps starting at birth or even earlier, which results in the commission of crime by some individuals and not by others.

Of Immediate Concern

Vipers in the Desert

Strange things were happening in the woods. Last November agent Jose Wall of the Bureau of Alcohol, Tobacco and Firearms in Phoenix got disturbing information from people who had been through nearby Tonto National Forest. A deer hunter said he had been stopped by a group of men dressed in camouflage and armed with guns. They warned him to turn back, saying they were "security" and hinting they were with the government. The hunter didn't believe them. But something about their eyes, not to mention their weapons made him think arguing would be imprudent. He ran into other people forced to retreat by the armed men—a Boy Scout troop. After the hunter's call, agent Wall drove out to Tonto. Near an abandoned mine, he found a crater almost big enough to swallow a car. It was recent. Someone had been using powerful explosives (1)

In July 1996, Alcohol, Tobacco and Firearms agents uncovered a plot by members of "Team Viper" to blow up seven buildings in Phoenix, Arizona, using the same mixture of chemicals used in the Oklahoma City bombing. (1) The agents found an arsenal of two machine guns, six rifles, two pistols, grenades, fuses, blasting caps, and 56 boxes stuffed with 11,463 rounds of ammunition, as well as hundreds of pounds of the chemicals ammonium nitrate and nitromethane, which can be mixed to make a bomb. (1) Group members were charged in federal court for offenses including illegal possession of a machine gun and conspiracy to teach bombing techniques to provoke civil disorder. (2) The Vipers are white, largely blue collar, with no significant criminal records, and stuck in dead-end low-paying jobs. They include two janitors, a used-furniture salesman, a telephone company billing representative, an air conditioner repairman, a doughnut baker, an engineer, and a bouncer at a local topless bar. The Vipers reflect the demographics of the antigovernment paramilitary movement. (2) Indeed, in some respects the Vipers are seemingly like many other Americans; in other respects, however, they are extremely different. One member of the group, Dean Pleasant, used to paint grenades with camouflage designs and leave them on the lawn to dry. His roommate, Randy Nelson, slept each night below a Browning machine gun he had mounted over his bed, to which he had given the name "Shirley." (2)

FBI agent Bruce Gebhardt, agent in charge of the Phoenix office, cautioned about the potential danger of a group such as the Vipers. "A lot of these individuals are copycats and wannabes. They hear the rhetoric of one and repeat it to the other. Are they really expressing their First Amendment rights? There's a line here we have to watch very closely." (1)

What may be most alarming about the Vipers is their obsession with guns that drew them together. This obsession is also driving some of them to devise schemes aimed at the disruption, if not the destruction, of a government based on the rule of law and the right to bear arms.

Sources

1. Christopher John Farley, "A Nest of Vipers," *Time*, July 15, 1996, pp. 24–25.
2. James Brooke, "Volatile Mix in Viper Militia: Hatred plus a Love for Guns," *New York Times*, July 5, 1996, p. 1.

Questions for Discussion

1. What is it that makes members of groups like the Vipers feel they have a legitimate organization and a legitimate cause?
2. Where should government draw the limit on the legal possession of armament: Super rifles? Machine guns? Mortars? Heavy artillery? Tanks? Submarines?

Let us analyze the following rather typical scenario: In the maximum-security unit of a Midwestern penitentiary is an inmate we will call Jeff. He is one of three robbers who held up a check-cashing establishment. During the robbery, another of the robbers killed the clerk. Jeff has been sentenced to life imprisonment.

Born in an inner-city ghetto, Jeff was the third child of an unwed mother. He had a succession of temporary "fathers." By age 12 he had run away from home for the first time, only to be brought back to his mother, who really did not care much whether he returned or not. He rarely went to school because, he said, "all the guys were bigger." At age 16, after failing two grades, Jeff dropped out of school completely and hung around the streets of his deteriorated, crime-ridden neighborhood. He had no job. He had no reason to go home, since usually no one was there.

One night he was beaten up by members of a local gang. He joined a rival gang for protection and soon began to feel proud of his membership in one of the toughest gangs in the neighborhood. Caught on one occasion tampering with parking meters and on another trying to steal a car CD player, he was sentenced to two months in a county correctional institution for boys. By the age of 18 he had moved from petty theft to armed robbery.

Many people reading the story of Jeff would conclude that he deserves what is coming to him and that his fate should serve as a warning to others. Other people would say that with his background, Jeff did not have a chance. Some may even marvel at Jeff's ability to survive at all in a very tough world.

To the criminologist, popular interpretations of Jeff's story do not explain the process of breaking laws in Sutherland's terms. Nor do these interpretations explain why people in general break a certain law. Sutherland demanded scientific rigor in researching and explaining the process of breaking laws. As we will see later in the book (Parts II and III), scientists have thoroughly explored Jeff's story and the stories of other lawbreakers. They ask: Why are some people prone to commit crime and others are not? There is no agreement on the answer as yet. Researchers have approached the question from different perspectives. Some have examined delinquents (juvenile offenders) and criminals from a biological perspective in order to determine whether some human beings are constitutionally more prone to yield to opportunities to commit criminal acts. Are genes to blame? Hormones? Diet? Others have explored the role played by moral development and personality. Is there a criminal personality? (These questions are discussed in Chapter 4.)

Most contemporary criminologists look to such factors as economic and social conditions, which can produce strain among social groups and lead to law-breaking (Chapter 5). Others point to subcultures committed to violent or illegal activities (Chapter 6). Yet another argument is that the motivation to commit crime is simply part of human nature. So some criminologists examine the ability of social groups and institutions to make their rules effective (Chapter 7).

The findings of other scholars tend to show that law-breaking depends less on what the offender does than on what society, including the criminal justice system, does to the offender (Chapter 8). This is the perspective of the labeling, conflict, and radical theorists, who have had great influence on criminological thinking since the 1970s.

Scholars have also researched the question of why people who are inclined to break laws engage in particular acts at particular times. They have demonstrated that opportunity plays a great role in the decision to commit a crime. Opportunities are suitable targets inadequately protected. In these circumstances, all that is required for a crime to be committed is a person motivated to offend. These claims are made by criminologists who explain crime in terms of two perspectives: routine activities and rational choice (Chapter 9).

SOCIETY'S REACTION TO THE BREAKING OF LAWS

Criminologists' interest in understanding the process of breaking a law (or any other social norm) is tied to understanding society's reaction to deviance. The study of reactions to law-breaking demonstrates that society has always tried to control or prevent norm breaking.

In the Middle Ages, the wayfarer entering a city had to pass the gallows, on which the bodies of criminals swung in the wind. Wayfarers had to enter through gates in thick walls, and the drawbridges were lowered only during the daylight hours; at nightfall the gates were closed. In front of the town hall, stocks and pillory warned dishonest vendors and pickpockets. Times have changed, but perhaps less than we think. Today penitentiaries and jails dot the countryside. Teams of work-release convicts work along highways under guard. Signs proclaim "Drug-Free School Zone," and decals on doors announce "Neighborhood Crime Watch." Police patrol cars are as visible as they are audible.

These overt signs of concern about crime provide us with only a surface view of the apparatus society has created to deal with law-breaking; they tell us little of the research and policy making that have gone into the creation of the apparatus. Criminologists have done much of the research on society's reaction to the breaking of laws, and the results have influenced policy making and legislation aimed at

---

:// **Crime Surfing**

http://www.crime.about.com/newsissues/crime/mpchat.htm

Would you like to join a chat room for ongoing discussions of current crime and justice issues?

crime control. The research has also revealed that society's reaction to law-breaking has often been irrational, arbitrary, emotional, politically motivated, and counterproductive.

Research on society's reaction to the breaking of laws is more recent than research on the causes of crime. It is also more controversial. For some criminologists, the function of their research is to assist government in the prevention or repression of crime. Others insist that such a use of science only supports existing power structures that may be corrupt. The position of most criminologists is somewhere in between. Researchers often discover inhumane and arbitrary practices and provide the database and the ideas for a humane, effective, and efficient **criminal justice system.**

Criminology and the Criminal Justice System

The term "criminal justice system" is relatively new. It became popular only in 1967, with the publication of the report of the President's Commission on Law Enforcement and Administration of Justice, *The Challenge of Crime in a Free Society*. The discovery that various ways of dealing with law-breaking form a system was itself the result of criminological research. Research into the functioning of the system and its component parts, as well as into the work of functionaries within the system, has provided many insights over the last few decades.

Scientists who study the criminal justice system are frequently referred to as "criminal justice specialists." This term suggests a separation between criminology and criminal justice. In fact, the two fields are closely interwoven. Scholars of both disciplines use the same scientific research methods. They have received the same rigorous education, and they pursue the same goals. Both fields rely on the cooperation of many other disciplines, including sociology, psychology, political science, law, economics, management, and education. Their origins, however, do differ. Criminology has its roots in European scholarship, though it has undergone refinements, largely under the influence of American sociology. Criminal justice is a recent American innovation.

The two fields are also distinguished by a difference in focus. Criminology generally focuses on scientific studies of crime and criminality, whereas criminal justice focuses on scientific studies of decision-making processes, operations, and such justice-related concerns as the efficiency of police, courts, and corrections systems; the just treatment of offenders; the needs of victims; and the effects of changes in sentencing philosophy.

The United States has well over 50 criminal justice systems—those of the 50 states and of the federal government, the District of Columbia, Puerto Rico, Guam, the U.S. Virgin Islands, American Samoa, the Commonwealth of the Northern Mariana Islands, Palau, and the military. They are very similar: All are based on constitutional principles and on the heritage of the common law. All were designed to cope with the problem of crime within their territories, on the assumption that crime is basically a local event calling for local response. Crimes that have an interstate or international aspect are under the jurisdiction of federal authorities, and such offenses are prosecuted under the federal criminal code.

The Global Approach to the Breaking of Laws

Until fairly recently there was rarely any need to cooperate with foreign governments, because crime had few international connections. This situation has changed drastically: Crime, like life itself, has become globalized, and responses to law-breaking have inevitably extended beyond local and national borders. In the first three and a half decades after World War II, from 1945 until the late 1970s, the countries of the world gradually became more interdependent. Commercial relations among countries increased. The jet age brought a huge increase in

---

:// Crime Surfing

http://www.albany.edu/sourcebook

If you want to know more about the criminal justice system, its characteristics, its function, its cost, and its impact, go to the "Sourcebook of Criminal Justice Statistics."

In Placentia, California residents clamor for protection of children from convicted and released child molesters. Public protests have led to a flood of local laws regarding the identification of where these ex-offenders are residing.

international travel and transport. Satellite communications facilitated intense and continuous public and private relationships. The Internet added the final touch to globalization.

Beginning in the 1980s, the internationalization of national economies accelerated sharply, and with the collapse of Marxism in Eastern Europe in the 1990s, a global economy is being created. These developments, which turned the world into what has been called a "global village," have also had considerable negative consequences. As everything else in life became globalized, so did crime. Transnational crimes, with which we began this chapter, suddenly boomed. Then there are the truly international crimes—those that are proscribed by international law—such as crimes against the peace and security of mankind, genocide, and war crimes. But even many apparently purely local crimes, whether local drug crime or handgun violence, now have international dimensions. In view of the rapid globalization of crime, we devote an entire chapter (Chapter 14) to the international dimensions of criminology. In addition, a "Window to the World" box in each chapter explores the international implications of various topics.

RESEARCH INFORMS POLICY

Skeptics often ask: With so many criminologists at work in the United States, and so many studies conducted over the last half century, why do we have so much crime, why is some of it increasing, and why do new forms of crime emerge constantly? There are several answers. Crime rates go up and down. Through the 1990s and recently, crime has actually been decreasing. The popular perception that the crime problem is increasing rests on a fear of crime that is fueled by media portrayals. Obviously, the various elements of the mass media are very competitive, and such competitiveness determines the focus on crime. Sensational reports often sell newspapers and TV programs. Politicians, in turn, seek security in office by catering to public perceptions of crime, rather than to its reality. They therefore propose and enact measures that respond to popular demands and that often are more symbolic than result-oriented. At the moment, this means ever harsher and more punitive measures for dealing with the crime problem.

Few criminologists believe that at present enough research exists to justify such an approach. In fact, some criminological research demonstrates the futility of escalating punishments and often points to measures of quite a different nature as more promising, more humane, and more cost-beneficial. So why do criminologists not make themselves heard? The answer is that criminologists are social scientists, not politicians. Criminologists are not voted into Congress or to the presidency or a governorship. Yet criminologists have served on virtually every federal and state commission dealing with problems of crime or criminal justice. But just as the Pentagon cannot declare war, criminologists cannot dictate national or state crime-control policies. They can, however, provide pertinent research findings that inform national policy making.[22] Recently, for example, the attorney general of the United States asked criminologists to formulate policy recommendations based on their research findings in areas such as delinquency prevention, drug control, global crime, youth violence, and violence against women.[23] In subsequent chapters that deal with the causes of crime, we continue this discussion under the heading "Theory Informs Policy."

REVIEW

Very little happens on earth that does not concern criminology. Yet criminology as a science is only a century old. Edwin H. Sutherland provided the most widely accepted definition: "The body of knowledge regarding crime as a social phenomenon. It includes within its scope the process of making laws, of breaking laws, and of reacting toward the breaking of laws."

Criminologists study behavior that violates all social norms, including laws. They distinguish between two conflicting views of the history of criminal law: the consensus view, which regards lawmaking as the result of communal agreement about what is to be prohibited, and the conflict view, according to which laws are imposed by those with power over those without power.

The breaking of laws (the subject to which much of this book is devoted) is not merely a formal act that may lead to arrest and prosecution, but an intricate process by which some people violate some laws under some circumstances. Many disciplines contribute to understanding the process of breaking laws or other norms, but as yet there is no consensus on why people become criminals. Society has always reacted to law-breaking, although the scientific study of law-breaking is of very recent origin. Today criminologists analyze the methods and procedures society uses in reacting to crime; they evaluate the success or failure of such methods; and on the basis of their research, they propose more effective and humane ways of controlling crime.

Criminologists have discovered that the various agencies society has created to deal with law-breaking constitute a system that, like any other system, can be made more efficient. Research on the system depends on the availability of a variety of data, especially statistics. The gathering and analysis of statistics on crime and criminal justice are among the primary tasks of criminologists. The effectiveness of their work depends on reliable data.

The province of criminology today is the entire world: Every aspect of life, including crime, has become increasingly globalized in recent years as a result of both rapid advances in technology and economic integration.

Criminology is a politically sensitive discipline. Its findings inform public policy. While criminologists cannot dictate what the branches of government—the legislative, the judicial, and the executive—should do about crime, their research findings are being used increasingly in making governmental decisions.

CRIMINOLOGY & PUBLIC POLICY

Crime waves always carry with them calls for more law enforcement authority. What happened on September 11, 2001, was, among other things, a crime wave—that one day caused the number of homicides in America in 2001 to be 20 percent higher than the year before. It is no surprise, then, that even before the fires in the rubble that was the World Trade Center burned themselves out, some politicians were calling for broader powers for law enforcement and greater restrictions on citizens, all in the effort to fight this particular crime wave.

That is not a bad thing. Law enforcement authority naturally varies with the nature and size of the crime problems police must combat. A glance at the recent history of criminal procedure shows as much. Most legal restrictions on policing date from the criminal procedure revolution of the 1960s, which itself can be seen as a consequence of the low-crime 1950s. Higher crime rates led to cutbacks in those legal protections in the 1970s and 1980s, just as lower crime rates have led to some expansion in the past few years. In short, Fourth and Fifth Amendment rights have varied with crime before, and they will probably do so in the future, as they must if the law is to reflect a sensible balance between the social need for order and individuals' desire for privacy and liberty. The terrorist attacks on New York and Washington raised the demands on law enforcement. Those increased demands have already led to some increases in law enforcers' legal authority, and that trend will—and probably should—continue, at least for a while. (Source: William J. Stuntz, "Local Policing after Terror," *Yale Law Journal*, **111** (2002): 2137.)

Questions for Discussion Sutherland's broad definition of criminology (see p. 3) includes a critical examination of the criminal justice response to crimes. Following the spirit of his definition, how should we fashion and refashion our criminal justice system in response to the threat of terrorism in the United States? Should we increasingly delegate the responsibility for investigating and combating terrorism to local law enforcement agencies? How then do we control the flow of intelligence data?

One of the most significant questions concerns the extent to which our response to 9/11 will jeopardize the constitutional rights of U.S. citizens. How much freedom are you willing to give up in the name of law enforcement?

YOU BE THE CRIMINOLOGIST

How would you teach the ideal course on criminology? (Don't answer until you have completed the course!)

KEY TERMS

The numbers next to the terms refer to the pages on which the terms are defined.

conflict model (15)
consensus model (14)
crime (13)
criminal justice system (18)
criminologist (12)
criminology (12)
deviance (13)
social norms (13)

CHAPTER 2 Counting Crime and Measuring Criminal Behavior

The Ingredients of Crime
  The Seven Basic Requirements
  The Act Requirement
  The Legality Requirement
  The Harm Requirement
  The Causation Requirement
  Mens Rea: The "Guilty Mind" Requirement
  The Concurrence Requirement
  The Punishment Requirement

The Defenses

Typologies of Crime

Measuring Crime
  Methods of Collecting Data
  Ethics and the Researcher

The Nature and Extent of Crime
  Police Statistics
  Victimization Surveys
  Self-Report Surveys

Measuring Characteristics of Crime
  Crime Trends
  Locations and Times of Criminal Acts
  Severity of Crime

Measuring Characteristics of Criminals
  Age and Crime
  Gender and Crime
  Social Class and Crime
  Race and Crime

REVIEW

CRIMINOLOGY & PUBLIC POLICY

YOU BE THE CRIMINOLOGIST

KEY TERMS

Boxes
  From the Pages of The New York Times: Can Politics Influence Crime Data?
  Of Immediate Concern: Why Does Crime Drop?
  Window to the World: Measuring World Crime

Special Features
  Did You Know?
  Crime Surfing

KEY TERMS

aging-out phenomenon
birth cohort
case study
crimes against property
crimes against the person
criminal careers
data
experiment
felonies
field experiment
hypothesis
Index crimes
longitudinal studies
mens rea
misdemeanors
nonparticipant observation
participant observation
population
primary data
random sample
sample
secondary data
self-report surveys
strict liability
survey
theory
torts
variables
victimization surveys
violations

Many large police departments conduct weekly crime control strategy sessions or COMPSTAT (Computerized Statistics) meetings to increase the flow of information between police executives and the commanders of operational units

In one of many versions of Aesop's fable about the three blind men and the elephant, a circus comes to town, and the residents of a home for the blind are invited to "experience" an elephant. When one blind man is led to the elephant, he touches one of its legs. He feels its size and shape. Another man happens to touch the tail, and still another feels the trunk. Back at their residence they argue about the nature of the beast. Says the first man, "An elephant is obviously like the trunk of a tree." "No," says the second, "it's like a rope." "You're both wrong," says the third. "An elephant is like a big snake." All three are partly right, for each has described the part of the animal he has touched.

Assessment of the nature and extent of crime often suffers from the same shortcomings as the three blind men's assessments of the elephant. Researcher A may make assessments on the basis of arrest records. Researcher B may rely on conviction rates to describe crime. Researcher C may use the number of convicts serving prison sentences. None of the researchers, however, may be in a position to assess the full nature and extent of crime; each is limited by the kinds of data he or she uses.

Questions about how crime is measured and what those measurements reveal about the nature and extent of crime are among the most important issues in contemporary criminology. Researchers, theorists, and practitioners need information in order to explain and prevent crime and to operate agencies that deal with the crime problem. We begin this chapter with an explanation of the ingredients that all crimes share. We then look at the objectives and methods of collecting information on specific types of crimes. Next, we will consider the limitations of the information sources criminologists most frequently use to estimate the nature and extent of crime in the United States. We then explore measurement of the characteristics of crimes and criminals.

THE INGREDIENTS OF CRIME

Before we begin to measure specific crimes, we will examine the part of criminal law that deals with the common legal ingredients, or elements, found in all crimes. With few exceptions, if any one of these elements is not present, no crime has been committed. All the defenses available to a person charged with a crime allege that at least one of these elements is not present.

The Seven Basic Requirements

The American criminal law scholar Jerome Hall has developed the theory that a human event, in order to qualify as a crime, must meet seven basic requirements:[1]

1. The act requirement
2. The legality requirement
3. The harm requirement
4. The causation requirement
5. The mens rea requirement
6. The concurrence requirement
7. The punishment requirement[2]

The Act Requirement

Law scholars have long agreed that one fundamental ingredient of every crime is a human act. In this context, what is an "act"? Suppose a sleepwalker, in a trance, grabs a stone and hurls it at a passerby, with lethal consequences. The law does not consider this event to be an act; before any human behavior can qualify as an act, there must be a conscious interaction between mind and body, a physical movement that results from the determination or effort of the actor. Thus a reflex or convulsion, a bodily movement that occurs during unconsciousness or sleep, conduct that occurs during hypnosis or results from hypnotic suggestion, or a bodily movement that is not determined by the actor, as when somebody is pushed by another person, are behaviors that are not considered voluntary acts.[3] It is only when choices are overpoweringly influenced by forces beyond our control that the law will consider behavior irrational and beyond its reach.

Act versus Status The criminal law, in principle, does not penalize anyone for a status or condition. Suppose the law made it a crime to be more than 6 feet tall or to have red hair. Or suppose the law made it a crime to be a member of the family of an army deserter or to be of a given religion or ethnic background. That was exactly the situation in the Soviet Union under Stalin's penal code, which made it a crime to be related to a deserter from the Red Army.[4]

There is thus more to the act requirement than the issue of a behavior's being voluntary and rational: There is the problem of distinguishing between act and status. A California law made it a criminal offense, subject to a jail term, to be a drug addict. In *Robinson v. California* the U.S. Supreme Court held that statute to be unconstitutional. By making a status or condition a crime, the statute violated the Eighth Amendment to the U.S. Constitution, which prohibits "cruel and unusual punishments." Addiction, the Court noted, is a condition, an illness, much like leprosy or venereal disease.[5]

Failure to Act The act requirement has yet another aspect. An act requires the interaction of mind and body. If only the mind is active and the body does not move, we do not have an act: Just thinking about punching someone in the nose is not a crime (Figure 2.1). We are free to think. But if we carry a thought into physical action, we commit an act, which may be a crime.

Then there is the problem of omission, or failure to act. If the law requires that convicted sex offenders register with the police, and such a person decides not to fill out the registration form, that person is guilty of a crime by omission. But he has acted! He told his hand not to pick up that pen, not to fill out the form. Inaction may be action when the law clearly spells out what one has to do and one decides not to do it.

The law in most U.S. states imposes no duty to be a Good Samaritan, to offer help to another person in distress. The law requires action only if one has a legal duty to act. Lifeguards, for example, are contractually obligated to save

PART I Understanding Criminology   25

FIGURE 2.1

© 1962 *The Saturday Evening Post.* Reprinted by permission of the Saturday Evening Post.

bathers from drowning; parents are obligated by law to protect their children; law enforcement officers and firefighters are required to rescue people in distress.

The Legality Requirement

Marion Palendrano was charged with, among other things, being a "common scold" because she disturbed "the peace of the neighborhood and of all good and quiet people of this State." Mrs. Palendrano moved that the charge be dismissed, and the Superior Court of New Jersey agreed with her, reasoning:

1. Such a crime cannot be found anywhere in the New Jersey statute books. Hence there is no such crime, although, long ago, the common law of England may have recognized such a crime.

2. "Being a common scold" is so vague a concept that to punish somebody for it would violate constitutional due process: "We insist that laws give the person of ordinary intelligence a reasonable opportunity to know what is prohibited, so

that he may act accordingly," ruled the court.[6]

If we want a person to adhere to a standard, the person has to know what that standard is. Thus we have the ancient proposition that only conduct that has been made criminal by law before an act is committed can be a crime. Police, prosecutors, and courts are not interested in the billions of acts human beings engage in unless such acts have previously been defined by law as criminal. The law is interested only in an act (*actus*) that is guilty, evil, and prohibited (*reus*).

The Harm Requirement

Every crime has been created to prevent something bad (a given harm) from happening. Murder is prohibited because we don't want people to be killed. This detrimental consequence that we are trying to avoid is called *harm*. If the specified harm has not been created by the defendant's act, the crime is not complete. Just think of would-be assassin John W. Hinckley, Jr., who tried to kill President Reagan. He shot Reagan, but the president did not die. The harm envisioned by the law against murder had not been accomplished. (Hinckley could have been found guilty of attempted murder, but he was acquitted by reason of insanity.)

From a criminological perspective, most crimes are grouped by the harm that each entails. Offenses against the person involve harm to an individual, and offenses against property involve damage to property or loss of its possession.

The Causation Requirement

What is the act of hitting a home run? Of course it is a hit that allows a batter to run to first, second, and third base, and then back to home plate. Actually, it is

> **Did You Know?**
>
> . . . that the concept of guilt (guilty mind, mens rea) is so central to our sense of justice that we symbolized it in the pre-Christian era with the goddess of justice (*justice*) and her scales—to measure guilt and punishment? In the Christian era *Justitia* became a symbol of justice, sometimes referred to as a saint, but certainly no longer a goddess. She is now the lady justice.

The posting of "pooper-scooper" regulations has had its effect. Most inner city residents consider the failure to "pick up" to be a sign of disrespect and a violation of custom.

much more complicated than that. It starts with the decision to swing a bat, at a certain angle, with a particular intensity, in a specific direction, in order to cause a home run. Suppose that at a San Diego Padres home game, the batter hits a ball unusually high into the air. A passing pelican picks it up, flies off with it, and then drops it into the bleachers. Has the batter hit a home run? We doubt it.

It's the same in crime. Causation requires that the actor achieve the result (the harm) through his or her own effort. Suppose that A, in an effort to kill B, wounds him and that B actually dies when the ambulance carrying him to the hospital collides with another vehicle. Despite B's death, A did not succeed in her personal attempt to kill B. Thus the act of murder is incomplete, although A may be guilty of an attempt to kill. The causation requirement, then, holds that a crime is not complete unless the actor's conduct necessarily caused the harm without interference by somebody else, and that it is the proximate cause of the act.[7]

Mens Rea: The "Guilty Mind" Requirement

Every crime, according to tradition, requires **mens rea,** a "guilty mind." Let us examine the case of Ms. Lambert. She was convicted in Los Angeles of an offense created by city ordinance: having lived in the city without registering with the police as a person previously convicted of a crime. Ms. Lambert had no idea that Los Angeles had such a registration requirement. Nor could she possibly have known that she was required to register. She appealed all the way to the U.S. Supreme Court, and she won. Said the Court: "Where a person did not know [of the prohibition] (s)he may not be convicted consistent with due process."[8]

Of course, to blame Ms. Lambert for violating the Los Angeles city ordinance would make no sense. Ms. Lambert had no notion that she was doing something wrong by living in Los Angeles and not registering herself as a convicted person. With Ms. Lambert's case we have reached a fundamental point: No one can be guilty of a crime unless he or she acted with the knowledge of doing something wrong. This principle always has existed. It is implicit in the concept of crime that the perpetrator know the wrongfulness of the act. It is not required that the perpetrator know the penal code or have personal feelings of guilt. It is enough that the perpetrator knows that he or she had no right to do what he or she did and decided to do it anyway.[9]

Anyone who violently attacks another person, takes another's property, invades another's home, forces intercourse, or forges a signature on someone else's check knows rather well that he or she is doing something wrong. All these examples of mens rea entail an intention to achieve harm or a knowledge that the prohibited harm will result. For some crimes, however, less than a definite intention suffices: reckless actions by which the actors consciously risk causing a prohibited harm (for example, the driver who races down a rain-slicked highway or the employer who sends his employees to work without safety equipment, knowing full well that lives are thereby being endangered).

Strict liability is an exception to the mens rea requirement. There is a class of offenses for which legislatures or courts require no showing of criminal intent or mens rea. For these offenses, the fact that the actor makes an innocent mistake and proceeds in good faith does not affect criminal liability. Strict-liability offenses range all the way from distributing adulterated food to passing a red light. Typically, these offenses are subject to small penalties only, but in a few cases substantial punishments can be and have been imposed.

The Concurrence Requirement

The concurrence requirement states that the criminal act must be accompanied by an equally criminal mind. Suppose a striker throws a stone at an office window in order to shatter it, and a broken piece of glass pierces the throat of a secretary, who bleeds to death. Wanting to damage property deserves condemnation, but of a far lesser degree than wanting to kill. Act and intent did not concur in this case, and the striker should not be found guilty of murder. The law has created many exceptions to the concurrence requirement, one of which, the felony murder rule, we discuss in Chapter 10.

The Punishment Requirement

The last ingredient needed to constitute a crime is that of punishment. An illegal act coupled with an evil mind (criminal intent or mens rea) still does not constitute a crime unless the law subjects it to a punishment. If a sign posted in the park states "Do not step on the grass" and you do it anyway, have you committed a criminal offense? Not unless there is a law that subjects that act to punishment. Otherwise it is simply an improper or inconsiderate act.

The punishment requirement, more than any of the others, helps us differentiate between crimes (which are subject to punishments) and **torts,** civil wrongs for which the law does not prescribe punishment but merely grants the injured party the right to recover damages.

The nature and severity of punishments also help us differentiate between grades of crime. Most penal codes recognize three degrees of severity: **Felonies** are severe crimes, subject to punishments of a year or more in prison or to capital punishment. **Misdemeanors** are less severe crimes, subject to a maximum of one year in jail. (For crimes of both grades, fines can also be imposed as punishments.) **Violations** are minor offenses, normally subject only to fines.

> **Did You Know?**
>
> . . . that in England, 200 or more years ago, all felonies were subject to capital punishment? If all felons had, in fact, been executed, England would have lost most of its male population. So, to save fellow citizens from the gallows, juries refused to convict and judges invented (or expanded) defenses to felony charges.

THE DEFENSES

You will soon see that we measure the amount of crime at various stages of the criminal process. For example: How many crimes are reported to the police? For how many of these crimes have convictions been obtained? There is a huge discrepancy. Far fewer convictions have been obtained than crimes reported or even prosecuted. There are several reasons for this discrepancy. One of the principal reasons is that not all elements of the crime charged could be proven in court. And why not? Because frequently the defendant has offered one of a number of defenses to the offense charged. Each of these defenses simply negates the existence of one (or more) of the elements of the offense charged.

Let us take the insanity defense as an example. When the defendant pleads the existence of a mental disease or defect (a psychiatric question), he claims that he could not have acted (did not appreciate the nature and quality of the act—consequently no *actus reus*) or he could not form the requisite mens rea (did not appreciate the wrongfulness of the act).[10]

The defense of infancy could have been worked out similarly. But instead, it was decided at common law that nobody under age 7 should be deemed capable of acting rationally or to have the requisite mens rea. At age 14 all youngsters are deemed to have that capacity. The defense of infancy varies widely among the states.

Let us look at the defense of mistake of fact. Here the defendant claims that by reason of a factual error (e.g., taking someone else's coat believing it to be one's own) she did not, and could not, realize that she did something wrong. Hence, there was no mens rea (or sometimes not even the requisite *actus reus*).

In some situations the defendant's defense is that the element of wrongfulness was lacking (the legality requirement). Normally, touching another person without consent amounts to assault and battery. The police officer's defense is that the law requires that he touch others without consent. Therefore, what is normally illegal has become legal (the defense of public duty). Other defenses, such as duress, necessity, self-defense, and defense of property, all work pretty much on the same principle—they negate an essential element of the offense charged.

TYPOLOGIES OF CRIME

The general term "crimes" covers a wide variety of types of crimes, with their own distinct features. Murder and arson, for example, both are crimes. They have the same seven general elements, including a criminal intent (mens rea) and a harm element. But these elements take different forms in different crimes. In murder the criminal intent takes the form of intending to kill another human being wrongfully, while in arson the intent is that of wrongfully burning the property of another. Lawyers and criminologists have searched for a system of grouping the many types of crimes into coherent, rational categories, for ease of understanding, of learning, and of finding them in the law books, and for purposes of studying them from both a legal and a criminological perspective. Such categorizations are called "typologies."

Here are some examples: The ancient Romans classified their crimes as those against the gods and those against other human beings. As late as the eighteenth century, some English lawyers simply listed crimes alphabetically. The French of the early nineteenth century created a typology with three categories: serious crimes (which we would call "felonies"), medium serious crimes (which we would call "misdemeanors"), and crimes of a petty character (which we would call "violations"). The more serious crimes were grouped into categories based on the harm those crimes entailed, such as harm against life, against physical integrity, against honor, against property, and so on.

Nowadays the French categorization is generally accepted worldwide, although lawyers and criminologists may differ on the desirability of lumping various crime types together into categories. Lawyers, after all, may be much more interested in the procedural consequences that flow from the categorizations, while criminologists may be much more concerned with criminological implications for studying different types of perpetrators and devising schemes of crime prevention.

There are also political considerations in devising a typology. For example, the criminal codes of the former communist countries had large categories of political crimes, which were given the most prominent place in those codes. They included many crimes that in Western democracies are grouped in other categories, such as property crimes or crimes against the person, or that may have no counterpart at all.

The typology we have chosen for this book seeks to accommodate both the established legal typology—for example, that used in the Model Penal Code—and the criminological objectives that are so important for the study of crime from a sociological and behavioral perspective. These categories are:

- Violent crimes
- Crimes against property
- White collar and corporate crime
- Drug-, alcohol-, and sex-related crimes

We discuss these categories in Part III.

MEASURING CRIME

There are three major reasons for measuring characteristics of crimes and criminals. First of all, researchers need to collect and analyze information in order to test theories about why people commit crime. One criminologist might record the kinds of offenses committed by people of different ages; another might count the number of crimes committed at different times of the year. But without ordering these observations in some purposeful way, without a **theory**, a systematic set of principles that explain how two or more phenomena are related, scientists would be limited in their ability to make predictions from the data they collect.

The types of data that are collected and the way they are collected are crucial to the research process. Criminologists analyze these data and use their findings to support or refute theories. In Part II we examine several theories (including the one outlined briefly here) that explain why people commit crime, and we will see how these theories have been tested.

One theory of crime causation, for example, is that high crime rates result from the wide disparity between people's goals and the means available to them for reaching those goals. Those who lack legitimate opportunities to achieve their goals (primarily, people in the lower class) try to reach them through criminal means. To test this theory, researchers might begin with the **hypothesis** (a testable proposition that describes how two or more factors are related) that lower-class individuals engage in more serious crimes and do so more frequently than middle-class individuals. (See "Social Class and Crime" later in this chapter.) Next they would collect facts, observations, and other pertinent information—called **data**—on the criminal behavior of both lower-class and middle-class individuals. A finding that lower-class persons commit more crimes would support the theory that people commit crimes because they do not have legitimate means to reach their goals.

The second objective of measurement is to enhance our knowledge of the characteristics of various types of offenses. Why are some more likely to be committed than others? What situational factors, such as time of day or type of place, influence the commission of crime? Experts have argued that this information is needed if we are to prevent crime and develop strategies to control it (Chapter 9 deals with this subject).

Measurement has a third major objective: Criminal justice agencies depend on certain kinds of information to facilitate daily operations and to anticipate future needs. How many persons flow through county jails? How many will receive prison sentences? Besides the questions that deal with the day-to-day functioning of the system (number of beds, distribution and hiring of personnel), other questions affect legislative and policy decisions. For instance, what effect does a change in law have on the amount of crime committed? Consider legislation on the death penalty. Some people claim that homicides decrease when a death penalty is instituted. Others claim that capital punishment laws make no difference. Does fear of crime go down if we put more police officers in a neighborhood? Does drug smuggling move to another entry point if old access routes are cut off? These and other potential changes need to be evaluated—and evaluations require measurement.

Methods of Collecting Data

Given the importance of data for research, policy making, and the daily operation and planning of the criminal justice system, criminologists have been working to perfect data collection techniques. Through the years these methods have become increasingly more sophisticated.

Depending on what questions they are asking, criminologists can and do collect their data in a variety of ways: through survey research, experiments, observation, and case studies. One of the most widely used methods is survey research, which is a cost-effective method of measuring characteristics of groups. Experimental studies are difficult and costly to conduct, and for that reason they are used infrequently. But they have been, and still are, an important means of collecting data on crime. Participant observation involves the direct participation of the researcher in the activities of the people who are the subjects of the research. A variation of this technique is nonparticipant observation, in which the researcher collects data without joining in the activity. Another way to collect information about crime, and especially about criminal careers, is to examine biographical and autobiographical accounts of individual offenders (the case-study method).

Data can be found in a wide variety of sources, but the most frequently used sources are statistics compiled by government agencies, private foundations, and businesses. Familiarity with the sources of data and the methods used to gather data will help in understanding the studies we discuss throughout this book. The facts and observations researchers gather for the purpose of a particular study are called **primary data.** Those they find in government sources, or data that were previously collected for a different investigation, are called **secondary data.**

Surveys Most of us are familiar with surveys—in public opinion polls, marketing research, and election-prediction studies. Criminologists use surveys to obtain quantitative data. A **survey** is the systematic collection of respondents' answers to questions asked in questionnaires or interviews; interviews may be conducted face-to-face or by telephone. Generally, surveys are used to gather information about the attitudes, characteristics, or behavior of a large group of persons, who are called the **population** of the survey. Surveys conducted by criminologists measure, for example, the amount of crime, attitudes toward police or toward the sentencing of dangerous offenders, assessment of drug abuse, and fear of crime.

Instead of interviewing the total population under study, most researchers interview a representative subset of that population—a **sample.** If a sample is carefully drawn, researchers can generalize the results from the sample to the population. A sample determined by random selection, whereby each person in the population to be studied has an equal chance of being selected, is called a **random sample.**

Surveys are a cost-effective method, but they have limitations. If a study of drug use by high school students were done one time only, the finding of a relationship between drug use and poor grades would not tell us whether drug use caused bad grades, whether students with bad grades turned to drugs, or whether bad grades and drug-taking resulted from some other factor, such as lack of a stable family.

The year 2000 census started when Harold Johnson visited the Eskimo village of Unalkleet, Alaska, on January 19, 2000. The U.S. Census will provide information on all Americans, their lifestyles and problems, including, through random survey done in cooperation with the Bureau of Justice Statistics, data on crime victimization.

Experiments The **experiment** is a technique used in the physical and biological sciences, and in the social sciences as well. An investigator introduces a change into a process and makes measurements or observations in order to evaluate the effects of the change. Through experimentation, scientists test hypotheses about how two or more **variables** (factors that may change) are related. The basic model for an experiment involves changing one variable, keeping all other factors the same (controlling them, or holding them constant), and observing the effect of that change on another variable. If you change one variable while keeping all other factors constant and then find that another variable changes as well, you may safely assume that the change in the second variable was caused by the change in the first.

Despite experimental evidence that the Scared Straight experience may be counterproductive, the program continues at East Jersey State Prison (formerly Rahway State Prison). Here, a member of the Lifer's group appears in a Scared Straight 1999 video. The film is an update of the original Scared Straight video that shows how inmates give young people in trouble a taste of prison life.

Most experiments are done in laboratories, but it is possible to do them in real-world, or field, settings (hence the name **field experiment**). A field experiment was done at New Jersey's Rahway State Prison to test the hypothesis that if youngsters were shown the horrors of prison, they would not commit crimes. The object was to scare young people out of crime; consequently, the project became known as "Scared Straight!" Several agencies were asked to propose male juveniles for the experiment. All were given a series of tests to determine their attitudes toward crime, punishment, prison, the police, and so forth. Afterward some of the juveniles were randomly assigned to the experimental group, which would actually go to the prison. The rest were assigned to a control group, which would not go.

After the experimental group had participated in the program, both groups were again given the same attitude tests to find out if the prison experience had changed the attitudes of the experimental group. Six months later the juvenile records of the two groups were checked to find out how many of the youths in both groups had committed crimes during the six-month period. Had fewer of the youngsters who had supposedly been scared straight been arrested than those who had not made the prison visit? No, according to James Finckenauer's analysis. In fact, many more of the boys in the experimental group had been arrested than had boys in the control group, and the boys in the experimental group also tended to commit more serious offenses than those in the control group.[11]

Experiments in the real world are costly and difficult to carry out, but they have the advantage of increasing scientists' ability to establish cause and effect.

Participant and Nonparticipant Observation Researchers who engage in participant and nonparticipant observation use methods that provide detailed descriptions of life as it actually is lived—in prisons, gangs, and other settings.

Observation is the most direct means of studying behavior. Investigators may play a variety of roles in observing social situations. When they engage in **nonparticipant observation,** they do not join in the activities of the groups they are studying; they simply observe the activities in everyday settings and record what they see. Investigators who engage in **participant observation** take part in many of the activities of the groups in order to gain acceptance, but they generally make clear the purpose of their participation. Anne Campbell, a criminologist who spent two years as a participant observer of the lifestyles of girl gang members, explains:

> My efforts to meet female gang members began with an introduction through the New York City Police Department's Gang Crimes Unit. Through one of their plain-clothes gang liaison officers, John Galea, I was introduced first to the male gang members of a number of Brooklyn gangs. On being reassured that I "only" wanted to talk to the female members, the male leaders gave their OK and I made arrangements to meet with the girls' leaders or "godmothers." At first they were guarded in their disclosures to me. They asked a lot about my life, my background and my reasons for wanting to hang out with them. Like most of us, however, they enjoyed talking about themselves and over the period of six months that I spent with each of three female gangs they opened up a good deal—sitting in their kitchens, standing on the stoops in the evenings or socializing at parties with allied gangs.[12]

Observations of groups in their natural setting afford the researcher insights into behavior and attitudes that cannot be obtained through such techniques as surveys and experiments.

Case Studies A **case study** is an analysis of all pertinent aspects of one unit of study, such as an individual, an institution, a group, or a community. The sources of information are documents such as life histories, biographies, diaries, journals, letters, and other records. A classic demonstration of criminologists' use of the case-study method is found in Edwin Sutherland's *The Professional Thief*, which is based on interviews with a professional thief.

Sutherland learned about the relationship between amateur and professional thieves, how thieves communicate, how they determine whether to trust each other, and how they network. From discussions with the thief and an analysis of his writings on topics selected by the researcher, Sutherland was able to draw several conclusions that other techniques would not have yielded. For instance, a person is not a professional thief unless he is recognized as such by other professional thieves. Training by professional thieves is necessary for the development of the skills, attitudes, and connections required in the "profession."[13] One of the drawbacks of the case-study method is that the information given by the subject may be biased or wrong and by its nature is limited. For these reasons it is difficult to generalize from one person's story—in this instance—to all professional thieves.

Using Available Data in Research Besides collecting their own data, researchers often depend on secondary data collected by private and public organizations. The police, the courts, and corrections officials, for example, need to know the number of persons passing through the criminal justice system at various points in order to carry out day-to-day administrative tasks and to engage in long-range planning. It is not always feasible to collect new data for a research project, nor is it necessary to do so when such vast amounts of relevant information are already available.

To study the relationship between crime and variables such as average income or single-parent households, one might make use of the Uniform Crime Reports (see "Police Statistics" later in this chapter), together with information found in the reports of the Bureau of the Census. Various other agencies, among them the Federal Bureau of Prisons, the Drug Enforce-

---

:// Crime Surfing

www.jrsainfo.org/ibrrc/index.html

The Justice Research and Statistics Association (JRSA) is a national nonprofit group of state-level statistical analysis centers. The group gathers data from across the country, conducts studies on criminal justice issues, and helps people find information on topics relating to criminal justice programs and research. The JRSA website discusses the National Incident-Based Reporting System (NIBRS).

ment Agency, the Treasury Department, and the Labor Department, are also excellent sources of statistics useful to criminologists. At the international level, UN world crime surveys contain information on crime, criminals, and criminal justice systems in countries on all continents.

Researchers who use available data can save a great deal of time and expense. However, they have to exercise caution in fitting data not collected for the purpose of a particular study into their research. Many official records are incomplete or the data have been collected in such a way as to make them inadequate for the research. It is also frequently difficult to gain permission to use agency data that are not available to the public because of a concern about confidentiality.

Ethics and the Researcher

In the course of their research, criminologists encounter many ethical issues. Chief among such issues is confidentiality. Consider the dilemma faced by a group of researchers in the late 1960s. In interviewing a sample of 9,945 boys born in 1945, the team collected extensive self-reported criminal histories of offenses the boys had committed before and after they turned 18. Among the findings were four unreported homicides and 75 rapes. The researchers were naturally excited about capturing such interesting data. More important, the researchers had feelings of grave concern. How should they handle their findings?

Should the results of these interviews be published?
Could the failure of the research staff to disclose names be considered the crime of obstructing justice?
Does an obligation to society as a whole to release the names of the offenders transcend a researcher's obligation to safeguard a subject's confidentiality?
What is the best response to a demand by the police, a district attorney, or a court for the researcher's files containing the subjects' names?
Should criminologists be immune to prosecution for their failure to disclose the names of their subjects?
Is it possible to develop a technique that can ensure against the identification of a subject in a research file?[14]

Such questions have few clear-cut answers. When researchers encounter these problems, however, they can rely on standards for ethical human experimentation. Human-experimentation review committees at most universities and government agencies check all proposals for research projects to ensure the protection of human subjects. In addition, researchers are required to inform their subjects about the nature of the study and to obtain written and informed agreement to participate.

Because of heightened awareness of the ethical issues involved in human experimentation—particularly in correctional institutions, where coercion is difficult to avoid—the field of criminology and criminal justice is in the process of adopting formal codes of ethics. The guidelines include full reporting of experimental findings, honoring commitments made to respondents, not misleading respondents, and protecting respondents' confidentiality. Special provisions for what are called "vulnerable populations" (e.g., the illiterate, the mentally ill, children, those of low social status, and those under judicial or penal supervision) include taking appropriate steps to secure informed consent and to avoid invasions of privacy.[15] In the end, however, as Seth Bloomberg and Leslie Wilkins have noted, "the responsibility for safeguarding human subjects ultimately rests with the researcher.... A code of ethics may provide useful guidelines, but it will not relieve the scientist of moral choice."[16]

THE NATURE AND EXTENT OF CRIME

As we have seen, criminologists gather their information in many ways. The methods they choose depend on the questions they want answered. To estimate the nature and extent of crime in the United States, they rely primarily on the Uniform Crime Reports, data compiled by the police; on the National Crime Victimization Survey, which measures crime through reports by victims; and on various self-report surveys, which ask individuals about criminal acts

FIGURE 2.2 The process of bringing crime to the attention of police.

Act or situation
↓
1. Perception
↓
2. Definition
↓
3. Reporting
↓
4. Redefinition
↓
5. Recording
↓
Recorded crime known to the police

Source: R. F. Sparks, H. G. Genn, and D. J. Dodd, *Surveying Victims: A Study of the Measurement of Criminal Victimization, Perceptions of Crime, and Attitudes to Criminal Justice* (Chichester, Eng.: Wiley, 1977), p. 6.

they have committed, whether or not these acts have come to the attention of the authorities.

Official statistics gathered from law enforcement agencies provide information available on the crimes actually investigated and reported by these agencies. But not all crimes appear in police statistics. In order for a criminal act to be "known to the police," the act first must be *perceived* by an individual (the car is not in the garage where it was left). It must then be *defined*, or classified, as something that places it within the purview of the criminal justice system (a theft has taken place), and it must be *reported* to the police. Once the police are notified, they classify the act and often *redefine* what may have taken place before *recording* the act as a crime known to the police (Figure 2.2). Information about criminal acts may be lost at any point along this processing route, and many crimes are never discovered to begin with.

Police Statistics

In 1924 the director of the Bureau of Investigation, J. Edgar Hoover, initiated a campaign to make the bureau responsible for gathering national statistics. With support from the American Bar Association (ABA) and the International Association of Chiefs of Police (IACP), the House of Representatives in 1930 passed a bill authorizing the bureau (later renamed the Federal Bureau of Investigation, or FBI) to collect data on crimes known to the police. These data are compiled into reports called the Uniform Crime Reports (UCR). At present approximately 17,000 city, county, and state law enforcement agencies, which cover 95 percent of the total population, voluntarily contribute information on crimes brought to their attention. These agencies represent over 254 million U.S. inhabitants, with higher representation in large urban areas (97 percent) than in smaller cities (90 percent) or rural areas (87 percent). If the police verify that a crime has been committed, that crime goes into the report, whether or not an arrest has been made. Each month, reporting agencies provide data on offenses in 29 categories.

Part I and Part II Offenses The UCR divide offenses into two major categories: Part I and Part II. Part I offenses include eight crimes, which are aggregated as **crimes against the person** (criminal homicide, forcible rape, robbery, and aggravated assault) and **crimes against property** (burglary, larceny-theft, motor vehicle theft, and arson). Collectively, Part I offenses are called **Index crimes.** Because they are serious, these crimes tend to be reported to the police more reliably than others and therefore can be used in combination as an index, or indicator, of changes over time. All other offenses, except traffic violations, are Part II crimes. These 21

> **Did You Know?**
>
> . . . that the average American's risk of being murdered in any given year is about 1 in 15,000, much lower than the annual risk of dying of heart disease (1 in 340), cancer (1 in 500), or stroke (1 in 1,700); of being killed in an accident (1 in 2,900) or a car crash (1 in 5,000); of succumbing to AIDS (1 in 11,000) or breast cancer (if you are female) (1 in 5000); or of committing suicide (1 in 10,000).

The New York Times

Can Politics Influence Crime Data?

Two agencies within the U.S. Department of Justice are concerned with compiling crime data: the Bureau of Justice Statistics (BJS), the United States' primary source of criminal justice statistics, and the National Institute of Justice (NIJ), the only federal agency solely dedicated to researching crime control and justice issues. Since the attacks on the World Trade Center, however, criminal justice experts say they have become increasingly concerned that the attorney general and the Justice Department are moving to exert political control over these previously independent agencies.

Both the BJS and the NIJ, until recently, have been independent of the attorney general and have been allowed to release reports and make research grants without clearing them through the attorney general's office. But in October 2001, the U.S.A. PATRIOT Act was passed, a sweeping antiterrorism mea-sure that removed much of the freedom the directors of the Bureau of Justice Statistics and the National Institute of Justice had long enjoyed, giving their authority to the assistant attorney general for the Office of Justice Programs, who said that there was a need to "centralize control over these agencies" due to the terrorist attacks. The result of this change is that all statistical reports and decisions about research grants must now go through the assistant attorney general, and then on to the attorney general, for clearance.

The dispute about control of crime statistics came to the attention of the public when someone from the Justice Department leaked a major report from the BJS to the Associated Press. The report, which indicated a 9 percent decrease in violent crimes in 2001, had been held up for two months awaiting review by the Justice Department. Leaking a report goes against the guidelines of the National Research Council, which emphasizes that for a federal statistical agency to maintain credibility, all data must be widely and promptly released and "perceived to be free of political interference." The leak gave the statistics a political taint, as data showing a drop in crime is always beneficial to the administration.

Another change in policy came through a directive to BJS and NIJ employees not to talk to journalists and to refer media callers to a public affairs officer, to ensure that the Justice Department "speaks with one voice" on crime issues. However, Alfred Blumstein, professor of statistics and criminology at Carnegie Mellon University, and one of the founders of the BJS, rebutted this statement, saying, "Sometimes statistics and research findings will be in conflict with Justice Department policy, so requiring a single voice will undermine the independence of statistics and research."

Source

Fox Butterfield, "Some Experts Fear Political Influence on Crime Data Agencies," *The New York Times*, Sept. 22, 2002.

Questions for Discussion

1. Should crime statistics and the agencies that produce them be "centrally controlled" by the government? Does the threat of terrorism justify the control of this kind of information?
2. What measures might be taken to prevent the Justice Department's abuse of power in overseeing the gathering and release of such statistics?

---

crimes include fraud, embezzlement, weapons offenses, vandalism, and simple assaults.

Crime Rates To analyze crime data, experts frequently present them as crime rates. Crime rates are computed by the following formula:

$$\text{Crime rate} = \frac{\text{number of reported crimes}}{\text{total population}} \times 100{,}000$$

Crime rates may be computed for groups of offenses (such as the Index crimes or crimes against the person) or for specific offenses (such as homicide). If we say, for example, that the homicide rate is 10.2, we mean that there were 10.2 homicides for every 100,000 persons in the population under consideration (total U.S. population, say, or all males in the United States). Expressing the amount of crime in terms of rates over time shows whether an increase or a decrease in crime results from a change in the population or a change in the amount of crime committed.

In addition to data on reported crimes, the UCR include the number of offenses cleared by arrest. Crimes may be cleared in one of two ways: by the arrest, charging, and turning over to the courts of at least one person for prosecution; or by disposition of a case when an arrest is not possible, as when the suspect has died or fled the jurisdiction.

> **:// Crime Surfing**
>
> http://www.crime.org/
>
> Examine this annotated list of links to websites that have data on crime and explanations of what crime data are, where they come from, and how accurate they are likely to be.

Besides reported crimes and crimes cleared by arrest, the reports contain data on characteristics of crimes (such as geographical location, time, and place), characteristics of criminals (such as gender, age, and race), and distribution of law enforcement personnel. We shall look at what these statistics reveal about the characteristics of crime and criminals in more detail later, but first we must recognize their limitations.

Limitations of the Uniform Crime Reports

Despite the fact that the UCR are among the main sources of crime statistics, their research value has been questioned. The criticisms deal with methodological problems and reporting practices. Some scholars argue, for example, that figures on reported crime are of little use in categories such as larceny, in which a majority of crime is not reported. The statistics present the amount of crime known to law enforcement agencies, but they do not reveal how many crimes have actually been committed. Another serious limitation is the fact that when several crimes are committed in one event, only the most serious offense is included in the UCR; the others go unreported. At the same time, when certain other crimes are committed, each individual act is counted as a separate offense. If a person robs a group of six people, for example, the UCR list one robbery (Figure 2.3). But if a person assaults six people, the UCR list six assaults. UCR data are further obscured by the fact that they do not differentiate between completed acts and attempted acts.

Police reports to the FBI are voluntary and vary in accuracy. In a study conducted on behalf of the Police Foundation, Lawrence Sherman and Barry Glick found that while the UCR require that arrests be recorded even if a suspect is released without a formal charge, all 196 departments surveyed recorded an arrest only after a formal booking procedure.[17] In addition, police departments may want to improve their image by showing that their crime rate has either declined (meaning the streets are safer) or risen (justifying a crackdown on, say, prostitution).[18] New record-keeping procedures can also create significant changes (the New York robbery rate appeared to increase 400 percent in one year).[19] Many fluctuations in crime rates may therefore be attributable to events other than changes in the actual numbers of crimes committed.

Finally, the UCR data suffer from several omissions. Many arsons go unreported because not all fire departments report to the UCR.[20] Federal cases go unlisted. Most white-collar offenses are omitted because they are reported not to the police but to regulatory authorities, such as the Securities and Exchange Commission and the Federal Trade Commission.

To deal with the limitations of the UCR, in 1986 the International Association of Chiefs of Police, the National Sheriffs' Association, and the state-level UCR programs joined forces with the FBI.[21] A new reporting system was developed, called the "National Incident-Based Reporting System" (NIBRS). Reporting to the NIBRS is voluntary and coexists with the UCR. The NIBRS is a major attempt to improve the collection of crime data. But it deals only with crimes that come to the attention of the police. What about crimes that remain unreported? For what is called the "dark figure of crime," we have to rely on victimization data and self-report studies.

Victimization Surveys

Victimization surveys measure the extent of crime by interviewing individuals about their experiences as victims. The Bureau of the Census, in cooperation with the Bureau of Justice Statistics, collects information annually about persons and households that have been victimized. The report is called the "National Crime Victimization Survey" (NCVS). Researchers for the NCVS estimate the total number of crimes committed by asking respondents from a national sample of approximately 43,000 households, representing 80,000 persons over the age of 12 (parental permission is needed for those under 14 years old), about their experiences as victims during a specific time period. Interviewers visit (or sometimes telephone) the homes selected for the sample. Each housing

PART I **Understanding Criminology**

FIGURE 2.3 Counting crime in the Uniform Crime Reports

One offense

Six offenses

unit remains in the sample for three years. Every six months 10,000 households are rotated out of the sample and replaced by a new group.

The NCVS measures the extent of victimization by rape, robbery, assault, larceny, burglary, personal theft, and motor vehicle theft. Note that two of the UCR Part I offenses—criminal homicide and arson—are not included (see Table 2.1).[22] Homicide is omitted because the NCVS covers only crimes whose victims can be interviewed. The designers of the survey also decided to omit arson, a relative newcomer to the UCR, because measuring it with some validity by means of a victimization survey was deemed to be too difficult. Part II offenses have been excluded altogether because many of them are considered victimless (prostitution, vagrancy, drug abuse, drunkenness) or because victims are willing participants (gambling, con games) or do not know they have been victimized (forgery, fraud).

The survey covers characteristics of crimes such as time and place of occurrence, number of offenders, use of weapons, economic loss, and time lost from work; characteristics of victims, such as gender, age, race, ethnicity, marital status, household composition, and educational attainment; perceived characteristics of offenders, such as age, gender, and race; circumstances surrounding the offenses and their effects, such as financial loss and injury; and patterns of police reporting, such as rates of reporting and reasons for reporting and for not reporting. Some questions also encourage interviewees to discuss family violence.

Limitations of Victimization Surveys While victimization surveys give us information about crimes that are not reported to the police, these data, too, have significant limitations. The NCVS covers crimes in a more limited way than the UCR; the NCVS includes only 7 offenses, whereas there are 8 offenses in Part I of the UCR and an additional 21 in Part II. Although the NCVS is conducted by trained interviewers, some individual variations in interviewing and recording style are inevitable, and as a result, the information recorded may vary as well.

TABLE 2.1 How Do the Uniform Crime Reports and the National Crime Victimization Survey Differ?

	Uniform Crime Reports	National Crime Victimization Survey
Offenses measured	Homicide Rape Robbery (personal and commercial) Assault (aggravated) Burglary (commercial and household) Larceny (commercial and household) Motor vehicle theft Arson	Rape Robbery (personal) Assault (aggravated and simple) Household burglary Larceny Personal theft Motor vehicle theft
Scope	Crimes reported to the police in most jurisdictions; considerable flexibility in developing small-area data	Crimes both reported and not reported to police; all data are for the nation as a whole; some data are available for a few large geographical areas
Collection method	Police department reports to FBI	Survey interviews; periodically measures the total number of crimes committed by asking a national sample of 43,000* households representing 80,000* persons over the age of 12 about their experiences as victims of crime during a specified period
Kinds of information	In addition to offense counts, provides information on crime clearances, persons arrested, persons charged, law enforcement officers killed and assaulted, and characteristics of homicide victims	Provides details about victims (such as age, race, sex, education, and income, and whether the victim and offender were related to each other) and about crimes (such as time and place of occurrence, whether or not reported to police, use of weapons, occurrence of injury, and economic consequences)
Sponsor	Department of Justice, Federal Bureau of Investigation	Department of Justice, Bureau of Justice Statistics

*Figures have been updated.

Source: Adapted from U.S. Department of Justice, Bureau of Justice Statistics, *Report to the Nation on Crime and Justice*, 2d ed. (Washington, D.C.: U.S. Government Printing Office, 1988), p. 11; U.S. Department of Justice, Bureau of Justice Statistics, *Criminal Victimization 1997* (Washington, D.C.: U.S. Government Printing Office, December 1998), pp. 1–2.

Since the NCVS is based on personal reporting, it also suffers from the fact that memories may fade over time; so some facts are forgotten while others are exaggerated. Moreover, some interviewees may try to please the interviewer by fabricating crime incidents.[23] Respondents also have a tendency to telescope events—that is, to move events that took place in an earlier time period into the time period under study. Like the UCR, the NCVS records only the most serious offense committed during an event in which several crimes are perpetrated.

Self-Report Surveys

Another way to determine the amount and types of crime actually committed is to ask people to report their own criminal acts in a confidential interview or, more commonly, on an anonymous questionnaire. These investigations are called **self-report surveys**.

Findings of Self-Report Surveys Self-reports of delinquent and criminal behavior have produced several important findings since their development in the 1940s. First, they quickly refuted the conventional wisdom that only a small percentage of the general population commits crimes. The use of these measures over the last several decades has demonstrated very high rates of law-violating behavior by seemingly law-abiding people. Almost everyone, at some point in time, has broken a law.

In 1947, James S. Wallerstein and Clement J. Wyle questioned a group of 1,698 individuals on whether or not they had committed any of 49 offenses that were serious enough to require a maximum sentence of not less than one year. They found that over 80 percent of the men reported committing malicious mischief, disorderly conduct, and larceny. More than 50 percent admitted a history of crimes including reckless driving and driving while intoxicated, indecency, gambling, fraud, and tax evasion. The authors acknowledged the lack of scientific rigor of their study. No attempt was made to ensure a balanced or representative cross section of the individuals surveyed.[24] However, these findings do suggest that the distinction between criminals and noncriminals may be more apparent than real.

Studies conducted since the 1940s have provided a great deal more information. They suggest a wide discrepancy between official and self-report data as regards the age, race, and gender of offenders.[25] Unrecorded offenders commit a wide variety of offenses, rather than specializing in one type of offense.[26] It also appears that only one-quarter of all serious, chronic juvenile offenders are apprehended by the police. Moreover, an estimated 90 percent of all youths commit delinquent or criminal acts, primarily truancy, use of false identification, alcohol abuse, larceny, fighting, and marijuana use.[27]

From 1991 to 1993, the first International Self-Report Delinquency (ISRD) study was conducted in Finland, Great Britain, the Netherlands, Belgium, Germany, Switzerland, Portugal, Spain, Italy, Greece, the United States, and New Zealand. Each country used the same questionnaire, which had been translated into the respective languages. The studies used various sampling techniques, so the results from each country are not strictly comparable. Nonetheless, the findings support much of what is found in the self-report literature. Boys commit about twice as many offenses as girls. The peak age of offending in the participating countries is 16 to 17 years. Violence is strongly related to lower educational levels. No relationship was found between socioeconomic status and delinquency. Drug use seems related to leaving school early and unemployment. School failure is related to violent offenses.[28]

Limitations of Self-Report Surveys Self-report surveys have taught us a great deal about criminality. But they, like the other methods of data collection, have drawbacks. The questionnaires are often limited to petty acts, such as truancy, and therefore do not represent the range of criminal acts that people may commit. Michael Hindelang, Travis Hirschi, and Joseph Weis argue that researchers who find discrepancies with respect to gender, race, and class between the results produced by official statistics and those collected by self-report methods are in fact measuring different kinds of behavior rather than different amounts of the same behavior. They suggest that if you take into account the fact that persons who are arrested tend to have committed more serious offenses and to have prior records (criteria that affect decisions to arrest), then the two types of statistics are quite comparable.[29]

Another drawback of self-reports is that most of them are administered to high school or college students, so the information they yield applies only to young people attending school. And who can say that respondents always tell the truth? The information obtained by repeated administration of the same questionnaire to the same individuals might yield different results. Many self-report measures lack validity; the data obtained do not correspond with some other criterion (such as school records) that measures the same behavior. Finally, samples may be biased. People who choose not to participate in the studies may have good reason for not wanting to discuss their criminal activities.

Each of the three commonly used sources of data—police reports, victim surveys, and self-report surveys—adds a different dimension to our knowledge of crime. All of them are useful in our search for the characteristics of crimes, criminals, and victims.

MEASURING CHARACTERISTICS OF CRIME

Streets in Charlotte, North Carolina, with tranquil names—Peaceful Glen, Soft Wind, Gentle Breeze—were killing lanes.[30] The city that had hoped to displace Atlanta as the "Queen City of the South" had 115 homicides in 1992, more than double the number it had six years earlier. It seemed that the city was out of control. Experts pointed to drugs and to a growing number of swap shops and flea markets that served as unregulated outlets for buying guns as the reasons

FIGURE 2.4 National Crime Victimization Survey and Uniform Crime Reports: A comparison of number of crimes reported. (a) National Crime Victimization Survey: Total number of victimizations, 2000. (b) Uniform Crime Reports: Total number of Index offenses, 2000.

National Crime Victimization Survey (Number of offenses)
Total = 25,893,000

- Larceny: 14,916,000
- Assault: 5,330,000
- Burglary: 3,444,000
- Motor vehicle theft: 937,000
- Robbery: 732,000
- Personal theft: 274,000
- Rape/sexual assault: 261,000

(a)

Uniform Crime Reports (Number of offenses)
Total = 11,605,751

- Larceny/theft: 6,965,957
- Burglary: 2,049,946
- Motor vehicle theft: 1,165,559
- Aggravated assault: 910,744
- Robbery: 407,842
- Forcible rape: 90,186
- Murder/nonnegligent manslaughter: 15,517

(b)

Source: (a) Adapted from U.S. Department of Justice, Bureau of Justice Statistics, *Criminal Victimization 2000* (Washington D.C.: U.S. Government Printing Office, June 2001), p. 3; (b) Adapted from U.S. Department of Justice, Federal Bureau of Investigation, *Crime in the United States, 2000* (Washington D.C.: U.S. Government Printing Office, 2001), p. 67.

---

for the high number of homicides. Most of the killings took place in a 26-square-mile area inhabited primarily by low-income African American families. Fortunately, within 8 years the situation reversed itself. In 2000 the number of homicides in Charlotte was reduced to 74.[31] This information not only gives us general insights into the crime problem in Charlotte, but also enables us to examine the changes in the homicide rate over time, the high-risk areas, and the racial and economic composition of those areas, to provide a full picture of the crime history.

Criminologists use these kinds of data about crimes in their research. Some investigators, for example, may want to compare drug use to crime in major cities. Others may want to explain a decrease or an increase in the crime rate in a single city (Charlotte), in a single neighborhood (the impoverished inner city), or perhaps in the nation as a whole.

Crime Trends

One of the most important characteristics of any crime is how often it is committed. From such figures we can determine crime trends, the increases and decreases of crime over time. The UCR show that about 11.6 million Index crimes (excluding arson) were reported to the police in 2000 (Figure 2.4b). Of the total number of Index crimes, violent crimes make up a small portion—12 percent—with a murder rate of 5.5 per 100,000. Most Index crimes are property offenses (88 percent), and 67 percent of the property offenses are larcenies.[32]

The 2000 NCVS presents a somewhat different picture (Figure 2.4a). Though the data presented in the NCVS and the UCR are not entirely comparable because the categories differ, the number of crimes reported to the police and the number reported in the victimization survey are clearly far apart. According to the

FIGURE 2.5 Uniform Crime Reports: Rate of all Index crimes per 100,000 population, 1960–1994.

Source: U.S. Department of Justice, Federal Bureau of Investigation, *Crime in the United States, 1975; 1980; 1992; 1994; 1997; 2000* (Washington D.C.: U.S. Government Printing Office, 1976, 1981, 1993, 1995, 1998, 2001), pp. 41, 49, 58, 67.

NCVS, there were over 25 million victimizations. Indeed, the NCVS reports more thefts than the total number of UCR Index offenses.[33]

According to UCR data, the crime rate increased slowly between 1930 and 1960. After 1960 it began to rise much more quickly. This trend continued until 1980 (Figure 2.5), when the crime rate rose to 5,950 per 100,000. From that peak the rate steadily dropped until 1984, when there were 5,031.3 crimes per 100,000. After that year the rate rose again until 1991. Since then, it has decreased every year, to 4,124.0 in 2000, the lowest rate since 1972.[34] The NCVS also shows that the victimization rate peaked from 1979 to 1981, but that in the 5-year span from 1993 to 1998, the victimization rates for all crimes dropped.[35] This trend continued for 2000.

The gradual decline in the crime rate after 1980 is an important phenomenon that requires a bit more analysis. One important factor is the age distribution of the population. Given the fact that young people tend to have the highest crime rate, the age distribution of the population has a major effect on crime trends. After World War II, the birthrate increased sharply in what is known as the "baby boom." The baby-boom generation reached its crime-prone years in the 1960s, and the crime rate duly rose. As the generation grew older, the crime rate became more stable and in the 1980s began to decline. Some researchers claim that the children of the baby boomers may very well expand the ranks of the crime-prone ages once again and that crime will again increase.

During the period when the baby-boom generation outgrew criminal behavior, U.S. society was undergoing other changes. We adopted a get-tough crime-control policy, which may have deterred some people from committing crimes. Mandatory prison terms meant judges had less discretion in sentencing, and fewer convicted felons were paroled. In addition, crime-prevention programs, such as Neighborhood Watch groups, became popular. These and other factors have been suggested to explain why the crime rate dropped, but we have no definitive answers.

Locations and Times of Criminal Acts

Statistics on the characteristics of crimes are important not only to criminologists who seek to know why crime occurs but also to those who want to know how to prevent it (Chapter 9). Two

> **:// Crime Surfing**
> http://www.albany.edu/sourcebook
>
> The "Sourcebook of Criminal Justice Statistics" is an excellent place to look for official data on all parts of the criminal justice system. Go to this website to find the most recent arrest data for the area in which you live. Which three offenses have the most arrests?

Of Immediate Concern

Why Does Crime Drop?

It has been a few years since the dramatic drop in the rate for violent crime in New York City and many other jurisdictions across the country. Criminologists in policing circles have spent much of that time trying to understand why this drop occurred and debating various explanations. The number of ideas about what accounted for the decline in violent crime in the mid-1990s is growing as more researchers carry out studies to examine this phenomenon closely. Here are some opinions and findings:

- University of Chicago economist Steven Levitt and Stanford University law professor John Donohue III argue that legalizing abortion in 1973 (as a consequence of the *Roe v. Wade* decision) may account for as much as half of the drop in crime. This notion has generated a torrent of criticism from those on both sides of the abortion debate, as well as from some criminologists, who say the research does not examine other factors that may explain the drop in crime.(1)
- On the basis of data from the NCVS, Warren Friedman estimates that Americans devote almost 4 billion hours each year to "organized safety activity." He argues that what ordinary people contribute in these grassroots efforts is overlooked by most researchers, with their focus on punishment, police, and prisons. Crime prevention at the community level may well have had an important impact on the decline of violent crime.(2)
- In a study comparing alcohol consumption with homicide rates, researchers concluded that declining alcohol consumption is related to the drop in murders in the United States. They argue that violent crime may be reduced and prevented through "tighter regulation of alcohol availability, taxation, and restrictions on the age of purchase."(3)
- University of New Mexico criminologist Gary LaFree argues that changes in the "legitimacy of social institutions" explain the rapid changes in street-crime trends over the past 50 years. Declining crime rates in the 1990s, he asserts, may be the result of increased trust in political institutions, increased economic well-being, increased viable alternatives to the traditional two-parent family, as well as increased support for criminal justice, welfare, and educational institutions.(4)
- George Kelling and William Bratton (the latter who was the New York City police commissioner during one of the most dramatic drops in that city's crime rate) claim that the decline in violent crime is largely a result of a change in police tactics and strategies. Rather than focusing on serious crimes, the police began to address disorderly behavior and so-called quality-of-life offenses (such as public drunkenness and vagrancy). When these seemingly petty crimes were brought under control, citizens felt less fearful, and hard-core criminals found it more difficult to move into certain communities. In addition, New York City was one of the first places in the country to implement COMPSTAT, a process involving ongoing analysis of crime data and accountability for crime reduction at the precinct level.(5)
- In his decade-long ethnographic study of several Brooklyn communities, Rick Curtis concluded that one explanation for the drop in violent crime was that the people themselves took back their neighborhoods. Young people "shared a conviction that they would not succumb to the same fate that nearly erased the previous generation." They turned away from the things that would put them in danger: the open-market sale of

Crackdown on quality of life offenses. Here New York City police officers removed the homeless from Tomkins Square.

---

statistics of use in prevention efforts are those on *where* crimes are committed and *when* they are committed.

Most crimes are committed in large urban areas rather than in small cities, suburbs, or rural areas. This pattern can be attributed to a variety of factors—population density, age distribution of residents, stability of the population, economic conditions, and the quality of law enforcement, to name but a few. The statistics for Charlotte, North Carolina, for example, show that most arrests took place in the poverty-ridden ghetto areas. The fact that the majority of those arrests were made in neighborhoods where drug dealers were visibly present on the streets fits the national picture.

42

drugs, rampant violence, and hard-drug use.(6)
- Other criminologists point to the stabilization of the drug markets in inner cities. In business management parlance, drug markets are said to have "matured," which translates into fewer conflicts between rival drug dealers and fewer drug-related murders. Because this type of murder accounts for so many of the homicides occurring in cities, maturation of the drug market could explain a significant part of the drop in murder rates. In addition, the crack epidemic of the 1980s has largely subsided. There seems to have been a switch among users from cocaine, which agitates the user, to heroin, which mellows the user.(7)
- One school of thought holds that demographic changes, specifically a temporary dip in the high-crime population aged 18 to 24, can account for some of the drop in violent crime.(8)
- Another theory is that the most dangerous criminals are now in prison. In New York State alone, the number of felons behind bars is nearly 70,000, almost three times what it was 15 years ago.(9)

It has been said that criminologists are luckier than economists. Economists are judged on their ability to predict the future of the economy, while criminologists just have to explain what happened after the fact.(10) But explaining is harder than it seems, and the stakes can be high. The better that criminologists become at understanding past crime rates, the better they will be at predicting future crime rates. The implications of these predictions can be huge. Criminologists' predictions about crime patterns in the future can mean changes in, for example, policing strategies, the length of prison sentences, the amount of money to be earmarked for rehabilitation and child welfare programs, and politicians' and citizens' attitudes about crime and crime policy.

Sources

1. Erica Goode, "Linking Drop in Crime to Rise in Abortion," *New York Times,* Aug. 20, 1999, p. 14.
2. Warren Friedman, "Volunteerism and the Decline of Violent Crime," *Journal of Criminal Law and Criminology,* **88** (1999): 1453–1474.
3. Robert Nash Parker and Randi S. Cartmill, "Alcohol and Homicide in the United States 1934–1995—or One Reason Why U.S. Rates of Violence May Be Going Down," *Journal of Criminal Law and Criminology,* **88** (1999): 1369–1398.
4. Gary LaFree, "Social Institutions and the Crime 'Bust' of the 1990s," *Journal of Criminal Law and Criminology,* **88** (1999): 1325–1386.
5. George L. Kelling and William J. Bratton, "Declining Crime Rates: Insiders' Views of the New York City Story," *Journal of Criminal Law and Criminology,* **88** (1999): 1217–1232.
6. Richard Curtis, "The Improbable Transformation of Inner-City Neighborhoods: Crime, Violence, Drugs and Youth in the 1990s," *Journal of Criminal Law and Criminology,* **88** (1999): 1233–1276.
7. Clifford Krauss, "The Mystery of New York, the Suddenly Safer City," *New York Times,* July 23, 1995, p. 4A.
8. Gregory Beals and Evan Thomas, "A Crimebuster's Fall," *Newsweek,* Apr. 8, 1996, p. 42.
9. Camille Graham Camp and George M. Camp, *The Corrections Yearbook 1998* (Middletown, Conn.: Criminal Justice Institute, Inc., 1998), p. 6.
10. Michael D. Maltz, "Which Homicides Decreased? Why?" *Journal of Criminal Law and Criminology,* **88** (1999): 1489–1495.

Questions for Discussion

1. Why is there so much disagreement about what has caused the drop in violent crime? Do you think criminologists have vested interests in one explanation over another?
2. Is it possible for the police to have the great impact on crime that Kelling and Bratton claim? To what extent is crime something that can be controlled by the police?
3. Crime rates continue to drop across the country. Have you noticed any changes in your community in the past few years that may be a result of lower crime rates? For example, are there more businesses in downtown areas, do the streets seem safer, is there less drug-related violence?

NCVS data tell us the safest place to be is at home, although we are likely to be victimized when we are in familiar territory. In 1995, only one-quarter of violent crimes took place near or at the victim's home. Almost three-quarters of violent crimes occurred within 5 miles of home. Common locations for violent crimes are streets other than those near the victim's home (19 percent), at school (14 percent), or at a commercial establishment (12 percent).[36]

As for the time of day when crimes are committed, NCVS data reveal that over 57 percent of all violent crimes involving strangers are committed at night, between 6 P.M. and 6 A.M. Household crimes follow the same pattern: Of crimes committed within a known period, 70 per-

FIGURE 2.6 Serious juvenile crime by time of day. On school days serious juvenile crimes cluster in the hours immediately after the close of school. On school days, serious violent crimes by juveniles peak at 3 P.M.

On nonschool days the temporal pattern of juvenile violence is similar to the overall pattern for adults; juvenile violence peaks at night on nonschool days.

Note: Serious violent crimes include murder, violent sex assaults, robbery, and aggravated assault.

Source: Analyses of the FBI's *National Incident-Based Reporting System master files* for the years 1991–1996 [machine-readable data files], as cited in *Juvenile Offenders and Victims: 1999 National Report.*

cent of household larcenies and 75 percent of motor vehicle thefts are committed at night. Most personal thefts, however, are committed during the day. For juveniles, 19 percent of violent crimes occur in the four hours (3 P.M. to 7 P.M.) immediately after the close of school (Figure 2.6).[37]

Nationwide crime rates also vary by season. Personal and household crimes are more likely to be committed during the warmer months of the years, perhaps because in summer people spend more time outdoors, where they are more vulnerable to crime.[38] People also often leave doors and windows open when they go out in warm weather.

Did You Know?
... that in one-third of all sexual assaults reported to police, the victim was under the age of 12?

Severity of Crime

We have seen that crime rates vary by time and place. They also vary in people's perception of their severity. To some extent, legislation sets a standard of severity by the punishments it attaches to various crimes. But let us take a critical look at such judgments.

Do you believe that skyjacking an airplane is a more serious offense than smuggling heroin? Is forcible rape more serious than kidnapping? Is breaking into a home and stealing $1,000 more serious than using force to rob a person of $10? A yes answer to all three questions conforms with the findings of the National Survey of Crime Severity, which in 1977 measured public perceptions of the seriousness of 204 events, from planting a bomb that killed 20 people to playing hooky from school.[39]

The survey, conducted by Marvin E. Wolfgang and his colleagues, found that individuals generally agree about the relative seriousness of specific crimes (Table 2.2). In ranking severity, people seem to base their decisions on such factors as the ability of victims to protect themselves, the amount of injury and loss suffered, the type of business or organization from which property is stolen, the relationship between offender and victim, and (for drug offenses) the types of drugs involved. Respondents generally agreed that violent crime is more serious than property crime. They also considered white-collar crimes, such as engaging in consumer fraud, cheating on income taxes, polluting, and accepting bribes, to be as serious as many violent and property crimes.

MEASURING CHARACTERISTICS OF CRIMINALS

Information on the characteristics of crimes is not the only sort of data analyzed by criminologists. They also want to know the characteristics of the people who commit those crimes.

Behind each crime is a criminal or several criminals. Criminals can be differentiated by age, ethnicity, gender, socioeconomic level, and other criteria. These characteristics enable us to group criminals into categories, and it is these categories that researchers find useful. They study the various offender groups to determine why some people are more likely than others to commit crimes or particular types of crimes. It has been estimated that 12.2 million arrests

PART I **Understanding Criminology**

TABLE 2.2 How Do People Rank the Severity of Crime?

Severity Score	Ten Most Serious Offenses	Severity Score	Ten Least Serious Offenses
72.1	Planting a bomb in a public building. The bomb explodes and 20 people are killed.	1.3	Two persons willingly engage in a homosexual act.
52.8	A man forcibly rapes a woman. As a result of physical injuries, she dies.	1.1	Disturbing the neighborhood with loud, noisy behavior.
		1.1	Taking bets on the numbers.
43.2	Robbing a victim at gunpoint. The victim struggles and is shot to death.	1.1	A group continues to hang around a corner after being told to break up by a police officer.
39.2	A man stabs his wife. As a result, she dies.	0.9	A youngster under 16 years old runs away from home.
35.7	Stabbing a victim to death.	0.8	Being drunk in public.
35.6	Intentionally injuring a victim. As a result, the victim dies.	0.7	A youngster under 16 years old breaks a curfew law by being out on the street after the hour permitted by law.
		0.6	Trespassing in the backyard of a private home.
33.8	Running a narcotics ring.	0.3	A person is a vagrant. That is, he has no home and no visible means of support.
27.9	A woman stabs her husband. As a result, he dies.		
26.3	An armed person skyjacks an airplane and demands to be flown to another country.	0.2	A youngster under 16 years old plays hooky from school.
25.8	A man forcibly rapes a woman. No other physical injury occurs.		

Source: Adapted from Marvin E. Wolfgang, Robert Figlio, Paul E. Tracey, and Simon I. Singer, *National Survey of Crime Severity* (Washington, D.C.: U.S. Government Printing Office, 1985).

were made in 2000 for all criminal offenses except traffic violations. Figure 2.7 shows how these arrests were distributed among the offenses. During the 10 years between 1991 and 2000, the number of arrests for Crime Index offenses fell 25.3 percent. Let us take a close look at the characteristics of the persons arrested.[40]

Age and Crime

Six armed men who have been called the "over-the-hill gang" were arrested trying to rob an elegant bridge and backgammon club in midtown New York City. The robbery began at 10:25 P.M. when the men, wearing rubber gloves and ski masks and armed with two revolvers, a shotgun, and a rifle, forced the customers and employees to lie down in a back room while they loaded a nylon bag with wallets, players' money, and the club's cash box. A club worker slipped out a side door to alert police, who arrived within minutes. They surprised and disarmed one member of the gang, a 48-year-old, whom they found clutching a .22-caliber revolver. They took a .38-caliber revolver from another gang member, 41 years old.

During the scuffle with the officers, one suspect tried to escape, fell, and broke his nose. The officers then found and arrested a 40-year-old man standing in the hallway with a 12-gauge Winchester shotgun. Meanwhile, the other gang members abandoned their gloves and masks and lay down among the people they had robbed. One of the suspects, aged 72, who wore a back brace, complained of chest and back pain as police locked handcuffs on him. He was immediately hospitalized.[41]

In another case, 94-year-old career criminal Wesley (Pop) Honeywood, from Jacksonville, Florida, was sentenced to seven years after he pointed an unloaded gun at another man who warned him not to eat grapes growing in the man's yard. Mr. Honeywood was given the option to go to a nursing home

:// Crime Surfing

www.uncjin.org

The United Nations Crime and Justice Information Network (UNCJIN) is a resource for investigating crime and criminal justice systems in various countries around the world. The URL above will take you to reported crime data for many countries. Use these data to determine whether other countries have crime patterns similar to those of the United States.

FIGURE 2.7 Distribution of total number of arrests, 2000 (estimated).

PART I OFFENSES

Key:
- Violent crime
  - Murder and manslaughter
  - Forcible rape
  - Robbery
  - Aggravated assault } 625,132
- Property crime
  - Burglary
  - Larceny-theft
  - Motor vehicle theft
  - Arson } 1,620,928

PART II OFFENSES

Key:
- Other assaults 1,312,169
- Forgery, counterfeiting, fraud, embezzlement 473,338
- Sex, drugs, gambling 1,683,807
- Alcohol-related offenses 2,791,967
- Disorderly conduct, vagrancy 671,282
- Other offenses 4,719,592
  - stolen property • suspicion
  - vandalism • curfew
  - weapons • runaways
  - crimes v. family • other (except traffic)

Source: U.S. Department of Justice, Federal Bureau of Investigation, *Crime in the United States, 2000* (Washington, D.C.: U.S. Government Printing Office, 2001), p. 216.

---

instead of prison, but he resisted, saying, "If I go to jail, I may be out in a couple of years. If I go to a nursing home, I may be there the rest of my life."[42]

These cases are extraordinary for at least two reasons. First, in any given year approximately half of all arrests are of individuals under the age of 25; and second, gang membership is ordinarily confined to the young. Though juveniles (people under the age of 18) constitute about 8 percent of the population, they account for almost one-third of the arrests for Index crimes. Arrest rates begin to decline after age 30 and taper off to about 2.6 percent or less from age 50 on (Figure 2.8).[43] In fact, although people aged 65 and over constitute 12.6 percent of the population, they make up fewer than 1 percent of arrests.[44] This decline in criminal activities with age is known as the **aging-out phenomenon.** The reasons for it have sparked a lively scientific debate. Michael Gottfredson and Travis Hirschi contend there is a certain inclination to commit crimes which peaks in the middle or late teens and then declines throughout life. This relationship between crime and age does not change, "regardless of sex, race, country, time, or offense."[45]

Crime decreases with age, the researchers add, even among people who commit frequent offenses. Thus differences in crime rates found among young people of various groups, such as males and females or lower class and middle class, will be maintained throughout the life cycle. If lower-class youths are three times more likely to commit crimes than middle-class youths, for instance, then 60-year-old lower-class

Measuring World Crime

In the early 1970s, the General Assembly of the United Nations requested the Secretary-General to conduct a global survey on the prevalence of crime in Member States. Governments may have had various reasons for wanting to know the amount of crime in the world, but they all seemed to agree that crime impedes national development and imposes great burdens on individual victims.

The UN Crime Prevention and Criminal Justice Branch (now called the Centre for International Crime Prevention) surveyed all Member States by means of a questionnaire. This exercise has been repeated every five years so that by now, statistical information about the extent of crime (and the operations of criminal justice systems) is available for the period from 1970 to the present. The number of participating countries has increased over the years, from 72 to over 100. Many difficulties had to be overcome to obtain data and to assess their validity, such as national differences in the definitions of crimes, varying methods of reporting and recording those to be considered, as well as a variety of factors which prompt officials to under- or overstate the amount of some crimes. Victimization surveys and self-report studies, which have been conducted more recently, have helped in the analysis of the prevalence of crime.

While it is impossible to present the global picture here, a few statistical snapshots are indicative of the challenges posed by the UNCJS to statisticians and policy makers. The figure depicts the percentages of various crime types reported globally.

The global picture shows property crime to account for most criminality. Obviously, patterns vary somewhat from country to country, and from region to region.

In sample years from all five world crime surveys, a global comparison of homicide rates grouped by developing countries versus industrialized countries reveals a startling development, namely, a complete reversal of incident rates. In 1974, developing countries had over twice as many homicides as industrialized countries. By 1994, industrialized countries had twice as many homicides as the more rural developing countries.

This trend gives criminologists, statisticians, and policy makers much to think about: What accounts for this enormous shift to homicides in industrialized countries? Would one not have expected a far greater rise in homicides in developing countries, where ethnic strife and civil wars are exacting a great toll in lives? They must also address other startling findings in the never-ending effort to track down crime's root causes, to determine the relation between crime and socioeconomic development, and to evaluate the interplay between official (public) crime-prevention efforts and other forms of social control. Ultimately, they must devise policy guidelines that will be useful to nations and communities in dealing with the problem of crime *now,* before it victimizes more of the world's citizens and their countries.

Crime types reported to the UNCJS, 1994.

- Theft 50%
- Burglary 20%
- Drug-related 7%
- Fraud 7%
- Assault 7%
- Robbery 6%
- Other 3%

Source: Fifth United Nations Crime and Justice Survey Global Report on Crime and Justice.

Source

Graeme Newman, ed., *Global Report on Crime and Justice* (New York: United Nations; Oxford: Oxford University Press, 1999).

Questions for Discussion

1. Since every country has its own notions on what constitutes crime and how a particular crime is defined, how would you go about making statistical information received from 100 or more countries comparable?
2. Why would governments under- or overstate their "official" crime rates?
3. What methods can a statistician use to obtain a true picture of crime rates?

FIGURE 2.8 Violent Crime Index arrests by age.

Violent Crime Index arrests per 100,000 population

[Graph showing two curves labeled "1997" and "1980", peaking around ages 18–20 at approximately 975 and 750 respectively, declining with age from 10 to 65.]

Source: Analysis of arrest data from an unpublished FBI report for 1980 and the FBI's *Crime in the United States 1997* and population data from the Bureau of the Census for 1980 from *Current Population Reports*, P25–1095 and for 1997 from *Estimates of the Population of States by Age, Sex, Race, and Hispanic Origin: 1997* [machine-readable data file], as cited in *Juvenile Offenders and Victims: 1999 National Report.*

persons will be three times more likely to commit crimes than 60-year-old middle-class persons, though crimes committed by both lower-class and middle-class groups will constantly decline.[46] According to this argument, all offenders commit fewer crimes as they grow older because they have less strength, less mobility, and so on.

James Q. Wilson and Richard Herrnstein support the view that the aging-out phenomenon is a natural part of the life cycle.[47] Teenagers may become increasingly independent of their parents yet lack the resources to support themselves; they band together with other young people who are equally frustrated in their search for legitimate ways to get money, sex, alcohol, and status. Together they find illegitimate sources. With adulthood, the small gains from criminal behavior no longer seem so attractive. Legitimate means open up. They marry. Their peers no longer endorse law-breaking. They learn to delay gratification. Petty crime is no longer adventurous. It is at this time that the aging-out process begins for most individuals. Even the ones who continue to commit offenses will eventually slow down with increasing age.

The opposing side in this debate, sometimes called the "life-course perspective," argues that the decrease in crime rates after adolescence does not imply that the number of crimes committed by all individual offenders declines. In other words, the frequency of offending may go down for most offenders, but some chronic active offenders may continue to commit the same amount of crime over time. Why might this be so? Because the factors that influence any individual's entrance into criminal activity vary, the number and types of offenses committed vary, and the factors that eventually induce the individual to give up criminal activity vary.[48]

According to this argument, the frequency of criminal involvement, then, depends on such social factors as economic situation, peer pressure, and lifestyle; and it is these social factors that explain the aging-out phenomenon. A teenager's unemployment, for example, may have very little to do with the onset of criminal activity because the youngster is not yet in the labor force and still lives at home. Unemployment may increase an adult's rate of offending, however, because an adult requires income to support various responsibilities. Thus the relationship between age and crime is not the same for all offenders. Various conditions during the life cycle affect individuals' behavior in different ways.[49]

To learn how the causes of crime vary at different ages, Alfred Blumstein and his colleagues suggest that we study **criminal careers**, a concept that describes the onset of criminal activity, the types and amount of crime committed, and the termination of such activity.[50] **Longitudinal studies** of a particular group of people over time should enable researchers to uncover the factors that distinguish criminals from noncriminals and those that differentiate criminals in regard to the number and kinds of offenses they commit.

Those who are involved in research on criminal careers assume that offenders who commit 10 crimes may differ from those who commit 1 or 15. They ask: Are the factors that cause the second offense the same ones that cause the fourth or the fifth? Do different factors move one offender from theft to rape or from assault to shoplifting? How many persons in a **birth cohort** (a group of people born in the same year) will become criminals? Of those, how many will become career criminals (chronic offenders)?

In the 1960s, researchers at the Sellin Center of the University of Pennsylvania began a search for answers. Their earliest publication, in 1972, detailed the criminal careers of 9,945 boys (a cohort) born in Philadelphia in 1945. Marvin Wolfgang, Robert Figlio, and Thorsten Sellin obtained their data from school records and official police reports. Their major findings were that 35 percent of the boys had had contact with the police before reaching their 18th birthday; of those boys, 46 percent were one-time offenders and 54 percent were repeat offenders. Of those with police contact, 18 percent had committed five or more offenses; they represented 6 percent of the total. The "chronic 6 percent," as they are now called, were responsible for more than half of all the offenses committed, including 71 percent of the homicides, 73 percent of the rapes, 82 percent of the robberies, and 69 percent of the assaults.[51]

Research continued on 10 percent of the boys in the original cohort until they reached the age of 30. This sample was divided into three groups: those who had records of offenses only as juveniles, those who had records only as adults, and those who were persistent offenders with both juvenile and adult records. Though they made up only 15 percent of the follow-up group, those who had been chronic juvenile offenders made up 74 percent of all the arrests. Thus chronic juvenile offenders do indeed continue to break laws as adults.[52]

The boys in the original cohort were born in 1945. Researchers questioned whether the same behavior patterns would continue over the years. Criminologist Paul Tracy and his associates found the answer in a second study, which examined a cohort of 13,160 males born in 1958. The two studies show similar results. In the second cohort, 33 percent had had contact with the

> **Did You Know?**
>
> . . . that one in every three delinquents with a history of violent offenses has a juvenile court record before reaching age 14?

Two very old inmates in the geriatric unit at Estelle Prison, Huntsville, Texas: an increasing burden for custodial care.

police before reaching their 18th birthday, 42 percent were one-time offenders, and 58 percent were repeat offenders. Chronic delinquents were found in both cohorts. The chronic delinquents in the second cohort, however, accounted for a greater percentage of the cohort—7.5 percent. They also were involved in more serious and injurious acts than the previous group.

The 1945 cohort study did not contain females, so no overall comparisons can be made over time. But comparing females and males in the 1958 cohort, we see significant gender differences. Of the 14,000 females in the cohort, 14 percent had had contact with the police before age 18. Among the female delinquents, 60 percent were one-time offenders, 33 percent were repeat offenders, and 7 percent were chronic offenders. Overall, female delinquency was less frequent and less likely to involve serious charges.[53]

In another longitudinal study, researchers followed about 4,000 youngsters in Denver, Pittsburgh, and Rochester, New York, for five years, 1988 through 1992. By the age of 16, over half the youngsters admitted to committing violent criminal acts. According to Terence P. Thornberry, the principal investigator in Rochester, chronic offenders also accounted for a high percentage of all violent offenses: 15 percent of the youths in the sample were responsible for 75 percent of the acts.[54]

The policy implications of such findings are clear. If a very small group of offenders is committing a large percentage of all crime, the crime rate should go down if we incarcerate those offenders for long periods of time. Many jurisdictions around the country are developing sentencing policies to do just that, but such policies are quite controversial.

Gender and Crime

Except for such crimes as prostitution, shoplifting, and welfare fraud, males traditionally commit more crimes than females at all ages. According to the UCR for 2000, the arrest ratio is typically about 4 male offenders to 1 female offender.[55] The NCVS of 1999 reports a wider gap: For personal crimes of violence involving a single offender, 82 percent of victims perceived the gender of the offender as male.[56]

Since the 1960s, however, there have been some interesting developments in regard to gender and crime data. In 1960 females accounted for 11 percent of the total number of arrests across the country. They now account for about 22 percent. And while the female arrest rate is still much lower than that of males, the rate of increase for women has risen faster than the rate for men (Figure 2.9 shows juvenile rates).[57]

Self-report surveys, which show more similarities in male and female criminal activity than official reports do, find that males commit more offenses than females. However, several of these studies suggest that gender differences in crime may be narrowing. They demonstrate that the patterns and causes of male and female delinquent activity are becoming more alike.[58] John Hagan and his associates agree, but only with respect to girls raised in middle-class egalitarian families in which husband and wife share similar positions of power at home and in the workplace. They argue that girls raised in lower-class, father-dominated households grow up in a cult of domesticity that reduces their freedom and thus the likelihood of their delinquency.[59] Researchers Merry Morash and Meda Chesney-Lind disagree. In a study of 1,427 adolescents and their caretakers, they found gender differences in delinquency between girls and boys regardless of the type of family in which the youngsters were raised.[60]

Because women traditionally have had such low crime rates, the scientific community and the mass media had generally ignored the subject of female criminality. Both have tended to view female offenders as misguided children who are an embarrassment rather than a threat to society. Only a handful of the world's criminologists have deemed the subject worthy of independent study. Foremost among them was Cesare Lombroso (whom we shall meet again in Chapter 3). His book *The Female Offender* (coauthored by William Ferrero), which appeared in 1895, detailed the physical abnormalities that would predestine some girls to be criminal from birth.[61] Lombroso's findings on male criminals, however, have not stood the test of later scientific research, and his por-

FIGURE 2.9 Juvenile male and female arrest rates.

Property Crime Index arrest rate	1981	1997
Male	3,895	3,242
Female	931	1,298

Aggravated assault arrest rate	1981	1997
Male	229	385
Female	44	105

While juvenile male arrest rates for Property Crime Index offenses declined during the 1990s, the female rate increased. Between 1981 and 1997, male juvenile property crime rates declined 17 percent, while female rates increased 39 percent.

While male arrest rates for aggravated assault leveled off between 1992 and 1995, female arrest rates continued to increase. In 1997, male arrest rates for aggravated assault were nearly four times the female rates. Between 1981 and 1997, female arrest rates increased twice as much as male rates increased.

Note: Arrest rates are arrests per 100,000 males or females ages 10 to 17.

Source: Analyses of arrest data from unpublished FBI reports for 1980 through 1994 and the FBI's *Crime in the United States* reports for 1995, 1996, and 1997 and population data from the Bureau of the Census for 1980 through 1989 from *Current Population Reports*, P25–1095 and for 1990 through 1997 from *Estimates of the Population of States by Age, Sex, Race, and Hispanic Origin: 1990–1997* [machine-readable data files], as cited in *Juvenile Offenders and Victims: 1999 National Report*.

trayal of the female criminal has been found to be similarly inaccurate.

A little over a generation later, in the 1930s, Sheldon and Eleanor Glueck launched a massive research project on the biological and environmental causes of crime, with a separate inquiry into female offenders. Their conclusions were decidedly sociological. They said, in essence, that in order to change the incidence of female criminality, there would have to be a change in the social circumstances in which females grow up.[62]

Otto Pollack shared the Gluecks' views on sociological determinants. In 1952 he proposed that female crime has a "masked character" that keeps it from being properly recorded or otherwise noted in statistical reports. Protective attitudes toward women make police officers less willing to arrest them, make victims less eager to report their offenses, make district attorneys less enthusiastic about prosecuting them, and make juries less likely to find them guilty. Moreover, Pollack noted that women's social roles as homemakers, child rearers, and shoppers furnish them with opportunities for concealed criminal activity and with victims who are the least likely to complain and/or cooperate with the police. He also argued that female crime was limited by the various psychological and physiological characteristics inherent in the female anatomy.[63]

A quarter century after Pollack's work, two researchers, working independently, took a fresh look at female crime in light of women's new roles in society. In 1975 Freda Adler posited that as social and economic roles of women changed in the legitimate world, their participation in crime would also change. According to this argument, the temptations, challenges, stresses, and strains to which women have been

Mary Kay Letourneau, 35 years old, the teacher who had sex with a 13-year-old student and gave birth to his child, is sentenced to six months in jail in a Seattle, Washington, court (Nov. 1997). Ms. Letourneau had pleaded guilty to second degree child rape. Shortly after her release from jail, she resumed her relationship with the boy and was sentenced to seven years in prison for violating the conditions of her release. (She subsequently had a second child with the boy.) The boy, now 19 years old, recently sued the Highline School District and the Des Moines, Washington, police department for nearly $2 million, claiming the authorities did not do enough to protect him. In May 2002, the suit was dismissed.

increasingly subjected in recent years cause them to act or react in the same manner in which men have consistently reacted to the same stimuli. In other words, equalization of social and economic roles leads to similar behavior patterns, both legal and illegal, on the part of both men and women. To steal a car, for example, one needs to know how to drive. To embezzle, one needs to be in a position of trust and in control of funds. To get into a bar fight, one needs to go to a bar. To be an inside trader on Wall Street, one needs to be on the inside.[64]

Rita Simon has taken a similar position. She, too, has argued that female criminality has undergone changes. But these changes, according to Simon, have occurred only in regard to certain property crimes, such as larceny/theft and fraud/embezzlement. Women are becoming more involved in these crimes because they have more opportunities to commit them. Simon hypothesizes that since the propensity of men and women to commit crime is not basically different, as more women enter the labor force and work in a much broader range of jobs, their property crime rate will continue to go up.[65]

Some criminologists have challenged the views of Adler and Simon. Many questions have been asked about the so-called new female criminal. Does she exist? If so, does she commit more crimes than the old female criminal did? What types of crimes? Is she still involved primarily in offenses against property, or has she turned to more violent offenses? Researchers differ on the answers. Some contend that the extent of female criminality has not changed through the years but that crimes committed by women are more often making their way into official statistics simply because they are more often reported and prosecuted. In other words, the days of chivalry in the criminal justice system are over.[66]

Others argue that female crime has indeed increased, but they attribute the increase to nonviolent, petty property offenses that continue to reflect traditional female gender roles.[67] Moreover, some investigators claim, the increased involvement in these petty property offenses suggests that women are still economically disadvantaged, still suffering sexism in the legitimate marketplace.[68] Other researchers support the contention of Adler and Simon that female roles have changed and that these changes have indeed led women to commit the same kinds of crimes as men, violent as well as property offenses.[69]

Though scholars disagree on the form and extent of female crime, they do seem to agree that the crimes women commit are closely associated with their socioeconomic position in society. The controversy has to do with whether or not that position has changed. In any case, the association between gender and crime has become a recognized area of concern in the growing body of research dealing with contemporary criminological issues.[70]

Social Class and Crime

Researchers agree on the importance of age and gender as factors related to crime, but they disagree strongly about whether social class is related to crime. First of all, the term "class" can have many meanings. If "lower class" is defined by income, then the category might include graduate students, unemployed stockbrokers, pensioners, welfare mothers, prison inmates, and many others who have little in common except low income. Furthermore, "lower class" is often defined by the low prestige associated with blue-collar occupations. Some delinquency studies determine the class of young people by the class of their fathers, even though the young people may have jobs quite different from those of their fathers.

Another dispute focuses on the source of statistics used by investigators. Many researchers attribute the relatively strong association between class and crime found in arrest statistics to class bias on the part of the police. If the police are more likely to arrest a lower-class suspect than a middle-class suspect, they say, arrest data will show more involvement of lower-class people in criminality whether or not they are actually committing more crimes. When Charles Tittle, Wayne Villemez, and Douglas Smith analyzed 35 studies of the relationship between social class and crime rates in 1978, they found little support for the claim that crime is primarily a lower-class phenomenon. An update of that work, which evaluates studies done between 1978 and 1990, again found no pervasive relationship.[71]

Many scholars have challenged such conclusions. They claim that when self-report studies are used for analysis, the results show few class differences because the studies ask only about trivial offenses. Delbert Elliott and Suzanne Ageton, for example, looked at serious crimes among a national sample of 1,726 young people ages 11 to 17. According to the youths' responses to a self-report questionnaire, lower-class young people were much more likely than

Martin Frankel was arrested at this luxury Hamburg, Germany, hotel on charges of money laundering and wire fraud in the amount of $350 million.

middle-class young people to commit such serious crimes as burglary, robbery, assault, and sexual assault.[72] A follow-up study concluded that middle-class and lower-class youths differed significantly in both the nature and the number of serious crimes they committed.[73]

Controversies remain about the social class of people who commit crimes. There is no controversy, however, about the social class of people in prison. The probability that a person such as Chan Desaigoudar, former chief executive officer of California Micro Devices, who was convicted of insider trading, will get a prison sentence is extremely low. Desaigoudar does not fit the typical profile of the hundreds of thousands of inmates of our nation's jails and prisons. He is educated. Only 28 percent of prison inmates have completed high school.[74] His income was that of a high-ranking corporate officer. The average yearly income of jail inmates who work is $5,600. He had a white-collar job. Eighty-five percent of prison inmates are blue-collar workers. He committed a white-collar offense. Only 18 percent of those convicted of such offenses go to prison for more than one year, whereas 39 percent of the violent offenders and 26 percent of the property offenders do.[75] Finally, Chan Desaigoudar is white in a criminal justice system where blacks are disproportionately represented.

Race and Crime

Statistics on race and crime show that while African Americans constitute 12 percent of the population, they account for 30.4 percent of all arrests for Index crimes.[76] Other statistics confirm their disproportionate representation in the criminal justice system. Fifty percent of black urban males are arrested for an Index crime at least once during their lives, compared with 14 percent of white males. The likelihood that any man will serve time in jail or prison is estimated to be 18 percent for blacks and 3 percent for whites. Moreover, the leading cause of death among young black men is murder.[77]

These statistics raise many questions. Do blacks actually commit more crimes? Or are they simply arrested more often? Are black neighborhoods under more police surveillance than white neighborhoods? Do blacks receive differential treatment in the criminal justice system? If blacks commit more crimes than whites, why?

Some data support the argument that there are more African Americans in the criminal justice system because bias operates from the time of arrest through incarceration. Other data support the argument that racial disparities in official statistics reflect an actual difference in criminal behavior. Much of the evidence comes from the statistics of the NCVS, which are very similar to the statistics on race found in arrest data. When interviewers asked victims about the race of offenders in violent crimes, 28 percent identified the assailants as black.[78] Similarly, while self-report data demonstrate that less-serious juvenile offenses are about equally prevalent among black and white youngsters, more serious ones are not: Black youngsters report having committed many more Index crimes than do whites of comparable ages.[79]

If the disparity in criminal behavior suggested by official data, victimization studies, and self-reports actually exists, and if we are to explain it, we have to try to discover why people commit crimes. A history of hundreds of years of abuse, neglect, and discrimination against black Americans has left its mark in the form of high unemployment, residence in socially disorganized areas, one-parent households, and negative self-images.

In 1968, in the aftermath of the worst riots in modern American history, the National Advisory Commission on Civil Disorders alluded to the reasons blacks had not achieved the successes accomplished by other minority groups that at one time or another were discriminated against as well. European immigrants provided unskilled labor needed by industry. By the time blacks migrated from rural areas to cities, the U.S. economy was changing and soon there was no longer much demand for unskilled labor. Immigrant groups had also received economic advantages by working for local political organizations. By the time blacks moved to the cities, the political machines no longer had the power to offer help in return for votes. Though both immigrants and blacks arrived in cities with little money, all but the very youngest members of the cohesive immigrant family contributed to the family's income. As slaves, however, black persons had been forbidden to marry, and the unions they formed were subject to disruption at the owner's convenience and therefore tended to be unstable. We will have more to say about the causal factors associated with high crime rates and race in Chapters 5 and 6.

REVIEW

Researchers have three main objectives in measuring crime and criminal behavior patterns. They need (1) to collect and analyze data to test theories about why people commit crime, (2) to learn the situational characteristics of crimes in order to develop prevention strategies, and (3) to determine the needs of the criminal justice system on a daily basis. Data are collected by surveys, experiments, nonparticipant and participant observation, and case studies. It is often cost effective for researchers to use repositories of information gathered by public and private organizations for their own purposes. The three main sources of data for measuring crime are the Uniform Crime Reports, the National Crime Victimization Survey, and self-report questionnaires. Though each source is useful for some purposes, all three have limitations.

By measuring the characteristics of crime and criminals, we can identify crime trends, the places and times at which crimes are most likely to be committed, and the public's evaluation of the seriousness of offenses. Current controversies concerning offenders focus on the relationship between crime and age throughout the life cycle, the changing role of women in crime, and the effects of social class and race on the response of the criminal justice system. Crime is an activity disproportionately engaged in by young people, males, and minorities.

CRIMINOLOGY & PUBLIC POLICY

Police defend their racially disparate practices by saying that, generally, minorities commit more crimes than whites. They also hold that enforcement of criminal laws that are violated by whites and minorities in roughly even numbers (for example, narcotics violations) is disproportionate because the location and social impact of the same types of crimes justifies a more aggressive response in minority communities. They argue that current practices work: Aggressive policing and targeting of minority communities have led to significant seizures of contraband, weapons, and fugitives—and a reduction in crime.

In the wake of September 11 events, advocates of racial and ethnic profiling point to the need for heightened suspicion regarding the activities of young Arabic men. The arrests and detention of hundreds of people after the terrorist attacks has created considerable controversy—many of these people would not have been subject to this treatment were it not for ethnic characteristics, and the government has not yet provided evidence linking them to terrorist activities. Furthermore, it is not likely that ethnic profiling will be any more useful or constitutional than racial profiling. In the area in which racial profiling has been most controversial—narcotics enforcement—proponents' arguments do not withstand empirical and legal scrutiny. For example, the data do not indicate a minority-dominated drug trade. National drug abuse studies show that minorities possess and use drugs only slightly more frequently than whites do. "The typical cocaine user is white, male, a high school graduate employed full-time, and living in a small metropolitan area or suburb," former drug czar William Bennett has said.

Arrest statistics are also misleading. New Jersey's attorney general pointed out that these statistics are "a self-fulfilling prophecy where law enforcement agencies rely on arrest data that they themselves generated as a result of the discretionary allocation of resources and targeted drug enforcement efforts." Empirical evidence from reviews of car stops and searches supports this view. On the New Jersey Turnpike, 10.5 percent of contraband seized during traffic stops came from white drivers and 13.5 percent from African American drivers. In Maryland, searches on I-95 resulted in "find rates" that were roughly equal by race. In both states, mostly small amounts of drugs were seized, indicating possession for personal use. Millions of drivers use these highways each day, yet so few stops or searches of motorists—black or white—result in contraband seizures that it's hard to justify stopping large numbers of African-Americans so the police can make the occasional seizure. The logic behind racial profiling is faulty, as Ira Glasser, former executive director of the Americal Civil Liberties Union, has said:

> Even if most of the drug dealers in the Northeast corridor or in any particular neighborhood or city are black or Latino, it does not follow that most blacks and Latinos are drug dealers. . . . Think about it for a minute. Most players in the NBA are black. But if you were trying to get a team together, you wouldn't go out in the street and round up random African-Americans.
>
> It's a very simple, logical fallacy. The fact that most drug dealers are X does not mean that most X are drug dealers. In policing, as in many areas of contemporary American life, race matters—and it matters a lot. The substantial racial disparities documented in stop, frisk, and search practices cannot be fully explained or rationalized by crime patterns, police deployment, or policing tactics. (Source: David Rudovsky, "Breaking the Pattern of Racial Profiling," *Trial*, August 2002.)

Questions for Discussion Crime data are often discussed in racial terms. As we note on page 54, these data raise a host of questions including, as Prof. Rudovsky notes, the way in which people of color are treated by police. Is racial profiling justifiable? Ever? If the answer is yes, how effective must the profiling be to remain justified? If the answer is no, do the events of 9/11 suggest a justification for other forms of ethnic profiling?

YOU BE THE CRIMINOLOGIST

Your agency has been asked by the mayor's office to develop a program to reduce youth violence. Of course, you must first determine the extent of youth violence before going out into the field to talk to people. You plan to use information that is publicly available. What specifically will you measure, and what data will you use?

KEY TERMS

The numbers next to the terms refer to the pages on which the terms are defined.

aging-out phenomenon (46)
birth cohort (48)
case study (32)
crimes against property (34)
crimes against the person (34)
criminal careers (48)
data (29)
experiment (30)
felonies (27)
field experiment (31)
hypothesis (29)
Index crimes (34)
longitudinal studies (48)
mens rea (26)
misdemeanors (27)
nonparticipant observation (32)
participant observation (32)
population (30)
primary data (30)
random sample (30)
sample (30)
secondary data (30)
self-report surveys (38)
strict liability (27)
survey (30)
theory (29)
torts (27)
variables (30)
victimization surveys (36)
violations (27)

CHAPTER 3
Schools of Thought throughout History

Classical Criminology
  The Historical Context
  Cesare Beccaria
  Jeremy Bentham's Utilitarianism
  The Classical School: An Evaluation

Positivist Criminology

Biological Determinism: The Search for Criminal Traits
  Lombroso, Ferri, Garofalo: The Italian School
  A Return to Biological Determinism

Psychological Determinism
  Pioneers in Criminal Psychology
  Psychological Studies of Criminals

Sociological Determinism
  Adolphe Quételet and André Michel Guerry
  Gabriel Tarde
  Émile Durkheim

Historical and Contemporary Criminology: A Time Line

REVIEW

CRIMINOLOGY & PUBLIC POLICY

YOU BE THE CRIMINOLOGIST

KEY TERMS

Boxes
  Window to the World: *Stone Age Crime and Social Control*
  Of Immediate Concern: *Utilitarianism Gone Astray*
  From the Pages of The New York Times: *Who's Responsible?*

Special Features
  Crime Surfing
  Did You Know?

KEY TERMS
anomie
atavistic stigmata
born criminal
classical school
eugenics
laws of imitation
phrenology
physiognomy
positivist school
somatotype school
utilitarianism

Painter Vincent van Gogh portrayed himself among the inmates in *The Prison Courtyard*, 1890. Oil on canvas. The Pushkin Museum of Fine Art, Moscow, Russia.

Criminologists traditionally consider that their field has its origins as a science in the eighteenth century, when Cesare Beccaria established what came to be known as the "classical school of criminology." But when we look at what some much earlier thinkers had to say about crime, we may have to reconsider this assumption. Take a look at this quotation:

"Children now love luxury. They have bad manners, contempt for authority. They show disrespect for elders. They contradict their parents, chatter before company, cross their legs and tyrannize their teachers."[1] This may appear to be a modern description of delinquent youth, but Socrates made this observation over 2300 years ago.

Scholars, philosophers, and poets have speculated about the causes of crime and possible remedies since ancient times, and modern criminology owes much to the wisdom the ancient philosophers displayed. The philosophical approach culminated in the middle of the eighteenth century in the **classical school of criminology.** It is based on the assumption that individuals choose to commit crimes after weighing the consequences of their actions. According to classical criminologists, individuals have free will. They can choose legal or illegal means to get what they want; fear of punishment can deter them from committing crime; and society can control behavior by making the pain of punishment greater than the pleasure of the criminal gains.

Public punishment: painting depicts beheading of the king's wife Marie Antoinette at the guillotine, October 16, 1793.

The classical school did not remain unchallenged for long. In the early nineteenth century great advances were made in the natural sciences and in medicine. Physicians in France, Germany, and England undertook systematic studies of crimes and criminals. Crime statistics became available in several European countries. There emerged an opposing school of criminology, the **positivist school.** This school posits that human behavior is determined by forces beyond individual control and that it is possible to measure those forces. Unlike classical criminologists, who claim that people rationally choose to commit crime, positivist criminologists view criminal behavior as stemming from biological, psychological, and social factors.

The earliest positivist theories centered on biological factors, and studies of those factors dominated criminology during the last half of the nineteenth century. In the twentieth century, biological explanations were ignored (and even targeted as racist after World War II). They did not surface again until the 1970s, when scientific advances in psychology shifted the emphasis from defects in criminals' bodies to defects in their minds. Throughout the twentieth century, psychologists and psychiatrists have played a major role in the study of crime causation. A third area of positivist criminology focuses on the relation of social factors to crime. Sociological theories, developed in the second half of the nineteenth century and advanced throughout the twentieth, continue to dominate the field of criminology today.

An understanding of the foundations of modern criminology helps us understand contemporary developments in the field. Let us begin with the developments that led to the emergence of the classical school.

CLASSICAL CRIMINOLOGY

In the late eighteenth to the mid-nineteenth centuries, during what is now called the "neoclassical period," the classical culture of the ancient Mediterranean was rediscovered. This was also a period of scientific discoveries and the founding of new scholarly disciplines. One of these was criminology, which developed as an attempt to apply rationality and the rule of law to brutal and arbitrary criminal justice processes.

Stone Age Crime and Social Control

On a fine Thursday afternoon in September 1991, vacationers from Germany, on an alpine hiking trip, spotted a head protruding from the glacial ice. They hurried to a nearby guest house and reported their find to the innkeeper, who promptly called both the Italian and the Austrian police. It became immediately apparent that this corpse was no ordinary mountain casualty. Rather, this was an ancient mountain casualty. Experts were brought in from Austrian universities, and the body was freed from its icy embrace. It was dubbed "Oetzi," after the Oetztal Alps of the discovery.

Oetzi is 5,300 years old, a robust young man, 25 to 30 years old at the time of his death. Completely mummified, he was found in the position in which he had placed himself, in a crevice, probably to escape a snowstorm. He was fully dressed, in an unlined fur robe. Originally fashioned with great skill, the robe was badly repaired with sinew and plant fiber, suggesting that he could not have relied on the services of his wife or the village seamstress for some time. Oetzi had placed his equipment by his side, most of it of the best Stone Age craftsmanship. What is surprising is that he did not carry with him a ready-to-shoot bow.

Investigators determined that Oetzi was an outdoor type, a shepherd who sought refuge in the crevice, froze to death, and was preserved for five millennia by permafrost and glacial ice. But what was Oetzi doing at 3,210 meters (nearly 10,000 feet) above sea level on a fall day? Obviously, he was not a herder since he was far above the grazing range of a herd. Nor was he a trader trying to cross the Alps in the fall. So what was he doing up there, where nothing grows and where it is hard to breathe? One answer, based on all the evidence available so far, is that Oetzi may have been an outlaw.

Oetzi was a Late Stone Age (Neolithic) man, likely to have come from a herding community of, at most, 200 persons. Robert Carneiro of the American Museum of Natural History has figured out that a community of 200 produces 20,000 one-on-one disagreement possibilities. Oetzi may have had such interpersonal problems.

The tasks of social control even within such a small community stagger the imagination. Fighting could have erupted within the community. Jealousy could be engendered about who deserves more respect as the best hunter, the best storyteller, the best healer, or the wisest person. A dispute could have happened over the distribution of food or the sharing of tools.

The evidence about Neolithic society permits us to conclude that these societies had no institution that we could compare with modern criminal justice, although they had problems that today might be referred to a criminal justice system. How were such problems solved? Minor problems were dealt with by the use of shaming, by dispute resolution, by compensation, and by sacrifices. Major unforgivable offenses led to casting out the wrongdoers: They would be declared outlaws. They had to leave camp instantly, without gathering weapons or tools, and flee to the wilderness. Oetzi fits the description of such an outlaw, literally, a person cast outside the protection of the laws, the customs, and the protection of his group, to take to the wilderness and perhaps to die there. If Oetzi was a criminal banished from his village, the punishment clearly was effective.

Oetzi, who was preserved in the glacial crevice in which he died five thousand years ago.

Source

Adapted from Gerhard O. W. Mueller and Freda Adler, "The Emergence of Criminal Justice: Tracing the Route to Neolithic Times," in *Festskrift till Jacob W. F. Sundberg*, eds. Erik Nerep and Wiweka Warnling Nerep (Stockholm: Jurisförlaget, 1993), pp. 151–170.

Questions for Discussion

1. For purposes of improving modern crime-control techniques, can we learn anything from Stone Age societies?
2. What crimes do you think might result in the banishment of one of the members of such a community?

The work of criminology's founders—scholars like Cesare Beccaria and Jeremy Bentham—became known as "classical criminology."

The Historical Context

Classical criminology grew out of a reaction against the barbaric system of law, punishment, and justice that existed before the French Revolution of 1789. Until that time, there was no real system of criminal justice in Europe. There were crimes against the state, against the church, and against the crown. Some of these crimes were specified; some were not. Judges had discretionary power to convict a person for an act not even legally defined as criminal.[2] Monarchs often issued what were called in French *lettres de cachet,* under which an individual could be imprisoned for almost any reason (disobedience to one's father, for example) or for no reason at all.

Many criminal laws were unwritten, and those that had been drafted, by and large, did not specify the kind or amount of punishment associated with various crimes. Arbitrary and often cruel sentences were imposed by judges who had unbounded discretion to decide questions of guilt and innocence and to mete out punishment. Due process in the modern sense did not exist. While there was some official consensus on what constituted crime, there was no real limit to the amount and type of legal sanction a court could command. Punishments included branding, burning, flogging, mutilating, drowning, banishing, and beheading.[3] In England a person might receive the death penalty for any of more than 200 offenses, including what we today call petty theft.

Public punishments were popular events. When Robert-François Damiens was scheduled to be executed on March 2, 1757, for the attempted murder of Louis XV, so many people wanted to attend the spectacle that window seats overlooking the execution site were rented for high prices. Torture to elicit confessions was common. A criminal defendant in France might be subjected to the *peine forte et dure,* which consisted of stretching him on his back and placing over him an iron weight as heavy as he could bear. He was left that way until he died or spoke. A man would suffer these torments and lose his life in order to avoid trial and therefore conviction so that his lands and goods would not be confiscated and would be preserved for his family. This proceeding was not abolished until 1772.[4]

Even as Europe grew increasingly modern, industrial, and urban in the eighteenth century, it still clung to its medieval penal practices. With prosperity came an increasing gulf between the haves and the have-nots. Just before the French Revolution, for example, a Parisian worker paid 97 percent of his daily earnings for a 4-pound loaf of bread.[5] Hordes of unemployed people begged by day and found shelter under bridges by night. One of the few ways in which the established upper class could protect itself was through ruthless oppression of those beneath it, but ruthless oppression created more problems. Social unrest grew. And as crime rates rose, so did the brutality of punishment. Both church and state became increasingly tyrannical, using violence to conquer violence.

The growing educated classes began to see the inconsistency in these policies. If terrible tortures were designed to deter crime, why were people committing even more crimes? Something must be wrong with the underlying reasoning. By the mid-eighteenth century, social reformers were beginning to suggest a more rational approach to crime and punishment. One of them, Cesare Beccaria, laid the foundation for the first school of criminology—the classical school.

Cesare Beccaria

Cesare Bonesana, Marchese di Beccaria (1738–1794), was rather undistinguished as a student. After graduating with a law degree from the University of Pavia, he returned home to Milan and joined a group of articulate and radical intellectuals. Disenchanted with contemporary European society, they organized themselves into the Academy of Fists, one of many young men's clubs that flourished in Italy at the time. Their purpose was to discover what reforms would be needed to modernize Italian society.

In March 1763 Beccaria was assigned to prepare a report on the prison system. Pietro Verri,

Cesare Beccaria, the young Italian nobleman-dissident who became the father of modern criminology with his monograph, *On Crimes and Punishment*.

Did You Know?

. . . that it took the 26-year-old Cesare Beccaria just nine months to write *On Crimes and Punishment*, the brief book that has influenced criminology all over the world? And did you know that he published the book anonymously out of fear that the authorities, with their interest in perpetuating the existing brutal system, would persecute him?

the head of the Academy of Fists, encouraged him to read the works of English and French philosophers—David Hume (1711–1776), John Locke (1632–1704), Claude Adrien Helvétius (1715–1771), Voltaire (1694–1778), Montesquieu (1685–1755), and Jean-Jacques Rousseau (1712–1778). Another member of the academy, the protector of prisons, revealed to him the inhumanities that were possible under the guise of social control. Beccaria learned well. He read, observed, and made notes on small scraps of paper. These notes, Harry Elmer Barnes has observed, were destined to "assure to its author immortality and would work a revolution in the moral world" upon their publication in July 1764 under the title *Dei delitti e delle pene (On Crimes and Punishment)*.[6] Beccaria presented a coherent, comprehensive design for an enlightened criminal justice system that was to serve the people rather than the monarchy.

The climate was right: With the publication of this small book, Cesare Beccaria became the "father of modern criminology." The controversy between the rule of men and the rule of law was at its most heated. Some people defended the old order, under which judges and administrators made arbitrary or whimsical decisions. Others fought for the rule of law, under which the decision making of judges and administrators would be confined by legal limitations. Beccaria's words provided the spark that ultimately ended medieval barbarism.

According to Beccaria, the crime problem could be traced not to bad people but to bad laws. A modern criminal justice system should guarantee all people equal treatment before the law. Beccaria's book supplied the blueprint. That blueprint was based on the assumption that people freely choose what they do and are responsible for the consequences of their behavior. Beccaria proposed the following principles:

- *Laws should be used to maintain the social contract.* "Laws are the conditions under which men, naturally independent, united themselves in society. Weary of living in a continual state of war, and of enjoying a liberty, which became of little value, from the uncertainty of its duration, they sacrificed one part of it, to enjoy the rest in peace and security."

- *Only legislators should create laws.* "The authority of making penal laws can only reside with the legislator, who represents the whole society united by the social compact."

- *Judges should impose punishment only in accordance with the law.* "[N]o magistrate then, (as he is one of the society), can, with justice inflict on any other member of the same society punishment that is not ordained by the laws."

- *Judges should not interpret the laws.* "Judges, in criminal cases, have no right to interpret the penal laws, because they are not legislators. . . . Every man hath his own particular point of view, and, at different times, sees the same objects in very different lights. The spirit of the laws will then be the result of the good or bad logic of the judge; and this will depend on his good or bad digestion."

- *Punishment should be based on the pleasure/pain principle.* "Pleasure and pain are the only springs of actions in beings endowed with sensibility. . . . If an equal punishment be ordained for two crimes that injure society in different degrees, there is nothing to deter men from committing the greater as often as it is attended with greater advantage."

- *Punishment should be based on the act, not on the actor.* "Crimes are only to be measured by the injuries done to the society. They err, therefore, who imagine that a crime is greater or less according to the intention of the person by whom it is committed."

- *The punishment should be determined by the crime.* "If mathematical calculation could be applied to the obscure and infinite combinations of human actions, there might be a corresponding scale of punishments descending from the greatest to the least."

- *Punishment should be prompt and effective.* "The more immediate after the commission of a crime a punishment is inflicted, the more just and useful it will be. . . . An immediate punishment is more useful; because the smaller the interval of time between the punishment and the crime, the stronger and more lasting will be the association of the two ideas of crime and punishment."

- *All people should be treated equally.* "I assert that the punishment of a nobleman should in no wise differ from that of the lowest member of society."

- *Capital punishment should be abolished.* "The punishment of death is not authorized by any right; for . . . no such right exists. . . . The terrors of death make so slight an impression, that it has not force enough to withstand the forgetfulness natural to mankind."

- *The use of torture to gain confessions should be abolished.* "It is confounding all relations to expect . . . that pain should be the test of truth, as if truth resided in the muscles and fibres of a wretch in torture. By this method the robust will escape, and the feeble be condemned."

- *It is better to prevent crimes than to punish them.* "Would you prevent crimes? Let the laws be clear and simple, let the entire force of the nation be united in their defence, let them be intended rather to favour every individual than any particular classes. . . . Finally, the most certain method of preventing crime is to perfect the system of education."[7]

Perhaps no other book in the history of criminology has had so great an impact. Beccaria's ideas were so advanced that Voltaire, the great French philosopher of the time, who wrote the commentary for the French version, referred to Beccaria as "brother."[8] The English version appeared in 1767; by that time, three years after the book's publication, it had already gone through six Italian editions and several French editions.

After the French Revolution, Beccaria's basic tenets served as a guide for the drafting of the French penal code, which was adopted in 1791. In Russia, Empress Catherine II (the Great) convened a commission to prepare a new code and issued instructions, written in her own hand, to translate Beccaria's ideas into action. The Prussian King Friedrich II (the Great) devoted his reign to revising the Prussian laws according to Beccaria's principles. Emperor Joseph II had a new code drafted for Austria-Hungary in 1787—the first code to abolish capital punishment. The impact of Beccaria's treatise spread across the Atlantic as well: It influenced the first 10 amendments to the U.S. Constitution (the Bill of Rights).

> **:// Crime Surfing**
>
> www.utm.edu/research/iep/b/beccaria.htm
>
> If Beccaria were alive today, what arguments would he use in a debate on capital punishment?

Utilitarianism Gone Astray

Few people can be credited for their contribution to Anglo-American criminal law philosophy as much as Jeremy Bentham (1748–1832), the foremost spokesperson for the utilitarian approach to the management of people in general, and criminals and potential criminals in particular. Above all, he is remembered for his proposition that the purpose of all legislation is to achieve "the greatest happiness of the greatest number." Punishments, he argued, should be no greater (nor less) than necessary to achieve government's purpose to control crime.(1)

According to Princeton University professor Peter Singer, utilitarianism—the greatest good of the greatest number—implies that a child born with incurable birth defects should be killed, as its life would impose a far greater emotional and financial burden on its family and the community, than its death.(2) Thus Singer argues that "some infanticide is not even as important as, say, killing a happy cat."(3) Among his principal examples for justifiable infanticide are babies born with Down's syndrome. Singer's argument fails to take into account the many adults with Down's syndrome who take a bus to work every day, earn a salary, and pay taxes on their earnings.(2)

Putting aside the difficulty of making a prognosis about a baby's chance to have a productive and content life, how would society determine where to put the limit on legalizing infanticide? Justice Holmes ruled in *Buck v. Bell* that "three generations of imbeciles are enough" in upholding a state statute that mandated the sterilization of "imbeciles" with a family record of imbecility.(4) By those utilitarian standards, killing *all* imbecile babies would be even more cost-beneficial. Should a similar mandate apply to three generations of criminals, as determined by convictions? And would society not be better off (in terms of cost-benefit calculations) if it were to get rid of *all* troublemakers? Would Professor Singer go that far?

Bentham had nothing of that sort in mind when he set forth his utilitarian principles. In fact, he was not even an advocate of capital punishment, considering it to be "unfrugal" and "irremissible."(1)

To demonstrate his utilitarianism, Jeremy Bentham decreed that upon his death (June 6, 1832), his body be dissected in the presence of his friends and the skeleton be reconstructed, supplied with a wax head to replace the original (to be mummified), dressed in his own clothes, and placed upright in a glass case so that he, himself, could be useful as a reminder of his principles. Until recently, once a year at meetings of the Bentham Society in London, Bentham's body was wheeled out and celebrated with a feast.

Demonstrators picket Princeton University over its appointment of a controversial bioethics professor, Peter Singer, in Princeton, New Jersey, April 1999.

Sources

1. Jeremy Bentham, *An Introduction to the Principles of Morals and Legislation* (1789; New York: Haffner Library of Classics, 1948), esp. pp. 197, 200.
2. Peter Singer, *Rethinking Life and Death: The Collapse of Our Traditional Ethics* (New York: St. Martin's Press, 1996); *How Are We to Live? Ethics in an Age of Self-Interest* (New York: Prometheus Books, 1995).
3. George F. Will, "Life and Death at Princeton," *Newsweek,* Sept. 13, 1999, pp. 80–81.
4. *Buck v. Bell,* 274 U.S. 200, 207 (1927).

Questions for Discussion

1. According to utilitarian principles, is capital punishment preferable to a life sentence?
2. Should abortion be legalized when a baby can be profiled (by family history) as a high risk for a life in crime?
3. Can you think of a way to use utilitarian principles to reduce the use and duration of imprisonment?

Jeremy Bentham's Utilitarianism

Legal scholars and reformers throughout Europe proclaimed their indebtedness to Beccaria, but none owed more to him than the English legal philosopher Jeremy Bentham (1748–1832). Bentham had a long and productive career. He inspired many of his contemporaries, as well as criminologists of future generations, with his approach to rational crime control.

Bentham devoted his life to developing a scientific approach to the making and breaking of laws. Like Beccaria, he was concerned with achieving "the greatest happiness of the greatest number."[9] His work was governed by utilitarian principles. **Utilitarianism** assumes that all human actions are calculated in accordance with their likelihood of bringing happiness (pleasure) or unhappiness (pain). People weigh the probabilities of present and future pleasures against those of present and future pain.

Bentham proposed a precise pseudomathematical formula for this process, which he called "felicific calculus." According to his reasoning, individuals are "human calculators" who put all the factors into an equation in order to decide whether or not a particular crime is worth committing. This notion may seem rather whimsical today, but at a time when there were over 200 capital offenses, it provided a rationale for reform of the legal system.[10] Bentham reasoned that if prevention was the purpose of punishment, and if punishment became too costly by creating more harm than good, then penalties needed to be set just a bit in excess of the pleasure one might derive from committing a crime, and no higher. The law exists in order to create happiness for the community. Since punishment creates unhappiness, it can be justified only if it prevents greater evil than it produces. Thus, Bentham suggested, if hanging a man's effigy produced the same preventive effect as hanging the man himself, there would be no reason to hang the man.

Sir Samuel Romilly, a member of Parliament, met Jeremy Bentham at the home of a mutual friend. He became interested in Bentham's idea that the certainty of punishment outweighs its severity as a deterrent against crime. On February 9, 1810, in a speech before Parliament, he advocated Benthamite ideas:

> So evident is the truth of that maxim that if it were possible that punishment, as the consequence of guilt, could be reduced to an absolute certainty, a very slight penalty would be sufficient to prevent almost every species of crime.[11]

Although conservatives prevented any major changes during Romilly's lifetime, the program of legislative pressure he began was continued by his followers and culminated in the complete reform of English criminal law between 1820 and 1861. During that period the number of capital offenses was reduced from 222 to 3: murder, treason, and piracy. Gradually, from the ideals of the philosophers of the Age of Enlightenment and the principles outlined by the scholars of the classical school, a new social order was created, an order that affirmed a commitment to equal treatment of all people before the law.

The Classical School: An Evaluation

Classical criminology had an immediate and profound impact on jurisprudence and legislation. The rule of law spread rapidly through Europe and the United States. Of no less significance was the influence of the classical school on penal and correctional policy. The classical principle that punishment must be appropriate to the crime was universally accepted during the nineteenth and early twentieth centuries. Yet the classical approach had weaknesses. Critics attacked the simplicity of its argument: The responsibility of the criminal justice system was simply to enforce the law with swiftness and certainty and to treat all people in like fashion, whether the accused were paupers or nobles; government was to be run by the rule of law rather than at the discretion of its officials. In other words, the punishment was to fit the crime, not the criminal. The proposition that human beings had the capacity to choose freely between good and evil was accepted without question. There was no need to ask why people behave as they do, to seek a motive, or to ask about the specific circumstances surrounding criminal acts.

During the last half of the nineteenth century, scholars began to challenge these ideas. Influenced by the expanding search for scientific explanations of behavior in place of philosophical ones, criminologists shifted their attention from the act to the actor. They argued that people did not choose of their own free will to commit crime; rather, factors beyond their control were responsible for criminal behavior.

POSITIVIST CRIMINOLOGY

During the late eighteenth century, significant advances in knowledge of both the physical and the social world influenced thinking about crime. Auguste Comte (1798–1857), a French sociologist, applied the modern methods of the physical sciences to the social sciences in his six-volume *Cours de philosophie positive (Course in Positive Philosophy),* published between 1830 and 1842. He argued that there could be no real knowledge of social phenomena unless it was based on a positivist (scientific) approach. Positivism alone, however, was not sufficient to bring about a fundamental change in criminological thinking. Not until Charles Darwin (1809–1882) challenged the doctrine of creation with his theory of the evolution of species did the next generation of criminologists have the tools with which to challenge classicism.

The turning point was the publication in 1859 of Darwin's *Origin of Species*. Darwin's theory was that God did not make all the various species of animals in two days, as proclaimed in Genesis 1:20–26, but rather that the species had evolved through a process of adaptive mutation and natural selection. The process was based on the survival of the fittest in the struggle for existence. This radical theory seriously challenged traditional theological teaching. It was not until 1871, however, that Darwin publicly took the logical next step and traced human origins to an animal of the anthropoid group—the ape.[12] He thus posed an even more serious challenge to a religious tradition that maintained that God created the first human in his own image (Genesis 1:27).

The scientific world would never be the same again. The theory of evolution made it possible to ask new questions and to search in new ways for the answers to old ones. New biological theories replaced older ones. Old ideas that demons and animal spirits could explain human behavior were replaced by knowledge based on new scientific principles. The social sciences were born.

The nineteenth-century forces of positivism and evolution moved the field of criminology from a philosophical to a scientific perspective. But there were even earlier intellectual underpinnings of the scientific criminology that emerged in the second half of the nineteenth century.

BIOLOGICAL DETERMINISM: THE SEARCH FOR CRIMINAL TRAITS

Throughout history a variety of physical characteristics and disfigurements have been said to characterize individuals of "evil" disposition. In the earliest pursuit of the relationship between biological traits and behavior, a Greek scientist who examined Socrates found his skull and facial features to be those of a person inclined toward alcoholism and brutality.[13] The ancient Greeks and Romans so distrusted red hair that actors portraying evil persons wore red wigs. Through the ages cripples, hunchbacks, people with long hair, and a multitude of others were viewed with suspicion. Indeed, in the Middle Ages laws indicated that if two people were suspected of a crime, the uglier was the more likely to be guilty.[14]

The belief that criminals are born, not made, and that they can be identified by various physical irregularities is reflected not only in scientific writing but in literature as well. Shakespeare's Julius Caesar states:

> Let me have men about me that are fat;
> Sleek-headed men, and such as sleep o' nights.
> Yond Cassius has a lean and hungry look;
> He thinks too much: such men are dangerous.

Although its roots can be traced to ancient times, it was not until the sixteenth century that the Italian physician Giambattista della Porta (1535–1615) founded the school of human **physiognomy,** the study of facial features and their relation to human behavior. According to Porta,

A criminological examination according to an 1890 caricature.

a thief had large lips and sharp vision. Two centuries later Porta's efforts were revived by the Swiss theologian Johann Kaspar Lavater (1741–1801).[15] They were elaborated by the German physicians Franz Joseph Gall (1758–1828) and Johann Kaspar Spurzheim (1776–1832), whose science of **phrenology** posited that bumps on the head were indications of psychological propensities.[16] In the United States these views were supported by the physician Charles Caldwell (1772–1853), who searched for evidence that brain tissue and cells regulate human action.[17] By the nineteenth century, the sciences of physiognomy and phrenology had introduced specific biological factors into the study of crime causation.

Lombroso, Ferri, Garofalo: The Italian School

Cesare Lombroso (1835–1909) integrated Comte's positivism, Darwin's evolutionism, and the many pioneering studies of the relation of crime to the body. In 1876, with the publication of *L'uomo delinquente (The Criminal Man)*, criminology was permanently transformed from an abstract philosophy of crime control through legislation to a modern science of investigation into causes. Lombroso's work replaced the concept of free will, which had reigned for over a century as the principle that explained criminal behavior, with that of determinism. Together with his followers, the Italian legal scholars Enrico Ferri and Raffaele Garofalo, Lombroso developed a new orientation, the Italian, or positivist, school of criminology, which seeks explanations for criminal behavior through scientific experimentation and research.

Cesare Lombroso After completing his medical studies, Cesare Lombroso served as an army physician, became a professor of psychiatry at the University of Turin, and later in life accepted an appointment as professor of criminal anthropology. His theory of the "born criminal" states that criminals are a lower form of life, nearer to their apelike ancestors than noncriminals in traits and dispositions. They are distinguishable from noncriminals by various **atavistic stigmata**—physical features of creatures at an earlier stage of development, before they became fully human.

He argued that criminals frequently have huge jaws and strong canine teeth, characteristics common to carnivores who tear and devour meat raw. The arm span of criminals is often greater than their height, just like that of apes, who use their forearms to propel themselves

PART I **Understanding Criminology** 69

This depiction of the human brain appeared in an 1890s scientific book, *How to Read Character: A New Illustrated Hand-Book of Physiology, Phrenology and Physiognomy for Students and Examiners.*

FIG. 22.

SYMBOLICAL HEAD

ILLUSTRATING THE

NATURAL LANGUAGE OF THE FACULTIES.

along the ground. An individual born with any five of the stigmata is a **born criminal**. This category accounts for about a third of all offenders.

The theory became clear to Lombroso "one cold grey November morning" while he pored over the bones of a notorious outlaw who had died in an Italian prison:

> This man possessed such extraordinary agility, that he had been known to scale steep mountain heights bearing a sheep on his shoulders. His cynical effrontery was such that he openly boasted of his crimes. On his death . . . I was deputed to make the post-mortem, and on laying open the skull I found . . . a distinct depression . . . as in inferior animals.

Lombroso was delighted by his findings:

> This was not merely an idea, but a revelation. At the sight of that skull, I seemed to see all of a sudden, lighted up as a vast plain under a flaming sky the problem of the nature of the criminal—an atavistic being who reproduces in his person the ferocious instincts of primitive humanity.[18]

Criminal women, according to Lombroso, are different from criminal men. It is the prostitute who represents the born criminal among them:

> We also saw that women have many traits in common with children; that their moral sense is different;

they are revengeful, jealous, inclined to vengeance of a refined cruelty.... When a morbid activity of the psychical centres intensifies the bad qualities of women ... it is clear that the innocuous semi-criminal present in normal women must be transformed into a born criminal more terrible than any man.... The criminal woman is consequently a monster. Her normal sister is kept in the paths of virtue by many causes, such as maternity, piety, weakness, and when these counter influences fail, and a woman commits a crime, we may conclude that her wickedness must have been enormous before it could triumph over so many obstacles.[19]

To the born criminal, Lombroso added two other categories, insane criminals and criminoloids. *Insane criminals* are not criminal from birth; they become criminal as a result of some change in their brains which interferes with their ability to distinguish between right and wrong.[20] *Criminoloids* make up an ambiguous group that includes habitual criminals, criminals by passion, and other diverse types.

Most scientists who followed Lombroso did not share his enthusiasm or his viewpoint. As happens so often in history, his work has been kept alive more by criticism than by agreement. The theory that criminals were lodged on the lower rungs of the evolutionary ladder did not stand up to scientific scrutiny. But the fact that Lombroso measured thousands of live and dead prisoners and compared these measurements with those obtained from control groups (however imperfectly derived) in his search for determinants of crime changed the nature of the questions asked by the generations of scholars who came after him.

His influence continues in contemporary European research; American scientists, as the criminologist Marvin Wolfgang says, use him "as a straw man for attack on biological analyses of criminal behavior."[21] Thorsten Sellin has noted: "Any scholar who succeeds in driving hundreds of fellow-students to search for the truth, and whose ideas after half a century possess vitality, merits an honorable place in the history of thought."[22] At his death, true to his lifetime pursuits, Lombroso willed his body to the laboratory of legal medicine and his brain to the Institute of Anatomy at the University of Turin, where for so many years the father of empirical criminology had espoused biological determinism.[23]

Enrico Ferri The best known of Lombroso's associates was Enrico Ferri (1856–1929). Member of Parliament, accomplished public lecturer, brilliant lawyer, editor of a newspaper, and esteemed scholar, Ferri had published his first major book by the time he was 21. By age 25 he was a university professor. Although Ferri agreed with Lombroso on the biological bases of criminal behavior, his interest in socialism led him to recognize the importance of social, economic, and political determinants.

Ferri was a prolific writer on a vast number of criminological topics. His greatest contribution was his attack on the classical doctrine of free will, which argued that criminals should be held morally responsible for their crimes because they must have made a rational decision to commit these acts. Ferri believed criminals could not be held morally responsible because they did not choose to commit crimes but, rather, were driven to commit them by conditions in their lives. He did, however, stress that society needed protection against criminal acts and that it was the purpose of the criminal law and penal policy to provide that protection.

Although he advocated conventional punishments and even the death penalty for individuals he assumed would never be fit to live in society, he was more interested in controlling crime through preventive measures—state control of the manufacture of weapons, inexpensive housing, better street lighting, and so forth. Ferri claimed that strict adherence to preventive measures based on scientific methods would eventually reduce crime and allow people to live together in society with less dependence on the penal system. Toward the end of his life he proudly admitted that he was an idealist, a statement with which generations of scholars have agreed. Though his prescription for crime reduction was overly optimistic, Ferri's importance to the development of mod-

> **Did You Know?**
>
> ... that certain Nazi anthropologists and physicians made use of Lombroso's ideas about born criminals? They proposed "scientific" classification of Arians and non-Arians (and ultimately death or denial of civil rights to non-Arians) on the basis of skull measurements.

ern criminology is undisputed. "When Enrico Ferri died on April 12, 1929," writes Thorsten Sellin, "one of the most colorful, influential figures in the history of criminology disappeared."[24]

Raffaele Garofalo Another follower of Lombroso was the Italian nobleman, magistrate, senator, and professor of law Raffaele Garofalo (1852–1934). Like Lombroso and Ferri, Garofalo rejected the doctrine of free will and supported the position that the only way to understand crime was to study it by scientific methods. Influenced by Lombroso's theory of atavistic stigmata, in which he found many shortcomings, Garofalo traced the roots of criminal behavior not to physical features but to their psychological equivalents, which he called "moral anomalies." According to this theory, natural crimes are found in all human societies, regardless of the views of lawmakers, and no civilized society can afford to disregard them.[25]

Natural crimes, according to Garofalo, are those that offend the basic moral sentiments of probity (respect for the property of others) and piety (revulsion against the infliction of suffering on others). An individual who has an organic deficiency in these moral sentiments has no moral constraints against committing such crimes. Garofalo argued that these individuals could not be held responsible for their actions. But, like Ferri, he also emphasized that society needed protection and that penal policy should be designed to prevent criminals from inflicting harm.[26]

Influenced by Darwinian theory, Garofalo suggested that the death penalty could rid society of its maladapted members, just as the natural selection process eliminated maladapted organisms. For less-serious offenders, capable of adapting themselves to society in some measure, other types of punishments were preferable: transportation to remote lands, loss of privileges, institutionalization in farm colonies, or perhaps simply reparation. Clearly, Garofalo was much more interested in protecting society than in defending the individual rights of offenders.

Challenges to Lombrosian Theory Although Lombroso, Ferri, and Garofalo did not always agree on the causes of criminal behavior

Dr. Cesare Lombroso (1836–1909), professor of criminal anthropology at Turin University, founder of the Positivist School of Criminology.

or on the way society should respond to it, their combined efforts marked a turning point in the development of the scientific study of crime. These three were responsible for developing the positivist approach to criminality, which influences criminology to the present day. Nevertheless, they had their critics. By using the scientific method to explore crime causation, they paved the way for criminologists to support or refute the theories they had created. The major challenge to Lombrosian theory came from the work of Charles Buckman Goring.

From 1901 until 1913 Charles Buckman Goring (1870–1919), a medical officer at Parkhurst Prison in England, collected data on 96 traits of more than 3,000 convicts and a large control group of Oxford and Cambridge university students, hospital patients, and soldiers. Among his research assistants was a famous statistician, Karl Pearson. When Goring had completed his examinations, he was armed with enough data to refute Lombroso's theory of the anthropological criminal type. Goring's report to the scientific community proclaimed:

> From a knowledge only of an undergraduate's cephalic [head] measurement, a better judgment could be given as to whether he were studying at an English or Scottish university than a prediction could be made as to whether he would eventually become a university professor or a convicted felon.[27]

This evaluation still stands as the most cogent critical analysis of Lombroso's theory of the born criminal. Although Goring rejected the claim that specific stigmata identify the criminal, he was convinced that poor physical condition plus a defective state of mind were determining factors in the criminal personality.

A Return to Biological Determinism

After Goring's challenge, Lombrosian theory lost its academic popularity for about a quarter century. Then in 1939 Ernest Hooten (1887–1954), a physical anthropologist, reawakened an interest in biologically determined criminality with the publication of a massive study comparing American prisoners with a noncriminal control group. He concluded:

> [I]n every population there are hereditary inferiors in mind and in body as well as physical and mental deficients.... Our information definitely proves that it is from the physically inferior element of the population that native born criminals from native parentage are mainly derived.[28]

Like his positivist predecessors, Hooten argued for the segregation of those he referred to as the "criminal stock," and he recommended their sterilization as well.[29]

The Somatotype School In the search for the source of criminality, other scientists, too, looked for the elusive link between physical characteristics and crime. The **somatotype school of criminology**, which related body build to behavior, became popular during the first half of the twentieth century. It originated with the work of a German psychiatrist, Ernst Kretschmer (1888–1964), who distinguished three principal types of physiques: (1) the asthenic—lean, slightly built, narrow shoulders; (2) the athletic—medium to tall, strong, muscular, coarse bones; and (3) the pyknic—medium height, rounded figure, massive neck, broad face. He then related these physical types to various psychic disorders: pyknics to manic depression, asthenics and athletics to schizophrenia, and so on.[30]

Kretschmer's work was brought to the United States by William Sheldon (1898–1977), who formulated his own group of somatotypes: the *endomorph*, the *mesomorph*, and the *ectomorph*. Sheldon's father was a dog breeder who used a point system to judge animals in competition, and Sheldon worked out a point system of his own for judging humans. Thus one could actually measure on a scale from 1 to 7 the relative dominance of each body type in any given individual. People with predominantly mesomorph traits (physically powerful, aggressive, athletic physiques), he argued, tend more than others to be involved in illegal behavior.[31] This finding was later supported by Sheldon Glueck (1896–1980) and Eleanor Glueck (1898–1972), who based their studies of delinquents on William Sheldon's somatotypes.[32]

By and large, studies based on somatotyping have been sharply criticized for methodological flaws, including nonrepresentative selection of their samples (bias), failure to account for cultural stereotyping (our expectations of how muscular, physically active people should react), and poor statistical analyses. An anthropologist summed up the negative response of the scientific community by suggesting that somatotyping was "a New Phrenology in which the bumps on the buttocks take the place of the bumps on the skulls."[33] After World War II, somatotyping seemed too close to eugenics (the science of controlled reproduction to improve hereditary qualities), and the approach fell into disfavor. During the 1960s, however, the discovery of an extra sex chromosome in some criminal samples (see Chapter 4) revived interest in this theory.

Inherited Criminality During the period when some researchers were measuring skulls and bodies of criminals in their search for the physical determinants of crime, others were arguing that criminality was an inherited trait passed on in the genes. To support the theory, they traced family histories. Richard Dugdale (1841–1883), for example, studied the lives of more than a thousand members of the family he called "Jukes." His interest in the family began when he found six related people in a jail in upstate New York. Following one branch of the family, the descendants of Ada Jukes, whom he referred to as the "mother of criminals," Dugdale found among the thousand of descendants 280 paupers, 60 thieves, 7 murder-

Dugdale and others identified the Jukes clan as determined by heredity to be criminals, imbeciles and paupers. Research since then has shown that the methodology was flawed and many conclusions were fabricated.

ers, 40 other criminals, 40 persons with venereal disease, and 50 prostitutes.

His findings indicated, Dugdale claimed, that since some families produce generations of criminals, they must be transmitting a degenerate trait down the line.[34] A similar conclusion was reached by Henry Goddard (1866–1957). In a study of the family tree of a Revolutionary War soldier, Martin Kallikak, Goddard found many more criminals among the descendants of Kallikak's illegitimate son than among the descendants of his son by a later marriage with "a woman of his own quality."[35]

These early studies have been discredited primarily on the grounds that genetic and environmental influences could not be separated. But in the early twentieth century they were taken quite seriously. On the assumption that crime could be controlled if criminals could be prevented from transmitting their traits to the next generation, some states permitted the sterilization of habitual offenders. Sterilization laws were held constitutional by the U.S. Supreme Court in a 1927 opinion written by Justice Oliver Wendell Holmes, Jr., which included the following well-known pronouncement:

It is better for all the world, if instead of waiting to execute degenerate offspring for crime, or to let them starve for their imbecility, society can prevent those who are manifestly unfit from continuing their kind. . . . Three generations of imbeciles are enough.[36]

Clearly the early positivists, with their focus on physical characteristics, exerted great influence. They were destined to be overshadowed, though, by investigators who focused on psychological characteristics.

PSYCHOLOGICAL DETERMINISM

On the whole, scholars who investigated criminal behavior in the nineteenth and early twentieth centuries were far more interested in the human body than in the human mind. During that period, however, several contributions were made in the area of psychological explanations of crime. Some of the earliest contributions came from physicians interested primarily in the legal responsibility of the criminally insane. Later on, psychologists entered the field and applied their

FROM THE PAGES OF The New York Times

Who's Responsible?

For more than two centuries, scholars, psychologists, and criminologists have been debating the question of whether people with mental deficiencies should be held fully responsible for their crimes, especially when the death penalty is involved. In June 2002, the U.S. Supreme Court barred the execution of mentally retarded inmates, stating that "today our society views mentally retarded offenders as categorically less culpable than the average criminal."

The decision was based on the case of a Virginia man, Daryl Atkins, with an IQ of 59, who was convicted of committing a murder and robbery at the age of 18. The generally accepted definition of mental retardation is an IQ of approximately 70, accompanied by limitations on abilities like communication or caring for oneself. Fifteen countries of the European Union filed a brief on behalf of Mr. Atkins, and a group of American diplomats told the Court that executing the retarded was out of step with the rest of the world. Amnesty International reported that since 1995, only three countries had executed mentally retarded people: Kyrgyzstan, Japan, and the United States.

The Court made its ruling based on the majority's view that a "national consensus" now rejected such executions as cruel and unusual punishment, as put forward in the Eighth Amendment of the Constitution.

In another case, decided in November 2002, the Supreme Court granted a last-minute reprieve to a death-row inmate who suffers from severe mental illness, halting his execution at 5:59 P.M., one minute before the inmate was scheduled to be led to the death chamber. In 1994, James Blake Colburn raped and murdered a woman he knew. Although he had a history of psychiatric problems, including chronic paranoid schizophrenia and 15 suicide attempts, the jury sentenced him to death. The Court granted the stay "pending the timely filing and disposition of a petition for writ of certiorari," or a request for the Court to review the case. That means they did not ban the execution of the mentally ill; instead they gave Mr. Colburn's attorneys more time to prove that he had not been given a fair trial or appropriate sentence.

Source

Linda Greenhouse, "The Supreme Court: The Death Penalty; Citing 'National Consensus,' Justices Bar Death Penalty for Retarded Defendants," *The New York Times,* June 21, 2002; and Jim Yardley, "Court Stays Execution of Mentally Ill Texan," *The New York Times,* Nov. 7, 2002. Reprinted with permission.

Questions for Discussion

1. Where do we draw the line on who is responsible for his or her own behavior and who is not? Should this be determined on a case-by-case basis, or can laws cover such instances "across the board"?
2. The U.S. Supreme Court banned the execution of retarded offenders, not because it found the practice morally or legally wrong, but because it found a "national consensus" that such executions were excessive and inappropriate. Can you think of ways that such a method of determination might have both positive and negative effects?
3. James Blake Colburn was executed on March 26, 2003. Do you believe that inmates with serious mental illness should be put to death?

---

new testing techniques to the study of offenders (see Chapter 4).

Pioneers in Criminal Psychology

Isaac Ray (1807–1881), acknowledged to be America's first forensic psychiatrist, was interested throughout his life in the application of psychiatric principles to the law. He is best known as the author of *The Medical Jurisprudence of Insanity,* a treatise on criminal responsibility that was widely quoted and influential.[37] In it he defended the concept of moral insanity, a disorder first described in 1806 by the French humanitarian and psychiatrist Philippe Pinel (1745–1826).[38] "Moral insanity" was a term used to describe persons who were normal in all respects except that something was wrong with the part of the brain that regulates affective responses. Ray questioned whether we could hold people legally responsible for their acts if they had such an impairment, because such people committed their crimes without an intent to do so.

Born in the same year as Lombroso, Henry Maudsley (1835–1918), a brilliant English medical professor, shared Ray's concerns about criminal responsibility. According to Maudsley, some people may be considered either "insane or criminal according to the standpoint from which they are looked at." He believed that for many persons crime is an "outlet in which their unsound tendencies are discharged; they would go mad if they were not criminals."[39] Most of Maudsley's attention focused on the borderline between insanity and crime.

Psychological Studies of Criminals

Around the turn of the twentieth century, psychologists used their new measurement techniques to study offenders. The administering of intelligence tests to inmates of jails, prisons, and other public institutions was especially popular at that time, because it was a period of major controversy over the relation of mental deficiency to criminal behavior. The new technique seemed to provide an objective basis for differentiating criminals from noncriminals.

In 1914 Henry H. Goddard (1866–1957), research director of the Vineland, New Jersey, Training School for the Retarded, examined some intelligence tests that had been given to inmates and concluded that 25 to 50 percent of the people in prison had intellectual defects that made them incapable of managing their own affairs.[40] This idea remained dominant until it was challenged by the results of intelligence tests administered to World War I draftees, whose scores were found to be lower than those of prisoners in the federal penitentiary at Leavenworth. As a result of this study and others like it, intelligence quotient (IQ) measures largely disappeared as a basis for explaining criminal behavior.

SOCIOLOGICAL DETERMINISM

During the nineteenth and early twentieth centuries, some scholars began to search for the social determinants of criminal behavior. The approach had its roots in Europe in the 1830s, the time between Beccaria's *On Crimes and Punishment* and Lombroso's *The Criminal Man*.

Adolphe Quételet and André Michel Guerry

The Belgian mathematician Adolphe Quételet (1796–1874) and the French lawyer André Michel Guerry (1802–1866) were among the first scholars to repudiate the classicists' free-will doctrine. Working independently on the relation of crime statistics to such factors as poverty, age, sex, race, and climate, both scholars concluded that society, not the decisions of individual offenders, was responsible for criminal behavior.

The first modern criminal statistics were published in France in 1827. Guerry used those statistics to demonstrate that crime rates varied with social factors. He found, for example, that the wealthiest region of France had the highest rate of property crime but only half the national rate of violent crime. He concluded that the main factor in property crime was opportunity: There was much more to steal in the richer provinces.

Quételet did an elaborate analysis of crime in France, Belgium, and Holland. After analyzing criminal statistics, which he called "moral statistics," he concluded that if we look at overall patterns of behavior of groups across a whole society, we find a startling regularity of rates of various behaviors. According to Quételet:

> We can enumerate in advance how many individuals will soil their hands in the blood of their fellows, how many will be frauds, how many prisoners; almost as one can enumerate in advance the births and deaths that will take place.[41]

By focusing on groups rather than individuals, he discovered that behavior is indeed predictable, regular, and understandable. Just as the physical world is governed by the laws of nature, human behavior is governed by forces external to the individual. The more we learn about those forces, the easier it becomes to predict behavior. A major goal of criminological research, according to Quételet, should be to identify factors related to crime and to assign to them their "proper degree of influence."[42] Though neither he nor Guerry offered a theory of criminal behavior, the fact that both studied social factors scientifically, using quantitative research methods, made them key figures in the subsequent development of sociological theories of crime causation.

Gabriel Tarde

One of the earliest sociological theories of criminal behavior was formulated by Gabriel Tarde (1843–1904), who served 15 years as a provincial judge and then was placed in charge of France's national statistics. After an extensive analysis of these statistics, he came to the following conclusion:

> The majority of murderers and notorious thieves began as children who had been abandoned, and the true seminary of crime must be sought for upon each public square or each crossroad of our towns, whether they be small or large, in those flocks of pillaging street urchins who, like bands of sparrows, associate together, at first for marauding, and then for theft, because of a lack of education and food in their homes.[43]

Tarde rejected the Lombrosian theory of biological abnormality, which was popular in his time, arguing that criminals were normal people who learned crime just as others learned legitimate trades. He formulated his theory in terms of **laws of imitation**—principles that governed the process by which people became criminals. According to Tarde's thesis, individuals emulate behavior patterns in much the same way that they copy styles of dress. Moreover, there is a pattern to the way such emulation takes place: (1) Individuals imitate others in proportion to the intensity and frequency of their contacts; (2) inferiors imitate superiors—that is, trends flow from town to country and from upper to lower classes; and (3) when two behavior patterns clash, one may take the place of the other, as when guns largely replaced knives as murder weapons.[44] Tarde's work served as the basis for Edwin Sutherland's theory of differential association, which we shall examine in Chapter 5.

Émile Durkheim

Modern criminologists take two major approaches to the study of the social factors associated with crime. Tarde's approach asks how individuals become criminal. What is the process? How are behavior patterns learned and transmitted? The second major approach looks at the social structure and its institutions. It asks how crime arises in the first place and how it is related to the functioning of a society. For answers to these questions, scholars

Émile Durkheim (1858–1917), one of the founders of sociology.

begin with the work of Émile Durkheim (1858–1917).

Of all nineteenth-century writers on the relationship between crime and social factors, none has more powerfully influenced contemporary criminology than Durkheim, who is universally acknowledged as one of the founders of sociology. On October 12, 1870, when Durkheim was 12 years old, the German army invaded and occupied his hometown, Epinal, in eastern France. Thus at a very early age he witnessed social chaos and the effects of rapid change, topics with which he remained preoccupied throughout his life. At the age of 24 he became a professor of philosophy, and at 29 he joined the faculty of the University of Bordeaux. There he taught the first course in sociology ever to be offered by a French university.

By 1902 he had moved to the University of Paris, where he completed his doctoral studies. His *Division of Social Labor* became a landmark work on the organization of societies. According to Durkheim, crime is as normal a part of society as birth and death. Theoretically, crime could disappear altogether only if all members of society had the same values, and such standardization is neither possible nor desirable. Furthermore, some crime is in fact necessary if a society is to progress:

> The opportunity for the genius to carry out his work affords the criminal his originality at a lower level. . . . According to Athenian law, Socrates was a criminal, and his condemnation was no more than just. However, his crime, namely, the independence of his thought, rendered a service not only to humanity but to his country.[45]

Durkheim further pointed out that all societies have not only crime but sanctions. The rationale for the sanctions varies in accordance with the structure of the society. In a strongly cohesive society, punishment of members who deviate is used to reinforce the value system—to remind people of what is right and what is wrong—thereby preserving the pool of common belief and the solidarity of the society. Punishment must be harsh to serve these ends. In a large, urbanized, heterogeneous society, on the other hand, punishment is used not to preserve solidarity but rather to right the wrong done to a victim. Punishment thus is evaluated in accordance with the harm done, with the goal of restitution and reinstatement of order as quickly as possible. The offense is not considered a threat to social cohesion, primarily because in a large, complex society criminal events do not even come to the attention of most people.

The most important of Durkheim's many contributions to contemporary sociology is his concept of **anomie**, a breakdown of social order as a result of a loss of standards and values. In a society plagued by anomie (see Chapter 5), disintegration and chaos replace social cohesion.

> **:// Crime Surfing**
>
> www.runet.edu/~lridener/DSS/INDEX.HTML
>
> According to Durkheim, what role does religion play in society?

HISTORICAL AND CONTEMPORARY CRIMINOLOGY: A TIME LINE

Classical criminologists thought the problem of crime might be solved through limitations on governmental power, the abolition of brutality, and the creation of a more equitable system of justice. They argued that the punishment should fit the crime. For over a century this perspective dominated criminology. Later on, positivist criminologists influenced judges to give greater consideration to the offender than to the gravity of the crime when imposing sentences. The current era marks a return to the classical demand that the punishment correspond to the seriousness of the crime and the guilt of the offender. Table 3.1 presents a chronology of all the pioneers in criminology we have discussed.

As modern science discovered more and more about cause and effect in the physical and social universes, the theory that individuals commit crimes of their own free will began to lose favor. The positivists searched for determinants of crime in biological, psychological, and social factors. Biologically based theories were popular in the late nineteenth century, fell out of favor in the early part of the twentieth, and emerged again in the 1970s (see Chapter 4) with studies of hormone imbalances, diet, environmental contaminants, and so forth. Since the studies of criminal responsibility in the nineteenth century centering on the insanity defense and of intelligence levels in the twentieth century, psychiatrists and psychologists have continued to play a major role in the search for the causes of crime, especially after Sigmund Freud developed his well-known theory of human personality (Chapter 4). The sociological perspective became popular in the 1920s and has remained the predominant approach of criminological studies. (We will examine contemporary theories in Chapters 5 through 9.)

TABLE 3.1 Pioneers in Criminology: A Chronology

Classical Criminology

Free Will

Cesare Beccaria (1738–1794). Devised the first design for comprehensive, enlightened criminal justice system based on law
Jeremy Bentham (1748–1832). Developed utilitarian principles of punishment

Positivist Criminology

Biological Determinism

Giambattista della Porta (1535–1615). Was the founder of the school of physiognomy, which is the study of facial features and their relation to human behaviors
Johann Kaspar Lavater (1741–1801). Espoused a biological approach to crime causation; developed phrenology
Franz Joseph Gall (1758–1828). Espoused a biological approach to crime causation; further developed phrenology
Charles Caldwell (1772–1853). Was a physician who searched for evidence that brain tissue and cells regulate human behavior
Johann Kaspar Spurzheim (1776–1832). Espoused a biological approach; continued studies of phrenology
Charles Darwin (1809–1882). Formulated theory of evolution, which changed explanations of human behavior
Cesare Lombroso (1835–1909). Saw determinism as explanatory factor in criminal behavior; posited the "born criminal"; father of modern criminology
Richard Dugdale (1841–1883). Related criminal behavior to inherited traits (Jukes family)
Raffaele Garofalo (1852–1934). Traced roots of criminal behavior to "moral anomalies" rather than physical characteristics
Enrico Ferri (1856–1929). Produced first penal code based on positivist principles; replaced moral responsibility with social accountability
Ernest Hooten (1887–1954). Related criminality to hereditary inferiority
Ernst Kretschmer (1888–1964). Introduced the somatotype school of criminology
William Sheldon (1898–1977). Related body types to illegal behavior

Psychological Determinism

Isaac Ray (1807–1881). Questioned whether those who were "morally insane" could be held legally responsible for their acts
Henry Maudsley (1835–1918). Pioneered criteria for legal responsibility
Henry H. Goddard (1866–1957). Related criminal behavior to intelligence (Kallikak family)

Social Determinism

Adolphe Quételet (1796–1874). Was one of the first to repudiate classical free-will doctrine; studied social determinants of behavior
Auguste Comte (1798–1857). Brought modern scientific methods from physical to social sciences
André Michel Guerry (1802–1866). Was one of the first to repudiate free-will doctrine; related crime statistics to social factors
Gabriel Tarde (1843–1904). Explained crime as learned behavior
Émile Durkheim (1858–1917). Was one of the founders of sociology; developed theory of anomie and idea that crime is normal in all societies
Charles Buckman Goring (1870–1919). Used empirical research to refute Lombroso's theory of criminal types
Sheldon Glueck (1896–1980) and *Eleanor Glueck* (1898–1972). Espoused primarily social causes of delinquency, but also psychological and biological explanations

REVIEW

In the history of criminology from ancient times to the early twentieth century, its many themes at times have clashed and at times have supported one another. There is no straight-line evolutionary track that we can follow from the inception of the first "criminological" thought to modern theories. Some scholars concentrated on criminal law and procedure; others, on criminal behavior. Some took the biological route; others, the psychological; still others, the sociological. And the work of some investigators has encompassed a combination of factors. Toward the end of the nineteenth century a discipline began to emerge.

Tracing the major developments back in time helps us understand how criminology grew into the discipline we know today. Many of the issues that appear on the intellectual battlefields as we enter the twenty-first century are the same issues our academic ancestors grappled with for hundreds, indeed thousands, of years. With each new clash, some old concepts died, while others were incorporated within competing doctrinal boundaries, there to remain until the next challenge. The controversies of one era become the foundations of knowledge for the next. As societies develop and are subjected to new technologies, the crime problem becomes ever more complex. So do the questions it raises. In Part II we will see how twentieth-century theorists have dealt with those questions.

CRIMINOLOGY & PUBLIC POLICY

The execution methods debate is played out by legislative decision-makers, who oftentimes turn a blind eye to the concerns of those who actually have to kill. In turn, a considerable portion of doctors, nurses, and other medical personnel willingly participate in executions. Prison officials face the worst of both worlds: They have limited political clout by which to make their choices known and minimal guidance provided by those who make the choices for them. The process is made all the more perplexing because those who report the problems with the system—media witnesses—have questionable credibility when experts attempt to use their accounts in court. "As a result," in Foucault's words, "justice no longer takes public responsibility for the violence that is bound up with its practice." The system becomes literally and symbolically unobservable. In the context of applying execution methods, when justice becomes unobservable, it ceases to exist.

(*Source:* Deborah W. Denno, "When Legislatures Delegate Death: The Troubling Paradox behind State Uses of Electrocution and Lethal Injection and What It Says about Us," *Ohio State Law Journal,* **63** (2002): 63.)

Questions for Discussion Beccaria voiced concerns over bad laws (see p. 63). He made an inspired call for an end to medieval barbarism. Punishment should be prompt and effective. Capital punishment should be abolished—and so, too, should the use of torture. Debate over the death penalty in recent years has turned on concerns over executing innocents, the mentally ill, and the insane. Much has been written about the racial application of the death penalty as well. Professor Denno raises a very different concern: Are the methods we use to execute inmates justifiable? Interestingly, Professor Denno raises this concern about the use of lethal injection—considered to be the most humane of the methods of execution. If you agree with her reasoning, do you come to the conclusion that all methods of execution should be abolished?

YOU BE THE CRIMINOLOGIST

A historical society has invited you to represent criminology in a discussion group made up of experts from various disciplines. The topic is: How do the foundations of your discipline help us to understand contemporary developments in the field? What would you discuss?

KEY TERMS

The numbers next to the terms refer to the pages on which the terms are defined.

anomie (77)
atavistic stigmata (68)
born criminal (69)
classical school of criminology (59)
eugenics (72)
laws of imitation (76)
phrenology (68)
physiognomy (67)
positivist school of criminology (60)
somatotype school of criminology (72)
utilitarianism (66)

PART II

Explanations of Crime and Criminal Behavior

Having explored the history of criminology, the early explanations of criminal behavior, and the scientific methods used by criminologists, we turn now to contemporary theories and research. Current explanations of criminal behavior focus on biological, psychological, social, and economic factors. Biological and psychological theories assume that criminal behavior results from underlying physical or mental conditions that distinguish criminals from noncriminals (Chapter 4). These theories yield insight into individual cases, but they do not explain why crime rates vary from place to place and from one situation to another.

Sociological theories seek to explain criminal behavior in terms of the environment. Chapter 5 examines strain and cultural deviance theories, which focus on the social forces that cause people to engage in criminal behavior. Both theories assume that social class and criminal behavior are related. Strain theorists argue that people commit crimes because they are frustrated by not being able to achieve their goals through legitimate means. Cultural deviance theorists claim that crime is learned in socially disorganized neighborhoods where criminal norms are transmitted from one generation to the next. In Chapter 6 we examine subcultures that have their own norms, beliefs, and values, which differ significantly from those of the dominant culture. Chapter 7 explains how people remain committed to conventional behavior in the face of frustration, poor living conditions, and other criminogenic factors. In Chapter 8 we discuss three theoretical perspectives that focus on society's role in creating criminals and defining them as such. Finally, in Chapter 9 we explain why offenders choose to commit one offense rather than another at a given time and place.

CHAPTER 4 Psychological and Biological Perspectives

Psychology and Criminality
  Psychological Development
  Moral Development
  Maternal Deprivation and Attachment Theory
  Learning Aggression and Violence
  Personality

Mental Disorders and Crime
  Psychological Causation

Biology and Criminality
  Modern Biocriminology
  Genetics and Criminality
  The Controversy over Violence and Genes
  The IQ Debate
  Biochemical Factors
  Neurophysiological Factors

Crime and Human Nature
  Criticisms of Biocriminology
  An Integrated Theory

REVIEW

CRIMINOLOGY & PUBLIC POLICY

YOU BE THE CRIMINOLOGIST

KEY TERMS

Boxes
  From the Pages of *The New New York Times*: *The Apple Doesn't Fall Far*
  Of Immediate Concern: *The Taboo Crime of Parricide*
  Window to the World: *Censoring TV Violence*

Special Features
  Crime Surfing
  Did You Know?

KEY TERMS
attachment
behavioral modeling
biocriminology
chromosomes
conditioning
cortical arousal
differential association-reinforcement
dizygotic (DZ) twins
ego
extroversion
fundamental psycholegal error
hypoglycemia
id
minimal brain dysfunction (MBD)
monozygotic (MZ) twins
neuroticism
psychoanalytic theory
psychopathy
psychosis
psychoticism
social learning theory
superego

> "I am the most cold-blooded sonofabitch you'll ever meet."
> Ted Bundy, serial killer

The official word came from the Director of the FBI on October 25, 2002, that the suburban Washington, D.C., snipers were found sleeping in their car at a highway rest stop. After 19 separate sniper attacks and 13 deaths, John Allen Muhammad and John Lee Malvo were in custody awaiting trial. Muhammad, a 41-year-old Gulf War veteran, is a twice-divorced convert to Islam. Less is known about 17-year-old Malvo who, it appears, was substantially influenced by Muhammad.[1]

Muhammad's family members are simply baffled: "I can't imagine what would have gone on in his life," asks Muhammad's aunt Yvonne Crawford, "that would make John even think about doing this, if he's the one."[2] Criminologists immediately offered explanations, most grounded in psychological and biological theories.

Over time, criminologists learned much more about Malvo, the young triggerman. In custody Malvo confessed that the motive for the shootings stemmed from a desire to terrorize the community, ultimately forcing the authorities to pay money in exchange for an end to the shootings.

Malvo bragged about his shooting prowess, telling investigators that he shot some of his victims in the head just for the effect. The shootings were precision military operations, Malvo boasted, laughingly pointing to body parts where victims were hit. If given the opportunity I would do it all again, Malvo said.

Did Malvo readily accept his fate? Not the prospect of going to prison. "You can't build a jail strong enough to hold me. . . . Kill me. I don't care. Torture me. . . . Nothing bothers me. . . . Get rid of me."[2]

> **Did You Know?**
>
> ...that there are as many as 50 serial killers living (and killing) in the United States today?

In the United States, explanations of criminal behavior have been dominated by sociological theories. These theories focus on lack of opportunity and the breakdown of the conventional value system in urban ghettos, the formation of subcultures whose norms deviate from those of the middle class, and the increasing inability of social institutions to exercise control over behavior. Criminological texts have treated psychological and biological theories as peripheral, perhaps because criminology's disciplinary allegiance is to sociology. When psychological theories were first advanced to explain criminal behavior, their emphasis was largely psychoanalytic, so they may have seemed not quantitative enough to some criminologists.[3] Others may have considered the early work of Lombroso, Goring, and Hooten too scientifically naive to be taken seriously.

Sociological theories focus on crime rates of groups that experience frustration in their efforts to achieve accepted goals, not on the particular individual who becomes a criminal. Sociological theories cannot explain how one person can be born in a slum, be exposed to family discord and abuse, never attend school, have friends who are delinquents, and yet resist opportunities for crime, while another person can grow up in an affluent suburban neighborhood in a two-parent home and end up firing a gun at the president. In other words, sociologists do not address individual differences.[4] Instead, psychologists and biologists are interested in finding out what may account for individual differences.

It is clear that psychological, biological, and sociological explanations are not competing to answer the same specific questions. Rather, all three disciplines are searching for answers to different questions, even though they study the same act, status, or characteristic. We can understand crime in a society only if we view criminality from more than one level of analysis: why a certain individual commits a crime (psychological and biological explanations) and why some groups of individuals commit more or different criminal acts than other groups (sociological explanations).

Serial killers stop murdering when they are caught or killed.

Sociological theory and empirical research often ignore such factors as personality and human biology, almost as if they were irrelevant. And psychological theory often focuses on the individual, with little regard for the fact that while each one of us comes into the world with certain predispositions, from the moment we are born we interact with others in complex situations that influence our behavior.

PSYCHOLOGY AND CRIMINALITY

Psychologists have considered a variety of possibilities to account for individual differences—defective conscience, emotional immaturity, inadequate childhood socialization, maternal deprivation, poor moral development. They study how aggression is learned, which situations promote violent or delinquent reactions, how crime is related to personality factors, and how various mental disorders are associated with criminality.

Psychological Development

The **psychoanalytic theory** of criminality attributes delinquent and criminal behavior to at least three possible causes:

- A conscience so overbearing that it arouses feelings of guilt
- A conscience so weak that it cannot control the individual's impulses
- The need for immediate gratification

Consider the case of Richard. Richard was 6 when he committed his first delinquent act: He stole a comic book from the corner drugstore. Three months before the incident, his father, an alcoholic, had been killed in an automobile accident, and his mother, unable to care for the family, had abandoned the children.

For the next 10 years the county welfare agency moved Richard in and out of foster homes. During this time he actively pursued a life of crime, breaking into houses during daylight hours and stealing cars at night. By age 20, while serving a 10-year prison sentence for armed robbery, he had voluntarily entered psychoanalysis. After two years, Richard's analyst suggested three reasons for his criminality:

1. Being caught and punished for stealing made him feel less guilty about hating both his father for dying and thus abandoning him as well as his mother for deliberately abandoning him.

2. Stealing did not violate his moral and ethical principles.

3. Stealing resulted in immediate gratification and pleasure, both of which Richard had great difficulty resisting.

Sigmund Freud (1856–1939), the founder of psychoanalysis, suggested that an individual's psychological well-being is dependent on a healthy interaction among the id, ego, and superego—the three basic components of the human psyche. The **id** consists of powerful urges and drives for gratification and satisfaction. The **ego** is the executive of the personality, acting as a moderator between the superego and id. The **superego** acts as a moral code or conscience. Freud proposed that criminality may result from an overactive superego or conscience. In treating patients, he noticed that those who were suffering from unbearable guilt

"The first human who hurled an insult instead of a stone was the founder of civilization."

Sigmund Freud

committed crimes in order to be apprehended and punished.[5] Once they had been punished, their feelings of guilt were relieved. Richard's psychoanalyst suggested that Richard's anger over his father's death and his mother's abandonment created unconscious feelings of guilt, which he sought to relieve by committing a crime and being punished for it.

The psychoanalyst also offered an alternative explanation for Richard's persistent criminal activities: His conscience was perhaps not too strong, but too weak. The conscience, or superego, was so weak or defective that he was unable to control the impulses of the id. Because the superego is essentially an internalized parental image, developed when the child assumes the parents' attitudes and moral values, it follows that the absence of such an image may lead to an unrestrained id and thus to delinquency.[6]

Psychoanalytic theory suggests yet another explanation for Richard's behavior: an insatiable need for immediate reward and gratification. A defect in the character formation of delinquents drives them to satisfy their desires at once, regardless of the consequences.[7] This urge, which psychoanalysts attribute to the id, is so strong that relationships with people are important only so long as they help satisfy it. Most analysts view delinquents as children unable to give up their desires for instant pleasure.

The psychoanalytic approach is still one of the most prominent explanations for both normal and asocial functioning. Despite criticism,[8] three basic principles still appeal to psychologists who study criminality:

1. The actions and behavior of an adult are understood in terms of childhood development.
2. Behavior and unconscious motives are intertwined, and their interaction must be unraveled if we are to understand criminality.
3. Criminality is essentially a representation of psychological conflict.

In spite of their appeal, psychoanalytic treatment techniques devised to address these principles have been controversial since their introduction by Freud and his disciples. The controversy has involved questions about improvement following treatment and, perhaps more important, the validity of the hypothetical conflicts the treatment presupposes.

Moral Development

Consider the following moral dilemma:

> In Europe, a woman is near death from a special kind of cancer. There is one drug that the doctors think might save her. It is a form of radium that a druggist in the same town has recently discovered. The drug is expensive to make, and the druggist is charging ten times that cost. He paid $200 for the radium and is charging $2,000 for a small dose of the drug. The sick woman's husband, Heinz, goes to everyone he knows to borrow the money, but he can get together only $1,000. He tells the druggist that his wife is dying and asks him to sell the drug more cheaply or to let him pay later. The druggist says, "No, I discovered the drug and I'm going to make money from it." Heinz is desperate and considers breaking into the man's store to steal the drug for his wife.[9]

This classic dilemma sets up complex moral issues. While you may know that it is wrong to steal, you may believe that this is a situation in which the law should be circumvented. Or is it always wrong to steal, no matter what the circumstances? Regardless of what you decide, the way you reach the decision about whether or not to steal reveals much about your moral development.

The psychologist Lawrence Kohlberg, who pioneered moral developmental theory, has found that moral reasoning develops in three phases.[10] In the first, the preconventional level, children's moral rules and moral values consist of dos and don'ts to avoid punishment. A desire to avoid punishment and a belief in the superior power of authorities are the two central reasons for doing what is right. According to the theory, until the ages of 9 to 11, children usually reason at this level. They think, in effect, "If I steal, what are my chances of getting caught and being punished?"

Adolescents typically reason at the conventional level. Here individuals believe in and have adopted the values and rules of society. Moreover, they seek to uphold these rules. They think, in effect, "It is illegal to steal and therefore I should not steal, under any circumstances." Finally, at the postconventional level, individuals examine customs and social rules according to their own sense of universal human rights, moral principles, and duties. They think, in effect, "One must live within the law, but certain universal ethical principles, such as respect for human rights and for the dignity of human life, supersede the written law when the two conflict." This level of moral reasoning is generally seen in adults after the age of 20. (See Table 4.1.)

According to Kohlberg and his colleagues, most delinquents and criminals reason at the preconventional level. Low moral development or preconventional reasoning alone, however, does not result in criminality. Other factors, such as the presence or the absence of significant social bonds, may play a part. Kohlberg has argued that basic moral principles and social norms are learned through social interaction and role playing. In essence, children learn how to be moral by reasoning with others who are at a higher level of moral development.[11]

Students of Kohlberg have looked at practical applications of his theory. What would happen, for instance, if delinquents who were poor moral reasoners were exposed to individuals who reasoned at a higher level? Joseph Hickey, William Jennings, and their associates designed programs for Connecticut and Florida prisons and applied them in school systems throughout the United States. The "just-community intervention" approach involves a structured educational curriculum stressing democracy, fairness, and a sense of community. Above all, the focus is on the growth and development of moral reasoning. A series of evaluations of just-community programs has revealed significant improvement in moral development.[12]

Maternal Deprivation and Attachment Theory

In a well-known psychological experiment, infant monkeys were provided with the choice between two wire "monkeys." One, made of uncovered cage wire, dispensed milk. The other, made of cage wire covered with soft fabric, did not give milk. The infant monkeys in the experiment gravitated to the warm cloth monkey, which provided comfort and security even though it did not provide food. What does this have to do with criminality? Research has demonstrated that a phenomenon important to social development takes place shortly after the birth of any mammal: the construction of an emotional bond between the infant and its mother. The strength of this emotional bond, or **attachment**, will determine, or at least materially affect, a child's ability to form attachments in the future. In order to form a successful attachment, a child needs a warm, loving, and interactive caretaker.

Studies of Attachment The British psychiatrist John Bowlby has studied both the need for warmth and affection from birth onward and the consequences of not having it. He has proposed a theory of attachment with seven important features:

- *Specificity.* Attachments are selective, usually directed to one or more individuals in some order of preference.
- *Duration.* Attachments endure and persist, sometimes throughout the life cycle.
- *Engagement of emotion.* Some of the most intense emotions are associated with attachment relationships.
- *Ontogeny (course of development).* Children form an attachment to one primary figure in the first nine months of life. That principal attachment figure is the person who supplies the most social interaction of a satisfying kind.
- *Learning.* Though learning plays a role in the development of attachment, Bowlby finds that attachments are the products not of rewards or reinforcements, but of basic social interaction.
- *Organization.* Attachment behavior follows cognitive development and interpersonal maturation from birth onward.
- *Biological function.* Attachment behavior has a biological function—survival. It is

TABLE 4.1 Kohlberg's Sequence of Moral Reasoning

Level	Stage	Sample Moral Reasoning In Favor of Stealing	Sample Moral Reasoning Against Stealing
Level 1: Preconventionl morality. At this level, the concrete interests of the individual are considered in terms of rewards and punishments.	Stage 1: Obedience and punishment orientation. At this stage, people stick to rules in order to avoid punishment, and there is obedience for its own sake.	If you let your wife die, you will get in trouble. You'll be blamed for not spending the money to save her, and there'll be an investigation of you and the druggist for your wife's death.	You shouldn't steal the drug because you'll be caught and sent to jail if you do. If you do get away, your conscience will bother you, thinking how the police will catch up with you at any minute.
	Stage 2: Reward orientation. At this stage, rules are followed only for one's own benefit. Obedience occurs because of rewards that are received.	If you do happen to get caught, you could give the drug back and you wouldn't get much of a sentence. It wouldn't bother you much to serve a little jail term, if you have your wife when you get out.	You may not get much of a jail term if you steal the drug, but your wife will probably die before you get out, so it won't do much good. If your wife dies, you shouldn't blame yourself; it wasn't your fault she had cancer.
Level 2: Conventional morality. At this level, moral problems are approached by an individual as a member of society. People are interested in pleasing others by acting as good members of society.	Stage 3: "Good boy" morality. Individuals at this stage show an interest in maintaining the respect of others and doing what is expected of them.	No one will think you're bad if you steal the drug, but your family will think you're an inhuman husband if you don't. If you let your wife die, you'll never be able to look anybody in the face again.	It isn't just the druggist who will think you're a criminal; everyone else will too. After you steal it, you'll feel bad, thinking how you've brought dishonor on your family and yourself; you won't be able to face anyone again.
	Stage 4: Authority and social-order-maintaining morality. People at this stage conform to society's rules and consider that "right" is what society defines as right.	If you have any sense of honor, you won't let your wife die just because you're afraid to do the only thing that will save her. You'll always feel guilty that you caused her death if you don't do your duty to her.	You're desperate and you may not know you're doing wrong when you steal the drug. But you'll know you did wrong after you're sent to jail. You'll always feel guilty for your dishonesty and lawbreaking.
Level 3: Postconventional morality. People at this level use moral principles which are seen as broader than those of any particular society.	Stage 5: Morality of contract, individual rights, and democratically accepted law. People at this stage do what is right because of a sense of obligation to laws which are agreed upon within society. They perceive that laws can be modified as part of changes in an implicit social contract.	You'll lose other people's respect, not gain it, if you don't steal. If you let your wife die, it will be out of fear, not out of reasoning. So you'll just lose self-respect and probably the respect of others too.	You'll lose your standing and respect in the community and violate the law. You'll lose respect for yourself if you're carried away by emotion and forget the long-range point of view.
	Stage 6: Morality of individual principles and conscience. At this final stage, a person follows laws because they are based on universal ethical principles. Laws that violate the principles are disobeyed.	If you don't steal the drug, if you let your wife die, you'll always condemn yourself for it afterward. You won't be blamed and you'll have lived up to the outside rule of the law, but you won't have lived up to your own standards of conscience.	If you steal the drug, you won't be blamed by other people, but you'll condemn yourself because you won't have lived up to your own conscience and standards of honesty.

Source: Adapted from Robert S. Feldman, *Understanding Psychology* (New York: McGraw-Hill, 1987), p. 378.

found in almost all species of mammals and in birds.[13]

Bowlby contends that a child needs to experience a warm, intimate, and continuous relationship with either a mother or a mother substitute in order to be securely attached. When a child is separated from the mother or is rejected by her, anxious attachment results. Anxious attachment affects the capacity to be affectionate and to develop intimate relationships with others. Habitual criminals, it is claimed, typically have an inability to form bonds of affection:

> More often than not the childhoods of such individuals are found to have been grossly disturbed by death, divorce, or separation of the parents, or by other events resulting in disruption of bonds, with an incidence of such disturbance far higher than is met with in any other comparable group, whether drawn from the general population or from psychiatric casualties of other sorts.[14]

Considerable research supports the relationship between anxious attachment and subsequent behavioral problems:

- In a study of 113 middle-class children observed at 1 year of age and again at 6 years, researchers noted a significant relationship between behavior at age 6 and attachment at age 1.[15]
- In a study of 40 children seen when they were 1 year old and again at 18 months, it was noted that anxiously attached children were less empathetic, independent, compliant, and confident than securely attached children.[16]
- Researchers have noted that the quality of one's attachment correlates significantly with asocial preschool behavior—being aggressive, leaving the group, and the like.[17]

Family Atmosphere and Delinquency Criminologists also have examined the effects of the mother's absence, whether because of death, divorce, or abandonment. Does her absence cause delinquency? Empirical research is equivocal. Perhaps the most persuasive evidence comes from longitudinal research conducted by Joan McCord, who has investigated the relationship between family atmosphere (such as parental self-confidence, deviance, and affection) and delinquency.

In one study, she collected data on the childhood homes of 201 men and their subsequent court records in order to identify family-related variables that would predict criminal activity. Such variables as inadequate maternal affection and supervision, parental conflict, the mother's lack of self-confidence, and the father's deviance were significantly related to the commission of crimes against persons and/or property. The father's absence by itself was not correlated with criminal behavior.[18]

Other studies, such as those by Sheldon and Eleanor Glueck and the more recent studies by Lee N. Robins, which were

> **:// Crime Surfing**
>
> www.ncjrs.org
>
> Material deprivation can be related to delinquent behavior. What happens to deprived (often abused and neglected) children? Is there a cycle of violence?

> **Did You Know?**
>
> ... that, while evidence is lacking that deprivation directly causes delinquency, research on the impact of family-based crime-prevention programs is promising? Programs that target family risk factors in multiple settings (ecological contexts) have achieved success. (See Table 4.2.)

Experiments with young monkeys and surrogate mothers reveal the power of attachment in behavioral development. Here a frightened baby rhesus monkey holds on to a terry-cloth mother.

TABLE 4.2 Family-Based Crime Prevention by Ecological Context

Ecological Context	Program	Prevention Agent
Home	Regular visits for emotional, informational, instrumental, and educational support for parents of preschool (or older) children	Nurses, teachers, paraprofessionals, preschool teachers
	Foster care outplacement for the prevention of physical and sexual abuse or neglect	Family services, social workers
	Family preservation of families at risk of outplacement of child	Private family-preservation teams
	Personal alarm for victims of serious domestic violence	Police
	In-home proactive counseling for domestic violence	Police, social workers
Preschool	Involvement of mothers in parent groups, job training, parent training	Preschool teachers
School	Parent training	Psychologists, teachers
	Simultaneous parent and child training	Psychologists, child care workers, social workers
Clinics	Family therapy	Psychologists, psychiatrists, social workers
	Medication—psychostimulants for treatment of hyperactivity and other childhood conduct disorders	Psychiatrists, psychologists, pediatricians
Hospitals	Domestic violence counseling	Nurses, social workers
	Low-birthweight baby mothers' counseling and support	Nurses, social workers
Courts	Prosecution of batterers	Police, prosecutors
	Warrants for unarrested batterers	Police, prosecutors
	Restraining orders or "stay away" order of protection	Police, prosecutors, judges, victims' advocates
	Hot line notification of victim about release of incarcerated domestic batterer	Probation, victim advocates
Battered women's shelters	Safe refuge during high-risk two to seven days' aftermath of domestic assault; counseling; hot lines	Volunteers, staff

carried out in schools, juvenile courts, and psychiatric hospitals, suggest a moderate to strong relation between crime and childhood deprivation.[19] However, evidence that deprivation directly causes delinquency is lacking.[20]

So far we have considered psychological theories that attribute the causes of delinquency or criminality to unconscious problems and failures in moral development. Not all psychologists agree with these explanations of criminal behavior. Some argue that human behavior develops through learning. They say that we learn by observing others and by watching the responses to other people's behavior (on television or in the movies, for instance) and to our own. Social learning theorists reject the notion that internal functioning alone makes us prone to act aggressively or violently.

Learning Aggression and Violence

Social learning theory maintains that delinquent behavior is learned through the same psychological processes as any other behavior. Behavior is learned when it is reinforced or rewarded; it is not learned when it is not reinforced. We learn behavior in various ways: observation, direct experience, and differential reinforcement.

Observational Learning Albert Bandura, a leading proponent of social learning theory, argues that individuals learn violence and aggression through **behavioral modeling**: Children learn how to behave by fashioning their behavior after that of others. Behavior is socially transmitted through examples, which come primarily from the family, the subculture, and the mass media.[21]

Psychologists have been studying the effects of family violence (Chapter 10) on children. They have found that parents who try to resolve family controversies by violence teach their children to use similar tactics. Thus a cycle of violence may be perpetuated through generations. Observing a healthy and happy family environment tends to result in constructive and positive modeling.

FROM THE PAGES OF The New York Times

The Apple Doesn't Fall Far

The Bogle family is famous in the Willamette Valley of Oregon. To be more precise, they're infamous throughout the state. That's because, by official count, 28 members of the Bogle family—parents, children, and grandchildren—have been arrested, convicted, and sent to prison. This criminal dynasty began when Rooster Bogle moved to Oregon from Texas, where he had already served hard time in prison. He then taught his children to be criminals; by the time the boys were 10 years old, they were breaking into liquor stores and stealing tractor-trailer trucks.

"Rooster raised us to be outlaws," said Tracey Bogle, the youngest of Rooster's children. "There is a domino effect in a family like ours. What you're raised with, you grow to become. You don't escape."

The Bogles may be an extreme example, but criminal justice experts have long observed that crime often runs in families. Justice Department figures show that 47 percent of inmates in state prisons have a parent or other close relative who has also been incarcerated. And, says Allen J. Beck of the Bureau of Justice Statistics, half of all juveniles in custody have a father, mother, or other close relative who has been in jail or prison.

Until recently, states paid little attention to these kinds of family ties. But in 2002, Oregon officials began asking all newly admitted inmates if they have a relative who has been incarcerated and whether they themselves have children. If they have relatives who have been locked up, the state is offering them increased services in areas like drug and alcohol treatment and mental health counseling, and courses in preventing domestic violence. In addition, Oregon has begun trying to keep track of inmates' children.

Fay Gentle, the training and transition coordinator for the Oregon Department of Corrections, says that there are a number of reasons a "clan" like the Bogles ends up in jail. Many of these families suffer from poverty, abuse, neglect, and drug use. But to Ms. Gentle, a critical reason is simply that children learn to imitate their parents. "Instead of learning appropriate behavior, they are learning how to cheat, lie, steal, and manipulate. Kids are so eager to please, they imitate their parents."

There is hope, however, even in the Bogle family. Daughter Tammie Bogle Stuckey has not only stayed out of prison, she now helps run five halfway houses for newly released inmates—many of whom come from her own family. She had to kick her own son out of her program for violating the terms of his parole. She wasn't entirely sorry, however. "I am actually relieved when he is in jail or prison," Tammie said, "cause I know he's not out trying to get himself killed."

Source

Source: Fox Butterfield, "Father Steals Best: Crime in an American Family," *New York Times,* Aug. 21, 2002.

Question for Discussion

1. If you were a state official, what kinds of programs would you put in place for inmates who come from crime-oriented families? Should this kind of family history be considered when sentencing such criminals?
2. What can be done to stop the cycle of family crime? Should children of criminals be taken away from their families, for example? Does targeting these children violate their rights in any way?

To understand the influence of the social environment outside the home, social learning theorists have studied gangs, which often provide excellent models of observational learning of violence and aggression. They have found, in fact, that violence is very much a norm shared by some people in a community or gang. The highest incidence of aggressive behavior occurs where aggressiveness is a desired characteristic, as it is in some subcultures.

Observational learning takes place in front of the television set and at the movies, as well. Children who have seen others being rewarded for violent acts often believe that violence and aggression are acceptable behaviors.[22] And today children can see a lot of violence. The psychologist Leonard Eron has argued that the "single best predictor of how aggressive a young man would be when he was 19 years old was the violence of the television programs he preferred when he was 8 years old."[23]

Results from the three-year landmark *National Television Violence Study* initiated in 1994 suggest that the problem is one not only of violence, but also of the portrayal of violence—the absence of consequences for violent acts and the glamorization of violence.[24] (See Figure 4.1.)

Of Immediate Concern

The Taboo Crime of Parricide

Mark Martone was 16 when he shot his father to death. [He] remembers abuse back to age five, when he told his dad he was scared of the dark. "Oh, Jesus Christ," said the parent in disgust. Then he led the terrified boy down to the cellar, handcuffed his arms over a rafter, turned off the light and shut the door. Mark dangled in silence for hours. When Mark was nine, his father held the boy's hand over a red-hot burner as punishment for moving a book of matches on a bureau. And when he was 15, his dad, angered by a long-distance phone bill, stuck a gun in his son's mouth and "told me he was going to blow my brains out."(1)

Sylvester Hobbs III, a 20-year-old, said to be depressed and withdrawn, stabbed and killed his stepfather and wounded his mother.(2)

Eleven-year-old identical twins were charged with murdering their father and attempting to kill their mother and 16-year-old sister in their house.(3)

James Brian Hill, 28, said he was defending his own life when he killed his father, who had previously assaulted his mother.(2)

Carlton Akee Turner Jr., 19, killed his parents because his father was said to be abusive.(2)

An estimated 5.7 million children in the United States are physically, mentally, and sexually abused by their parents annually, and the problem is not lessening. Of those millions of children, maybe a few hundred each year fight back with the ultimate weapon: They kill the abusive parent. In the past such children were regarded as particularly evil, and the law reserved the most terrible forms of capital punishment for parricides. With the growing understanding of the horrors of child abuse, however, these youths are being treated with increasing sympathy. "They know what they're doing is wrong," comments a psychologist at the University of Virginia. "But they are desperate and helpless, and they don't see alternatives."(1)

The typical case involves a 16- to 18-year-old from a white middle-class family. Sons are more likely than daughters to commit murder, and the victim is more likely to be a father than a mother. While children who kill nonabusive parents usually display some sign of mental disorder, the killers of abusive parents generally are seen as well adjusted.(4)

The increasing sympathy for these teenagers has led to verdicts of not guilty by reason of self-defense or guilty of reduced charges (for example, manslaughter instead of first-degree murder). A battered-child-syndrome defense sometimes is successful, but the killings do not usually fit the typical idea of self-defense: Most happen when the parent is in a vulnerable position instead of in the middle of an attack on the child. But mental health experts think that treatment is more appropriate than punishment for children who kill their abusive parents. "These kids don't need to be locked up for our protection," says one attorney and psychologist. "Some may benefit in the sense that they've been able to atone and overcome some guilt. But beyond that, it's really Draconian."(1)

CHARACTERISTICS ASSOCIATED WITH ADOLESCENT PARRICIDE OFFENDERS

1. Patterns of family violence exist (parental brutality and cruelty toward child and/or toward one another).
2. Adolescent's attempts to get help from others fail.
3. Adolescent's efforts to escape family situation fail (e.g., running away, thoughts of suicide, suicide attempts).
4. Adolescent is isolated from others/fewer outlets.
5. Family situation becomes increasingly intolerable.
6. Adolescent feels increasingly helpless, trapped.
7. Adolescent's inability to cope leads to loss of control.
8. Prior criminal behavior is minimal or nonexistent.
9. Gun is available.
10. Homicide victim is alcoholic.
11. Evidence to suggest dissociative state in some cases.
12. Victim's death perceived as relief to offender/family; initial absence of remorse.

Sources

1. Hannah Bloch and Jeanne McDowell, "When Kids Kill Abusive Parents," *Time,* Nov. 23, 1992, p. 60.
2. Nancy Calaway, "Spotlight Intensifies on Children Who Murder Parents; Recent Focus on Crime Doesn't Mean It's Increasing, Analyst Says," *Dallas Morning News,* Aug. 30, 1999, p. 1A.
3. Anne Saker, "Twin Boys Face Trial in Father's Killing," (Raleigh, N.C.) *News and Observer,* Aug. 1, 1999, p. A1.
4. Kathleen M. Heide, *Why Kids Kill Parents* (Columbus: Ohio State University Press, 1992), pp. 40–41.

Questions for Discussion

1. If you were on a jury, would you be willing to consider that what appears to be cold-blooded murder might have been a form of self-defense for a battered child?
2. An attorney specializing in parricide feels that such cases "open a window on our understanding of child abuse." How would you go about determining which of millions of child abuse cases are likely to lead to parricide for which a standard defense should be recognized?

Source: Excerpted from Kathleen M. Heide, *Why Kids Kill Parents* (Columbus: Ohio State University Press, 1992), table 3.1, pp. 40–41.

PART II Explanations of Crime and Criminal Behavior

FIGURE 4.1 Overall television industry averages: three-year comparisons.

Category	Measure	Year 1	Year 2	Year 3
	% of Programs with Violence	58	61	61
VIOLENT PROGRAMS	% with an Anti-Violence Theme	4	4	3
	% that show Long-Term Negative Consequences	16	13	16
	% with Violence in Realistic Settings	51	55	55
	% with "Bad" Characters who go Unpunished	37	39	45
VIOLENT SCENES	% with No Remorse, Criticism or Penalty for Violence	73	75	71
	% with Blood and Gore	15	14	14
	% with Humor	39	43	42
VIOLENT INTERACTIONS	% that show No Pain	58	55	51
	% with Unrealistically Low Levels of Harm	35	40	34
	% with use of a Gun	25	23	26
	% with Repeated Behavioral Violence	58	58	61
	% with Perpetrators who are Attractive	37	40	39
	% with Lethal Violence	52	52	54

Source: J. Federman, ed., *National Television Violence Study*, vol. 3 (Santa Barbara: University of California, Center for Communications and Social Policy, 1998).

Direct Experience What we learn by observation is determined by the behavior of others. What we learn from direct experience is determined by what we ourselves do and what happens to us. We remember the past and use its lessons to avoid future mistakes. Thus we learn through trial and error. According to social learning theorists, after engaging in a given behavior, most of us examine the responses to our actions and modify our behavior as necessary to obtain favorable responses. If we are praised or rewarded for a behavior, we are likely to repeat it. If we are subjected to verbal or physical punishment, we are likely to refrain from such behavior. Our behavior in the first instance and our restraint in the second are said to be "reinforced" by the rewards and punishments we receive.

The psychologist Gerald Patterson and his colleagues examined how aggression is learned by direct experience. They observed that some passive children at play were repeatedly victimized by other children but were occasionally successful in curbing the attacks by counteraggression. Over time, these children learned defensive fighting, and eventually they initiated fights. Other passive children, who were rarely observed to be victimized, remained submissive.[25] Thus children, like adults, can learn to be aggressive and even violent by trial and error.

While violence and aggression are learned behaviors, they are not necessarily expressed until they are elicited in one of several ways. Albert Bandura describes the factors that elicit behavioral responses as "instigators." Thus social learning theory describes not only how aggression is acquired but also how it is instigated. Consider the following instigators of aggression:

- *Aversive instigators*. Physical assaults, verbal threats, and insults; adverse reductions in conditions of life (such as impoverishment) and the thwarting of goal-directed behavior
- *Incentive instigators*. Rewards, such as money and praise
- *Modeling instigators*. Violent or aggressive behaviors observed in others
- *Instructional instigators*. Observations of people carrying out instructions to engage in violence or aggression
- *Delusional instigators*. Unfounded or bizarre beliefs that violence is necessary or justified[26]

Differential Reinforcement In 1965 the criminologist C. Ray Jeffery suggested that learning theory could be used to explain criminality.[27] Within one year Ernest Burgess and Ronald Akers combined Bandura's psychologically based learning theory with Edwin Sutherland's sociologically based differential association theory

Thomas Junta, a six foot, 270 pound truck driver, demonstrates how he shook the coach of his son's hockey team, Michael Costin, after practice. A resulting fight led to Costin's death. Junta was convicted of involuntary manslaughter on January 25, 2002, and sentenced to 6 to 10 years in prison.

Window to the World

Censoring TV Violence

On December 19, 1996, the U.S. television industry announced a voluntary TV ratings system. All TV shows are now rated as follows:

- TV-Y, material suitable for children of all ages. Show contains little or no violence, strong language, or sexual content.
- TV-Y7, material suitable for children 7 and older.
- TV-G, material suitable for all audiences.
- TV-PG, parental guidance is suggested. Program may contain infrequent coarse language, limited violence, some suggestive sexual dialogue and situations.
- TV-14, material may be inappropriate for children under 14. Program may contain sophisticated themes, strong language, and sexual content.
- TV-M, for mature audiences only. Program may contain profane language, graphic violence, and explicit sexual content.

What prompted this unprecedented move? Many Americans had for some time been concerned about the ever increasing amount of violence on television and its effects on children.(1)

SOCIAL CONTROL VERSUS CENSORSHIP

While many people saw the networks' plans for ratings as a disappointingly small contribution to a big problem, others began worrying about freedom of expression. Representative Edward J. Markey pushed for a plan that would require "V-block" computer chips in all new TV sets—the chip would allow parents to block all V-rated (violent) shows. V-chips are now mandatory on all television sets with screens 13 inches and larger.(1) "I am totally opposed to the government getting involved in any way that infringes on the First Amendment," argues Jack Valenti, president of the Motion Picture Association of America.(1) " 'That's getting awfully close to censorship,' frets Peggy Charren, founder of Action for Children's Television."(2)

If such warnings and "zappings" do constitute censorship, the United States is ahead of other countries. In Egypt, both radio and television are owned by the state, and all broadcasts are supervised by the government.(3) In Singapore, television also is state-controlled.(4) India, despite being open to satellite-dish broadcasting, was still using its government-run network in 1992 to censor the violence that occurred during religious riots across the country.(5) Indonesia's government announced in 1993 that censoring all materials citizens could watch on private and foreign networks had become "too onerous a task" for its National Film Censorship Board; it stated that the people themselves should judge what to watch and should avoid "morally unsuitable" programs, such as those containing pornography and violence.(6)

The Chinese Example

Perhaps China provides the most prominent example of the use of television for social control: "In the hands of Chinese media experts, TV is both an instrument to instill terror and obedience and an educational tool," wrote *Newsday* reporter Thomas Collins after the Tiananmen Square protests. "The . . . important thing was to control and limit what a billion Chinese people would believe had happened."(7) According to Collins, the event was portrayed as follows:

Rather than a demonstration for democratic reforms involving millions of people throughout the country, the protests were the work of a handful of "counter-revolutionaries" and "hoodlums." Instead of the massacre of hundreds, possibly thousands of students and workers, the Chinese populace is being told that the only casualties were soldiers. No students were killed.

Sources

1. Ann Scott, "The Role of Washington in Curbing Youth Violence," *Christian Science Monitor,* May 6, 1999, p. 2.
2. Harry F. Waters, "Networks under the Gun," *Newsweek,* July 12, 1993, pp. 64–66.
3. "Middle East Watch Report," *Middle East News Network,* Nov. 17, 1991.
4. "Singapore: Opening Up to a Little Sex and Nudity," *Inter Press Service,* Apr. 15, 1991.
5. Molly Moore, "Satellite TV Shows Asia a World beyond Reach of State Censors," *Washington Post,* Apr. 10, 1993, p. A12.
6. "Indonesia to Revamp Film Censorship," *Straits Times,* Apr. 29, 1993, p. 13.
7. Thomas Collins, "In China, the Carnage That Never Was," *Newsday,* June 14, 1989, p. 67.

Questions for Discussion

1. Research suggests an association between children's exposure to TV violence and the likelihood that they will resolve their own conflicts by violent means. Are we then justified in censoring TV violence?
2. Suppose censorship were imposed. How could we then measure the impact of censorship on rates of violent crime?

(Chapter 5) to produce the theory of **differential association-reinforcement.** This theory suggests that (1) the persistence of criminal behavior depends on whether or not it is rewarded or punished, and (2) the most meaningful rewards and punishments are those given by groups that are important in an individual's life—the peer group, the family, teachers in school, and so forth. In other words, people respond more readily to the reactions of the most significant people

95

With 15,577 fans watching, rookie Joe Thornton took on the 6-foot-2, 217-pound Canucks forward Dave Scatchard who just ran him into the boards near the penalty box after some words were exchanged. What was the reaction of the fans? Violent fights are the highlight of hockey games. Fans, young and old, cheered Thornton for standing up to Scatchard.

in their lives. If criminal behavior elicits more positive reinforcement or rewards than punishment, such behavior will persist.[28]

Social learning theory helps us understand why some individuals who engage in violent and aggressive behavior do so: They learn to behave that way. But perhaps something within the personality of a criminal creates a susceptibility to aggressive or violent models in the first place. For example, perhaps criminals are more extroverted, irresponsible, or unsocialized than noncriminals. Or perhaps criminals are more intolerant and impulsive or have lower self-esteem.

Personality

Four distinct lines of psychological research have examined the relationship between personality and criminality.[29] First, investigators have looked at the differences between the personality structures of criminals and noncriminals. Most of this work has been carried out in state and federal prisons, where psychologists have administered personality questionnaires such as the Minnesota Multiphasic Personality Inventory (MMPI) and the California Psychological Inventory (CPI) to inmates. The evidence from these studies shows that inmates are typically more impulsive, hostile, self-centered, and immature than noncriminals.[30]

Second, a vast amount of literature is devoted to the prediction of behavior. Criminologists want to determine how an individual will respond to prison discipline and whether he or she will avoid crime after release. The results are equivocal. At best, personality characteristics seem to be modest predictors of future criminality.[31] Yet when they are combined with such variables as personal history, they tend to increase the power of prediction significantly.[32]

Third, many studies examine the degree to which normal personality dynamics operate in criminals. Findings from these studies suggest that the personality dynamics of criminals are often quite similar to those of noncriminals. Social criminals (those who act in concert with others), for example, are found to be more sociable, affiliative, outgoing, and self-confident than solitary criminals.[33]

Finally, some researchers have attempted to quantify individual differences between types and groups of offenders. Several studies have compared the personality characteristics of first-time offenders with those of repeat or habitual criminals. Other investigators have compared violent offenders with nonviolent offenders, and murderers with drug offenders. In addition, prison inmates have been classified according to personality type.[34]

In general, research on criminals' personality characteristics has revealed some important associations. However, criminologists have been skeptical of the strength of the relationship of personality to criminality. A review of research on that relationship published in 1942 by Milton Metfessel and Constance Lovell dismissed personality as an important causal factor in criminal behavior.[35] In 1950 Karl Schuessler and Donald Cressey reached the same conclusion.[36] Twenty-seven years later, Daniel Tennenbaum's updated review agreed with earlier assessments. He found that "the data do not reveal any significant differences between criminal and noncriminal psychology.... Personality testing has not differentiated criminals from noncriminals."[37]

Despite these conclusions, whether or not criminals share personality characteristics continues to be debated. Are criminals in fact more aggressive, dominant, and manipulative than noncriminals? Are they more irresponsible? Clearly, many criminals are aggressive; many have manipulated a variety of situations; many assume no responsibility for their acts. But are such characteristics common to all criminals? Samuel Yochelson and Stanton Samenow addressed these questions. In *The Criminal Personality*, this psychiatrist-psychologist team described their growing disillusion with traditional explanations of criminality.

From their experience in treating criminals in the Forensic Division of St. Elizabeth's Hospital in Washington, D.C., they refuted psychoanalysts' claims that crime is caused by inner conflict. Rather, they said, criminals share abnormal thinking patterns that lead to decisions to commit crimes. Yochelson and Samenow identified as many as 52 patterns of thinking common to the criminals they studied. They argued that criminals are angry people who feel a sense of superiority, expect not to be held accountable for their acts, and have a highly inflated self-image. Any perceived attack on their glorified self-image elicits a strong reaction, often a violent one.[38]

Other researchers have used different methods to study the association between criminality and personality. For example, criminologists have reviewed the findings of a large sample of studies that use the California Psychological Inventory. Their research revealed a common personality profile: The criminals tested showed remarkable similarity in their deficient self-control, intolerance, and lack of responsibility.[39]

Though studies dealing with personality correlates of criminals are important, some psychologists are concerned that by focusing on the personalities of criminals in their search for explanations of criminal behavior, investigators may overlook other important factors, like the complex social environment in which a crime is committed.[40] A homicide that began as a barroom argument between two intoxicated patrons who backed different teams to win the Super Bowl, for example, is very likely to hinge on situational factors that interact with the participants' personalities.

Eysenck's Conditioning Theory For over 20 years Hans J. Eysenck has been developing and refining a theory of the relationship between personality and criminality that considers more than just individual characteristics.[41] His theory has two parts. First, Eysenck claims that all human personality may be seen in three dimensions—psychoticism, extroversion, and neuroticism. Individuals who score high on measures of **psychoticism** are aggressive, egocentric, and impulsive. Those who score high on measures of **extroversion** are sensation-seeking, dominant, and assertive. High scorers on scales assessing **neuroticism** may be described as having low self-esteem, excessive anxiety, and wide mood swings. Eysenck has found that when criminals respond to items on the Eysenck Personality Questionnaire (EPQ), they uniformly score higher on each of these dimensions than do noncriminals.

The second part of Eysenck's theory suggests that humans develop a conscience through **conditioning.** From birth, we are rewarded for social behavior and punished for asocial behavior. Eysenck likens this conditioning to training a dog. Puppies are not born house trained. You have to teach a puppy that it is good to urinate and defecate outside your apartment or house by pairing kind words and perhaps some tangible reward (such as a dog treat) with successful outings. A loud, angry voice will convey disapproval and disappointment when mistakes are made inside.

In time most dogs learn and, according to Eysenck, develop a conscience. But as Eysenck also has noted, some dogs learn faster than others. German shepherds acquire good "bathroom habits" faster than basenjis, who are most difficult to train. It is argued that the same is true of humans; there are important individual differences. Criminals become conditioned slowly and appear to care little whether or not their asocial actions bring disapproval.

Eysenck has identified two additional aspects of a criminal's poor conditionability. First, he has found that extroverts are much more difficult to condition than introverts and thus have greater difficulty in developing a conscience. Youthful offenders tend to score highest on measures of extroversion. Second, differences in conditionability are dependent on certain physiological factors, the most important of which is **cortical arousal,** or activation of the cerebral cortex.

The cortex of the brain is responsible for higher intellectual functioning, information processing, and decision making. Eysenck found that individuals who are easily conditionable and develop a conscience have a high level of cortical arousal; they do not need intense external stimulation to become aroused. A low level of cortical arousal is associated with poor conditionability, difficulty in developing a conscience, and need for external stimulation.

MENTAL DISORDERS AND CRIME

It has been difficult for psychiatrists to derive criteria that would help them decide which offenders are mentally ill. According to psychiatrist Seymour L. Halleck, the problem lies in the evolving conceptualization of mental illness. Traditionally, the medical profession viewed mental illness as an absolute condition or status—either you are afflicted with **psychosis** or you are not. Should such a view concern us? Halleck suggests that it should. "Although this kind of thinking is not compatible with current psychiatric knowledge," he writes, "it continues to exert considerable influence upon psychiatric practice. . . . As applied to the criminal, it also leads to rigid dichotomies between the 'sick criminal' and the 'normal criminal.' "[42]

Halleck and other psychiatrists, such as Karl Menninger, conceptualize mental functioning as a process.[43] Mental illness should not be considered apart from mental health—the two exist on the same continuum. At various times in each of our lives we move along the continuum from health toward illness.[44] For this reason, a diagnosis of "criminal" or "mentally ill" may overlook potentially important gradations in mental health and mental illness. This issue is perhaps no more apparent than in the insanity defense, which calls for proof of sanity or insanity and generally does not allow for gradations in mental functioning (see Chapter 2).

Estimates vary, but between 20 and 60 percent of state correctional populations suffer from a type of mental disorder that in the nineteenth century was described by the French physician Philippe Pinel as *manie sans délire* ("madness without confusion"), by the English physician James C. Prichard as "moral insanity," and by Gina Lombroso Ferrero as "irresistible atavistic impulses." Today such mental illness is called **psychopathy,** sociopathy, or antisocial personality—a personality characterized by the inability to learn from experience, lack of warmth, and absence of guilt.

The psychiatrist Hervey Cleckley views psychopathy as a serious illness even though patients may not appear to be ill. According to Cleckley, psychopaths appear to enjoy excellent mental health; but what we see is only a "mask of sanity." Initially, they seem free of any kind of mental disorder and appear to be reliable and honest. After some time, however, it becomes clear that they have no sense of responsibility whatsoever. They show a disregard for truth, are insincere, and feel no sense of shame, guilt, or humiliation. Psychopaths lie and cheat without hesitation and engage in verbal as well as physical abuse without any thought. Cleckley describes the following case:

> A sixteen-year-old boy was sent to jail for stealing a valuable watch. Though apparently . . . untouched by his situation, after a few questions were asked he began to seem more like a child who feels the unpleasantness of his position. He confessed that he had worried much about masturbation, saying he had been threatened and punished severely for it and told that it would cause him to become "insane."
>
> He admitted having broken into his mother's jewelry box and stolen a watch valued at $150.00. He calmly related that he exchanged the watch for 15 cents' worth of ice cream and seemed entirely satisfied with what he had done. He readily admitted that his act was wrong, used the proper words to express his intention to cause no further trouble, and, when asked, said that he would like very much to get out of jail.
>
> He stated that he loved his mother devotedly. "I just kiss her and kiss her ten or twelve times when she comes to see me!" he exclaimed with shallow zeal. These manifestations of affection were so artificial, and, one would even say, unconsciously artificial, that few laymen would be convinced that any feeling, in the ordinary sense, lay in them. Nor was his mother convinced.
>
> A few weeks before this boy was sent to jail he displayed to his mother some rifle cartridges. When asked what he wanted with them he explained that they would fit the rifle in a nearby closet. "I've tried them," he announced. And in a lively tone added, "Why, I could put them in the gun and shoot you. You would fall right over!" He laughed and his eyes shone with a small but real impulse.[45]

Psychologists also have found that psychopaths, like Hans Eysenck's extroverts, have a low internal arousal level; thus psychopaths constantly seek external stimulation, are less susceptible to learning by direct experience (they do not modify their behavior after they are punished), are more impulsive, and experience far less anxiety than nonpsychopaths about any adverse consequences of their acts.[46] Some psychiatrists consider "psychopathy" to be an artificial label for an antisocial personality.[47] To Eysenck and others, it is a major behavioral category that presents significant challenges. Eysenck sums up this view by writing that the psychopath poses the riddle of delinquency. If we could solve the riddle, then we would have a powerful weapon to fight the problem of delinquency.[48]

> **:// Crime Surfing**
>
> www.psych.org/public_info/insanity.cfm
>
> Interested in the insanity defense? Go to the American Psychiatric Association's website.

John Dupont, heir to the Dupont fortune, who imagined himself to be the Christ child, the Dali Lama, and the crown prince of Russia, killed the Olympic wrestler he had hired as a coach. Dupont was found guilty but mentally ill at trial and was sentenced to 13 to 30 years in prison.

Psychological Causation

With all this discussion of possible psychological correlates of criminal behavior, it is easy to make what Stephen Morse calls the **fundamental psycholegal error.** This error in thinking or mistaken belief occurs when we identify a cause for criminal behavior and then assume that it naturally follows that any behavior resulting from that "cause" must be excused by law. Think about the kinds of defenses to criminal charges raised by lawyers and ask yourself whether Professor Morse is correct. (See Table 4.3.)

Consider, for example, the likelihood of psycholegal error in cases where lawyers have raised an insanity defense. Park Dietz, a highly regarded forensic psychiatrist, was interviewed recently and revealed just how easy it is to confuse the cause of criminal behavior with an appropriate and legally justifiable defense.

Interviewer: . . . Many defense attorneys argue that sick deeds are born in sick minds, and you have difficulty with that.

PD [Park Dietz]: With rare exceptions, people are responsible for what they do. Killers seldom meet the legal standard for insanity, which is quite different from the way most people use the word every day. Killers may be *disturbed,* but that doesn't necessarily mean that they can't tell right from wrong or are compelled to maim or murder.

Interviewer: But what about someone like Jeffrey Dahmer? People say, "If he wasn't crazy, who is?"

PD: He was certainly *disturbed,* but he knew what he was doing was wrong. He tried to conceal his victims' bodies. He also wore a condom while having sex with the corpses, which indicates that the intensity of his sexual urge was less than many teenagers experience in backseats with their girlfriends.

TABLE 4.3 Defenses Sometimes Attempted by Defense Lawyers

Defense	Description of Defense
The Twinkie defense (hypoglycemia—too much sugar)	Because he lost his job as a San Francisco supervisor, Dan White gorged on junk food—Twinkies, Coca-Cola, candy. Depressed, he sneaked a gun into City Hall. After killing Mayor Moscone, he killed a leader of the gay community, Supervisor Milk, in 1978.
Defendants or victims with multiple personalities	Many psychiatric experts agree that the disorder exists but disagree on how common it is. If a woman with multiple personalities complains of rape, the defendant might argue that consent to sex was given by one of the personalities. A defendant with multiple personalities might argue that he or she could not control the bad personality.
Sleepwalking and other forms of automatism (unconsciousness)	Automatism is a state in which a person is capable of action but is not conscious of what he or she is doing. This defense is statutorized in some states, including California, and held to be an affirmative defense separate from the insanity defense. *Fulcher v. State,* 633 P.2d 142, 29 CrL 2556 (Wyo. 1981)
Cultural disorientation	Some immigrants to the United States bring with them cultural practices that are in conflict with our criminal codes. For example, some continue the ancient traditions of the medicinal use of opium, the practice of capturing young brides, and the ritual slaughtering of animals. In 1985 when a young Japanese mother of two children learned that her husband was having an affair with another woman, she walked into the Pacific Ocean with her children to commit suicide (*oy ako shinju*). She was saved but the children drowned.
Premenstrual syndrome (PMS) and tension	PMS, a form of emotional and physical stress, afflicts some women before their monthly periods. In certain cases, such stress is so severe that it seriously disrupts the women's lives. In 1982, a British Appeal Court held that PMS could not be used as a defense to a criminal charge but could be used in mitigation to lessen sentences.
Television intoxication	In the 1978 case of *Zamora v. State,* 361 So.2d 776 (Fla. 1978), the defendant was convicted after arguing temporary insanity from "involuntary subliminal television intoxication."
XYY chromosome defense	Everyone has chromosomes. Some have either too few or too many, causing abnormalities. Some scientists believe that the abnormality of the supermale, or XYY in males, can cause such men to exhibit antisocial or criminal conduct. The XYY syndrome is not recognized as a defense unless the requirements of the insanity test of the state are met.

Source: Adapted from Thomas J. Gardner and Terry M. Anderson, *Criminal Law: Principles and Cases* (Belmont, Calif.: Wadsworth, 2000), pp. 100–101.

Interviewer: Still, doesn't that elude the bigger issue, his frame of reference? If I believe that little green men are descending from outer space and the only way to get rid of them is to sprinkle blue cheese on the lawn, and I go out and sprinkle cheese, that would be logical rational behavior given my overarching belief.

PD: And if that were a *crime,* you'd be insane for it.

Interviewer: But Dahmer doesn't fall into that category? It seems to me that while his separate actions may seem rational, he's operating under the idea that he can turn strangers into companions by killing and eating them. Why isn't that insane?

PD: If Dahmer had had the delusion that he'd have companions for life if he killed them and ate them, and that that was somehow a good thing and not *criminal,* that would make him insane. But those weren't the facts at all. Even the defense experts agreed that Dahmer knew it was wrong. In fact, Dahmer was so offended by the idea of killing that he had to get himself drunk to overcome his aversion to doing the killing. It's that point that proves that he did not have an irresistible impulse to kill.[49]

Jeffrey Dahmer murderd more than 17 boys and men before his capture. He was beaten to death by a fellow inmate on November 28, 1994.

BIOLOGY AND CRIMINALITY

Within the last two decades, biologists have followed in the tradition of Cesare Lombroso, Raffaele Garofalo, and Charles Goring in their search for answers to questions about human behavior. Geneticists, for example, have argued that the predisposition to act violently or aggressively in certain situations may be inherited. In other words, while criminals are not born criminal, the predisposition to be violent or commit crime may be present at birth.

To demonstrate that certain traits are inherited, geneticists have studied children born of criminals but reared from birth by noncriminal adoptive parents. They wanted to know whether the behavior of the adoptive children was more similar to that of their biological parents than to that of their adoptive parents. Their findings play an important role in the debate on heredity versus environment. Other biologists, sometimes called "biocriminologists," take a different approach. Some ask whether brain damage or inadequate nutrition results in criminal behavior. Others are interested in the influence of hormones, chromosomal abnormalities, and allergies. They investigate interactions between brain and behavior, and between diet and behavior.

> **Did You Know?**
>
> ... that a recent study published in the *Annals of Internal Medicine* concluded that there is a strong association between low cholesterol levels and violence?

Modern Biocriminality

Biocriminology is the study of the physical aspects of psychological disorders.[50] It has been known for some time that adults who suffer from depression show abnormalities in brain waves during sleep, experience disturbed nervous system functioning, and display biochemical abnormalities. Research on depressed children reveals the same physical problems; furthermore, their adult relatives show high rates of depression as well. In fact, children whose parents suffer from depression are more than four times more likely than the average child to experience a similar illness.[51] Some researchers believe depression is an inherited condition that manifests itself in psychological and physical disturbances. The important point is that until only recently, physicians may have been missing the mark in their assessment and treatment of depressed children and adults by ignoring the physiological aspects.

Criminologists who study sociology and psychology to the exclusion of the biological sciences may also be missing the mark in their efforts to discover the causes of crime. Recent research has demonstrated that crime does indeed have psychobiological aspects similar to those found in studies of depression—biochemical abnormalities, abnormal brain waves, nervous system dysfunction. There is also evidence that strongly suggests a genetic predisposition to criminality.[52]

The resurgence of interest in integrating modern biological advances, theories, and principles into mainstream criminology began two decades ago. The sociobiological work of Edward Wilson on the interrelationship of biology, genetics, and social behavior was pivotal.[53] So were the contributions of C. Ray Jeffery, who argued that a biosocial interdisciplinary model should become the major theoretical framework for studying criminal behavior.[54]

Criminologists once again began to consider the possibility that there are indeed traits that predispose a person to criminality and that these traits may be passed from parent to child through the genes. Other questions arose as well. Is it possible, for instance, that internal biochemical imbalances or deficiencies cause antisocial behavior? Could too much or too little sugar in the bloodstream increase the potential for aggression? Or could a vitamin deficiency or some hormonal problem be responsible? We will explore the evidence for a genetic predisposition to criminal behavior, the relationship between biochemical factors and criminality, and neurophysiological factors that result in criminal behavior.

Genetics and Criminality

Today the proposition that human beings are products of an interaction between environmental and genetic factors is all but universally accepted.[55] We can stop asking, then, whether nature or nurture is more important in shaping us; we are the products of both. But what does the interaction between the two look like? And what concerns are raised by reliance on genetics to the exclusion of environmental factors? Consider the example of the XYY syndrome.

The XYY Syndrome Chromosomes are the basic structures that contain our genes—the biological material that makes each of us unique. Each human being has 23 pairs of inherited chromosomes. One pair determines gender. A female receives an X chromosome from both mother and father; a male receives an X chromosome from his mother and a Y from his father. Sometimes a defect in the production of sperm or egg results in genetic abnormalities. One type of abnormality is the XYY chromosomal male. The XYY male receives two Y chromosomes from his father rather than one. Approximately 1 in 1,000 newborn males in the general population has this genetic composition.[56] Initial studies done in the 1960s found the frequency of XYY chromosomes to be about 20 times greater than normal XY chromosomes among inmates in maximum-security state hospitals.[57] The XYY inmates tended to be tall, physically aggressive, and frequently, violent.

Supporters of these data claimed to have uncovered the mystery of violent criminality. Critics voiced concern over the fact that these studies were done on small and unrepresentative samples. The XYY syndrome, as this condition became known, received much public attention because of the case of Richard Speck. Speck, who in 1966 murdered eight nurses in Chicago, initially was diagnosed as an XYY chromosomal male. However, the diagnosis later turned out to be wrong. Nevertheless, public concern was aroused: Were all XYY males potential killers?

Studies undertaken since that time have discounted the relation between the extra Y chromosome and criminality.[58] Although convincing evidence in support of the XYY hypothesis appears to be slight, it is nevertheless possible that aggressive and violent behavior is at least partly determined by genetic factors. The problem is how to investigate this possibility. One difficulty is separating the external or environmental factors, such as family structure, culture, socioeconomic status, and peer influences, from the genetic predispositions with which they begin to interact at birth.

A particular individual may have a genetic predisposition to be violent but be born into a wealthy, well-educated, loving, and calm familial environment. He may never commit a violent act. Another person may have a genetic predisposition to be rule-abiding and nonaggressive yet be born into a poor, uneducated, physically abusive, and unloving family. He may commit violent criminal acts. How, then, can we determine the extent to which behavior is genetically influenced? Researchers have turned to twin studies and adoption studies in the quest for an answer.

Twin Studies To discover whether or not crime is genetically predetermined, researchers have compared identical and fraternal twins. Identical, or **monozygotic (MZ), twins** develop from a single fertilized egg that divides into two embryos. These twins share all their genes. Fraternal, or **dizygotic (DZ), twins** develop from two separate eggs, both fertilized at the same time. They share about half of their genes. Since the prenatal and postnatal family environments are, by and large, the same, greater behavioral similarity between identical twins than between fraternal twins would support an argument for genetic predisposition.

In the 1920s a German physician, Johannes Lange, found 30 pairs of same-sex twins—13 identical and 17 fraternal pairs. One member of each pair was a known criminal. Lange found that in 10 of the 13 pairs of identical twins, both twins were criminal; in 2 of the 17 pairs of fraternal twins, both were criminal.[59] The research techniques of the time were limited, but Lange's results were nevertheless impressive.

Many similar studies have followed. The largest was a study by Karl Christiansen and Sarnoff A. Mednick that included all twins born between 1881 and 1910 in a region of Denmark, a total of 3,586 pairs. Reviewing serious offenses only, Christiansen and Mednick found that the chance of there being a criminal twin when the other twin was a criminal was 50 percent for identical twins and 20 percent for same-sex fraternal twins.[60] Such findings lend support to the hypothesis that some genetic influences increase the risk of criminality.[61] A more recent American study conducted by David C. Rowe and D. Wayne Osgood reached a similar conclusion.[62]

While the evidence from these and other twin studies looks persuasive, we should keep in mind the weakness of such research. It may not be valid to assume a common environment for all twins who grow up in the same house at the same time. If the upbringing of identical twins is much more similar than that of fraternal twins, as it well may be, that circumstance could help explain their different rates of criminality.

Adoption Studies One way to separate the influence of inherited traits from that of environmental conditions would be to study infants separated at birth from their natural parents and placed randomly in foster homes. In such cases we could determine whether the behavior of the adopted child resembled that of the natural parents or that of the adoptive parents, and by how much. Children, however, are adopted at various ages and are not placed randomly in foster homes. Most such children are matched to their foster or adoptive parents by racial and religious criteria. And couples who adopt children may differ in some important ways from other couples. Despite such shortcomings, adoption studies do help us expand our knowledge of genetic influences on human variation.

The largest adoption study conducted so far was based on a sample of 14,427 male and female adoptions in Denmark between 1924 and 1947. The hypothesis was that criminality in the biological parents would be associated with an increased risk of criminal behavior in the child. The parents were considered criminal if either the mother or the father had been convicted of a felony. The researchers had sufficient information on more than 4,000 of the male children to assess whether or not both the biological and the adoptive parents had criminal records. Mednick and his associates reported the following findings:

- Of boys whose adoptive and biological parents had no criminal record, 13.5 percent were convicted of crimes.
- Of boys who had criminal adoptive parents and noncriminal biological parents, 14.7 percent were convicted of crimes.
- Of boys who had noncriminal adoptive parents and criminal biological parents, 20 percent were convicted of crimes.
- Of boys who had both criminal adoptive parents and criminal biological parents, 24.5 percent were convicted of crimes.[63]

These findings support the claim that the criminality of the biological parents has more influence on the child than does that of the adoptive parents. Other research on adopted children has reached similar conclusions. A major Swedish study examined 862 adopted males and 913 adopted females. The researchers found a genetic predisposition to criminality in both sexes, but an even stronger one in females. An American study of children who were put up for adoption by a group of convicted mothers supports the Danish and Swedish findings on the significance of genetic factors.[64]

Results of adoption studies have been characterized as "highly suggestive" or "supportive" of a genetic link to criminality. But how solid is this link? There are significant problems with adoption studies. One is that little can be done to ensure the similarity of adopted children's environments. Of even greater concern to criminologists, however, is the distinct possibility of mistaking correlation for causation. In other words, there appears to be a significant correlation between the criminality of biological parents and adopted children in the research we have reviewed, but this correlation does not prove that the genetic legacy passed on by a criminal parent causes an offspring to commit a crime.

So far, research has failed to shed any light on the nature of the biological link that results in the association between the criminality of parents and that of their children. Furthermore, even if we could identify children with a higher-than-average probability of committing offenses as adults on the basis of their parents' behavior, it is unclear what we could do to prevent these children from following the parental model.

The Controversy over Violence and Genes

At the same time that advances in research on the biological bases of violence shed new light on crime, attacks on such research are calling its usefulness into question. Government-sponsored research plans have been called racist, a conference on genetics and crime was canceled after protests, and a session on violence and heredity at a recent American Association for the Advancement of Science meeting became "a politically correct critique of the research."[65]

Few involved in such research expect to find a "violence gene"; rather, researchers are looking for a biological basis for some of the behaviors associated with violence. As one explanation put it:

> Scientists are . . . trying to find inborn personality traits that might make people more physically aggressive. The tendency to be a thrill seeker may be one such characteristic. So might "a restless impulsiveness, an inability to defer gratification." A high threshold for anxiety or fear may be another key trait. . . . such people tend to have a "special biology," with lower-than-average heart rates and blood pressure.[66]

No one yet has found any direct link between genes and violence. In fact, Sarnoff Mednick, the psychologist who conducted adoption studies of criminal behavior in Denmark, found no evidence for the inheritance of violence. "If there were any genetic effect for violent crimes, we would have picked it up," says Mednick, whose study included 14,427 men.

The controversy over a genetic basis for violent behavior seems to deal less with actual research findings than with the implications of such findings. For example, Harvard psychologist Jerome Kagan predicts that in 25 years biological and genetic tests will make it possible to identify the 15 children in every 1,000 who may have violent tendencies. Of those 15, only 1 will actually become violent. The ethical question, then, is what to do with this knowledge. "Do we tell the mothers of all 15 that their kids might be violent?" he asks. "How are the mothers then going to react to their children if we do that?"[67]

A recent National Academy of Science (NAS) report on violence recommended finding better ways to intervene in the development of children who could become violent, and it listed risk factors statistically linked to violence: hyperactivity, poor early grades, low IQ, fearlessness, and an inability to defer gratification, for example.[68]

What frightens those opposed to biological and genetic research into the causes of violence is the thought of how such research could be used by policy makers. If a violent personality can be shown to be genetically determined, crime-prevention strategies might try to identify "potential criminals" and to intervene before their criminal careers begin and before anyone knows if they would ever have become criminals. "Should genetic markers one day be found for tendencies . . . that are loosely linked to crime," explains one researcher, "they would probably have little specificity, sensitivity or explanatory power: most people with the markers will not be criminals and most criminals will not have the markers."[69] On the other hand, when environment—poverty, broken homes, and other problems—is seen as the major cause of violence, crime prevention takes the shape of improving social conditions rather than labeling individuals.

A middle-of-the-road approach is proposed by those who see biological research as a key to helping criminals change their behavior. "Once you find a biological basis for a behavior, you can try to find out how to help people cope," says one such scholar. "Suppose the link is impulsivity, an inability to defer gratification. It might be you could design education programs to teach criminals to readjust their time horizon."[70]

The IQ Debate

A discussion of the association between genes and criminality would be incomplete without paying at least some attention to the debate over IQ and crime. Is an inferior intelligence inherited, and if so, how do we account for the strong relationship between IQ and criminality?

The Research Background Nearly a century ago scientists began to search for measures to determine people's intelligence, which they believed to be genetically determined. The first test to gain acceptance was developed by a French psychologist, Alfred Binet. Binet's test measured the capacity of individual children to perform tasks or solve problems in relation to the average capacity of their peers.

Between 1888 and 1915, several researchers administered intelligence tests to incarcerated criminals and to boys in reform schools. Initial studies of the relationship between IQ and crime revealed some surprising results. The psychologist Hugo Munsterberg estimated that 68 percent of the criminals that he tested were of low IQ. Using the Binet scale, Henry H. Goddard found that between 25 and 50 percent of criminals had low IQs.[71] What could account for such different results?

Edwin Sutherland observed that the tests were poor and there were too many variations among the many versions administered. He reasoned that social and environmental factors caused delinquency, not low IQ.[72] In the 1950s the psychologist Robert H. Gault added to Sutherland's criticism. He noted particularly that it was "strange that it did not occur immediately to the pioneers that they had examined only a small sample of caught and convicted offenders."[73]

For more than a generation the question about the relationship between IQ and criminal behavior was not studied, and the early inconsistencies remained unresolved. Then in the late 1970s the debate resumed.[74] Supporters of the view that inheritance determines intelligence once again began to present their arguments. The psychologist Arthur Jensen suggested that race was a key factor in IQ differences; Richard J. Herrnstein, a geneticist, pointed to social class as a factor.[75] Both positions spurred a heated debate in which criminologists soon became involved. In 1977 Travis Hirschi and Michael Hindelang evaluated the existing literature on IQ and crime.[76] They cited the following three studies as especially important:

- Travis Hirschi, on the basis of a study of 3,600 California students, demonstrated that the effect of a low IQ on delinquent behavior is more significant than that of the father's education.[77]
- Marvin Wolfgang and associates, after studying 8,700 Philadelphia boys, found a strong relationship between low IQ and delinquency, independent of social class.[78]
- Albert Reiss and Albert L. Rhodes, after an examination of the juvenile court records of 9,200 white Tennessee schoolboys, found IQ to be more closely related to delinquency than is social class.[79]

Hirschi and Hindelang concluded that IQ is an even more important factor in predicting crime than is either race or social class. They found significant differences in intelligence between criminal and noncriminal populations within like racial and socioeconomic groups. A lower IQ increases the potential for crime within each group. Furthermore, they found that IQ is related to school performance. A low IQ ultimately results in a youngster's associating with similar nonperformers, dropping out of school, and committing delinquent acts. Hirschi and Hindelang's findings were confirmed by James Q. Wilson and Richard Herrnstein but rejected by criminologist Deborah Denno, who conducted a prospective investigation of 800 children from birth to age 17.[80] Her results failed to confirm a direct relationship between IQ and delinquency.

The Debate: Genetics or Environment? The debate over the relationship between IQ and crime has its roots in the controversy over whether intelligence is genetically or environmentally determined. IQ tests, many people believe, measure cultural factors rather than the innate biological makeup of an individual.[81] Studies by psychologists Sandra Scarr and Richard Weinberg of black and white adopted children confirmed that environment plays a significant role in IQ development. They found that both black and white children adopted by white parents had comparable IQs and performed similarly.[82] With evidence of cultural bias and environmental influence, why not abandon the use of intelligence tests? The answer is simple: They do predict performance in school and so have significant utility. It appears that this debate will be with us for a long time to come.

Biochemical Factors

Biocriminologists' primary focus has been on the relationship between criminality and biochemical and neurophysical factors. Biochemical factors include food allergies, diet, hypoglycemia, and hormones. Neurophysical factors include brain lesions, brain wave abnormalities, and minimal brain dysfunction.

Food Allergies In 1993, by the time Rachel was 2 years old, she displayed a pattern of behavior that went way beyond the "terrible twos." Without warning, her eyes would glaze over, her speech would develop a lisp, and she'd kick and hit and thrash about wildly until her mother swaddled her tightly and she fell asleep, exhausted. She even developed a "kitty-cat" routine, complete with meowing, stalking, and growling, that often went on for hours.

When Rachel's sister Emma was born later that year, she nursed poorly and never slept through the night. After their mother introduced baby corn into her diet, Emma experienced severe intestinal distress, for which she was hospitalized. After a battery of medical tests proved inconclusive, she was sent home, but the symptoms continued intermittently, without apparent reason.

The following year, in desperation, their mother had Rachel and Emma, then 3 years and 15 months, tested for food allergies. Both showed marked sensitivity to corn, wheat, sugar, preservatives, and dairy products. After those foods were eliminated, Emma's health and well-being improved, and Rachel's perplexing and worrisome behavior all but disappeared.[83]

Over the last decade researchers have investigated the relation between food allergies and aggression and antisocial behavior. In fact, since 1908 there have been numerous medical reports indicating that various foods cause such reactions as irritability, hyperactivity, seizures, agitation, and behavior that is "out of character."[84] Investigators have identified the following food components as substances that may result in severe allergic reactions:

Phenylethylamine (found in chocolate)
Tyramine (found in aged cheese and wine)
Monosodium glutamate (used as a flavor enhancer in many foods)
Aspartame (found in artificial sweeteners)
Xanthines (found in caffeine)

Each of these food components has been associated with behavioral disorders, including criminality.

Diet

- Susan had been charged with 16 offenses, including criminal damage, solvent abuse, and vehicle theft, by the time she was 13. She had no friends, showed no affection toward her parents, and frequently hit her mother. Her schoolwork deteriorated, and she played truant most days. After six months on a changed diet, which excluded burgers, bananas, and chocolate, the number of her offenses dropped to zero. And for the first time since she was a young child, Susan gave her mother a hug.

- Craig, 15, vandalized his home several times and committed numerous petty crimes. He was a bully and was virtually impossible to teach. And his 8-year-old brother was beginning to follow in his footsteps. Both were put on a special diet, cutting out fizzy drinks and sweets, and including more green vegetables and fresh fruit. Within months, says their mother, both were more pleasant and easier to deal with. But Craig has since quit the diet and has reoffended. The bullying and the violence have started again.

- Graham, an 11-year-old, turned from an uncontrollable delinquent into a normal, pleasant boy when pizzas, baked beans,

The National Council Against Health Fraud is critical of the diet-crime link. "Valid evidence is lacking to support the claim that diet is an important determinant in the development of violence and criminal behavior" (see www.ncahf.org).

and chocolate in his diet were replaced by fresh vegetables, coconut milk, and carrots. He became less aggressive and argumentative and, reportedly, was "happy" for the first time in his life. Graham's schoolwork improved, and he began to make friends.

Anecdotal reports, in addition to more scientific investigations, link criminality to diets high in sugar and carbohydrates, to vitamin deficiency or dependency, and to excessive food additives.

Criminologist Stephen Schoenthaler conducted a series of studies on the relation between sugar and the behavior of institutionalized offenders. In these investigations inmates were placed on a modified diet that included very little sugar. They received fruit juice in place of soda and vegetables instead of candy. Schoenthaler found fewer disciplinary actions and a significant drop in aggressive behavior in the experimental group.[85] Some individuals charged with crimes have used this finding to build a defense like that of Dan White.

In 1979, San Francisco city supervisor Dan White was on trial for the murder of his fellow supervisor, Harvey Milk, and Mayor George Moscone. White defended himself with testimony on the impact of sugar on his behavior. The testimony showed that when White was depressed, he departed from his normal, healthy diet and resorted to high-sugar junk food, including Twinkies, Coca-Cola, and chocolates. Thereafter, his behavior became less and less controllable. The jury found White guilty of manslaughter, rather than murder, due to diminished capacity. White served five years in prison and committed suicide after his release. His defense was promptly dubbed the "junk-food defense," "Dan White's defense," or the "Twinkie defense."

Most subsequent attempts to use the junk-food defense have failed. In a 1989 Ohio case (*Johnson*), it was ruled that the defense may not be used to establish diminished capacity. In 1990, a Cape Cod man was unsuccessful when he defended himself on a charge of stealing (and eating) 300 candy bars (*Callanan*). Nor did this defense (Twinkie and soda pop) succeed in a murder case in Ohio (*McDonald*, 1988). But in a 1987 Florida case, a defendant (*Rosenthal*) was acquitted of drunk-driving charges on evidence that consumption of chocolate mousse after half a glass of sherry caused an unusual blood sugar reaction.

Other researchers have looked for the causes of crime in vitamin deficiencies. One such study found that 70 percent of criminals charged with serious offenses in one Canadian jurisdiction had a greater-than-normal need for vitamin B_6.[86] Other studies have noted deficiencies of vitamins B_3 and B_6 in criminal population samples.

Some investigators have examined the effects of food additives and food dyes on behavior. Benjamin Feingold has argued that between 30 and 60 percent of all hyperactivity in children may be attributable to reactions to food coloring.[87] There is additional support for this hypothesis.[88] Some studies have suggested that a diet deficient in protein may be responsible for violent aggression.

Let us look at the association between the consumption of tryptophan, an amino acid (a protein building block), and crime rates. Tryptophan is a normal component of many foods. Low levels of it have been associated with aggression and, in criminal studies, an increased sensitivity to electric shock. Anthony R. Mawson and K. W. Jacobs reasoned that diets low in tryptophan would be likely to result in higher levels of violent crime, particularly violent offenses such as homicide.

They hypothesized that because corn-based diets are deficient in tryptophan, a cross-national comparison of countries should reveal a positive relationship between corn consumption and homicide rates. Mawson and Jacobs obtained homicide data from the United Nations and the mean per capita corn intake rates of 53 foreign countries from the U.S. Department of Agriculture. They discovered that countries whose per capita rates of corn consumption were above the median had significantly higher homicide rates than countries whose diets were based on wheat or rice.[89]

Hypoglycemia What prompted an otherwise loving father to throw his 20-month-old daughter into a nearby lake? Neighbors knew that something was amiss when they noticed

22-year-old Joe Holt climb on the roof of his duplex in a quiet Orlando suburb. Joe then proceeded to dance, touching power lines in the course of his pantomime. No one sounded the alarm, however, until he disappeared into his lakeside apartment, returning momentarily with his daughter Ashley in his arms. The police arrived on the scene to find Joe in a state of agitation and Ashley facedown in Lake Apopka. Seated in the back of a squad car, handcuffed, the bewildered Joe had no recollection of the preceding events. When his blood was tested, he had a glucose level of 20 milligrams per deciliter of blood. The average is 80 to 120 milligrams. Joe was suffering from severe hypoglycemia. According to a sheriff's spokesman, "He had virtually no thought process."[90]

Hypoglycemia is a condition that occurs when the level of sugar in the blood falls below an acceptable range. The brain is particularly vulnerable to hypoglycemia, and such a condition can impair its function. Symptoms of hypoglycemia include anxiety, headache, confusion, fatigue, and even aggressive behavior. As early as 1943, researchers linked the condition with violent crime, including murder, rape, and assault. Subsequent studies found that violent and impulsive male offenders had a higher rate of hypoglycemia than noncriminal controls.

Consider the work of Matti Virkkunen, who has conducted a series of studies of habitually violent and psychopathic offenders in Finland. In one such study done in the 1980s he examined the results of a glucose tolerance test (used to determine whether hypoglycemia is present) administered to 37 habitually violent offenders with antisocial personalities, 31 habitually violent offenders with intermittent explosive disorders, and 20 controls. The offenders were found to be significantly more hypoglycemic than the controls.[91]

Hormones Experiments have shown that male animals are typically more aggressive than females. Male aggression is directly linked to male hormones. If an aggressive male mouse is injected with female hormones, he will stop fighting.[92] Likewise, the administration of male hormones to pregnant monkeys results in female offspring who, even three years after birth, are more aggressive than the daughters of non-injected mothers.[93]

While it would be misleading to equate male hormones with aggression and female hormones with nonaggression, there is some evidence that abnormal levels of male hormones in humans may prompt criminal behavior. Several investigators have found higher levels of testosterone (the male hormone) in the blood of individuals who have committed violent offenses.[94] Some studies also relate premenstrual syndrome (PMS) to delinquency and conclude that women are at greater risk of aggressive and suicidal behavior before and during the menstrual period. After studying 156 newly admitted adult female prisoners, Katherina Dalton concluded that 49 percent of all their crimes were committed either in the premenstrual period or during menstruation.[95] Recently, however, critics have challenged the association between menstrual distress and female crime.[96]

Neurophysiological Factors

In England in the mid-1950s, a father hit his son with a mallet and then threw him out of a window, killing him instantly. Instead of pleading insanity, as many people expected him to do, he presented evidence of a brain tumor, which, he argued, resulted in uncontrollable rage and violence. A jury acquitted him on the grounds that the brain tumor had deprived him of any control over and knowledge of the act he was committing.[97] Brain lesions or brain tumors have led to violent outbursts in many similar cases. Neurophysiological studies, however, have not focused exclusively on brain tumors; they have included a wide range of investigations: MRI studies of cerebral structure, brain wave studies, clinical reports of minimal brain dysfunction, and theoretical explorations into the relationship between the limbic system and criminality.[98]

EEG Abnormalities Sam recalled that his wife Janet looked slightly different and that the house smelled funny and he felt out of sorts. During an intimate moment in bed Janet made a funny remark, after which Sam flew into a rage, choked her, and slashed her throat. When

Andrea Yates, convicted of drowning her children in a bathtub, was sentenced to life in prison in March, 2002. Yates pleaded not guilty by reason of insanity—claiming postpartum psychosis and postpartum depression.

he came to his senses, he immediately went to the police and admitted to the crime, although he had little memory of his violent acts. Can EEG tracings explain the behavior of this young U.S. Marine who had returned home on leave? Subsequent tracings were found to be abnormal—indicative of an "intermittent explosive disorder." After reviewing this evidence, the court reduced Sam's charges from first-degree murder to manslaughter.

The EEG (electroencephalogram) is a tracing made by an instrument that measures cerebral functioning by recording brain wave activity with electrodes placed on the scalp. Numerous studies that have examined the brain activity of violent prisoners reveal significant differences between the EEGs of criminals and those of noncriminals. Other findings relate significantly slow brain wave activity to young offenders and adult murderers.[99] When Sarnoff A. Mednick and his colleagues examined the criminal records and EEGs of 265 children in a birth cohort in Denmark, they found that certain types of brain wave activity, as measured by the EEG, enabled investigators to predict whether convicted thieves would steal again.[100]

When Jan Volavka compared the EEGs of juvenile delinquents with those of comparable nondelinquents, he found a slowing of brain waves in the delinquent sample, most prominently in those children convicted of theft. He concluded that thievery "is more likely to develop in persons who have a slowing of alpha frequency than in persons who do not."[101]

Minimal Brain Dysfunction Minimal brain dysfunction (MBD) is classified as "attention deficit hyperactivity disorder."[102] MBD produces such asocial behavioral patterns as impulsivity, hyperactivity, aggressiveness, low self-esteem, and temper outbursts. The syndrome is noteworthy for at least two reasons. First, MBD may explain criminality when social theories fail to do so—that is, when neighborhood, peer, and familial associations do not suggest a high risk of delinquency. Second, MBD is an easily overlooked diagnosis. Parents, teachers, and clinicians tend to focus more on the symptoms of a child's psychopathology than on the possibility of brain dysfunction, even though investigators have repeatedly found high rates of brain dysfunction in samples of suicidal adolescents and youthful offenders.[103]

CRIME AND HUMAN NATURE

The criminologist Edward Sagarin has written:

> In criminology, it appears that a number of views . . . have become increasingly delicate and sensitive, as if all those who espouse them were inherently evil, or at least stupidly insensitive to the consequences of their research. . . . In the study of crime, the examples of unpopular orientations are many. Foremost is the link of crime to the factors of genes, biology, race, ethnicity, and religion.[104]

Criticisms of Biocriminology

What is it about linking biology and criminality that makes the subject delicate and sensitive?

Why is the concept so offensive to so many people? One reason is that biocriminologists deny the existence of individual free will. The idea of predisposition to commit crimes fosters a sense of hopelessness. But this criticism seems to have little merit. As Diana H. Fishbein has aptly noted, the idea of a "conditioned free will" is widely accepted.[105] This view suggests that individuals make choices in regard to a particular action within a range of possibilities that is "preset" yet flexible. When conditions permit rational thought, one is fully accountable and responsible for one's actions. It is only when conditions are somehow disturbed that free choice is constricted. The child of middle-class parents who has a low IQ might avoid delinquent behavior. But if that child's circumstances changed so that he lived in a lower-class, single-parent environment, he might find the delinquent lifestyle of the children in the new neighborhood too tempting to resist.

Critics have other concerns as well. Some see a racist undertone to biocriminological research. If there is a genetic predisposition to commit crime and if minorities account for a disproportionate share of criminal activity, are minorities then predisposed to commit crime? In Chapter 2 we learned that self-reports reveal that most people have engaged in delinquent or criminal behavior. How, then, do biocriminologists justify their claim that certain groups are more prone than others to criminal behavior? Could it be that the subjects of their investigations are only criminals who have been caught and incarcerated? And is the attention of the police disproportionately drawn to members of minority groups?

How do biocriminologists account for the fact that most criminologists see the structure of our society, the decay of our neighborhoods, and the subcultures of certain areas as determinants of criminality? Are biocriminologists unfairly deemphasizing social and economic factors? (In Chapters 5 through 9 we review theories that attribute criminality to group and environmental forces.)

These issues raise a further question that is at the core of all social and behavioral science: Is human behavior the product of nature (genetics) or nurture (environment)? The consensus among social and behavioral scientists today is that the interaction of nature and nurture is so pervasive that the two cannot be viewed in isolation.

Supporters of biocriminology also maintain that recognizing a predisposition to crime is not inconsistent with considering environmental factors. In fact, some believe that predispositions are triggered by environmental factors. Even if we agree that some people are predisposed to commit crime, we know that the crime rate would be higher in areas that provide more triggers. In sum, while some people may be predisposed to certain kinds of behavior, most scientists agree that both psychological and environmental factors shape the final forms of those behaviors.

An Integrated Theory

In recent years the debate has found a new forum in integrated biocriminological theories, such as the one proposed by James Q. Wilson and Richard Herrnstein. These scholars explain predatory street crime by showing how human nature develops from the interplay of psychological, biological, and social factors. It is the interaction of genes with environment that in some individuals forms the kind of personality likely to commit crimes. The argument takes into account such factors as IQ, body build, genetic makeup, impulsiveness, ability to delay gratification, aggressiveness, and even the drinking and smoking habits of pregnant mothers.

According to Wilson and Herrnstein, the choice between crime and conventional behavior is closely linked to individual biological and psychological traits and to such social factors as family and school experiences. Their conclusion is that "the offender offends not just because of immediate needs and circumstances, but also because of enduring personal characteristics, some of whose traces can be found in his behavior from early childhood on."[106] In essence, they argue that behavior results from a person's perception of the potential rewards and/or punishments that go along with a criminal act. If the potential reward (such as money) is greater than the expected punishment (say, a small fine), the chance that a crime will be committed increases.

REVIEW

When psychologists have attempted to explain criminality, they have taken four general approaches. First, they have focused on failures in psychological development—an overbearing or weak conscience, inner conflict, insufficient moral development, and maternal deprivation, with its concomitant failure of attachment. Second, they have investigated the ways in which aggression and violence are learned through modeling and direct experience. Third, they have investigated the personality characteristics of criminals and found that criminals tend to be more impulsive, intolerant, and irresponsible than noncriminals. Fourth, psychologists have investigated the relationship of criminality to such mental disorders as psychosis and psychopathy.

Biocriminologists investigate the biological correlates of criminality, including a genetic predisposition to commit crime. The XYY syndrome, though now generally discounted as a cause of criminality, suggests that aggressive and violent behavior may be at least partly determined by genetic factors. Studies of the behavior of identical and fraternal twins and of the rates of criminality among adopted children with both criminal and noncriminal biological and adoptive parents tend to support this hypothesis. Investigators have also found a strong correlation between low IQ and delinquency. Criminologists are still debating what public policy issues are raised by the possible role of genetics in crime.

Biocriminologists' most recent and perhaps most important discovery is the relation of criminal behavior to biochemical factors (food allergies, dietary deficiencies, hormonal imbalances) and neurophysiological factors (EEG abnormalities and minimal brain dysfunction). Most scientists agree that if some people are biologically predisposed to certain behaviors, both psychological and environmental factors shape the forms of those behaviors.

CRIMINOLOGY & PUBLIC POLICY

Sexual predators fall into the gap between criminal and civil confinement.

They are routinely held fully responsible and blameworthy for their behavior because they almost always retain substantial capacity for rationality, they remain entirely in touch with reality, and they know the applicable moral and legal rules. Consequently, even if their sexual violence is in part caused by a mental abnormality, they do not meet the usual standards for an insanity defense. For the same reason, they do not meet the usual nonresponsibility standards for civil commitment and retain the competence to make rational decisions about treatment. Moreover, in most cases in which civil commitment is justified, most states no longer maintain routine, indefinite, involuntary civil commitment but instead tend to limit the permissible length of commitment.

To fill the gap, Kansas and a substantial minority of other states have adopted a form of indefinite, involuntary civil commitment that applies to "sexually violent predators who have a mental abnormality or personality disorder." The Kansas definition of a sexually violent predator, which is similar to those that other states have adopted, is "any person who has been convicted of or charged with a sexually violent offense and who suffers from a mental abnormality or personality disorder which makes the person likely to engage in repeat acts of sexual violence." The state may impose this form of civil commitment not only when a person has been charged with or convicted of a sexual offense but also after an alleged predator has completed a prison term for precisely that type of sexually violent conduct. Commitment is for an indefinite period, and thus potentially for life, although an annual review of the validity of the commitment is required. (Source: Stephen J. Morse. "Uncontrollable Urges and Irrational People," *Virginia Law Review*, **88** (2002) 1025.)

Questions for Discussion How should crminologists view the commitment of "sexual predators" to mental institutions for an indefinite term after serving time in prison? Does this commitment amount to a second round of punishment? If not, and little treatment takes place, how is this additional term of incapacitation justified? Should sexual predators be diverted from the criminal justice system in the first place? All of these questions raise serious concerns with the problem of mentally ill offenders in the criminal justice system.

PART II Explanations of Crime and Criminal Behavior

YOU BE THE CRIMINOLOGIST

For many years psychologists searched for the criminal personality, a common set of personality characteristics associated with criminals. If you were asked to assist in this effort, what methods would you use to capture the criminal personality? Would you use objective personality inventories? If you were successful, what would you do with your findings? How could this common personality profile be used in the criminal justice system?

KEY TERMS

The numbers next to the terms refer to the pages on which the terms are defined.

attachment (87)
behavioral modeling (90)
biocriminology (101)
chromosomes (102)
conditioning (98)
cortical arousal (98)
differential association-reinforcement (95)
dizygotic (DZ) twins (103)
ego (85)
extroversion (97)
fundamental psycholegal error (100)
hypoglycemia (109)
id (85)
minimal brain dysfunction (MBD) (110)
monozygotic (MZ) twins (103)
neuroticism (97)
psychoanalytic theory (85)
psychopathy (98)
psychosis (98)
psychoticism (97)
social learning theory (90)
superego (85)

CHAPTER 5
Strain and Cultural Deviance Theories

The Interconnectedness of Sociological Theories

Anomie: Émile Durkheim
  The Structural-Functionalist Perspective
  Anomie and Suicide

Strain Theory
  Merton's Theory of Anomie
  Modes of Adaptation
  Tests of Merton's Theory
  Evaluation: Merton's Theory
  Institutional Imbalance and Crime
  General Strain Theory
  Theory Informs Policy

Cultural Deviance Theories
  The Nature of Cultural Deviance
  Social Disorganization Theory
  Tests of Social Disorganization Theory
  Evaluation: Social Disorganization Theory
  Theory Informs Policy
  Differential Association Theory
  Tests of Differential Association Theory
  Evaluation: Differential Association Theory
  Theory Informs Policy
  Culture Conflict Theory

REVIEW

CRIMINOLOGY & PUBLIC POLICY

YOU BE THE CRIMINOLOGIST

KEY TERMS

Boxes
  Window to the World: *A Social System Breaks Down*
  From the Pages of *The New York Times*: *A Head Start Really Does Help*
  Of Immediate Concern: *Cults—Culture Conflict—Crime*

Special Features
  Crime Surfing
  Did You Know?

KEY TERMS
accommodate
conduct norms
cultural deviance theories
cultural transmission
culture conflict theory
deviance
differential association theory
general strain theory
social disorganization theory
strain theory

Growing up on a vacant lot in a Bronx slum: What are their chances?

The early decades of the twentieth century brought major changes to American society. One of the most significant was the change in the composition of the populations of cities. Between 1840 and 1924, 45 million people—Irish, Swedes, Germans, Italians, Poles, Armenians, Bohemians, Russians—left the Old World; two-thirds of them were bound for the United States.[1] At the same time, increased mechanization in this country deprived many American farmworkers of their jobs and forced them to join the ranks of the foreign-born and the black laborers who had migrated from the South to northern and midwestern industrial centers. During the 1920s large U.S. cities swelled with five million new arrivals.[2]

Chicago's expansion was particularly remarkable: Its population doubled in 20 years. Many of the new arrivals brought nothing with them except what they could carry. The city offered them only meager wages, 12-hour working days in conditions that jeopardized their health, and tenement housing in deteriorating areas. Chicago had other problems as well. In the late 1920s and early 1930s it was the home of major organized crime groups, which fought over the profits from the illegal production and sale of liquor during Prohibition (as we shall see in Chapter 10).

Teeming with newcomers looking for work, corrupt politicians trying to buy their votes, and bootleggers growing more influential through sheer firepower and the political strength they controlled, Chicago also had a rapidly rising crime rate. The city soon became an inviting urban laboratory for criminologists, who began to challenge the then predominant theories of crime causation, which were based on biological and psychological factors. Many of these criminologists were associated with the University of Chicago, which has the oldest sociology program in the United States (begun in 1892). By the 1920s these criminologists began to measure scientifically the amount of criminal behavior and its relation to the social turmoil Chicago was experiencing. Since that time, sociological theories have remained at the forefront of the scientific investigation of crime causation.

115

THE INTERCONNECTEDNESS OF SOCIOLOGICAL THEORIES

The psychological and biological theories of criminal behavior (Chapter 4) share the assumption that such behavior is caused by some underlying physical or mental condition that separates the criminal from the noncriminal. They seek to identify the kind of person who becomes a criminal and to find the factors that caused the person to engage in criminal behavior. These theories yield insight into individual cases, but they do not explain why crime rates vary from one neighborhood to the next, from group to group, within large urban areas, or within groups of individuals. Sociological theories seek the reasons for differences in crime rates in the social environment. These theories can be grouped into three general categories: strain, cultural deviance, and social control.[3]

The strain and cultural deviance theories formulated between 1925 and 1940, and still popular today, focus on the social forces that cause people to engage in criminal activity. These theories laid the foundation for the subcultural theories we discuss in Chapter 6. Social control theories (Chapter 7) take a different approach: They are based on the assumption that the motivation to commit crime is part of human nature. Consequently, social control theories seek to discover why people do not commit crime. They examine the ability of social groups and institutions to make their rules effective.

Strain and cultural deviance theories both assume that social class and criminal behavior are related, but they differ about the nature of the relationship. **Strain theory** argues that all members of society subscribe to one set of cultural values—that of the middle class. One of the most important middle-class values is economic success. Since lower-class persons do not have legitimate means to reach this goal, they turn to illegitimate means in desperation. **Cultural deviance theories** claim that lower-class people have a different set of values, which tend to conflict with the values of the middle class. Consequently, when lower-class persons conform to their own value system, they may be violating conventional or middle-class norms.

ANOMIE: ÉMILE DURKHEIM

Imagine a clock with all its parts finely synchronized. It functions with precision. It keeps perfect time. But if one tiny weight or small spring breaks down, the whole mechanism will not function properly. One way of studying a society is to look at its component parts in an effort to find out how they relate to each other. In other words, we look at the structure of a society to see how it functions. If the society is stable, its parts operating smoothly, the social arrangements are functional. Such a society is marked by cohesion, cooperation, and consensus. But if the component parts are arranged in such a way as to threaten the social order, the arrangements are said to be dysfunctional. In a class-oriented society, for example, the classes tend to be in conflict.

The Structural-Functionalist Perspective

The structural-functionalist perspective was developed by Émile Durkheim (1858–1917) before the end of the nineteenth century.[4] At the time, positivist biological theories, which relied on the search for individual differences between criminals and noncriminals, were dominant. So at a time when science was searching for the abnormality of the criminal, Durkheim was writing about the normality of crime in society. To him, the explanation of human conduct, and indeed human misconduct, lies not in the individual but in the group and the social organization. It is in this context that he introduced the term "anomie," the breakdown of social order as a result of the loss of standards and values.[5]

Throughout his career, Durkheim was preoccupied with the effects of social change. He believed that when a simple society develops into a modern, urbanized one, the intimacy needed to sustain a common set of norms declines. Groups become fragmented, and in the absence of a common set of rules, the actions and expectations of people in one sector may clash with those of people in another. As behavior becomes unpredictable, the system gradually breaks down, and the society is in a state of anomie.

Anomie and Suicide

Durkheim illustrated his concept of anomie in a discussion, not of crime, but of suicide.[6] He suggested several reasons why suicide was more common in some groups than in others. For our purposes, we are interested in the particular form of suicide he called "anomic suicide." When he analyzed statistical data, he found that suicide rates increased during times of sudden economic change, whether that change was major depression or unexpected prosperity. In periods of rapid change people are abruptly thrown into unfamiliar situations. Rules that once guided behavior no longer hold.

Consider the events of the 1920s. Wealth came easily to many people in those heady, prosperous years. Toward the end, through July, August, and September 1929, the New York stock market soared to new heights. Enormous profits were made from speculation. But on October 24, 1929, a day history records as Black Thursday, the stock market crashed. Thirteen million shares of stock were sold. As more and more shares were offered for sale, their value plummeted. In the wake of the crash, a severe depression overtook the country and then the world. Banks failed. Mortgages were foreclosed. Businesses went bankrupt. People lost their jobs. Lifestyles changed overnight. Many people were driven to sell apples on street corners to survive, and they had to stand in mile-long breadlines to get food to feed their families. Suddenly the norms by which people lived were no longer relevant. People became disoriented and confused. Suicide rates rose.

It is not difficult to understand rising suicide rates in such circumstances, but why would rates also rise at a time of sudden prosperity? According to Durkheim, the same factors are at work in both situations. What causes the problems is not the amount of money available but the sudden change. Durkheim believed that human desires are boundless, an "insatiable and bottomless abyss."[7] Since nature does not set such strict biological limits on the capabilities of humans as it does on those of other animals, he argued, we have developed social rules that put a realistic cap on our aspirations. These regulations are incorporated into the individual conscience and thus make it possible for people to feel fulfilled.

But with a sudden burst of prosperity, expectations change. When the old rules no longer determine how rewards are distributed among members of society, there is no longer any restraint on what people want. Once again the system breaks down. Thus, whether sudden change causes great prosperity or great depression, the result is the same—anomie.

STRAIN THEORY

A few generations after Durkheim, the American sociologist Robert Merton (1910–2002) also related the crime problem to anomie. But his conception differs somewhat from Durkheim's. The real problem, Merton argued, is created not by sudden social change but by a social structure that holds out the same goals to all its members without giving them equal means to achieve them. This lack of integration between what the culture calls for and what the structure permits, the former encouraging success and the latter preventing it, can cause norms to break down because they no longer are effective guides to behavior.

Merton borrowed the term "anomie" from Durkheim to describe this breakdown of the normative system. According to Merton:

> It is only when a system of cultural values extols, virtually above all else, certain common symbols of success for the population at large while its social structure rigorously restricts or completely eliminates access to approved modes of acquiring these symbols for a considerable part of the same population, that antisocial behavior ensues on a considerable scale.[8]

From this perspective, the social structure is the root of the crime problem (hence the approach Merton takes is sometimes called a "structural explanation"). "Strain theory," the name given by contemporary criminologists to Merton's explanation of criminal behavior, assumes that people are law-abiding but when

Window to the World

A Social System Breaks Down

The American anthropologist Kenneth Good committed—for anthropologists—the unpardonable sin of marrying a young woman of the tribe he studied, the Yanomamö. The young bride returned with her husband to suburban Pennsylvania in 1988, and there they raised their children.(1) But in 1993 the Yanomamö wife slipped back into the Amazon jungle to live among her own people.

Who are the Yanomamö?

When another anthropologist Robert Carneiro went to the Amazon jungle in 1975 to study the Yanomamö, he found them to be a remote, stone-age, people dedicated to frequent intervillage warfare.(2)

Indeed, the Yanomamö are the last major remaining Stone Age people on earth, living their lives in harmony with nature, but also engaging in tribal warfare, according to their customs.

But all went awry in the 1980s, when gold was discovered in the Yanomamö territory.(3) As many as 40,000 prospectors had invaded by 1987, clearing the jungle for airstrips, bringing diseases—venereal and others—against which the Yanomamö had no immunity, importing modern weapons to replace Stone Age clubs, and raising the homicide rate.(4) What once was a nation of 100,000 was reduced to 22,000 (9,400 in Brazil; 12,600 in Venezuela). A severe drought in the late 1990s added to the suffering of the Yanomamös, who use ancient incantations to bring rain as well as to quench forest fires and to drive out invaders.(2)

Help is under way and more is promised. The United Nations sent an emergency team of firefighters to deal with the forest fires. The Brazilian government clamped down on encroachments by rogue miners. The

A Yanomamö man with the trappings of modern civilization.

U.S. Congress made some assistance available to protect the rain forests, but did not designate preservation of the Yanomamö territory and lifestyle a priority.

Too little, too late? The Yanomamö's traditional way of life has broken down. The chances that they can withstand the attack of the Western culture invasion are slim. The large deposits of gold, diamonds, tin, and other minerals in the soil of their land will continue to attract invaders, with their attack on the traditional culture. Yanomamös are dying faster than ever before, hunting and fishing are increasingly difficult, alcohol and prostitution are taking their toll, firearms are escalating the death rate, and infant mortality is 24 times that of the United States.(5)

What are we to do about the Yanomamö? It does not seem possible to transplant Yanomamö into suburban New Jersey. Forcing modern capitalism on them is even more destructive.

Should we just build a fence around the Yanomamö territory and allow them to live their accustomed lifestyle? The spectre of an entrepreneur flying in tourists in jumbo jets and charging admission to view "unspoiled," stone-aged Yanomamö is just too daunting.

Are we witnessing a genocide in the making?

Are you wondering about the Yanomamö wife? Well, you can see her adorned with tribal decoration in a photo at the American Museum of Natural History, Amazon exhibit.

Sources

1. Kenneth Good with David Chernoff, *Into the Heart* (New York: Simon and Schuster, 1991).
2. Robert L. Carneiro, "War and Peace: Alternating Realities in Human History," in *Studying War—Anthropological Perspectives,* ed. S. P. Reyna and R. E. Downs (Langhorn, PA: Gordon and Breach, 1994), pp. 3–27.
3. Lynne Wallis, "Quiet Genocide: Miners Seeking Precious Metals Are Causing Deaths of the Yanomami," *Ottawa Citizen,* June 28, 1993, p. A6.
4. "Aid for an Ancient Tribe," *Newsweek,* Apr. 9, 1990, p. 34.
5. "Genocide in the Amazon," *Newsweek,* Aug. 30, 1993, p. 61.

Questions for Discussion

1. As the Yanomamö culture is being destroyed, how would you expect the tribe's traditional ways of dealing with crime to be affected? Explain.
2. What measures might be effective in protecting indigenous peoples in all parts of the world from suffering a fate similar to that of the Yanomamö?

under great pressure will resort to crime. Disparity between goals and means provides that pressure.

Merton's Theory of Anomie

Merton argued that in a class-oriented society, opportunities to get to the top are not equally distributed. Very few members of the lower class ever get there. His anomie theory emphasizes the importance of two elements in any society: (1) cultural aspirations, or goals that people believe are worth striving for, and (2) institutionalized means or accepted ways to attain the desired ends. If a society is to be stable, these two elements must be reasonably well integrated; in other words, there should be means for individuals to reach the goals that are important to them. Disparity between goals and means fosters frustration, which leads to strain.

Merton's theory explains crime in the United States in terms of the wide disparities in income among the various classes. Statistics clearly demonstrate that such disparities exist. American families had a median income of $42,148 in 2000. While 12 percent of all families had incomes above $100,000, 11.3 percent were below the federal government's poverty level—$17,603 for a family of four. 7.5 percent of whites, 22 percent of blacks, and 21 percent of Hispanics were living below the poverty level, and 16 percent of the poor were children.[9]

It is not, however, solely wealth or income that determines people's position on a social ladder that ranges from the homeless to the very, very rich who live on great estates. In 1966 Oscar Lewis described the "culture of poverty" that exists in inner-city slums. It is characterized by helplessness, apathy, cynicism, and distrust of social institutions such as schools and the police.[10] A few years later Gunnar Myrdal argued that there is a worldwide "underclass, whose members lack the education and skills necessary to compete with the rest of society."[11] And in 1987, William Julius Wilson depicted the ranks of the underclass as the "truly disadvantaged." This group of urban inner-city dwellers is at the bottom of the ladder. Basic institutions such as the school and the family have deteriorated. There is little community cohesion. The people remain isolated—steeped in their own ghetto culture and the anger and aggression that accompany their marginal existence.[12]

The United States In our society opportunities to move up the social ladder exist, but they are not equally distributed. A child born to a single, uneducated, 13-year-old girl living in a slum has practically no chance to move up, whereas the child of a middle-class family has a better-than-average chance of reaching a professional or business position. Yet all people in the society share the same goals. And those goals are shaped by billions of advertising dollars spent each year to spread the message that everyone can drive a sports car, take a well-deserved exotic vacation, and record the adventure with a camcorder.

The mystique is reinforced by instant lottery millionaires, the earnings of superstar athletes, and rags-to-riches stories of such people as Ray Kroc. Kroc, a high school dropout, believed that a 15-cent hamburger with a 10-cent bag of French fries could make dining out affordable for low-income families; his idea spread quickly through the United States—and to 116 other countries with 24,500 McDonald's restaurants and their golden arches all over the world. Superstar athletes are another example of American icons. Consider the NBA's Michael Jordan. At age 21 he had a rookie contract of $6 million over seven years, which increased to the $25 million salary range per season plus $40 million in commercial endorsements. And now in retirement he has yet another multimillion-dollar venture—the famous Michael Jordan's Restaurants in Chicago and in New York, where guests can dine and buy an array of memorabilia in his bustling boutiques. In like manner, record-setting home-run hitter Sammy Sosa already makes over $9 million in salary and $8 million in endorsements. Sosa, now in his 30s, worked as a shoeshine boy in the Dominican Republic to help support his fatherless family.

> **Did You Know?**
>
> . . . that according to the Institute for Research on Poverty, in 2000, 31.1 million Americans lived in poverty. Blacks and Hispanics were more than twice as likely to live in poverty than whites.

Sammy Sosa takes a few minutes before a game in Seattle (June 2000) to greet Cubs' fans, Kerry and Sammy Lepse. Kerry, left, was named after Cubs' Kerry Wood and Sammy, middle, was named after Sosa.

Though Merton argued that lack of legitimate means for everyone to reach material goals like these does create problems, he also made it clear that the high rate of deviant behavior in the United States cannot be explained solely on the basis of lack of means.

India The world has produced class systems that are more rigid than our own, and societies that place much stricter limitations on people's ability to achieve their goals, without causing the problems the United States faces. In the traditional society of India, for example, the untouchables at the bottom of the caste system are forbidden by custom (although no longer by law) even to enter the temples and schools used by those above them, while those at the top enjoy immense privileges.

All Hindu castes fall within a hierarchy, each one imposing upon its members duties and prohibitions covering both public and private life. People of high status may give food to people of lower status, for example, but may not receive food from them. One may eat in the home of a person of lower status, but the food must be cooked and served by a person of equal or higher status. Members of such a rigid system clearly face many more restraints than we do. Why, then, does India not have a very high crime rate?

The answer lies in the fact that Indians learn from birth that all people do not and cannot aspire to the same things. In the United States, the egalitarian principle denies the existence of limits to upward mobility within the social structure.[13] In reality, everyone in society experiences some pressures and strains, and the amounts are inversely related to position in the hierarchy: the lower the class, the higher the strain.

Modes of Adaptation

To be sure, not everyone who is denied access to a society's goals becomes deviant. Merton outlined five ways in which people adapt to society's goals and means. Individuals' responses (modes of adaptation) depend on their attitudes toward the cultural goals and the institutional means of attaining those goals. The options are conformity, innovation, ritualism, retreatism, and rebellion (see Table 5.1).

Merton does not tell us how any one individual chooses to become a drug pusher, for example, and another chooses to work on an assembly line. Instead, he explains why crime rates are high in some groups and low in others.

Conformity Conformity is the most common mode of adjustment. Individuals accept

PART II Explanations of Crime and Criminal Behavior   121

TABLE 5.1 A Typology of Modes of Individual Adaptation

Mode of Adaptation	Culture Goals*	Institutionalized Means*
Conformity	+	+
Innovation	+	−
Ritualism	−	+
Retreatism	−	−
Rebellion	±	±

*+ = acceptance; − = rejection; ± = rejection and substitution.
Source: Robert K. Merton, *Social Theory and Social Structure* (New York: Free Press, 1957), p. 140.

both the culturally defined goals and the prescribed means for achieving those goals. They work, save, go to school, and follow the legitimate paths. Look around you in the classroom. You will see many children of decent, hardworking parents. After college they will find legitimate jobs. Some will excel. Some will walk the economic middle path. But all those who are conformists will accept (though not necessarily achieve) the goals of our society and the means it approves for achieving them.

Innovation Individuals who choose the adaptation of innovation accept society's goals, but since they have few legitimate means of achieving them, they design their own means for getting ahead. The means may be burglary, robbery, embezzlement, or a host of other crimes. Youngsters who have no parental attention, no encouragement in school, no way to the top—no future—may scrawl their signatures on subway cars and buildings and park benches in order to achieve recognition of a sort. Such illegitimate forms of innovation are certainly not restricted to the lower classes, as evidenced by such crimes as stock manipulation, sale of defective products, and income tax evasion.

Ritualism People who adapt by ritualism abandon the goals they once believed to be within reach and resign themselves to their present lifestyles. They play by the rules; they work on assembly lines, hold middle-management jobs, or follow some other safe routine. Many workers have been catching a bus at the same street corner at the same hour every day for 20 years or more. They have long forgotten why, except that their jobs are where their paychecks come from. Their great relief is a two-week vacation in the summer.

Retreatism Retreatism is the adaptation of people who give up both the goals (can't make it) and the means (why try?) and retreat into the world of drug addiction or alcoholism. They have internalized the value system and therefore are under internal pressure not to innovate. The retreatist mode allows for an escape into a nonproductive, nonstriving lifestyle. Some members of the antiwar movement of the 1960s opted to drop out entirely. The pressure was too great; the opportunities were unacceptable. They became addicts or followers of occult religions.

Rebellion Rebellion occurs when both the cultural goals and the legitimate means are rejected. Many individuals substitute their own goals (get rid of the establishment) and their own means (protest). They have an alternate scheme for a new social structure, however ill-defined. Many of the so-called militias operating in America today, ranging in size from two to several hundred persons, have lost faith in the legitimacy of the U.S. government and are trying to establish their own alternative quasi-governmental structures.

Merton's theory of how the social structure produces strain that may lead to deviant behavior is illustrated in Figure 5.1. His theory has challenged researchers for half a century.

Tests of Merton's Theory

Merton and his followers (Chapter 6) predict that the greatest proportion of crime will be found in the lower classes because lower-class people have the least opportunity to reach their goals legitimately. Many research studies designed to test the various propositions of strain theory focus on the association between social class and delinquency (an association that evokes considerable controversy). Some studies report a strong inverse relationship: As class goes up, crime rates go down. Others find no association at all between the two variables (Chapter 2).

FIGURE 5.1 Modes of deviant behavior.

```
Common success          Unequal distribution    Disjunction of       Lower class       Pressure          Deviant
goals (e.g., acquisition → of means to achieve → goals and means  →  faced with    →   resolved by   →   behavior
of wealth) of all         goals (limited jobs     creates anomic      strain            alternative
members of society        and education)          condition                             solutions
```

```
Retain goals, reject means      Innovation      criminal behavior
Reject goals, reject means  →   Retreatism  →   drop out into drugs, alcohol, vagrancy
Create new goals, create        Rebellion       revolutionary activity
new means
```

Social Class and Crime The controversy over the relationship between social class and crime began when researchers, using self-report questionnaires, found more serious and more frequent delinquency among lower-class boys than among those of higher classes.[14] In Chapter 2 we saw that other researchers seriously questioned those findings.[15] When Charles Tittle and his colleagues attempted to clarify the relationship by analyzing 35 empirical studies, they concluded that "class is not now and has not been related to criminality in the recent past."[16] Summarizing the research literature on social class and crime, Gary Jensen and Kevin Thompson wrote: "The safest conclusion concerning class structure and delinquency is the same one that has been proposed for several decades: Class, no matter how defined, contributes little to explaining variation in self-reports of common delinquency."[17]

Once again there was a critical reaction. A summary of more than 100 projects concluded that "lower-class people do commit those direct interpersonal types of crime which are normally handled by the police at a higher rate than middle-class people."[18] But if low social status creates frustration that pushes people to commit crime, why don't all the people in the lowest class commit crimes, or drop out into the drug world, or become revolutionaries? Since they clearly do not, there must be some limitations to the causal relationship between crime and social class.

Nikos Passas answers the question by pointing out that not all those persons exposed to the same problems respond in the same way. In fact, not all people perceive the same situation as a problem. He explains that anomie theorists base their arguments on rates of crime, rather than on individual behavior.[19]

Terence Thornberry and Margaret Farnsworth argue that there is no simple connection between class and crime. The relationship, they say, is highly complex; it involves race, seriousness of the offense, education of family and offender, and many other factors.[20] Researchers have also found that low social status promoted delinquency by increasing individuals' strain and by decreasing educational and occupational aspirations, whereas high social status promoted individuals' delinquency by increasing risk taking and decreasing conventional values.[21]

According to a number of studies, we may be able to learn more about the relationship between social class and crime if we look closely at specific types of offenses rather than at aggregate crime (or delinquency) rates. Take homicide, for example: In a study of 190 U.S. cities with populations of 100,000 or more, it was found that both income inequality and poverty are related to homicide rates. The researchers argue that the relationship can be explained "through the legitimate desires of impoverished persons to reduce deprivation and through their decreased ability to compete for legitimate employment."[22] In two large cross-national studies, two teams of Canadian researchers explored the relationship between income inequality and national homicide rates.[23] Both teams reported results that support strain theory. When opportunities or means for success are not provided equally to all members of society (as indicated by crime rates), pressure is exerted on some members of that society to engage in deviant behavior (in this case, homicide). Further analyses by one of the teams showed that the effects of inequality on homicide may be even more pronounced in more democratic societies. The researchers commented: "Income inequality might be more likely to generate violent behavior in more democratic societies because of the coexistence of high material inequality and an egalitarian value system."[24]

David Brownfield also related social class to specific offenses, in this instance to fistfights and brawls among teenagers.[25] His information came from two sources: the Richmond Youth Study, conducted at the University of California at Berkeley, and the Community Tolerance Study, done by a team of researchers at the University of Arizona. Brownfield's analysis of questionnaires completed by 1,500 white male students in California and 1,300 white male students in Arizona suggests a very strong relation between poverty—as measured by unemployment and welfare assistance—and violent behavior. He concluded that the general public expresses much hostility against the "disreputable poor," a term used by David Matza to describe people who remain unemployed for a long time, even during periods of full employment.[26] In fact, Brownfield suggests, many people hold them in contempt. (He cites a *New York Times*/CBS poll that found that over half of all the respondents believed that most people on welfare could get along without it if they only tried.) This hostility causes the "disreputable poor" to build up frustration, which is made worse by the lack of such fundamental necessities as food and shelter. Such a situation breeds discontent—and violence.

John Hagan argues that youngsters who grow up in a culture where friends are delinquent, parents are criminals, and drug abuse is common, and where early experiences with delinquent activities are widespread, become "embedded" in behaviors that result in later adult unemployment. They are excluded from employment by events that begin early in life. Of course, youngsters can become equally "embedded" in a culture of middle-class values, economic stability, and early work experiences—the foundation for job stability and career success.[27]

Race and Crime Yet another question that relates to strain theory concerns the relationship between racial inequality and violent crime. Judith and Peter Blau studied data from 125 metropolitan areas in the United States.[28] Their primary finding was that racial inequality—as measured by the difference in socioeconomic status between whites and nonwhites—is associated with the total rate of violent crime. The conclusion fits well with Merton's theory.

The Blaus argued that in a democratic society that stresses equal opportunities for individual achievement but in reality distributes resources on the basis of race, there is bound to be conflict. The most disadvantaged are precisely those who cannot change their situation through political action. In such circumstances, the frustrations created by racial inequalities tend to be expressed in various forms of aggression, such as violent crime. Several researchers have supported these findings. But not all researchers are in agreement.

John Braithwaite examined Uniform Crime Report statistics for a sample of 175 American cities. He compared the rates of violent crime with racial inequality, as measured by the incomes of black families and the incomes of all other families in his sample cities. He concluded that racial inequality does not cause specific crime problems.[29] Perhaps the crucial point is not whether one actually has an equal chance to be successful but rather, how one perceives one's chances. According to this reasoning, people who feel the most strain are those who have not only high goals but also low expectations of reaching them. So far, however, research has not supported this contention.

Evaluation: Merton's Theory

The strain perspective developed by Merton and his followers has influenced both research and theoretical developments in criminology.[30] Yet, as popular as this theory remains, it has been questioned on a variety of grounds.[31] By concentrating on crime at the lower levels of the socioeconomic hierarchy, for example, it neglects

At a Los Angeles welfare agency, masses of adults and children just sit and wait.

crime committed by middle- and upper-class people. Radical criminologists (see Chapter 8), in fact, claim that strain theory "stands accused of predicting too little bourgeois criminality and too much proletarian criminality."[32]

Other critics question whether a society as heterogeneous as ours really does have goals on which everyone agrees. Some theorists argue that American subcultures have their own value systems (Chapter 6). If that is the case, we cannot account for deviant behavior on the basis of Merton's cultural goals. Other questions are asked about the theory. If we have an agreed-upon set of goals, is material gain the dominant one? If crime is a means to an end, why is there so much useless, destructive behavior, especially among teenagers?

No matter how it is structured, each society defines goals for its members. The United States is far from being the only society in which people strive for wealth and prestige. Yet, while some people in other cultures have limited means for achieving these goals, not all these societies have high crime rates. Two such societies—Japan and Switzerland—are among the most developed and industrialized in the world. Although the United States has quite a bit in common with them, it does not share their very low crime rates.[33]

Despite the many critical assessments, strain theory, as represented primarily by Merton's formulation of anomie, has had a major impact on contemporary criminology. It dominated the delinquency research of the 1950s and 1960s. During the 1970s the theory lost its dominant position as criminologists paid increasing attention to how crime and delinquency were related to individuals' loss of attachment to their social institutions—the family, the school, or the government (see Chapter 7). Then, in the mid-1980s and continuing unabated into the 2000s, there was a resurgence of interest in empirical research and theorizing based on strain concepts.

Institutional Imbalance and Crime

In their book *Crime and the American Dream*, Steven Messner and Richard Rosenfeld agree with Merton that the material success goal is pervasive in American culture. In essence, the American dream is quite clear—succeed by any means necessary, even if those means are illegitimate.[34] The American dream, then, encourages high crime rates. Messner and Rosenfeld expand on Merton's ideas on the relationships among culture, social structure, anomie, and crime rates. High crime, they contend, is more than a matter of striving for monetary gains. It also results from the fact that our major social institutions do not have the capacity to control behavior. These institutions fail to counterbalance the ethos of the American dream. The dominance of economic institutions manifests itself in three ways: devaluation of other institutions, their accommodation to economic institutions, and the penetration of economic norms.

• *The devaluation of noneconomic roles and functions.* Performance in the economic world takes precedence over performance in other institutional settings: Noneconomic functions are devalued. Education is important, for example, only because it promises economic gains. Learning for its own sake is relatively unimportant. In the context of the family, the home owner is more important than the homemaker. In politics, too, there is a devaluation: If a citizen does not vote, there may be mild disapproval; if an adult citizen does not work, he or she loses status.

• *The accommodation of other institutions to economic needs.* In situations where institutions compete, noneconomic ones **accommodate**.

From the Pages of The New York Times

A Head Start Really Does Help

In the longest study of its kind, researchers at the University of Wisconsin tracked 1,500 school children from the age of 5 to the age of 20, and announced their results in the May 2001 *Journal of the American Medical Association.* The conclusion? Poor children who attend intensive preschool classes are more likely to graduate from high school and less likely to be arrested than poor children who have not participated in such programs.

The study followed 989 children who were living at or below the poverty level. Their educational careers were compared with 550 other children from the same neighborhoods who did not attend any preschool at all, or who attended schools with less intensive programs. The study found that 16.9 percent of those who graduated from the Chicago preschool program had been arrested for juvenile crimes, while 25.1 percent of those who did not attend preschool had been arrested. They also found that 49.7 percent of the Chicago preschool students graduated from high school, as compared to 38.5 percent of those with little or no preschool experience.

Edward Ziglar, a founder of the Head Start program in the 1960s, commented that the Chicago findings "contradict the naysayers who believe that public schools cannot be fixed or that poor children cannot be helped because of nature or nurture."

The caveat, however, is that the programs must be highly structured and that parents must be involved in order to achieve the desired results. The children studied all attended child-care centers run by the public school system of Chicago, which require parents to participate in their children's homework assignments. The Center also helps families arrange medical care and social services.

In other words, they focus on more than just learning to read. Arthur J. Reynolds, professor of social work at Wisconsin, added, "You've got to put parents in classrooms, as well as kids." Outside of the classroom, teachers are responsible for working with parents or guardians, helping them with projects like finding family photographs children might use to make a journal.

"We're providing a foundation for academic success," said Armando Almendarez, chief officer for early education at the Chicago public schools. "We know that success is tied to what is happening in the home environment, and that we can impact that environment."

Source

Adapted from Jacques: Steinberg, "Gains Found for the Poor in Rigorous Preschool," *The New York Times,* May 9, 2001. Reprinted with permission.

Questions for Discussion

1. Although this study shows positive results, there are several contributing factors. One of the most important seems to be family participation. Many federal programs—including Head Start—concentrate more on reading skills. Should federal guidelines be put in place to require more parental input in all federally funded child-care programs?
2. What do these findings say about nature versus nurture? About how to design child-care programs that are effective in preventing future crime?

Family life is generally dominated by work schedules. Individuals go to school primarily to get a "good" job. Once out of school, those who return usually do so to get a better job. In political accommodation, government strives to maintain an environment hospitable to business.

- *The penetration of economic norms.*
Penetration of economic norms into those of other institutions is widespread. Spouses become partners in "managing" the home, businesspeople/politicians campaign for public office claiming they will "run the country like a corporation," and economic terms such as "accountability" are adopted by educators.

Messner and Rosenfeld contend that as long as there is a disproportionate emphasis on monetary rewards, the crime problem will increase. In fact, if economic opportunities increase, there may be an increase in the preoccupation with material success. Crime will decrease only when noneconomic institutions have the capacity to control behavior.[35]

Freda Adler's study of 10 countries with low crime rates supports this argument. She demonstrates that where economic concerns have not devalued informal social control institutions such as family, community, or religion, crime rates are relatively low and stable. This finding held for nonindustrialized *and* highly industrialized societies.[36]

General Strain Theory

Sociologist Robert Agnew substantially revised Merton's theory in order to make it more broadly explanatory of criminal behavior.[37] The reformulation is called **general strain theory**. Agnew argues that failure to achieve material goals (the focal point of Merton's theory) is not the only reason for committing crime. Criminal behavior may also be related to the anger and frustration that result when an individual is treated in a way he or she does not want to be treated in a social relationship. General strain theory explains the range of strain-producing events.

• *Strain caused by failure to achieve positively valued goals.* This type of strain is based on Merton's view that lower-class individuals are often prevented from achieving monetary success goals through legitimate channels. When people do not have the money to get what they want, some of them turn to illegitimate means to get it.

• *Stress caused by the removal of positively valued stimuli from the individual.* This type of strain results from the actual or anticipated loss of something or someone important in one's life: death of a loved one, breakup with a boyfriend/girlfriend, divorce of parents, move to a new school. Criminal behavior results when individuals seek revenge against those responsible, try to prevent the loss, or escape through illicit drug use.

• *Strain caused by the presentation of negative stimuli.* The third major source of strain involves stressful life situations. Adverse situations and events may include child abuse, criminal victimization, bad experiences with peers, school problems, or verbal threats. Criminal behavior in these situations may result when an individual tries to run away from the situation, end the problem, or seek revenge.[38]

According to Agnew, each type of strain increases an individual's feelings of anger, fear, or depression. The most critical reaction for general strain theory is anger, an emotion that increases the desire for revenge, helps justify aggressive behavior, and stimulates individuals into action.

General strain theory acknowledges that not all persons who experience strain become criminals. Many are equipped to cope with their frustration and anger. Some come up with rationalizations ("don't really need it anyway"); others use techniques for physical relief (a good workout at the gym); and still others walk away from the condition causing stress (get out of the house). The capacity to deal with strain depends on personal experience throughout life. It involves the influence of peers, temperament, attitudes, and, in the case of pressing financial problems, economic resources. Recent empirical tests show preliminary support for general strain theory.[39] By broadening Merton's concepts, general strain theory has the potential to explain a wide range of criminal and delinquent behavior, including aggressive acts, drug abuse, and property offenses, among individuals from all classes in society.

Theory Informs Policy

Strain theory has helped us develop a crime-prevention strategy. If, as the theory tells us, frustration builds up in people who have few means for reaching their goals, it makes sense to design programs that give lower-class people a bigger stake in society.

Head Start It was in the 1960s that President Lyndon Johnson inaugurated the Head Start program as part of a major antipoverty campaign. The goal of Head Start is to make children of low-income families more socially competent, better able to deal with their present environment and their later responsibilities. The youngsters get a boost (or a head start) in a one-year preschool developmental program that is intended to prevent them from dropping out of society. Program components include community and parental involvement, an 8-to-1 child/staff ratio, and daily evaluation and involvement of all the children in the planning of and responsibility for their own activities.

Since a one-year program could not be expected to affect the remainder of a child's life, Project Follow Through was developed in an effort to provide the same opportunities for Head Start youngsters during elementary school. What began as a modest summer experience for half a million preschool children has expanded into a year-round program that provides educational and social services to millions of young people and their families. This, then, is a program clearly intended to lower stress in the group most likely to develop criminal behavior.

Some research findings do indicate that the program has had a certain measure of success. In 1997 the National Head Start Association awarded special recognition to newly elected U.S. Representative Loretta Sanchez as a model of success for the Head Start program. She is the first member of Congress to have been a Head Start child. Sanchez, who could not speak until age 4, recalls how Head Start gave her a jump start to a graduate degree in business and to running a successful financial consulting firm.[40] Yet successes of individual Head Start programs are unevenly distributed over the country, depending largely on program and staff quality. Even supporters warn that Head Start's success rates can improve only if these funds are carefully aimed at program improvement, rather than enlargement.

Perry Preschool Project Another program that tried to ameliorate the disparity between goals and means in society was the Perry Preschool Project, begun in 1962 on the south side of Ypsilanti, Michigan. Its purpose was to develop skills that would give youngsters the means of getting ahead at school and in the workplace, thereby reducing the amount and seriousness of delinquent behavior. Overall, 123 black children 3 and 4 years old participated for two years, five days a week, two and half hours a day. The program provided a teacher for every five children, weekly visits by a teacher to a child's home, and a follow-up of every child annually until age 11 and thereafter at ages 14, 15, and 19.

There is little doubt about the effectiveness of the project. By age 19, the participants did better in several areas than a group that had not participated:

- Employment rates doubled.
- Rates of postsecondary education doubled.
- Teenage pregnancy was cut in half.
- The high school graduation rate was one-third higher.
- Arrest rates were 40 percent lower.[41]

Job Corps Yet another survivor of President Johnson's War on Poverty is the federal Job Corps program. It aims at "the worst of the worst," as Senator Orrin Hatch of Utah said.[42] The program enables neglected teenagers—otherwise headed for juvenile detention or jail—to master work habits that they did not learn at home. In 2003, 70,000 young people were serving in the Job Corps. Most of them had enlisted on the basis of recruitment posters, like those distributed by the armed forces. The average length of stay in the corps is just short of a year, at an annual cost of $18,831. That sounds expensive, but juvenile detention costs $29,600 a year—and residential drug treatment centers cost $19,000. Since its inception in 1964 the program has served 1.8 million people.[43]

Over two-thirds of former Job Corps members get jobs, and 17 percent go on to higher education. Research has shown that the Job Corps returns $1.46 for every dollar spent, because of increased tax revenue and decreased cost of welfare, crime, and incarceration. Over two-thirds of Job Corps members come from minorities; over 80 percent are high school dropouts (see Figure 5.2).

In a report to the United States Congress on which programs prevent crime, researchers at the University of Maryland classified the Job Corps program as "promising." Its potential for success includes the resocialization of youth through prosocial role models; a residential requirement that reduces contact with antisocial groups; and the vocational focus and attachment to the job market.[44]

CULTURAL DEVIANCE THEORIES

The programs that emanate from strain theory attempt to give underprivileged children ways to achieve middle-class goals. Programs based on cultural deviance theories concentrate on teaching middle-class values.

Strain theory attributes criminal behavior in the United States to the striving of all citizens to conform with the conventional values of the middle class, primarily financial success. Cultural deviance theories attribute crime to a set of values that exist in disadvantaged

FIGURE 5.2 A Profile of Job Corps members.

Racial Makeup	%
Asian-Pacific Islander	2.3%
American Indian	3.8
Hispanic	17.2
White	28.6
Black	48

	Job Corps	Entire U.S.
From families on public assistance	40.2%	5.6%
Annual family income	$5,803	$42,652
High school dropouts	82.3%	12.1%

Source: Adapted from Jane Gross, "Remnant of the War on Poverty, Job Corps Is Still a Quiet Success," *New York Times*, Feb. 17, 1992, p. A14, updated (http://jobcorpswork.org).

neighborhoods. Conformity with the lower-class value system, which determines behavior in slum areas, causes conflict with society's laws. Both strain and cultural deviance theories locate the causes of crime in the marginalized position of those at the lowest stratum in a class-based society.

Scholars who view crime as resulting from cultural values that permit, or even demand, behavior in violation of the law are called "cultural deviance theorists." The three major cultural deviance theories are social disorganization, differential association, and culture conflict. **Social disorganization theory** focuses on the development of high-crime areas in which there is a disintegration of conventional values caused by rapid industrialization, increased immigration, and urbanization. **Differential association theory** maintains that people learn to commit crime as a result of contact with antisocial values, attitudes, and criminal behavior patterns. **Culture conflict theory** states that different groups learn different conduct norms (rules governing behavior) and that the conduct norms of some groups may clash with conventional middle-class rules.

All three theories contend that criminals and delinquents in fact do conform—but to norms that deviate from those of the dominant middle class. Before we examine the specific theories that share the cultural deviance perspective, we need to explore the nature of cultural deviance.

The Nature of Cultural Deviance

When you drive through rural Lancaster County in Pennsylvania, or through Holmes County in Ohio, or through Elkhart and Lagrange Counties in Indiana, in the midst of fertile fields and well-tended orchards, you will find isolated villages with prosperous and well-maintained farmhouses but no electricity. You will see the farmers and their families traveling in horse-drawn buggies, dressed in homespun clothes, and wearing brimmed hats. These people are Amish. Their ancestors came to this country from the German-speaking Rhineland region as early as 1683 to escape persecution for their fundamentalist Christian beliefs. Shunning motors, electricity, jewelry, and affiliation with political parties, they are a *nonconformist* community within a highly materialistic culture.

Motorcycle gangs made their appearance shortly after World War II. The Hell's Angels was the first of many gangs to be established in slum areas of cities across the country. To become a member of this gang, initiates are subjected to grueling and revolting degradations. They are conditioned to have allegiance only to the gang. Contacts with middle-class society are usually antagonistic and criminal. Motorcycle gangs finance their operations through illegal activities, such as dealing drugs, running massage parlors and gambling operations, and selling stolen goods. The members' code of loyalty to one another and to their national and local

Man with a Hitler tattoo on his back sells white power books at a Ku Klux Klan cross-burning rally in Hico, Texas. Deviant hate groups such as these exist throughout the United States and in many foreign countries.

Cultural deviance theorists argue that our society is made up of various groups and subgroups, each with its own standards of right and wrong. Behavior considered normal in one group may be considered deviant by another. As a result, those who conform to the standards of cultures considered deviant are behaving in accordance with their own norms but may be breaking the law—the norms of the dominant culture.

You may wonder whether the Hell's Angels are outcasts in the slum neighborhoods where they live. They are not. They may even be looked up to by younger boys in places where toughness and violence are not only acceptable but appropriate. Indeed, groups such as the Hell's Angels may meet the needs of youngsters who are looking for a way to be important in a disorganized ghetto that offers few opportunities to gain status.

:// Crime Surfing
www.streetgangs.com/bibliography/gangbib.html
Learn more about gangs and street crimes.

groups makes the gangs extremely effective criminal organizations.

The normative systems of the Amish and the bikers are at odds with the conventional norms of the society in which they live. Both deviate from middle-class standards. Sociologists define **deviance** as any behavior that members of a social group define as violating their norms. As we can see, the concept of deviance can be applied to noncriminal acts that members of a group view as peculiar or unusual (the lifestyle of the Amish) or to criminal acts (behavior that society has made illegal). The Hell's Angels fit the expected stereotype of deviance as negative; the Amish culture demonstrates that deviance is not necessarily bad, just different.

Social Disorganization Theory

Scholars associated with the University of Chicago in the 1920s became interested in socially disorganized Chicago neighborhoods where criminal values and traditions replaced conventional ones and were transmitted from one generation to the next. In their classic work *The Polish Peasant in Europe and America,* W. I. Thomas and Florian Znaniecki described the difficulties Polish peasants experienced when they left their rural life in Europe to settle in an industrialized city in America.[45] The scholars compared the conditions the immigrants had left in Poland with those they found in Chicago. They also investigated the immigrants' assimilation.

Older immigrants, they found, were not greatly affected by the move because they managed, even within the urban slums, to continue living as they had lived in Poland. But the second generation did not grow up on Polish farms; these people were city dwellers and they were American. They had few of the old Polish

FIGURE 5.3 Social disorganization.

| Rapid changes in industrialization or urbanization or increased immigration | → | Decline in the effectiveness of institutional and informal social control forces in communities or neighborhoods; that is, social disorganization. | → | Development of delinquency areas, as exemplified by high rates of delinquency and the existence of delinquent traditions and values in specific geographical areas or neighborhoods |

Source: Donald J. Shoemaker, *Theories of Delinquency*, 2d ed. (New York: Oxford University Press, 1990), p. 82.

traditions but were not yet assimilated into the new ones. The norms of the stable, homogeneous folk society were not transferable to the anonymous, materially oriented urban settings. Rates of crime and delinquency rose. Thomas and Znaniecki attributed this result to *social disorganization*—the breakdown of effective social bonds, family and neighborhood associations, and social controls in neighborhoods and communities. (See Figure 5.3.)

The Park and Burgess Model Thomas and Znaniecki's study greatly influenced other scholars at the University of Chicago. Among them were Robert Park and Ernest Burgess, who advanced the study of social disorganization by introducing ecological analysis into the study of human society.[46] Ecology is the study of plants and animals in relation to each other and to their natural habitat, the place where they live and grow. Ecologists study these interrelationships, how the balance of nature continues, and how organisms survive. Much the same approach is used by social ecologists, scholars who study the interrelationships of people and their environment.

In their study of social disorganization, Park and Burgess examined area characteristics instead of criminals for explanations of high crime rates. They developed the idea of natural urban areas, consisting of concentric zones extending out from the downtown central business district to the commuter zone at the fringes of the city. Each zone had its own structure and organization, its own cultural characteristics and unique inhabitants (Figure 5.4). Zone I, at the center, called the Loop because the downtown business district of Chicago is demarcated by a loop of the elevated train system, was occupied by commercial headquarters, law offices, retail establishments, and some commercial recreation. Zone II was the zone in transition, where the city's poor, unskilled, and disadvantaged lived in dilapidated tenements next to old factories. Zone III housed the working class, people whose jobs enabled them to enjoy some of the comforts the city had to offer at its fringes. The middle class—professionals, small-business owners, and the managerial class—lived in Zone IV. Zone V was the commuter zone of satellite towns and suburbs.

Shaw and McKay's Work Clifford Shaw and Henry McKay, two researchers at Chicago's Institute for Juvenile Research, were particularly interested in the model Park and Burgess had created to demonstrate how people were distributed spatially in the process of urban growth. They decided to use the model to investigate the relationship between crime rates and the various zones of Chicago. Their data, found in 55,998 juvenile court records covering a period of 33 years, from 1900 to 1933, indicated the following:

- Crime rates were differentially distributed throughout the city, and areas of high crime rates had high rates of other community problems, such as truancy, mental disorders, and infant mortality.
- Most delinquency occurred in the areas nearest the central business district and decreased with distance from the center.
- Some areas consistently suffered high delinquency rates, regardless of the ethnic makeup of the population.

FIGURE 5.4 Park and Burgess's conception of the "natural urban areas" of Chicago.

Source: Robert E. Park, Ernest W. Burgess, and R. D. McKenzie, *The City* (Chicago: University of Chicago Press, 1925), p. 55.

- High-delinquency areas were characterized by a high percentage of immigrants, nonwhites, and low-income families and a low percentage of home ownership.
- In high-delinquency areas there was a general acceptance of nonconventional norms, but these norms competed with conventional ones held by some of the inhabitants.[47]

Shaw and McKay demonstrated that the highest rates of delinquency persisted in the same areas of Chicago over the extended period from 1900 to 1933, even though the ethnic composition changed (German, Irish, and English at the turn of the century; Polish and Italian in the 1920s; an increasing number of blacks in the 1930s). This finding led to the conclusion that the crucial factor was not ethnicity but, rather, the position of the group in terms of economic status and cultural values. Finally, through their study of three sets of Cook County juvenile court records—1900 to 1906, 1917 to 1923, and 1927 to 1933—they learned that older boys were associated with younger boys in various offenses and that the same techniques for committing delinquent acts had been passed on through the years. The evidence clearly indicated to them that delinquency was socially learned behavior.

transmitted from one generation to the next in disorganized urban areas.[48] This phenomenon is called **cultural transmission.**

Tests of Social Disorganization Theory

Social disorganization, like early strain theory, was overshadowed in the 1970s by social control theorists who turned to explanations of why people do *not* break laws in the face of poor social environments with few means of becoming successful. While these explanations still have widespread impact on the scholarly community, the 1980s and 1990s saw a major resurgence of interest in how neighborhoods affect people's lives. Modern-day social ecologists have once again begun to focus on the interrelationship between individuals and their environment. What are the consequences of rising crime rates in a neighborhood? Ralph Taylor suggests separating these consequences into three categories: psychological and social, behavioral, and economic.[49]

Psychological and Social Effects Life in physically deteriorated neighborhoods with their rat-infested buildings, graffiti-ridden streets, trash-strewn vacant lots, boarded-up windows, and openly conducted drug selling, takes its psychological toll on residents.[50] They feel less emotional investment in their communities, mistrust their neighbors, and harbor increasing desires to "get out." Frustration mounts because they are unable to do so. Many parents are so worried about violence on their streets that they confine their youngsters to the home except for school attendance. Young people refer to this confinement as "lockdown" (a term used to describe the locking of prison cells for security reasons). This desperate move to protect their children from getting hurt physically has had harmful psychological effects. According to one professor of developmental psychology, in a world where a simple altercation can end as an assault, or even a murder,[51] these "protected" children are at a disadvantage. When they eventually go back on the streets, they don't know how to survive.

Researchers are questioning whether people living in socially disorganized neighborhoods become more fearful. The answer is, they usually do.[52] When word of victimization begins to spread, fear can reach epidemic proportions. Residents begin to stay off the streets, abandoning them to the gangs, drug sellers, and others involved in illicit activities. Fear becomes greatest in communities undergoing rapid age and racial-composition changes.[53]

Fear increases when there is a perception that the police care little about a neighborhood. Douglas Smith looked at police behavior and characteristics of 60 neighborhoods in three large U.S. cities (Rochester, New York; St. Louis, Missouri; Tampa/St. Petersburg, Florida). His major findings suggest that police officers are less likely to file reports of crime incidents in high-crime areas than in low-crime areas and that they are more likely to assist residents and initiate contacts with suspicious-looking people in low-crime neighborhoods.[54]

Dina Rose and Todd Clear link social disorganization to high incarceration rates. They suggest that when large numbers of males are removed through incarceration, local social, political, and economic systems in already disorganized communities become even weaker. In these areas children are more likely to experience lack of supervision, more single-parent families, and few effective guardians. The researchers do not advocate policies that allow those who threaten the personal safety of residents to be on the streets. But, they argue, there are many offenders who can be regulated in the community through various neighborhood-based approaches monitored by collaborative efforts of the police, probation and parole officers, and local groups, leaders, and residents. This crime-control strategy, one that ties the offender to the community, could then strengthen, rather than weaken, already socially disorganized neighborhoods.[55]

Behavioral Effects A 1999 report on an ongoing research project that focuses on 343 urban neighborhoods in Chicago shows that residents overall consider substance abuse and fistfighting "very wrong" to "extremely wrong." Broken down by racial and ethnic groups, minority-group members were more intolerant of deviance than were whites.[56] Regardless of the level of residents' intolerance, however, widespread

Cults—Culture Conflict—Crime

As the Hale-Bopp comet streaked through the sky over California on March 26, 1997, 39 members of the computer-related cult Gate of Heaven committed suicide at their luxurious Rancho Santa Fe, California, estate. The victims, males between 18 and 24 years old, fully expected to be conveyed to heaven by a waiting spacecraft.(1)

A cult is defined as "... a great devotion to a person, idea, object, [or] movement; ... a usually small group of people characterized by such devotion" (*Merriam Webster's Collegiate® Dictionary*, Tenth Edition). Most cults are marked by

- A dynamic leader.
- The willingness of members to surrender their worldly possessions.
- Strict obedience to the leader.
- A communal social structure, with its own set of norms and values that are in conflict with those of conventional societies.

Experts estimate that there are 1,000 to 2,000 cults in America with as many as four to six million members.

Criminologists are interested primarily in destructive cults, such as these:

- An Indian cult has its devotees "marry" their little daughters to a goddess. Upon reaching puberty, the little girls are sold into prostitution for about $200 each.(2)
- Members of the Japanese cult Aun Shinrikyo launched a nerve gas attack in the Tokyo subway system—for unknown reasons—killing 12 and injuring over 5,000 (March 20, 1995).
- The Reverend Jim Jones led his cult followers to death at their Jonestown, Guyana, encampment: 914 died; those who refused to take the poison were shot (November 18, 1978).

Shoko Asahara, leader of the Japanese cult Aun Shinrikyo.

- The Solar Temple cult followers committed 74 murder/suicides in Canada and in Switzerland (1994–1997).
- Of the 107 members of the cult group of David Koresh—called the Branch Davidians—80 died (most committed suicide) in a standoff with federal authorities in Waco, Texas (April 1993).(3)

Some governments (China, Germany, and Russia) have outlawed some cults. The Vatican has issued a strong report exhorting the Church to fulfill the spiritual needs of the people to keep them from seeking salvation in cults.(4) The debate in America centers on First Amendment religious freedom. However, that constitutional clause does not protect criminally destructive forms of religious expression. What governments, theologians, and criminologists have in common is their determination to bring alienated members of society into the mainstream to keep them out of destructive cults.

Sources

1. Shirley Levung, "Deaths May Be Work of Religious Cult, Expert Says," *Boston Globe,* Mar. 27, 1997, p. A15.
2. "India Sex Cult's 'Handmaidens' Join Tribute to Hindu Goddess, Secret Society Forces Girls Who 'Marry' Yelamma into Prostitution," *Toronto Star,* Jan. 23, 1997, p. A16.
3. Richard Lacayo, "Cult of Death," *Time,* Mar. 15, 1993, p. 36; Sophfionia Scott Gregory, "Children of a Lesser God," *Time,* May 17, 1993, p. 54.
4. E. J. Dionne, "Vatican, Taking Some Blame, Cites Threat of Cults," *New York Times,* May 4, 1986, p. A10.

Questions for Discussion

1. Where and how can we draw the line between those cults that engage in violations of the criminal law (such as murder, arson, incitation to suicide, rape, child abuse, and prostitution) and those that have not (yet) committed any criminal act and therefore enjoy First Amendment privileges?
2. Both theologians and criminologists advocate narrowing the gap between conduct norms of deviant cultures (cults, sects) and the rules of mainstream society. How could either group practically accomplish that goal?

Of Immediate Concern

deviance in a community generally tends to make people limit their participation in efforts to "clean up" the neighborhood. There are, however, communities that fight back with community patrols, anticrime programs, and various activities to protect children. Many would prefer to move away, but few do. Factors besides crime come into play: low income, stage of life cycle, an affordable place to live, or location of employment.[57] Those moving in usually do so because it is the only place they can find an inexpensive place to live.[58]

Economic Effects Crime problems in a community influence assessments of property values by realtors and lenders. Research in Boston suggests that a 5 percent decrease in crime could bring in $7 million to $30 million in increased tax revenue.[59] In another investigation, researchers asked about the impact of Atlantic City casinos and the related increased crime rate on real estate in three southern New Jersey counties.[60] They found a sizable drop in house values. Those communities most accessible to Atlantic City suffered the worst economic consequences.

Middle- and working-class people tend to escape the urban ghetto, leaving behind the most disadvantaged. When you add to those disadvantaged the people moving in from outside who are also severely disadvantaged, over time these areas become places of concentrated poverty, isolated from the mainstream.

Some social ecologists argue that communities, like people, go through life cycles. Neighborhood deterioration precedes rising crime rates. When crime begins to rise, neighborhoods go from owner-occupied to renter-occupied housing, with a significant decline in the socioeconomic status of residents and an increase in population density. Later in the community life cycle, there is a renewed interest on the part of investors in buying up the cheap real estate with the idea of renovating it and making a profit (gentrification).[61]

> **:// Crime Surfing**
> www.ojp.usdoj.gov/bjs/
>
> Is the association between victimization levels and neighborhoods supported by recent survey data?

Evaluation: Social Disorganization Theory

Though their work has made a significant impact, social ecologists have not been immune to challenges. Their work has been criticized for its focus on how crime patterns are transmitted, not on how they start in the first place. The approach has also been faulted for failing to explain why delinquents stop committing crime as they grow older, why most people in socially disorganized areas do not commit criminal acts, and why some bad neighborhoods seem to be insulated from crime. Finally, critics claim that this approach does not come to grips with middle-class delinquency.

Clearly, however, modern criminology owes a debt to social disorganization theorists, particularly to Shaw and McKay, who in the 1920s began to look at the characteristics of people and places and to relate both to crime. There is now a vast body of research for which they laid the groundwork.

Theory Informs Policy

Theorists of the Chicago school were the first social scientists to suggest that most crime is committed by normal people responding in expected ways to their immediate surroundings, rather than by abnormal individuals acting out individual pathologies. If social disorganization is at the root of the problem, crime control must involve social organization. The community, not individuals, needs treatment. Helping the community, then, should lower its crime rate.

The Chicago Area Project Social disorganization theory was translated into practice in 1934 with the establishment of the Chicago Area Project (CAP), an experiment in neighborhood reorganization. The project was initiated by the Institute for Juvenile Research, at which Clifford Shaw and Henry McKay were working. It coordinated the existing community support groups—local schools, churches, labor unions, clubs, and merchants. Special efforts were made to control delinquency through recreational facilities, summer camps, better law enforcement, and the upgrading of neighborhood schools, sanitation, and general appearance.

In 1994 this first community-based delinquency-prevention program could boast 60 years of achievement. South Chicago remains an area of poverty and urban marginalization, dotted with boarded-up buildings and signs of urban decay, though the pollution from the nearby steel mills is under control. But the Chicago Area Project (CAP) initiated by Shaw and McKay is as vibrant as ever, with its three-pronged attack on delinquency: direct service, advocacy, and community involvement. Residents, from clergy to gang members, are working with CAP to keep kids out of trouble, to help those in trouble, and to clean up the neighborhoods. "In fact, in those communities where area projects have been in operation for a number of years, incidents of crime and delinquency have decreased."[62]

Operation Weed and Seed and Others

Operation Weed and Seed is a federal, state, and local effort to improve the quality of life in targeted high-crime urban areas across the country. The strategy is to "weed" out negative influences (drugs, crime) and to "seed" the neighborhoods with prevention and intervention. The key components of the strategy are:

- *Enhanced coordination.* The analysis of neighborhood problems and the development of a law enforcement/community plan to deal with them.
- *Weeding.* The concentrated effort of law enforcement to weed out drug traffickers, violent offenders, and other criminals through arrest, prosecution, adjudication, and supervision.
- *Community policing.* The involvement of police officers in helping the community solve its problems. By increasing the trust of the community, police and prosecutors join with residents and businesses as partners in enforcing the laws.
- *Seeding.* The focus on eliminating harmful behavior through human services that include youth activities, adult literacy classes, and neighborhood revitalization efforts.

When the program began in 1991 there were three target areas—Kansas City, Missouri; Trenton, New Jersey; and Omaha, Nebraska. By 1999 the number of target areas had increased to 200 sites. An eight-state evaluation showed that the effectiveness of Operation Weed and Seed varied by the original severity of the crime problems, the strength of the established network of community organizations, early seeding with constant weeding, active leadership of key community members, and the formation of partnerships among local organizations.[63]

Another community action project has concentrated on revitalizing a Puerto Rican slum community. Sister Isolina Ferre worked for 10 years in the violent Navy Yard section of Brooklyn, New York. In 1969 she returned to Ponce Plaza, a poverty-stricken area in Ponce, Puerto Rico, infested with disease, crime, and unemployment. The area's 16,000 people had no doctors, nurses, dentists, or social agencies. The project began with a handful of missionaries, university professors, dedicated citizens, and community members who were willing to become advocates for their neighborhood. Among the programs begun were a large community health center, Big Brother/Big Sister programs for juveniles sent from the courts, volunteer tutoring, and recreational activities to take young people off the streets. Young photographers of Ponce Plaza, supplied with a few cameras donated by friends at Kodak, mounted an exhibit at the Metropolitan Museum of Art in New York. Regular fiestas have given community members a chance to celebrate their own achievements as well.[64]

> **Did You Know?**
>
> ... that preventing one youth from leaving school and turning to a life of crime and drugs saves society approximately $2 million?

Programs based on social disorganization theory attempt to bring conventional social values to disorganized communities. They provide an opportunity for young people to learn norms other than those of delinquent peer groups. Let us see how such learning takes place.

Differential Association Theory

What we eat, what we say, what we believe—in fact, the way we respond to any situation—

Latin Kings gang member teaches gang hand symbols to a child. Social interactions like these are learned and transmitted from one generation to the next.

depends on the culture in which we have been reared. In other words, to a very large extent, the social influences that people encounter determine their behavior. Whether a person becomes law-abiding or criminal, then, depends on contacts with criminal values, attitudes, definitions, and behavior patterns. This proposition underlies one of the most important theories of crime causation in American criminology—differential association.

Sutherland's Theory In 1939 Edwin Sutherland introduced differential association theory in his textbook *Principles of Criminology*. Since then scholars have read, tested, reexamined, and sometimes ridiculed this theory, which claimed to explain the development of all criminal behavior. The theory states that crime is learned through social interaction. People come into constant contact with "definitions favorable to violations of law" and "definitions unfavorable to violations of law." The ratio of these definitions—criminal to noncriminal—determines whether a person will engage in criminal behavior.[65] In formulating this theory, Sutherland relied heavily on Shaw and McKay's findings that delinquent values are transmitted within a community or group from one generation to the next.

Sutherland's Nine Propositions Nine propositions explained the process by which this transmission of values takes place:

1. Criminal behavior is learned.
2. Criminal behavior is learned in interaction with other persons in a process of communication. A person does not become a criminal simply by living in a criminal environment. Crime is learned by participation with others in verbal and nonverbal communications.
3. The principal part of the learning of criminal behavior occurs within intimate personal groups. Families and friends have the most influence on the learning of deviant behavior. Their communications far outweigh those of the mass media.
4. When criminal behavior is learned, the learning includes (a) techniques of committing the crime, which are sometimes very complicated, sometimes very simple, and (b) the specific direction of motives, drives, rationalizations, and

attitudes. Young delinquents learn not only how to shoplift, crack a safe, pick a lock, or roll a joint but also how to rationalize and defend their actions. One safecracker accompanied another safecracker for one year before he cracked his first safe.[66] In other words, criminals, too, learn skills and gain experience.

5. The specific direction of motives and drives is learned from definitions of the legal codes as favorable or unfavorable. In some societies an individual is surrounded by persons who invariably define the legal codes as rules to be observed, while in others he or she is surrounded by persons whose definitions are favorable to the violation of the legal codes. Not everyone in our society agrees that the laws should be obeyed; some people define them as unimportant. In American society, where definitions are mixed, we have a culture conflict in relation to legal codes.

6. A person becomes delinquent because of an excess of definitions favorable to violation of law over definitions unfavorable to violation of law. This is the key principle of differential association. In other words, learning criminal behavior is not simply a matter of associating with bad companions. Rather, learning criminal behavior depends on how many definitions we learn that are favorable to law violation as opposed to those that are unfavorable to law violation.

7. Differential associations may vary in frequency, duration, priority, and intensity. The extent to which associations and definitions will result in criminality is related to the frequency of contacts, their duration, and their meaning to the individual.

8. The process of learning criminal behavior by association with criminal and anticriminal patterns involves all the mechanisms that are involved in any other learning. Learning criminal behavior patterns is very much like learning conventional behavior patterns and is not simply a matter of observation and imitation.

9. While criminal behavior is an expression of general needs and values, it is not explained by those general needs and values, since noncriminal behavior is an expression of the same needs and values. Shoplifters steal to get what they want. Others work to get money to buy what they want. The motives—frustration, desire to accumulate goods or social status, low self-concept, and the like—cannot logically be the same because they explain both lawful and criminal behavior.

Tests of Differential Association Theory

Since Sutherland presented his theory more than 50 years ago, researchers have tried to determine whether his principles lend themselves to empirical measurement. James Short tested a sample of 126 boys and 50 girls at a training school and reported a consistent relationship between delinquent behavior and frequency, duration, priority, and intensity of interactions with delinquent peers.[67] Similarly, Travis Hirschi demonstrated that boys with delinquent friends are more likely to become delinquent.[68] Research on seventh- and eighth-grade students attending Rochester, New York, public schools in the late 1980s and early 1990s shows that gang membership is strongly associated with peer delinquency and the amount of delinquency and drug use.[69] Mark Warr demonstrated that while the duration of delinquent friendships over a long period of time has a greater effect than exposure over a short period, it is recent friendships rather than early friendships that have the greatest effect on delinquency.[70]

Adults have also been the subjects of differential association studies. Two thousand residents of New Jersey, Oregon, and Iowa were asked such questions as how many people they knew personally had engaged in deviant acts and how many were frequently in trouble. They were also asked how often they attended church (assumed to be related to definitions unfavorable to the violation of law). This differential association scale correlated significantly with such crimes as illegal gambling, income tax cheating, and theft.[71]

Evaluation: Differential Association Theory

Many researchers have attempted to validate Sutherland's differential association theory. Others have criticized it. Much of the criticism stems from errors in interpretation. Perhaps this type of error is best demonstrated by the critics who ask why it is that not everyone in heavy, prolonged contact with criminal behavior patterns becomes a criminal. Take, for argument's sake, corrections officers, who come into constant contact with more criminal associations than noncriminal ones. How do they escape from learning to be law violators themselves?

The answer, of course, is that Sutherland does not tell us that individuals become criminal by associating with criminals or even by association with criminal behavior patterns. He tells us, rather, that a person becomes delinquent because of an "excess of definitions favorable to violation of law over definitions unfavorable to violation of law." The key word is "definitions." Furthermore, unfavorable definitions may be communicated by persons who are not robbers or murderers or tax evaders. They may, for example, be law-abiding parents who, over time, define certain situations in such a way that their children get verbal or nonverbal messages to the effect that antisocial behavior is acceptable.

Several scholars have asked whether the principles of differential association really explain all types of crime. They might explain theft, but what about homicide resulting from a jealous rage?[72] Why do some people who learn criminal behavior patterns not engage in criminal acts? Why is no account taken of nonsocial variables, such as a desperate need for money? Furthermore, while the principles may explain how criminal behavior is transmitted, they do not account for the origin of criminal techniques and definitions. In other words, the theory does not tell us how the first criminal became a criminal.

Differential association theory suggests there is an inevitability about the process of becoming a criminal. Once you reach the point where your definitions favorable to law violation exceed your definitions unfavorable to law violation, have you crossed an imaginary line into the criminal world? Even if we could add up the definitions encountered in a lifetime, could scientists measure the frequency, priority, duration, and intensity of differential associations?

Despite these criticisms, the theory has had a profound influence on criminology.[73] Generations of scholars have tested it empirically, modified it to incorporate psychologically based learning theory (see Chapter 4), and used it as a foundation for their own theorizing (Chapter 6). The theory has also had many policy implications.

Theory Informs Policy

If, according to differential association theory, a person can become criminal by learning definitions favorable to violating laws, it follows that programs that expose young people to definitions favorable to conventional behavior should reduce criminality. Such educational efforts as Head Start and the Perry Preschool Project have attempted to do just that. The same theory underlies many of the treatment programs for young school dropouts and pregnant teenagers.

An innovative Ohio program is trying to break the vicious cycle between poverty–welfare–school dropout–drugs–delinquency and teenage pregnancy. This program, LEAP (for learning, earning, and parenting), provides financial rewards for teenage single parents to stay in, or return to, school and deductions from the welfare checks of those who do not participate in education. A 1993 evaluation found that the program, which costs the state very little, has been moderately successful. Success appears to increase with increased counseling and aid services. Several states have instituted similar "learnfare" programs (for example, Virginia, Florida, Maryland, and Oklahoma), while others are considering this option.[74]

Recently, schools in Chicago, New York, Boston, Los Angeles, Tucson, and Washington have introduced conflict resolution into the curriculum. These programs zero in on teaching youngsters to deal with problems nonviolently. For example, by role-playing situations, children practice how to respond when someone insults or challenges them. In the Chicago area alone, 5,000 students are going through this antiviolence program, which is supported by the National Institute of Mental Health.[75]

Culture Conflict Theory

Differential association theory is based on the learning of criminal (or deviant) norms or attitudes. Culture conflict theory focuses on the source of these criminal norms and attitudes. According to Thorsten Sellin, **conduct norms**—norms that regulate our daily lives—are rules that reflect the attitudes of the groups to which each of us belongs.[76] Their purpose is to define what is considered appropriate or normal behavior and what is inappropriate or abnormal behavior.

Sellin argues that different groups have different conduct norms and that the conduct norms of one group may conflict with those of another. Individuals may commit crimes by conforming to the norms of their own group if that group's norms conflict with those of the dominant society. According to this rationale, the main difference between a criminal and a noncriminal is that each is responding to different sets of conduct norms.

Examples of groups with values significantly deviating from those of the surrounding majority include MOVE, an African American group concerned with issues like police brutality, animal rights, and African heritage. MOVE, located in a house on Osage Street in Philadelphia, alienated its neighbors by loud and profanity-laced loudspeaker messages. Mutual animosity escalated. Some MOVE members armed themselves. A police officer was killed.

San Francisco 49ers' Terrell Owens, left, and Lee Harris reach for a loose ball during the "Hoops That Help" celebrity basketball game on June 19, 1999, at Selland Arena in Fresno, California. The charity event raises money for the Community Intervention and Assistance Foundation, which provides scholarships, job training, and housing.

Ultimately, the police, armed with arrest warrants for some members, entered the area. The group did not surrender. The police attacked: 10,000 rounds of ammunition were fired, and a bomb was dropped from a police helicopter. All but two of the MOVE members died, and all the houses on the street went up in flames.

The last chapter in the MOVE drama was not written until February 1997, when the City of Philadelphia agreed to pay more than $500,000 each to the estates of MOVE founders John Africa and Frank James—after having spent over $30 million to rebuild the houses destroyed by the police bombing, and to settle lawsuits by the estates of nine other MOVE members who had perished.

Another example—far more criminal—was the Solar Temple, founded by a former Gestapo officer, which flourished in Switzerland and Canada. This mystic cult attracted wealthy members who "donated" all their property to the cult, perhaps $93 million in all; much of it was spent for the personal benefit of two cult leaders. Cult members were heavily armed (and engaged in arms trading) in anticipation of the end of the world. Their end of the world came in the fall of 1994, when the two cult leaders murdered nearly all their followers and then committed suicide.

Sellin distinguishes between primary and secondary conflicts. "Primary conflict" occurs when norms of two cultures clash. A clash may occur at the border between neighboring cultural areas; a clash may occur when the law of one cultural group is extended to cover the territory of another; or it may occur when members of one group migrate to another culture. In a widening gap between cultural norms and generations, Southeast Asian immigrant children are running away from home in increasing numbers. They often run into an informal nationwide network of "safe houses." No one knows how many runaways there are, but it is estimated that at least one-third of all refugee families have had at least one child vanish for days, months, or even longer.

"Secondary conflict" arises when a single culture evolves into a variety of cultures, each with its own set of conduct norms. This type of conflict occurs when the homogeneous societies of simpler cultures become complex societies in which the number of social groupings multiplies constantly and norms are often at odds. Your college may make dormitory living mandatory for all freshmen, for example, but to follow the informal code of your peer group, you may seek the freedom of off-campus housing. Or you may have to choose whether to violate work rules by leaving your job half an hour early to make a mandatory class or to violate school rules by walking into class half an hour late. Life situations are frequently controlled by conflicting norms, so no matter how people act, they may be violating some rule, often without being aware that they are doing so.

MOVE members and neighbors watch their houses burn after aerial and ground attacks by the Philadelphia police, May 1985. Over the next 11 years the city paid more than $30 million to rebuild homes and settle lawsuits of cult members and their families.

In the next chapter, which deals with the formation and operation of subcultures, we will expand the discussion of the conflict of norms. We will also examine the empirical research that seeks to discover whether there is indeed a multitude of value systems in our society and, if so, whether and how they conflict.

REVIEW

Contemporary criminologists tend to divide the sociological explanation of crime into three categories: strain, cultural deviance, and social control. The strain and cultural deviance perspectives focus on the social forces that cause people to engage in deviant behavior. They assume that there is a relationship between social class and criminal behavior. Strain theorists argue that all people in society share one set of cultural values and that since lower-class persons often do not have legitimate means to attain society's goals, they may turn to illegitimate means instead. General strain theory, a revision of Merton's theory, relates criminal behavior to the anger that results when an individual is treated in a way he or she does not want to be treated in a social relationship. Cultural deviance theorists maintain that the lower class has a distinctive set of values and that these values often conflict with those of the middle class.

Cultural deviance theories—social disorganization, differential association, and culture conflict—relate criminal behavior to the learning of criminal values and norms. Social disorganization theory focuses on the breakdown of social institutions as a precondition for the establishment of criminal norms. Differential association theory concentrates on the processes by which criminal behavior is taught and learned. Culture conflict theory focuses on the specifics of how the conduct norms of some groups may clash with those of the dominant culture.

CRIMINOLOGY & PUBLIC POLICY

"In American society, personal worth tends to be evaluated on the basis of what people have achieved rather than who they are or how they relate to others in social networks. 'Success' is to a large extent the ultimate measure of social worth. Quite understandably, then, there are pervasive cultural pressures to achieve at any cost. A strong achievement orientation, at the level of basic cultural values, thus cultivates and sustains a mentality that 'its not how you play the game; it's whether you win or lose.'" (Source: Richard Rosenfeld and Steven F. Messner, "Crime and the American Dream: An Institutional Analysis," in *The Legacy of Anomie: Advances in Criminological Theory*, F. Adler and W. S. Laufer (eds. New Brunswick, N.J.: Transaction, 1999).)

Questions for Discussion Robert Merton's notion of strain may be traced to the same values upon which the American Dream rests, in particular a strong achievement orientation. What are the ramifications of such a theoretical premise? What kind of social programs address this orientation? Do programs grounded in this success orientation promote an unrealistic and unattainable goal?

YOU BE THE CRIMINOLOGIST

A major funding agency has given a large grant for changing the quality of life in a high-crime inner-city neighborhood where residents are afraid to let their children play outside. You are the project director. Whom would you hire as consultants? Would you work with law enforcement? And, finally, what would be your goals, and how would you reach them?

KEY TERMS

The numbers next to the terms refer to the pages on which the terms are defined.

accommodate (124)
conduct norms (139)
cultural deviance theories (116)
cultural transmission (132)
culture conflict theory (128)
deviance (129)
differential association theory (128)
general strain theory (126)
social disorganization theory (128)
strain theory (116)

CHAPTER 6
The Formation of Subcultures

The Function of Subcultures

Subcultural Theories of Delinquency and Crime
  The Middle-Class Measuring Rod
  Corner Boy, College Boy, Delinquent Boy
  Tests of Cohen's Theory
  Evaluation: Cohen's Theory

Delinquency and Opportunity
  Tests of Opportunity Theory
  Evaluation: Differential Opportunity Theory

The Subculture of Violence
  Tests of the Subculture of Violence
  Evaluation: The Subculture of Violence Theory

Focal Concerns: Miller's Theory
  Tests of Miller's Theory
  Evaluation: Miller's Theory

Gangs at the Turn of the 21st Century
  Guns and Gangs

Female Delinquent Subcultures
  Early Research
  Recent Studies

Middle-Class Delinquency Explanations

Theory Informs Policy
  MOBY
  Other Programs
  Getting Out: Gang Banging or the Morgue

REVIEW

CRIMINOLOGY & PUBLIC POLICY

YOU BE THE CRIMINOLOGIST

KEY TERMS

Boxes
  From the Pages of *The New York Times*: *Street Gangs of New York: From the 1860s to the 1960s*
  Of Immediate Concern: *The Girls in the Gang*
  Window to the World: *America's Changing Ethnic Gangs*

Special Features
  Crime Surfing
  Did You Know?

KEY TERMS
differential opportunity theory
reaction formation
subculture
subcultures of violence

Ethinic gangs, like this Hispanic group, are growing in numbers and size across the United States.

In Fresno, California, the Mongolian Boys Society, a Hmong gang, terrorized, assaulted, and forced girls as young as 12 into prostitution. Hmong gangs are also springing up in Denver, Colorado, where gang members lure Asian girls into motel rooms by offering them a ride and a chance to "party." The gang members do not release the girls until they have had sex with a number of customers. Hmong gang members also kidnapped and gang-raped a 20-year-old University of Colorado student. Vietnamese gangs in Atlanta smuggle young women and girls into the United States. The cost of the trip, including the promise of legal employment in America, is $40,000. If they are unable to pay the fee, they are forced to be sex slaves in illegal brothels until the amount of passage is paid off, an equivalent of about 600 sex acts.[1]

While Asian gangs represent only a minority of gangs in the United States, their rapid spread to cities such as Denver, as well as to smaller communities, including suburbs and rural areas, demonstrates the increasing prevalence of gangs outside major cities such as New York, Los Angeles, and Chicago. Nationwide, 23 cities had known street gangs in 1961. In 1999, the National Youth Gang Center surveyed over 2,600 cities, towns, and counties and found 26,000 gangs and 840,500 gang members.[2]

Gang violence, too, is on the rise. Reports about juvenile gang activities fill the files of police departments, juvenile courts, and adult courts as well. How did these groups get started in American society? What keeps them going?

143

THE FUNCTION OF SUBCULTURES

Strain theorists explain criminal behavior as a result of the frustrations suffered by lower-class individuals deprived of legitimate means to reach their goals. Cultural deviance theorists assume that individuals become criminal by learning the criminal values of the groups to which they belong. In conforming to their own group standards, these people break the laws of the dominant culture. These two perspectives are the foundation for subcultural theory, which emerged in the mid-1950s.

A **subculture** is a subdivision within the dominant culture that has its own norms, beliefs, and values. Subcultures typically emerge when people in similar circumstances find themselves isolated from the mainstream and band together for mutual support. Subcultures may form among members of racial and ethnic minorities, among prisoners, among occupational groups, among ghetto dwellers. Subcultures exist within a larger society, not apart from it. They therefore share some of its values. Nevertheless, the lifestyles of their members are significantly different from those of individuals in the dominant culture.

SUBCULTURAL THEORIES OF DELINQUENCY AND CRIME

Subcultural theories in criminology had been developed to account for delinquency among lower-class males, especially for one of its most important expressions—the teenage gang. According to subcultural theorists, delinquent subcultures, like all subcultures, emerge in response to special problems that members of the dominant culture do not face. Theories developed by Albert Cohen and by Richard Cloward and Lloyd Ohlin are extensions of the strain, social disorganization, and differential association theories. They explain why delinquent subcultures emerge in the first place (strain), why they take a particular form (social disorganization), and how they are passed on from one generation to the next (differential association).

The explanations of delinquency developed by Marvin Wolfgang and Franco Ferracuti and by Walter Miller are somewhat different from those mentioned above. These theorists do not suggest that delinquency begins with failure to reach middle-class goals. Their explanations are rooted in culture conflict theory. The subculture of violence thesis argues that the value systems of some subcultures demand the use of violence in certain social situations. This norm, which affects daily behavior, conflicts with conventional middle-class norms. Along the same lines, Miller suggests that the characteristics of lower-class delinquency reflect the value system of the lower-class culture and that the lower-class values and norms conflict with those of the dominant culture.

Although Miller contends that the lower-class culture as a whole—not a subculture within it—is responsible for criminal behavior in urban slums, his theory is appropriate to our discussion because it demonstrates how the needs of young urban males are met by membership in a street gang. Miller's street gangs, like those of Cohen and of Cloward and Ohlin, condone violent criminal activity as one of the few means of attaining status in a slum.

The Middle-Class Measuring Rod

Albert Cohen was a student of Robert Merton and of Edwin Sutherland, both of whom had made convincing arguments about the causes of delinquency. Sutherland persuaded Cohen that differential association and the cultural transmission of criminal norms led to criminal behavior. From Merton he learned about structurally induced strain. Cohen combined and expanded these perspectives to explain how the delinquent subculture arises, where it is found within the social structure, and why it has the particular characteristics that it does.[3]

According to Cohen, delinquent subcultures emerge in the slum areas of large American cities. They are rooted in class differentials in parental aspirations, child-rearing practices, and classroom standards. The relative position of a youngster's family in the social structure determines the problems the child will have to face throughout life.

PART II Explanations of Crime and Criminal Behavior   145

FIGURE 6.1 The process of reaction formation among delinquent boys.

Working-class socialization + Middle-class values of success → Lower-class failure in the school system (among many) → Loss of self-esteem and increased feelings of rejection → School dropout and association with delinquent peers (among some) → Increased hostility and resentment toward middle-class standards and symbols, thus reaction formation → Improved self-image in a gang context and through negative and malicious delinquent behavior

Source: Donald J. Shoemaker. *Theories of Delinquency: An Examination of Explanations of Delinquent Behavior*, 3d ed. (New York: Oxford University Press, 1996), p. 107.

Lower-class families who have never known a middle-class lifestyle, for example, cannot socialize their children in a way that prepares them to enter the middle class. The children grow up with poor communication skills, lack of commitment to education, and an inability to delay gratification. Schools present a particular problem. There, lower-class children are evaluated by middle-class teachers on the basis of a middle-class measuring rod. The measures are based on such middle-class values as self-reliance, good manners, respect for property, and long-range planning. By such measures, lower-class children fall far short of the standards they must meet if they are to compete successfully with middle-class children. Cohen argues that they experience status frustration and strain, to which they respond by adopting one of three roles: corner boy, college boy, or delinquent boy.

Corner Boy, College Boy, Delinquent Boy

"Corner boys" try to make the best of bad situations. The corner boy hangs out in the neighborhood with his peer group, spending the day in some group activity, such as gambling or athletic competition. He receives support from his peers and is very loyal to them. Most lower-class boys become corner boys. Eventually, they get menial jobs and live a conventional lifestyle.

There are very few "college boys." These boys continually strive to live up to middle-class standards, but their chances for success are limited because of academic and social handicaps.

"Delinquent boys" band together to form a subculture in which they can define status in ways that to them seem attainable. Cohen claims that even though these lower-class youths set up their own norms, they have internalized the norms of the dominant class and they feel anxious when they go against those norms. To deal with this conflict, they resort to **reaction formation,** a mechanism that relieves anxiety through the process of rejecting with abnormal intensity what one wants but cannot obtain. These boys turn the middle-class norms upside down, thereby making conduct right in their subculture precisely because it is wrong by the norms of the larger culture (Figure 6.1).

Consequently, their delinquent acts serve no useful purpose. They do not steal things to eat them, wear them, or sell them. In fact, they often discard or destroy what they have stolen. They appear to delight in the discomfort of others and in breaking taboos. Their acts are directed against people and property at random, unlike the goal-oriented activities of many adult criminal groups. The subculture is typically characterized by short-run hedonism, pure pleasure seeking, with no planning or deliberation about what to do, nor where or when to do it. The delinquents hang out on the street corner until someone gets an idea; then they act impulsively, without considering the consequences. The group's autonomy is all-important. Its members are loyal to each other and resist any attempts on the part of family, school, or community to restrain their behavior.

Tests of Cohen's Theory

Criminological researchers generally agree that Cohen's theory is responsible for major advances in research on delinquency.[4] Among them are researchers who have found a relationship between delinquency and social status in our society (Chapter 5). Much evidence also supports Cohen's assumption that lower-class children perform more poorly in school than middle-class children.[5] Teachers often expect them to perform less ably than their middle-class students, and this expectation is one of the components of poor performance.

Researchers have demonstrated that poor performance in school is related to delinquency. When Travis Hirschi studied more than 4,000 California schoolchildren, he found that youths who were academically incompetent and performed poorly in school came to dislike school. Disliking it, they rejected its authority; rejecting its authority, they committed delinquent acts (Chapter 7).[6] Delbert Elliott and Harwin Voss also investigated the relationship between school and delinquency. They analyzed annual school performance and delinquency records of 2,000 students in California from ninth grade to one year after the expected graduation date. Their findings indicated that those who dropped out of school had higher rates of delinquency than those who graduated. They also found that academic achievement and alienation from school were closely related to dropping out of school.[7]

Boredom in class, as demonstrated by this ninth-grade student, may lead to dropout and delinquency.

From analysis of the dropout-delinquency relationship among over 5,000 persons nationwide, G. Roger Jarjoura concluded that while dropouts were more likely to engage in delinquent acts than graduates, the reason was not always simply the fact that they had dropped out. Dropping out because of a dislike for school, poor grades, or financial reasons was related to future involvement in delinquency; dropping out because of problems at home was not. Dropping out for personal reasons such as marriage or pregnancy was significantly related to subsequent violent offending.[8] All these findings support Cohen's theory. Other findings, however, do not.

In a study of 12,524 students in Davidson County, Tennessee, Albert Reiss and Albert Rhodes found only a slight relationship between delinquency and status deprivation.[9] This conclusion was supported by the research of Marvin Krohn and his associates.[10] Furthermore, several criminologists have challenged Cohen's claim that delinquent behavior is purposeless.[11] They contend that much delinquent behavior is serious and calculated and often engaged in for profit.[12] Oth-

PART II Explanations of Crime and Criminal Behavior   147

ers have also questioned the consistency of the theory: Cohen argues that the behavior of delinquent boys is a deliberate response to middle-class opinion; yet he also argues that the boys do not care about the opinions of middle-class people.[13]

Evaluation: Cohen's Theory

Researchers have praised and criticized Cohen's work. Cohen's theory answers a number of questions left unresolved by the strain and cultural deviance theories. It explains the origin of delinquent behavior and why some youths raised in the same neighborhoods and attending the same schools do not become involved in delinquent subcultures. His concepts of status deprivation and the middle-class measuring rod have been useful to researchers. Yet his theory does not explain why most delinquents eventually become law-abiding even though their position in the class structure remains relatively fixed. Some criminologists also question whether youths are driven by some serious motivating force or whether they are simply out on the streets looking for fun.[14] Moreover, if delinquent subcultures result from the practice of measuring lower-class boys by a middle-class measuring rod, how do we account for the growing number of middle-class gangs?

Other questions concern the difficulty of trying to test the concepts of reaction formation, internalization of middle-class values, and status deprivation, among others. To answer some of his critics, Cohen, with his colleague James Short, expanded the idea of delinquent subcultures to include not only lower-class delinquent behavior but also such variants as middle-class delinquent subcultures and female delinquents.[15] Cohen took Merton's strain theory a step further by elaborating on the development of delinquent behavior. He described how strain actually creates frustration and status deprivation, which in turn foster the development of an alternative set of values that give lower-class boys a chance to achieve recognition. Since the mid-1950s Cohen's theory has stimulated not only research but the formulation of new theories.

Multicultural macho advertisements appeal to young males concerned with showing toughness through masculinity. This billboard suggests that Converse sneakers are not for kids' playgrounds.

DELINQUENCY AND OPPORTUNITY

Like Cohen's theory, the theory of differential opportunity developed by Richard Cloward and Lloyd Ohlin combines strain, differential association, and social disorganization concepts.[16] Both theories begin with the assumption that conventional means to conventional success are not equally distributed among the socioeconomic classes, that lack of means causes frustration for lower-class youths, and that criminal behavior is learned and culturally transmitted. Both theories also agree that the common solution to shared problems leads to

FIGURE 6.2 Factors leading to development of three types of delinquent gangs.

```
┌─────────────────────────────┐      ┌─────────────────────────────┐
│ Limited access to legitimate│─────▶│ Feeling of frustration and  │
│ means of achieving desired  │      │ deprivation, leading to gang│
│ economic success            │      │ formation                   │
└─────────────────────────────┘      └─────────────────────────────┘
              │                                       │
              ▼                                       │
┌─────────────────────────────┐      ┌─────────────────────────────┐
│ Predominance of one of three│      │ Stable, integrated conventional│
│ types of gangs, depending on│─────▶│ and criminal systems = criminal,│
│ the integration of          │      │ theft gang                  │
│ conventional adult and      │      └─────────────────────────────┘
│ criminal adult value and    │      ┌─────────────────────────────┐
│ behavior systems in a       │─────▶│ Nonintegrated systems, absence│
│ neighborhood                │      │ of criminal organization,   │
└─────────────────────────────┘      │ instability = conflict, violent gang│
                                     └─────────────────────────────┘
                                     ┌─────────────────────────────┐
                                     │ In either type of neighborhood,│
                                     │ double failure, residual    │
                                     └────▶│ adolescence = retreatist "gang,"│
                                     │ or, more accurately, retreatist│
                                     │ response                    │
                                     └─────────────────────────────┘
```

Source: Donald J. Shoemaker, *Theories of Delinquency: An Examination of Explanations of Delinquent Behavior*, 3rd ed. (New York: Oxford University Press, 1996), p. 115.

the formation of delinquent subcultures. They disagree, however, on the content of these subcultures. As we have noted, norms in Cohen's delinquent subcultures are right precisely because they are wrong in the dominant culture. Delinquent acts are negative and nonutilitarian. Cloward and Ohlin disagree; they suggest that lower-class delinquents remain goal-oriented. The kind of delinquent behavior they engage in depends on the illegitimate opportunities available to them.

According to Cloward and Ohlin's **differential opportunity theory**, delinquent subcultures flourish in lower-class areas and take the particular forms they do because opportunities for illegitimate success are no more equitably distributed than those for conventional success. Just as means—opportunities—are unequally distributed in the conventional world, opportunities to reach one's goals are unequally distributed in the criminal world. A person cannot simply decide to join a theft-oriented gang or, for that matter, a violence-oriented one. Cloward and Ohlin maintain that the types of subcultures and of the juvenile gangs that flourish within them depend on the types of neighborhoods in which they develop (Figure 6.2).

In areas where conventional and illegitimate values and behavior are integrated by a close connection of illegitimate and legitimate businesses, "criminal gangs" emerge. Older criminals serve as role models. They teach youngsters the kinds of people to exploit, the necessary criminal skills, the importance of loyal relationships with criminal associates, and the way to make the right connections with shady lawyers, bail bondsmen, crooked politicians, and corrupt police officers. Adolescent members of criminal gangs, like adult criminals in the neighborhood, are involved in extortion, fraud, theft, and other activities that yield illegal income.

This type of neighborhood was described by one of its members in a classic work published in 1930:

> Stealing in the neighborhood was a common practice among the children and approved by the parents. Whenever the boys got together they talked about robbing and made more plans for stealing. I hardly knew any boys who did not go robbing. The

little fellows went in for petty stealing, breaking into freight cars, and stealing junk. The older guys did big jobs like stickups, burglary, and stealing autos. The little fellows admired the "big shots" and longed for the day when they could get into the big racket. Fellows who had "done time" were the big shots and looked up to and gave the little fellows tips on how to get by and pull off big jobs.[17]

Neighborhoods characterized by transience and instability, Cloward and Ohlin argue, offer few opportunities to get ahead in organized criminal activities. This world gives rise to "conflict gangs," whose goal is to gain a reputation for toughness and destructive violence. Thus "one particular biker would catch a bird and then bite off its head, allowing the blood to trickle from his mouth as he yelled 'all right!'"[18] It is the world of the warrior: Fight, show courage against all odds, defend and maintain the honor of the group. Above all, never show fear.

Violence is the means used to gain status in conflict gangs. Conventional society's recognition of the "worst" gangs becomes a mark of prestige, perpetuating the high standards of their members. Conflict gangs emerge in lower-class areas where neither criminal nor conventional adult role models exercise much control over youngsters.

A third subcultural response to differential opportunities is the formation of "retreatist gangs." Cloward and Ohlin describe members of retreatist gangs as double failures because they have not been successful in the legitimate world and have been equally unsuccessful in the illegitimate worlds of organized criminal activity and violence-oriented gangs. This subculture is characterized by a continuous search for getting high through alcohol, atypical sexual experiences, marijuana, hard drugs, or a combination of these.

The retreatist hides in a world of sensual adventure, borrowing, begging, or stealing to support his habit, whatever it may be. He may peddle drugs or work as a pimp or look for some other deviant income-producing activity. But the income is not a primary concern; he is interested only in the next high. Belonging to a retreatist gang offers a sense of superiority and well-being that is otherwise beyond the reach of these least successful dropouts.

Not all lower-class youngsters who are unable to reach society's goals become members of criminal, conflict, or retreatist gangs. Many choose to accept their situation and to live within its constraints. These law-abiding youngsters are Cohen's corner boys.

Tests of Opportunity Theory

Cloward and Ohlin's differential opportunity theory presented many new ideas, and a variety of studies emerged to test it empirically.

The first of Cloward and Ohlin's assumptions—that blocked opportunities are related to delinquency—has mixed support. Travis Hirschi, for example, demonstrated that "the greater one's acceptance of conventional (or even quasi-conventional) success goals, the less likely one is to be delinquent, regardless of the likelihood these goals will someday be attained."[19] In other words, the youngsters who stick to hard work and education to get ahead in society are the least likely to become delinquent, no matter what their real chances of reaching their goals. John Hagedorn disagrees. In late 1992 and early 1993, he conducted interviews with 101 founding members of 18 gangs in Milwaukee. His conclusion: "Most of those we were trying to track appeared to be on an economic merry-go-round, with continual movement in and out of the secondary labor market. Although their average income from drug sales far surpassed their income from legal employment, most Milwaukee male gang members apparently kept trying to find licit work."[20] There is also evidence that both gang and nongang boys believe the middle-class values of hard work and scholastic achievement to be important. Gang boys, however, are more ready to approve of a wide range of behaviors, including aggressive acts and drug use.[21]

The second assumption of differential opportunity theory—that the type of lower-class gang depends on the type of neighborhood in which it emerges—has also drawn the attention of criminologists. Empirical evidence suggests that gang behavior is more versatile and involves a wider range of criminal and noncriminal acts than the patterns outlined by Cloward and Ohlin. Ko-lin Chin's research on New York

Three suspected members of the Crips, a gang reputed for its toughness and violence, hit the pavement after being chased by SAPD officers and deputies of the Baxar County Gang Unit. The suspects' names were being checked through computers for any outstanding warrants. All three were arrested.

gangs in 1993 demonstrates that Chinese gangs are engaged in extortion, alien smuggling, heroin trafficking, and the running of gambling establishments and houses of prostitution.[22] A recent report from the Denver Youth Survey showed that while the most frequent form of illegal activity is fighting with other gangs, gang members are also involved in robberies, joyriding, assaults, stealing, and drug sales.[23]

Research does, however, support Cloward and Ohlin's argument that criminal gangs emerge in areas where conventional and illegitimate behavior have a close connection with illegitimate and legitimate businesses. Chinatowns in America, for example, are social, economic, political, and cultural units.[24] All types of organizations, including those that dominate illegal activities, play an important role in the maintenance of order in the community. The illegitimate social order has control of territorial rights, gambling places, heroin trafficking, alien smuggling, and loan-sharking. The illegal order defines who is in control of particular restaurants, retail shops, garment factories, and the like. Business owners pay a "membership fee" for protection. Adult criminals maintain control of youth gang members by threatening to exclude them from work that pays well. They also resolve conflicts, provide recreational facilities, lend money, and give the young gang members a chance to climb the illegitimate career ladder within the criminal organization. Gang activities are closely supervised by their leaders, who work with the adult crime groups. Elaborate initiation rites are conducted by an adult the youngsters call "uncle"—the link between the gang and the adult sponsoring organization.

Gang members (1,015) from California, Illinois, Iowa, Michigan, and Ohio also reported having a variety of legal and illegal income sources, collective gang "treasuries," and mostly adult leaders.[25] Their businesses include dance clubs, billiard halls, and stereo, liquor, jewelry, grocery, cellular phone/beeper, and auto repair shops. They also sell illegal goods: $268 for a 9-mm Glock semiautomatic pistol, $42 for a box of cartridges, $882 for 1 ounce of cocaine, and $155 for a stolen 12-gauge shotgun.[26] These gangs operate somewhat like a union for the underground economy. Members attend meetings, pay dues, follow rules, have their own language, and make collective expenditures (for guns, funerals, attorneys).

From Stephen Moore, *Investigating Deviance*, Unwin Hyman Ltd., 1988. Copyright © 1988 Stephen Moore. Reprinted with permission.

Evaluation: Differential Opportunity Theory

For three decades criminologists have reviewed, examined, and revised the work of Cloward and Ohlin.[27] One of the main criticisms is that their theory is class-oriented. If, as Cloward and Ohlin claim, delinquency is a response to blocked opportunities, how can we explain middle-class delinquency? Another question arises from contradictory statements. How can delinquent groups be nonutilitarian, negativistic, and malicious (Cohen)—and also goal-oriented and utilitarian? Despite its shortcomings, however, differential opportunity theory has identified some of the reasons lower-class youngsters may become alienated. Cloward and Ohlin's work has also challenged researchers to study the nature of the subcultures in our society. Marvin Wolfgang and Franco Ferracuti have concentrated on one of them—the subculture of violence.

THE SUBCULTURE OF VIOLENCE

Like Cohen, and like Cloward and Ohlin, Marvin Wolfgang and Franco Ferracuti turned to subcultural theory to explain criminal behavior among lower-class young urban males. All three theories developed by these five researchers assume the existence of subcultures made up of people who share a value system that differs from that of the dominant culture. And they assume that each subculture has its own rules or conduct norms that dictate how individuals should act under varying circumstances. The three theories also agree that these values and norms persist over time because they are learned by successive generations. The theories differ, however, in their focus.

Cohen and Cloward and Ohlin focus on the origin of the subculture, specifically, culturally induced strain. The thrust of Wolfgang and Ferracuti's work is culture conflict. Furthermore, the earlier theories encompass all types of delinquency and crime; Wolfgang and Ferracuti concentrate on violent crime. They argue that in some subcultures behavior norms are dictated by a value system that demands the use of force or violence.[28] Subcultures that adhere to conduct norms conducive to violence are referred to as **subcultures of violence.**

Violence is not used in all situations, but it is frequently an expected response. The appearance of a weapon, a slight shove or push, a derogatory remark, or the opportunity to wield power undetected may very well evoke an aggressive reaction that seems uncalled for to middle-class people. Fists rather than words settle disputes. Knives or guns are readily available, so confrontations can quickly escalate. Violence is a pervasive part of everyday life. Child-rearing practices (hitting), gang activities (street wars), domestic quarrels (battering), and social events (drunken brawls) are all permeated by violence.

Violence is not considered antisocial. Members of this subculture feel no guilt about their aggression. In fact, individuals who do not resort to violence may be reprimanded. The value system is transmitted from generation to generation, long after the original reason for the violence has disappeared. The pattern is very hard to eradicate.

When Wolfgang and Ferracuti described population groups that are likely to respond violently to stress, they posed a powerful question to the criminal justice system. How does one go about changing a subcultural norm? This question becomes increasingly significant with the merging of the drug subculture and the subculture of violence.

Did You Know?

. . . that L.A. Gang warfare claimed over 600 lives in 2002?

Tests of the Subculture of Violence

Howard Erlanger, using nationwide data collected for the President's Commission on the Causes and Prevention of Violence, found no major differences in attitudes toward violence by class or race. Erlanger concluded that though members of the lower class show no greater approval of violence than middle-class persons do, they lack the sophistication necessary to settle grievances by other means.[29] The subculture of violence thesis has also generated a line of empirical research that looks at regional differences in levels of violent crime.

The South (as you will see in Chapter 10) has the highest homicide rate in the country. Some researchers have attributed this high rate to subcultural values.[30] They argue that the Southern subculture of violence has its historical roots in an exaggerated defense of honor by Southern gentlemen, mob violence (especially lynching), a military tradition, the acceptance of personal vengeance, and the widespread availability and use of handguns.[31]

The problem with many of these studies is that it is difficult to separate the effects of economic and social factors from those of cultural values. Several researchers have sought to solve this problem. Colin Loftin and Robert Hill, for example, using a sophisticated measure of poverty, found that economic factors, not cultural ones, explained regional variation in homicide rates.[32] Similarly, others suggest that high homicide rates and gun ownership may have a great deal to do with socioeconomic conditions, especially racial inequality in the South.[33]

Researchers who support the subculture of violence thesis point to statistics on characteristics of homicide offenders and victims: Lower-class, inner-city black males are disproportionately represented in the FBI's Uniform Crime Reports. In addition:

- The majority of the offenders are young, most in their 20s but many in their late teens.
- Typically, the offender and the victim know each other.
- The offender and the victim are usually in the same age group and of the same race.[34]

Furthermore, in a study of 556 males interviewed at age 26, 19 percent of the respondents, all inner-city males, reported having been shot or stabbed. These victimizations were found to be highly correlated with both self-reported offenses and official arrest statistics. In fact, the best single predictor of committing a violent act was found to be whether or not the individual had been a victim of a violent crime. Though most people in the dominant society who are shot or stabbed do not commit a criminal act in response, it appears that many inner-city males alternate the roles of victim and offender in a way that maintains the values and attitudes of a violent subculture.[35]

Evaluation: The Subculture of Violence Theory

Though empirical evidence remains inconclusive, the subculture of violence theory is supported by the distribution of violent crime in American society.[36] The number of gangs and the violence associated with their activities are growing.[37] Jeffrey Fagan noted that "drug use is widespread and normative" among gangs.[38] Gang warfare, which takes the lives of innocent bystanders in ghetto areas, is a part of life in most of the impoverished, densely populated neighborhoods in such major cities as Los Angeles, New York, Chicago, Miami, Washington, D.C., and Atlanta, and in smaller disintegrating urban centers as well. For example, over the three years between 1985 and 1988, Jamaican "posses"—gangs transplanted from Kingston, Jamaica, to the United States—have been involved in 1,400 homicides.[39]

Though not all persons in these subcultures follow the norm of violence, it appears that a dismaying number of them attach less and less importance to the value of human life and turn increasingly to violence to resolve immediate problems and frustrations. (We return to this issue later in the chapter.)

FOCAL CONCERNS: MILLER'S THEORY

All the theorists we have examined thus far explain criminal and delinquent behavior in terms of subcultural values that emerge and are perpetuated from one generation to the next in lower-class urban slums. Walter Miller reasons differently. According to Miller:

> In the case of "gang" delinquency, the cultural system which exerts the most direct influence on behavior is that of the lower-class community itself—a long-established, distinctively patterned tradition with an integrity of its own—rather than a so-called "delinquent subculture" which has arisen through conflict with middle-class culture and is oriented to the deliberate violation of middle-class norms.[40]

To Miller, juvenile delinquency is not rooted in the rejection of middle-class values; it stems from lower-class culture, which has its own value system. This value system has evolved as a response to living in disadvantaged neighborhoods characterized by single-parent households (Figure 6.3). Gang norms are simply the adolescent expression of the lower-class culture

Rapper 50 Cent, pictured here in February 2003, expressed his values with his debut record "Get Rich or Die Tryin," which sold 892,000 copies in four days.

in which the boys have grown up. This lower-class culture exists apart from the middle-class culture, and it has done so for generations. The value system, not the gang norms, generates delinquent acts.

Miller has identified six focal concerns, or areas, to which lower-class males give persistent attention: trouble, toughness, smartness, excitement, luck, and autonomy. Concern over *trouble* is a major feature of lower-class life. Staying out of trouble and getting into trouble are daily preoccupations. Trouble can get a person into the hands of the authorities, or it can result in prestige among peers. Lower-class individuals are often evaluated by the extent of their involvement in activities such as fighting, drinking, and sexual misbehaving. In this case, the greater the involvement or the

FIGURE 6.3 Many children live in poverty, often residing in single-parent households where the head of the household does not have a job.

Percentage of Children Living in Poverty or with No Working Parent

Living Arrangement	No Working Parent	Living in Poverty
Both parents	14%	10%
Single parent	34	43
Mother	37	47
Father	19	22

Source: Juvenile Offenders and Victims: 1999 National Report (Washington, D.C.: Office of Juvenile Justice and Delinquency Prevention, 1999), pp. 6, 8.

more extreme the performance, the greater the prestige or "respect" the person commands.

These young men are almost obsessively concerned with *toughness*; the code requires a show of masculinity, a denial of sentimentality, and a display of physical strength. Miller argues that this concern with toughness is related to the fact that a large proportion of lower-class males grow up in female-dominated households and have no male figure from whom to learn the male role. They join street gangs in order to find males with whom they can identify.

Claude Brown's classic 1965 autobiography, *Manchild in the Promised Land,* illustrates the concerns about trouble and toughness among adolescents growing up in an urban slum:

> My friends were all daring like me, tough like me, dirty like me, ragged like me, cursed like me, and had a great love for trouble like me. We took pride in being able to hitch rides on trolleys, buses, taxicabs and in knowing how to steal and fight. We knew that we were the only kids in the neighborhood who usually had more than ten dollars in their pockets.... Somebody was always trying to shake us down or rob us. This was usually done by the older hustlers in the neighborhood or by storekeepers or cops.... We accepted this as a way of life.[41]

Another focal concern is *smartness*—the ability to gain something by outsmarting, outwitting, or conning another person. In lower-class neighborhoods youngsters practice outsmarting each other in card games, exchanges of insults, and other trials. Prestige is awarded to those who demonstrate smartness.

Many aspects of lower-class life are related to another focal concern, the search for *excitement*. Youngsters alternate between hanging out with peers and looking for excitement, which can be found in fighting, getting drunk, and using drugs. Risks, danger, and thrills break up the monotony of their existence.

Fate, particularly *luck,* plays an important role in lower-class life. Many individuals believe that their lives are subject to forces over which they have little control. If they get lucky, a rather drab life could change quickly. Common discussions center on whether lucky numbers come up, cards are right, or dice are good. Brown recalls:

> After a while [Mama] settled down, and we stopped talking about her feelings, then somebody came upstairs and told her she had hit the numbers. We just forgot all about her feelings. I forgot about her feelings. Mama forgot about her feelings. Everybody did. She started concentrating on the number. This was the first time she'd had a hit in a long time. They bought some liquor. Mama and Dad started drinking: everyone started making a lot of noise and playing records.[42]

Miller's last focal concern, *autonomy,* stems from the lower-class person's resentment of external controls, whether parents, teachers, or police. This desire for personal freedom is ex-

FIGURE 6.4 The relationship between delinquency and lower-class focal concerns.

Lower-class focal concerns + Female-dominated households → Desire of lower-class male adolescents to seek male identity and status in "one-sex peer-unit" street-corner gangs → Behavior in accordance with lower-class focal concerns → Behavior that is often delinquent and criminal

Source: Donald J. Shoemaker, *Theories of Delinquency: An Examination of Explanations of Delinquent Behavior,* 3rd ed. (New York: Oxford University Press, 1996), p. 122.

FROM THE PAGES OF The New York Times

Street Gangs of New York: From the 1860s to the 1960s

In December of 2002, Martin Scorcese's long-awaited film, *Gangs of New York,* was released. It was based on a book by Herbert Asbury, written in 1928, about the gangs that existed in New York City in the late 1800s. These gangs caused major problems for law-abiding citizens, and were one of the precipitating factors behind the rise of a strong city-wide police force.

One of the most frightening times in New York City history (before September 11) occurred in 1863, when for three days gangs rioted and took over much of the city. Most of the members of the gangs were Irish workers who were angry at their plight in general (they lived in the most densely packed neighborhood in the world), and were specifically angry at the new National Conscription Act, which made virtually all able-bodied men eligible for the draft. The Act, however, allowed wealthy men to get out of service by paying a $300 fee—more than most lower-class workers made in a year. Historians report that 119 people were killed in the riots, and hundreds more were injured.

Gangs of ethnic origins continued to flourish in New York, brought to public attention again in the late 1950s and early 1960s with the musical *West Side Story.* In 1958, *The New York Times* wrote a seven-part, front-page series examining the antisocial behavior of adolescents in the "shook-up" generation. Some of these gang members attended a reunion of sorts in 1999. In the late 50s, photographer Bruce Davidson spent several months hanging out and photographing a street gang in Brooklyn. Forty years later, several gang members showed up to see an exhibit of these photos at the International Center of Photography.

The gang members recalled the violence of the time. They grew up in Brooklyn, and called themselves the Jokers and the Eighth Avenue Boys. Their fathers were factory workers who were frequently laid off, with no way to support their large families. Many came from homes with two alcoholic parents. It was a place, said one former gang member, where "a kid wished he was dead a million times." They didn't have guns then, but if they had, several former gang members said, they probably would have used them. They fought instead with chains and pipes, knives and baseball bats. Many of the gang members were long since dead. Some died in jail, some died from drugs, some from alcohol, and some from bullets that eventually became the weapon of choice.

There were, however, signs that gang life doesn't necessarily lead to death and destruction. Among the living gang members, who struggled long and hard to fight their way out of poverty and addiction, were two retired police officers, an electrician, a retired transit worker, a hospital administrator, a singer, and an addiction counselor. Most have children who grew up in New Jersey or on Long Island, and who knew nothing of gangs, except from the papers and dad's stories over dinner.

Source

Geoffrey C. Ward, "Gangs of New York," *The New York Times,* October 6, 2002. Blaine Harden, "With Brass-Knuckled Tales, 50's Street Gang Looks Back," *The New York Times,* February 15, 1999. Reprinted with permission.

Questions for Discussion

1. Obviously, gangs in New York (or anywhere else for that matter) are not a modern phenomenon. The gangs described in the story above—both in the 1860s and the 1960s—came from lower, working-class families. How does this support Albert Cohen's "delinquent boys" theory? How do the circumstances not support the part of the theory that says their delinquent acts serve no useful purpose?
2. What can we make of the fact that many of the gang members went on to get good jobs and raise middle-class families with middle-class lifestyles and values?

---

pressed often in such terms as "No one can push me around" and "I don't need nobody."[43]

According to Miller, status in every class is associated with the possession of qualities that are valued. In the lower class the six focal concerns define status. It is apparent that by engaging in behavior that affords status by these criteria, many people will be breaking the laws of the dominant society (Figure 6.4).

Tests of Miller's Theory

An obvious question is whether in our urban, heterogeneous, secular, technologically based society any isolated pockets of culture are still to be found. The pervasiveness of mass advertising, mass transit, and mass communication makes it seem unlikely that an entire class of people could be unaware of the dominant value system. Empirical research on opportunity theory has found that lower-class boys share the conventional success goals of the dominant culture. This finding suggests that the idea of isolation from the dominant system does not fit with reality. Empirical research has also found, however, that while gang boys may support middle-class values, they are willing to deviate from them. If an opportunity arises to gain prestige in a fight, gang boys are willing to take the chance that their act will not result in punishment.

Most empirical tests of values question young people on their attachment to middle-class values. Stephen Cernovich expanded this type of research by investigating attachment to lower-class focal concerns.[44] He found that toughness, excitement, trouble, and pleasure seeking were related to self-reported delinquency in all classes. His findings also showed that boys of all classes were committed to delayed gratification, hard work, and education. Cernovich concluded that it is values, rather than class, that are associated with delinquency.

Evaluation: Miller's Theory

Criminologists have been disturbed by Miller's assumption that the lower-class lifestyle is generally focused on illegal activity. In making such an assumption, they say, Miller disregards the fact that most people in the lower class do conform to conventional norms. Moreover, some criminologists ask, if lower-class boys are conforming to their own value system, why would they suffer guilt or shame when they commit delinquent acts?[45]

Perhaps the best support for Miller's ideas is found in qualitative, rather than quantitative, accounts of life in a lower-class slum. In our discussion of cultural deviance and subcultural theories we noted that the values and norms that define behavior in these areas do not change much over time or from place to place. Successive generations have to deal with the same problems. They typically demonstrate similar responses. Angela D'Arpa-Calandra, a former probation officer who now directs a Juvenile Intensive Supervision program, says she recently walked into a New York courtroom and "saw a mother and grandmother sitting with the 14-year-old offender. 'I had the grandmother in criminal court in 1963,' D'Arpa-Calandra says. 'We didn't stop it there. The grandmother was 14 when she was arrested. The mother had this child when she was 14. It's like a cycle we must relive.'"[46]

By and large, descriptions of life in poverty-stricken areas, whether written by people who have lived in them or by people who have studied them, reveal dreary routine, boredom, constant trouble, and incessant problems with drugs, alcohol, and crime. As the father tells his son in Eugene O'Neill's autobiographical play *Long Day's Journey into Night*, "There was no damned romance in our poverty."[47] There still isn't. In 1993, the *New York Times* ran a series of profiles of youth in poverty:

> Derrick White rides through the crumbling asphalt roads of the Hurt Village housing project where he played tag among the steel clotheslines and shot baskets through bent and wobbly hoops. He passes the trash bins where men with black plastic bags mine for cans to sell to a recycling center. He passes the "dope track," where he saw a friend shot in the neck and killed.
>
> Beyond the project he passes the supermarket that refused him a job interview because, he believes, his address marks him as a project kid.[48]

GANGS AT THE TURN OF THE 21ST CENTURY

In Los Angeles:
A 7-year-old boy was slain and his 10-month-old brother seriously injured by stray bullets as members of the Crips gang opened fire in a parking lot to avenge shootings that had occurred two hours earlier.[49]

In New York:
An 11-year-old boy was killed as two gang members bicycled up to a crowded playground and opened fire. The goal was to kill a member of a rival gang.[50]

In Washington, D.C.:
An 18-year-old pleaded guilty to first-degree murder of a 12-year-old boy. He beat and shot the victim whom he had warned to stay out of the gang war. When the warning was not heeded, he concluded that the victim "wanted to be dead."[51]

Violence and police raids are part of everyday life in many inner-city housing projects.

In Santa Monica, California:
Within a 2-week period, gang wars left five people dead and three seriously injured. In the previous year Santa Monica had one homicide.[52]

The new subculture that emerged in the 1980s and continues into the new century combines violence, which has become more vicious than in earlier years, with big business in drug trafficking (Table 6.1).[53] It is estimated that one gang alone, the Eight Trey Gangster Crips, distributed hundreds of kilos of crack and cocaine worth over $10 million on the streets of Los Angeles and five other cities, as far east as Birmingham, Alabama, and Atlanta. The FBI reports that this network is only one of perhaps a hundred more operating across the country.[54] Rival gangs kill for more than simply turf. In cities around the world teenagers are driving BMWs with Uzi submachine guns concealed under the driver's seat and thousands of dollars in their pockets so that they can make bail at any moment. Movies like *Colors*, *American Me*, and *Boyz in the Hood* provide models for their activities.

Guns and Gangs

It is estimated that between 50 and 70 percent of gang members own or have access to weapons. In fact, gangs often judge each other by their firepower. Their arsenal of weapons includes sawed-off rifles and shotguns, semiautomatic weapons like the Uzi and the AK-47, all types of handguns, body armor, and explosives.[55] Gangs have "treasuries" to buy the sophisticated weapons that are now used on the street for resolving conflicts, for demonstrating bravery, for self-defense, and for protecting turf.

The National Center for Juvenile Justice and the FBI report that:

- From 1989 through 1997 nearly 20,000 juveniles were murdered in the United States.
- More than half of juvenile homicide victims are killed by a firearm.

:// Crime Surfing

www.ncjrs.org/html/ojjdp_yth_gang_prob_2001/summary.html

Would you like to find out more about the prevalence of gangs in various areas?

TABLE 6.1 Gang Control of Drug Distribution in Cities Across the United States

Level of Control	Percentage
All	1
More than half	29
Less than half	23
Less than one-fourth	41
None	6

Source: 1996 National Youth Gang Survey (Washington, D.C.: Office of Juvenile Justice and Delinquency Prevention, July 1999), p. 43.

- The percentage of juveniles killed with a firearm increased from 41 percent in 1980 to 56 percent in 1997.
- The juvenile arrest rate for weapons violations increased 44 percent from 1988 to 1997.[56]

Use of guns rather than knives and clubs turns violent events into life-and-death situations; gangs battle gangs in a kind of street guerrilla warfare. Drive-by shootings, in particular, have become a favored method of operation. A "drive-by" involves members of one gang driving into a rival gang's turf to shoot at someone, followed by a high-speed escape. Gang members take great pride in this hit-and-run technique. Often these encounters occur spontaneously, but they easily spiral into planned events. The sequence may be the following:

> A gang member shoots a rival gang member during an argument. The surviving rival or his friends get a gun and conduct a drive-by on the initial instigator or members of his gang at their home(s). During this retaliatory strike, a friend, family member or gang member is killed or seriously wounded. The original instigatory gang now views itself as the "passive victim" and sets out to get back at the new aggressor. This spiral which, in real time, can result in several drive-by shootings or other murders within a few hours, can and often does lead to protracted gang wars.[57]

> **:// Crime Surfing**
>
> www.dc.state.fl.us/pub/gangs/faq.html
>
> Find out more about types of gangs and their affiliations.

Some drive-bys are for "fun," some for defending gang honor, and others for getting rid of competition in the drug business.

FEMALE DELINQUENT SUBCULTURES

Traditionally, gang membership has been limited primarily to young, inner-city males. Theoretical and empirical studies in this area therefore focused on that population. More recently, however, gang membership has been changing. There are increasing numbers of white participants, members younger than 14, members older than 18, and females (see Table 6.2). Little was known about female subcultures. Researchers are now focusing more attention on the two types of female gangs—those that are affiliates of male gangs and those that consist of all females.

Early Research

In one of the few early studies, done in 1958, Albert Cohen and James Short suggested that female delinquent subcultures, like their male counterparts, were composed of members who had been frustrated in their efforts to achieve conventional goals (respectability, marriage, status). The girls had drifted into a subculture that offered them substitute status, albeit outside legitimate society. Drug use and prostitution became all but inevitable. Since the research that led to this finding was conducted among mostly lower-class black females, Cohen and Short admitted that their findings probably could not be generalized to all female delinquent subcultures.[58]

Recent Studies

Twenty-six years after these tentative findings, Anne Campbell published the first major work on the lifestyle of female gang members in New York. She spent two years with three gangs: one Hispanic (the Sex Girls), one black (the Five Percent Nation), and one racially mixed (the Sandman Ladies). Campbell's findings demonstrate that girls, like boys, join gangs for mutual support, protection, and a

TABLE 6.2 Demographic Profile of Gang Members, 1995

Total number	846,000
Sex	
Male	90%
Female	10
Race-ethnicity	
Hispanic	44%
Black	35
White	14
Asian	5
Other	2
Age	
14 or younger	16%
15–17	34
18–24	37
25 or older	13

Source: *Juvenile Offenders and Victims: 1999 National Report* (Washington, D.C.: Office of Juvenile Justice and Delinquency Prevention, 1999).

sense of belonging. They, too, gain status by living up to the value system of their gang. Campbell also noted that these youngsters will probably end up, as their mothers have, living on welfare assistance in a ghetto apartment. Men will come and go in their lives, but after their gang days the women feel they have lost their support group and are constantly threatened by feelings of isolation.[59]

Between 10 and 25 percent of gang members nationwide are female. In major cities the number is higher. Among 214 wards of the state of California in 1990, 32 percent were gang members, ages 14 to 21.[60] Among them they had 289 arrests. All but 3 of the women had been arrested for a violent crime—22 murders, 31 armed robberies, and 31 assaults with a deadly weapon.

Many of the female gangs are affiliates of male gangs, often offering support for the young men they refer to as their "homeboys." Initiation rites for females involve either a "jump-in, jump-out" in which they are beaten by four or five gang members or a "sex-in, sex-out" in which they have sexual relations with all male members.[61] Some female affiliate gangs, however, have their own initiation rites (which mimic male ceremonies but are usually much less violent) and their own gang colors. A strong allegiance exists among gang members. For many of these youngsters the gang takes the place of a family. Shorty, a member of Los Angeles's Tiny Diablas, had no family except a grandmother, who had given up on trying to control her. Shorty's mother, who had been a gang member, abandoned her at an early age. Her father overdosed on heroin and was identified by a tattoo of Shorty's name. Her aunt had a teardrop tattoo next to her eye, to signify one year in jail; her uncle had two teardrops. Such family ties are not unusual among gang members.[62]

Not all female gangs have male affiliates. In a study of crack sales and violence among gangs in San Francisco, researchers interviewed members of an all-female group, the Potrero Hill Posse (PHP).[63] This independent group was formed in the mid-1980s when the females realized that their gang-affiliated boyfriends were not distributing the profits and labor of their crack sales fairly. The PHP young women run "rock houses" (outlets for crack sales, lent by tenants who receive a small quantity of crack in return), procure other women to provide sex to male customers, and engage in a major shoplifting business that fills orders placed by people who do not want to pay retail prices.

Gang members rely on the gang for assistance ("Nobody will mess with me . . . because they know that I got back-up. I got back-up. I got my homegirls behind me. And whatever goes down with me, they are going to have to take up with them") and for status ("It [membership] means being bad, being tough, and being able to walk without . . . you know, everybody just respects me because they know I am one of the Potrero Hill Posse girls").[64]

Overall, according to gang research done as part of the Rochester Youth Development Study, the extent and nature of female participation has changed considerably over the last few decades. The findings show increased participation in gangs (in this study, about equal to that of males) and in gang-related activities, including serious delinquent acts and drug abuse.[65]

> **Did You Know?**
>
> . . . that 400,000 nonmarital teen births occurred in 2000?

Of Immediate Concern

The Girls in the Gang

Psychologist Anne Campbell studied female gangs in New York City and published her findings in her 1984 book, *The Girls in the Gang*. She summarizes some of her observations here:

> All the girls in the gang come from families that are poor. Many have never known their fathers. Most are immigrants from Puerto Rico. As children the girls moved from apartment to apartment as they were evicted or burned out by arsonists. Unable to keep any friends they managed to make and alienated from their mothers, whose lack of English restricted their ability to control or understand their daughters' lives, the girls dropped out of school early and grew up on the streets. In the company of older kids and street-corner men, they graduated early into the adult world. They began to use drugs and by puberty had been initiated into sexual activity. By fifteen many were pregnant. Shocked, their mothers tried to pull them off the streets. Some sent their daughters back to relatives in Puerto Rico while they had their babies. Abortion was out of the question in this Catholic world.
>
> Those who stayed had "spoiled their identity" as good girls. Their reputations were marred before they ever reached adulthood. On the streets, among the gang members, the girls found a convenient identity in the female gang. Often they had friends or distant relatives who introduced them as "prospects." After a trial period, they could undertake the initiation rite: they had to fight an established member nominated by the godmother. What was at issue was not winning or losing but demonstrating "heart," or courage. Gangs do not welcome members who join only to gain protection. The loyalty of other gang members has to be won by a clear demonstration of willingness to "get down," or fight.
>
> Paradoxically, the female gang goes to considerable lengths to control the sexual behavior of its members. Although the neighborhood may believe they are fast women, the girls themselves do not tolerate members who sleep around. A promiscuous girl is a threat to the other members' relationships with their boyfriends. Members can take a boyfriend from among the male gang members (indeed, they are forbidden to take one from any other gang) but they are required to be monogamous. A shout of "Whore!" is the most frequent cause of fistfights among the female members.
>
> On the positive side, the gang provides a strong sense of belonging and sisterhood. After the terrible isolation of their lives, the girls acquire a ready-made circle of friends who have shared many of their experiences and who are always willing to support them against hostile words or deeds by outsiders. Fighting together generates a strong sense of camaraderie and as a bonus earns them the reputation of being "crazy." This reputation is extremely useful in the tough neighborhoods where they live. Their reputation for carrying knives and for solidarity effectively deters outsiders from challenging them. They work hard at fostering their tough "rep" not only in their deeds but in their social talk. They spend hours recounting and embroidering stories of fights they have been in. Behind all this bravado it is easy to sense the fear they work so hard to deny. Terrified of being victims (as many of them have already been in their families and as newcomers in their schools), they make much of their own "craziness"—the violent unpredictability that frightens away anyone who might try to harm them.[1]

A portrait of Hispanic teen female members of the Pico Rivera gang with one member holding her child.

Campbell demonstrates the commonality of violence in the lives of female gang members in the early 1980s. Today there is a growing concern over the increasing prevalence and severity of violence in some areas of the country.[2] The number of female gang members and the extent of changes in the use of violence are, however, still debated among researchers.[3]

Sources

1. Written by Anne Campbell. Adapted from Anne Campbell, *The Girls in the Gang* (New York: Basil Blackwell, 1984).
2. John M. Hagedorn, "Gang Violence in the Postindustrial Era," in *Youth Violence, Crime and Justice: A Review of Research,* vol. 24, eds. Michael Tonry and Mark H. Moore (Chicago: University of Chicago Press, 1998), pp. 365–419.
3. Margaret O'Brien, "At Least 16,000 Girls in Chicago's Gangs More Violent than Some Believe, Report Says," *Chicago Tribune,* Sept. 17, 1999, p. 5.

Questions for Discussion

1. How similar are Campbell's female gangs to the male gangs described in this chapter? Are there any significant differences?
2. Would you expect female gangs to become as involved in criminal activity as male gangs? Why or why not?

MIDDLE-CLASS DELINQUENCY

In Tucson, Arizona, a white middle-class teenager wearing gang colors died, a victim of a drive-by shooting as he stood with black and Hispanic members of the Bloods gang.

At Antelope Valley High School in Lancaster, California, about 50 miles north of Los Angeles, 200 students threw stones at a policeman who had been called to help enforce a ban on the gang outfits that have become a fad on some campuses....

A member of the South Bay Family gang in Hermosa Beach, a 21-year-old surfer called Road Dog, who said his family owned a chain of pharmacies, put it this way: "This is the 90's, man. We're the type of people who don't take no for an answer. If your mom says no to a kid in the 90's, the kid's just going to laugh." He and his friends shouted in appreciation as another gang member lifted his long hair to reveal a tattoo on a bare shoulder: "Mama tried."[66]

FIGURE 6.5 Jurisdictions reporting active gangs. Although the majority of gangs are in major cities, they are becoming more common in less-populated areas.

Area	Percentage
Rural areas	25%
Small cities	34%
Suburbs	57%
Big cities	74%

Source: *Juvenile Offenders and Victims: 1999 National Report* (Washington, D.C.: Office of Juvenile Justice and Delinquency Prevention, 1999), p. 78.

Most people think of gangs as synonymous with inner-city slums, low-income housing projects, turf wars, and a membership that often comes into conflict with law enforcement. But now gang lifestyle is moving to suburbia.[67] (See Figure 6.5.) Affluent youngsters are joining established gangs such as the Crips and the Bloods or forming their own gangs, sometimes referred to as "yuppie gangs."[68] Their activities can be as harmless as adherence to a particular dress code or as violent as a drive-by shooting. Experts have identified several types of suburban gangs.[69]

Delinquent Gangs. Delinquent gangs are similar to most inner-city gangs. Criminal activities include physical assaults, theft, burglary, and distribution of illegal drugs. The members seek money, peer recognition, the thrill of high-risk behavior, or even protection: "If you want to be able to walk the mall, you have to know you've got your boys behind you."[70] They typically adopt hand signals used by inner-city gangs.

Hate Gangs. These gangs, such as skinheads, attach themselves to an ideology that targets racial and ethnic groups. Physical assaults and even murder are justified by their belief system. Their numbers are growing rapidly. In 1988 there were 1,000 to 1,500 skinheads operating in 12 states. By June 1993, the number was close to 3,500, spread across 40 states.[71] According to the FBI, 9,730 hate crimes were committed by neo-Nazis, skinheads, and other right-wing extremist groups in 2001. Because of the difficulties in gathering hate-crime statistics, this number is considered only a small percentage of the actual figure.[72]

Satanic Gangs. These groups are affiliated with the controversial satanic cults. Their practices include the worship of specific gods, desecration of graveyards, use of a Ouija board to predict the future, ritualistic drug consumption, animal sacrifice, various witchcraft and pagan rituals, and submission to sexual abuse or pain. The common element for these gangs is heavy-metal music. (The name of one heavy-metal group, KISS, stands for Kids [or Knights] in Satan's Service.)[73] Satanic gang members can be identified by their dress: metal-spiked wrist cuffs, belts, anti-Christian items, and T-shirts labeled with heavy-metal band names such as Iron Maidens, Venom, Judas Priest, and Dio.[74]

HATE is shown by demeanor and facial expressions of Denver skinheads at a demonstration against Martin Luther King Day.

Explanations

Most explanations of middle-class delinquency are extensions of subcultural explanations of lower-class delinquency. Albert Cohen, for example, suggested that changes in the social structure have weakened the value traditionally associated with delay of gratification.[75] Some criminologists say that a growing number of middle-class youngsters no longer believe that the way to reach their goals is through hard work and delayed pleasure. They prefer reaping profits from quick drug sales or shoplifting goods that attract them. Behavior has become more hedonistic and more peer-oriented. While most of this youth subculture exhibits nondelinquent behavior, sometimes the pleasure-seeking activities have led to delinquent acts. Bored and restless, these youngsters seek to break the monotony with artificial excitement and conspicuous indulgence: fast cars, trendy clothes, alcohol, drugs, and sexual activity. Experts note that many affluent gang members come from broken, unstable, or extremely dysfunctional homes. Their problems stem from divorce, separation, physical or sexual abuse, or a drug- or alcohol-addicted parent.[76]

THEORY INFORMS POLICY

Subcultural theory assumes that individuals engage in delinquent or criminal behavior because (1) legitimate opportunities for success are blocked and (2) criminal values and norms are learned in lower-class slums. The theory was translated into action programs during the 1960s. Two presidents, John F. Kennedy and Lyndon Johnson, directed that huge sums of money be spent on programs to help move lower-class youths into the social mainstream.

MOBY

The best-known program, Mobilization for Youth (MOBY), was based on opportunity theory. It provided employment, social services, teacher training, legal aid, and other crime-prevention services to an area on New York's Lower East Side. The cost was over $12 million. MOBY ultimately became highly controversial. Many people accused it of being too radical, especially when neighborhood participants became involved in rent strikes, lawsuits charging discrimination, and public demonstrations. News of the conflict between supporters and opponents, and between the staff and the neighborhood it served, reached Congress, which made it clear that the point of the project was to reduce delinquency, not to reform society. Little was done to evaluate the program's success. The project was eventually abandoned, and the commission that had established it ceased to exist. The political climate had changed, and federal money was no longer available for sweeping social programs. However, MOBY's failure does not disprove the opportunity theory on which it was based. In 1995 the Office of Juvenile Justice and Delinquency Prevention (OJJDP) launched the Comprehensive Gang Model, a pilot project based on the same principles as MOBY. It is too early to say whether or not the Comprehensive Gang Model will succeed where MOBY failed, but the OJJDP project reflects the use of pilot projects and research in developing programs.[77]

Other Programs

Many other programs based on subcultural theory have attempted to change the attitudes and behavior of ghetto youngsters who have spent most of their lives learning unconventional street norms. Change is accomplished by setting up an extended-family environment for high-risk youths, one that provides positive role models, academic and vocational training, strict rules for behavior, drug treatment, health care, and other services. For many youths these programs provide the first warm, caring living arrangement they have ever had. One such program is the House of Umoja (a Swahili word for "unity") in Philadelphia.

At any given time about 25 black male teenage offenders live together as "sons" of the founder, Sister Fattah. Each resident signs a contract with Umoja obligating himself to help in the household, become an active part of the family group, study, and work in one of the program's businesses (a restaurant, a moving company, a painting shop) or elsewhere. By many measures this program is successful.

Programs similar to Umoja spread throughout the country; they include Argus in New York's South Bronx; Violent Juvenile Offender Research and Development programs in Chicago, Dallas, New Orleans, Los Angeles, and San Diego; and Neighborhood Anticrime Self-Help programs in Baltimore, Newark, Cleveland, Boston, Miami, and Washington, D.C. All have the same mission: to provide a bridge from a delinquent subcultural value system to a conventional one.[78]

Other means have been used to break up delinquent subcultures. Street workers, many of them former gang members (called "OGs," for "original gangsters"), serve as a "street-smart diplomatic corps" in many of the poorest ghettos in the country.[79] In Los Angeles, where gang members control many streets, the OGs work for the Community Youth Gang Service (a government-funded agency). Five nights a week more than 50 of these street workers cover the city, trying to settle disputes between rival gangs and to discourage nonmembers from joining them. They look for alternatives to violence, in baseball games, fairs, and written peace treaties. During a typical evening the street workers may try to head off a gang fight:

> *Parton* [*street worker*]: Hey, you guys, Lennox is going to be rollin' by here. . . .
> *Ms. Diaz* [*street worker*]: You with your back to the street, homeboy. They goin' to be lookin' for this car, some burgundy car.
> *Boy:* If they want to find me, they know where I'm at.
> *Ms. Diaz:* I'm tellin' you to be afraid of them. There are some girls here. You better tell them to move down the street. . . . We are goin' back over there to try to keep them there. Don't get lazy or drunk and not know what you're doin'. I know you don't think it's serious, but if one of your friends gets killed tonight, you will.
> *Boy:* It's serious, I know.
> *Ms. Diaz:* We're goin' to keep them in their 'hood, you just stay in yours for a while.
> *Boy:* All right.[80]

After two hours of negotiation, the fight was called off. There was plenty of work left for the team. They would continue the next day to help the gang members find jobs.

Window to the World

America's Changing Ethnic Gangs

Irish, Italian, and Puerto Rican inner-city gangs have been replaced or augmented by gangs reflecting the new waves of immigrants to America, who seek the protection and group loyalty that gang membership traditionally was thought to have provided.

Most Mexican gang members, for example, are migrants from rural areas where gangs do not exist. At home they had family support. That support all but vanishes when they find themselves in the ghetto neighborhoods of American cities. Other Latin American and Caribbean cultures are also represented in the American gang structure. Jamaican gangs, specializing in the drug and weapons trade, are known for their violence. Colombian gangs have engaged in multiple armed robberies in several states, focusing on jewelers and other businesses. The Colombians have established an arsenal of technologically advanced equipment to commit their robberies and to escape detection. They even use cosmetic surgery to alter their appearances and change their fingerprints. Asian gangs, among them Vietnamese, Korean, Cambodian, Laotian, and Chinese, have sprung up on both coasts and in the middle of the country. Other groups hail from the Pacific Islands. The Tongan Crips gangsters and Sons of Samoa, demonstrating their macho values, have spread fear in once quiet, pastoral Utah. The Vietnamese have established a reputation as "housebreakers"; they burglarize the homes of other, wealthier Vietnamese immigrants.

Chinese gangs have been the greatest surprise for American law enforcement. Traditionally, Chinese-Americans were considered particularly law-abiding. This picture changed drastically with the easing of immigration restrictions that allowed larger numbers of younger Chinese from the mainland, as well as Taiwan and Hong Kong, into the country. These new arrivals have formed gangs.

Chinese gangs, although small in number (an estimated 2,000 members nationwide), engage in the smuggling of illegal Chinese immigrants by the tens of thousands annually. Often these immigrants are enslaved until the transportation fee (presently about $30,000 per person) has been paid off. These gangs also engage in major heroin trafficking and protection of the gambling clubs popular in Chinese communities. Their main business is extortion. Their strength, and tradition of ferocious violence, derives from their affiliation with Chinese secret societies known as "Triads."

The end of the cold war and the collapse of the Soviet Union have opened new windows of opportunity for Russian entrepreneurs—legal and illegal. A thriving Russian colony in Brighton Beach, New York, is the seat of Russian gangs as ruthless as those of any other ethnic origin. They smuggle gold and Russian army surplus—often passing the goods off as high-grade Japanese products. They deal in bootlegged gasoline. They use extortion and murder to strengthen their operations. Some of the gang leaders are experienced criminals with long histories of economic offenses in Russia. Russians call them "thieves-in-law."

Gangs made up of immigrant Albanians and former Yugoslavians have been committing burglaries along the East Coast since the early 1990s. Their targets are retail shops, banks, and automated teller machines. They specialize in supermarket safes because these stores generally have a great deal of cash on hand. Their techniques are highly sophisticated, not the run-of-the-mill break and enter. The burglars rarely carry guns; every detail is carefully planned (oxygen tanks may be brought for their safe-cracking torches); and they are equipped with an arsenal of tools, gloves, and walkie-talkies. Often they cut phone lines to set off alarms, wait until the police come and go, and then strike.

Some gangs have ties to their homelands; others are independent. Some are national; others are strictly local. Some have memberships of young adults; others, of teenagers. Some are involved in the sale and use of drugs and arms; others are geared primarily toward survival in tough neighborhoods. Indeed, if ethnic gangs have any common characteristic beyond a membership of a single ethnic group, it is probably the diversity of patterns of formation and operation. That diversity is likely to continue as the country's ever changing immigrant populations result in the emergence of new gangs.

Source

Jayson Blair, "Killing of Ex-Officer Is Linked to Gang on Nationwide Robbery Spree," *New York Times,* Sept. 12, 1999, p. 37.

Questions for Discussion

1. Dealing with gangs may require infiltrating them. What if there are no young police officers from the gangs' ethnic groups? What else can be done?
2. Are there ways of dealing with ethnic gangs outside the criminal justice system? What of the role of elders, who are highly respected in many ethnic cultures?

PART II Explanations of Crime and Criminal Behavior

Getting Out: Gang Banging or the Morgue

The most difficult problem that counselors and street workers face is the power of gangs over their members. Gangs, through loyalty and terror, make it almost impossible for members to quit. Many gang members would gladly get out, but any move to leave leads to gang banging or the morgue. A Wichita, Kansas, group, the church-sponsored Project Freedom, has created an "underground railroad," a network of local contacts that leads families with gang members to anonymity and freedom out of state.[81]

Gangs, once a local problem, have become a national concern. The federal antigang budget goes primarily to police and prosecution. In 1992 the Department of Justice spent $500 million on law enforcement, while the Department of Health and Human Services spent $40 million on prevention programs over a three-year period.[82] Experts agree that unless we put more money into educational and socioeconomic programs, there is little likelihood that America's gang problems will lessen as we enter the twenty-first century.

REVIEW

In the decade between the mid-1950s and mid-1960s, criminologists began to theorize about the development and content of youth subcultures and the gangs that flourish within them. Some suggested that lower-class males, frustrated by their inability to meet middle-class standards, set up their own norms by which they could gain status. Often these norms clashed with those of the dominant culture. Other investigators have refuted the idea that delinquent behavior stems from a rejection of middle-class values. They claim that lower-class values are separate and distinct from middle-class values and that it is the lower-class value system that generates delinquent behavior.

Gangs of the 1990s show increasing violence and reliance on guns. They are involved in large profit-making activities such as drug distribution. The number of homicides is rising.

Explanations of female delinquent subcultures and middle-class delinquency are an extension of subcultural explanations of lower-class delinquency. While the theories of reaction formation, the subculture of violence, and differential opportunity differ in some respects, they all share one basic assumption—that delinquent and criminal behaviors are linked to the values and norms of the areas where youngsters grow up.

CRIMINOLOGY & PUBLIC POLICY

"Many aspects of female gang functioning and the lives of female gang members remain a mystery because relatively few researchers have considered female gangs worthy of study. In addition, researchers face serious obstacles to the study of female gangs and, because of these obstacles, they often settle for unrepresentative samples. Gangs are highly suspicious of researchers and cooperate with them only under unusual circumstances. Female gang members, in particular, have been averse to talking about sexual abuse, whether it occurred at home or within the gang . . . . Unfortunately, female gang members have received little programmatic attention." (Source: Joan Moore and John Hagedorn, *Female Gangs: A Focus on Research* (Washington, D.C.: OJJDP, 2001).)

Questions for Discussion Can you conceive of other reasons why female gangs have been overlooked? After reviewing the work of Prof. Anne Campbell (p. 160), what kinds of programs do you suppose would help female gang members make a transition to prosocial activities and lifestyles? In what ways must these programs differ from those proposed for male gang members?

YOU BE THE CRIMINOLOGIST

You are a consultant called in to address the rise in female gang activity and violence. On what theory or theories would you base your intervention? Are the theories based on male delinquency sufficient? Are gender-based theories necessary?

KEY TERMS

The numbers next to the terms refer to the pages on which the terms are defined.

differential opportunity theory (148)

reaction formation (145)

subculture (144)

subcultures of violence (151)

CHAPTER 7
Social Control Theory

What Is Social Control?

Theories of Social Control
  The Microsociological Perspective: Hirschi
  Social Bonds
  Empirical Tests of Hirschi's Theory
  Evaluation: Hirschi's Social Control Theory

Social Control and Drift

Personal and Social Control
  Failure of Control Mechanisms
  Stake in Conformity

Containment Theory
  Empirical Tests of Containment Theory
  Evaluation: Containment Theory

Recent Theoretical Explorations
  Developmental/Life Course Theory
  Integrated Theory
  General Theories

Theory Informs Policy
  Family
  School
  Neighborhood

REVIEW

CRIMINOLOGY & PUBLIC POLICY

YOU BE THE CRIMINOLOGIST

KEY TERMS

Boxes
  Of Immediate Concern: *Defying Convention and Control: "In Your Face"*
  From the Pages of *The New York Times*: *Social Control—Punishing the Cheat*
  Window to the World: *Nations with Low Crime Rates*

Special Features
  Crime Surfing
  Did You Know?

KEY TERMS
attachment
belief
commitment
conformity
containment theory
direct control
drift
indirect control
internalized control
involvement
macrosociological studies
microsociological studies
social control theory
synnomie

North Korean Communist Party in May Day Stadium as 100,000 spectators witness a 25,000 person display of political might.

Obedience, respect for authority, shared goals and values, commitment to and investment in custom and convention—this is the glue that makes a successful sports team, no less a powerful social order.

In William Golding's novel *Lord of the Flies,* a group of boys are stranded on an island far from civilization. Deprived of any superior authority—all the grown-ups, their parents, their teachers, the government, that have until now determined their lives—they begin to decide on a structure of government for themselves. Ralph declares: "We can't have everybody talking at once. We'll have to have 'Hands up' like at school. . . . Then I'll give him the conch."

"Conch?"

"That's what this shell is called. I'll give the conch to the next person to speak. He can hold it when he's speaking!" . . .

Jack was on his feet.

"We'll have rules!" he cried excitedly. "Lots of rules!"[1]

But do rules alone guarantee the peaceful existence of the group? Who and what ensure compliance with the rules? Social control theorists study these questions.

Strain theories, as we noted, study the question of why some people violate norms, for example, by committing crimes. Social control theorists are interested in learning why people conform to norms. Control theorists take it for granted that drugs can tempt even the youngest schoolchildren; that truancy can lure otherwise good children onto a path of academic failure and lifetime unemployment; that petty fighting, petty theft, and recreational drinking are attractive features of adolescence and young adulthood. They ask why people conform in the face of so much temptation and peer pressure. The answer is that juveniles and adults conform to the law in response to certain controlling forces in their lives. They become criminals when the controlling forces are weak or absent.

WHAT IS SOCIAL CONTROL?

What are those controlling forces? Think about the time and energy you have invested in your school, your job, your extracurricular activities. Think about how your academic or vocational ambition would be jeopardized by persistent delinquency. Think about how the responsibility of homework has weighed you down, setting limits on your free time. Reflect on the quality of your relationships with your family, friends, and acquaintances and on how your attachment to them has encouraged you to do right and discouraged you from doing wrong.

Social control theory focuses on techniques and strategies that regulate human behavior and lead to conformity, or obedience to society's rules—the influences of family and school, religious beliefs, moral values, friends, and even beliefs about government. The more involved and committed a person is to conventional activities and values and the greater the attachment to parents, loved ones, and friends, the less likely that person is to violate society's rules and to jeopardize relationships and aspirations.

The concept of social control emerged in the early 1900s in a volume by E. A. Ross, one of the founders of American sociology. According to Ross, belief systems, rather than specific laws, guide what people do and universally serve to control behavior. Since that time, the concept has taken on a wide variety of meanings. Social control has been conceptualized as representing practically any phenomenon that leads to conformity. The term is found in studies of laws, customs, mores, ideologies, and folkways describing a host of controlling forces.[2]

Is there danger in defining social control so broadly? It depends on your perspective. To some sociologists, the vagueness of the term—its tendency to encompass almost the entire field of sociology—has significantly decreased its value as a concept.[3] To others, the value of social

Learning to play by the rules: the Harlem Little League team was challenged at the Little League World Series at Williamsport, Pennsylvania, August 2002, for having outside players on their team.

168

control lies in its representation of a mechanism by which society regulates its members. According to this view, social control defines what is considered deviant behavior, what is right or wrong, and what is a violation of the law.

Theorists who have adopted this orientation consider laws, norms, customs, mores, ethics, and etiquette to be forms of social control. Donald Black, a sociologist of law, noted: "Social control is found whenever people hold each other to standards, explicitly or implicitly, consciously or not: on the street, in prison, at home, at a party."[4]

If an example would help, consider that as recently as 20 years ago there were no legal restrictions, norms, or customs regulating the smoking of cigarettes in public places. The surgeon general's declaration in 1972 that secondhand smoke poses a health hazard ushered in two decades of controls over behavior that not too long ago was considered sociable—if not sophisticated and suave.

At present most states have laws restricting or banning smoking in public places. Los Angeles became the 32nd city in California to outlaw smoking in all its restaurants.[5] In April 2003, New York City did the same. The U.S. Supreme Court followed, holding that it is "cruel and unusual punishment" to expose prison inmates to levels of tobacco smoke that place their health at risk. Laws, norms, customs, and etiquette relating to smoking exert strong controls over this behavior.

THEORIES OF SOCIAL CONTROL

Why is social control conceptualized in such different ways? Perhaps because social control has been examined from both a macrosociological and a microsociological perspective. Macrosociological studies explore formal systems for the control of groups:

- The legal system, laws, and particularly, law enforcement
- Powerful groups in society
- Social and economic directives of governmental or private groups

These types of control can be either positive—that is, they inhibit rule-breaking behavior by a type of social guidance—or negative—that is, they foster oppressive, restrictive, or corrupt practices by those in power.[6]

The microsociological perspective is similar to the macrosociological approach in that it, too, explains why people conform. Microsociological studies, however, focus on informal systems. Researchers collect data from individuals (usually by self-report methods), are often guided by hypotheses that apply to individuals as well as groups, and frequently make reference to or examine a person's internal control system.

The Microsociological Perspective: Hirschi

Travis Hirschi has been the spokesperson of the microsociological perspective since the publication of his *Causes of Delinquency* in 1969. He is not, however, the first scholar to examine the extent of individual social control and its relationship to delinquency. In 1957 Jackson Toby introduced the notion of individual "commitment" as a powerful determining force in the social control of behavior.[7] Scott Briar and Irving Piliavin extended Toby's thesis by advancing the view that the extent of individual commitment and conformity plays a role in decreasing the likelihood of deviance. They noted that the degree of an adolescent's commitment is reflected in relationships with adult authority figures and with friends and is determined in part by "belief in God, affection for conventionally behaving peers, occupational aspirations, ties to parents, desire to perform well at school, and fear of material deprivations and punishments associated with arrest."[8]

Briar and Piliavin were not entirely satisfied with control dimensions alone, however, and added another factor: individual motivation to be delinquent. This motivation may stem from a person's wish to "obtain valued goods, to portray courage in the presence of, or to belong to, peers, to strike out at someone who is disliked, or simply to get his kicks."[9]

Hirschi was less interested in the source of an individual's motivation to commit delinquent acts than in the reasons people do not commit such acts. He claimed that social control theory explains conformity and adherence to rules, not deviance. It is thus not a crime-causation theory in a strict sense but a theory of prosocial behavior used by criminologists to explain deviance.

Social Bonds

Hirschi posited four social bonds that promote socialization and conformity: attachment, commitment, involvement, and belief. The stronger these bonds, he claimed, the less likelihood of delinquency.[10] To test this hypothesis, he administered a self-report questionnaire to 4,077 junior and senior high school students in California (see Table 7.1) that measured both involvement in delinquency and the strength of the four social bonds. Hirschi found that weakness in any of the bonds was associated with delinquent behavior.

Attachment. The first bond, attachment, takes three forms: attachment to parents, to school (teachers), and to peers. According to Hirschi, youths who have formed a significant attachment to a parent refrain from delinquency because the consequences of such an act might jeopardize that relationship. The bond of affection between a parent and a child thus becomes a primary deterrent to criminal activities.[11] Its strength depends on the depth and quality of parent-child interaction. The parent-child bond forms a path through which conventional ideals and expectations can pass. This bond is bolstered by:

- The amount of time the child spends with parents, particularly the presence of a parent at times when the child is tempted to engage in criminal activity
- The intimacy of communication between parent and child
- The affectional identification between parent and child[12]

Next Hirschi considered the importance of the school. As we saw in Chapter 6, Hirschi linked inability to function well in school to delinquency through the following chain of events: Academic incompetence leads to poor school performance; poor school performance results in a dislike of school; dislike of school leads to rejection of teachers and administrators

TABLE 7.1 Items from Travis Hirschi's Measure of Social Control

1. In general, do you like or dislike school?
   A. Like it
   B. Like it and dislike it about equally
   C. Dislike it

2. How important is getting good grades to you personally?
   A. Very important
   B. Somewhat important
   C. Fairly important
   D. Completely unimportant

3. Do you care what teachers think of you?
   A. I care a lot
   B. I care some
   C. I don't care much

4. Would you like to be the kind of person your father is?
   A. In every way
   B. In most ways
   C. In some ways
   D. In just a few ways
   E. Not at all

5. Did your mother read to you when you were little?
   A. No
   B. Once or twice
   C. Several times
   D. Many times, but not regularly
   E. Many times, and regularly
   F. I don't remember

6. Do you ever feel that "there's nothing to do"?
   A. Often
   B. Sometimes
   C. Rarely
   D. Never

Source: Travis Hirschi, *Causes of Delinquency* (Berkeley: University of California Press, 1969).

as authorities. The result is delinquency. Thus attachment to school depends on a youngster's appreciation for the institution, perception of how he or she is received by teachers and peers, and level of achievement in class.

Hirschi found that attachment to parents and school overshadows the bond formed with peers:

> As was true for parents and teachers, those most closely attached to or respectful of their friends are least likely to have committed delinquent acts. The relation does not appear to be as strong as was the case for parents and teachers, but the ideas that delinquents are unusually dependent upon their peers, that loyalty and solidarity are characteristic

PART II **Explanations of Crime and Criminal Behavior**

of delinquent groups, that attachment to adolescent peers fosters nonconventional behavior, and that the delinquent is unusually likely to sacrifice his personal advantage to the "requirements of the group" are simply not supported by the data.[13]

Commitment. Hirschi's second group of bonds consists of commitment to or investment in conventional lines of action—that is, support of and participation in social activities that tie the individual to the society's moral or ethical code. Hirschi identified a number of stakes in conformity or commitments: vocational aspirations, educational expectations, educational aspirations.

Many programs and institutions currently strive to nurture and encourage such aspirations. One such institution is the Pioneer Academy of Electronics, established soon after the 1992 riots in South-Central Los Angeles. Founded on "academic rigor, real work opportunities, decision-making responsibilities, a teacher who serves as a mentor, and a peer group that reinforces positive behavior," the Pioneer Academy gives inner-city high school students an opportunity to immerse themselves in something other than everyday gang activity. The academy's commitment to providing one-on-one interaction and training has changed the aspirations and work ethic of its students. Gilbert Ybarra, a prospective graduate, attests to its positive impact. Before enrollment in the academy, Gilbert opted for play over work, an attitude that was reflected in his high school grades and attendance. Soon thereafter, he was a proud and confident leader among his peers, excelling in his vocational pursuits, and aspiring to be the first in his family to attend college.[14]

Though Hirschi's theory is at odds with the competing theories of Albert Cohen and Richard Cloward and Lloyd Ohlin (Chapter 6), Hirschi provided empirical support for the notion that the greater the aspiration and expectation, the more unlikely delinquency becomes. Also, "students who smoke, those who drink, and those who date are more likely to commit delinquent acts; ... the more the boy is involved in adult activities, the greater his involvement in delinquency."[15]

Involvement. Hirschi's third bond is involvement, or preoccupation with activities that promote the interests of society. This bond is derived from involvement in school-related activities (such as homework) rather than in working-class adult activities (such as smoking and drinking). A person who is busy doing conventional things has little time for deviant activities.

With this premise in mind, several regional schools will soon be following the example set by Parrot Middle School in Southwest Florida. Parrot Middle School currently offers its students an invaluable service. As part of an after-school program that provides counseling and tutoring services, students have been given the opportunity to participate in a diverse range of recreational courses, including martial arts, gymnastics, home economics, computer basics, and art. The program is designed to provide constructive pastimes for youths formerly left unsupervised during the interim between the end of the school day and that of the typical workday.[16]

Belief. "This type of prejudice insults me as an individual, but I am helpless because I can't vote. Then again, it's not as if any of the new legislation is affecting me, right? Why should I have any say in my own life? After all, I'm just a teen."

Jeff Lofvers's sentiments reflect much of Florida's teenage population. As of July 1, 1996, the state of Florida enacted a curfew restricting late-night driving for all licensed drivers under the age of 18. Between the hours of 11 P.M. and 6 A.M., 16-year-olds cannot legally drive, unless accompanied by a licensed driver at least 21 years old. The same applies to 17-year-olds between 1 A.M. and 6 A.M. "It amazes me that my friends and I can walk around town

---

:// Crime Surfing

www.street-soldiers.org/

Hirschi identified four social bonds that promote socialization: attachment, commitment, involvement, and belief. How do the programs and resources of the Omega Boys Club promote a commitment to conventional lines of action?

These girl scouts on a canoe trip in the Tampa area show teamwork—attachment to peers: one of Hirschi's ways of fighting delinquency.

as late as we want, yet we're not allowed to be safely locked in our cars past 11 P.M.," protested one angry teen. And another's defiant response when asked to comment on the anticipated effectiveness of this law? "[I]f they (legislators) are trying to trap us in our homes, it won't work."[17]

The last of the bonds, **belief,** consists of assent to the society's value system. The value system of any society entails respect for its laws and for the people and institutions that enforce them. The results of Hirschi's survey lead to the conclusion that if young people no longer believe laws are fair, their bond to society weakens, and the probability that they will commit delinquent acts increases.

Empirical Tests of Hirschi's Theory

Hirschi's work has inspired a vast number of studies. We can examine only a small selection of some of the more significant research.

Michael Hindelang studied rural boys and girls in grades 6 through 12 on the East Coast. His self-report delinquency measure and questionnaire items were very similar to those devised by Hirschi. Hindelang found few differences between his results and those of Hirschi. Two of those differences, however, were significant. First, he found no relationship between attachment to mother and attachment to peers. Hirschi had observed a positive relationship (the stronger the attachment to the mother, the stronger the attachment to peers). Second, involvement in delinquency was positively related to attachment to peers.[18] Hirschi had found an inverse relationship (the stronger the attachment to peers, the less the involvement in delinquency).

In another study, criminologists administered a self-report questionnaire to 3,056 male and female students in three Midwestern states. The researchers were critical of Hirschi's conceptualization of both commitment and involvement, finding it difficult to understand how he separated the two. Serious involvement, they argued, is quite unlikely without commitment. They combined commitment and involvement items and ended up with only three bonds: attachment, commitment, and belief.[19]

The study related these bonds to alcohol and marijuana use, use of strong drugs, minor delinquent behavior, and serious delinquent behavior. The results suggested that strong social bonds were more highly correlated with less-serious deviance than with such delinquent acts as motor vehicle theft and assault. Also, the social bonds were more predictive of deviance in girls than in boys. Moreover, criminologists who conducted this study noticed that the commitment bond (now joined with involvement) was more significantly correlated with delinquent behavior than were attachment and belief.

Other researchers administered questionnaires to 2,213 10th-grade boys at 86 schools, seeking to answer three questions: First, are Hirschi's four bonds distinct entities? Second, why did Hirschi name only four bonds? Third, why were some factors that are related to educational and occupational aspiration (such as ability and family socioeconomic status) omitted from his questionnaire? The researchers constructed new scales for measuring attachment, commitment, involvement, and belief. They used a self-report measure to assess delinquency. These researchers found little that is independent or distinctive about any of the bonds.[20]

Robert Agnew provided the first longitudinal test of Hirschi's theory by using data on 1,886 boys in the 10th and 11th grades. Eight social control scales (parental attachment, grades, dating index, school attachment, involvement, commitment, peer attachment, and belief) were examined at two periods in relation to two self-report scales (one measuring total delinquency and the other measuring seriousness of delinquency). Agnew found the eight control scales to be strongly correlated with the self-reported delinquency, but the social control measures did little to predict the extent of future delinquency reported at the second testing. Agnew concluded that the importance of Hirschi's control theory has probably been exaggerated.[21]

Most of the recent empirical work on Hirschi's theory explores the relationship between social bonds and other competing theories.[22] Researchers have discovered that the explanatory power of social control theory is enhanced dramatically when joined with other structural and process theories.

Evaluation: Hirschi's Social Control Theory

While social control theory has held a prominent position in criminology for several decades, it is not without weaknesses. For example, social control theory seeks to explain delinquency, not adult crime. It concerns attitudes, beliefs, desires, and behaviors that, though deviant, are often characteristic of adolescents. This is unfortunate because there has long been evidence that social bonds are also significant explanatory factors in postadolescent behavior.[23]

Questions also have been raised about the bonds. Hirschi claims that antisocial acts result from a lack of affective values, beliefs, norms, and attitudes that inhibit delinquency. But these terms are never clearly defined.[24] Critics have also faulted Hirschi's work for other reasons:

- Having too few questionnaire items that measure social bonds
- Failing to describe the chain of events that results in defective or inadequate bonds
- Creating an artificial division of socialized versus unsocialized youths
- Suggesting that social control theory explains why delinquency occurs, when in fact it typically explains no more than 50 percent of delinquent behavior and only 1 to 2 percent of the variance in future delinquency[25]

Despite the criticisms, Hirschi's work has made a major contribution to criminology. The mere fact that a quarter-century of scholars have tried to validate and replicate it testifies to its importance.

Furthermore, research using and extending Hirschi's constructs has become increasingly sophisticated. Recent research coming from the Rochester Youth Development Study, for example, has considered not only the role of weakened bonds to family and school in promoting delinquency but also the role of delinquent behavior in attenuating the strength of those very bonds. Criminologists have refined Hirschi's constructs so that the effects of social control on delinquency, as well as the effects of delinquency on social control, are considered.[26]

Finally, Hirschi's conception of social bonds has complemented competing explanations of group-level criminality such as gang behavior (see discussion of subcultural theories in Chapter 6). Social control is now discussed in relation to community, family, school, peer group, and individual-level factors (see Table 7.2).

TABLE 7.2 Risk Factors for Youth Gang Membership
How powerful is social control theory? Consider the premise of this theory in relation to the risk factors for gang membership.

Domain	Risk Factors
Community	Social disorganization, including poverty and residential mobility Organized lower-class communities Underclass communities Presence of gangs in the neighborhood Availability of drugs in the neighborhood Availability of firearms Barriers to and lack of social and economic opportunities Lack of social capital Cultural norms supporting gang behavior Feeling unsafe in neighborhood; high crime Conflict with social control institutions
Family	Family disorganization, including broken homes and parental drug/alcohol abuse Troubled families, including incest, family violence, and drug addiction Family members in a gang Lack of adult male role models Lack of parental role models Low socioeconomic status Extreme economic deprivation, family management problems, parents with violent attitudes, sibling antisocial behavior
School	Academic failure Low educational aspirations, especially among females Negative labeling by teachers Trouble at school Few teacher role models Educational frustration Low commitment to school, low school attachment, high levels of antisocial behavior in school, low achievement test cores, and identification as being learning disabled
Peer group	High commitment to delinquent peers Low commitment to positive peers Street socialization Gang members in class Friends who use drugs or who are gang members Friends who are drug distributors Interaction with delinquent peers
Individual	Prior delinquency Deviant attitudes Street smartness; toughness Defiant and individualistic character Fatalistic view of the world Aggression Proclivity for excitement and trouble *Locura* (acting in a daring, courageous, and especially crazy fashion in the face of adversity) Higher levels of normlessness in the context of family, peer group, and school Social disabilities Illegal gun ownership Early or precocious sexual activity, especially among females Alcohol and drug use Drug trafficking Desire for group rewards, such as status, identity, self-esteem, companionship, and protection Problem behaviors, hyperactivity, externalizing behaviors, drinking, lack of refusal skills, and early sexual activity Victimization

Source: James C. Howell, *Youth Gangs: An Overview* (Washington, D.C.: U.S. Department of Justice, 1998).

SOCIAL CONTROL AND DRIFT

In the 1960s David Matza developed a different perspective on social control that explains why some adolescents drift in and out of delinquency. According to Matza, juveniles sense a moral obligation to be bound by the law. A "bind" between a person and the law, something that creates responsibility and control, remains in place most of the time. When it is not in place, the youth may enter into a state of **drift**, or a period when he or she exists in limbo between convention and crime, responding in turn to the demands of each, flirting now with one, now with the other, but postponing commitment, evading decision. Thus, the person drifts between criminal and conventional actions.[27]

If adolescents are indeed bound by the social order, how do they justify their delinquent acts? The answer is that they develop techniques to rationalize their actions. These techniques are defense mechanisms that release the youth from the constraints of the moral order:

- Denial of responsibility. ("It wasn't my fault; I was a victim of circumstances.")
- Denial of injury. ("No one was hurt, and they have insurance, so what's the problem?")
- Denial of the victim. ("Anybody would have done the same thing in my position—I did what I had to do given the situation.")
- Condemnation of the condemner. ("I bet the judge and everyone on the jury has done much worse than what I was arrested for.")
- Appeal to higher loyalties. ("My friends were depending on me and I see them every day—what was I supposed to do?")[28]

Empirical support for drift theory has not been clear. Some studies show that delinquents consider these rationalizations valid,[29] while other research suggests that they do not. Later investigations also demonstrate that delinquents do not share the moral code or values of nondelinquents.[30]

PERSONAL AND SOCIAL CONTROL

Over the last 40 years support has increased for the idea that both social (external) and personal (internal) control systems are important forces in keeping individuals from committing crimes. In other words, Hirschi's social bonds and Matza's drift paradigm may not be enough by themselves to explain why people do not commit crimes.

Failure of Control Mechanisms

Albert J. Reiss, a sociologist, was one of the first researchers to isolate a group of personal and social control factors. According to Reiss, delinquency is the result of (1) a failure to internalize socially accepted and prescribed norms of behavior; (2) a breakdown of internal controls; and (3) a lack of social rules that prescribe behavior in the family, the school, and other important social groups.

To test these notions, Reiss collected control-related data on 1,110 juvenile delinquents placed on probation in Cook County (Chicago), Illinois. He examined three sources of information: (1) a diverse set of data on such variables as family economic status and moral ideals and/or techniques of control by parents during childhood; (2) community and institutional information bearing on control, such as residence in a delinquency area and home ownership; and (3) personal control information, such as ego or superego controls, from clinical judgments of social workers and written psychiatric reports. Reiss concluded that measures of both personal and social control seem "to yield more efficient prediction of delinquent recidivism than items which are measures of the strength of social control."[31]

Stake in Conformity

Imagine that your earliest childhood memory conjures up the sound of splintering wood as the police break down your front door, and the image of your grandmother being led away in handcuffs. You are 4 years old. What impact would such an image have on you? What if

Of Immediate Concern

Defying Convention and Control: "In Your Face"

The Lambeau Leap, the Ickey Shuffle, the Fun Bunch, and the Sack Dance. Perhaps you were fortunate enough to watch "Monday Night Football" and see a Green Bay Packer leap into a row of Cheesehead fans. Or maybe you have joined others in amazement as Ickey Woods shuffled across the artificial turf, moving side to side, as he passed the football back and forth—to himself. Who could forget the celebratory moves of the Washington Redskins' wide receivers after a touchdown—a collective and well-choreographed high five. What could be worse (or better) than the New York Jets' Mark Gastineau strutting, stomping, swaggering, gyrating, and wildly pounding his chest in delight over his unparalleled accomplishments?(1) The answer is the cut throat.

The cut throat, also known as the slash, is a simple and less elegant move—just run your hand across your throat in a symbolic gesture that, to Brett Favre, Ricky Watters, Akili Smith, and Keyshawn Johnson, means nothing more than "you cannot stop me" and "in your face." To the National Football League (NFL), however, it means more. The gesture is nothing less than a taunt that crosses the line. This is the line drawn between aggression, confidence, pride, celebration, and sportsmanship on one side—all necessary and important characteristics of the game—and a clear breach of contract between the offending players and fans on the other side. Football players, like their brothers in baseball and hockey, are expected to fight hard to win, to be brutal when necessary, to break bones and teeth when given no other choice, but all within a game that has a set of conventional rules—rules that reflect agreed-upon values; a strong and intractable commitment to the fans, who pay to watch, admire, and fantasize about playing in a game that is uniquely American. This is a familiar pact.

This pact reflects the very social bonds that promote and sustain our conventional life. That is why all of these violations of convention are so very easy to spot, even when referees fail to throw down their penalty flags. One commentator noted with wonderful sarcasm that there is a reason we do not do the same as Brett, Ricky, Akili, and Keyshawn in "real life." Just imagine:

> There is nothing too mundane to lord over a co-worker today. Start with hanging your coat. Turn this nonevent into an in-your-face "gotcha." Scream "This is my house." Let everybody know that you cannot and will not be stopped from putting your coat on that hanger.
>
> If you work in retail—let's say the jewelry counter at a department store—slam the register shut after a transaction, stare at the lady in housewares and menacingly trace a dollar sign in the air. . . .
>
> If you work in an airport control tower, punctuate every safe landing by throwing off your headset so everybody can see your face more clearly. Point up in the sky. Thump your chest.
>
> If you're a surgeon, heckle the patient for needing anesthesia. Don't just remove the tonsils. Say, "I got your tonsils right here." Then spike them.(2)

None of this is done, of course, because places of work reflect our relational attachments, our commitment to convention, a valued involvement in being productive, and our contribution to a shared belief system. With all the effort it takes to succeed—along with the good fortune—few want to lose out on their investment. Few knowingly violate a shared and agreed-to set of values—especially one that has a national time-honored tradition.

Now that the NFL (known in some circles as the "No Fun League") has sent letters to all 31 teams warning owners that large fines and significant game penalties will follow the cut throat, will Brett, Ricky, Akili, and Keyshawn conform? Social control theorists would say yes. Not only for fear of fines, but for fear of breaching custom and violating convention, and for fear of losing the admiration of the fans.

Brett Favre challenging custom and convention by completing the cutthroat gesture.

Sources

1. Harriet Barovick et al., "Banned Zone," *Time,* Dec. 6, 1999, p. 37.
2. Bud Shaw, "For Many Pro Athletes, Showtime Is All about Me," (New Orleans) *Times-Picayune,* Dec. 12, 1999, p. 7c.

Questions for Discussion

1. As NFL commissioner, would you impose strict rules on this kind of behavior?
2. Can you think of a sport where custom and convention allow for even more significant demonstrations of individual pride?

your formative years were spent in an impoverished urban environment where your mother and grandmother sold heroin out of your living room, your closest friends were high school dropouts with criminal records, and your adolescent confrontations did not involve the school bully demanding your lunch money, but rather the neighborhood drug dealer stopping by to settle overdue debts? Where would you be today?

Six years after the publication of Reiss's study, Jackson Toby proposed a different personal and social control model. Toby discussed the complementary role of neighborhood social disorganization and an individual's own stake in conformity. He agreed that the social disorganization of the slums explains why some communities have high crime rates while others do not: In slums both the community and the family are powerless to control members' behavior. Thieves and hoodlums usually come from such neighborhoods. But a great many law-abiding youngsters come from slums as well. Toby questioned how a theory that explained group behavior could account for individual differences in response to a poor environment. In other words, how can the theory of social disorganization explain why only a few among so many slum youths actually commit crimes?[32]

According to Toby, the social disorganization approach can explain why one neighborhood has a much higher crime rate than another, but not why one particular individual becomes a hoodlum while another does not. What accounts for the difference is a differing stake in **conformity,** or correspondence of behavior to society's patterns, norms, or standards. One person may respond to conditions in a "bad" neighborhood by becoming hostile to conventional values, perhaps because he or she knows that the chances for legitimate success are poor. Another person in the same neighborhood may maintain his or her stake in conformity and remain committed to abiding by the law. Toby reminds us that when we try to account for crime in general, we should look at both group-level explanations (social disorganization) and individual-level explanations (stake in conformity).

CONTAINMENT THEORY

A broad analysis of the relationship between personal and social controls is found in Walter Reckless's presentation of containment theory.[33] **Containment theory** assumes that for every individual there exists a containing external structure and a protective internal structure, both of which provide defense, protection, or insulation against delinquency.

According to Reckless, "outer containment," or the structural buffer that holds the person in bounds, can be found in the following components:

- A role that provides a guide for a person's activities
- A set of reasonable limits and responsibilities
- An opportunity for the individual to achieve status
- Cohesion among members of a group, including joint activity and togetherness
- A sense of belongingness (identification with the group)
- Identification with one or more persons within the group
- Provisions for supplying alternative ways and means of satisfaction (when one or more ways are closed)[34]

"Inner containment," or personal control, is ensured by:

- A good self-concept
- Self-control
- A strong ego
- A well-developed conscience
- A high frustration tolerance
- A high sense of responsibility

Reckless suggests that the probability of deviance is directly related to the extent to which internal pushes (such as a need for immediate gratification, restlessness, and hostility), external pressures (such as poverty, unemployment, and blocked opportunities), and external pulls are controlled by one's inner and outer containment. The primary containment factor is found

The New York Times

FROM THE PAGES OF

Social Control—Punishing the Cheat

In January 2002, scientists conducted a study based on the theories of social control and the evolution of punishment. The type of criminal they chose to study was "the cheat": the transgressor of fair play, the violator of accepted norms, the sneak who smiles with Chicklet teeth while ladling from the community till.

The good news is that scientists conclude that human beings are more willing than any other species to work for the common good—to cooperate with nonkin and to help out strangers, sometimes at great cost to themselves, as the death of hundreds of rescue workers at the World Trade Center only too sadly showed. This kind of behavior, scientists say, could not have evolved without a corresponding readiness to catch, and to punish, the cheat.

Researchers now theorize that a willingness, even eagerness, to punish transgressors of social control is essential to the maintenance of social harmony. In an article entitled, "Altruistic Punishment in Humans," Dr. Ernst Fehr of the University of Zurich and Dr. Simon Gachter of the University of St. Gallen in Switzerland state that people will seek to punish a cheat even when the punishment is costly to them and offers them no material benefit.

The European scientists conducted an experiment in which a group of people contributed money to a community project. Each participant decided how much to contribute, which in turn determined how much would be divided amongst participants at the end. In some groups, participants could do nothing about people who did not contribute very much. In other groups, freeloaders could be punished. The punishment was that contributors put more money into the till—and the freeloader had to put in three times as much. So, in essence, contributors had to "pay" to punish the transgressor. Even so, 84 percent of the participants chose to punish the cheats at least once.

Another findings was that when the game was carried out under no-punishment conditions, cooperation among group members quickly broke down, and participants contributed progressively less as the experiment went on. But when the opportunity to punish and be punished was applied, individual contributions rose sharply, and cooperation among group members grew stronger and stronger.

Scientists like Dr. Fehr have concluded that the drive to punish selfish transgressors is a basic human predilection, although this drive varies considerably in different cultures. As a rule, said Dr. Fehr, the more closely a society's economy is based on market rather than kinship ties, the more prevalent the use of altruistic punishment to bring others into line. In other words, the more likely a person is to be negotiating with nonrelatives—and hence the higher the chances that selfish freeloaders will seek to infiltrate the system—the more important it becomes that everybody play by the rules.

Source

Natalie Angier, "The Urge to Punish Cheats: It Isn't Merely Vengeance," *New York Times,* Jan. 22, 2002. Reprinted with permission.

Questions for Discussion

1. How do you explain the fact that most people were willing to punish the cheaters—even though it meant that they had to give up some of their hard-earned money themselves?
2. Why do you think that cooperation among participants broke down when they were not allowed to punish transgressors?

---

in self-concept, or the way one views oneself in relation to others, and to the world as well. A strong self-concept, coupled with some additional inner controls (such as a strong conscience and sense of responsibility), plus outer controls, makes delinquency highly unlikely.

Table 7.3 shows how the probability of deviance changes as an individual's inner and outer containment weakens. But why is it important to examine inner and outer controls simultaneously? Consider John, a college freshman, who had extensive community ties and strong family attachments and was valedictorian of his high school class. He also was a dealer in cocaine. All efforts to explain John's drug selling would prove disappointing if measures of social control were used alone. In other words, according to Hirschi's social control theory, John should be a conformist—he should focus his efforts on becoming a pharmacist or teacher. Containment theory, on the other hand, would be sensitive to the fact that John, while socially controlled and bonded by external forces, had a poorly developed self-concept, had an immature or undeveloped conscience, and was extremely impulsive. In short, he was driven to selling drugs as a result of a poor set of inner controls.

PART II   Explanations of Crime and Criminal Behavior

TABLE 7.3 The Probability of Deviance as Indicated by Inner and Outer Containment*

Outer Containment (Social Control)	Inner Containment (Personal Control)	
	Strong	Weak
Strong	+ +	+ −
Weak	+ −	− −

*+ + = very low; + − = average; − − = very high.

Source: Adapted from Walter C. Reckless, "A Non-Causal Explanation: Containment Theory," Excerpta Criminologia, **2** (1962): 131–132.

The idea that both internal and external factors are involved in controlling behavior has interested a number of scholars. Francis Ivan Nye, for example, developed the notion that multiple control factors determine human behavior. He argued that **internalized control,** or self-regulation, was a product of guilt aroused in the conscience when norms have been internalized. **Indirect control** comes from an individual's identification with noncriminals and a desire not to embarrass parents and friends by acting against their expectations.

Nye believes that social control involves "needs satisfaction," by which he means that control depends on how well a family can prepare the child for success at school, with peers, and in the workplace. Finally, **direct control**, a purely external control, depends on rules, restrictions, and punishments.[35]

Other researchers have looked at direct controls in different ways. Parental control, for example, may depend on such factors as a broken home, the mother's employment, and the number of children in the family; such factors indicate some loss of direct control. Once again we find mixed results. Some studies indicate very little relationship between a broken home and delinquency, except for minor offenses such as truancy and running away.[36] The same can be said about the consequences of a mother's employment and family size.[37] A national study of 1,886 males concluded, however, that direct parental control as measured by strictness and punitiveness is indeed correlated with delinquent behavior, and the study warned us not to dismiss this fact lightly. But the question remains open.[38]

Empirical Tests of Containment Theory

"Not when you're 15 and live in a crowded apartment with seven siblings, all younger than 6. Not when your mom has no job, is coming off drugs and belongs to the same gang as you, your drug-addicted dad, and all your relatives belong to. Not when you have to dress so carefully for the trip to class each day, because one mistake could kill. Does Calvin Klein know his

At a wilderness camp in Florida, adolescent probationers learn positive values at a program characterized by its rules and restrictions.

logo means 'Crips Killer' in Southeast L.A.? Green means you deal drugs. The wrong belt buckle or shoelace knot is big trouble if you meet rival gangs on your way."[39]

How can a child living in this neighborhood grow up to be a good, law-abiding citizen? How is he or she protected from the crime-producing influences lurking around each corner? To answer these questions, Reckless and his associates had high school teachers in a high-crime neighborhood nominate boys they believed would neither commit delinquent acts nor come into contact with police and juvenile court.

The 125 "good boys" scored high on a social responsibility test and low on a delinquency-proneness test. These boys avoided trouble, had good relations with parents and teachers, and had a good self-concept. They thought of themselves as obedient. Reckless concluded that nondelinquent boys follow conventional values even in bad neighborhoods if they maintain a positive self-image. It is this positive self-image that protects them. In a follow-up study the research team compared good boys with those nominated by teachers as "bad boys" (those they believed were headed for trouble). The good boys scored better on parental relation, self-image, and social responsibility tests. Far more of the bad boys had acquired police and juvenile court records.[40]

> **Did You Know?**
>
> ... that most criminologists favor social control theory as an explanation of criminal behavior?

Evaluation: Containment Theory

Containment theory, like Hirschi's social control theory, has received significant criticism.[41] The most damaging has come from Clarence Schrag, who contends that the terminology used is vague and poorly defined, that the theory is difficult to test empirically, and that the theory fails to consider why some poorly contained youths commit violent crimes while others commit property crimes.[42] These criticisms are not easy to answer. And because little empirical research has been done to test the findings of Reckless and his colleagues over the intervening 30 years, there is little evidence of the validity of containment theory.

TABLE 7.4 Examples of Recent Theoretical Explanations

Life Course/Developmental Theory	
Farrington	A combination of multiple personal (e.g., impulsivity), social (e.g., poor parental supervision), and environmental (e.g., low income) factors are associated with crime over the course of a lifetime.
Thornberry	Crime is a function of a dynamic social process that is determined by learning variables (e.g., association with delinquent peers), boundary variables (e.g., attachment and commitment to conventional activities), as well as social class, race, and gender.
Moffitt	Life-course-persistent offending is explained by faulty interactions between children and their parents, resulting in poor self-control and impulsivity. Adolescent-limited offending is traced to social mimicry, antisocial reinforcements, and models.
Le Blanc	An integrative, multilayered control theory that borrows heavily from competing perspectives explains criminality, the criminal, and the criminal event in both static and developmental terms.
Laub and Sampson	Crime causation must be viewed developmentally—in the context of the turning points in a criminal career.
Integrated Theory	
Weis	Crime results from an interaction between diminished social controls and influences from delinquent peers.
Elliott	Delinquency is traced to strain, weak social bonds, and deviant subcultures.
General Theory	
Hirschi and Gottfredson	Individual differences in crime commission may be attributed to levels of self-control.

RECENT THEORETICAL EXPLANATIONS

Over the past several years a number of attempts have been made to reconceptualize social control by joining, merging, and testing of different theoretical hypotheses and propositions.[43] As Table 7.4 reveals, theoretical criminologists have relied on social control theory to propose developmental, integrated, and general theories of crime.

PART II Explanations of Crime and Criminal Behavior

The best predictor of crime in adulthood, according to theorists, is weak social controls as a child. What are the prospects for Nathaniel Abraham, an 11-year-old boy from Michigan, who was convicted as an adult of murder. He was sentenced to a juvenile detention center until age 21, after which he will be freed.

Developmental/Life Course Theory

All developmental theories share one thing in common: explanations for why offending starts (onset), why it continues (continuance), why it becomes more frequent or serious (escalation), why it de-escalates (de-escalation), and why, inevitably, it stops (desistance). Rather than focusing exclusively on childhood, adolescence, young adulthood, or adulthood, these theories consider each developmental period in relation to the life span of an offender. In an extension of Hirschi's theory to the "life course," for example, Robert J. Sampson and John H. Laub found that family, school, and peer attachments were most strongly associated with delinquency from childhood to adolescence (through age 17).[44] From the transition to young adulthood through the transition to middle adulthood, attachment to work (job stability) and family (marriage) appears most strongly related to crime causation. Sampson and Laub found evidence that these positive personal and professional relationships build a "social capital" in otherwise vulnerable individuals that significantly inhibits deviance over time.

Another life-course theory combines control with learning theory (Chapter 4). Terence Thornberry argues that the potential for delinquency begins with the weakening of a person's bonds to the conventional world (parents, school, and accepted values). For this potential to be realized, there must be a social setting in which to learn delinquent values. In this setting, delinquents seek each other out and form common belief systems. There is nothing static about this kind of learning. Criminality, according to Thornberry, is a function of a dynamic social process that changes over time.[45]

David Farrington's work with the data from the Cambridge Study of Delinquent Development reveals different explanations for the general tendency to engage in crime (long-term variables) over time, as well as the influences that prompt an individual, at any given time, to engage in crime (short-term variables) (Table 7.4). The former include impulsivity, low empathy, and belief systems favorable to law violation. The latter consider momentary opportunities and situationally induced motivating factors, such as alcohol consumption and boredom.[46]

In one of the most elegant developmental theories to date, Marc LeBlanc employs social control theory to provide both static (pertaining to a particular time and place) and dynamic (occurring over time) explanations of criminality (the total number of infractions), the criminal (personal characteristics of an offender), and the crime (the criminal event). To construct his models, LeBlanc borrows from a host of disciplines (see Figure 7.1).

Integrated Theory

Integrated theory combines a criminological theory, such as differential association, with a number of social controls. Delbert Elliott and his colleagues have integrated the social bonds of Hirschi's theory of social control with strain theories. These researchers suggest that limited or blocked opportunities and a subsequent failure to achieve cultural goals would weaken or even destroy bonds to the conventional or social order. In other words, even if someone establishes strong bonds in childhood, a series of negative experiences in school, in the community, and at home, along with blocked access to opportunity, would be likely to lead to a weakening of those social bonds. As strain weakens social bonds, the chance of delinquency increases.[47]

Joseph Weis has proposed a social development model of crime which is an elegant integration of social control and social learning theory. He proposes that delinquency is minimized when youths who are at risk to commit crime have the opportunity to engage in conforming activities and are rewarded for doing so. Consistent reinforcement maximizes the social bonds which, in turn, diminish associations with delinquent peers and reduce crime.[48]

General Theories

In *A General Theory of Crime,* Travis Hirschi and Michael Gottfredson propose a new model of personal and social control—one designed to explain an individual's propensity to commit crime.[49] Hirschi and Gottfredson claim that their model, unlike earlier conceptualizations, explains the tendency to commit all crimes,

FIGURE 7.1 Control theory at the level of the criminality.

Source: Marc LeBlanc, "A Generic Control Theory of the Criminal Phenomenon: The Structural and Dynamic Statements of an Integrative Multilayered Control Theory," in *Developmental Theories of Crime and Delinquency: Advances in Criminological Theory*, ed. T. P. Thornberry, vol. 7 (1997), p. 238.

from crimes of violence such as robbery and sexual assault to white-collar offenses such as mail fraud and federal securities violations.[50]

This "general theory" of propensity to commit crimes, shown in Figure 7.2, assumes that offenders have little control over their own behavior and desires. When the need for momentary pleasure and immediate gratification outweighs long-term interests, crime occurs. In short, crime is a function of poor self-control.

What leads to poor self-control? Inadequate socialization and poor child-rearing practices, coupled with poor attachment, increase the probability of impulsive and uncontrolled acts. According to Hirschi and Gottfredson individ-

FIGURE 7.2 The Hirschi-Gottfredson self-control model. Hirschi and Gottfredson's model assumes that poor self-control is an intervening variable that explains all crime, as well as differences in crime rates, by age, gender, and race.

```
Ineffective                                    Criminal acts
child-rearing      →    Poor         →
practices and           self-control
inadequate                            →        Noncriminal acts
socialization                                  that result in harm
                                               (drinking, smoking,
                                               accidents)
```

uals with low self-control also tend to be involved in noncriminal events that result in harm, such as drinking, smoking, and most types of accidents, including auto crashes, household fires, and unwanted pregnancies.

Evidence in support of this theory is mixed. In the analysis of interviews and breathalyzer tests, one study found a definite association between self-control and DUI.[51] Equivocal results, however, were obtained by other researchers who examined interview data from a sample of college students, high school students, adults from Oklahoma City, residents of a Canadian province, and residents of a large southwestern U.S. city.[52] Additional research is establishing the usefulness of this general theory of crime.[53]

It is important to remember that all of these recent explanations of criminality share one common variable—the social bonds that are at the foundation of social control theory. The ingredients of social control theory have been used quite effectively over the last decade as building blocks for these recent developments.

THEORY INFORMS POLICY

Social control theory tells us that people commit crimes when they have not developed adequate attachments, have not become involved in and committed to conventional activities, and have not internalized the rules of society (or do not care about them). Efforts to prevent crime must therefore include the teaching of conventional values.

It is also necessary to find ways to strengthen individual bonds to society, commitment to the conventional order, and involvement in conventional activities. One way is to strengthen the institutions that socialize people and continue to regulate their behavior throughout life—the family, the school, and the workplace.[54]

Family

Experimental school-based parent training programs are offered in many states. The major premise of these programs is that a child's bond to a family is crucial. To develop this bond, parents learned to provide opportunities that would help the child participate and succeed in a social unit such as the school (by demonstrating good study habits, for example) and to reinforce conformity or punish violations of the group's norms. Results suggest that these initiatives decrease children's aggressiveness and increase parental skills.[55]

School

A program called PATHE (Positive Action Through Holistic Education) operates in middle schools and high schools around the United States. Its object is to reduce delinquency by strengthening students' commitment to school and attachment to conforming members—in other words, by bonding young people to the conventional system.

PATHE brings together students, school staff, and community members to plan and implement a program designed to foster a better school climate (encourage more open discussion), improve academic skills, and prepare students for careers. Evaluations of the program reveal higher grades, better attendance, fewer dropouts, and increased commitment to education.[56]

Neighborhood

Historically, church and family have helped protect and maintain the social order in neighborhoods and instill a sense of pride and comfort in residents. This is no longer the case in many areas. The neighborhood as an institu-

Window to the World

Nations with Low Crime Rates

Most criminologists devote their efforts to learning why people commit crime and why there is so much crime. A few have looked at the question from the opposite perspective: In places with little crime, what accounts for the low crime rate? Using the United Nations' first World Crime Survey (1970–1975), Freda Adler studied the two countries with the lowest crime rates in each of five general cultural regions of the world(1):

Western Europe: Switzerland and the Republic of Ireland

Eastern Europe: The former German Democratic Republic (East Germany) and Bulgaria

Arab countries: Saudi Arabia and Algeria

Asia: Japan and Nepal

Latin America: Costa Rica and Peru(2)

This is an odd assortment of countries. They seem to have little in common. Some are democratic, others authoritarian. Some are republics, others monarchies. Some were ruled by dictators, others by communal councils. Some are rural, others highly urbanized. Some are remote and isolated; others are in the political mainstream. Some are highly religious, some largely atheistic. Some have a very high standard of living, others a very low one. What explains their common characteristic of low crime rates?

Investigations slowly revealed a common factor in all 10 countries: Each appeared to have an intact social control system, quite apart from whatever formal control system (law enforcement) it had. Here are brief descriptions of the types of social control systems identified:

Western Europe: Switzerland fostered a strong sense of belonging to and participating in the local community.(3) The family was still strong in the Republic of Ireland, and it was strengthened by shared religious values.

Workers in Japan showing solidarity in an early morning exercise ritual.

---

tion of informal social control has been very much weakened. Various agencies have tried to reverse this trend with programs to prevent juvenile crime that are implemented through neighborhood-based organizations, for example, in Chicago, Dallas, Los Angeles, New Orleans, New York, and San Diego. Federally funded programs seek to reduce crime by strengthening neighborhood cohesion. Programs assess the needs of residents and then set up crisis intervention centers, mediation (between youngsters and school, family, or police, and between warring gangs), youth training, supervision programs, and family support systems.

Program evaluations reveal that serious juvenile crime decreases.[57] Hundreds of such community crime-prevention projects around the country have been organized by government agencies, private persons, and religious groups.[58] They have made a local impact, but they have not been able to change the national crime rate. The most successful models, however, may offer a plan for crime prevention on a broader, perhaps even a national, scale.

Eastern Europe: The former German Democratic Republic involved all youths in communal activities, organized by groups and aimed at having young people excel for the glory of self and country. In Bulgaria, industrialization focused on regional industry centers so that the workers would not be dislodged from their hometowns, which served as continuing social centers.

Arab countries: Islam continued to be strong as a way of life and exercised a powerful influence on daily activities, especially in Saudi Arabia. Algeria had, in addition, a powerful commitment to socialism in its postindependence era, involving the citizens in all kinds of commonly shared development activities.

Asia: Nepal retained its strong family and clan ties, augmented by councils of elders that oversaw the community and resolved problems. Highly industrialized Japan had lost some of the social controls of family and kinship, but it found a substitute family in the industrial community, to which most Japanese belonged: Mitsubishi might now be the family that guides one's every step.

Latin America: Costa Rica spent all the funds that other governments devoted to the military on social services and social development, caring for and strengthening its families. Peru went through a process of urbanization in stages: Village and family cohesion marked the lives of people in the countryside, and this cohesion remained with the people as they migrated from Andean villages to smaller towns and then to the big city, where they were received by and lived surrounded by others from their own hometowns.

The study concluded that **synnomie**, a term derived from the Greek *syn* meaning "with" and *nomos* meaning "norms," marked societies with low crime rates.

Sources

1. United Nations, *Report of the Secretary General on Crime Prevention and Control*, A/32/199 (popularly known as the First U.N. World Crime Survey) (New York: United Nations, 1977).
2. Freda Adler, *Nations Not Obsessed with Crime* (Littleton, Colo.: Fred B. Rothman, 1983).
3. Marshall B. Clinard, *Cities with Little Crime: The Case of Switzerland* (Cambridge, Mass.: Cambridge University Press, 1978).

Questions for Discussion

1. People in the United States work in factories, live in family groups, go to church, and join youth groups. Why do these institutions not function effectively as forms of social control to keep the crime rate low?
2. How could government or community decision makers use the information presented by this study to help solve crime problems in the United States?

As our understanding of control theory evolves, so will our appreciation of the effects of control interventions. If nothing else, it is fair to say that social control programs and interventions are proliferating and may be found in every state. Here are just a few examples:

Homebuilders (Tacoma, Washington). A family preservation program that seeks to keep at-risk children at home[59]

Families First (Michigan). A program that strengthens vulnerable families[60]

S.W.E.A.T. Team (Bridgeport, Connecticut). A project that employs teenagers to create new activities for children who may be tempted into joining gangs or selling drugs[61]

Learnfare (Ohio, Virginia, Florida, Maryland, and Oklahoma). Programs that provide financial and social support for teenage welfare mothers who attend school[62]

Table 7.5 lists programs that Boston, Massachusetts, has initiated since 1982.

Crime-prevention programs like those initiated in Boston, Massachusetts, over the past decade have met with significant success. Most of these efforts are grounded in principles of social control.

TABLE 7.5 Violence-Prevention Programs in Boston (Listed by Start Date)

1982	1990
Boston City Hospital Violence Prevention Program	Mayor's Safe Neighborhood Initiative
	Teens against Gang Violence
1985	Citizens for Safety
Friends for Life—PSA Campaign Ad Council of Boston	**1992**
WEATOC Teen Theatre Group Adds Violence Prevention to Its Repertoire	WBZ-TV Stop the Violence Campaign
	Ten-Point Coalition
1986	**1994**
South Boston Boys and Girls Club—Friends for Life Clubs and Violence Prevention Programs	Louis D. Brown Peace Curriculum
	Community Policing in Boston
	Adolescent Wellness Program
1987	**1995**
Violence Prevention Curriculum for Adolescents Published for Distribution	Ceasefire
1989	**1996**
Gang Peace	Strike Force

Source: Boston Police Department, as cited in *What Can the Federal Government Do to Decrease Crime and Revitalize Communities?* (Washington, D.C.: National Institute of Justice, 1998), p. 60.

REVIEW

The term "social control" has taken on a wide variety of meanings. In general, it describes any mechanism that leads to conformity to social norms. Mainstream studies of social control take one of two approaches. Macrosociological studies focus on formal systems of social control. Most contemporary criminological research takes the microsociological approach, which focuses on informal systems. Travis Hirschi's social control theory has had a long-lasting impact on the scholarly community. Hirschi identified four social bonds that promote adherence to society's values: attachment, commitment, involvement, and belief. The stronger these bonds, Hirschi claimed, the less the likelihood of delinquency.

According to the containment theory of Walter Reckless, every person has a containing external structure (a role in a social group with reasonable limits and responsibilities and alternative means of attaining satisfaction). In addition, each individual has a protective internal structure that depends on a good self-concept, self-control, a well-developed conscience, a tolerance for frustration, and a strong sense of responsibility.

Most investigators today believe that personal (inner) controls are as important as social (external) controls in keeping people from committing crimes. Albert Reiss found that personal controls reinforce social controls. Jackson Toby stressed the importance of a stake in conformity in keeping a person from responding to social disorganization with delinquent behavior. Recent efforts to integrate social control theories with other theories have resulted in developmental, integrated, and general theories of crime. All share one common variable—the social bonds that constitute social control theory.

As part of an effort to reduce delinquency, a variety of programs at the local and regional levels help parents, schools, and neighborhood groups develop social controls.

CRIMINOLOGY & PUBLIC POLICY

In recent years lawmakers at both the state and federal levels have passed legislation increasing penalties for criminal offenses, particularly violent crimes. These actions came in response to public concerns about crime and the belief that many serious offenders are released from prison too soon. Many such laws have come under the gen-

eral label of "three strikes and you're out." The purpose of these laws is simple: Offenders convicted repeatedly of serious offenses should be removed from society for long periods of time, in many cases for life. For many years most states have had provisions in their laws that included enhanced sentencing for repeat offenders. Yet between 1993 and 1995, 24 states and the federal government enacted new laws using the "three strikes" moniker, with similarly labeled bills introduced in a number of other states.

The rapid expansion of three-strikes laws, regardless of how they are defined, reflects the perception that existing laws did not adequately protect public safety in their application and/or outcome, that exceptional incidents had occurred that the new laws would address, or that the intent of current laws was being frustrated by other factors such as prison crowding. Whether the perception was accurate and what the impact will be of the new laws are questions that cannot yet be answered. (Source: John Clark, James Austin, and D. Alan Henry, *Three Strikes and You're Out: A Review of State Legislation* (Washington, D.C.: NIJ, 1997).

Questions for Discussion Three-strikes laws can be harsh. Offenders committing petty thefts as their third strike may in some jurisdictions, for example, receive 25 or more years in prison as courts and prosecutors take their prior record into consideration. Such sentences were upheld by the U.S. Supreme Court in 2003. What concerns with three-strikes laws are raised by recent extensions to Hirschi's notion of social control—life course theories of offending? If the fundamental rationale of three-strikes laws is to protect the community from habitual offenders, are life course theories supportive? If we know what best predicts future offending, and programs may be created to address these causal factors, why rely on long prison sentences?

YOU BE THE CRIMINOLOGIST

The desire for stability, involvement, belief, and conformity can have a dark side. Consider how mechanisms of social control, narrowly conceived, can support new religious, political, and psychosocial cults or sects. How does social control theory help explain the attraction to Heaven's Gate, the Aum Supreme Truth, the Order of the Solar Temple, or the Branch Davidians?

KEY TERMS

The numbers next to the terms refer to the pages on which the terms are defined.

attachment (170)
belief (172)
commitment (171)
conformity (177)
containment theory (177)
direct control (179)
drift (175)
indirect control (179)
internalized control (179)
involvement (171)
macrosociological studies (169)
microsociological studies (169)
social control theory (168)
synnomie (185)

CHAPTER 8
Labeling, Conflict, and Radical Theories

Labeling Theory
　The Origins of Labeling Theory
　Basic Assumptions of Labeling Theory
　Labeling in the 1960s
　Empirical Evidence for Labeling Theory
　Evaluation: Labeling Theory

Conflict Theory
　The Consensus Model
　The Conflict Model
　Conflict Theory and Criminology
　Empirical Evidence for the Conflict Model

Radical Theory
　The Intellectual Heritage of Marxist Criminology
　Engels and Marx
　Willem Adriaan Bonger
　Georg Rusche and Otto Kirchheimer
　Radical Criminology since the 1970s
　Evaluation: Marxist Criminological Theory
　Emerging Explanations

REVIEW

CRIMINOLOGY & PUBLIC POLICY

YOU BE THE CRIMINOLOGIST

KEY TERMS

Boxes
　From the Pages of The New York Times: *Racial Profiling Labeling Before the Fact*
　Of Immediate Concern: *The Rights of the Poorest*
　Window to the World: *The Forgotten Criminology of Genocide*

Special Features
　Crime Surfing
　Did You Know?

KEY TERMS
conflict theory
consensus model
due process
equal protection
labeling theory
penologists
radical criminology
social interactionists

LAPD officers wearing riot gear in a standoff against protestors outside the Democratic National Convention in Los Angeles, California, August 2000.

Each era of social and political turmoil has produced profound changes in people's lives. Perhaps no such era was as significant for criminology as the 1960s. A society with conservative values was shaken out of its complacency when young people, blacks, women, and other disadvantaged groups demanded a part in the shaping of national policy. They saw the gaps between philosophical political demands and reality: Blacks had little opportunity to advance; women were kept in an inferior status; old politicians made wars in which the young had to die. Rebellion broke out, and some criminologists joined it.

These criminologists turned away from theories that explained crime by characteristics of the offender or of the social structure. They set out to demonstrate that individuals become criminals because of what people with power, especially those in the criminal justice system, do. Their explanations largely reject the consensus model of crime, on which all earlier theories rested. Their theories not only question the traditional explanations of the creation and enforcement of criminal law but blame that law for the making of criminals. (See Table 8.1.)

It may not sound so radical to assert that unless an act is made criminal by law, no person who performs that act can be adjudicated a criminal. The exponents of contemporary alternative explanations of crime grant that much. But, justifiably, they also ask: Who makes these laws in the first place? And why? Is breaking such laws the most important criterion for being a criminal? Are all people who break these laws criminals? Do all members of society agree that those singled out by the criminal law to be called "criminals" are criminals and that others are not?

TABLE 8.1 Comparison of Four Criminological Perspectives

Perspective	Origin of Criminal Law	Causes of Criminal Behavior	Focus of Study
Traditional/consensus	Laws reflect shared values.	Psychological, biological, or sociological factors.	Psychological and biological factors (Chap. 4); unequal opportunity (Chap. 5); learning criminal behavior in disorganized neighborhoods (Chap. 5); subculture values (Chap. 6); social control (Chap. 7).
Labeling	Those in power create the laws, decide who will be the rule breakers.	The process that defines (or labels) certain persons as criminals.	Effects of stigmatizing by the label "criminal"; sociopolitical factors behind reform legislation; origin of laws; deviant behavior (Chap. 8).
Conflict	Powerful groups use laws to support their interests.	Interests of one group do not coincide with needs of another.	Bias and discrimination in criminal justice system; differential crime rates of powerful and powerless; development of criminal laws by those in power; relationship between rulers and ruled (Chap. 8).
Radical (Marxist)	Laws serve interests of the ruling class.	Class struggle over distribution of resources in a capitalist system.	Relationship between crime and economics; ways in which state serves capitalist interests; solution to crime problem based on collapse of capitalism (Chap. 8).

LABELING THEORY

The 1950s was a period of general prosperity and pride for Americans. Yet some social scientists, uneasy about the complacency they saw, turned their attention to the social order. They noted that some of the ideals the United States had fought for in World War II had not been achieved at home. Human rights existed on paper but were often lacking in practice. It was clear that blacks continued to live as second-class citizens. Even though the Fourteenth Amendment to the Constitution guaranteed blacks equal rights, neither the law of the country nor the socioeconomic system provided them with equal opportunities.

Nowhere was this fact more apparent than in the criminal justice system. Social scientists and liberal lawyers pressed for change, and the Supreme Court, under Chief Justice Earl Warren, responded. In case after case the Court found a pervasive influence of rules and customs that violated the concepts of **due process,** under which a person cannot be deprived of life, liberty, or property without lawful procedures, and **equal protection,** under which no one can be denied the safeguards of the law. The result of hundreds of Supreme Court decisions was that both black and white citizens now were guaranteed the right to counsel in all criminal cases, freedom from self-incrimination, and other rights enumerated in the first 10 amendments to the Constitution. Nevertheless, a great deal of social injustice remained.

In this social climate, a small group of social scientists, known as "labeling theorists," began to explore how and why certain acts were defined as criminal or, more broadly, as deviant behavior and others were not, and how and why certain people were defined as criminal or deviant. These theorists viewed criminals not as inherently evil persons engaged in inherently wrong acts but, rather, as individuals who had had criminal status conferred upon them by both the criminal justice system and the community at large.

Viewed from this perspective, criminal acts themselves are not particularly significant; the social reaction to them, however, is. Deviance and its control involve a process of social definition in which the response of others to an individual's behavior is the key influence on subsequent behavior and on individuals' views of themselves. The sociologist Howard S. Becker has written:

Deviance is not a quality of the act the person commits, but rather a consequence of the application by others of rules and sanctions to an "offender." The deviant is one to whom that label has successfully been applied; deviant behavior is behavior that people so label.[1]

In focusing on the ways in which social interactions create deviance, **labeling theory** declares that the reactions of other people and the subsequent effects of those reactions create deviance. Once it becomes known that a person has engaged in deviant acts, he or she is segregated from conventional society, and a label ("thief," "whore," "junkie") is attached to the transgressor. This process of segregation creates "outsiders" (as Becker called them), or outcasts from society, who begin to associate with others like themselves.[2]

As more people begin to think of these people as deviants and to respond to them accordingly, the deviants react to the response by continuing to engage in the behavior society now expects of them. Through this process their self-images gradually change as well. So the key factor is the label that is attached to an individual: "If men define situations as real, they are real in their consequences."[3]

The Origins of Labeling Theory

The intellectual roots of labeling theory can be traced to the post–World War I work of Charles Horton Cooley, William I. Thomas, and George Herbert Mead. These scholars, who viewed the human self as formed through a process of social interaction, were called **social interactionists.** In 1918 Mead compared the impact of social labeling to "the angel with the fiery sword at the gate who can cut one off from the world to which he belongs."[4]

Labeling separates the good from the bad, the conventional from the deviant. Mead's interest in deviance focused on the social interactions by which an individual becomes a deviant. The person is not just a fixed structure whose action is the result of certain factors acting upon it. Rather, social behavior develops in a continuous process of action and reaction.[5] The way we perceive ourselves, our self-concept, is built not only on what we think of ourselves but also on what others think of us.

Somewhat later, the historian Frank Tannenbaum (1893–1969) used the same argument in his study of the causes of criminal behavior. He described the creation of a criminal as a process: Breaking windows, climbing onto roofs, and playing truant are all normal parts of the adolescent search for excitement and adventure. Local merchants and others who experience these activities may consider them a nuisance or perhaps even evil. This conflict is the beginning of the process by which the evil act transforms the transgressor into an evil individual. From that point on, the evil individuals are separated from those in conventional society. Given a criminal label, they gradually begin to think of themselves as they have been officially defined.

Tannenbaum maintained that it is the process of labeling, or the "dramatization of evil," that locks a mischievous boy into a delinquent role ("the person becomes the thing he is described as being"). Accordingly, "the entire process of dealing with young delinquents is mischievous insofar as it identifies him to himself and to the environment as a delinquent person."[6] The system starts out with a child in trouble and ends up with a juvenile delinquent.

Basic Assumptions of Labeling Theory

In the 1940s the sociologist Edwin Lemert elaborated on Tannenbaum's discussion by formulating the basic assumptions of labeling theory.[7] He reminded us that people are constantly involved in behavior that runs the risk of being labeled delinquent or criminal. But although many run that risk, only a few are so labeled. The reason, Lemert contended, is that there are two kinds of deviant acts: primary and secondary.[8]

"Primary deviations" are the initial deviant acts that bring on the first social response. These acts do not affect the individual's self-concept. It is the "secondary deviations," the acts that follow the societal response to the primary deviation, that are of major concern. These are the acts that result from the change in self-concept brought about by the labeling process.[9] The scenario goes somewhat like this:

1. An individual commits a simple deviant act (primary deviation)—throwing a stone at a neighbor's car, for instance.

2. There is an informal social reaction: The neighbor gets angry.
3. The individual continues to break rules (primary deviations)—he lets the neighbor's dog out of the yard.
4. There is increased, but still primary, social reaction: The neighbor tells the youth's parents.
5. The individual commits a more serious deviant act—he is caught shoplifting (still primary deviation).
6. There is a formal reaction: The youth is adjudicated a "juvenile delinquent" in juvenile court.
7. The youth is now labeled "delinquent" by the court and "bad" by the neighborhood, by his conventional peers, and by others.
8. The youth begins to think of himself as "delinquent"; he joins other unconventional youths.
9. The individual commits another, yet more serious, deviant act (secondary deviation)—he robs a local grocery store with members of a gang.
10. The individual is returned to juvenile court, has more offenses added to his record, is cast out further from conventional society, and takes on a completely deviant lifestyle.

According to Lemert, secondary deviance sets in after the community has become aware of a primary deviance. Individuals experience "a continuing sense of injustice, which [is] reinforced by job rejections, police cognizance, and strained interaction with normals."[10] In short, deviant individuals have to bear the stigma of the "delinquent" label, just as English and American convicts, as late as the eighteenth century, bore stigmas, in the form of an M for murder or a T for thief, burned or cut into their bodies to designate them as persons to be shunned.[11] Once such a label is attached to a person, a deviant or criminal career has been set in motion. The full significance of labeling theory was not recognized, either in Europe or in the United States, until political events provided the opportunity.[12]

Labeling in the 1960s

The 1960s witnessed a movement among students and professors to join advocacy groups and become activists in the social causes that were rapidly gaining popularity on college campuses across the nation, such as equal rights for minorities, liberation for women, and peace for humankind. The protests took many forms—demonstrations and rallies, sit-ins and teach-ins, beards and long hair, rock music and marijuana, dropping out of school, burning draft cards.

Arrests of middle-class youths increased rapidly; crime was no longer confined to the ghettos. People asked whether arrests were being made for behavior that was not really criminal. Were the real criminals the legislators and policy makers who pursued a criminal war in Vietnam while creating the artificial crime of draft card burning at home? Were the real criminals the National Guardsmen who shot and killed campus demonstrators at Kent State University? Labeling theorists made their appearance and provided answers. The sociologist Kai Erickson has put it well:

> Deviance is not a property inherent in certain forms of behavior; it is a property conferred upon these forms by audiences which directly or indirectly witness them. The critical variable in the study of deviance, then, is the social audience rather than the individual actor, since it is the audience which eventually determines whether or not any episode or behavior or any class of episodes is labeled deviant.[13]

Edwin Schur, a leading labeling theorist of the 1960s, elaborated on Erickson's explanation:

> Human behavior is deviant to the extent that it comes to be viewed as involving a personally discreditable departure from a group's normative expectation, and it elicits interpersonal and collective reactions that serve to "isolate," "treat," "correct," or "punish" individuals engaged in such behavior.[14]

Schur also expanded on Lemert's secondary deviance with his own concept of "secondary elaboration," by which he meant that the effects of the labeling process become so significant that individuals who want to escape from their deviant groups and return to the conventional

Kent State University protestor grieving over body of fellow student shot and killed by National Guardsmen, Ohio, 1970.

world find it difficult to do so. Schur points to members of the gay and drug cultures.[15] The strength of the label, once acquired, tends to exclude such people permanently from the mainstream culture.[16] Schur found that involvement in activities that are disapproved of may very well lead to more participation in deviance than one had originally planned, and so increase the social distance between the person labeled deviant and the conventional world.[17]

The labeling theorists then asked: Who makes the rules that define deviant behavior, including crime? According to Howard Becker, it is the "moral entrepreneurs"—the people whose high social position gives them the power to make and enforce the social rules by which members of society have to live. By making the rules that define the criminal, Becker argues, certain members of society create outsiders.

The whole process thus becomes a political one, pitting the rule makers against the rule breakers. Becker goes even further, suggesting that people can be labeled simply by being falsely accused. As long as others believe that someone has participated in a given deviant behavior, that individual will experience negative social reaction. People can also suffer the effects of labeling when they have committed a deviant act that has not been discovered. Since most people know how they would be labeled if they were caught, these secret deviants may experience the same labeling effects as those who have been caught.[18]

Empirical Evidence for Labeling Theory

Empirical investigations of labeling theory have been carried out by researchers in many disciplines using a variety of methodologies. One group of investigators arranged to have eight sane volunteers apply for admission to various mental hospitals. In order to get themselves admitted, the subjects claimed to be hearing voices, a symptom of schizophrenia. Once admitted to the hospital, however, they behaved normally. The experiences of these pseudopatients clearly reveal the effects of labeling.

> **Did You Know?**
>
> ... that the American Civil Liberties Union (ACLU) has taken a strong stance against racial profiling? The practice of racial profiling allows police officers to stop a pedestrian or a motorist simply because that person fits a set of characteristics—for example, young black males—associated with certain types of criminal activity. To educate and inform the public about this form of labeling, the ACLU has prepared a pocket-sized card with information on handling such police encounters.

Doctors, nurses, and assistants treated them as schizophrenic patients. They interpreted the normal everyday behavior of the pseudopatients as manifestations of illness. An early arrival at the lunchroom, for example, was described as exhibiting "oral aggressive" behavior; a patient seen writing something was referred to as a "compulsive note-taker." Interestingly enough, none of the other patients believed the pseudopatients were insane; they assumed they were researchers or journalists. When the subjects were discharged from the hospital, it was as schizophrenics "in remission."

The findings support criminological labeling theory. Once the sane individuals were labeled schizophrenic, they were unable to eliminate the label by acting normally. Even when they supposedly had recovered, the label stayed with them in the form of "schizophrenia in remission," which implied that future episodes of the illness could be expected.[19]

Researchers have also looked at how labels affect people and groups with unconventional lifestyles, whether prohibited by law or not—"gays," "public drunks," "junkies," "strippers," "streetwalkers."[20] The results of research, no matter what the group, were largely in conformity: "Once a _____, always a _____." Labeling by adjudication may have lifelong consequences. Richard Schwartz and Jerome Skolnick, for example, found that employers were reluctant to hire anyone with a court record even though the person had been found not guilty.[21]

The criminologist Anthony Platt has investigated how certain individuals are singled out to receive labels. Focusing on the label "juvenile delinquent," he shows how the social reformers of the late nineteenth century helped create delinquency by establishing a special institution, the juvenile court, for the processing of troubled youths. The Chicago society women who lobbied for the establishment of juvenile courts may have had the best motives in trying to help immigrants' children who, by their standards, were out of control. But by getting the juvenile court established, they simply widened the net of state agencies empowered to label some children as deviant.

The state thus aggravated the official problem of juvenile delinquency, which until then had been a neighborhood nuisance handled by parents, neighbors, priests, the local grocer, or the police officer on the street. Juvenile delinquency, according to Platt, was invented. Through its labeling effect, it contributed to its own growth.[22]

The criminologist William Chambliss also studied the question of the way labels are distributed. Consider the following description:

> Eight promising young men [the Saints]—children of good, stable, white upper-middle-class families, active in school affairs, good pre-college students—were some of the most delinquent boys at Hanibal High School. . . . The Saints were constantly occupied with truancy, drinking, wild driving, petty theft and vandalism. Yet not one was officially arrested for any misdeed during the two years I observed them.
>
> This record was particularly surprising in light of my observations during the same two years of another gang of Hanibal High School students, six lower-class white boys known as the Roughnecks. The Roughnecks were constantly in trouble with police and community even though their rate of delinquency was about equal with that of the Saints.[23]

What accounts for the different responses to these two groups of boys? According to Chambliss, the crucial factor is the social class of the boys, which determined the community's reaction to their activities. The Roughnecks were poor, outspoken, openly hostile to authority, and highly visible because they could not afford cars to get out of town. The Saints, on the other hand, had reputations for being bright, they acted apologetic when authorities confronted

FROM THE PAGES OF

The New York Times

Racial Profiling: Labeling Before the Fact

It's one thing to be labeled a criminal after you've broken the law, but what happens when you're targeted for arrest before you've done anything? For years, blacks and Latinos have complained that they were being stopped and searched for no reason except the color of their skin. After September 11th, racial profiling became an even stronger subject of debate.

In fact, racial profiling has been a controversial subject in law enforcement for many years. In came into the national spotlight in April 1998, when four black and Latino men were shot in New Jersey during a traffic stop—an incident that raised public awareness of allegations that state police officers pulled people over simply because of their race.

Four years later, New Jersey state prosecutors decided to dismiss criminal charges in 86 cases involving people who said that state troopers singled them out because of the color of their skin. All of the dismissed cases were related to charges involving drugs, weapons, or other forms of contraband, and prosecutors said that all convictions would be purged from the defendants' records.

The dismissals were welcomed by lawyers representing those who said they were singled out because of racial profiling. There were also many critics of the decision, including Kenneth J. McClelland, president of the state troopers' fraternal association, who said, "The state is going to put drug dealers and thugs who were found to be breaking the law back on the streets, based on nothing but political correctness."

Some of the cases involved people who were already serving prison sentences, including Emory Gibson, who had already served eight years behind bars for possession with intent to distribute cocaine. He was a passenger in the car in which the cocaine was found. A review of the case, however, found that the troopers who stopped Mr. Gibson and the two other men stopped minorities almost exclusively.

Source

Richard Lezin Jones, "New Jersey Prosecutors Cite Racial Profiling in Dismissal of 86 Criminal Cases," *New York Times*, April 20, 2002. Reprinted with permission.

Questions for Discussion

1. A number of people of Middle Eastern and Asian descent are suing various airlines. They claim they were kicked off flights—after they had passed vigorous security checks—only because a passenger or flight attendant felt uncomfortable with them on board. None of the people had done anything wrong, yet they were all asked to get off the planes. Is racial profiling justified in these situations?
2. What affect might such racial profiling have on you in a similar situation? How would you feel? Would it cause you to behave any differently in the future?

---

them, they held school offices, they played on athletic teams, and they had cars to get them out of town. Their behavior went undiscovered, unprocessed, and unpunished.

Chambliss's research reveals what many believe is the inherent discrimination in the juvenile justice system that causes the police and courts to identify the behavior of some as delinquent more so than others. These criminologists state that young minority males are more likely to be arrested and officially processed. This is also true of members of the lower economic classes. Those with wealth or political power, on the other hand, are more likely to be given simply a warning. In this way a Roughneck who spends all his time around other Roughnecks, but does not engage in criminal behavior, would be more likely to be arrested and processed than a Saint who was engaged in illegal activity. Research also seems to indicate that the level of seriousness of the crime committed and the prior record of the individual committing the crime have much influence on delinquency processing.

Up to this point, the contentions of labeling theorists and the evidence they present provide a persuasive argument for the validity of labeling theory. But despite supportive scientific evidence, labeling theory has been heavily criticized.

Evaluation: Labeling Theory

Critics ask: Why is it that individuals, knowing they might be labeled, get involved in socially disapproved behavior to begin with? Most labeled persons have indeed engaged in some act that is considered morally or legally wrong.[24] According to sociologist Ronald Akers, the impression is sometimes given that people are passive actors in a process by which the bad system bestows a derogatory label, thereby declaring them unacceptable, or different, or untouchable.[25] Critics suggest that the labels may identify real behavior rather than create it. After all, many delinquents have in fact had a long history of deviant behavior, even though they have never been caught and stigmatized. These critics question the overly active role labeling theory has assigned to the community and its criminal justice system and the overly passive role it has assigned to offenders.

Some criminologists also question how labeling theory accounts for individuals who have gone through formal processing but do not continue deviant lifestyles. They suggest that punishment really does work as a deterrent.[26] The argument is that labeling theorists are so intent on the reaction to behavior that they completely neglect the fact that someone has defied the conventions of society.[27] The criminologist Charles Wellford reminds us that, by and large, offenders get into the hands of authorities because they have broken the law. Furthermore, the decisions made about them are heavily influenced by the seriousness of their offenses. He concludes:

> The assumption that labels are differentially distributed, and that differential labelling affects behavior, is not supported by the existing criminological research. In sum, one should conclude that to the degree that these assumptions can be taken to be basic to the labelling perspective, the perspective must be seriously questioned; and criminologists should be encouraged to explore other ways to conceptualize the causal process of the creation, perpetuation, and intensification of criminal and delinquent behavior.[28]

While most critics believe that labeling theorists put too much emphasis on the system, others of a more radical or Marxist persuasion believe that labeling theorists have not gone far enough. They claim that the labeling approach concentrates too heavily on "nuts, sluts, and perverts," the exotic varieties of deviants who capture public imagination, rather than on "the unethical, illegal and destructive actions of powerful individuals, groups, and institutions of our society."[29] We will look at this argument more closely in a moment.

Empirical evidence that substantiates the claims of labeling theory has been modest. All the same, the theory has been instrumental in calling attention to some important questions, particularly about the way defendants are processed through the criminal justice system. Labeling theorists have carried out important scientific investigations of that system which complement the search of more traditional criminologists for the causes of crime and delinquency.

Some of the criticism of labeling theory can best be countered by one of its own proponents. Howard Becker explains that labeling is intended not as a theory of causation but, rather, as a perspective, "a way of looking at a general area of human activity, which expands the traditional research to include the process of social control."[30] Labeling theory has provided this perspective; it has also spawned further inquiry into the causes of crime.

In a recent extension of labeling theory to a developmental control theory, Sampson and Laub conclude that some delinquency persists because of the reactions that offenders receive to their criminal behavior. Add significant socioeconomic disadvantage, and the result is often a breakdown in social control.[31]

CONFLICT THEORY

Labeling theorists are as well aware as other criminologists that some people make rules and some break them. Their primary concern is the consequences of making and enforcing rules. One group of scholars has carried this idea further by questioning the rule-making process itself. They claim that a struggle for power is a basic feature of human existence. It is by means of such power struggles that various interest groups manage to control lawmaking and law enforcement.[32] To understand the theoretical approach of these conflict theorists, we must go back to the traditional approach, which views crime and criminal justice as arising from communal consensus.

Among recent targets of "anti-capitalist," "anti-imperialist" demonstrators is the International Monetary Fund (IMF), from which many developing countries had to borrow for development. These demonstrators want these debts to be cancelled.

In Durkheim's words, "We can . . . say that an act is criminal when it offends strong and defined states of the collective conscience."[33] Consensus theorists view society as a stable entity in which laws are created for the general good. The laws' function is to reconcile and to harmonize most of the interests that most members of a community cherish, with the least amount of sacrifice.

Deviant acts not only are part of the normal functioning of society but in fact are necessary, because when the members of society unite against a deviant, they reaffirm their commitment to shared values. Durkheim captured this view:

> We have only to notice what happens, particularly in a small town, when some moral scandal has been committed. They stop each other on the street, they visit each other, they seek to come together to talk of the event and to wax indignant in common. From all the similar impressions which are exchanged, for all the temper that gets itself expressed, there emerges a unique temper, more or less determinate according to the circumstances, which is everybody's without being anybody's in particular. That is the public temper.[34]

Societies in which citizens agree on right and wrong and the occasional deviant serves a useful purpose are scarce today. Such societies could be found among primitive peoples at the very beginning of social evolution. By and large, consensus theory recognizes that not everyone can agree on what is best for society. Yet consensus theory holds that conflicting interests can be reconciled by means of law.[35]

The Consensus Model

Sometimes members of a society consider certain acts so threatening to community survival that they designate these acts as crimes. If the vast majority of a group's members share this view, the group has acted by consensus. This is the **consensus model** of criminal lawmaking. The model assumes that members of society by and large agree on what is right and wrong and that law is the codification of these agreed-upon social values. The law is a mechanism to settle disputes that arise when individuals stray too far from what the community considers acceptable.

The Conflict Model

With this view of the consensus model, we can understand and evaluate the arguments of the **conflict theorists**. In the 1960s, while labeling theorists were questioning why some people were designated as criminals, another group of scholars began to ask who in society has the power to make and enforce the laws. Conflict theory, already well established in the field of sociology, thus became popular as an explanation of crime and justice as well.

Like labeling theory, **conflict theory** has its roots in rebellion and the questioning of values.

Of Immediate Concern

The Rights of the Poorest

The poorest and least powerful have had little influence on the making of laws and on society's reaction to the breaking of laws. Somehow, the poorest have to survive in a society on which they have no apparent impact. In recent years court cases in New York have served as the battleground over what for some is a basic question of survival: Do the poor have a constitutional right to beg?

YES-NO-YES: COURT RULINGS

Yes, said New York federal district court judge Leonard Sand in January 1990, they have a right to panhandle in subway cars.(1) His ruling was overturned by the federal court of appeals in May of the same year, thus denying citizens the right to beg in the New York City subway system.(2) In 1993, when the question concerned the rights of the poor to beg in city streets and public parks, a federal court of appeals decided in favor of the poor.(3)

What did the justices consider in their efforts to decide whether beggars are criminals? Sand's novel ruling stated that panhandling is a form of free speech protected by the First Amendment. "A true test of one's commitment to constitutional principles," he wrote, "is the extent to which recognition is given to the rights of those in our midst who are the least affluent, least powerful and least welcome."(1) The case he decided grew out of attempts by the Metropolitan Transit Authority (MTA) to crack down on panhandling in New York City subway cars and stations. The Legal Action Center for the Homeless had filed a class action against the MTA on behalf of homeless panhandlers.

The court of appeals, in reversing the decision of the district court, criticized the lower court for overlooking the concerns of the MTA's millions of riders. It said that "whether intended as so, or not, begging in the subway often amounts to nothing less than assault, creating in the passengers the apprehension of imminent danger."(2)

CRITICAL COMMENTARY

Judge Sand's ruling created a spate of mostly virulent comments focusing on the judiciary's right to rule on the conduct of those dispossessed of power. One critic, Jill Adler, responded to these attacks:

> Judges as the ultimate guardians and interpreters of the Constitution have been charged with the duty of insuring that its fundamental guarantees such as freedom of speech and assembly are not abridged by the government. In this capacity they may sometimes be required to make unpopular decisions.

It is at least arguable that panhandling or begging is a form of symbolic speech—if only because it may be the only avenue of expression open to those society has shunned. Time, place, and manner restrictions, while undoubtedly an important protection for the community, can also be a convenient means of ignoring constitutional guarantees. They will not, however, make the homeless disappear.(4)

Model legislation suggests an increasing interest in curtailing aggressive panhandling by establishing reasonable time, place, and manner restrictions that will not run afoul of the First Amendment. Consider the selected provisions listed below from the Center for Community Interests' (CCI) model legislation on aggressive begging. You should know that CCI calls itself the "common-sense counter to the ACLU—without going to the other extreme."

Section 2. Prohibited acts.

A. No person shall solicit in an aggressive manner in any public place.
B. No person shall solicit on private or residential property without permission from the owner or other person lawfully in possession of such property.
C. No person shall solicit within twenty feet of public toilets.

But while labeling theorists and traditional criminologists focused on the crime and the criminal, including the labeling of the criminal by the system, conflict theorists questioned the system itself. The clash between traditional and labeling theorists, on the one hand, and conflict theorists, on the other, became ideological.

Conflict theorists asked: If people agree on the value system, as consensus theorists suggest, why are so many people in rebellion, why are there so many crimes, so many punitive threats, so many people in prison? Clearly conflict is found everywhere in the world, between one country and another, between gay rights and antigay groups, between people who view abortion as a right and others who view it as murder, between suspects and police, between family members, between neighbors. If the criminal law supports the collective communal interest, why do so many people deviate from it?

Conflict theorists answered that, contrary to consensus theory, laws do not exist for the collective good; they represent the interests of specific groups that have the power to get them enacted.[36] The key concept in conflict theory is power. The people who have political control in any given society are the ones who are able to make things happen. They have power. Conflict

Of Immediate Concern

Do aggressive panhandlers have a constitutional right to beg? Is asking for money "symbolic" speech protected by the First Amendment? Answers to these questions are increasingly difficult.

cle while such vehicle is located on any street, for the purpose of performing or offering to perform a service in connection with such vehicle or otherwise soliciting the sale of goods or services. Provided, however, that this paragraph shall not apply to services rendered in connection with emergency repairs requested by the operator or passenger of such vehicle.(5)

Sources

1. 729 F. Supp. 341 (S.D.N.Y. 1990).
2. 903 F.2d 146 (2d Cir. 1990).
3. Docket No. 92-9127, United States Court of Appeals for the Second Circuit, July 29, 1993.
4. Andrea Sachs, *Time*, Feb. 12, 1990, p. 55; Jill Adler, *International Herald Tribune*, Feb. 15, 1990, p. 9.
5. http://www.communityinterest.org/backgrounders/indbackg.htm

Questions for Discussion

1. Begging has been regulated throughout history in the United States, and many states currently have statutes that limit or ban begging. What do you suppose the U.S. Supreme Court will do to these statutes?
2. Do you agree that subway begging should be viewed as different from begging on the street?

D. No person shall solicit within twenty feet of any entrance or exit of any financial institution or check cashing business or within twenty feet of any automated teller machine without the consent of the owner of the property or another person legally in possession of such facilities. Provided, however, that when an automated teller machine is located within an automated teller machine facility, such distance shall be measured from the entrance or exit of the facility.

E. No person shall solicit an operator or other occupant of a motor vehi-

---

theory holds that the people who possess the power work to keep the powerless at a disadvantage. The laws thus have their origin in the interests of the few; these few shape the values, and the values, in turn, shape the laws.[37]

It follows that the person who is defined as criminal and the behavior that is defined as crime at any given time and place mirror the society's power relationships. The definitions are subject to change as other interests gain power. The changing of definitions can be seen in those acts we now designate as "victimless" crimes. Possession of marijuana, prostitution, gambling, refusing to join the armed forces—all have been legal at some times, illegal at others. We may ask, then, whether any of these acts is inherently evil. The conflict theorist would answer that all are *made* evil when they are so designated by those in power and thus defined as crimes in legal codes.

The legal status of victimless crimes is subject to change. But what about murder, a crime considered evil in all contemporary societies? Many conflict theorists would respond that the definition of murder as a criminal offense is also rooted in the effort of some groups to guard their power. A political terrorist may very well become a national hero.

199

Conflict theorists emphasize the relativity of norms to time and place: Capital punishment is legal in some states, outlawed in others; alcohol consumption is illegal in Saudi Arabia but not in the United States. Powerful groups maintain their interests by making illegal any behavior that might be a threat to them. Laws thus become a mechanism of control, or "a weapon in social conflict."[38]

Conflict Theory and Criminology

The sociologist George Vold (1896–1967) was the first theorist to relate conflict theory to criminology. He argued that individuals band together in groups because they are social animals with needs that are best served through collective action. If the group serves its members, it survives; if not, new groups form to take its place. Individuals constantly clash as they try to advance the interests of their particular group over those of all the others. The result is that society is in a constant state of conflict, "one of the principal and essential social processes upon which the continuing ongoing of society depends." For Vold, the entire process of lawmaking and crime control is a direct reflection of conflict between interest groups, all trying to get laws passed in their favor and to gain control of the police power.[39]

The sociologist Ralf Dahrendorf and the criminologist Austin Turk are major contemporary contributors to the application of conflict theory to criminology. To Dahrendorf, the consensus model of society is utopian. He believes that enforced constraint, rather than cooperation, binds people together. Whether society is capitalist, socialist, or feudal, some people have the authority and others are subject to it. Society is made up of a large number of interest groups. The interests of one group do not always coincide with the needs of another—unions and management, for instance.

Dahrendorf argues that social change is constant, social conflicts are ever-present, disintegration and change are ongoing, and all societies are characterized by coercion of some people by others. The most important characteristics of class, he contends, are power and authority. The inequities remain for him the lasting determinant of social conflict. Conflict can be either destructive or constructive, depending on whether it leads to a breakdown of the social structure or to positive change in the social order.[40]

Austin Turk has continued and expanded this theoretical approach. "Criminality is not a biological, psychological, or even behavioral phenomenon," he says, "but a social status defined by the way in which an individual is perceived, evaluated, and treated by legal authorities." Criminal status is defined by those he calls the "authorities," the decision makers. Criminal status is imposed on the "subjects," the subordinate class. Turk explains that this process works so that both authorities and subjects learn to interact as performers in their dominant and submissive roles. There are "social norms of dominance" and "social norms of deference." Conflict arises when some people refuse to go along and they challenge the authorities. "Law breaking, then, becomes a measure of the stability of the ruler/ruled relationship."[41] The people who make the laws struggle to hold on to their power, while those who do not make laws struggle to do so.

People with authority use several forms of power to control society's goods and services: police or war power, economic power, political power, and ideological power (beliefs, values).[42] The laws made by the "ins" to condemn or condone various behaviors help shape all social institutions—indeed, the entire culture. Where education is mandatory, for example, the people in power are able to maintain the status quo by passing on their own value system from one generation to the next.[43]

History seems to demonstrate that primitive societies, in their earliest phases of development, tend to be homogeneous and to make laws by consensus. The more a society develops economically and politically, the more difficult it becomes to resolve conflict situations by consensus. For an early instance of criminal lawmaking by the conflict model, we can go back to 1530, when King Henry VIII of England broke away from the Roman Catholic Church because the pope refused to annul Henry's marriage to Catherine of Aragon so that he could marry Anne Boleyn. Henry confiscated church property and closed all the monasteries. Virtually

Conflict: Pro-choice advocates confront right-to-life supporters over the explosive issue of abortion.

overnight, tens of thousands of people who had been dependent on the monasteries for support were cast out, to roam the countryside in search of a living. Most ended up as beggars. This huge army of vagrants posed a burden on and danger to the establishment. To cope with the problem, Parliament revived the vagrancy laws of 1349, which prohibited the giving of aid to vagrants and beggars. Thus the powerful, by controlling the laws, gained control over the powerless.[44]

Empirical Evidence for the Conflict Model

Researchers have tested several conflict theory hypotheses, such as those pertaining to bias and discrimination in the criminal justice system, differential crime rates of powerful and powerless groups, and the intent behind the development of the criminal law. The findings offer mixed support for the theory.

Alan Lizotte studied 816 criminal cases in the Chicago courts over a one-year period to test the assumption that the powerless get harsher sentences. His analysis relating legal factors (such as the offense committed) and extralegal factors (such as the race and job of the defendant) to length of prison sentence pointed to significant sentencing inequalities related to race and occupation.[45] When Freda Adler studied the importance of nonlegal factors in the decision making of juries, she found that the socioeconomic level of the defendants significantly influenced their judgment.[46]

While these and similar studies tend to support conflict theory by demonstrating class or racial bias in the administration of criminal justice, others, unexpectedly, show an opposite bias.[47] When we evaluate the contribution of conflict theory to criminological thought, we must keep in mind Austin Turk's warning that conflict theory is often misunderstood. The theory does not, he points out, suggest that most criminals are innocent or that powerful persons engage in the same amount of deviant behavior as do powerless persons or that law enforcers typically discriminate against people without power. It does acknowledge, however, that behaviors common among society's more disadvantaged members have a greater likelihood of being called "crime" than the activities in which the more powerful typically participate.[48]

Conflict theory does not attempt to explain crime; it simply identifies social conflict as a basic fact of life and as a source of discriminatory treatment by the criminal justice system of groups and classes that lack the power and status of those who make and enforce the laws. Once we recognize this, we may find it possible to change the process of criminalizing people to provide greater justice. Conflict theorists anticipate a guided evolution, not a revolution, to improve the existing criminal justice system.

RADICAL THEORY

While labeling and conflict theorists were developing their perspectives, social and political conditions in the United States and Europe were changing rapidly and drastically. The youth of America were deeply disillusioned about a political and social structure that had brought about the assassinations of John F. Kennedy, Robert Kennedy, and Martin Luther King Jr.; the war in Vietnam; and the Watergate debacle. Many looked for radical solutions to social problems, and a number of young criminologists searched for answers to the nation's questions about crime and criminal justice. They found their answers in Marxism, a philosophy born in similar social turmoil a century earlier.

The Intellectual Heritage of Marxist Criminology

The major industrial centers of Europe suffered great hardships during the nineteenth century. The mechanization of industry and of agriculture, heavy population increases, and high rates of urbanization had created a massive labor surplus, high unemployment, and a burgeoning class of young urban migrants forced into the streets by poverty. London is said to have had at least 20,000 individuals who "rose every morning without knowing how they were to be supported through the day or where they were to lodge on the succeeding night, and cases of death from starvation appeared in the coroner's lists daily."[49] In other cities conditions were even worse.

Engels and Marx

It was against this background that Friedrich Engels (1820–1895) addressed the effects of the Industrial Revolution. A partner in his father's industrial empire, Engels was himself a member of the class he attacked as "brutally selfish." After a two-year stay in England, he documented the awful social conditions, the suffering, and the great increase in crime and arrests. All these problems he blamed on one factor—competition. In *The Condition of the Working Class in England,* published in 1845, he spelled out the association between crime and poverty as a political problem:

> The earliest, crudest, and least fruitful form of this rebellion was that of crime. The working man lived in poverty and want, and saw that others were better off than he. . . . Want conquered his inherited respect for the sacredness of property, and he stole.[50]

Though Karl Marx (1818–1883) paid little attention to crime specifically, he argued that all aspects of social life, including laws, are determined by economic organization. His philosophy reflects the economic despair that followed the Industrial Revolution. In his *Communist Manifesto* (1848) Marx viewed the history of all societies as a documentation of class struggles: "Freeman and slave, patrician and plebeian, lord and serf, guildmaster and journeyman, in a word, oppressor and oppressed, stood in constant opposition to one another."[51]

Marx went on to describe the most important relationship in industrial society as that between the capitalist bourgeoisie, who own the means of production, and the proletariat, or workers, who labor for them. Society, according to Marx, has always been organized in such a hierarchical fashion, with the state representing not the common interest but the interests of those who own the means of production. Capitalism breeds egocentricity, greed, and predatory behavior; but the worst crime of all is the exploitation of workers. Revolution, Marx concluded, is the only means to bring about change, and for that reason it is morally justifiable.

Many philosophers before Marx had noted the link between economic conditions and social problems, including crime. Among them were Plato, Aristotle, Virgil, Horace, Sir Thomas More, Cesare Beccaria, Jeremy Bentham, André Guerry, Adolphe Quételet, and Gabriel Tarde (several of whom we met in Chapter 3). But

PART II   Explanations of Crime and Criminal Behavior   203

> **:// Crime Surfing**
> www.soci.niu.edu/~critcrim/dp/dp.html
>
> Do critical criminologists support the death penalty, or are they opposed?

none of them had advocated revolutionary change. And none had constructed a coherent criminological theory that conformed with economic determinism, the cornerstone of the Marxist explanation that people who are kept in a state of poverty will rebel by committing crimes. Not until 1905 can we speak of Marxist criminology.

Willem Adriaan Bonger

As a student at the University of Amsterdam, Willem Adriaan Bonger (1876–1940) entered a paper in a competition on the influence of economic factors on crime. His entry did not win; but its expanded version, *Criminality and Economic Conditions,* which appeared in French in 1905, was selected for translation by the American Institute of Criminal Law and Criminology. Bonger wrote in his preface, "[I am] convinced that my ideas about the etiology of crime will not be shared by a great many readers of the American edition."[52] He was right. Nevertheless, the book is considered a classic and is invaluable to students doing research on crime and economics.

Bonger explained that the social environment of primitive people was interwoven with the means of production. People helped each other. They used what they produced. When food was plentiful, everyone ate. When food was scarce, everyone was hungry. Whatever people had, they shared. People were subordinate to nature. In a modern capitalist society, people are much less altruistic. They concentrate on production for profit rather than for the needs of the community. Capitalism encourages criminal behavior by creating a climate that is less conducive to social responsibility. "We have a right," argued Bonger, "to say that the part played by economic conditions in criminality is predominant, even decisive."[53]

Willem Bonger died as he had lived, a fervent antagonist of the evils of the social order. An archenemy of Nazism and a prominent name on Hitler's list of people to be eliminated, he refused to emigrate even when the German army was at the border. On May 10, 1940, as the German invasion of Holland began, he wrote to his son: "I don't see any future for myself and I cannot bow to this scum which will now overmaster us."[54] He then took his own life. He left a powerful political and criminological legacy. Foremost among his followers were German socialist philosophers of the progressive school of Frankfurt.

Georg Rusche and Otto Kirchheimer

Georg Rusche and Otto Kirchheimer began to write their classic work at the University of Frankfurt. Driven out of Germany by Nazi persecution, they continued their research in exile in Paris and completed it at Columbia University in New York in 1939. In *Punishment and the Social Structure,* they wrote that punishments had always been related to the modes of production and the availability of labor, rather than to the nature of the crimes themselves.

Consider galley slavery. Before the development of modern sailing techniques, oarsmen were needed to power merchant ships; as a result, galley slavery was a punishment in antiquity and in the Middle Ages. As sailing techniques were perfected, galley slavery was no longer necessary, and it lost favor as a sanction. By documenting the real purposes of punishments through the ages, Rusche and Kirchheimer made **penologists,** who study the penal system, aware that severe and cruel treatment of offenders had more to do with the value of human life and the needs of the economy than with preventing crime.

The names Marx, Engels, Bonger, and Rusche and Kirchheimer were all but forgotten by mainstream criminologists of the 1940s and 1950s, perhaps because of America's relative prosperity and conservatism during those years. But when tranquillity turned to turmoil in the mid-1960s, the forgotten names provided the intellectual basis for American and European radical criminologists, who explicitly stated their commitment to Marxism.

Radical Criminology since the 1970s

Radical criminology (also called critical, new, and Marxist criminology) made its first public appearance in 1968, when a group of British sociologists organized the National Deviancy Conference (NDC), a group of more than 300 intellectuals, social critics, deviants, and activists of various persuasions. What the group members had in common was a basic disillusion with the criminological studies being done by the British Home Office, which they believed was system-serving and "practical." They were concerned with the way the system controlled people rather than with traditional sociological and psychological explanations of crime. They shared a respect for the interactionist and labeling theorists but believed these theorists had become too traditional. Their answer was to form a new criminology based on Marxist principles.

The conference was followed by the publication in 1973 of *The New Criminology*, the first textual formulation of the new radical criminology. According to its authors, Ian Taylor, Paul Walton, and Jock Young, it is the underclass, the "labor forces of the industrial society," that is controlled through the criminal law and its enforcement, while "the owners of labor will be bound only by a civil law which regulates their competition between each other." The economic institution, then, is the source of all conflicts. Struggles between classes always relate to the distribution of resources and power, and only when capitalism is abolished will crime disappear.[55]

About the time that Marxist criminology was being formulated in England, it was also developing in the United States, particularly at the School of Criminology of the University of California at Berkeley, where Richard Quinney, Anthony Platt, Herman and Julia Schwendinger, William Chambliss, and Paul Takagi were at the forefront of the movement. These researchers were also influenced by interactionist and labeling theorists, as well as by the conflict theories of Vold, Dahrendorf, and Turk.

Though the radical criminologists share the central tenet of conflict theory, that laws are created by the powerful to protect their own interests, they disagree on the number of forces competing in the power struggle. For Marxist criminologists, there is only one dominating segment, the capitalist ruling class, which uses the criminal law to impose its will on the rest of the people in order to protect its property and to define as criminal any behavior that threatens the status quo.[56] The leading American spokesperson for radical criminology is Richard Quinney. His earliest Marxist publications appeared in 1973: "Crime Control in Capitalist Society" and "There's a Lot of Us Folks Grateful to the Lone Ranger."[57]

The second of these essays describes how Quinney drifted away from capitalism, with its folklore myths embodied in individual heroes like the Lone Ranger. He asserts that:

> The state is organized to serve the interests of the dominant economic class, the capitalist ruling class; that criminal law is an instrument the state and the ruling class use to maintain and perpetuate the social and economic order; that the contradictions of advanced capitalism . . . require that the subordinate classes remain oppressed by whatever means necessary, especially by the legal system's coercion and violence; and that only with the collapse of capitalist society, based on socialist principles, will there be a solution to the crime problem.[58]

In *Class, State, and Crime*, Quinney proclaims that "the criminal justice movement is . . . a state-initiated and state-supported effort to rationalize mechanisms of social control. The larger purpose is to secure a capitalist order that is in grave crisis, likely in its final stage of development."[59] Quinney challenges criminologists to abandon traditional ways of thinking about causation, to study what could be rather than what is, to question the assumptions of the social order, and to "ultimately develop a Marxist perspective."[60]

Marxist theory also can be found in the writings of other scholars who have adopted the radical approach to criminology. William Chambliss and Robert Seidman present their version in *Law, Order, and Power*:

> Society is composed of groups that are in conflict with one another and . . . the law represents an institutionalized tool of those in power (ruling class) which functions to provide them with superior moral as well as coercive power in conflict.[61]

PART II Explanations of Crime and Criminal Behavior

They comment that if, in the operation of the criminal justice system by the powerful, "justice or fairness happen to be served, it is sheer coincidence."[62]

To Barry Krisberg, crime is a function of privilege. The rich create crimes to distract attention from the injustices they inflict on the masses. Power determines which group holds the privilege, defined by Krisberg as that which is valued by a given social group in a given historical time.[63] Herman and Julia Schwendinger supported this idea in their summary of the causes of delinquency. They stated that legal relations secure a capitalistic mode of production, while laws are created to secure the labor force. The bourgeoisie are always in a state of being threatened by the proletariats; therefore, while some laws may secure lower-class interests, capitalist interests underlie the basic constitutional laws. Laws in general, according to the Schwendingers, contradict their stated purpose. The Schwendingers went even further in proposing that the state fails to control delinquency because lower-class deviants supply factories with a ready pool of low-wage laborers.[64]

Anthony Platt, in a forceful attack on traditional criminology, has even suggested it would not be "too farfetched to characterize many criminologists as domestic war criminals" because they have "serviced domestic repression in the same way that economics, political science, and anthropology have greased the wheels and even manufactured some of the important parts of modern imperialism."[65]

He suggests that traditional criminology serves the state through research studies that purport to "investigate" the conditions of the lower class but in reality only prove, with their probes of family life, education, jobs, and so on, that the members of the lower class are in fact less intelligent and more criminal than the rest of us. Platt claims that these inquiries, based as they are on biased and inaccurate data, are merely tools of the middle-class oppressors.

A number of other areas have come under the scrutiny of Marxist criminologists.[66] They have studied how informal means of settling disputes outside courts actually extend the control of the criminal justice system by adjudicating cases that are not serious enough for the courts; how juvenile court dispositions are unfairly based on social class; how sentencing reform has failed to benefit the lower class; how police practices during the latter half of the nineteenth century were geared to control labor rather than crime; how rape victims are made to feel guilty; how penitentiary reform has benefited the ruling class by giving it more control over the lower class; and how capitalist interests are strengthened by private policing.[67]

Evaluation: Marxist Criminological Theory

Critiques of Marxist criminology range from support for the attention the approach calls to the crimes of the powerful to accusations that it is nothing more than a revival of the Robin Hood myth, in which the poor steal from the rich in order to survive.[68] By far the most incisive criticism is that of sociologist Carl Klockars, who points out that the division of society into social classes may have a beneficial effect, contrary to Marxist thought. Standards, he argues, are created by some people to inspire the remainder of society. In present-day America, Klockars claims, poverty has lost some of its meaning because luxuries and benefits are spread out over classes. To him, ownership and control of industry are two different things. Anyone who buys a share of stock, for example, can be an owner, while control is handled by bureaucrats who may or may not be owners.[69]

Class Interests versus Interest Groups Klockars attacks Marxists for focusing exclusively on class interests and ignoring the fact that society is made up of many interest groups. This Marxist bias has yielded results that are untrustworthy and predictable, ignore reality, explain issues that are self-evident (some businesspeople are greedy and corrupt), and do not explain issues that are relevant (why socialist states have crime).[70]

Not without a note of sympathy, Richard Sparks summed up the criticism when he said:

The organization Witness for Peace, a politically independent grass-roots organization, recently demonstrating against U.S. policies and corporate practices that contribute to poverty and oppression.

Marxist criminologists tend to be committed to praxis and the desire for radical social reform; but this commitment is not entailed by the scientific claims which Marxists make, and it has sometimes led to those claims being improperly suspect.[71]

Opposition to the new criminology follows many paths, but the most popular, in one way or another, is concerned with its oversimplification of causation by the exclusive focus on capitalism.[72] Critics also attack Marxist criminologists for their assertion that even by studying crime empirically, criminologists are supporting the status quo. That puts Marxist criminologists on the defensive, because if they are not ideologically in a position to expose their theories to empirical research or are unwilling to do so, their assertions will remain just that—assertions with no proof.[73]

Collapse of the Economic Order. Even sharper criticism of Marxist theory can be anticipated in the wake of the collapse of the Marxist economic order in the Soviet Union, Poland, Czechoslovakia, Hungary, the German Democratic Republic, Bulgaria, Albania, and Romania, as well as in countries in Africa and Latin America.[74] Many East European criminologists are no longer quoting Marx in their publications, which tend increasingly to focus on the classical rule-of-law concept. But Quinney has never seen the conditions in those countries as representative of Marxism. According to him, a true Marxist state has not yet been attained, but the ideal is worth pursuing.[75]

To the credit of radical criminologists, it must be said that they have encouraged their more traditional colleagues to look with a criti-

The Forgotten Criminology of Genocide

Why has criminology forgotten the systematic decimation of 1 1/2 million Armenians by the Young Turks during World War I, as well as the systematic killing of 6 million Jews and the extermination of another 5 million including Gypsies, political opponents, mentally ill, retarded, and other "inferior" peoples between 1941 and 1945? How could criminology have neglected an examination of the crimes against humanity that resulted in an estimated 7 million to 16 million deaths over the past 50 years since World War II? You would think that criminology, an academic field concerned with violence, aggression, power, and victimization, would focus on the crime of genocide.

If not in the violence literature, one would expect to find this scholarship in the efforts of conflict, critical, and Marxist theorists in their explanations of organized, state-sanctioned violence and oppression. Criminologists whose life's work is crime prevention also must regularly discuss the causal factors that lead to acts of genocide. If you search through every issue of the journals *Criminology* and *Journal of Criminal Law and Criminology* since their inception, however, you will find only one article on genocide, the most serious of all crimes, and that article was written over 40 years ago. So, why is there no criminology of genocide? Our answers to this question, regrettably, are inadequate.

1. *Genocide is a political act reflecting the will of sovereignty.* Genocide, it has been said, is a political rather than criminal act, most often employed to enhance a country's solidarity and unification. Decisions to liquidate, exterminate, and cleanse a minority population are matters of political policy reflecting the will of sovereignty. The immorality of genocide is tempered by a moral generosity to a sovereign's motivation. The effect of shrouding genocide in a political cloth is to see the annihilation of certain populations as something less than or different from a crime.(1)

2. *Genocide is a breach of international norms and international law.* Several years ago two groups of victims and representatives of victims from Bosnia-Herzegovina brought an action in federal court under the Alien Tort Claims Act against the president and leader of the Bosnian Serb forces for aggravated sexual assault, forced prostitution and impregnation, various acts of extreme torture, and mass execution.(2) The case carried significant symbolic value. Are acts of genocide torts or crimes, violations of international norms or international law? The answers to these questions are far from simple.

3. *Genocide is committed by the state.* Of the many revelations over the past 50 years, criminologists seem to have the most difficulty with the notion that an organization or entity, whether a corporation or nation-state, may commit a crime. When crimes are imputed from an individual to an inanimate entity, the intellectual challenge becomes: Should an individual be blamed as well? The equivocation with bringing those responsible for ethnic cleansing and planned mass murder to justice may be explained, at least in part, by a resistance to the notion that individuals within a "guilty" collective are to blame.

4. *The magnitude of victimization in genocide defies belief.* The extent of victimization and harm in genocide strains any assessment of seriousness. Who appreciates differences in seriousness when the offense is, for example, 100,000, 250,000, or 500,000 butchered Hutus or Tutsis?

How is it that so many people in countries around the world live in shadows of past genocides and seemingly choose to ignore it?

Is there a difference in judgments of offense seriousness between the planned killing of 6 million versus 7 million people?

5. *Problems arise regarding both denying and admitting atrocity.* Two prominent themes that emerge from the literature on genocide capture an ambivalence hard felt by some survivors and refugees of genocide. This ambivalence is captured in the titles of two recently published books on the Holocaust— Deborah Lipstadt's *Denying the Holocaust* and Lawrence L. Langer's *Admitting the Holocaust*.(3) The problem of admission is with the casting of genocide as a historical problem requiring serious study; the effects of intellectualizing mass torture and death; the packaging of the Holocaust neatly into a social science; and the elevation of

continued

Window to the World

Window to the World

The Forgotten Criminology of Genocide—continued

genocide to a respectable academic discipline of its own, with courses that fit a core curriculum and endow Holocaust professorships. The problem with denial comes from historical revisionists.

Many have commented that the field of criminology has matured. Unfortunately, it has done so without considering the most serious of all crimes.(4)

Sources

1. Irving Louis Horowitz, *Taking Lives: Genocide and State Power* (New Brunswick, NJ: Transaction, 1997).
2. *Kaic v. Karadzic*, 70 F.3d 232 (2d Cir. 1995).
3. Deborah Lipstadt, *Denying the Holocaust: The Growing Assault on Truth and Memory* (New York: Free Press, 1993); and Lawrence L. Langer, *Admitting the Holocaust: Collected Essays* (New York: Oxford, 1996).
4. William S. Laufer, "The Forgotten Criminology of Genocide," *Advances in Criminological Theory*, **8** (1999): 45–58.

Questions for Discussion

1. How satisfactory are these answers to you?
2. What could conflict and radical theorists contribute to this dialogue?

---

cal eye at all aspects of the criminal justice system, including the response of the system to both poor and rich offenders. Their concern is the exercise of power. They ask: Whose power? On whose behalf? For whose benefit? What is the legitimacy of that power? And who is excluded from the exercise of power, by whom, and why? Criminologists have had to address all these questions. Many may not have changed their answers, but the fact that the questions have been raised has ensured clearer answers than had been offered before.

Emerging Explanations

Over the last decade a number of important critical perspectives have emerged that are worthy of attention. These perspectives include radical feminist theory, left realism, abolitionist and anarchist criminology, and peacemaking criminology.

Radical Feminist Theory. One significant limitation to critical and Marxist work is an almost exclusive focus on crime committed by males. This limitation has been addressed only recently by both radical and socialist (Marxist) feminists. The former find the cause of crime in women to be male aggression, as well as men's attempts to control and subordinate women. The latter view female crime in terms of class, gender, and race oppression.[76]

Research by both radical and socialist feminists provides important insights into our conceptualization of law, social control, power relationships, and crime-causation theory. They include:

- Reframing the way in which rape is conceptualized (see Chapter 10)
- Acknowledging the fact that the way in which criminologists conceive of and define violence is male-centered
- Uncovering the relationship between male power, female economic dependency, and battery (for example, spouse abuse)
- Revealing the powerful effect of gender on justice processing[77]

Left Realism. Another critical perspective is left realism.[78] This school of thought emerged over the last decade as a response to the perception that radical criminologists (called "radical idealists" by left realists) place far too much weight on the evils of elite deviance, largely ignoring the fact that the disenfranchised lower classes are persistently victimized by street crime. Radical idealists, it is argued, have developed only weak crime-control strategies. Left realists, on the other hand, recognize street crime as an inevitable outcome of social and political deprivation. They seek a crime-control agenda, capable of being implemented in a capitalist system, that will protect the more vulner-

As the Marxist socioeconomic order was toppled, so was the statue of the founder of the KGB, Felix Dzerzhinsky, at the Moscow headquarters.

able members of the lower classes from crime and the fear of crime. The latter, according to left realists, has given conservative right-wing politicians a green light to promote a repressive law-and-order agenda.

Abolitionist and Anarchist Criminology. Both abolitionist and anarchist critical theories dispute the existing systems of supremacy. Abolitionism is very much like left realism in its rejection of state controls, as it focuses on the punitive response of segregative punishment. According to abolitionist theory, crime and punishment have a reciprocal effect on each other, with one causing the other. Abolitionist theory advocates the redistribution of power, by returning it to communities and individuals, in order to fix the existing power differential. Similar to this is the anarchist theory of criminology, which also believes that the destruction of communities by the state is at the root of crime. Anarchists, however, reject the sensible and organized opposition to this condition led by abolitionists, opting instead to wage the struggle with chaos and disorder.

Peacemaking Criminology. The most recently articulated critical perspective, peacemaking, promotes the idea of peace, justice, and equality in society. The current obsession with punishment and the war on crime suggests an orientation to criminology that only encourages violence. Peacemakers suggest that mutual aid, mediation, and conflict resolution, rather than coercive state control, are the best means to achieve a harmonious, peaceful society.[79] In short, peacemaking criminology advocates humanistic, nonviolent, and peaceful solutions to crime.

The peacemaking perspective is part of an intellectual and social movement toward restorative justice. What is restorative justice? According to Braithwaite restorative justice "means restoring victims, a more victim-centered criminal justice system, as well as restoring offenders and restoring community." This includes restoring:

- Property loss
- Sense of security
- Dignity
- Sense of empowerment
- Deliberative democracy
- Harmony based on a feeling that justice has been done
- Social support

REVIEW

Labeling theory, conflict theory, and radical theory offer alternative explanations of crime, in the sense that they do not restrict their inquiry to individual characteristics or to social or communal processes. These three theories examine the impact of lawmaking and law enforcement processes on the creation of offenders. The labeling and conflict theories, as critical as they are of the existing system of criminal justice, envisage a system made more just and equitable by reform and democratic processes; radical theory demands revolutionary change. With long historical antecedents, all three theories gained prominence in the 1960s and early 1970s, during an era of rebellion against social, political, and economic inequities.

Labeling theory does not presume to explain all crime, but it does demonstrate that the criminal justice system is selective in determining who is to be labeled a criminal. It explains how labeling occurs, and it blames the criminal justice system for contributing to the labeling process and, therefore, to the crime problem.

Conflict theory goes a step beyond labeling theory in identifying the forces that selectively decide in the first place what conduct should be singled out for condemnation—usually, so it is claimed, to the detriment of the powerless and the benefit of the powerful.

Radical theory singles out the relationship between the owners of the means of production and the workers under capitalism as the root cause of crime and of all social inequities. Radical theory demands the overthrow of the existing order, which is said to perpetuate criminality by keeping the oppressed classes under the domination of the capitalist ruling class.

All three theories have adherents and opponents. Research to demonstrate the validity of the theories has produced mixed results. More important, all these theories have challenged conventional criminologists to rethink their approaches and to provide answers to questions that had not been asked before.

CRIMINOLOGY & PUBLIC POLICY

The United States has a long history of denying convicted felons the right to vote. At common law, "when all felons were in principle subject to capital punishment," worrying about convicted felons' voting rights was almost nonsensical. Yet the expansion of the "concept of felony," accompanied by rising incarceration rates, has called into question the traditional practice of "disenfranchising" convicts for life. Today, one might be permanently disenfranchised for participating with others "in a course of disorderly conduct," "breaking a water pipe," "aiding or inducing another to engage in gambling," or aiding, abetting, or encouraging any "bull, bear, dog, or cock fight." Current estimates place the total number of disenfranchised felons and exfelons at approximately 3.9 million voting-age citizens. Of this number, approximately 1.4 million have completed their sentences. Over one-third of the total disenfranchised population are black men.

Recently, felon disenfranchisement laws have received considerable attention from a variety of studies and in the popular press. Some commentators discuss felon disenfranchisement in terms of altered electoral outcomes; others emphasize its effect on democratic representation. Still others focus on felon disenfranchisement's disparate impact, contending that such laws deny the vote to over 10 percent of the black voting-age population in 15 states.

No matter how one views the issue, it is difficult to deny that skyrocketing incarceration rates have raised the stakes of criminal disenfranchisement, altering the composition of the American electorate. Moreover, given this nation's history of voting discrimination, any process that disproportionately disenfranchises racial minorities should be cause for concern. (Source: "Developments in the Law: One Person, No Vote: The Laws of Felon Disenfranchisement," *Harvard Law Review,* **115** (2002): 1939.)

Questions for Discussion What is the justification for these laws? What do you suppose the effect is of taking away an ex-offender's voting rights? Does it unfairly contribute to the labeling of ex-offenders? What role does race play in the effect of these laws? Do you support law reform in this area? If so, what would you propose?

YOU BE THE CRIMINOLOGIST

What kind of crime-prevention program is suggested by critical, Marxist, and labeling theories? How would you go about designing such a program? How would you evaluate its effectiveness?

KEY TERMS

The numbers next to the terms refer to the pages on which the terms are defined.

conflict theory (197)
consensus model (197)
due process (190)
equal protection (190)
labeling theory (191)
penologists (203)
radical criminology (204)
social interactionists (191)

CHAPTER 9
Environmental Theory

Situational Theories of Crime
  Environmental Criminology
  Rational-Choice Perspective
  Routine-Activity Approach
  Practical Applications of
    Situational Theories of Crime

Theories of Victimization
  Lifestyle Theories
  Victim-Offender Interaction
  Repeat Victimization
  Hot Spots of Crime
  Geography of Crime
  Interrelatedness of Theories

Preventing Crimes against Places, People, and Valuable Goods
  Situational Crime Prevention
  Displacement

Theory Informs Policy

REVIEW

CRIMINOLOGY & PUBLIC POLICY

YOU BE THE CRIMINOLOGIST

KEY TERMS

Boxes
  Window to the World:
    Decresting the Lovebug, Worldwide
  From the Pages of *The New York Times*: *New York City Cracks Down on "Hot Spots"*
  Of Immediate Concern:
    Maximum-Security Schools

Special Features
  Crime Surfing
  Did You Know?

KEY TERMS
displacement
environmental criminology
rational choice
routine activity
target hardening
theories of victimization

At the Denver Colorado International Airport, security personnel are monitoring checkpoints throughout the facility.

In the Riverside, California, Superior Court, a victim who nearly bled to death after a brutal rape asked her attacker, "Do you think God loves me?" One hour with the "monster" and 90 minutes of jury deliberation, ended with a potential 82-year prison term.[1] Sizzler's Steak House in Arvada, Colorado, was twice victimized within a two-week period, apparently by the same "scruffy" white male in his mid 30s or early 40s. The assailant, who claimed to be armed with a Magnum revolver, is also a suspect in several other robberies in the area.[2] It happened in Paramus, New Jersey: Car thieves used a stolen limo, equipped with machinery to duplicate keys, to target cars at Garden State Plaza for their thefts. What a great location! There are three escape routes: Route 4, Route 17, and the Garden State Parkway."[3]

Here we have three different types of crime, committed in three different jurisdictions—California, Colorado, and New Jersey—involving three different types of harm: nonconsensual intercourse, the taking of property by force and violence, and the loss of automobiles. The prosecutors in these jurisdictions will know what to do. They will identify these crimes under their respective penal codes as sexual assault, robbery, and larceny, respectively, and they will file charges accordingly. But the criminologist, looking more deeply into these crime scenarios, will consider something in addition, something seemingly not of interest to the law, namely, that each of the three crimes occurs at a specific time, at a specific place. The presence of an offender is only one of the necessary components: crimes require many conditions that are independent of the offender, such as the availability of a person to be assaulted or of goods to be stolen.

The three scenarios enable us to see how, up to

213

the actual moment of the crime, the events were a part of everyday life: People sleep in their homes; cars break down, sometimes at odd hours; stores are open for business; and people own Hondas, which must be parked when not being driven. For a full understanding of crime, it is necessary to find out how offenders view the scenes and situations around them as they exercise an option to commit a crime.

In other chapters we have focused on factors explaining why individuals and groups engage in criminal behavior. Now we look at how, in recent years, some criminologists have focused on why offenders choose to commit one offense rather than another at a given time and place. They identify conditions under which those who are prone to commit crime will in fact do so. Current criminological research shows that both a small number of victims and a small number of places experience a large amount of all crime committed. Crimes are events. Criminals choose their targets. Certain places actually attract criminals. Think about the community you live in. Are there some places you hesitate to go to alone? If so, you recognize that some spaces are more dangerous than others. Are there areas that are safe during the day, but not at night? Crime has temporal patterns—some crimes happen more often at night than during the day; others happen more on the weekend than during the rest of the week. There are even what criminologists call seasonal patterns. Certain lifestyles increase people's chances of being victimized. For example, is a drunk person walking alone more likely to be attacked than a sober one? Although victims of crime rarely are to blame for their victimization, they frequently play a role in the crimes that happen to them.

In this chapter we discuss theories of crime and theories of victimization. We will demonstrate how various environmental, opportunity, and victimization theories are interrelated. We will also explore the prevention of crimes against people, places, and valuable goods, presenting current criminological research. In this discussion we include situational crime prevention, diffusion of benefits, routine precautions, and the theoretical and practical implications of focusing on the victims and targets of crime.

PART II Explanations of Crime and Criminal Behavior   215

SITUATIONAL THEORIES OF CRIME

Among the theories of crime that focus on the situation in which a crime occurs, three distinct approaches have been identified: environmental criminology, the rational-choice perspective, and the routine-activity approach. These theoretical approaches to crime are sometimes called "opportunity theories" because they analyze the various situations that provide opportunities for specific crimes to occur (see Table 9.1).

Environmental Criminology

Environmental criminology examines the location of a specific crime and the context in which it occurred in order to understand and explain crime patterns. They ask: Where and when did the crime occur? What are the physical and social characteristics of the crime site? What movements bring offender and target together at the crime site? Environmental criminologists want to know how physical "location in time and space" interacts with the offender, the target/victim, and the law that makes the crime an illegal act.[4]

Contrary to the established criminological theories that explain criminal motivation, environmental criminology begins with the assumption that some people are criminally motivated. Through mapping crimes on global, country, state, county, city, or site-specific levels,

TABLE 9.1 Ten Principles of Opportunity and Crime

1. Opportunities play a role in causing all crime.
2. Crime opportunities are highly specific.
3. Crime opportunities are concentrated in time and space.
4. Crime opportunities depend on everyday movements.
5. One crime produces opportunities for another.
6. Some products offer more tempting crime opportunities.
7. Social and technological changes produce new crime opportunities.
8. Opportunities for crime can be reduced.
9. Reducing opportunities does not usually displace crime.
10. Focused opportunity reduction can produce wider declines in crime.

Source: Marcus Felson and Ronald V. Clarke, *Opportunity Makes the Thief: Practical Theory for Crime Prevention*, Police Research Series Paper 98 (London: Home Office, 1998), p. 9.

New York Police Department Compstat: Crime mapping is now a powerful tool in the fight against crime. Police departments around the country are developing sophisticated mapping programs to track crime trends, "hot spots," and the pattern of offending.

such as a particular building or plot of land, environmental criminologists can see crime patterns. They then relate these crime patterns to the number of targets; to the offender population; to the location of routine activities, such as work, school, shopping, or recreation; to security; and to traffic flow.

Mapping crimes and analyzing the spatial crime patterns is not new (Chapter 3). In the nineteenth century, Guerry examined the spatial patterning of crime through his comparison of conviction rates in various regions in France.[5] Quételet tried to establish links between seasonal differences and the probability of committing crime. He found, for instance, that property crimes increase in the winter months in France, whereas "the violence of the passions predominating in summer, excites to more frequent personal collisions" and a rise in crimes against persons (Chapter 3).[6] Contemporary research takes a more focused, crime-specific approach.

Rational-Choice Perspective

The **rational-choice** perspective, developed by Ronald Clarke and Derek Cornish, is based on two main theoretical approaches.[7] The first of these—utilitarianism—was addressed in Chapter 3. It assumes that people make decisions with the goal of maximizing pleasure and minimizing pain. The second basis for the rational-choice perspective is traditional economic choice theory, which argues that people evaluate the options and choose what they believe will satisfy their needs. According to this perspective, a person decides to commit a particular crime after concluding that the benefits (the pleasure) outweigh the risks and the effort (the pain).[8]

The rational-choice perspective assumes that people make these decisions with a goal in mind, and that they are made more or less intelligently and with free will. This contrasts with the theories of criminality that have an underlying assumption that when people commit a crime, forces beyond their control drive them. Rational choice implies a limited sense of rationality. An offender does not know all the details of a situation; rather, he or she relies on cues in the environment or characteristics of targets. This means the offender may not be able to calculate the costs and benefits accurately, and in hindsight, the decision may seem foolish. Further, an offender may have an impaired ability to make wise choices, perhaps because of intoxication from drugs or alcohol.

According to the rational-choice perspective, most crime is neither extraordinary nor the product of a deranged mind. Most crime is quite ordinary and committed by reasoning individuals who decide that the chances of getting caught are low and the possibilities for a relatively good payoff are high. Since the rational-choice perspective treats each crime as a specific event and focuses on analyzing all its components, it looks at crime in terms of an offender's decision to commit a *specific* offense at *a particular* time and place.

A variety of factors (or characteristics) come into play when an offender decides to commit a crime. These factors are called *choice structuring properties*. With the emphasis of rational-choice theory on analyzing each crime on a crime-specific basis, each particular type of crime has its own set of choice structuring properties (Figure 9.1). Those for sexual assault differ from those for computer crime, and those for burglary differ from those for theft. Nevertheless, these properties tend to fall into the same seven categories. Thus, a potential thief, before committing a theft, is likely to consider the following aspects (categories):

- The number of targets and their accessibility
- Familiarity with the chosen method (for example, fraud by credit card)
- The monetary yield per crime
- The expertise needed
- The time required to commit the act
- The physical danger involved
- The risk of apprehension

Characteristics fall into two distinct sets: those of the offender and those of the offense. The offender's characteristics include specific needs, values, learning experiences, and so on. The characteristics of the offense include the location of the target and the potential yield. According to rational-choice theory, involvement in crime depends on a personal decision made after one has weighed available information.

FIGURE 9.1 Event model (*example:* burglary in a middle-class suburb).

```
              DECISION
           To commit burglary
           /                \
  SELECTED                   REJECTED
  (MIDDLE-CLASS) AREA        (MIDDLE-CLASS) AREA
  Easily accessible,         Unfamiliar; distant,
  few police patrols;        neighborhood watch,
  low security housing,      no public transport
  larger gardens
      |                          |
  BURGLED HOME               NOT BURGLED
  No one at home;            Nosy neighbors,
  especially affluent,       burglar alarm,
  detached,                  no rear access,
  patio doors,               visible from street;
  bushes and other cover,    window locks; dog
  corner site
```

Source: Adapted from Ronald V. Clarke and Derek B. Cornish, "Modeling Offenders' Decisions: A Framework for Research and Policy," in *Crime and Justice*, vol. 6, eds. Michael Tonry and Norval Morris (Chicago: University of Chicago, 1985), p. 169.

Rational-choice theory, unlike traditional theories, is not concerned with strategies of overall crime prevention. (It leaves those problems to others.) Rather, it is concerned with reducing the likelihood that any given offense will be committed by somebody "involved" in criminal activity. This theory, therefore, has its greatest potential in developing strategies to frustrate perpetrators and to prevent them from committing a crime then and there. It has its greatest challenge in demonstrating that such prevention will not lead to the commission of the intended crime later on, or to the commission of other crimes (displacement). We turn to both of these issues shortly.

> **Did You Know?**
>
> ... that many of the things we do every day protect us from being victims of crime? Simple things like locking our doors, hiding our purses and wallets under the car seat, not flashing money in public, and avoiding places that make us feel unsafe are known as routine precautions. These small behaviors probably prevent more crime than police, courts, and corrections put together.

Routine-Activity Approach

According to Lawrence Cohen and Marcus Felson, a crime can occur only if there is someone who intends to commit a crime (likely offender), something or someone to be victimized (a suitable target), and no other person present to prevent or observe the crime (the absence of a capable guardian) (Figure 9.2). Later revisions added a fourth element—no person to control the activities of the likely offender (personal handler). When a suitable target that is unguarded comes together in time and space with a likely offender who is not "handled," the potential for a crime is there.[9] This explanation is called the **routine-activity** approach. It does not explore the factors that influence the offender's decision to commit a crime. Instead, Cohen and Felson focus on the routine or everyday activities of people, such as going to work, pursuing recreation, running errands, and the like. It is through routine activities that offenders come into contact with suitable victims and targets.

The routine-activity approach began with an analysis of crime rate increases in the post–World War II era (1947 to 1974), when socioeconomic conditions had improved in America. The increase was puzzling, since the general public (and some criminologists) expected crime rates to decrease with an increase in prosperity. But the authors of the routine-activity approach demonstrated that certain technological changes and alterations in the workforce create new crime opportunities. They referred to increases in female participation in the labor force, out-of-town travel, automobile usage, and technological advances as factors that account for higher risks of predatory victimization. Further advances in technology create further opportunities for the commission of crime. For example,

FIGURE 9.2 Components of a criminal event: the model of the routine-activity approach.

Window to the World

Decresting the Lovebug, Worldwide

It happened long before rational choice and routine activities had been created. Environmental design and situational crime prevention had yet to be invented. Yet there were Volkswagen Beetles the world over.

By 1961 Volkswagen (VW) had produced more than four million of these cars, fondly known as lovebugs, according to a popular movie of that time. Close to one million were being driven in America, and the rest all over the world. On their hoods, these cars had the distinctive crest of the town of their manufacture: Wolfsburg.

It so happens that soon after the Beetles reached the American market, they lost their crests. Research conducted in 1961 established that 80 percent of the Beetles in the United States had been decrested. The question naturally arose: Who did it (and why)? Police statistics were useless, since VW owners did not feel inclined to report a loss amounting to a little over $3, even though some cars had body damage (the result of removal) many times that amount. Nor did VW owners report the loss to their insurance companies—the value being below the deductible.

The researchers got the help of industry. VW of America made available its sales figures for replacement crests. These figures, statistically analyzed, showed an amazing pattern: The crest thefts started in the east and traveled west within a little over two years. The thefts also traveled from the outer perimeters of cities to the suburbs (in less time).

Research established that decrestings were highest in the neighborhood of junior high schools. In collaboration with junior high school administrators and police officials, it was learned that many students had amassed quantities of VW crests (but not those of other motor vehicles). Some were wearing them as necklaces; others had presented them to girlfriends.

Further statistical analysis showed that the fad—for that is what it seemed to be—had spread all over the world—except Brazil. It turned out that VW Beetles manufactured in Brazil were not adorned with the Wolfsburg crest, but with the totally different crest of São Paulo, which apparently was not attractive to pubescent males.

A copy of the research report was sent to the VW company. Now everybody knows how reluctant VW was to change its lovebug. But it did: Within a few months the Beetles rolled off VW's assembly line without the crest, but with a slightly longer chrome strip. Problem solved, no more decrestings, no more body damage to the hood.

Source

Gerhard O. W. Mueller, *Delinquency and Puberty: Examination of a Juvenile Delinquency Fad* (New York: Criminal Law Education and Research Center, 1971; Fred B. Rothman, Distr.).

Top photo: VW with crest popular with young males. Bottom photo: De-crested VW.

Questions for Discussion

1. Which of the theories discussed in this chapter best explains the decresting of VW Beetles?
2. What can and should manufacturers of any product do at the design stage to prevent their products from becoming the targets (or instruments) of crime?

---

as television sets, VCRs, personal and laptop computers, and CD players have become more common and lighter to carry, they have become attractive targets for thieves and burglars. The chance that a piece of property will become the target of a theft is based on the value of the target and its weight.[10] One need only compare the theft of washing machines and of electronic goods. Although both washing machines and electronic goods (such as television sets, laptop computers, and compact disc players) are expensive, washing machines are so heavy that their value is estimated at $4 per pound, compared with roughly $400 per pound for a laptop computer. And, of course, cellular phones have increasingly been subject to theft, for resale, for unauthorized telephone use, and for the facilitation of other crimes. Thus, cellular phones, as

A male thief shoplifts from a music store by stuffing CDs into his pants as an employee appears to be guarding the merchandise.

useful as they are in helping potential crime victims feel more secure, are also used increasingly by drug dealers to reduce the risk of having their calls traced.[11] It may be concluded that while technological developments help society run more smoothly, they also create new targets for theft, make old targets more suitable, or create new tools for criminals to use in committing their crimes. As people's daily work and leisure activities change with time, the location of property and personal targets also changes.

The logic of the routine-activity argument is straightforward: Routine patterns of work, play, and leisure time affect the convergence in time and place of motivated offenders who are not "handled," suitable targets, and the absence of guardians. If one component is missing, crime is not likely to be committed. And if all components are in place and one of them is strengthened, crime is likely to increase. Even if the proportions of motivated offenders and targets stay the same, changes in routine activities alone—for example, changes of the sort we have experienced since World War II—will raise the crime rate by multiplying the opportunities for crime. This approach has helped explain, among other things, rates of victimization for specific crimes, rates of urban homicide, and "hot spots"—areas that produce a disproportionate number of calls to police.[12]

Practical Applications of Situational Theories of Crime

The trio of approaches discussed here—environmental criminology, rational choice, and routine activities—often work together to explain why a person may commit a crime in a particular situation. We look now at how these theories of crime are used to explain specific varieties of crime, and how the ideas that arise from these theories have practical applications.

Burglars and Burglary. Criminologists are increasingly interested in the factors that go into a decision to burglarize: the location or setting of the building, the presence of guards or dogs, the type of burglar alarms and external lighting, and so forth. Does a car in the driveway or a radio playing music in the house have a significant impact on the choice of home to burglarize? George Rengert and John Wasilchick conducted extensive interviews with suburban burglars in an effort to understand their techniques. They found significant differences with respect to several factors:[13]

Thomas Crown (portrayed by Pierce Brosnan) crafted an extremely clever and well-planned theft of a painting from a well-guarded museum. Of course, not all burglars are so affluent and calculative.

- *The amount of planning* that precedes a burglary. Professional burglars plan more than do amateurs.
- The extent to which a burglar engages in *systematic selection of a home.* Some burglars examine the obvious clues, such as presence of a burglar alarm, a watchdog, mail piled up in the mailbox, newspapers on a doorstep. More experienced burglars look for subtle clues, for example, closed windows coupled with air conditioners that are turned off.
- The extent to which a burglar pays *attention to situational cues.* Some burglars routinely choose a corner property because it offers more avenues of escape, has fewer adjoining properties, and offers visibility.

Rengert and Wasilchick have also examined the use of time and place in burglary (Figure 9.3). Time is a critical factor to burglars, for three reasons:

- They must minimize the time spent in targeted places so as not to reveal their intention to burglarize.
- Opportunities for burglary occur only when a dwelling is unguarded or unoccupied, that is, during daytime. (Many burglars would call in sick so often that they would be fired from their legitimate jobs; others simply quit their jobs because the jobs interfered with their burglaries.)
- Burglars have "working hours"; that is, they have time available only during a limited number of hours (if they have a legitimate job).

Before committing their offenses, burglars take into account familiarity with the area, fear of recognition, concern over standing out as somebody who does not belong, and the possibility (following some successful burglaries) that a particular area is no longer cost-beneficial. Season, too, plays an important role. One experienced burglar stated that because neighborhoods are populated with children in the summer, he opted for winter months: "The best time to do crime out here is between 8:00 and 9:00 [A.M.]. All the mothers are taking the kids to school. I wait until I see the car leave. By the time she gets back, I've come and gone."[14]

Recent research demonstrates how important it is for burglars to have prior knowledge of their targets. They obtain such knowledge by

FIGURE 9.3 Crime day of burglar #26.

Source: George Rengert and John Wasilchick, *Suburban Burglary: A Time and a Place for Everything* (Springfield, Ill.: Charles C Thomas, 1985), p. 35.

knowing the occupants, by being tipped off about the occupants, or by observing the potential target.[15] Some burglars even acquire jobs that afford them the opportunity to observe their potential victims' daily activities; others gain access to the interior of a house, search for valuable goods, and steal them at a later date.

Robbers and Robberies. Richard Wright and Scott Decker conducted in-depth interviews with street robbers and found that they frequently victimize other street-involved individuals—drug dealers, drug users, and gang members—people who, because they are criminals themselves, are unlikely to go to the police. These people are also targeted because they are believed to have a lot of money, jewelry, and other desirable items. Street robbers report that they sometimes specifically target people whom they do not like, or people who have hurt or offended them in the past. When women are targeted, it is because robbers believe they will not resist and are not armed. On the other hand, women are not the desirable targets men are because robbers think women do not carry as much money.[16]

Criminologists also study whether commercial robbers operate the same way as street robbers in their selection of targets. Robbers who target business establishments are interested in some of the same factors that concern burglars. Perpetrators carefully examine the location of the potential robbery, the potential gain, the capability of security personnel, the possibility of intervention by bystanders, and the presence of guards, cameras, and alarms.[17]

Criminologists have found that potential victims and establishments can do quite a bit to decrease the likelihood of being robbed. Following a series of convenience-store robberies in Gainesville, Florida, in 1985, a city ordinance required store owners to clear their windows of signs that obstructed the view of the interior, to position cash registers where they would be visible from the street, and to install approved electronic cameras. Within a little over a year, convenience-store robberies had decreased 64 percent.[18] We will return to this discussion later in this chapter.

Hot Products. Why do thieves decide to steal some things and not others? What makes targets attractive? We have examined how burglars select which homes to burglarize, but once they have broken into a residence, how do they decide what to steal? When robbers target victims, they do so believing their chances of making off with something valuable are greater than their chances of not being successful in the robbery attempt. But what is it about things that makes them valuable to robbers? Cohen and Felson argued that items are attractive if they are visible, easy to take away, valuable, and accessible.[19] Twenty years later, Ronald Clarke expanded this idea with his discussion of hot products—those consumer goods that are attractive to thieves. Using an acronym (CRAVED) to organize this idea, Clarke claims that goods are attractive if they are concealable, removable, available, valuable, enjoyable, and disposable (i.e., can be easily fenced). This approach takes into account what thieves do with goods after they are stolen, because that factor

This woman, walking alone in a dark, deserted area, demonstrates how a victim can play a significant part in a criminal event.

figures into their decisions about the attractiveness of items.[20]

College Campus Crime. Crime on college campuses follows patterns that routine-activity theorists would expect, that is, if you engage in a risky and deviant lifestyle, your risk is significantly increased. Students who party frequently and use recreational drugs regularly are at risk. You are more likely to be a victim of property crime if you are a male aged 17 to 20. If you live in an all-female dorm, you are less likely to experience a theft. Not surprisingly, students who spend several nights per week on campus and full-time students are more vulnerable to property crime than part-time students or those who do not spend as many nights on campus. With respect to target attractiveness, people who spend large amounts of money on nonessential items have a higher risk of on-campus theft than those who spend less.[21]

THEORIES OF VICTIMIZATION

Although the victim is mentioned in many theories of crime, direct consideration of the role that victims play in the criminal event has been of secondary significance. As a result of the "missing victim" in basic criminology, **theories of victimization** have recently been developed for the purpose of understanding crime from the victim's perspective, or with the victim in mind.

The history of victims in criminology can be traced to Hans von Hentig's first article on the subject of victims, in 1941, in which he postulated that crime was an "interaction of perpetrator and victim."[22] Von Hentig, a highly respected scientist, had been a victim of Nazi persecution. It was that experience that made him focus on the significance of the victim. By carefully gathering and analyzing information, he demonstrated that tourist resorts were attractive to criminals who wanted to prey on unsuspecting vacationers. Von Hentig, through his book *The Criminal and His Victim*, published in 1948, founded the criminological subdiscipline of victimology, which examines the role played by the victim in a criminal incident.[23] Nevertheless, it must be acknowledged that the term "victimology" is a year older than von Hentig's book. The term was coined in 1947 by the Romanian lawyer Beniamin Mendelsohn, in a lecture before the Romanian Psychiatric Association in Bucharest, entitled "New Bio-Psycho-Social Horizons: Victimology."[24] In 1948, Frederic Wertham, an American psychiatrist, first used the term "victimology" in America.[25]

According to Canadian criminologist Ezzat Fattah, "von Hentig insisted that many crime victims contribute to their own victimization be it by inciting or provoking the criminal or by creating or fostering a situation likely to lead to the commission of the crime."[26] Thus, the entire event is regarded as crucial, because criminal behavior involves both the action of the offender and interaction between offender and victim. Nor is it tenable to regard "criminals and victims . . . as different as night and day," because there is an undeniable link between offending and victimization.[27] Many offenders are victimized repeatedly, and victims are frequently offenders.

Such findings may be deemed highly controversial in a time when victims' rights groups have been active, and successful, in securing rights for victims of crimes. It must be understood, however, that *guilt* is not shared by offender and victim. Criminal guilt belongs to the perpetrator of a crime—and it must be proved at trial beyond a reasonable doubt. The victim is free of guilt. Victimology, however, can demonstrate how potential victims, by acting differently, can decrease the risk of being victimized.[28]

We turn now to a discussion of the dominant victimological theories.

Lifestyle Theories

A *lifestyle theory of victimization* was developed by Michael Hindelang, Michael Gottfredson, and James Garofalo in 1978. It argues that because of changing roles (working mother versus homemaker) and schedules (a child's school calendar), people lead different lifestyles (work and leisure activities). Variations in lifestyle affect the number of situations with high victimization risks that a person experiences.[29] The kinds of people someone associates with, such as coworkers, friends, and sexual partners, also affect victimization rates. For instance, someone who has a drug dealer or an insider trader as a friend has a greater chance of being victimized than a person who associates only with law-abiding people. (The similarity of the lifestyle theory of victimization and the routine-activities approach is quite apparent.)

The lifestyle theory of victimization centers on a number of specific propositions that outline the essence of the theory and signal directions for future research:[30]

Proposition 1: The probability of suffering a personal victimization is directly related to the amount of time that a person spends in public places (e.g., on the street, in parks), and particularly in public places at night.

Proposition 2: The probability of being in public places, particularly at night, varies as a function of lifestyle.

Proposition 3: Social contacts and interactions occur disproportionately among individuals who share similar lifestyles.

Proposition 4: An individual's chances of personal victimization are dependent upon the extent to which the individual shares demographic characteristics with offenders [such as young urban males].

Proposition 5: The proportion of time that an individual spends among nonfamily members varies as a function of lifestyle.

Proposition 6: The probability of personal victimization, particularly personal theft, increases as a function of the proportion of the time that an individual spends among nonfamily members [such as a young man who works a double shift at a factory versus a middle-aged woman who stays home to take care of an elderly parent].

Proposition 7: Variations in lifestyle are associated with variations in the ability of individuals to isolate themselves from persons with offender characteristics [being able to leave high-crime urban areas for sheltered suburbs].

Proposition 8: Variations in lifestyle are associated with variations in the convenience, the desirability, and vincibility of the person as a target for a personal victimization [people who pass within the view of offenders, seem to have what the offender wants, appear unable to resist, or would probably not report the crime to the police].

Both the lifestyle theory of victimization and the routine-activity approach present some basic guidelines for reducing one's chances of victimization. And just as these theories themselves tend to embody common sense, so do the preventive measures derived from them. For instance, people in American society are told not to drive while intoxicated, not to smoke or abuse alcohol or drugs, and not to eat too much greasy food. All these messages are intended to reduce the risks of dying in a motor vehicle accident, or from lung or liver cancer, or from an overdose, or from a heart attack. Although public-service messages designed to protect health may not always be heeded, people do not see them as "blaming the victim." Similarly, messages to prevent criminal victimization, like not walking alone and not frequenting deserted or unfamiliar places late at night, should not be viewed as overly restrictive and intrusive, or as blaming victims who did not heed the advice. The messages directed at preventing victimization are based on theory and research and merely promote living and acting responsibly to ensure a more crime-free existence.

Victim-Offender Interaction

Marvin Wolfgang, one of the preeminent criminologists of his time, studied homicides in Philadelphia during the 1950s. He found that many of the victims had actually brought upon themselves the attack that led to their murder (see Chapter 10 for further discussion of Wolfgang's work). He coined the term "victim precipitation" to refer to situations where victims initiate the confrontations that lead to their death. Wolfgang estimated that as many as one-quarter to one-half of intentional homicides are victim-precipitated.[31] James Tedeschi and Richard Felson put forward a theory of "coercive actions," which stresses that the way victims and offenders interact plays a large role in violent crime.[32] They argue that people commit violence purposefully. In other words, people don't just lose control. When they are violent, it is with a particular goal in mind. They make a decision to be violent (note the similarity between this theory and the rational-choice perspective) and tend to choose targets who are less powerful than themselves. In unarmed attacks, males are more likely to injure their opponents, while females are more likely to be injured. Gender is not the determinant as much as body size.[33] There are also victims who instigate attacks by irritating others. Schoolyard bullies are a good example.[34]

Repeat Victimization

Not unlike the lifestyle theory of victimization, theories of repeat victimization also focus on the specific characteristics of situations in order to determine which factors account for the initial, as well as for repeat, victimization.[35] Theories of repeat victimization, also called "multiple victimization," dispel the myth that crime is uniformly distributed. Research shows that a small number of people and places account for a large amount of the crimes committed. For example, an analysis of the British Crime Survey (a victimization survey) from 1982 to 1992 found that between 24 and 38 percent of all victims of property and personal crime experienced five or more such offenses in a little over a year.[36]

The research literature on repeat victimization is increasing rapidly. A study of police calls for service from 34 fast-food restaurants in San Antonio, Texas, from 1990 to 1992 found that fast-food restaurants had the greatest chance of repeat police calls for service within one week of the last call. Thereafter, the number of calls decreases as the time between calls increases.[37] Similar findings have been made in research on the repeat risks of burglary.[38] Risks of a repeat burglary are highest immediately after a previous burglary. In their analysis of repeat victimization for crimes ranging from the repeated physical and sexual abuse of children to repeated credit card fraud, researchers concluded that the rational-choice theory of offender decision making is useful in understanding repeat victimization. Offenders choose targets based on the knowledge they gained in the previous victimization about the risks and rewards of a particular offense.[39]

Formulating strategies to deal with repeat victimizations would certainly be cost-beneficial. Resources could be concentrated on relatively few targets. Unfortunately, police recording systems are not designed to keep track of repeat victimizations. To overcome this problem, several innovative researchers have created their own databases, starting a whole new line of research, called "hot-spots" research.

Hot Spots of Crime

In 1989, Lawrence Sherman, Patrick Gartin, and Michael Buerger published the results of a study that immediately excited the profession. They had analyzed 911 calls for police assistance in Minneapolis, Minnesota, for the period December 15, 1985, to December 15, 1986. After plotting the more than 320,000 calls on a map, they discovered that 3 percent of the addresses and intersections in the city were the subject of 50 percent of the calls received.[40]

This graffiti-covered, seedy neighborhood in Manhattan, with its bars, walk-in hotels, and liquor stores represents a prime "hot spot" for crime.

They also found that certain types of crime were committed in specific places—for example, all auto thefts at 2 percent of all places. The researchers conclude that attempts to prevent victimization should be focused not on victims, but on the places themselves by making them less vulnerable to crime. Change places, not people! We should identify neighborhood hot spots, reduce social disorder and physical "incivilities," and promote housing-based neighborhood stabilization.[41]

Geography of Crime

Recently, new research based on the idea of hot spots has come into existence. It is labeled "geography of crime." Researchers found that more crime occurs around high schools[42] and blocks with bars,[43] liquor stores,[44] the city center,[45] and abandoned buildings.[46] Higher crime in areas that border high schools and bars is readily explainable: High schools contain a highly crime-prone age group. Bars attract, among others, offenders.[47] Abandoned buildings that are open and unsecured attract illegal users. In city centers there are more opportunities to commit crime and generally fewer social controls in place.

A study on the vulnerability of ports and marinas to vessel and equipment theft found that the proximity of a port or marina to a high-crime area is significant in predicting boat theft.[48] Research on drug markets in Jersey City, New Jersey, shows that areas with illicit drug markets account for a disproportionate amount of arrests and calls for police service.[49] In sum, the discovery that a large amount of crime occurs at a small number of places, and that such places have distinct characteristics, has led criminologists to explain crime in terms of not only who commits it, but also where it is committed.[50]

Interrelatedness of Theories

Environmental criminology, the rational-choice perspective, and the routine-activity approach focus on the interactions among the victim (or target), the offender, and the place. Recently, there has been an integration of these theories of crime with theories of victimization.[51] For example, one study using the lifestyle theory of victimization and the routine-activity approach explores how drinking routines are linked with victimization.[52] It found that alcohol contributed to victimization by making potential victims less able to protect themselves (more suitable targets). Motivated offenders also knew where to find their targets (in bars). Although the evidence on the relationships of alcohol, lifestyle,

FROM THE PAGES OF The New York Times

New York City Cracks Down on "Hot Spots"

When Rudolph Giuliani was mayor of New York City, he instituted many "quality of life" initiatives to make the city safer for its citizens. He put one such program in place during his second term, after several revelers were injured or died in violent fights or after overdosing on drugs while in nightclubs. That led him to form a task force known as March, for Multi Agency Response to Community Hotspots.

The administration of his successor, Mayor Michael Bloomberg, reported in November 2002 that it was reviving this program, and accelerating a crackdown of New York City's night life industry as part of the administration's attempts to remain vigilant about crime prevention. In October, the city announced that it would vigorously enforce its noise code, aimed in part at bars and clubs with noisy patrons who spill into the city's streets.

Robert F. Messner, an assistant police commissioner who runs the Civil Enforcement Division of the Police Department, said that "If you listen to stories about what led to this homicide or what led to this assault, you would be surprised how many stem from nightclubs." City officials insist that their goal is not to put nightclubs out of business, but rather to enforce the city's cabaret laws—established in 1926—which restrict clubs to certain areas of the city and lay out strict safety standards for any club applying for a cabaret license.

Club owners argue that the emphasis should not be on city regulations, but on the State Liquor Authority. They say that state officials issue liquor licenses and are loath to revoke them, making it too easy for clubs that are closed down due to drug use and violence to reopen. Bloomberg officials said they planned to review carefully how the State Liquor Authority conducts its business. However, John Feinblatt, the city's criminal justice coordinator, which oversees the March program, stated that its enforcement effort would continue to grow, saying "Rolling back is not on the table."

Source

Adapted from: Jennifer Steinhauer, "City Cracks Down on Nightclubs and May Revise Its Policies," *The New York Times*, November 10, 2002. Reprinted with permission.

Questions for Discussion

1. The City of New York is trying to achieve a balance between enforcing its current laws and recognizing that nightlife is an important industry in New York. Laws currently prohibit dancing in clubs that do not have a cabaret license—and getting one can be a long, drawn-out process. One club owner, who has been fined and her club shut down several times for allowing dancing, compared the situation to the movie *Footloose*, which depicted a small town where public dancing was prohibited. What do you think of the cabaret law in terms of hot spots of crime?
2. If you were a city official, what steps might you take to prevent the kinds of crimes that are often committed in areas where such clubs exist?

---

and increased risks of victimization is not conclusive, this research represents an important attempt at testing the interaction of lifestyle and routine-activity theories.

A further study on the relationship of alcohol and risks of victimization focuses specifically on the "suitable target" portion of routine-activity theory as it relates to sexual assault against women on college campuses.[53] It found that women who were sexually victimized went out more often and drank more when they were out than other women. Moreover, many of the women surveyed had experienced "uncomfortable advances in a bar or restaurant" or "on the street" or had "received obscene or threatening phone calls." In sum, by successfully combining theories of crime, like routine-activity theory, with lifestyle theory, situational factors (e.g., alcohol), and place considerations (e.g., bars and college settings) to examine victimization rates, criminological research has added a new dimension to explaining crime.[54]

PREVENTING CRIMES AGAINST PLACES, PEOPLE, AND VALUABLE GOODS

Situational crime prevention seeks to protect places, people, and valuable goods from victimization. It is rooted in the 1971 work of C. Ray Jeffery's "crime prevention through environmental design" (CPTED)[55] and in Oscar Newman's concept of defensible space.[56] CPTED posits that envi-

PART II Explanations of Crime and Criminal Behavior

TABLE 9.2 Sixteen Techniques of Situational Prevention

Increasing Perceived Effort	Increasing Perceived Risks	Reducing Anticipated Rewards	Inducing Guilt or Shame
1. *Target hardening:* Slug-rejector device, Steering locks, Bandit screens	5. *Entry/exit screening:* Automatic ticket gates, Baggage screening, Merchandise tags	9. *Target removal:* Removable car radio, Women's refuges, Phone card	13. *Rule setting:* Harassment codes, Customs declaration, Hotel registrations
2. *Access control:* Parking lot barriers, Fenced yards, Entry phones	6. *Formal surveillance:* Burglar alarms, Speed cameras, Security guards	10. *Identifying property:* Property marking, Vehicle licensing, Cattle branding	14. *Strengthening moral condemnation:* "Shoplifting is stealing", Roadside speedometers, "Bloody-idiots drink and drive"
3. *Deflecting offenders:* Bus stop placement, Tavern location, Street closures	7. *Surveillance by employees:* Pay phone location, Park attendants, CCTV systems	11. *Reducing temptation:* Gender-neutral phone lists, Off-street parking	15. *Controlling disinhibitors:* Drinking-age laws, Ignition interlock, Server intervention
4. *Controlling facilitators:* Credit card photo, Caller ID, Gun controls	8. *Natural surveillance:* Defensible space, Street lighting, Cab driver ID	12. *Denying benefits:* Ink merchandise tags, PIN for car radios, Graffiti cleaning	16. *Facilitating compliance:* Improved library checkout, Public lavatories, Trash bins

Source: Ronald V. Clarke and Ross Homel, "A Revised Classification of Situational Crime Prevention Techniques," in *Crime Prevention at a Crossroads,* ed. Steven P. Lab (Cincinnati, Ohio: Anderson, 1997).

> **:// Crime Surfing**
> www.preventingcrime.org/report/chapter7.htm
>
> John Eck, contributing to *Crime Prevention: What Works, What Doesn't, What's Promising,* compiled an extremely comprehensive literature review of research into the effectiveness of situational-crime-prevention strategies.

ronments can be altered, often at little expense, to decrease victimizations. "Defensible space" refers to improved architectural designs, particularly of public housing, in order to provide increased security. Design can enhance surveillance, reduce offenders' escape possibilities, and give residents a feeling of ownership that encourages them to protect their own space.[57] CPTED and defensible space have converged with rational choice and routine activity to form a new approach called "situational crime prevention."

Situational Crime Prevention

Rational-choice theory provides the foundation for designing situational-crime-prevention techniques and their classification (Table 9.2). Situational crime prevention consists of the knowledge of how, where, and when to implement a specific measure that will alter a particular situation in order to prevent a crime from occurring. The routine-activity approach also aims at situational crime prevention by reducing the opportunities for likely offenders to commit crimes. Techniques include protecting suitable targets (making them less suitable) and increasing the presence of capable guardians. Measures such as steering-column locks, vandal-resistant construction, enhanced street lighting, and improved library checkout systems demonstrably decrease opportunities for crime. These are **target-hardening** techniques.

Rational-choice theorists have recently reviewed their situational-crime-prevention techniques. They have added aspects of the offender's *perception* of a crime opportunity (Table 9.3) to the catalog of relevant factors, as well as the element of guilt or shame.[58] The addition of the category of "perception" of opportunity was self-evident. After all, offenders act only in accordance with what they perceive. The addition of a category called "inducing guilt or shame," on the other hand, is a significant expansion of rational choice.[59] Techniques that induce guilt or shame include the installation of signs saying "shoplifting is stealing" or

TABLE 9.3 Ten Factors Considered by Commercial Burglars in Suburban Philadelphia

1. *Revenues generated by burglary:*
   Is there a high "payoff"?
2. *Chances of being caught:*
   Can I get away with it?
3. *Location of target:*
   Is the target near a major road or thoroughfare? Commercial burglars like remote targets.
4. *Corner lot:*
   Is the target at the corner? Corner properties are easier to get into and out of.
5. *Shopping mall:*
   Is the target in a mall? Malls and large retail stores are ideal targets.
6. *Concentration of businesses:*
   Are there other businesses around? The more commercial establishments around, the greater the likelihood of burglary.
7. *Burglar alarm:*
   Is there a visible alarm or alarm sign?
8. *Exterior lighting:*
   How dark is the area around the target?
9. *Length of time the establishment has been in business:*
   Is this a new store? New commercial establishments are prime targets.
10. *Retail store:*
    Is the target retail? Retail is preferred over wholesale.

Source: Simon Hakim and Yochanan Shachmurove, "Spatial and Temporal Patterns of Commercial Burglaries: The Evidence Examined," *American Journal of Economics and Sociology,* **55** (1996): 443–456.

other measures calculated to prevent common crimes by increasing the personal and social cost in terms of shaming—especially after being caught in the act. For instance, if a high school student is leaving the school library with friends and the library checkout system detects a copy of *Rolling Stone* in his book bag (a magazine that is not allowed to leave the library), two things are expected to happen. First, the librarian will make the student surrender the magazine. Second, the student may be so embarrassed by having the librarian search his book bag while his friends stand by that he will not try to steal anything from the library again.

There are a number of successful examples of situational crime prevention. For example, situational-crime-prevention techniques have been successfully implemented to prevent crime at Disney World, to stop auto theft, to deter robberies at convenience stores, and to lessen crime in parking facilities.

The Phantom Crime Prevention at Disney World. Disney World, home of Donald Duck, Mickey and Minnie Mouse, Goofy, and their friends, provides us with an example of environmental/situational crime prevention. Illegal behavior is successfully controlled, yet in an environment that does not have the sterile, fortresslike appearance so often associated with security. How has this been accomplished?[60]

The intricate web of security and crowd control (not visible to the untrained eye) starts at the parking lot with advice to lock your car and remember that you have parked at a particular lot, for example, "Donald Duck 1." With friendly greetings of "have a good time," watchful eyes surround visitors on the rubber-wheeled train into never-never land. Crowd control is omnipresent, yet unobtrusive. Signs guide you through the maze of monorails, rides, and attractions. Physical barriers prevent injury and regulate the movement of adults and children alike. Mickey Mouse and Goofy monitor movements. Flower gardens, pools, and fountains are pretty to look at; they also direct people toward particular locations. Yet with all these built-in control strategies, few visitors realize the extent to which their choices of movement and action are limited.

Situational Prevention: Auto Theft. Let us return to the car theft scenario at the beginning of this chapter to illustrate how action research works in the case of car theft.[61] First, the Paramus Police Department collected information on the specific

> **Did You Know?**
>
> ... that sometimes stealing might result from over-socialization and embarrassment rather than from undersocialization? Research into shoplifting from drugstores shows that the items most commonly stolen include condoms and other birth-control products, as well as medications, such as Preparation H, for "intimate conditions." Similarly, librarians surveyed said that books about sex are among the most stolen items from libraries, apparently because "readers were too embarrassed to borrow such stock legitimately."

Even Goofy is part of the Disney crime prevention and control strategy, making Disneyland and Disney World some of the safest locations in the United States.

models and makes of the cars stolen, as well as the particular locations of the thefts. The Toyota Land Cruiser, Toyota 4Runner, and Mitsubishi Montero were the sport utility vehicles preferred by the thieves, while any Honda and the Toyota Camry were the favored cars. Second, information provided by the National Insurance Crime Bureau (see Table 9.4) indicated that some of these makes and models are the most targeted vehicles for theft not only in malls in Bergen County, New Jersey, but throughout the nation.

With this information, situational-crime-prevention practitioners analyze the vehicles and the specific situational factors that lead to their being targeted for theft. They then devise measures to block the opportunities that give rise to the theft of these particular vehicles, for example, side window panels that are particularly vulnerable, or key codes in the gas tank compartment (the thief simply writes down the key code and gets a replacement of the "lost" car key).[62]

Devising situational prevention measures, however, is usually not as easy as suggesting to a car manufacturer that the key code be placed in a more secure place. It is important that a researcher also analyze the type of offenders who steal cars (Table 9.5).

Convenience Stores. One of the most successful crime-prevention studies was the Tallahassee Convenience Store Study. In fact, it launched the concept of crime prevention through environmental design. It had long been known that convenience stores, like the 7-Eleven shops, had been prime robbery targets. Researchers studied the vulnerability of these stores

TABLE 9.4 Top 25 Most Commonly Stolen Vehicles in 2001

1. Toyoto Camry	13. Plymouth/Dodge Neon
2. Honda Accord	14. Pontiac Grand Am
3. Honda Civic	15. Nissan Sentra
4. Oldsmobile Cutlass/Supreme/Ciera	16. Ford Explorer
	17. Ford Mustang
5. Jeep Cherokee/Grand Cherokee	18. Oldsmobile Delta 88/Royale
6. Chevrolet Full Size C/K Pickup	19. Buick Le Sabre
	20. Ford Escort
7. Toyota Corolla	21. Cadillac Deville
8. Ford Taurus	22. Chevrolet Full Size Extended Cab Pickup
9. Chevrolet Caprice	
10. Ford F150 Pickup	23. Plymouth Voyager/Grand Voyager
11. Dodge Caravan/Grand Caravan	
	24. Nissan Maxima
12. Chevrolet Cavalier	25. Toyota Pickup

Source: http://www.nicb.org/uploaded_documents/pressreleases/top100stolen2001.pdf

Of Immediate Concern

Maximum-Security Schools

A rash of school shootings during the 1998–1999 academic year (see "School Shootings" in Chapter 10) caused great concern across the nation. Criminologists, police, educators, lawmakers, and parents struggled to figure out why these young men and boys decided to pick up firearms and destroy the lives of their teachers and classmates. Many blamed the easy access to guns; others pointed to the social isolation these students experienced; still others looked to broader sociological explanations.

Although you would not know it, given all the media coverage surrounding these school shooting incidents, as well as experts' premonitions of doom and gloom, we are actually in the midst of a decline in violent crime in American schools. Thirty percent fewer students are carrying weapons to school than in 1991, and the number of student fights has also dropped. The number of school-related violent deaths is one-half what it was six years ago. During the 1997–1998 school year, only 34 students died in violent incidents in all the nation's schools. In fact, school is one of the safest places for young people, safer than the streets or even their homes. Young people are far more likely to die in alcohol-related automobile accidents (eight die per day, which represents 40 percent of all deaths of 16- to 20-year-olds), or from unintentional injury or suicide (10 and 13 percent, respectively, of deaths of those aged 10 to 24).(1) Even so, deaths related to school violence get much more press coverage—much of it sensationalized. As a result, parents, and the community at large, tend to panic.

Target hardening and situational crime prevention in schools are nothing new. Schools in certain parts of some cities have had metal detectors, doors with alarms, and locker searches for years. Then there are the other schools in towns few have heard of: places like Paducah, Conyers, and Littleton. The image of these suburban schools as

In some inner-city schools, security measurers rival those used in prison: metal detectors, drug-sniffing dogs, frequent searches for weapons, and surveillance cameras that monitor the movement of students in and out of classrooms.

in great detail, assessing risks as well as losses, in terms of lives and property. The researchers recommended that stores have two or more clerks on duty, post "limited cash" signs, increase exterior lighting, and restrict escape routes and potential hiding places for robbers. The study led to the passage of the Florida Convenience Store Security Act (1990), which made certain security measures mandatory.[63] Convenience-store robberies in Florida have dropped by two-thirds.

Parking Facilities.[64] Parking garages are said to be dangerous places: Individuals are alone in a large space, there are many hiding places, the amount of valuable property (cars and their contents) is high, they are open to the public, an safe havens has been shattered. Although the likelihood of a shooting in any particular school is small, officials are not taking any chances. Interestingly, the prevention measures listed below fall squarely into Clarke and Homel's situational-crime-prevention model (see Table 9.2).

Access control
- Intercom systems are being used at locked doors to buzz in visitors.(2)
- Students have to flash or swipe computerized identification cards to get into school buildings.
- Perimeter fences delineate school property and secure cars after hours.

Controlling facilitators
- Students in Deltona, Florida, get an extra set of books to leave at home. The schools have banned backpacks and dismantled lockers to eliminate places to stash weapons. Other school districts are encouraging see-through lockers and backpacks.
- After the Littleton, Colorado, incident, school boards across the country banned trench coats and other oversized garments, apparently to prevent students from hiding weapons on their bodies or in their clothing.

Entry/exit screening
- Handheld and walk-through metal detectors keep anyone with a weapon from entering schools.

Formal surveillance
- Uniformed police officers and private security guards, some of them armed, patrol school halls.
- Schools are installing surveillance cameras in hallways and on school buses.

Surveillance by employees (or, in this case, students)
- Students are carrying small notebooks so that they can log and then report overheard threats.

Identifying property
- Tiny microfilm is hidden inside expensive school property so that it can be identified if stolen.

On the fact of it, these measures seem to make good sense. They can prevent people from bringing weapons into schools and keep unauthorized people out. They increase the ability of school officials to detect crime, identify evildoers, and prevent criminal incidents from happening. But have school officials and others gone too far? Diana Philip is the director of the American Civil Liberties Union of Texas for the northern region, which has filed several lawsuits against schools. She observes that "over the summer, we have had school boards putting together the most restrictive policies we have ever seen. A lot of them are in clear violation of the Fourth Amendment, which guarantees freedom from unreasonable searches."(3)

Chicago Tribune columnist Steve Chapman argues that schools treat students as "dangerous, incorrigible, undeserving of respect" or privacy. He asks, "What's the difference between school and prison? At school, you don't get cable TV."(4)

Sources
1. *Violence in School: The Facts,* Office of the Attorney General, State of Illinois, found at http://www.ag.state.il.us/program/school/facts.htm, Oct. 30, 1999.
2. Jacques Steinberg, "Barricading the School Door," *New York Times,* Aug. 22, 1999, New York section, p. 5.
3. S. C. Gwynne, "Is Anyplace Safe?" *Time,* Aug. 23, 1999 [http://www.pathfinder.com/magazine/time, accessed February 10, 2000].
4. Walter Olson, "Dial 'O' for Outrage: The Sequel—Tales from an Overlawyered America," *Reason,* November 1999, pp. 54–56.

Questions for Discussion
1. Do you think there would be as much concern over school violence if these shooting incidents had happened in urban schools? Why are people more upset when crime happens in places they perceive to be safe (such as in the suburbs)?
2. Does your high school or college campus have any security measures in place? If so, how do they fit into Clarke and Homel's 16 techniques of situational prevention?
3. Is there a point where security measures in schools become so extreme that they can no longer be justified? Have we reached that point yet?

Of Immediate Concern

---

offender's car can go unnoticed, and lighting is usually poor. Yet statistics indicate that because of the small amount of time and the relatively limited number of trips that each person takes to and from parking facilities, an individual's chances of being raped, robbed, or assaulted in a parking facility are very low. Nevertheless, the fear of victimization in these facilities is high. Efforts to improve conditions include better lighting, stairways and elevators that are open to the air or glass-enclosed, ticket-booth personnel monitoring drivers exiting and entering, color-coded signs designating parking areas, elimination or redesign of public restrooms, panic buttons and emergency phones, closed-circuit television, and uniformed security personnel.

TABLE 9.5 Typologies of Frequent Auto Theft Offenders

Acting-out Joyrider
- Most emotionally disturbed of the offenders—derives status from having his peers think he is crazy and unpredictable.
- Engages in outrageous driving stunts—dangerous to pursue—possesses a kamikaze attitude.
- Vents anger via car—responsible for large proportion of the totaled and burned cars.
- Least likely to be deterred—doesn't care what happens.

Thrill-seeker
- Heavily into drugs—doing crime is a way to finance the habit—entices others to feel the "rush" of doing crime.
- Engages in car stunts and willful damage to cars, but also steals them for transportation and to use in other crimes.
- Steals parts for sale in a loosely structured friendship network.
- Thrill-seeking behavior likely to be transferred to other activities and might be directed to legitimate outlets.

Instrumental Offender
- Doing auto theft for the money—most active of the offenders (five or more cars a week) but the smallest proportion of the sample—connected to organized theft operations.
- Rational, intelligent—does crimes with least risk—may get into auto theft from burglary—thinks about outcomes.
- Doing crime while young offender status affords them lenient treatment—indicate that they will quit crime at age 18.

Source: Zachary Fleming, Patricia Brantingham, and Paul Brantingham, "Exploring Auto Theft in British Columbia," in *Crime Prevention Studies*, vol. 3, ed. Ronald V. Clarke (Monsey, N.Y.: Criminal Justice Press, 1994), p. 62.

> **://Crime Surfing**
> www.crimereduction.gov.uk/
>
> This crime-prevention guide by the Home Office in Britain includes details about how one can avoid becoming a crime victim. The Home Office and its staff conduct extensive research on the effectiveness of situational-crime-prevention strategies.

Displacement

One important question concerning crime-prevention measures remains. What will happen, for example, if these measures do prevent a particular crime from being committed? Will the would-be offender simply look for another target? Crime-prevention strategists have demonstrated that **displacement**—the commission of a quantitatively similar crime at a different time or place—does not always follow. German motorcycle helmet legislation demonstrates the point. As a result of a large number of accidents, legislation that required motorcyclists to wear helmets was passed and strictly enforced. It worked: Head injuries decreased. But there were additional, unforeseen consequences. Motorcycle theft rates decreased dramatically.[65] The risks of stealing a motorcycle became too high because a would-be offender could not drive it away without wearing a helmet. At this point researchers expected to see a rise in the numbers of cars or bikes stolen. They did not. In other words, there was very little displacement. Of course, some offenders will look for other crime opportunities, but many others will quit for some time, perhaps forever.

THEORY INFORMS POLICY

The study of targets and victims is crucial to preventing crime. Understanding how offenders make decisions helps policy makers allocate resources efficiently. For example, if it is possible to significantly reduce convenience-store robbery by relatively simple measures, isn't it better to spend time and money doing those things rather than trying to prevent crime by focusing exclusively on troubled people (who

PART II Explanations of Crime and Criminal Behavior   233

THE FAR SIDE By GARY LARSON

Inconvenience stores

may or may not rob convenience stores anyway)? If we know that repeat victimization can be prevented by intervening with high-risk people and properties, isn't that the most cost-beneficial way to proceed?

We usually think of crime policy as being made by governments, for only they can control the police, courts, and corrections. Decisions about crime prevention, on the other hand, can be made by small communities, neighborhoods, schools, businesses, and individuals. We discussed how simple precautions lower the risk of convenience-store robbery. This knowledge not only encouraged governments to pass certain laws mandating that stores take those precautions, but led many in private industry to adopt the measures as well. Knowledge about crime prevention is especially valuable to all people because everyone can use these tools to reduce the chances of being a victim. Having discussed the application of theories of crime to conventional crime, we are left with the question whether these theories are also applicable to unconventional crimes, like terrorism.

REVIEW

This chapter focuses on situational theories of crime. These theories, which assume that there are always people motivated to commit crime, try to explain why crimes are being committed by a particular offender against a particular target. They analyze opportunities and environmental factors that prompt a potential perpetrator to act.

We discussed the three most prominent situational approaches to crime: environmental criminology, the rational-choice perspective, and the routine-activity approach. We noted that they have merged somewhat, particularly insofar as all these approaches aim at preventing victimization by altering external conditions that are conducive to crime.

Theories of victimization view crime as the dynamic interaction of perpetrators and victims (at a given time and place). Here too the aim is to find ways for potential victims to protect themselves. Research into lifestyles, victim-offender interaction, repeat victimization, hot spots, and geography of crime has vast implications for crime control in entire cities or regions. Situational theories of crime and theories of victimization are interrelated.

CRIMINOLOGY & PUBLIC POLICY

The kind of terrorism we are talking about is different in many respects from other crimes such as murder, rape, and robbery. The difference is that terrorism is generally more calculated, more premediated, and more goal-oriented than impulsive crimes or crimes of passion. Criminal justice expert Philip Heymann has observed:

> As a crime, terrorism is different. Most crimes are the product of greed, anger, jealousy, or the desire for domination, respect, or position in a group, and not of any desire to "improve" the state of the world or of a particular nation. Most crimes do not involve—as part of the plan for accomplishing their objectives—trying to change the occupants of government postions, their actions, or the basic structures and ideology of a nation. Some would argue that violence carried out for political purpose is more altruistic; others would vigorously deny that. But all would agree that political violence is different from ordinary

crime, in that it is planned to force changes in government actions, people, structure, or even ideology as a means to whatever ends the perpetrators are seeking with whatever motivations drive them towards those ends. It is in that sense that the U.S. State Department definition says that the violence is usually "perpetrated for political reasons."

Terrorism—at least of the kind described by Heymann—is thus more, not less, subject to disincentive and deterrence techniques than most ordinary crimes. To be sure, some acts of terrorism are revenge-driven and impulsive, but most are carefully calculated to achieve a goal. Sometimes the goal will be specific and immediate, while other times it may be more general, long term, and apocalyptic. But whatever the object, if it becomes clear that it will be disserved by terrorism—that the cause will be worse off—then it will be only a matter of time until cosupporters of the cause turn against those who resort to terrorism. Without widespread support from within the cause they are seeking to promote, terrorists cannot long thrive. Certainly if there is widespread opposition to terrorism within the cause, it will soon dry up. (Source: Alan M. Dershowitz, *Why Terrorism Works* (New York: Yale University Press, 2002).)

Questions for Discussion What do rational-choice theorists have to contribute to the ongoing "war" against terrorism? Is terrorism rational? In what ways? What counterterrorist strategies can you think of that would be effective against terrorism committed against targets in the United States?

YOU BE THE CRIMINOLOGIST

Imagine you are a security consultant working for a major department store chain. Recently, one of the stores, located in the downtown area of a large city, has experienced very high levels of shoplifting and employee theft. You must design a comprehensive program to protect merchandise from theft by customers and by people who work at the store. First, identify some of the store's most vulnerable areas (it may help to visit a local department store to observe how it operates). Then, using the 16 techniques of situational crime prevention as a model, prepare a list of prevention strategies.

KEY TERMS

The numbers next to the terms refer to the pages on which the terms are defined.

displacement (232)

environmental criminology (215)

rational choice (215)

routine activity (217)

target hardening (227)

theories of victimization (222)

PART III

Types of Crimes

The word "crime" conjures up many images: mugging and murder, cheating on taxes, and selling crack. Penal codes define thousands of different crimes. These crimes are grouped into convenient and comprehensive categories, for access and understanding.

In this part we are examining the specific categories of crimes. Violent crimes (Chapter 10) are crimes against the person, ranging from assault to homicide. Many of these crimes have been well established for centuries, though modern codes have transformed them, however slightly. Most of the crimes against property (Chapter 11) have been well-defined over the centuries. Yet, recent developments in commerce and technology have prompted legislatures to define new forms of crimes against property. With a spate of corporate scandals, reports of white-collar and corporate crime (Chapter 12) fill the pages of newspapers and news magazines. In this chapter we discuss how white-collar crime and corporate crime are defined and measured. The corporate criminal law is described in some detail, with a focus on corporate liability and corporate sanctions. The chapter concludes with references to the prosecution of Arthur Andersen, LLP, once one of the top five accounting firms in the United States. After criminal indictment and conviction for obstruction of justice, Andersen suffered the ultimate punishment—corporate capital punishment—or the death of a corporation. In the next chapter (Chapter 13), we address the controversial types of crime related to drug and alcohol trafficking and consumption, as well as those violating the sexual mores of the establishment. Finally, the occurrence of these types of crime is discussed in comparison with their occurrence elsewhere in the world (Chapter 14). This chapter is concerned with comparative criminology and, inevitably, the emergence of transnational and international criminality.

CHAPTER 10
Violent Crimes

Homicide
 Murder
 Manslaughter
 The Extent of Homicide
 The Nature of Homicide
 A Cross-National Comparison of Homicide Rates

Assault

Family-Related Crimes
 Spouse Abuse
 Child Abuse
 Abuse of the Elderly

Rape and Sexual Assault
 Characteristics of the Rape Event
 Who Are the Rapists?
 Rape and the Legal System
 Community Response

Kidnapping

Robbery
 Characteristics of Robbers
 The Consequences of Robbery

Organized Crime
 The History of Organized Crime
 The Structure and Impact of Organized Crime
 The New Ethnic Diversity in Organized Crime

Emerging Problems
 Terrorism
 Hate Crimes
 Militias
 Violence in Schools

Violence and Gun Control
 The Extent of Firearm-Related Offenses
 Youth and Guns
 Controlling Handgun Use
 The Gun-Control Debate

REVIEW

CRIMINOLOGY & PUBLIC POLICY

YOU BE THE CRIMINOLOGIST

KEY TERMS

Boxes
 Window to the World: *The Business of Organized Crime*
 Of Immediate Concern: *An Epidemic of Hate Crimes?*
 From the Pages of The New York Times: *Does the Brady Law Work?*

Special Features
 Crime Surfing
 Did You Know?
 Theory Connects

KEY TERMS

aggravated assault
assault
battery
Federal Witness Protection Program
felony murder
homicide
involuntary manslaughter
justifiable homicide
kidnapping
Mafia
malice aforethought
manslaughter
mass murder
murder
negligent homicide
Racketeer Influenced and Corrupt Organizations (RICO) Act
rape
robbery
serial murder
simple assault
sociopaths
stranger homicide
terrorism
victim precipitation
voluntary manslaughter

Mark of violence: One of the first shots in a sniper spree that numbed the Washington D.C. area in October 2002.

To millions of Americans few things are more pervasive, more frightening, more real today than violent crime and the fear of being assaulted, mugged, robbed, or raped. The fear of being victimized by criminal attack has touched us all in some way. People are fleeing their residences in cities to the expected safety of suburban living. Residents of many areas will not go out on the street at night. Others have added bars and extra locks to windows and doors in their homes. Bus drivers in major cities do not carry cash because incidents of robbery have been so frequent. In some areas local citizens patrol the streets at night to attain the safety they feel has not been provided. . . .

There are numerous conflicting definitions of criminal violence as a class of behavior. Police, prosecutors, jurists, federal agents, local detention officials, and behavioral scientists all hold somewhat different viewpoints as to what constitute acts of violence. All would probably agree, however, as the police reports make abundantly clear, that criminal violence involves the use of or the threat of force on a victim by an offender.[1]

237

The penal law defines types of violent crime, and each is distinguished by a particular set of elements. We concentrate on criminological characteristics: the frequency with which each type of violent crime is committed, the methods used in its commission, and its distribution through time and place. We also examine the people who commit the offense and those who are its victims. If we can determine when, where, and how a specific type of crime is likely to be committed, we will be in a better position to reduce the incidence of that crime by devising appropriate strategies to prevent it.

We begin with homicide, since the taking of life is the most serious harm one human being can inflict on another. Serious attacks that fall short of homicide are assaults of various kinds, including serious sexual assault (rape) and the forceful taking of property from another person (robbery). Other patterns of violence are not defined as such in the penal codes but are so important in practice as to require separate discussion. Family-related violence and terrorism, both of which encompass a variety of crimes, fall into this category.

HOMICIDE

Homicide is the killing of one human being by another. Some homicides are sanctioned by law. In this category of **justifiable homicide,** we find homicides committed by law enforcement officers in the course of carrying out their duties (see Chapter 10), homicides committed by soldiers in combat, and homicides committed by a home owner who has no recourse other than to kill an intruder who threatens the lives of family members. Criminologists are most interested in *criminal homicides*—unlawful killings, without justification or excuse. Criminal homicides are subdivided into three separate categories: murder, manslaughter, and negligent homicide.

Murder

At common law, **murder** was defined as the intentional killing of another person with **malice aforethought.** Courts have struggled with an exact definition of "malice." To describe it, they have used such terms as "evil mind" and "abandoned and malignant heart." Actually, malice is a very simple concept. It is the defendant's awareness that he or she had no right to kill but intended to kill anyway.[2]

Originally the malice had to be "aforethought": The person had to have killed after some contemplation, rather than on the spur of the moment. The concept eventually became meaningless because some courts considered even a few seconds sufficient to establish forethought. The dividing line between planned and spur-of-the-moment killings disappeared. But many legislators believed contemplation was an appropriate concept, because it allowed us to distinguish the various types of murder. They reintroduced it, calling it "premeditation and deliberation." A premeditated, deliberate, intentional killing became murder in the first degree; an intentional killing without premeditation and deliberation became murder in the second degree.

States that had the death penalty reserved it for murder in the first degree. Some state statutes listed particular means of committing murder as indicative of premeditation and deliberation, such as killing by poison or by lying in wait. More recently the charge of murder in the first degree has been reserved for the killing of a law enforcement officer or of a corrections officer and for the killing of any person by a prisoner serving a life sentence. Among the most serious forms of murder is *assassination,* the killing of a head of state or government or of an otherwise highly visible figure.

A special form of murder, **felony murder,** requires no intention to kill. It requires, instead, the intention to commit some other felony, such as robbery or rape, and the death of a person during the commission of, or flight from, that felony. Even accomplices are guilty of felony murder when one of their associates has caused a death. For example, while A and B are holding up a gas station attendant, A fires a warning shot, and the bullet ricochets and kills a passerby. Both A and B are guilty of felony murder. The rule originated in England centuries ago, when death sentences were imposed for all felonies, so it made no difference whether a perpetrator actually intended to kill or merely to rob. Most states today apply the felony murder rule only when the underlying felony is a life-endangering one, such as arson, rape, or robbery.

Manslaughter

Manslaughter is the unlawful killing of another person without malice. Manslaughter may be either voluntary or involuntary.

Voluntary Manslaughter. **Voluntary manslaughter** is a killing committed intentionally but without malice—for example, in the heat of passion or in response to strong provocation. Persons who kill under extreme provocation cannot make rational decisions about whether they have a right to kill or not. They therefore act without the necessary malice.[3]

Just as passion, fright, fear, or consternation may affect a person's capacity to act rationally, so may drugs or alcohol. In some states a charge of murder may be reduced to voluntary manslaughter when the defendant was so grossly intoxicated as not to be fully aware of the implications of his or her actions. All voluntary-manslaughter cases have one thing in common: The defendant's awareness of the unlawfulness of the act was dulled or grossly reduced by shock, fright, consternation, or intoxication.

Involuntary Manslaughter A crime is designated as **involuntary manslaughter** when

Yolanda Manuel, mother of seven-year-old sexual assault and murder victim Sherrice Iverson, speaks at a rally on U.C. Berkeley campus, 1998. The rally was staged to protest the presence, on the Berkeley campus, of sophomore David Cash, who watched and did nothing as a friend Jeremy Strohmeyer dragged Sherrice into a Las Vegas casino bathroom stall where he killed her.

a person has caused the death of another unintentionally but recklessly by consciously disregarding a substantial and unjustifiable risk that endangered another person's life. Many states have created an additional category, **negligent homicide,** to establish criminal liability for grossly negligent killing in situations where the offender assumed a lesser risk.

Manslaughter plays an increasingly prominent role in our society, with its high concentrations of population, high-tech risks, and chemical and even nuclear dangers. The reach of the crime of involuntary manslaughter was clearly demonstrated in the 1942 Coconut Grove disaster in Boston, in which 491 people perished because of a nightclub owner's negligence in creating fire hazards. The nightclub was overcrowded, it was furnished and decorated with highly flammable materials, and exits were blocked. The court ruled that a reasonable person would have recognized the risk. If the defendant is so "stupid" as not to have recognized the risk, he is nevertheless guilty of manslaughter.[4]

The Extent of Homicide

Social scientists who look at homicide have a different perspective from that of the legislators who define such crimes. Social scientists are concerned with rates and patterns of criminal activities. (For a rank ordering of violent crime rates, see Table 10.1.)

Homicide Rates in the United States Today
The American murder rate always has been high. It reached a peak in 1980 and has been declining erratically since then. In 2001, our population of just over 267 million experienced 15,980 murders and nonnegligent homicides (as reported to the police), or 5.6 per 100,000 of the population.[5] This is the lowest the murder rate has been since 1967, when the murder rate was 7 murders per 100,000 of the population. This rate is not equally distributed over the whole country: Murder rates are higher in the southern and western states (6.7 and 5.5 per 100,000, respectively) than in the northeastern and midwestern states (4.2 and 5.3 per 100,000, respectively).[6]

Your chance of becoming a murder victim is much higher if you are male than if you are female: Of all murder victims, 77 percent are male, 23 percent female. Age plays a role—45 percent of all murder victims are between the ages of 20 and 34; so does race—50 percent of all murder victims are white, 47.5 percent are black, and the remaining 2.5 percent are of other ethnic origins.[7]

Ninety-one percent of the black murder victims were slain by black offenders, and 84 percent of the white murder victims were killed by white offenders. Intentional criminal homicide apparently is an intraracial crime. But it is not an intragender crime. The data show that males were most often killed by males (88 percent), and 9 out of 10 female victims were murdered by males.[8]

TABLE 10.1 Where Does Your State Rank According to Rates of Violent Crime (per 100,000 Population)?

Rank	State	1999 Violent Crime* Rate
	United States, total	524.7
1	District of Columbia	1,627.7
2	Florida	854.0
3	South Carolina	847.1
4	New Mexico	834.5
5	Maryland	743.4
6	Delaware	734.0
7	Louisiana	732.7
8	Illinois	732.5
9	Tennessee	694.9
10	Alaska	631.5
11	California	627.2
12	New York	588.8
13	Michigan	574.9
14	Nevada	570.0
15	Texas	560.3
16	Arizona	551.2
17	Massachusetts	551.0
18	North Carolina	542.1
19	Georgia	534.0
20	Oklahoma	508.2
21	Missouri	500.2
22	Alabama	490.2
23	Nebraska	430.2
24	Arkansas	425.2
25	Pennsylvania	420.5
26	New Jersey	411.9
27	Kansas	382.8
28	Washington	377.3
29	Oregon	374.9
30	Indiana	374.6
31	West Virginia	350.6
32	Mississippi	349.3
33	Connecticut	345.6
34	Colorado	340.5
35	Ohio	316.4
36	Virginia	314.7
37	Kentucky	300.6
38	Rhode Island	286.6
39	Iowa	280.0
40	Utah	275.5
41	Minnesota	274.0
42	Wisconsin	245.9
43	Idaho	244.9
44	Hawaii	235.0
45	Wyoming	232.3
46	Montana	206.5
47	South Dakota	167.4
48	Vemoni	113.8
49	Maine	112.2
50	New Hampshire	96.5
51	North Dakota	66.9

Note: Violent crime is defined as murder and nonnegligent manslaughter, robbery, aggravated assault, and forcible rape.*

Source: Adapted from Sourcebook of Criminal Justice Statistics, 2000 (Albany, N.Y.: State University of New York at Albany, 2000), p. 290.

Yet another victim of the infamous Washington D.C. area snipers. This scene of the 2002 murder rampage is the Silver Spring post office located next to the Leisure World retirement community.

Homicide Rates Over Time Researchers have asked what happens to homicide rates over time when the composition of the population changes. What is the effect, for example, of a change in the racial composition of a city? Roland Chilton, using data on offenses committed in Chicago between 1960 and 1980 and census data for those years, found that about 20 percent of the total increase in homicide rates could be explained by increases in the nonwhite male population.[9] The same correlation is found in most major cities in the United States. Chilton argues that the problem will remain because of the poverty and demoralization of the groups involved. We can even expect that it will get worse if municipal governments are unable to improve the schools, reduce unemployment, and extend social services.

In a 1996 article, "Work," sociologist William Julius Wilson explains why America's ghettos have descended into "ever-deeper poverty and misery." According to him:

> For the first time in the 20th century, a significant majority of adults in many inner-city neighborhoods are not working in a typical week. Inner cities have always featured high levels of poverty, but the current levels of joblessness in some neighborhoods are unprecedented. For example, in the famous black-belt neighborhood of Washington Park on Chicago's South Side, a majority of adults had jobs in 1950; by 1990, only 1 in 3 worked in a typical week. High neighborhood joblessness has a far more devastating effect than high neighborhood poverty. A neighborhood in which people are poor but employed is different from a neighborhood in which people are poor and jobless. Many of today's problems in the inner-city neighborhoods—crime, family dissolution, welfare—are fundamentally a consequence of the disappearance of work.[10]

Until conditions change, what has been poignantly referred to as "the subculture of exasperation" will continue to produce a high homicide rate among nonwhite inner-city males.[11] Coramae Mann has found that although black women make up about 11 percent of the female population in the United States, they are arrested for three-fourths of all homicides committed by females. She argues that given such a disproportionate involvement in violent crime, one has to question whether the subculture of exasperation alone is entirely responsible.[12] But so few studies have been done on the subject that we cannot reach any definitive conclusion. Other investigators agree that homicide rates cannot be explained solely by such factors as poverty; the rates are also significantly associated with cultural approval of a resort to violence.

The Nature of Homicide

Let us take a closer look at killers and their victims and see how they are related to each other. In the 1950s Marvin Wolfgang studied homicide situations, perpetrators, and victims in the Philadelphia area. Victims and offenders were predominantly young black adults of low socioeconomic status. The offenses were committed in the inner city; they occurred primarily in the home of the victim or offender, on weekends, in the evening hours, and among friends or acquaintances.

A mural made in honor of the memory of more than 140 children killed between 1995 and 2000 by a mass murderer in Pereira, Colombia.

Building on the pioneering work of Hans von Hentig,[13] Wolfgang found that many of the victims had actually initiated the social interaction that led to the homicidal response, in a direct or subliminal way. He coined the term **victim precipitation** for such instances, which may account for as many as a quarter to a half of all intentional homicides. In such cases it is the victim who, by insinuation, bodily movement, verbal incitement, or the actual use of physical force, initiates a series of events that results in his or her own death. For example:

> During an argument in which a male called a female many vile names, she tried to telephone the police. He grabbed the phone from her hands, knocked her down, kicked her, and hit her with a tire gauge. She ran to the kitchen, grabbed a butcher knife, and stabbed him in the stomach.[14]

A study by Richard Felson and Steven Messner found that victim precipitation is more often seen in cases where women kill their husbands as opposed to incidents in which men kill their wives. However, males tend to be more violent than females in their killing methods.[15]

Other studies have provided additional insight into the patterns of homicide. Robert Silverman and Leslie Kennedy demonstrated that gender relationships, age, means of commission of the act, and location vary with relational distance, from closest relatives (lovers, spouses) to total strangers.[16]

Margaret Zahn and Philip Sagi have developed a model that distinguishes among homicides on the basis of characteristics of victims, offenders, location, method of attack, and presence of witnesses. They conclude that all these characteristics and variables serve to differentiate four categories of homicides: (1) those within the family, (2) those among friends and acquaintances, (3) stranger homicides associated with felonies, and (4) stranger homicides not associated with felonies.[17]

Did You Know?

... that between 1980 and 1997, nearly 38,000 juveniles were murdered in the United States?

Stranger Homicides The rate of **stranger homicide**—a killing in which killer and victim have had no known previous contact was 13.1 percent in 2001.[18] Marc Riedel, however, found these stranger homicide rates to be considerably understated. The true figures, according to Riedel, ranged from 14 to 29 percent.[19] Furthermore, the impact of stranger homicides on the quality of urban life—especially the fear of crime they engender—is far greater than their relatively small numbers would suggest.[20]

Relatives and Acquaintances Most homicides occur among relatives and acquaintances.[21] One study found that 44 percent of the victims were in intimate relationships with their killers, 26 percent were friends and acquaintances, 11 percent were the offender's own children, and only 7.5 percent were strangers. Of these homicides, those in which women killed their mates have received particular attention. Criminologists take special interest in the factors behind such crimes.[22] Researchers have found a high incidence of long-term abuse suffered by women who subsequently kill their mates.[23] They also suggest that mate homicides are the result of a husband's efforts to control his wife and the wife's efforts to retain her independence.[24]

Other recent trends are also noteworthy: One study found an increase in women who kill in domestic encounters, more planned killings, and less acceptance of self-defense as a motive in such cases.[25] Children are also at risk of death at the hands of family members. Research suggests that as the age of the child victim increases, so does the level of violence used to fatally injure the child.[26] Also, the closer the family relation to the victim (e.g., mother and child), the more passive the form of homicide (e.g., asphyxiation or abandonment), whereas the more distant a relative is to the victim, the more violent the method used (e.g., stabbing).[27] In most murders of a child under age 15, a family member killed the child, while murder victims aged 15 to 17 are more likely to be killed by an acquaintance of the victim or by someone unknown to the law enforcement authorities.[28] Whether killed by a family member or an acquaintance, boys are more often the victims of violent deaths than are girls.[29]

Young and Old Perpetrators Not surprisingly, the very young and the elderly have low homicide rates. In 2001, 114 homicide charges were placed against youngsters under 15, but this figure does not include the number of homicides in which the young killers were dealt with by juvenile courts or welfare agencies. Of the 9,426 persons of all ages arrested for homicide in 2001, 957 were under 18. The elderly, too, are underrepresented among killers. People age 55 and older accounted for only 2.8 percent of all murders in 2001.[30]

Homicide without Apparent Motive In most homicides, the killer has a motive or a reason for killing the victim. Popular fiction tells us that detectives tend to consider a case solved if they can establish the motive. But research shows that in a substantial number of murders, the motive remains unclear. The "unmotivated" murderers are a puzzle—and they constitute 25 percent of all homicide offenders.

Though in most respects the killers without motive are similar to those who kill for a reason, they are more likely to have "(1) no history of alcohol abuse; (2) a recent release from prison; (3) claims of amnesia for the crime; (4) denial of the crime; and (5) a tendency to exhibit psychotic behavior following the crime and to be assessed not guilty of the crime due to mental illness."[31]

Mass and Serial Murders Criminological researchers have paid special attention to two types of murder that are particularly disturbing to the community: **serial murder,** the killing of several victims over a period of time, and **mass murder,** the killing of multiple victims in one event or in very quick succession. Between 1970 and 1993 U.S. police knew of approximately 125 cases of multiple homicides. The literature on the subject is enormous.[32] Some recent serial murderers have become infamous.

Theodore "Ted" Bundy, law student and former crime commission staff member, killed between 19 and 36 young women in the northwestern states and Florida. David Berkowitz, the "Son of Sam," killed 6 young women in New York. Douglas Clark, the "Sunset Strip killer," killed between 7 and 50 prostitutes in Hollywood. The "Green River killer" of Seattle may have killed more than 45 victims. In the Midwest, Jeffrey Dahmer preserved, and took Polaroid photographs of, the mutilated body parts of his 11 to 17 victims; and on Long Island, Joel Rifkin collected souvenirs—a shoe, an earring, a driver's license—from the more than 13 streetwalkers he claimed as his victims.

In just one week in June 1996, two men, both suspected of being serial killers, were captured in New York City. Heriberto Seda, 28, lived a largely solitary life, except for those moments when he would emerge from the apartment he shared with his mother and sister. In two separate crime waves (in 1990, then again during 1992 and 1993), the self-proclaimed Zodiac Killer allegedly shot 8 people, killing 3 (Chapter 4). Larry Stevens, 31, who also lived with his mother, would allegedly trick old people into letting him into their homes. He would beat them or throw them downstairs, and then rob them. He is suspected of killing at least 2 elderly persons.[33]

Pedro Alonso Lopez, however, is considered the deadliest serial killer of all time, having killed over 300 people in Colombia, Peru, and Ecuador. Lopez has been dubbed the "Monster of the Andes."[34] In 1999, suspected serial killer Angel Leonicio Reyes Maturino Resendez was finally captured. Resendez was referred to as the "railroad killer" since all his slayings occurred near railroad tracks.[35]

Although the most notorious serial killers are men, female serial killers do exist. They are considered to be more difficult to apprehend and to have more complex motivations than their male counterparts.[36]

Throughout the 1990s an unusual number of mass murders occurred. In 1991, an unemployed young man drove his pickup through the glass window of a Texas café and opened fire with a semiautomatic pistol, leaving 22 dead. James Huberty walked into a McDonald's in California and killed 20 people. Colin Ferguson boarded a train where he killed 6 and wounded 17 in the Long Island massacre of 1993. In 1996, Thomas Hamilton entered a school in Dunblane, Scotland, shot and killed 16 kindergarten students and their teacher, and wounded 12 others.[37] In 1998, 5 of the 16 persons shot at a Jonesboro, Arkansas, middle school died. In 1999, there were 15 victims of a massacre at Columbine High School in Littleton, Colorado, and 7 victims of a mass shooting at a Baptist church in Fort Worth, Texas. Other 1999 incidents include 3 dead in Pelham, Alabama; 12 dead in Atlanta, Georgia; and 2 dead in Salt Lake City, Utah. In 2000, 7 masked gunmen entered a Philadelphia crack house and shot 10 people, killing 7. In 2001, unprecedented terror attacks on the World Trade Center in New York City killed thousands and sent shock waves throughout the world. In 2002, a New Jersey policeman went on a shooting rampage, killing 5 people before killing himself. Other incidents in 2002 included 18 killed in a school shooting in Erfurt, Germany; 5 children drowned in Texas; 5 killed in Los Angeles; 4 killed in San Bruno, California; and 3 killed in Long Beach, California. Most recently, the two

Serial killer Richard Kuklinski, known as the Iceman, appears relaxed as he pleads guilty to fatally shooting a New York police officer 23 years ago.

"Beltway" snipers, John Muhammed and John Lee Malvo, have been linked to 19 shootings and 13 deaths—in Washington, D.C., Maryland, Virginia, Louisiana, Georgia, and Alabama.

Recently, there has been an increase in mass murders in the workplace. From 1992 to 1996, more than 1,000 workplace homicides occurred annually.[38] San Franciscan failed businessman Gian Luigi Ferri, who blamed lawyers for his problems, burst into the 34th-floor law office where he had been a client and, with two pistols, killed 8 persons working in the firm. Disgruntled employee Paul Calder returned eight months after being fired to kill 3 and wound 2 at a Tampa insurance company. In 1999, day trader Mark O. Barton, after losing over $100,000 in the stock market in almost two months, bludgeoned his wife and 2 children to death. He then drove to an office complex in the Buckhead district of Atlanta. There he opened fire inside two brokerage firms where he had been employed. Barton killed a total of 13 people before committing suicide as police were closing in on him.[39] The U.S. Postal Service, where 38 employees died violently between 1986 and 1993, continues to look into ways to reduce employer-employee tension, especially when layoffs are imminent.[40]

It is popularly believed that multiple murderers are mentally ill; their offenses, after all, are often quite bizarre. In many such cases psychiatrists have found severe pathology.[41] Yet juries are reluctant to find these offenders not guilty by reason of insanity. Albert Fish, who cooked and ate the children he murdered, died in the electric chair.[42] Edmund Kemper, who killed hitchhikers as well as his own mother (he used her head as a dartboard), received a life term.[43]

The criminologists Jack Levin and James Fox do not agree with the hypothesis that all mass and serial murderers are mentally diseased (for example, psychotic) and therefore legally insane or incompetent. On the contrary, they say, serial killers are **sociopaths,** persons who lack internal controls, disregard common values, and have an intense desire to dominate others. But psychological characteristics alone cannot explain the actions of these people. They are also influenced by the social environment in which they function: the openness of our society, the ease of travel, the availability of firearms, the lack of external controls and supervision, and the general friendliness and trust of Americans in dealing with each other and with strangers.[44]

The American public is fascinated with the phenomena of mass and serial murder.[45] Levin and Fox suggest that the recent increase in mass and serial murders, despite a general decline in the murder rate, is to some extent attributable to the publicity given to mass murders and the resulting copycat phenomenon, the repetition of a crime as a result of the publicity it receives.[46] When one person killed at random by poisoning Tylenol capsules with cyanide, others copied the idea. This phenomenon has prompted experts to recommend that the media cooperate with the criminal justice system when the circumstances demand discretion.[47] Yet cooperation may be hard to achieve when media help is needed to alert the public to a health hazard (as in the Tylenol cases). In any event, the First Amendment's guarantee of freedom of the press does not permit controls.

Gang Murder Up to this point we have dealt largely with homicides committed by single offenders. But what about homicides by gangs of offenders? Are there any differences between the two types? On the basis of an analysis of data contained in 700 homicide investigation files, researchers found that "gang homicides differ both qualitatively and quantitatively from nongang homicides. Most distinctly, they differ with respect to ethnicity [more likely to be intraethnic], age [gang killers are five years younger], number of participants [2½ times as many participants], and relationship between the participants [gang killers are twice as likely not to know their victims]."[48] But similarities can also be seen. The causes of gang homicides, like those of single offenders, are often attributable to social disorganization, economic inequality, and deprivation.[49]

Since the 1950s the nature of gang murder has changed dramatically. As we discuss in Chapter 6, besides the major increase in killings, gang homicides have also gotten more brutal.

Drive-by and crossfire shootings of intended victims and innocent bystanders are no longer uncommon. From 1989 to 1993, there were 6,327 drive-by shootings, 9,053 people shot at, and 590 homicides; 47 percent of the people shot at and 23 percent of the homicide victims were innocent bystanders.[50] In Brooklyn, New York, all three brothers in one family fell victim to street violence. Motives also have changed through the years. Once, gang wars, with a few related homicides, took place over "turf," territory that members protected, with knives, rocks, or metal chains as weapons. Now the wars are over drugs, and the weapons are assault rifles and semiautomatic guns.[51]

A Cross-National Comparison of Homicide Rates

The criminal homicides we have been discussing are those committed in the United States. By comparing homicide rates in this country with those of other countries, we can gain a broader understanding of that crime. In the World Crime Survey ending with the year 1995, the United Nations revealed that the average rate of intentional homicide was 7.2 per 100,000 for developed (industrialized western) countries and 3.5 per 100,000 for developing countries.[52] The survey figures demonstrate that with the recent decline in U.S. homicide rates to 5.6 per 100,000 from 9 per 100,000 in 1994, the United States no longer has the highest rate among industrialized countries.[53] Recent data, however, show that the number of homicides per 100,000 children under age 15 in the United States was 5 times the number in the other countries combined. The rate of child homicides involving firearms was 16 times greater in the United States than in the other countries combined (Figure 10.1).[54]

One cross-national study found a moderate association between inequality of income and rate of homicide. It likewise revealed a relationship between a youthful population and the homicide rate. The analysis, the study concluded, "suggests that

Did You Know?

...that in 1997, on average about six juveniles were murdered daily in the United States?

FIGURE 10.1 Firearm-related homicide rates for children. The U.S. rate is more than twice that of Finland, the country with the next highest rate.

United States
Finland
Israel
France
Austria
Australia
Norway
Germany
Switzerland
Italy
Canada
Belgium
Sweden
England and Wales

0.0 0.1 0.2 0.3 0.4 0.5 0.6 0.7 0.8 0.9 1.0
Firearm-related deaths per 100,000 juveniles ages 0–14

Note: Countries with no firearm-related homicide for children: Denmark, Hong Kong, Ireland, Japan, Kuwait, the Netherlands, Northern Ireland, Scotland, Singapore, Taiwan, and Spain.

Source: Adapted from Centers for Disease Control and Prevention's rates of homicide, suicide, and firearm-related deaths among children—26 industrialized countries, as cited in *Juvenile Offenders and Victims: 1999 National Report.*

homicide rates are higher in poorer countries, in more culturally diverse countries, in countries which spend less on defense, in less-democratic societies, and in countries where fewer young people are enrolled in school."[55] Another researcher who compared the homicide rates in 76 countries with the rate in the United States found that when he took into consideration the differences in the age and sex distributions of the various populations, the United States had a higher rate than all but 15 countries,[56] most of which were experiencing civil war or internal strife.

A comparison of homicide rates with historical and socioeconomic data from 110 nations over a five-year period led researchers to the following conclusions:

- Combatant nations experience an increase in homicides following cessation of hostilities (violence has come to be seen as a legitimate means of settling disputes).

Anger at street encounters often escalates to assault, or even homicide. In San Francisco, California a crowd gathers as a street argument develops.

- The largest cities have the highest homicide rates; the smallest have the lowest homicide rates; but, paradoxically, as a city grows, its homicide rate per capita does not.
- The availability of capital punishment does not result in fewer homicides and in fact often results in more; abolition of capital punishment decreases the homicide rate.[57]

We have seen that murder rates are not distributed equally among countries or within a single country, or even within neighborhoods. As noted earlier, in the United States, homicide rates tend to be higher in the West and the South.[58] A greater proportion of males, young people, and blacks are perpetrators and victims of homicide, which tends to be committed against someone the killer knows, at or near the home of at least one of the persons involved, in the evening or on a weekend. Gang murders are increasing dramatically. A number of experts have found that homicides are related to the everyday patterns of interactions in socially disorganized slum areas.[59]

ASSAULT

The crimes of homicide and serious assault share many characteristics. Both are typically committed by young males, and a disproportionate number of arrestees are members of minority groups. Assault victims, too, often know their attackers. Spatial and temporal distributions are also quite comparable. Assault rates, like those of homicide, are highest in urban areas, during the summer months, in the evening hours, and in the South.

Though the patterns are the same, the legal definitions are not. A murder is an act that causes the death of another person and that is intended to cause death. An **assault** is an attack on another person that is made with apparent ability to inflict injury and that is intended to frighten or to cause physical harm. (An attack that results in touching or striking the victim is called a **battery**.) Modern statutes usually recognize two types of assault: A **simple assault** is one that inflicts little or no physical hurt; a felonious assault, or **aggravated assault,** is one in which the perpetrator inflicts serious harm on the victim or uses a deadly weapon.

Criminologists have looked closely at situations in which assaults are committed. One researcher identified six stages of a confrontational situation that leads to an assault:

1. One person insults another.
2. The insulted person perceives the significance of the insult, often by noting the reactions of others present, and becomes angry.

3. The insulted person contemplates a response: fight, flight, or conciliation. If the response chosen is a fight, the insultee assaults the insulter then and there. If another response is chosen, the situation advances to stage 4.

4. The original insulter, now reprimanded, shamed, or embarrassed, makes a countermove: fight or flight.

5. If the choice is a fight, the insulter assaults (and possibly kills) the insultee.

6. The "triumphant" party either flees or awaits the consequences (for example, police response).[60]

We can see that crucial decisions are made at all stages, and that the nature of the decisions depends on the context in which they are made. At stage 1, nobody is likely to offer an insult in a peaceful group or situation. At stage 2, the witnesses to the scene could respond in a conciliatory manner. (Let us call this a conflict-resolution situation.) At stage 3, the insulted person could leave the scene with dignity. (A confrontational person would call it flight; a conflict-resolution-minded person would call it a dignified end to a confrontational situation.) Stage 4 is a critical stage, since it calls for a counterresponse. The original aggressor could see this as the last chance to avoid violence and withdraw with apologies. That would be the end of the matter. In a confrontational situation, however, the blows will be delivered now, if none have been dealt already.

A similar pattern was proposed by James Tedeschi and Richard Felson, who developed a theory of aggression as instrumental behavior—that is, goal-oriented behavior carried out intentionally with the purpose of obtaining something. This is a different way of thinking about aggression. For years, criminologists and psychologists have generally accepted that aggression (and the violence that often goes with it) happens when a person reaches a "breaking point." There is little premeditation or thought given to some aggressive or violent behavior. But for Tedeschi and Felson, all aggression occurs after the person has thought about it first, even though these thoughts may be disorganized or illogical and may last for just a fraction of a second.[61]

The National Crime Victimization Survey estimates that 4,038,000 simple assaults were committed in 2001. Assault is the most common of all violent crimes reported to the police. The number of aggravated assaults has risen in recent years, reaching 1,293,000 in 2001.[62] These figures, however, grossly underestimate the real incidence. Many people involved in an assault consider the event a private matter, particularly if the assault took place within the family or household. Consequently, until quite recently little was known about family-related violence. But the focus of recent research is changing that situation rapidly.

FAMILY-RELATED CRIMES

In 1962 five physicians exposed the gravity of the "battered child syndrome" in the *Journal of the American Medical Association*.[63] When they reviewed X-ray photographs of patients in the emergency rooms of 71 hospitals across the country over the course of a year, they found 300 cases of child abuse, of which 11 percent resulted in death and over 28 percent in permanent brain damage. Shortly thereafter, the women's movement rallied to the plight of the battered wife and, somewhat later, to the personal and legal problems of wives who were raped by their husbands.[64]

In the 1960s and 1970s various organizations, fighting for the rights of women and children, exposed the harm that results from physical and psychological abuse in the home. They demanded public action. They created public awareness of the extent of the problem. Psychologists, physicians, anthropologists, and social scientists, among others, increasingly focused attention on the various factors that enter into episodes of domestic violence. Such factors include the sources of conflict, arguments, physical attacks, injuries, and temporal and spatial elements.

Within three decades family violence, the "well-kept secret," has come to be recognized as a major social problem.[65] Family violence shares some of the characteristics of other forms of violence, yet the intimacy of marital, cohabita-

A spectator holds up a sign offering advice to Boston Red Sox batter Wilfredo Cordero, as he pinch-hits for Reggie Jefferson in a game with the Toronto Blue Jays. The fans at Fenway Park, Boston, greeted him with boos as he stepped up to the plate.

tional, or parent-child relationships sets family violence apart. The physical and emotional harm inflicted in violent episodes tends to be spread over longer periods of time and to have a more lasting impact on all members of the living unit. Moreover, such events tend to be self-perpetuating.

Spouse Abuse

In May 1998, Motley Crüe drummer Tommy Lee was sentenced to six months in jail and three years probation for battering his wife, former "Baywatch" beauty Pamela Anderson. Lee was also ordered to perform 200 hours of community service and donate $5,000 to a battered women's shelter. He had been arrested in February 1998 after Anderson called 911 to report a domestic dispute in which Lee had kicked her in the back while she was holding seven-week-old Dylan Jagger. Lee was charged with spousal abuse, child abuse, and unlawful possession of a firearm. As the result of a plea agreement, all charges except for the spousal abuse charge were dropped.

Media celebrity and former star athlete O. J. Simpson was convicted in 1989 of assaulting his wife, Nicole Brown Simpson. He served no time in prison, nor was he required to undergo counseling. On June 13, 1994, Nicole Brown Simpson and her friend Ronald Goldman were found lying dead in pools of their own blood, victims of a vicious knife attack. O. J. Simpson was accused of their murder. Following a lengthy, highly publicized, and much-discussed trial, O. J. Simpson was found not guilty by a jury of his peers. The verdict had a wide-reaching impact on various aspects of the criminal justice system. It also made abused women fear for their lives. Concerned that a man who was a convicted batterer could be found not guilty of killing his ex-wife, despite what was perceived by many as convincing evidence, they wondered if they could eventually share the same fate as Nicole Brown Simpson.[66]

The Extent of Spouse Abuse In a national sample of 6,002 households, Murray A. Straus and Richard J. Gelles found that about one of every six couples experiences at least one physical assault during the year.[67] While both husbands and wives perpetrate acts of violence, the consequences of their acts differ.[68] Men, who more often use guns, knives, or fists, inflict more pain and injury. About 60 percent of spousal assaults consist of minor shoving, slapping, pushing; the other 40 percent are considered severe: punching, kicking, stabbing, choking.[69] According to the National Institute of Justice, partner violence is strongly linked to a variety of mental illnesses, a background of family adversity, dropping out of school, juvenile aggression, drug abuse, long-term unemployment, and cohabitation and/or parenthood at a young age. Research also suggests that women who have children by the age of 21 are two times more likely to be victims of domestic violence than are women who are not mothers, and that men who father children by age 21 are three times more likely to be perpetrators of abuse as men who are not fathers.[70]

Researchers agree that assaultive behavior within the family is a highly underreported crime. Data from the National Crime Victimization Survey indicate:

- One-half of the incidents of domestic assault are not reported.
- The most common reason given for failure to report a domestic assault to the police was that the victim considered the incident a private matter.
- Victims who reported such incidents to the police did so to prevent future assaults.
- Though the police classified two-thirds of the reported incidents of domestic violence as simple assaults, half of them inflicted bodily injury as serious as, or more serious than, the injuries inflicted during rapes, robberies, and aggravated assaults.[71]

The Nature of Spouse Abuse Before we can understand spouse abuse, we need information about abusers. Some experts have found that interpersonal violence is learned and transmitted from one generation to the next.[72] Studies demonstrate that children who are raised by aggressive parents tend to grow up to be aggressive adults.[73] Other researchers have demonstrated how stress, frustration, and severe psychopathology take their toll on family relationships.[74] A few researchers have also explored the role of body chemistry; one investigation ties abuse to the tendency of males to secrete adrenaline when they feel sexually threatened.[75]

The relationship between domestic violence and the use of alcohol and drugs has also been explored. Abusive men with severe drug and alcohol problems are more likely to abuse their wives or girlfriends when they are drunk or high and to inflict more injury.[76]

Several studies of other societies demonstrate cultural support for the abuse of women. Moroccan researcher Mohammed Ayat reported that of 160 battered women, about 25 percent believed that a man who does *not* beat his wife must be under some magic spell; 8 percent believed that such a man has a weak personality and is afraid of his wife; 2 percent believed that he must be abnormal; and another 2 percent believed that he doesn't love her or has little interest in her.[77] Wife beating, then, appears to be accepted as a norm by over one-third of the women studied—women who are themselves beaten. It even appears to be an expected behavior. In fact, in a study of 90 cultures, spouse beating was rare or nonexistent in only 15.[78]

Spouse abuse has often been attributed to the imbalance of power between male and female partners. According to some researchers, the historical view of wives as possessions of their husbands persists even today.[79] Until recently, spousal abuse was perceived as a problem more of social service than of criminal justice.[80] Police responding to domestic disturbance calls typically do not make an arrest unless the assailant is drunk, has caused serious injury, or has assaulted the officers. Take, for example, the case of *Thurman v. Torrington*. Tracey Thurman had repeatedly requested police assistance because she feared her estranged husband. Even after he threatened to shoot her and her son, the police merely told her to get a restraining order. Eventually, the husband attacked Thurman, inflicting multiple stab wounds that caused paralysis from the neck down and permanent disfigurement. The police had delayed in responding to her call on that occasion, and the city of Torrington, Connecticut, was held liable for having failed to provide her with equal protection of the laws. In the suit that followed, Ms. Thurman was awarded $2.3 million in damages.[81]

The Thurman case is rare. The majority of assault incidents within the family either are unreported to the police or, if reported, are classified as simple assaults. By and large, the victims of family violence—those who are willing to look for help—have turned to crisis telephone lines and to shelters for battered women (safe havens that first appeared in the early 1970s to provide legal, social, and psychological services).

Whether informal interventions are as effective as the criminal justice system, however, is a matter of controversy.[82] In a study conducted some years ago, the Minneapolis Domestic Violence Experiment, three types of action were taken: (1) The batterer was arrested, (2) the partners were required to separate for a designated period of time, and (3) a mediator intervened between the partners. Over a six-month period the offenders who were arrested had the lowest recidivism rate (10 percent), those who were required to separate had the highest (24 percent), and those who submitted to mediation fell in between (19 percent).[83] More recently, a 1991 study revealed that neither short-custody arrests for domestic violence in inner-city areas nor longer-term arrests are effective in curbing domestic violence, especially in the long run.[84] Questions on the subject of spouse abuse still far outnumber answers. Personal, ethical, and moral concerns make the issue highly sensitive. Researchers, however, are seeking answers.

Child Abuse

Spouse abuse is closely related to child abuse. One-half to three-quarters of men who batter women also beat their children, and many sexually abuse them as well. Children are also injured as a result of reckless behavior on the part of their fathers while the latter are abusing their mothers. In fact, the majority of abused sons over 14 suffer injuries trying to protect their mothers.[85]

The Extent of Child Abuse Most of the available data on child abuse come from the National Child Abuse and Neglect Data System (NCANDS).[86] The data show that there were approximately 3,000,000 referrals of child abuse in 2000, affecting up to 5,000,000 children. Of these, 62 percent were sent to the welfare system. Child maltreatment occurs when a parent or parent substitute (e.g., a day-care provider) abuses or permits the abuse of a child. Maltreatment includes physical abuse, sexual abuse, emotional abuse (e.g., verbal assaults), physical neglect, emotional neglect (inadequate nurturing), and educational neglect. (See Table 10.2.)

TABLE 10.2 Major Findings of NIS-3 on Maltreated Children

Type of Maltreatment	Percentage of Maltreated Children
Physical neglect	47
Physical abuse	22
Emotional neglect	21
Emotional abuse	19
Sexual abuse	11
Educational neglect	14

Note: One child may experience more than one type of maltreatment.
Source: U.S. Department of Justice, OJJDP, Juvenile Offenders and Victims, 1999 National Report, p. 41.

The NCANDS reported that approximately 1,300 children died of abuse or neglect in the year 2000. Of these, 85 percent were younger than 6 years of age.[87] It is still very difficult, however, to measure the extent of child abuse. Maltreatment usually takes place in the home, and the child victims rarely notify the police.[88]

The Nature of Child Abuse When child abuse first began to be investigated in the early 1960s, the investigators were predominantly physicians, who looked at the psychopathology of the abusers. They discovered that a high proportion of abusers suffered from alcoholism, drug abuse, mental retardation, poor attachment, low self-esteem, or sadistic psychosis. Later the search for causes moved in other directions. Some researchers pointed out that abusive parents did not know how to discipline children or, for that matter, even how to provide for basic needs, such as nutrition and medical attention. Claims have been made that abusers have themselves been abused; to date, however, the evidence in regard to this hypothesis is mixed.[89]

The list of factors related to child abuse is long. We know, for example, that the rate of child abuse in lower-income families is high.[90]

Fatal child abuse cases attract media attention. Approximately 3,000 children died of abuse or neglect in 2000. Of these fatalities, 85% were younger than six years of age.

This finding is probably related to the fact that low-income parents have few resources for dealing with the stress to which they are subjected, such as poor housing and financial problems. When they cannot cope with their responsibilities, they may become overwhelmed. Moreover, the risk of abuse is twice as great for children living with single parents as for children living with both parents.[91] The rate of child abuse may also be related to the acceptance of physical responses to conflict situations in what has been termed the "subculture of violence" (Chapter 6). Moreover, since child abuse among poor families is likely to be handled by a public agency, these cases tend to appear in official statistics.

When child abuse is reported to the authorities, the case goes through the criminal justice system just like any other case. However, certain factors are associated with how, and to what extent, these types of cases are prosecuted. One study suggests that, particularly in the case of child sexual abuse, those offenders who are charged with abusing multiple victims are much more likely to be prosecuted than are offenders charged with abusing only one victim. Also, offenders who are strangers to the victim are more likely to be prosecuted than are offenders related to the victim. Cases in which serious abuse was involved and medical evidence of abuse existed were also more likely to be prosecuted.[92]

Some researchers have found that formal action—arrest and prosecution—is the most effective means for limiting repeat offenses in the case of battered wives. The situation seems to be different when children are involved. Several advocates for children oppose any involvement of the criminal justice system. They believe that the parent-child attachment remains crucial to the child's development, and they fear that punishment of parents can only be detrimental to the child's need for a stable family environment. Only in the most extreme cases would they separate children from parents and place them in shelters or in foster homes. The preference is to prevent child abuse by other means, such as self-help groups (Parents Anonymous), baby-sitting assistance, and crisis phone lines.

The results of various types of intervention are characterized by the title of a report on child maltreatment: "Half Full and Half Empty."[93] Rates of repeated abuse are high; yet some families have had positive results, and advances have been made in identifying the best treatment for various types of problems. Although our understanding of the problem has indeed increased, we need to know a great deal more about the offense before we can reduce its occurrence.[94]

Abuse of the Elderly

When the amendments to the Older Americans Act appeared in 1987, they brought with them a federal definition of elder abuse, neglect, and exploitation. The definition is used only as a guideline and not for enforcement purposes. State laws provide their own definitions of elder abuse, and these definitions vary across state jurisdictions. Nevertheless, three basic categories of elder abuse emerged: domestic elder abuse, institutional elder abuse, and self-neglect or self-abuse. Domestic elder abuse results when an older person is maltreated by a person who has a special relationship with the elder, such as a spouse, sibling, child, or friend. Institutional elder abuse occurs in the context of a residential facility, such as a nursing home, in which paid caregivers or other staff are the perpetrators.

Self-neglect or self-abuse occurs when elderly persons threaten their own health or safety by, for example, failing to provide themselves with proper amounts of food, clothing, shelter, and medication.[95]

Abuse of the elderly has become an area of special concern to social scientists. The population group that is considered to be elderly is variously defined. The majority of researchers consider 65 the age at which an individual falls into the category "elderly." As health care in the United States has improved, longevity has increased. The population of elderly people has grown larger over the decades: from 4 percent of the total population in 1900 to 12.6 percent in the 1990s.[96] Every day 1,000 more people join the ranks. It is estimated that by the year 2020, 20 percent of the population will be elderly.[97]

Elderly persons who are being cared for by their adult children are at a certain risk of abuse. The extent of the problem, however, is still largely unknown. The abused elderly frequently do not talk about their abuse for fear of the embarrassment of public exposure and possible retaliation by the abuser. Congressional hearings on domestic abuse estimate that between 500,000 and 2.5 million elderly people are abused annually.[98] Among the causes of such abuse are caregivers who themselves grew up in homes where violence was a way of life, the stress of caregiving in a private home rather than an institution, generational conflicts, and frustration with gerontological (old-age) problems of the care receiver, such as illness and senility.[99]

We can see that criminologists share a growing concern about family-related violence. Child abuse has received the attention of scholars for three decades. Spousal abuse has been studied for two decades. The abuse of the elderly has begun to receive attention much more recently. Family abuse is not new; our awareness of the size and seriousness of the problem is. The same could be said about yet another offense. It was not until the 1960s that women's advocates launched a national campaign on behalf of victims of rape. Since then, rape has become a major topic in criminological literature and research.

RAPE AND SEXUAL ASSAULT

The common law defined **rape** as an act of enforced intercourse by a man of a woman (other than the attacker's wife) without her consent. Intercourse includes any sexual penetration, however slight. The exclusion of wives from the crime of rape rested on several outdated legal fictions, among them the propositions that the marriage vows grant implicit permanent rights of sexual access and that spouses cannot testify against each other. The Hale Doctrine, written in the seventeenth century and recognized judicially in 1857 by the United States, stated specifically that "the husband cannot be guilty of a rape committed by himself upon his lawful wife, for by their mutual matrimonial consent and a contract the wife hath given up herself in this kind unto her husband which she cannot retract."[100] Older laws universally classify rape as a sex crime. But rape has always been much more than that. It is inherently a crime of violence, an exercise of power.

> **Theory Connects**
>
> **Rape and Sexual Assault**
>
> What theories of crime causation explain rape and sexual assault? Why do you suppose most of the theories discussed in Chapters 4 through 8 are generally unhelpful? Is the crime of rape or sexual assault that different from homicide, robbery, or even assault?

Oddly, as Susan Brownmiller forcefully argues, it really started as a property crime. Men as archetypal aggressors (the penis as a weapon) subjugated women by the persistent threat of rape. That threat forced each woman to submit to a man for protection and thus to become a wife, the property of a man. Rape then was made a crime to protect one man's property—his wife—from the sexual aggressions of other men.[101] But even that view regards rape as a violent crime against the person, one that destroys the freedom of a woman (and nowadays of a man as well) to decide whether, when, and with whom to enter a sexual relationship.

Well over a thousand books, scholarly articles, and papers have been produced on the topic of rape and sexual assault since the 1960s. Much that was obscure and poorly understood has now been clarified by research generated largely by the initiatives of the feminist movement, the National Center for the Prevention and Control of Rape (NCPCR), and other governmental and private funding agencies. While most of the crimes in our penal codes have more or less retained their original form, the law on rape has changed rapidly and drastically. The name of the crime, its definition, the rules of evidence and procedure, society's reaction to it—all have changed.[102] Nevertheless, Americans still regard rape as one of the most serious crimes.

Characteristics of the Rape Event

According to the Uniform Crime Reports, there were 90,491 forcible rapes in 2001. This figure represents 6 percent of the total number of violent crimes.[103] The incidence of rape dropped 9 percent between 1993 and 1997. Of all those arrested for forcible rape, 45 percent were under age 25; and 63 percent were white.[104] Most rapes are committed in the summer, particularly in July. Several decades ago, Menachem Amir demonstrated that close to half of all rapes in Philadelphia from 1958 to 1965 were committed by a person known to or even friendly with the victim.[105] Recent victimization data show that the situation has not changed: 48 percent of rapes are committed by men who know their victims.[106] The offender may even be the husband, who in some states can now qualify as a rapist. Nevertheless, marital rape is still minimized by the law. We know little about it except that it often occurs in marriages that are characterized by other forms of violence and in marriages involving alcoholic husbands.[107]

Recently researchers have developed a three-category typology of rape. Stranger rape occurs when the victim has had little or no prior contact with the offender. Predatory rape involves a man who, using deception or force, intends and plans to rape his victim, by pretending to engage in legitimate dating behavior. Date rape involves a legitimate dating situation turned bad, when force is eventually used to gain sex from a woman who is an unwilling participant.[108] In these situations the offenders sometimes use the date rape "drug of choice," Rohypnol, commonly referred to as "Roofies." Rohypnol falls into the same class of drugs as marijuana. It is a sedative which is said to be 10 times the strength of Valium. Twenty to thirty minutes after it is consumed, often after being dropped into a drink at a social gathering, this tasteless, odorless drug produces in its victim muscle relaxation, a slowing of psychomotor responses, and amnesia.[109] Some research indicates that as many as 25 percent of all female college students may have experienced rape.[110] Criminologists have difficulty estimating the frequency of date rape, but in all likelihood such rape has increased significantly. It is estimated that only one-tenth of the date rapes committed are reported to the police.

There is an arrest made for all types of forcible rape in about 50 percent of the cases.[111] Many stranger rapists remain at large because they commit their acts in ways that produce little tangible evidence as to their identities. They maintain a distance from the victim by not interacting with her before the attack. The serial rapist also attacks strangers, but because he finds his victims repeatedly in the same places, his behavior is more predictable and so leads to a better arrest rate.[112]

Who Are the Rapists?

Explanations of rape fall into two categories, psychological and sociocultural. While research in these areas has expanded over the last two decades, the causes of rape remain speculative.

Psychological Factors Several experts view rapists as suffering from mental illness or personality disorders. They argue that some rapists are psychotic, sociopathic, or sadistic, or that they feel deficient in masculinity. Most rapists show hostile feelings toward women, have histories of violence, and tend to attack strangers. They commit the offense because of anger, a drive for power (expressed as sexual conquest), or the enjoyment of maltreating a victim (sadism). Some rapists view women as sex objects whose role is to satisfy them.

Sociocultural Factors Psychological explanations assume that men who rape are maladjusted in some way. But several studies done in the 1980s demonstrate that rapists are indistinguishable from other groups of offenders.[113] These studies generally conclude that rape is culturally related to societal norms that approve of aggression as a demonstration of masculinity (as we saw in Chapter 6) or that rape is the mechanism by which men maintain their power over women.

The social significance of rape has long been a part of anthropological literature. A cross-cultural study of 95 tribal societies found that 47 percent were rape-free, 35 percent intermediate, and 18 percent rape-prone. In the rape-prone societies women had low status and little decision-making power, and they lived apart from men. The author of this study concluded: "Violence is socially, not biologically, programmed."[114]

Despite anthropologists' traditional interest in gender relationships, it was not until the feminist movement and radical criminology focused on the subject that the relationship of rape, gender inequality, and socioeconomic status was fully articulated. Writing from the Marxist perspective, which we explore in Chapter 9, Julia and Herman Schwendinger posited that "the impoverishment of the working class and the widening gap between rich and poor" create conditions for the prevalence of sexual violence.[115] A test of this hypothesis showed that while the incidence of sexual violence was not related to ethnic inequality, it was significantly related to general income inequality.[116]

A more recent study analyzed these findings and concluded that economic inequality was not the sole determinant of violent crime in our society. Forcible rape was found to be an added "cost" of many factors, including social disorganization.[117] In sum, many factors have been associated with the crime of rape: psychological problems, social factors, and even sociopolitical factors. Some experts suggest that boys are socialized to be aggressive and dominating, that the innate male sex drive leads to rape, and that pornography encourages men to rape by making sex objects of women, degrading women, and glamorizing violence against them. Rape has been explained in such a wide variety of ways that it is extremely difficult to plan preventive strategies and to formulate crime-control policy. Moreover, it has created major difficulties in the criminal justice system.

Rape and the Legal System

The difficulties of rape prosecutions have their roots in the English common law. Sir Matthew Hale, a seventeenth-century jurist, explained in *Pleas of the Crown* (1685, 1736) how a jury was to be cautious in viewing evidence of rape: "[It] must be remembered . . . that it is an accusation easily to be made and hard to be proved, and harder to be defended, by the party accused, tho never so innocent."[118] This instruction, which so definitively protects the defendant, has until recently been a mandatory instruction to juries in the United States. Along with many other legal and policy changes, many jurisdictions have now cast it aside. The requirement of particularly stringent proof in rape cases had always been justified by the seriousness of the offense and the heavy penalties associated with it, plus the stigma attached to such a conviction.

Difficulties of Prosecution Victims of rape have often been regarded with suspicion by the criminal justice system. The victim's testimony has not sufficed to convict the defendant, no matter how unimpeachable that testimony may have been. There had to be "corroborating evidence," such as semen, torn clothes, bruises, or eyewitness testimony.

Another major issue has been that of consent. Did the victim encourage, entice, or maybe even agree to the act? Was the attack forced? Did the victim resist? Martin Schwartz and Todd Clear sum up the reasons for such questions: "There is a widespread belief in our culture that women 'ask for it,' either individually or as a group." They compared rape victims to victims of other offenses: "Curiously, society does not censure the robbery victim for walking around with $10, or the burglary victim for keeping all of those nice things in his house, or the car theft victim for showing off his flashy new machine, just asking for someone to covet it."[119]

Sara Lively, 24, left, and Michelle Coler, 21, test their drinks for date-rape drugs at the Britannia Arms pub in San Jose, California, September 2002. Colleges around the country are buying millions of coasters that test for "date-rape" drugs in drinks.

Because defendants in rape cases so often claim that the victim was in some way responsible for the attack, rape victims in the courtroom tend to become the "accused," required to defend their good reputations, their propriety, and their mental soundness. The severity of the assault, the injuries the victim sustains, whether or not the assailant was a stranger, and the victim's social support network all play a role in terms of the rape reporting process.[120] Experts claim that as many as 60 percent of rapes are not reported.[121] In sum, so many burdens are placed on the victim that no one seriously wonders why so few rapes are reported and why so few men accused of rape are convicted.

Legislative Changes The feminist movement has had a considerable impact on laws and attitudes concerning rape in our country. The state of Michigan was a leader in the movement to reform such laws by creating, in 1975, the new crime of "criminal sexual conduct" to replace the traditional rape laws. It distinguishes four degrees of assaultive sexual acts, differentiated by the amount of force used, the infliction of injury, and the age and mental condition of the victim.

The new law is gender-neutral, in that it makes illegal any type of forcible sex, including homosexual rape. Other states have followed Michigan's lead. Schwartz and Clear have suggested that reform should go one step further. They argue that if rape were covered by the general assault laws rather than by a separate statute on sex crimes, the emphasis would be on the assault (the action of the offender) and not on the resistance (the action of the victim).

Recent legislation has also removed many of the barriers women encountered as witnesses in the courtroom. Thus in states with rape shield laws women are no longer required to disclose their prior sexual activity, and corroboration requirements have been reduced or eliminated; as noted earlier, some states have reversed two centuries of legal tradition by striking down the "marital rape exemption" so that a wife may now charge her husband with rape.[122] But law reform has limits. Unfortunately, prejudices die hard.

Community Response

Women's advocates have taken an interest not only in legislative reform but also in the community's response to the victims of rape. In 1970 the first rape-specific support project, the Bay Area Women Against Rape—a volunteer-staffed emergency phone information service—was established in Berkeley, California.[123] By 1973, similar projects had spread throughout the country. Run by small, unaffiliated groups, they handled crises, monitored agencies (hospitals, police, courts) that came in contact with victims, educated the public about the problems of victims, and even provided lessons in self-defense.

By the late 1970s the number of these centers and their activities had increased dramatically. The mass media reported on their successes. Federal and, later, state and local support for such services rose. As the centers became more professional, they formed boards of directors, prepared detailed budgets to comply with the requirements of funding agencies, hired social workers and mental health personnel, and developed their political action component. But even with increased support, the demand for the services of rape crisis centers far outweighs the available resources.

KIDNAPPING

Kidnapping, as such, was not recognized as a felony under English common law; it was a misdemeanor. Some forms of kidnapping were later criminalized by statute. In the eighteenth century, the most frequent form of kidnapping, according to the great legal scholar Sir William Blackstone, was stealing children and sending them to servitude in the American colonies. Other forms of kidnapping were the "crimping," or shanghaiing, of persons for involuntary service aboard ships and the abduction of women for purposes of prostitution abroad.

All these offenses have elements in common, and together they define the crime of **kidnapping:** abduction and detention by force or fraud and transport beyond the authority of the place where the crime was committed. It was not until the kidnapping of Charles Lindbergh's infant son in 1932 that comprehensive kidnapping legislation was enacted in the United States. In passing the federal kidnapping statute—the so-called Lindbergh act (now 18 U.S. Code [sec.] 1201)—Congress made it a felony to kidnap and transport a victim across a state or national border. The crime was subject to the death penalty, unless the victim was released unharmed.

In the United States kidnapping often involves the abduction of a child from one parent by the other. An interesting case recently appeared in the news. In October 1979, Stephen Fagan kidnapped his two daughters, Lisa (age 2) and Rachael (age 5), from Massachusetts and then moved to Florida. He told his daughters that their mother had died. It was not until 1998 that an anonymous tip led to his arrest in Florida, where he was living the high life as a socialite under the name Dr. William Martin. Fagan claimed that he took his daughters away from his ex-wife, Barbara Kurth, who he believed was an unfit and alcoholic mother. Kurth vehemently denied the allegation. Fagan was charged with kidnapping his daughters even though the crime had occurred 20 years earlier. In a plea agreement, Fagan was spared jail time; instead, he was fined $100,000 and received a suspended 3- to 5-year prison sentence. He must also serve probation for 5 years. The two daughters have stood by their father and have decided not to reunite with their mother.[124]

ROBBERY

Portland (April 26, 1999)—Ethan is shrieking. It would be funny, but he is bleeding from the scrotum, and that's just not funny. In the adrenaline rush, he has shoved his dad's gun into his waistband and accidentally shot himself. His best friend Tom has stopped the car, a Chevy Suburban they paid someone $80 to steal for what was supposed to be their big finale. The Oregon teens had planned a major heist, Ethan would later say, maybe half a million that they would tote in athletic bags from the money room at a Nordstrom department store. But that plan didn't work out; in fact, the whole night had gone right to hell. (Why didn't they stick to knocking over Burger Kings?) Tom had worked as a clerk at Nordstrom and—duh—someone recognized him when he and Ethan ambled in. So they walked out without taking a thing. They should have gone home, but after weeks of planning, they were primed. They settled on Rustica, a neighborhood Italian place with a nice sourdough. The petrified manager handed over $500, and it was in the heady aftermath that not far away Ethan shot himself.[125]

Typical robbers? No. Thomas Curtis and Ethan Thrower were two high school superstars who had their fun completing a string of armed robberies.

Robbery is the taking of property from a victim by force and violence or by the threat of violence. The Model Penal Code (Section 222.1) grades robbery as a felony of the second degree, commanding a prison term of up to 10 years. If the robber has intentionally inflicted serious physical injury or attempted to kill, the sentence may be as long as life. In reality, however, the average sentence upon conviction for one charge of robbery is 6 years.[126] In 1997, the number of robbery offenses was 497,950, or 186 robberies per 100,000 of the population, the lowest rate since 1985.[127]

Offenders display weapons, mostly guns and knives, in almost half of all robberies. Since 44 percent of all robberies net the perpetrator less than $50, the overall reporting rate for robbery is only slightly higher than 50 percent. Robberies of individuals occur most frequently on the street (61.3 percent). The remaining robberies take place in parking lots and garages (14 percent), in residences (9.3 percent), in commercial buildings (5.2 percent), in transit stations or on public transportation (3.8 percent), in nightclubs, bars, or restaurants (2.7 percent), and in miscellaneous establishments (3.7 percent).[128]

Characteristics of Robbers

Criminologists have classified the characteristics of robbers as well as the characteristics of robberies. John Conklin detected four types of robbers:

- The *professional robber* carefully plans and executes a robbery, often with many accomplices; steals large sums of money; and has a long-term, deep commitment to robbery as a means of supporting a hedonistic lifestyle.
- The *opportunistic robber* (the most common) has no long-term commitment to robbery; targets victims for small amounts of money ($20 or less); victimizes elderly women, drunks, cab drivers, and other people who seem to be in no position to resist; and is young and generally inexperienced.
- The *addict robber* is addicted to drugs, has a low level of commitment to robbery but a high level of commitment to theft, plans less than professional robbers but more than opportunistic robbers, wants just enough money for a fix, and may or may not carry a weapon.
- The *alcoholic robber* has no commitment to robbery as a way of life, has no commitment to theft, does not plan his or her robberies, usually robs people after first assaulting them, takes few precautions, and is apprehended more often than other robbers.[129]

According to the Uniform Crime Reports, 90 percent of those arrested for robbery in 1997 were males. Approximately 65 percent of the arrestees were under 25 years of age. In terms of race, blacks accounted for 57 percent of all robbery arrests, whites accounted for 41 percent, and all other races constituted the remaining 2 percent of all robbery arrests.[130]

The Consequences of Robbery

Robbery is a property crime as well as a violent crime. It is the combination of the motive for economic gain and the violent nature of robbery that makes it so serious.[131] An estimated $496 million was lost as a result of robbery in 1994 alone. The value of stolen property per incident averaged $801, and the average amount of money stolen ranged from $387 (from convenience stores) to $3551 (from banks).[132] Loss of money, however, is certainly not the only consequence of robbery. The million-odd robberies that take place each year leave psychological and physical trauma in their wake, not to mention the pervasive fear and anxiety that have contributed to the decay of inner cities.

Not all criminologists agree, however, that the high level of fear is warranted. After examining trends in robbery-homicide data from 52 of the largest cities in the United States, one researcher found "little support for the fears that there is a new breed of street criminals who cause more serious injuries and deaths in robberies. Very recent trends point in the other direction. Killing a robbery victim appears to be going out of fashion."[133]

ORGANIZED CRIME

It's enough to make John Gotti turn in his grave—the feds are administering the last rites to his once-powerful Gambino crime family.

Only five days after the godfather's funeral, FBI agents yesterday pounced on 14 alleged family members and associates wanted for murder and racketeering crimes stretching back to the late '80s—a time when the Gambinos ruled New York's gangland with iron fists.

"It's a whole different world than it was," U.S. Attorney Jim Comey said, pointing proudly to a pyramid chart of rubbed-out Gambino mobsters with black crosses stamped on their faces.

" 'This thing of ours'—La Cosa Nostra—is very, very different today."

The freshest black cross was on the head of one of the late Dapper Don's longest serving capos, Louis "Big Louie" Vallario, who was one of four men indicted for the 1989 execution of Staten Island businessman Fred Weiss.

One of the Gambinos' rising stars, Michael "Mikey Scars" DiLeonardo, was also arrested for the execution-style slaying. It was allegedly carried out as a favor to Gotti, who feared Weiss was cooperating with the feds.

Comey said the three indictments unsealed yesterday represented a "further dismantling of the Gambino family's leadership" and sent a signal that the feds will prevent the family from re-establishing its "violent, extortionate grip" over New York.

New York FBI assistant director Kevin Donovan described the busts as the "latest chapter in the decade-long saga of the decline of the Gambinos."

"Making money the mob way has always meant instilling fear through intimidation and violence, and it is not true that the victims of mob violence are just other mobsters," Donovan said.

Since Gotti was put away for the last time in June 1992, the Gambinos' grip over legitimate industries, such as garbage carting and the waterfront, has been pried loose.

And the family's ability to rebuild was dealt a further blow this month, when Peter Gotti, who took over from his ailing brother this year, was arrested along with 16 other soldiers and associates.

As part of the indictments unsealed yesterday, the feds claim to have busted a large-scale theft racket centered on a vegetable store in The Bronx, called Top Tomato. It was owned by Salvatore Sciandra, brother of Gambino member Carmine Sciandra, the indictment says.

Sciandra's wife, Margaret, and her mother, Mildred Scarpati, are also facing up to five years in prison after being charged with conspiracy to defraud Allstate Insurance by filing a bogus car-loss claim.

Three Gambino associates were also charged with extorting two Manhattan garment businesses.[134]

On St. Valentine's Day, 1929, while Al Capone vacationed in Florida his mobsters machine gunned their rivals in Chicago. The victims were lured to this garage (to buy prohibited liquor) where the hit men dressed in stolen police uniforms, and driving a stolen police car "raided" the place, told the victims to line up against the wall, and then opened fire.

Earlier we noted that all forms of organizational criminality have in common the use of business enterprises for illegal profit. We have recognized some significant problems not only with existing definitions and conceptualizations of white-collar and corporate crime but with the criminal justice response to such offenses. Similar problems arise in efforts to deal with organized crime. It, too, depends on business enterprises. And like corporate crime, organized crime comes in so many varieties that attempts to define it precisely lead to frustration.

The difficulty of gaining access to information on organized crime has also hindered attempts to conceptualize the problems posed by this kind of law violation. Finally, law enforcement efforts have been inadequate to control the influence of organized crime. As will be evident, a greater effort must be made to uncover the nature, pattern, and extent of organized crime.

John Gotti Jr., 35, acting head of New York City's Gambino crime family, assumed the reigns of the family firm in 1994. In 1999, "John Junior" worked a deal with federal prosecutors by pleading guilty to racketeering, extortion, and tax evasion. He was sentenced to six and one-half years, with parole eligibility in 2004.

The History of Organized Crime

Organized crime had its origin in the great wave of immigrants from southern Italy (especially from Sicily) to the United States between 1875 and 1920. These immigrants came from an environment that historically had been hostile to them. Suppressed by successive bands of invaders and alien rulers dating back some 800 years before Christ, Sicily was first coveted as a strategic location between major Mediterranean trade routes by the Greeks and Phoenicians. In later centuries Roman, Byzantine, Arab, Norman, German, Spanish, Austrian, and French soldiers all laid siege and claim to Sicily. Exploited by mostly absentee landlords with their armies, Sicilians had learned to survive by relying on the strength of their own families. Indeed, these families had undergone little change since Greco-Roman times, two millennia earlier.

A traditional Sicilian family has been described as an extended family, or clan; it includes lineal relations (grandparents, parents, children, grandchildren) and lateral relations through the paternal line—uncles, aunts, and cousins as far as the bloodline can be traced. This *famiglia* is hierarchically organized and administered by the head of the family, the *capo di famiglia* (the Romans called him *pater familias*), to whom all members owe obedience and loyalty. Strangers, especially those in positions of power in state or church, are not to be trusted. The importance of the family is evident in the famous Sicilian proverb: "*La legge é per l ricchi, La forca é per l poveri, E la giustizie é per l buffoni.*" (The law is for the rich, the gallows are for the poor, and justice is for the fools.) For Sicilians all problems are resolved within the family, which must be kept strong. Its prestige, honor, wealth, and power have to be defended and strengthened, sometimes through alliances with more distant kin.[135]

Throughout history these strong families have served each other and Sicily. Upon migration to the United States, members of Sicilian families soon found that the social environment in their new country was as hostile as that of the old. Aspirations were encouraged, yet legitimate means to realize them were often not available. And the new country seemed already to have an established pattern for achieving wealth and power by unethical means. Many of America's great fortunes—those of the Astors, the Vanderbilts, the Goulds, the Sages, the Stanfords, the Rockefellers, the Carnegies, the Lords, the Harrimans—had been made by cunning, greed, and exploitation.

As time passed, new laws were enacted to address conspiracies in restraint of trade and other economic offenses. Yet by the time the last wave of Sicilian immigrants reached the United States, the names of the great robber barons were connected with major universities, foundations, and charitable institutions.[136] At the local level, the Sicilian immigrants found themselves involved in a system of politics in which patronage and protection were dispensed by corrupt politicians and petty hoodlums from earlier immigrant groups—German, Irish, and Jewish. The Sicilian family structure helped its members survive in this hostile environment. It also created the organizational basis that permitted them to respond to the opportunity created when, on January 16, 1920, the Eighteenth Amendment to the Constitution outlawed the manufacture, sale, and transportation of alcoholic beverages.

Howard Abadinsky explains what happened:

> Prohibition acted as a catalyst for the mobilization of criminal elements in an unprecedented manner. Pre-prohibition crime, insofar as it was organized, centered around corrupt political machines, vice entrepreneurs, and, at the bottom, gangs. Prohibition unleashed an unparalleled level of competitive criminal violence and changed the order—the gang leaders emerged on top.[137]

During the early years of Prohibition, the names of the most notorious bootleggers, mobsters, and gangsters sounded German, Irish, and Jewish: Arthur Flegenheimer (better known as "Dutch Schultz"), Otto Gass, Bo and George Weinberg, Arnold Rothstein, John T. Nolen (better known as "Legs Diamond"), Vincent "Mad Dog" Coll, Waxey Gordon, Owney Madden, and Joe Rock. By the time Prohibition was repealed, Al Capone, Salvatore Luciana (better known as "Lucky Luciano"), Frank Costello, Johnny Torrio, Vito Genovese, Guiseppe Doto (better known as "Joe Adonis"), and many other Sicilians were preeminent in the underworld. They had become folk heroes and role models for young boys in the Italian ghettos, many of whom were to seek their own places in this new society.

Sicilian families were every bit as ruthless in establishing their crime empires as the earlier immigrant groups had been. They were so successful in their domination of organized crime that, especially after World War II, organized crime became virtually synonymous with the Sicilian Mafia.

The term "Mafia" appears to derive from an Arabic word denoting "place of refuge." The concept, which was adopted in Sicily during the era of Arab rule, gradually came to describe a mode of life and survival. Sicilians trace the word to a tale of revenge that took place on Easter Monday, 1282. On this day, a French soldier who was part of a band of marauding foreigners raped a Sicilian woman on her wedding day. Following the assault, bands of Sicilians went to the streets of Palermo to slaughter hundreds of Frenchmen, spurred on by the screams of the young girl's mother: "Ma fia, ma fia" ("My daughter, my daughter").[138]

Ultimately, the **Mafia** became the entirety of those Sicilian families that were loosely associated with one another in operating organized crime, both in America and in Sicily.[139] The first realistic depiction of the organization of the Mafia came with the testimony of Joseph Valachi before the Senate's McClellan Committee in 1963. Valachi, a disenchanted soldier in New York's Genovese crime family, was the first member of Italian organized crime to describe a quasi-military secret criminal syndicate. From that point on, the Mafia has also been referred to as *La Cosa Nostra*, literally translated as "this thing of ours."[140]

Despite Valachi's testimony and later revelations, some scholars still doubt the existence of a Sicilian-based American crime syndicate. To the criminologist Jay Albanese, for instance:

> [I]t is clear . . . that despite popular opinion which has for many years insisted on the existence of a secret criminal society called "the Mafia," which somehow evolved from Italy, many separate historical investigations have found no evidence to support such a belief.[141]

The Structure and Impact of Organized Crime

Americans have felt the impact of organized crime, and they have followed the media coverage of the mob wars and their victims with

Window to the World

The Business of Organized Crime

Have you ever asked yourself (or anyone else) what the world's largest business, is? Oil? Autos? Computers? Steel? It's none of these. Drug and arms trafficking by major crime syndicates take first and second place. (1) The United Nations estimates that the combined annual sales from organized crime range from $700 billion to $1000 billion annually Trafficking in narcotics alone exceeds $300 billion each year. (1, p. 22).

Much of the expansion of organized crime in recent years has been made possible by the fragile political and economic situation of developing and transitional countries. A prime example is post–cold war Russia. Enticed by the weakened judicial system, reduced law enforcement, and a susceptible bureaucracy, organized-crime groups such as the Russian and Sicilian Mafias have established a firm hold on the ex-Soviet states. Organized crime has moved in, shielded by the need for foreign capital investment. The Russian Mafia alone, with over three million members in 5700 gangs, controls approximately one-quarter of the commercial and retail banks; as well as tens of thousands of other legitimate businesses. Gangs traffic in everything from raw material to nuclear weapons.

The infiltration of organized crime into legitimate businesses poses a particularly significant threat to the emerging economic order, of transitional economies. Politically and economically, the Mafia is becoming part of the business culture in certain markets. "Instead of being a threat to the legal order, the Mafia is becoming its rival and even its replacement. Wherever and whenever the state fails to fulfill the basic needs of its people, this creates a vacuum which the criminals can exploit." (2)

The effects of the infiltration of organized crime are unmistakable. On November 21, 1994, member states of the United Nations gathered in Naples, Italy, at the World Ministerial Conference on Organized Crime. One conclusion was very clear. "Traditionally insular and clannish, the world powers of crime—the Hong Kong–based Triads, the Cali Cartel of Colombia, the Italian Mafia, the Japanese Yakuza, the Russian Vory v. Zakonye and affiliated newcomers, and rapidly expanding West African crime groups—are now making deals with each other and taking tentative steps to maximize their operations." (1) The cooperative nature of organized crime has changed the realities of law enforcement efforts. The policing of organized crime is no longer a regional or local endeavor. To control the effects of the single largest business in the world, law enforcement efforts must also be transnational and cooperative.

Among the steps called for at the conference:
- Global assessment and regular monitoring of organized transnational crime.
- New legislation, both substantive (against the crimes) and procedural (against the criminals).
- Special cooperative programs and preventive strategies.
- A concerted attack on money laundering to chip away at the economic advantage of organized transnational crime and criminals.

Here is why the steps are needed. Each national criminal group, as the table that follows shows, is allied with most of the others across the globe.

---

fascination. But little was known about the Mafia's actual structure in the United States until a succession of government investigations began to unravel its mysteries. The major investigations were conducted by the Committee on Mercenary Crimes, in 1932; the Special Senate Committee to Investigate Organized Crime in Interstate Commerce (the Kefauver crime committee), from 1950 to 1951; the Senate Permanent Subcommittee on Investigations (the McClellan committee), from 1956 to 1963; President Lyndon Johnson's Commission on Law Enforcement and Administration of Justice (the Task Force on Organized Crime), from 1964 to 1967; and the President's Commission on Organized Crime, which reported to President Reagan in 1986 and 1987.[142]

The findings of these investigations established the magnitude of organized crime in the United States. It had become an empire almost beyond the reach of government, with vast resources derived from a virtual monopoly on gambling and loan-sharking, drug trafficking, pornography and prostitution, labor racketeering, murder for hire, the control of local crime activities, and the theft and fencing of securities, cars, jewels, and consumer goods of all sorts.[143] Above all, it was found that organized crime had infiltrated a vast variety of legitimate businesses, such as stevedoring (the loading and unloading of ships), the fish and meat industries, the wholesale and retail liquor industry (including bars and taverns), the vending machine business, the securities and investment

Organization	Size	Major Activities	International Ties
Colombian cartels	Hundreds of men	Drug trafficking—manage entire cycle from production to distribution	U.S. and Sicilian Cosa Nostra, Chinese Triads, Japanese Yakuza
Chinese Triads (Hong Kong and Taiwan)	150,000 in 5 groups	Drugs, usury, illegal immigration, gambling, racketeering, prostitution, money laundering	Colombian cartels, Japanese Yakuza, U.S. groups
Russian Mafia	3 million in 5,700 gangs	Trafficking in everything—army weapons, nuclear materials, drugs, money laundering, prostitution, counterfeiting	Settlements in the U.S., Colombian cartels, Sicilian Cosa Nostra
Sicilian Cosa Nostra	5,000 members	International drug trafficking clearinghouse, money laundering on a grand scale, arms trafficking, extortion	U.S. Cosa Nostra, Colombian cartels, Mafia families in western Europe, Russian Mafia, Chinese Traids
U.S. Cosa Nostra	3,000 soldiers in 25 families	Drug and arms trafficking, illegal gambling, prostitution, extortion, business activities	Colombian cartels, Russian Mafia, Sicilian Cosa Nostra
Japanese Yakuza	60,000 full-time, 25,000 associates, in 1,246 clans	Amphetamine traffic in Asia and U.S., extortion, prostitution	Chinese Triads, Colombian cartels, German groups, Russian Mafia, U.S. Cosa Nostra

Sources

1. ANSA News Agency Dossier on Organized Crime, *U.N. World Ministerial Conference on Organized Transnational Crime,* Naples, Italy, Nov. 21–23, 1994.
2. "Russian Organized Crime," *Jane's Intelligence Review,* 8 (May 1, 1996): 195.

Questions for Discussion

1. Why is organized crime the world's largest business?
2. What efforts to control the rise of organized crime seem most promising?

---

business, the waste disposal business, and the construction industry.[144]

Specific legislation and law enforcement programs have allowed governmental agencies to assert some measure of control over organized crime. Cases have been successfully prosecuted under the **Racketeer Influenced and Corrupt Organizations (RICO) Act** of 1970.[145] This statute attacks racketeering activities by prohibiting the investment of any funds derived from racketeering in any enterprise that is engaged in interstate commerce. In addition, the **Federal Witness Protection Program,** established under the Organized Crime Control Act of 1970, has made it easier for witnesses to testify in court by guaranteeing them a new identity, thus protecting them against revenge. Currently 14,000 witnesses are in the program.[146]

The information provided by the governmental commissions, in combination with scholarly research, has established that the structure of an organized crime group is similar to that of a Sicilian family. Family members are joined by "adopted" members; the family is then aided at the functional level by nonmember auxiliaries.[147] The use of military designations such as *caporegima* ("lieutenant") and "soldier" does not alter the fact that a criminal organization is rather more like a closely knit family business enterprise than like an army.[148] On the basis of testimony presented by Joseph Valachi in 1963, the commission's Task Force on

Legal immigrants from Russia settled in Brighton Beach, Brooklyn by the tens of thousands. But among the hard-working legitimate settlers, hundreds have formed a Russian-American mafia.

Organized Crime was able to construct an organization chart of the typical Mafia, or Cosa Nostra, family (Figure 10.2).

Relations among the various families, which were formerly determined in ruthlessly fought gang wars, have more recently been facilitated by a loosely formed coordinating body called "the Commission." By agreement, the country has been divided into territorial areas of jurisdiction, influence, and operation. These arrangements are subject to revision from time to time, by mutual agreement. Likewise, rules of conduct have become subject to control or regulation by the heads of the various crime families. They consider, for example, to what extent each family should enter the hard-drug market, how much violence should be used, and how each will deal with public officials and the police.[149]

Informants at the "convention" of the so-called Apalachin conspirators provided a rare opportunity to learn about the way crime families reach agreement on their operations. On November 14, 1957, 63 of the country's most notorious underworld figures were arrested in Apalachin, New York, at or near the home of Joseph M. Barbara, a well-known organized-crime figure. Participants included New York's Vito Genovese, Carlo Gambino, Paul Castellano, and Joe Bonano. Also arrested were Florida's don, Santo Trafficante, Jr.; Sam ("Momo") Giancana of Chicago; Detroit boss Joe Zerilli; and the boss of the Buffalo rackets, Stefano Magaddino. Apparently, they had congregated at Barbara's home to settle a dispute among the families, which had three weeks earlier resulted in the assassination of Mangano family boss Albert Anastasia (the Mangano family was predecessor to

"I TAKE IT YOU'RE ALSO IN THE FEDERAL WITNESS-PROTECTION PROGRAM."

© Sidney Harris. Reprinted with permission of Sidney Harris.

PART III **Types of Crimes** 265

FIGURE 10.2 Organization chart of the typical Mafia family.

```
                          Boss
                           |
                           |──────── Consigliere
                           |           (Counselor)
                       Underboss
    ┌──────────┬──────────┼──────────┬──────────┐
 Caporegima Caporegima Caporegima Caporegima Caporegima
(Lieutenant)(Lieutenant)(Lieutenant)(Lieutenant)(Lieutenant)
                           |
                        Soldiers
              (Members grouped under
                    lieutenants)
   Corruption of police                Exercise of control
   and public officials                in multistate area
         Through threats, assault, and
         murder, enforce discipline over
         members, nonmembers, and
         fronts on orders from leader
                           |
              ┌────────────┴────────────┐
        Legitimate industry         Illegal activities
         Food products            Gambling (numbers, policy,
         Realty                      dice, bookmaking)
         Restaurants                Narcotics
         Garbage disposal           Loan-sharking
         Produce                    Labor racketeering
         Garment manufacturing      Extortion
         Bars and taverns           Alcohol
         Waterfront                 Others
         Securities
         Labor unions
         Vending machines
         Others
```

Source: President's Commission on Law Enforcement and Administration of Justice, *Task Force Report: Organized Crime* (Washington, D.C.: U.S. Government Printing Office, 1967), p. 9.

the largest contemporary crime family in the United States, the Gambino crime family) and the attempted murder in May 1957 of Francesco Castiglia, better known as Frank Costello, by the current godfather of the Genovese crime family, Vincent "The Chin" Gigante.

The presence of so many out-of-state license plates on brand new Cadillacs and Lincolns in this small upstate New York town caught the attention of New York State Police Sergeant Edgar Croswell, an amateur organized-crime buff. Croswell, already somewhat suspicious of the true nature of Barbara's business dealings, put in a call to federal authorities and arranged to have a roadblock set up to guard against any of the participants leaving without being questioned. The police presence didn't go unnoticed by the gangsters, who rushed to make a quick escape back to their fiefdoms.

The comical scene of men in silk suits and fedora hats running through the forest was enough for Croswell. He caught as many as he

The funeral procession of Chinatown crime boss Benny Ong, August 19, 1994. Ong was the undisputed leader of New York City's Chinese gangs.

could and placed them under arrest. None of the conspirators, however, publicly revealed the true nature of their meeting. Some suggested that, quite by coincidence, all had simply come to visit their sick friend Joe Barbara, who would die of a heart attack two years later. All were indicted and convicted for refusing to answer the grand jury's questions about the true purpose of the meeting. The convictions were subsequently reversed.[150]

Certain core business matters were decided at that meeting:

- Carlo Gambino was given the leadership of the New York crime family that still bears his name, a family made famous by the subsequent exploits of the late John Gotti.
- As a vote of confidence for Vito Genovese, Frank Costello was asked to go into semiretirement to pave the way for Genovese to take over the family that Lucky Luciano had started.
- A ban was placed on any "made man" trafficking in drugs. "If you deal, you die" was the slogan that resonated throughout organized crime as of the late 1950s.

Although widely ignored, the ban still exists today.

The activities of the Mafia appear to have shifted from the once extremely violent bootlegging and street crime operations to a far more sophisticated level of criminal activity.[151] Modern organized crime has assumed international dimensions.[152] It extends not only to international drug traffic, but also to such legitimate enterprises as real estate and trade in securities, as well as to many other lucrative business enterprises. This transition has been accomplished both by extortion and by entry with laundered money derived from illegitimate activity. It is tempting to wonder whether we may be witnessing the same kind of metamorphosis that occurred a century ago, when the robber barons became legitimate business tycoons and, ultimately, philanthropists.

The New Ethnic Diversity in Organized Crime

Organized crime is not necessarily synonymous with the Mafia. Other groups also operate in the United States. Foremost among them

FIGURE 10.3 Time line of New York City's Chinese gangs: 1960–1990.

Source: Ko-lin Chin, *Chinese Subculture and Criminality* (New York: Greenwood Press, 1990), p. 76.

are the Colombian crime families, whose brutality is unrivaled by any other organized-crime group, and Bolivian, Peruvian, and Jamaican crime families, which since the 1970s have organized the production, transportation, and distribution within the United States of cocaine and marijuana.

Another form of organized crime, initiated by disillusioned veterans of the Korean War and reinforced by veterans of Vietnam, appears in the outlaw motorcycle gangs. Among them are the Hell's Angels, the Pagans, the Outlaws, the Sons of Silence, and the Bandidos. All are organized along military lines; all are devoted to violence; all are involved in the production and distribution of narcotics and other drugs. Many members are also involved in other criminal activities, including extortion and prostitution, trafficking in stolen motorcycles and parts, and dealing in automatic weapons and explosives.

Among other organized groups engaged in various criminal activities are Chinese gangs (see Figure 10.3), the so-called Israeli Mafia, the recently emerging Russian-Jewish Mafia, Jamaican posses, and the "Tattooed Men" of Japan's Yakuza, whose Yamaguchi-Gumi family alone has over 56,000 members, or nearly 20 times the number of fully initiated Italian organized-crime members in all the crews of all the families in the United States. All these groups have demonstrated potential for great social disruption.[153]

EMERGING PROBLEMS

Some of the more pressing issues we face today include global terrorism, an increase in hate crimes nationwide, the spread of racist and antigovernment militias, and deadly shootings in American schools. In recent years, largely as a result of media attention, these crimes have had a dramatic impact on the public's perception that violence has reached epidemic proportions. In reality, these crimes account for an extremely low proportion of all violent crimes, and rates for two of them (terrorism and violence in schools) have even gone down.

Terrorism

Many of those who worked in the South and North Towers of the World Trade Center arrived like clockwork—6:30 A.M., 7:00 A.M., 7:30 A.M., 8:00 A.M., and 8:30 A.M. They poured in from all over the tristate area (New York, New Jersey, and Connecticut) by car, rail, bus, ferry, and foot to ascend the two most visible symbols of New York.

Every day the mall on the ground floor was a teaming mass of blue and white collar workers—all marching toward one of two towers. It was no different on the morning of September 11, 2001. Secretaries were already checking email at Nishi-Nippon Bank, Ltd., on the 102nd floor. Bond traders from Cantor Fitzgerald Securities were grabbing their morning coffee on the 105th floor. And waiters were setting the tables for a private function at the restaurant Windows on the World on the 107th floor.

Life was its usual fast pace for over 30,000 people working or visiting the World Trade Center. That is, until hijacked American Airlines Flight 11 crashed into the central core of the North Tower, raining a hail of debris over much of lower Manhattan. Witnesses said that the tall, sleek building literally swallowed the Boeing 767. Twenty-one minutes later, United Airlines Flight 175 collided into the South Tower, igniting a second fire that trapped helpless workers high above the New York City skyline. Desperate and with no means of escape, several hundred jumped to their tragic deaths.

At 10:00 A.M. the South Tower collapsed, the building imploding from the burning jet fuel and instantly killing thousands of workers, police, and firefighters. A thick and dark cloud enveloped Tribeca (the neighborhood in Manhattan represented by the *Tri*angle *Be*low *Ca*nal Street) like a fast moving volcano. Thousands ran from lower Manhattan with an understandable mix of panic, fear, anger, confusion, and hysteria.

In a matter of seconds, everything and everybody left behind were covered in ash. It was, as some described it, like hell breaking loose or hell on earth. After the thunderous crash of metal and concrete, the air had a strong and pungent smell of a chemical burn. The scene had all trappings of a movie set—a high-budget pyrotechnic war movie. Huge chunks of metal, tons of paper, and thick ash covered the deserted streets of a fallen city. Anyone approaching Liberty Street or West Street would see the unimaginable. Familiar landmarks were gone—buildings were no longer where they once were. Cars close to "Ground Zero" had literally melted to the ground from the heat of the fire and implosions.

People who had escaped from the North and South Towers, and those who emerged from adjoining buildings, were dazed. Some were in shock. Many were crying and consoling each other. Others were in desperate need of medical attention with first- and second-degree burns. People who were bleeding from falling debris and choking from fumes rushed from lower Manhattan toward the Brooklyn Bridge, up Church Street and West Broadway. Many were crowded onto ferries to New Jersey. Everything that was typical, normal, and usual no longer was.

Emergency personnel from all five boroughs of New York City raced toward Tribeca and Ground Zero in a frenzied effort to put out the fire, to save and comfort the injured, to rescue the trapped, to evacuate the surrounding area, to set up roadblocks, and to pray for the dead. Twenty-nine minutes after the South Tower disappeared, the North Tower followed. Once again, the building incinerated its victims.

Within less than two hours after the first plane hit the North Tower, emergency and rescue workers set up a triage area. All hospitals with trauma centers were immediately instructed to make room for thousands of victims. Empty stretchers and gurneys were brought to the sidewalk in front of Saint Vincents Hospital to speed the receipt of a mass of casualties. Only two hundred and fifty ambulances left the site of the World Trade Center.

Firefighters and rescue workers dotted the remnants of the twin towers, sifting through the

New York City firefighters carry their fatally injured department chaplain from the wreckage of the World Trade Center, on September 11, 2001. Chaplain Mychal Judge was crushed to death while giving a man his last rites.

sharp and twisted debris, hoping against hope for one miracle at a time. There were precious few. Families of the missing posted photos of lost love ones. Maybe someone had seen them—perhaps they were unconscious in a hospital or still alive buried in the rubble.

Less than one hour after the World Trade Center was attacked, American Airlines Flight 77 crashed into the western facade of the Pentagon, setting off an enormous fireball that shot way up in the sky. Black smoke filled the air, along with the smell of jet fuel. It was pandemonium.

Soon thereafter, another highjacked plane, United Airlines Flight 93, crashed at a rural part of Pennsylvania. The United States, it appeared, was under attack. The White House was quickly evacuated. Thirty-thousand commercial airline flights were grounded. Incoming international flights were diverted.

As these events were unfolding, President George W. Bush was in Sarasota, Florida, about to address a secondary school class about the importance of reading. President Bush addressed the nation that same evening, vowing to bring to justice those who committed these "despicable acts of terror."

The United States opted for a swift military response—called Operation Enduring Freedom. Both U.S. and British military operations commenced on October 7, 2001, against Afghanistan using aircraft and cruise missiles. Three carrier battle groups were promptly deployed, in addition to a sizable number of aircraft and special operations forces. The objectives of Operation Enduring Freedom are destruction of terrorist training camps in Afghanistan, the apprehension of Al Qaeda leaders, and the cessation of terrorist activities in Afghanistan. It remains to be seen whether an Al Queda-Iraqi connection will be substantiated now that U.S. forces have made their way into Baghdad.

Terrorism is a resort to violence or a threat of violence on the part of a group seeking to accomplish a purpose against the opposition of constituted authority. Crucial to the terrorists' scheme is the exploitation of the media to attract attention to the cause. Many clandestine organizations around the world have sought to draw attention to their causes—the Irish Republican Army (IRA), committed to the cause of uniting the British counties of Northern Ireland with the Republic of Ireland; Islamic fundamentalists committed to the protection of Islam in its purist form against any Western influence; various Palestinian factions opposed to Israeli occupation or to any Mideast peace settlement; radical groups all over the world seeking an end to capitalism or colonialism or the imposition of one or another form of totalitarian rule.

From the outset the member states of the United Nations have been concerned about international terrorism because it endangers or takes innocent lives and jeopardizes fundamental freedoms, such as the freedom to travel and to congregate for public events. The UN effort to control international terrorism concentrates on removal of the underlying grievances that provoke people to sacrifice human lives, including their own, in an attempt to effect radical changes.[154] This approach to the control of terrorism is not concerned with the individual motivations of terrorists. Some of them may be highly motivated idealists; others are recruited for substantial rewards. The control effort is directed, rather, at the conditions that give rise to terrorism and at the removal of such conditions.

To the extent that some grievances have been reduced by political action, such as the granting of independence to colonies and the political accord reached in Northern Ireland in November 1999, terrorism has declined. But other problems remain, especially in the Balkans, India, Central America, Africa, and the West Bank and Gaza Strip occupied by Israel. Crimes of a terrorist nature occur virtually every day and are likely to continue wherever the underlying problems are not resolved. Terrorist activities include but are not restricted to assassinations, hostage taking, and interference with or destruction of ships, aircraft, or means of land transport (see Table 10.3). When funding by clandestine supporters is not forthcoming, terrorists have carried out robberies to finance their operations.

The 1998 bombings of the U.S. embassies in Kenya and Tanzania, as well as the October, 2000 attack on the USS Cole, have increased American awareness of terrorist activities. The impact of the networking of international terrorist groups has become apparent.[155] Osama bin Laden, the reputed mastermind of the embassy bombings, is referred to as the "new model terrorist" and the "chief executive officer" of a network of terrorist groups. He is considered one of the most significant sponsors of Islamic extremist activities in the world today. In fact, bin Laden's so-called terrorist network is considered the most prominent threat to our national security in spite of the recent killing and capture of key Al Queda leaders and operatives. As of 2003, bin Laden remained a fugitive. His name is on the FBI's "Ten Most Wanted Fugitives" list, and the United States government has offered a $5 million reward for his capture.[156]

In August 1999, a series of bombings began in Moscow.[157] (See "Window to the World," Chapter 1.) Some researchers suggest that the 15 newly independent states of the former Soviet Union are replacing the Middle East as the primary generator of international terrorism. Of additional concern to the Russians is blood feud terrorism, or acts of retaliation perpetrated solely on the basis of satisfying a vengeance code of a blood feud or clan vendetta, in ethnic communities and regions.[158]

The Extent of Terrorism The incidence of terrorism may seem slight in the light of overall national crime statistics. But the worldwide destructive impact of such acts is considerable. So too are the costs of increased security to combat terrorism. The airline industry alone spends $500 million a year for security.[159] After the bombing of the U.S. embassy complex in Beirut, Lebanon, with the loss of the lives of 241 marines and sailors, the strengthening of U.S. embassy security all over the world cost well over $3 billion.

In one year alone (1985) terrorists were responsible for:

4 letter bombs
5 barricade-hostage incidents
9 hijackings
17 specific threats
54 kidnappings
70 attempted attacks
84 armed assaults
165 bombings and arsons

Of these crimes, 12 were committed in Belgium, 14 in Chile, 29 in Colombia, 12 in Cyprus, 35 in West Germany, 12 in France, 29 in Greece, 17 in Italy, 47 in Lebanon, 10 in Peru, 18 in Portugal, 15 in Spain, 10 in the United Kingdom, and 148 in other countries that experienced fewer than 10 incidents each. Regionally, western Europe was hardest hit (182), followed by the Middle East (70) and South America (62). The remaining incidents were spread all over the other regions, with Asia and the Far East suffering the fewest incidents. Of the targets, 151 were political, 80 were

PART III **Types of Crimes**   271

TABLE 10.3 Terrorist Events against Americans, 1983–2002

👤 = 10 deaths

October 23, 1983, a suicide terrorist in a TNT-laden truck blew up U.S. Marine Corps headquarters in Beirut, Lebanon, killing 241 marines and sailors. A second truck blew up a French paratrooper barracks two miles away, killing 58.

October 7, 1985, five hijackers seized the Italian cruiseliner Achille Lauro. They held some 400 persons for ransom and killed a wheelchair-bound American passenger.

April 2, 1986, a bomb exploded aboard TWA flight 840 at Athens airport, killing 4 Americans.

April 5, 1986, terrorists exploded a bomb in a West Berlin disco frequented by American service personnel, killing 2 and injuring 200. The incident prompted an American air strike against Libya in retaliation.

September 5, 1986, four Pakistani gunmen, followers of Abu Nidal, attempted to hijack a Pan Am 747 in Karachi, Pakistan. After keeping the plane on the runway overnight, the gunmen were overpowered by security; 21 passengers died.

December 21, 1988, terrorists exploded Pan Am flight 103, en route from Frankfurt, Germany, to New York, killing 270 passengers, crew, and people on the ground at Lockerbie, Scotland.

February 26, 1993, a terrorist bomb in the basement garage of the World Trade Center in New York City killed 6 people, injured over 1,000 people, and caused extensive damage to the building.

April 19, 1995, a bomb made of fertilizer and diesel fuel exploded in front of the Murrah Federal Building in Oklahoma City, killing 168 and injuring over 600.

November 13, 1995, 5 Americans and 2 Indians were killed and 60 injured when a car bomb exploded near a U.S.-run military training facility in Riyadh, Saudi Arabia. Four Saudi Muslim militants were later executed for the attack.

June 25, 1996, in Dhahran, Saudi Arabia, a truck bomb exploded in front of a U.S. military barracks; 19 Americans were killed, and 400 people were injured.

July 17, 1996, TWA flight 800, en route to Paris from New York City's JFK Airport, went down in a ball of fire into the ocean off Long Island. All 230 passengers and crew aboard were killed. (It appears to be a terrorist attack.)

Late December 1996, 12 letter bombs were mailed to the United States in holiday greeting cards bearing Alexandria, Egypt, postmarks. On January 2, 1997, several of these letter bombs were discovered in the mailrooms of the federal prison in Leavenworth, Kansas, and the Washington, D.C., offices of the Saudi Arabian newspaper Al-Hayat.

August 7, 1998, the American embassies in Kenya and Tanzania were bombed, killing a total of 224 people, including 12 Americans. Hundreds of others were wounded. Exiled Saudi businessman Osama bin Laden is suspected as the mastermind behind these attacks.

October 12, 2000, a small boat loaded with explosives rammed into the USS Cole at the Port of Aden in Yemen. The collision killed 17 sailors and injured 39.

September 11, 2001, 4 planes were hijacked. Two planes were crashed into the World Trade Center in New York City, one plane was crashed into the Pentagon in Washington, D.C., and another plane was crashed in Pennsylvania. Thousands lost their lives as a result of the attacks.

June 14, 2002, a suicide attacker crashed a bomb-laden vehicle into a guard post at the U.S. consulate in Karachi, Pakistan. The attack killed 11 and injured 45, including one U.S. marine.

Source: National Center for Health Statistics, World Health Organization, country reports, and media reports; *FBI Report on Terrorism in the United States,* U.S. Government Printing Office, 1997.

diplomatic, 79 were economic, and the remainder were seemingly random public places, specific persons, and various facilities.[160] It is noteworthy that 31 of the 408 terrorist acts were committed on behalf of governments.

Among the most active terrorist groups were the Islamic Jihad (35 acts), the Fatah Revolutionary Council (24), the West German Red Army Faction (19), the Portuguese Popular Forces of 25 April (15), and the Chilean Manuel Rodriguez Popular Front (14). In the course of these acts of terrorism, 265 persons were killed, among them 46 Americans, 16 French, 15 British, 11 Germans, 11 Italians, 10 Israelis, and 9 staff members of international organizations. The terrorists suffered fewer deaths.

International Efforts to Control Terrorism
Many years ago the world community agreed on three international conventions to combat terrorism:

- Convention on Offenses and Certain Other Acts Committed on Board Aircraft, signed at Tokyo on September 14, 1963.
- Convention for the Suppression of Unlawful Seizure of Aircraft, signed at The Hague on December 16, 1970.
- Convention for the Suppression of Unlawful Acts against the Safety of Civil Aviation, signed at Montreal on September 23, 1971.

These conventions, which provide for widespread international cooperation in the prevention of airplane hijacking and the pursuit and extradition (surrender to a requesting country) of offenders, produced a dramatic drop in the number of such incidents. Subsequently, the international community agreed on two further conventions to protect diplomats, their families, and their installations:

- Convention on the Prevention and Punishment of Crimes against Internationally Protected Persons, Including Diplomatic Agents, adopted by the General Assembly of the United Nations on December 14, 1973.
- International Convention against the Taking of Hostages, adopted by the General Assembly of the United Nations on December 17, 1979.[161]

It appears that by 1989 several governments that had been supporting "freedom fighters" (elsewhere called terrorist groups) had grown disenchanted with the groups' exercise of arbitrary violence against uninvolved civilian targets, such as airplane passengers, and had ceased to support such groups. In addition, the end of the cold war and breakup of the Soviet bloc have deprived many of these groups of funding; consequently, they are on the decline. Rising in their stead is a new type of terrorist group, more difficult to monitor, and perhaps even more dangerous. The old-style politically motivated mayhem has been replaced with ethnically and religiously inspired violence.

Recently, cults have sprung up whose members believe that a catastrophic war or natural disaster will land the "chosen few" in paradise. These doomsday cults can turn inward, leading to mass suicide or the murder of the membership. Eighty-six of David Koresh's followers at the Branch Davidian compound in Waco, Texas, died a fiery death after a lengthy siege by the FBI. It is still unclear whether the Branch Davidians set the compound on fire themselves, or if the FBI was responsible. Other groups direct their actions at outsiders. In Japan, the Aum Shinrikyo ("Supreme Truth") sect was implicated in the deadly sarin nerve gas attack on the Tokyo subway, which killed 10 and injured over 5,000. The leader of the sect, Shoko Asahara, preached about the end of the world and claimed that sarin would be a primary weapon in the "final world war."[162]

Hate Crimes

In June 1998, James Byrd, an African American, was dragged to his death in Jasper, Texas. Byrd was hitchhiking on a Saturday night when John William King and two friends chained him to their truck and pulled him, alive, for over 2 miles. His head was finally severed from his body. King, who was sentenced to death in March 1999, and his two friends were Ku Klux Klan (KKK) members.

An equally barbaric hate crime occurred in October 1998. Russell Henderson and Aaron

Mary Nell Verrett remembers her brother, James Byrd, Jr., who was brutally murdered in a hate crime in Jasper, Texas.

McKinney posed as homosexuals and lured gay college student Matthew Shepard out of a bar in Wyoming. They robbed, pistol-whipped, and burned him with cigarettes before leaving him tied to a fence in near freezing temperatures. Shepard died five days later in a hospital. The murder trial of Henderson and McKinney incited further displays of hate, with antigay demonstrators shouting and waving signs that read "God Hates Fags."[163] Only a few months later, in Alabama, Steven Mullins and Charles Butler lured Billy Jack Gaither, another gay male, out of a bar into a secluded area where they beat him and then dumped him into the trunk of their car. They drove about 15 miles, took him out of the trunk, and killed him with an ax handle. Mullins and Butler then placed Gaither's body on top of two old tires that they had set on fire.[164]

In August 1999, Buford O. Furrow, a former member of the Aryan Nation, walked into the lobby of the North Valley Jewish Community Center in the Granada Hills area of Los Angeles, shooting and wounding a receptionist, a camp counselor, and three children. After leaving the scene, Furrow carjacked a person's vehicle, drove to the residential area of Chutsworth, and shot Joseph Ileto, a Filipino American postman who was in the middle of making his rounds. Furrow later turned himself in.[165]

During the late 1990s, the United States experienced some of the most gruesome displays of hate-crime violence. According to the Uniform Crime Reports, there were 8,049 incidents of hate crimes, which involved 9,861 separate offenses reported from over 11,000 law enforcement agencies to the FBI. Of the 8,049 incidents, 4,710 were racially motivated, followed by 1,385 religiously motivated offenses, 1,102 offenses targeting victims because of their sexual preferences, 836 ethnically motivated offenses, and 12 disability-motivated offenses.[166] According to the Southern Poverty Law Center, the number of hate groups increased from 474 in 1997 to 537 in 1998.[167] It also appears that groups are recruiting more violent members to carry out their messages of hate nationwide. One of the most recent tools used to attract these members is the Internet. Since 1995, over 160 online hate sites have been identified.[168]

Although hate crimes make up only a small percentage of overall criminality, the viciousness of the acts and their impact on broad population groups give them prominence in the media and pose extraordinary challenges to the criminal justice system. Presently, some police departments are forming bias-crime units to further the investigation of these crimes.

Militias

Militias have come to the attention of the American public only within the last decade. Most of them are groups whose memberships consist of white, Christian, working- and middle-class Americans whose fundamental belief is that their constitutional right to bear arms (protected under the Second Amendment) is threatened. Members tend to have apocalyptic, paranoid views of U.S. politics and the

> **:// Crime Surfing**
>
> www.splcenter.org
>
> The Southern Poverty Law Center is a nonprofit organization that combats hate, intolerance, and discrimination through education and litigation. For more information, visit the center's website.

Of Immediate Concern

An Epidemic of Hate Crimes?

The media, academics, advocacy groups, and politicians have created what has been described as a hate-crime epidemic. But is the problem really as great as we have been led to believe? Consider that the media can shape public opinion and reinforce the idea that there is an epidemic through the use of these types of headlines:

- "A Cancer of Hatred Afflicts America"[1]
- "Rise in Hate Crimes Signals Alarming Resurgence of Bigotry"[2]

Books and articles are often inflammatory, argue James Jacobs and Jessica Henry.[3] The authors suggest that some scholars simply assume a grave problem exists, in spite of an overwhelming lack of evidence. This can be a dangerous assumption, for the idea of hate crime divides the community and becomes a self-fulfilling prophecy. "Crime sells—so does racism, sexism, and homophobia. Garden-variety crime has become mundane." [3]

Advocacy groups representing blacks, Jews, gays and lesbians, women, and the disabled have embraced the idea of a hate-crime epidemic, much of which is based on dubious statistics. For example, the 1997 Uniform Crime Reports show only 8,049 reported hate crimes, less than .001 percent of all reported crimes. Is this an epidemic?

Jacobs and Henry point out that American history shows attacks on racial and ethnic groups started from the moment European settlers arrived and made Native Americans a target. Historically, blacks, Jews, Catholics, and recent immigrants have also been targeted. The 1990s brought a greater intolerance for this behavior, but, Jacobs and Henry say, there still is no epidemic.

Yet it matters little whether the spate of hate crimes is real or merely perceived; significant developments have taken place in consequence. Throughout the 1980s, media reports of increasing numbers of hate-motivated crimes (also know as *bias crimes*) pressured states to adopt statutes dealing with such crimes. These statutes prohibit acts of ethnically or religiously based intimidation, enhance penalties for these crimes, or raise the level of the crime from a misdemeanor to a felony. In addition, many criminal justice agencies have developed programs for dealing with bias crime, and at the federal level the Hate Crimes Statistics Act of 1990 mandates that local law enforcement agencies compile data on such crimes.

As defined by the federal Hate Crimes Statistics Act of 1990, hate crimes are crimes that show evidence of prejudice against certain group characteristics. The act mandates the collection of data that show evidence of prejudice based on race, sexual orientation, ethnicity, or religion. The Hate Crime Statistics Act was later amended by the Violent Crime and Law Enforcement Act of 1994 to include crimes motivated by bias against persons with disabilities.

Many bias crimes fall into the categories of simple assaults, vandalism, and harassment. Because these are relatively less serious crimes, they ordinarily get little attention. They can, however, have a major impact on the community by increasing the level of fear and hostility between groups. So extra attention to them is warranted.

In the twenty-first century, two trends are likely to continue, with increased challenges for legislators, judges, and criminal justice specialists. First, legislatures are adding sentence enhancements for crimes committed with the motive of hate. Such statues allow or require judges to add additional prison time for those convicted of crimes committed with a hate motive. Second, the reach of hate-crime legislation is likely to be expanded. For example, under existing federal law, hate crimes can be prosecuted only if the hate (bias) is directed at religion, sexual orientation, national origin, color, and disability. But under the Hate Crime Prevention Act (of 1998) the reach has been expanded to any "violent act causing death or bodily injury 'because of the actual or *perceived* race, color, religion, national origin, sexual orientation, *gender,* or disability' of the victim [emphasis supplied]." This act likely will become law and be followed by similar state legislation.

Sources

1. Spencer Rumsey, "A Cancer of Hatred Afflicts America," *Newsday,* May 27, 1993, p. 129.
2. Benjamin J. Hubbard, "Commentary on Tolerance," *Los Angeles Times,* Apr. 4, 1993, p. B9.
3. James B. Jacobs and Jessica S. Henry, "The Social Construction of a Hate Crime Epidemic," *Journal of Criminal Law and Criminology,* **86** (1996): 366–391.

Questions for Discussion

1. Wisconsin's sentence-enhancement law was challenged by a defendant who claimed that his First Amendment (freedom of speech) rights were violated because the statute punishes offenders' bigoted beliefs and not just their acts. Do you agree with the U.S. Supreme Court decision to uphold the Wisconsin statute?
2. An FBI study found that intimidation was the most common type of hate crime, followed by vandalism and assault. Do you think these crimes are serious enough to warrant the extra attention they receive?

PART III **Types of Crimes** 275

"Michigan Militia" Paramilitary Group training, suspected in Oklamoma City car bombing.

federal government. Their antigovernment beliefs are intertwined with some forms of white supremacy. They believe leading Democratic politicians are "liberal elitists who betray traditional American values."[169] Members of these groups believe that the federal government is preparing for a war against its own citizens.[170] The movement is a collection of grassroots groups who call themselves Patriots, Militiamen, Freemen, Common-Law Advocates, and Strict Constitutionalists. Although they are often labeled "right-wing," members' backgrounds touch all points on the political spectrum. The movement is so fragmented that membership estimates are unreliable. The Southern Poverty Law Center says that members can be found in all 50 states.[171] Some estimates are that as many as 100,000 Americans are involved (Figure 10.4).[172]

Most militia groups are nonviolent. Members have a fondness for wearing battle fatigues, participating in paramilitary maneuvers, and stockpiling firearms. Yet there are growing indications of involvement in illegal activities. The Michigan Militia Corps, for example, one of the nation's largest, with an estimated membership of 10,000 to 12,000, has alleged ties to Timothy McVeigh and Terry Nichols, both charged in the Oklahoma City bombing.[173]

Yet long before this bombing focused attention on the radical right, the FBI had insiders and informants tracking the Freemen of Montana. The Freemen, 13 of whom were indicted for counterfeiting and tax fraud, are reported to have posted $1 million rewards on the heads of local officials, threatened to hang local judges, and intimidated potential jurors in a case against a Freeman. Using bits of the Constitution, the Bible, and the Magna Carta, they put together a doctrine that says the federal government has illegally usurped the common law and power of localities. They also reject the American flag. In their own courts, the Freemen have filed multimillion-dollar "liens" against government officials, and "subpoenaed" public officials to appear before their own grand juries.

For the Freemen, their 960-acre Cranfield County, Montana, farm is sovereign territory that has its own laws, courts, and officials. They also have an armory and a bank. According to federal indictments, the bank turned over $1.8 million in phony money orders and other financial instruments. These were used in fraudulent transactions with credit card companies, mail-order houses, and banks. In 1996, 26 of the antigovernment fanatics holed up in the Freemen's enclaves. Eighty-one days, and millions of dollars later, they all left the compound. The standoff was one of the longest armed sieges in U.S. history.

FIGURE 10.4 Beyond the fringe.

⌬ Neo-Nazi
K Klan
● Skinhead
■ Militia group

SOURCES: KLANWATCH, PSYTEP CORPORATION

Source: Gregory L. Vistica, "Extremism in the Ranks," *Newsweek,* Mar. 25, 1996, p. 36.

Violence in Schools

In the nineteenth century, school violence was seen in the form of teachers' inflicting abuse on students, primarily by slapping a student's hand with a ruler. Parents and members of the community looked upon this "violence" as a way to remind students that they must respect authority.

The mid-twentieth century brought a new look to school violence. By the 1950s students were viewed not as the victims but rather as the agents of violence. In response, schools with high levels of violence developed security plans.[174] While overall, violence in schools has decreased, media accounts of school shootings have caused a nationwide panic, and many Americans have lost faith in the ability of the educational system to keep children safe.

Consider the following incidents: it was 12:35 P.M. on March 24, 1998, when the fire alarm bell sounded at Westside Middle School in Jonesboro, Arkansas. The children filed out of their classrooms—as in so many previous drills—and exited into an open area. Then the rifle shots rang out. By 12:39 P.M., 15 students and teachers lay in pools of blood; 4 students and 1 teacher did not survive. The shots were fired from the perimeter of the school grounds by two assailants dressed in army fatigues who had been hiding in the shrubbery. The assailants, 11-year-old Andrew Golden and his 13-year-old accomplice, had planned the attack well. They had arrived in a stolen van, armed with 10 rifles and handguns, plenty of ammunition, and survival gear.[175] That was America's seventh school massacre in little over a year. School massacre eight was not far behind.

> Littleton, Colorado. (April 23, 1999)—"The school's in a panic, and I'm in the library," the teacher is desperately trying to explain to the police dispatcher as she begs for help. "I've got students down."
>
> "Under the table, kids!" she says now, directing her attention back to the students who, moments before, had been quietly studying in the library at Columbine High School. "Kids, under the table. Kids, stay on the floor.... Oh, God. Oh, God—kids,

Shocked Erfurt, Germany residents on April 26, 2002, have just learned of a high school shooting in which 18 died.

just stay down." The teacher's frantic voice, heard as gunfire reverberated in the background, was part of a tape recording released by the police today of some of the emergency calls placed on Tuesday as two students began their lethal rampage.[176]

This 911 call depicts the horror of April 20, 1999. Eric Harris, 18 years old, and Dylan Klebold, 17 years old, executed a massacre they had planned for a year, to occur on Hitler's birthday, at the Littleton, Colorado, Columbine High School. Harris and Klebold were members of a group who referred to themselves as the "Trenchcoat Mafia," a group reportedly known to dislike athletes and minorities. With four firearms and over 30 explosives, they killed 14 students, one teacher, and lastly, themselves.

The media made much of the fact that schools had been turned into killing fields. Fear gripped students and parents all over the country. In fact, shortly after the Columbine shootings, copycat crimes and attempts occurred. In Alberta, Canada, a 14-year-old boy wearing a three-quarter-length parka walked into W. R. Myers High School, whipped out a .22 caliber rifle, killed a 17-year-old boy, and critically wounded another. In Brooklyn, New York, five students were arrested for bragging about plans to blow up the school on graduation day. It was also no surprise when schools in Hillsborough, New Jersey, closed for one day after students began receiving email messages stating, "If you think what happened in Colorado was bad, wait until you see what happens in Hillsborough Middle School on Friday."[177] Yet another incident occurred on December 9, 1999, when a seventh-grade honor student opened fire on his classmates, wounding five, at the Fort Gibson Middle School in Fort Gibson, Oklahoma. Educators called for stricter security, and legislators responded to the media frenzy with proposals ranging from keeping students away from school during all but regular school hours to seeking the death penalty for 11-year-olds.

What is the reality? What do experts tell us? A National School Safety Center research report shows that the probability of being killed by lightning is twice as high as that of being killed at school.[178] And the *1998 Annual Report on School Safety*, the first report of its kind, proclaims that 90 percent of schools are free of serious, violent crime. The most common types of attacks are fights without weapons. This report also claims that there exists less than a 1-in-a-million chance of suffering a school-associated violent death.[179] Yet that is little consolation to the victims of school massacres and their families.

The public looks for scapegoats. Who did what wrong? And what happened to the days when throwing a spitball or an eraser got a

FIGURE 10.5 Students and guns: a better report card.

Student gun-related expulsions, 1997–98
Number of students expelled per 100,000

Number of cases: ■ 0–9 ■ 10–49 ☐ 50–99 ■ 100+

Wash. 17.8 | Ore. 22.6 | Idaho 16.2 | Mont. 9.7 | N.D. 0.8 | Minn. 4.8 | Wis. 6.5 | Mich. 5.3 | N.H. 2.2 | Maine 2.2 | Vt. 4.5 | Mass. 4.4 | N.Y. 2.8 | R.I. 5.8 | Pa. 9.1 | N.J. 2.8 | Conn. 1.6 | Ohio 5.7 | Ind. 5.7 | Ill. 3.8 | Iowa 5.5 | S.D. 32.7 | Wyo. 0.0 | Neb. 3.3 | Colo. 10.2 | Utah 1.8 | Nev. 11.5 | Calif. 6.1 | Ariz. 12.3 | N.M. 8.8 | Kans. 6.5 | Okla. 2.6 | Mo. 17.2 | Ark. 11.7 | La. 3.1 | Texas 10.7 | Miss. 8.5 | Ala. 10.5 | Ga. 14.2 | Fla. 6.1 | Tenn. 19.9 | Ky. 10.2 | W.Va. 5.5 | Va. 8.3 | N.C. 8.9 | S.C. 12.1 | Md. 6.9 | Dela. 22.6 | D.C. 5.4 | Alaska 12.2 | Hawaii 1.4

Students and Violence, 1997

8.5% said they have carried a weapon at school
7.4% said they were threatened or injured with a weapon at school
4.0% said they felt too unsafe to attend school

Students who said they have... carried a weapon / carried a gun (1993, 95, 97)

Source: Claudia Kalb, "Schools on the Alert," *Newsweek,* Aug. 23, 1999, p. 42.

student in big trouble? The answer must come from specialists in criminology. All too often, policy and legislation in matters of crime and criminal justice are the result of publicity given to emotion-charged media reports rather than of research data from scientific studies. Experts need to look into the causes of school violence. What do the events have in common? Some say that students are growing up with violence. One survey of inner-city children showed that 43 percent of 7- to 19-year-olds have witnessed a homicide.[180]

What can be done specifically, not only in the aftermath of such events, but also in terms of preventive measures? According to the 1994 Gun Free Schools Act, all schools that receive federal education funding must maintain policies mandating expulsion for any student caught bringing a firearm to school (Figure 10.5).[181] In addition, individual schools are making major changes. Following the shootings at Columbine, new security measures were instituted, including the installation of 16 color TV cameras to monitor both indoor and outdoor activities, the issuance of identification badges, the restriction of access to locked entryways, and the addition of another uniformed guard to patrol the hallways.[182] Other schools are suggesting the use of computer-coded identification badges.[183] Any way the situation is viewed, there is a noticeable shift from general security in schools to crisis management. Schools are also becoming more militaristic. In some California schools, there are random checks with metal-detector wands. Policies requiring uniforms, or at a minimum, the requirement of tucked-in shirts, are aimed at preventing the carrying of concealed weapons.[184] Still other responses to school violence include the implementation of lockdowns, detector dogs, and rent-a-cops. The entire situation begs the question: Is it truly necessary to turn schools into prisonlike structures? (See also "Of Immediate Concern" in Chapter 9.)

With the implementation of security measures comes an increase in safety, but at what

A former senior fire-arms executive and chief lobbyist of the American Shooting Sports Council, Robert A. Ricker, testified against corrupt practices of gun dealers, February 3, 2003.

VIOLENCE AND GUN CONTROL

The tragedies of the recent school shootings have fueled the gun-control debate. Estimates indicate that in the wake of the school massacres, more than 80 percent of Americans support stricter gun laws.[186] In fact, following the Columbine High School shooting in Colorado, the National Rifle Association was politely asked by various officials and concerned citizens to cancel its national meeting that was to be held in Denver, Colorado, only weeks after the shootings.[187]

Violence in the United States is frequently attributed to historical conditioning (the need of frontier people to survive in a hostile environment), social factors (poverty, inequities, and other inner-city problems), and the laxity of the criminal justice system (failure to apprehend and convict enough criminals and to imprison long enough those who are convicted). Some researchers have focused on one common element in a large proportion of violent crime: the availability of firearms in the United States.

One of the hottest and longest political and scholarly debates in our history centers on this point: Should and can Americans drastically restrict the availability of firearms, and would such controls substantially reduce the rate and severity of violent crime?

The Extent of Firearm-Related Offenses

It is difficult to be certain how many guns there are in the United States. Before 1850 less than 10 percent of U.S. citizens were believed to own guns, and between 1800 and 1845, only about 15 percent of all violent deaths were caused by guns.[188] The Bureau of Alcohol, Tobacco and Firearms estimates that from 1899 to

cost? The level of trust between administrators and students dwindles. Innocent and normally well-behaved students feel they are being targeted and their privacy is being invaded. The result could be increased levels of alienation, which in some cases lies at the root of most violence. Zero-tolerance policies for weapons, including guns, switchblades, pocketknives, box cutters, razors, ice picks, blackjacks, and chains, are a necessity.[185] High-tech solutions are clearly not the only alternative. Also needed are efforts aimed at increasing communication and interpersonal skills, availability of counseling, and guidance in relationship building. If there is one thing to learn from the recent school shootings, it is that no school is immune to violence. School violence is no longer a problem restricted to inner cities. It is a nationwide concern.

> **:// Crime Surfing**
>
> www.ojp.usdoj.gov/bjs/pub/pdf/iscso2.pdf
>
> The Bureau of Justice Statistics and the National Center for Education Statistics collaborate to produce the *Annual Report on School Safety* and *Indicators of School Crime and Safety*.

TABLE 10.4 Murdered Juveniles by Age, Gender, and Type of Weapon Used, 1980–1997

Weapon	Age of Victim 0–17	0–5	6–11	12–17	Victim Ages 0–17 Males	Females
Total	100%	100%	100%[†]	100%	100%	100%
Firearm	51	10	42	75	60	31
Knife/blunt object	14	11	19	15	13	17
Personal*	19	48	11	3	15	27
Other	16	30	28	7	12	25

- Three out of four murdered juveniles age 12 or older were killed with a firearm.
- Nearly half (48%) of all murdered children below age 6 were killed by offenders using only their hands, fists, or feet.
- Male murder victims were nearly twice as likely as female victims to be killed with a firearm.

Note: *Personal includes hands, fists, or feet.
[†]Detail may not total 100% because of rounding.
Source: Adapted from the FBI's *Supplementary Homicide Reports* for the years 1980–1997 [machine-readable data files], as cited in *Juvenile Offenders and Victims: 1999 National Report.*

1993, about 223 million guns became available in this country. It is unknown how many of these guns have been seized, destroyed, or lost, or do not work properly.[189] Current estimates indicate there are over 200 million firearms in circulation in the United States, including about 70 million handguns.[190] Half of the handguns are so-called Saturday-night specials (defined by the Bureau of Alcohol, Tobacco and Firearms as small weapons of .32 caliber or less with a barrel length of less than 3 inches and costing $50 or less). The supply of handguns increases by about 1.5 million each year.[191]

The Federal Bureau of Investigation has reported that a handgun is used in about half of all murders and one-third of rapes and robberies (Table 10.4). Two-thirds of police deaths in the line of duty are attributed to the use of handguns. Rates of crime involving guns are far lower in most other developed Western nations than in the United States.[192] According to the Task Force on Firearms of the National Commission on the Causes and Prevention of Violence, the rate of homicide by gun is 40 times higher in the United States than in England and Wales, and our rate of robbery by gun is 60 times higher.

The financial cost of gunshot injury and death, in terms of medical costs, lost productivity, and pain, suffering, and reduced quality of life, was estimated at over $60 billion each year. The Centers for Disease Control and Prevention estimates that approximately 96,000 persons in the United States sustained gun shot wounds in 1997.[193]

Youth and Guns

Three young thugs boarded a city bus in Queens yesterday, brandished guns like Wild West bandits and staged a frontier-style holdup. They strode up and down the aisle, fired shots into the roof, terrorized and robbed 22 passengers, struck a girl in the face with a gun butt and escaped with $300 in cash and fistfulls of jewelry.

The outlaws—one armed with a silver revolver and another with a pair of guns, while a third carried a book bag—made no effort to conceal their faces as they boarded the Q-85 bus at 8:30 A.M. at 140th Avenue and Edgewood Avenue in Springfield Gardens, a residential neighborhood just northeast of Kennedy International Airport.[194]

The "bandits" were three youths age 15 to 19. In a growing number of incidents across the United States, young people are using guns for robberies, gang warfare, initiation rites (drive-by shootings by wanna-be gang members), random shootings (in fact, James Jordan, father of former basketball star Michael Jordan, fell victim), and protection from their peers.[195]

Concern is mounting over adolescent illegal gun ownership and use. In 1995 the National Institute of Justice interviewed a sample of arrested individuals in Denver, the District of Columbia, Indianapolis, Los Angeles, Phoenix, St. Louis, and San Diego. The study found that juveniles are more likely than arrestees overall to commit crime with a gun. Of the juveniles interviewed, 20 percent said they carried a gun most or all of the time, 25 percent had stolen a

> **Theory Connects**
>
> **Youth and Guns**
>
> How do subculture theories of delinquency (Chapter 6) help explain gun ownership among the young? In particular, does the notion of reaction formation (p. 000) reveal why so many adolescents are drawn to the violence of gang life?

A powerful protest plea outside the Denver NRA convention in 1999.

gun, and 33 percent who owned a gun had used one in a crime (the percentages were considerably higher for gang members). Eighteen percent of the juveniles agreed that it was appropriate to use a gun "to shoot someone who disrespected you."[196]

Another study, of inner-city high schools in California, Illinois, Louisiana, and New Jersey, found a connection between involvement in drugs and gun carrying.[197] The same study sampled female students as well; 1 in 10 female students owned a gun at some time and roughly the same percentage carried a gun.[198]

Why have youths turned to guns? When asked, many of them respond the way three teenagers did: "You fire a gun and you can just *hear* the power. It's like *yeah*!" or "It became cool to say you could get a gun," or "Nobody messes with you if they think you may have a gun."[199] While there are many studies on adolescent violent behavior, there are few on adolescent illegal gun use. One of the few, a recent study of ninth- and tenth-grade boys, 14- and 15-year-olds, in Rochester, New York, found that most boys who owned illegal guns had friends who owned guns; over half of the illegal gun owners were gang members; and selling drugs was a prime motivation for carrying a gun. Moreover, illegal gun ownership, friends' gun ownership, gang membership, and drug use were closely related to gun crime, street crime, and minor delinquency.[200] Illegal firearms have traditionally been used by youths in low-income urban neighborhoods. The problem, like that of school shootings, is now spreading to the suburbs.

:// **Crime Surfing**

www.atf.treas.gov

The Bureau of Alcohol, Tobacco and Firearms provides information on firearms use, guns in circulation, and programs aimed at reducing the possession of illegal firearms.

Controlling Handgun Use

While most people agree that gun-related crime is a particularly serious part of our crime problem, there is little agreement on what to do about it. Some want prohibition. Others want comprehensive licensing and registrations.[201] Civic organizations and police associations call for more laws prescribing mandatory sentences for the illegal purchase, possession, or use of firearms. Close to 20,000 laws that regulate firearms already exist in the United States.

A variety of methods of controlling handgun use have been tried:

- In 1996 the Bureau of Alcohol, Tobacco and Firearms established the Youth Crime Gun Interdiction Initiative *to trace crime guns* (those illegally possessed or used in a crime) recovered by law enforcement. Between 1997 and 1998, 76,000 crime guns were traced. Almost half were recovered from persons under the age of 25.[202]

- A *prohibition against carrying guns* in public seemed to be related to a drop in gun

Kevin Hood shows his son Dakota, 5, how to handle a BB gun while his daughter Chelsie, 11, watches in the yard of their Greenfield, Indiana home. Kevin is an avid hunter and Chelsie has accompanied him on numerous hunting trips.

crimes in Boston[203] and a leveling off of handgun violence in Detroit.[204]

- In Kansas City, Missouri, a *police gun-confiscation program* was implemented in gun-crime hot spots in the target area, which had a murder rate 20 times the national average. Gun seizures in the target area increased by over 65 percent, while gun crimes decreased by 49 percent. Homicides were also significantly reduced in the target area.[205]

- Some states have passed what are referred to as *sentence-enhancement statutes:* The punishment for an offense is more severe if a person commits it under certain conditions, such as by using a gun. The Massachusetts law (1975) mandates a minimum sentence of one year's incarceration upon conviction for the illegal carrying of a firearm.[206] Michigan created a new offense—commission of a felony while possessing a firearm—and added a mandatory two-year prison sentence to the sentence received for the commission of the felony itself. The state mounted a widespread publicity campaign: "One with a gun gets you two," read the billboards and bumper stickers.[207]

Sentence enhancement has been studied in six U.S. cities. Homicides committed with firearms decreased in all six after sentence-enhancement laws took effect, although the decline in homicides was large in some cities and small in others. Researchers studying sentence enhancement point out that its effectiveness is related to how closely judges follow the law. An additional three years in prison may deter criminals from using guns, while an additional month may not.

- Project Exile began in Richmond, Virginia, in 1997. This program specifies that any time a gun is found on a person, whether a drug dealer, drug user, convicted felon, or suspect in a crime, the case will be tried under federal statutes in federal court. By moving gun offenses into the federal system, offenders face mandatory sentences of five years without parole. Prison time is increased for repeated or aggravated offenses. This project is advertised all over the city on billboards that in bold letters say, "An Illegal Gun Gets You five Years in Federal Prison." Since the implementation of this program, murders in Richmond have dropped significantly, from 140 in 1997 to 94 in 1998 and 32 in the first six months of 1999. Project Exile also led to the recovery of almost 500 illegal handguns, indictments against about 400 people on gun charges, and a conviction rate of 86 percent through trials and plea bargains.[208] This Virginia program is being mirrored in other cities as well, with anticipation of a similar effect.[209] The National Rifle Association supports this program, claiming that it is the best alternative to restrictive gun laws.[210]

- A *total ban on handguns* was tried in Washington, D.C., beginning in 1976. Both gun homicides and gun suicides dropped visibly after the ban took effect, while no change occurred in homicides and suicides not committed with guns.[211]

- Some communities have tried *buy-back programs*. St. Louis, San Francisco, Philadelphia, New York, and several other cities have embarked on such programs to reduce the number of handguns in circulation in the community. Police departments buy guns, no questions asked, for $50 each. In October 1991, the St. Louis Police Department bought 5,371 guns from citizens in 10 days. The Philadelphia police received 1,044 guns within a two-week period.

- *Federal legislation* has been passed in an attempt to prevent criminals from buying guns. The Brady Bill, named after James Brady, White House press secretary who was injured in the 1981 assassination attempt on President Ronald Reagan, went into effect on February 28, 1994. It calls for a five-day waiting period and a background check before a handgun can be purchased. Further, the bill prevents certain groups of people, such as convicted felons, fugitives from justice, illegal aliens, juveniles, and the mentally ill, from buying guns. Between February 1994, when the Brady Bill was first implemented, and the end of the interim period, November 1998, at which time the permanent provisions of the law became effective,[212] approximately 12.7 million background checks resulted in about 312,000 rejections, a rejection rate of 2.4 percent. The reasons for rejection varied: 63 percent of applicants were rejected as a result of prior felony convictions or current felony indictments; 10 percent of the applicants were rejected as a result of domestic violence misdemeanor convictions; and 3 percent of applicants were rejected as a result of the presence of domestic violence protection orders. During the interim period, the U.S. Department of Justice established the National Instant Criminal Background Check System, which indexes and accesses criminal justice agency databases that are used in the background check process. When the permanent provisions for the Brady act became effective, presale background checks were expanded to include not only handguns, but all other types of firearms as well.[213] Supporters of the Brady Bill claim this shows that fewer felons are managing to obtain handguns. Others argue that felons can still obtain handguns through illegal channels. James Q. Wilson, for example, says the real test of the Brady Bill is whether "felons have been stopped from buying guns and then killing people with them."

None of these methods resulted in drastic reductions in the number of handgun-related deaths, although some led to a small decrease. As two gun-control researchers point out, the important question to be answered with regard to gun control is this: How many deaths must be prevented by a gun-control method to justify its use? Very few of the millions of people who own guns commit crimes with them, and control policies will affect legitimate owners as well as criminals. David McDowall and Alan Lizotte ask:

> Is the legitimate happiness of 10 million gun owners worth the lives of 10,000 murder victims? One murder victim? In another context, is a highly restrictive measure that would save 200 lives better than a less restrictive measure that would save 100? There is no obvious answer to these questions, and different people will draw the line in different places.[214]

Perhaps we can learn from the countries with low gun-related homicide rates. Many citizens of Switzerland and Israel, for example, have army-issue firearms at their constant disposal by virtue of citizen-army requirements, yet these weapons are rarely used for homicides. What factors control the use of handguns in these countries? Many European countries and Canada maintain strict national gun laws. These countries often require that guns be registered,

From the Pages of The New York Times

Does the Brady Law Work?

When John Hinckley attempted to assassinate President Ronald Reagan in 1981, he wounded the president, along with two law enforcement officers and the White House press secretary, James Brady. Brady, who suffered a debilitating head wound, worked tirelessly for the next 12 years to institute gun control laws. In 1994, the Brady law went into effect; it requires background checks and a five-day waiting period for people who buy handguns from federally licensed firearms dealers. The question of the effectiveness of the Brady law has been debated ever since.

In August 2000, a study published in the *Journal of the American Medical Association* concluded that there was no evidence that the Brady law contributed to a reduction in homicide rates. The study's authors compared two sets of states: Thirty-two states that installed the law in 1994 and 18 states plus the District of Columbia, all of which have had Brady-style restrictions for much longer. The authors said that based on their statistical analysis, the decline in handgun homicide in the states that recently installed the Brady law would have been much more rapid if the law had really had an effect.

Advocates of gun control, however, say that the study is flawed. For instance, two studies done by Dr. Garen Wintemute, director of the Violence Prevention Research Program at the University of California at Davis, have found that California laws requiring background checks of convicted felons and criminals who committed violent misdemeanors reduced crimes committed with guns by 25 percent to 30 percent.

The National Rifle Association, which argues that laws don't stop criminals from getting guns, was delighted with the results of the 2000 study. However, even the study's authors acknowledge that a major reason the Brady law may not have been effective is that the law does not go far enough.

Source

Adapted from Fox, Butterfield, "Study Disputes Success of the Brady Law," *New York Times,* Aug. 2, 2000; and Fox, Butterfield, "July 30–August 5; Questions on Brady Law," *New York Times,* Aug. 6, 2000. Reprinted with permission.

Question for Discussion

1. The Brady law requires background checks only for those who buy handguns from federally licensed firearms dealers. It does not cover the unregulated market involving an estimated 30 to 40 percent of all gun sales, like gun shows and private transactions. Do you think the law should be extended to cover these venues? What would be your argument in its favor? What would be your argument against extending the scope of the law?

---

that owners be licensed, and that guns be stored with the greatest security. In some countries it is mandatory that a gun license applicant pass an examination on gun safety.[215] Even if comparative studies come up with useful findings, some researchers believe the political problems surrounding gun control in the United States will probably continue to hinder the development of nationwide, or even statewide, gun-control policies for some time to come.

The Gun-Control Debate

The battle line on gun control appears to be clearly drawn between the opponents of regulation (including the 3 million members of the National Rifle Association, or NRA, and their supporters) on the one hand and the advocates of control (including the 12 major law enforcement groups, the private organization Handgun Control, and three-quarters of the American public) on the other. The gun lobby likes to say that it is people who kill, not guns, so it is the people who use guns illegally who should be punished. To deter these people, gun enthusiasts say, we need to have stiffer penalties, including mandatory sentences that take these offenders off the streets.

Gun-control opponents often have bumper stickers that read, "When guns are outlawed, only outlaws will have guns." Moreover, most gun owners claim that it is their right to own firearms to protect their homes, especially when they lose confidence in the police and courts.[216] And by controlling guns, they say, the government intrudes in their private affairs. They interpret the Second Amendment to the Constitution as giving them an individual right "to keep and bear arms." Furthermore, the gun lobby maintains, people may wish to enjoy their guns as collectors or for sport and hunting.

FIGURE 10.6 Companies are trying to make safer guns.

A Smarter Gun for the Future
A fingerprint-enabled handgun, being developed by Oxford Micro Devices, will use a miniature electronic fingerprint-capture-and-verification device built into the handle of a gun to identify the owner and prevent unauthorized users.
1 The "latching solenoid" locks the gun's hammer and trigger, preventing unauthorized use.
2 On picking up the gun, the owner's middle finger covers a tiny red button activating the fingerprint unit on the side of the grip. The finger also wraps over the print sensor, which then scans the fingerprint.
3 An image-processor chip captures the image from the sensor and, with the memory chip and circuit board, identifies the fingerprint and unlocks the gun.

Source: "A Nationwide Backlash: State and Local Governments Are Taking Aim at the Gun Industry, Either by Enacting Legislation or by Filing Lawsuits," *Time*, Aug. 9, 1999, p. 28.

Another argument concerns what is called the *displacement effect:* People who are deterred by gun-control legislation from using guns to commit offenses will use some other weapon to achieve their goals. Or perhaps even more violent offenses will be committed if offenders can rely on the fact that the consequences of a non-firearm offense are less serious.

Finally, in the face of increasing random violence and a perceived inability of the police to safeguard citizens, more people are routinely carrying guns for self-protection. In many states, it is now becoming easier to do so, as more and more jurisdictions adopt "carrying-concealed-weapons" laws.[217]

Gun-control advocates compare our extremely high homicide rate to the much lower rates of other countries with tighter gun-control laws, including our neighbor Canada. They also argue that the availability of a gun makes homicide and suicide much more probable, because it is easier to produce death with a gun than with any other weapon. Moreover, they claim, better regulation or prohibition of gun ownership is a much faster way to lessen gun-related criminality than such long-term approaches as finding remedies for social problems. Researchers are testing the claims, but thus far no definitive conclusions have been reached.

In a related aspect of the gun-control debate, the gun industry finds itself under pressure. Many lawsuits have been filed against the gun industry on the basis that gun manufacturers have neglected to incorporate safety devices into their products. Gun makers are also cited with allowing their products to be marketed in such ways that both criminals and juveniles can easily obtain them for illicit use.[218] As a response to these lawsuits, many gun makers are attempting to install various safety devices on their products, including trigger locks and cable locks (Figure 10.6).

REVIEW

Murder, assaults of various kinds, rape, robbery, kidnapping—all share the common element of violence, though they differ in many ways: in the harm they cause, the intention of the perpetrator, the punishment they warrant, and other legal criteria. Social scientists have been exploring the frequency with which these crimes are committed in our society and elsewhere, their distribution through time and place, and the role played by circumstances, including the environment and behavior patterns, in facilitating or preventing them.

Such categories as mass murder, serial murder, gang murder, and date rape are shorthand designations for frequently occurring crime patterns that have not been specifically identified in penal codes. Another pattern of crime that also is not defined as such in the penal codes has become so important that it may be considered in conjunction with the other crimes of violence: family-related crime. This pattern encompasses a variety of violent crimes that include the abuse of spouses, children, and the elderly.

Some of the more pressing problems we face today are global terrorism, an increase in hate crimes nationwide, the spread of racist and antigovernment militias, and deadly shootings in American schools. The media attention given to these crimes has had a dramatic effect on the public's perception that violence has reached epidemic proportions.

The gun-control controversy demonstrates that both the definitions of crimes and the social and environmental characteristics associated with them must be studied in order to develop control and prevention strategies. Our violence-prone society will have to make serious choices if it is to reach that level of peaceful living achieved by many other modern societies.

CRIMINOLOGY & PUBLIC POLICY

Just how far is too far? Consider the next chapter of possible privacy invasion that the government has planned for us. With very little public fanfare, and insignificant media attention, the Pentagon's new Office of Information Awareness (OIA) is building a system called "Total Information Awareness" that would give the government access to an ultra-large-scale database of personal information from all communications (phone calls, emails, and web searches), to financial records, medical records, and travel history.

John Poindexter, former national security advisor (under President Ronald Reagan) and now head of OIA promotes the idea of a virtual centralized database that would serve as a central repository of information in our war against terrorism. (Source: http://www.darpa.MIL/iao/)

Questions for Discussion Should we be concerned that Total Information Awareness is a "Big Brother" program that may spy on innocent civilians? Without very specific limitations on its use, what is to prevent the OIA from expanding its program to gather information on targeted criminal organizations, political groups, and suspected insurgents?

YOU BE THE CRIMINOLOGIST

You are the superintendent of schools for your district. Your schools have not experienced any violent incidents, but because of the media hype surrounding the school shootings throughout the country, you are under pressure to take preventive measures. What actions would you take and what programs would you develop to make your schools safe and gun-proof? How would you implement these preventive measures? What are their advantages and disadvantages? How would you target your audience? What are the likely positive and negative reactions to the preventive measures?

KEY TERMS

The numbers next to the terms refer to the pages on which the terms are defined.

aggravated assault (247)

assault (247)

battery (247)

Federal Witness Protection Program (263)

felony murder (239)

homicide (238)
involuntary manslaughter (239)
justifiable homicide (238)
kidnapping (257)
Mafia (261)
malice aforethought (238)
manslaughter (239)
mass murder (243)
murder (238)
negligent homicide (239)
Racketeer Influenced and Corrupt Organizations (Rico) Act (263)
rape (253)
robbery (258)
serial murder (243)
simple assault (247)
sociopaths (245)
stranger homicide (242)
terrorism (269)
victim precipitation (242)
voluntary manslaughter (239)

CHAPTER 11
Crimes against Property

Larceny
   The Elements of Larceny
   The Extent of Larceny
   Who Are the Thieves?
   Shoplifting
   Art Theft
   Motor Vehicle Theft
   Boat Theft

Fraud
   Obtaining Property by False Pretenses
   Confidence Games and Frauds
   Check Forgery
   Credit Card Crimes
   Insurance Fraud

High-Tech Crimes: Concerns for Today and Tomorrow
   Characteristics of High-Tech Crimes
   Computers and the Internet: Types of Crime
   Characteristics of the High-Tech Criminal
   The Criminal Justice Problem

Burglary

Fencing: Receiving Stolen Property

Arson

Comparative Crime Rates

REVIEW

CRIMINOLOGY & PUBLIC POLICY

YOU BE THE CRIMINOLOGIST

KEY TERMS

Boxes
   Window to the World: *Crime on the Oceans: Whose Problem?*
   Of Immediate Concern: *Insurance Fraud on the Rise: New Jersey's Experience*
   From the Pages of *The New York Times*: *Whose Identity Is It Anyway?*

Special Features
   Crime Surfing
   Did You Know?
   Theory Connects

KEY TERMS

arson
burglary
check forging
confidence game
false pretenses, obtaining property by
fence
fraud
high-tech crime
larceny
shoplifting

A building engulfed in flames, May 1, 1992, in Los Angeles, California. As a result of the riots more than 50 died, over 4,000 were injured and property damage was over $1 billion.

The motion picture *The Gods Must Be Crazy* introduces us to a society of happy aborigines, remote from the hustle and bustle of modern life. Such tools as they have are shared and can easily be replaced from an abundance of sticks and stones.

High up, a "noisy bird" passes over the camp of these happy people. The pilot of the noisy bird casually throws an empty Coke bottle out of the cockpit. It lands in the middle of the camp. The aborigines stare at this foreign object. They handle it delicately and then discover what a useful object it is: It holds water; it can be used for rolling dough, for hammering, for many things. Everybody needs it and wants it. Fights ensue over who can have it. The peace and tranquillity of this little society are shattered. These people have discovered the concept of property, and they are experiencing all the troubles that go with the possession of property, including property crime.

The film has a happy ending. The aborigines finally get rid of the bottle, and life returns to normal.

We have explored some of the patterns of social interaction and the routine activities of daily life that set the stage for offenders to commit violent crimes and for other people—family members, acquaintances, strangers, airplane passengers—to become victims. We know that if we are to develop effective policies to prevent and control violent crime, we must have a thorough understanding of the characteristics of specific offenses; we need to know where, when, and how they are committed, and which individuals are most likely to commit them. The same is true for property offenses. To develop crime-prevention strategies, we need to study the characteristics that differentiate the various types of offenses which deprive people of their property.

Do such offenses as pocket-picking (pickpocketing), shoplifting, check forgery, theft by use of stolen credit cards, car theft, computer crimes, and burglary have different payoffs and risks? What kinds of resources are needed (weapons, places to sell stolen property)? Are any specific skills needed to carry out these offenses? The opportunities to commit property crime are all but unlimited. Studies demonstrate that if these opportunities are reduced, the incidence of crime is reduced as well.

The traditional property crimes are larceny (theft, or stealing); obtaining property by fraud of various sorts, including false pretenses, confidence games, forgery, and unauthorized use of credit cards; burglary, which does not necessarily involve theft; and arson, which not only deprives the owner of property but also endangers lives. New crime types, such as software piracy, online frauds, and computer viruses, are associated with high-technology equipment. We shall defer until Chapter 12 discussion of the crimes by which criminals deprive people of their property through organizational manipulations—individual white-collar crimes and corporate crimes.

LARCENY

Larceny (theft, stealing) is the prototype of all property offenses. It is also the most prevalent crime in our society; it includes such contemporary forms as purse-snatching, pickpocketing, shoplifting, art theft, and vehicle theft. In the thirteenth century, when Henry de Bracton set out to collect from all parts of England what was common in law—and thus common law—he learned to his surprise that there was no agreement on a concept of larceny. He found a confusing variety of ancient Germanic laws. So he did what he always did in such circumstances: He remembered what he had learned about Roman law from Professor Azo in Bologna, and simply inserted it into his new text of English law. Thus our common law definition of larceny is virtually identical with the concept in Roman law.[1]

The Elements of Larceny

Here are the elements of **larceny** (or theft, or stealing):

A trespassory
Taking and
Carrying away of
Personal property
Belonging to another
With the intent to deprive the owner of the property permanently

Each of these elements has a long history that gives it its meaning. The first element is perhaps the easiest. There must be a trespass. "Trespass," a Norman-French term, has a variety of meanings. In the law of larceny, however, it simply means any absence of authority or permission for the taking. Second, the property must be taken: The perpetrator must exert authority over the property, as by putting a hand on a piece of merchandise or getting into the driver's seat of the targeted car.

Third, the property must be carried away. The slightest removal suffices to fulfill this element: moving merchandise from a counter, however slightly; loosening the brakes of a car so that it starts rolling, even an inch. Fourth, the property in question, at common law, has to be personal property. (Real estate is not subject to larceny.) Fifth, the property has to belong to another, in the sense that the person has the right to possess that property. Sixth, the taker must intend to deprive the rightful owner permanently of the property. This element is present when the taker (thief) intends to deprive the rightful owner of the property forever. In many states, however, the law no longer requires proof that the thief intended to deprive the owner "permanently" of the property.

The Extent of Larceny

Larceny, except for the most petty varieties, was a capital offense in medieval England.[2] Courts interpreted all its elements quite strictly—that is, in favor of defendants—so as to limit the use of capital punishment. Only once did the courts expand the reach of larceny, when they ruled that a transporter who opens a box entrusted to him and takes out some items has committed larceny by "breaking bulk." For the other forms of deceptive acquisition of property, such as embezzling funds and obtaining property by false pretenses, Parliament had to enact separate legislation.

In the United States the rate of larceny is extraordinarily high. The UCR reported 7.1 million thefts in 2001, or a rate of 2,485 for each 100,000 of the population.[3] The NCVS figure, 14.3 million, is more than two times the UCR number, and neither figure includes automobile thefts.[4] The vast majority of thefts are, and always have been, committed furtively and without personal contact with the victims. Thefts involving personal contact—pickpocketing, purse-snatching, and other varieties of larceny—lag behind. Figure 11.1 shows the distribution of all larcenies known to the police in 2001. The estimated dollar value of stolen goods to victims nationally was over $5.2 billion.[5]

Who Are the Thieves?

Nobody knows exactly how many of the total number of thefts are committed by amateurs who lead rather conventional lives and how many are the work of professionals. According to some criminologists, the two types differ considerably.[6]

The Amateur Thief Amateur thieves are occasional offenders who tend to be opportunists. They take advantage of a chance to steal when little risk is involved. Typically, their acts are carried out with little skill, are unplanned, and result from some pressing situation, such as the need to pay the rent or a gambling debt.[7] In other words, amateurs resolve some immediate crisis by stealing. Most occasional offenders commit few crimes; some commit only one crime. Many are juveniles who do not go on to commit crimes in adulthood.

Amateur thieves do not think of themselves as professional criminals, nor are they recognized as such by those who do think of themselves as professionals. The lives of amateur thieves are quite conventional: Amateurs work, go to school, have conventional friends, and find little support or approval for their criminal behavior.

FIGURE 11.1 Distribution of larcenies known to police, 2001. (Because of rounding, figures may not total 100 percent.)

- .5% Purse-snatching
- .5% Pocket-picking
- .7% Coin machines
- 14% Shoplifting
- 4% Bicycles
- 26% From motor vehicles
- 13% From buildings
- 10% Motor vehicle accessories
- 31% All others

Source: Uniform Crime Reports, 2001.

> **Theory Connects**
>
> **Who Are the Thieves?**
>
> Situational theories of crime, such as rational choice and routine activities theories, suggest that offenders calculate the costs and benefits of committing crimes. In what ways do these theories explain the behavior of professional thieves?

The Professional Thief Professional thieves make a career of stealing. They take pride in their profession. They are imaginative and creative in their work and accept its risks. The most common crimes committed by professional thieves are pickpocketing, shoplifting, forgery, confidence swindling, and burglary. Professional thieves also are involved in art theft, auto vehicle theft, and fraud or theft by use of stolen or forged credit cards, among other crimes.

Thomas Bartholomew Moran, a professional thief who died in a Miami rescue mission in 1971, has been considered the best of American pickpockets. His career began in 1906, when, as a teenager, he started to pick women's purses. Under the careful guidance of Mary Kelly, a well-known pickpocket, he soon sharpened his skills until he could take wallets from pants, jeweled pins from clothing, and watches from vests without alerting the victims. He devoted his life to shoplifting, forgery, and other forms of theft. In 1912 he boarded the Titanic, with the intention of profiting handsomely from proximity to

> the more than 300 first-class passengers whose collective wealth exceeded $250 million. His immediate ambitions were dimmed, however, when the Titanic brushed an iceberg in the North Atlantic [and sank] only two hours and forty minutes later. But Moran was among the 705 passengers who managed to find space in one of the ship's twenty lifeboats, and his career in crime continued to flourish for the better part of the 59 remaining years of his life.[8]

The most influential study of professional thieves was conducted by Edwin Sutherland in 1937. Sutherland found that professional thieves share five characteristics:

1. They have well-developed technical skills for their particular mode of operation.
2. They enjoy status, accorded to them by their own subculture and by law enforcement.
3. They are bound by consensus, a sharing of values with their own peers.
4. Not only do they learn from each other, but they also protect each other.
5. They are organized, however loosely.[9]

Subsequent studies have tended to confirm Sutherland's findings.

Shoplifting

Shoplifting, the stealing of goods from retail merchants, is a very common crime; it constitutes about 15 percent of all larcenies. A recent survey in Spokane, Washington, revealed that every twelfth shopper is a shoplifter, and that men and women are equally likely to be offenders.[10] Perhaps shoplifting is so frequent because it is a low-risk offense, with a detection rate of perhaps less than 1 percent.[11] Shoppers are extremely reluctant to report shoplifters to the store management.[12] According to one study, of those apprehended for shoplifting, approximately 45.5 percent are actually prosecuted. It is also estimated that men are slightly more likely than women to be shoplifters, and that 41 percent of offenders are white, 29 percent are black, and 16 percent are Hispanic. More than half of shoplifting events occur between the hours of 12:00 P.M. and 6:00 P.M.[13] Interviews with 740 shoplifters in 50 Minneapolis stores revealed that almost half of those who expressed motivation for stealing said that they stole the merchandise because they liked it and did not have enough money to pay for it.[14] A study conducted in New South Wales with juvenile offenders in detention revealed that their reasons for shoplifting ranged from excitement, peer pressure, thrills, or fun; to obtaining clothes, food, or money for drugs or alcohol; to relieving boredom or stress.[15]

Mary Owen Cameron found that professional shoplifters largely conform to Sutherland's five characteristics but that amateurs do not. She estimates that of all shoplifters, only 10 percent are professionals—people who derive most of their income from the sale of stolen goods.[16] A broad range of motivations may lead to shoplifting. Among amateurs, need and greed as well as opportunity may precipitate the event.[17] Some researchers point to depression and other emotional disturbances and to the use of various prescription drugs.[18]

To most people, shoplifting is a rather insignificant offense. After all, how much can be stolen? On an individual basis, usually not very much: The average theft amount for each inci-

At the upscale Beverly Hills Saks Fifth Avenue on December 12, 2001, actress Winona Ryder is seen from a security surveillance tape released by the Los Angeles County Courts. On November 6, 2002, a jury found the two-time Oscar nominee guilty of grand theft and felony vandalism for stealing designer clothes worth about $5,000.

dent was roughly $61.[19] Taken together, however, all shoplifting incidents cost U.S. retail businesses over $18 billion every year.[20] In 1999, approximately $10 million worth of stolen merchandise was recovered. (See Table 11.1.)

As shoplifters decrease store profits, the price of goods goes up; stepped-up security adds even more to costs. Stores typically hire more and more security personnel, although it has been demonstrated that physical or electronic methods of securing merchandise are more cost effective than the deployment of guards.[21] It is only the amateur shoplifter who is deterred by the presence of guards or store personnel, not the professional.[22]

Given the significantly high costs of shoplifting to retailers, what can be done to reclaim what was stolen? One option, practiced quite often in the United Kingdom, is the use of civil recovery. Civil recovery is an administrative process that enables store owners to utilize the civil law in an attempt to collect restitution from shoplifters directly, whether the shoplifters are customers or store employees. This civil action operates parallel to the criminal process, meaning that stores can both report instances of shoplifting to the police and also file separate civil complaints against the shoplifters to obtain restitution. Those apprehended for shoplifting can then either pay the civil penalty imposed upon them or appear before a civil court. Research has shown that for amateur shoplifters (as opposed to professionals), the use of civil recovery does not have a significant impact on their initial offense, but does have an impact on preventing them from reoffending.[23]

Art Theft

At the high end of the larceny scale we find art theft. The public knows and seems to care little about art theft, yet it is as old as art itself. Looters have stolen priceless treasures from Egyptian tombs ever since they were built. As prices for antiques and modern art soar, the demand for stolen art soars. Mexico and other countries with a precious cultural heritage are in danger of losing their treasures to gangs of thieves who take what they can from archaeological sites, and leave the rest in ruins.

One of the most grandiose art thefts occurred on May 21, 1986, when a gang of Irish thieves invaded an estate in Ireland with commando precision and made off with 11 paintings, among them a Goya, two Rubenses, a Gainsborough, and a Vermeer.

Art theft, particularly the illicit trade in objects of cultural heritage, has increased significantly

TABLE 11.1 Most Frequently Shoplifted Items by Store Type

Type of Retailer	Merchandise
Auto parts	Hard parts
Bookstores	Electronics, CDs, cassettes, videos
Consumer electronics/computer stores	Portable CD players, car alarms, cordless phones
Department stores	Clothing: shirts
Discount stores	Clothing: undergarments, CDs
Drugstores/pharmacies	Cigarettes, batteries, over-the-counter remedies
Fashion merchandise stores	Sneakers
General merchandise stores	Earrings
Grocery stores/supermarkets	Over-the-counter remedies, health and beauty aids, cigarettes
Home centers/hardware stores	Assorted hand tools
Music stores	Compact discs
Shoe stores	Sneakers
Specialty stores	Bed sheets
Specialty apparel stores	Assorted clothes, shoes
Sporting goods stores	Nike shoes
Theme parks	Key chains, jewelry
Toy stores	Action figures
Video stores	Video games
Warehouse stores	Pens, movie videos

Source: Read Hayes, *1996 Retail Theft Trends Report: An Analysis of Customer Theft in Stores* (Winter Park, Fla.: Loss Prevention Specialists,

worldwide over recent years. Art thieves use a variety of means, including forms of shoplifting, burglary, and robbery, to either steal individual works of art, illegally export pieces of art, or pillage archaeological sites.[24] Despite the widespread incidence of art theft, nobody knows the overall cost. Some paintings are worth $50, others $5,000, and others $50 million. Tens of thousands of paintings and other art objects are missing.[25]

In response to the increasing problem of art theft, the Federal Bureau of Investigation (FBI) has created the National Stolen Art File, which consists of a computerized index of stolen art and other forms of cultural property. Once items are reported to either local law enforcement agencies within the United States or law enforcement agencies abroad, the FBI is notified and then incorporates images and physical descriptions of the objects, as well as information specific to the investigation of the particular art theft, into the National Stolen Art File index. The database that is created is used as an analytical tool to investigate and recover these items. According to the FBI, for an object to be entered into the National Stolen Art File, three specific criteria must be met. First, the object must be of artistic or historic significance. This includes fine arts, ethnographic objects, archaeological material, coins, stamps, musical instruments, and the like. Second, the stolen object in question must have a value of $2,000 or more. However, if the object is worth less than $2,000 but is associated with a major crime, the stolen object will meet the necessary criteria. Finally, the request for inclusion in the National Stolen Art File must be made by a law enforcement agency. Included in the request must be a description of the object, a photograph of the object, and if available, a police report and any other investigative information.[26]

Inasmuch as Hollywood movies are considered art, a new form of art theft has emerged—video piracy. Various video piracy rings exist throughout the country. They produce and sell bootleg tapes of films currently in movie theaters. Enforcement efforts have increased over the past few years. Recently, a New York–based piracy ring operating one of the largest video piracy operations along the East Coast was dismantled, resulting in 11 arrests and the confiscation of approximately 30,000 videotapes. This particular ring earned roughly $50,000 a week after producing and selling bootleg tapes of first-run films. The bootleg tapes sell for between $5 and $10 on the street. Those arrested were charged with trademark counterfeiting and failure to disclose the origin of a recording.[27]

People who commit larceny aim for places and objects that seem to offer the highest and most secure rewards. Our open, mercantile society affords an abundance of opportunities. While shoplifters need little expertise and a low level of professional connection, art thieves must have sophisticated knowledge of art and its value as well as good connections in the art world if they are to dispose of the items they steal. Art thieves methodically select the gallery from which they plan to steal objects of art, paying particular attention to the area in which the gallery is located, the floor of the gallery in which the art is housed, the showrooms with and without closed-circuit television (CCTV), and the number of visitors at the gallery at a particular time.[28] Other types of larceny, such as theft of automobiles and boats, require a moderate degree of skill—but more and more members of the general public are acquiring such skills.

Motor Vehicle Theft

Motor vehicle theft is the largest property crime in the United States. According to the UCR, approximately 1.2 million motor vehicles were stolen in the United States in 2001.[29] The value of motor vehicles stolen in 2001 was roughly $8.2 million, with the value of motor vehicles recovered approximately $5.1 million.[30]

In 2001, 74 percent of the vehicles stolen were passenger cars, 19 percent were trucks and buses, and 7 percent were other types of vehicles. The clearance rate (by arrest), as distinguished from the recovery rate of vehicles, is low—about 14 percent. Many cars are stolen during July and August, when schools are not in session. Thirty-nine percent of car thieves are youngsters under 18.[31] Most of their acts amount to *joyriding*, a type of larceny that lacks the element of "intent to deprive the owner of the property permanently." The thieves simply take the vehicle for momentary pleasure or transportation.

More recently, young car thieves have used stolen vehicles for racing, a show of status among peers, or for the "kick" of destroying them (Figure 11.2). At the other end of the spectrum are older, professional auto thieves who steal designated cars on consignment for resale in an altered condition (with identifying numbers changed) or for disposition in "chop shops," which strip the cars for the resale value of their parts.[32] Some estimate that a vehicle is worth three times its value when sold illegally for parts by professional car thieves.[33] In 2001 alone, more than 200,000 vehicles were illegally shipped abroad.[34] Table 11.2 describes the 10 areas in the United States with the highest vehicle theft rates in 2001. The types of vehicles stolen have changed over the years. It is interesting to note that sport utility vehicles and pickup trucks are becoming just as popular with thieves as they are with consumers. In fact, 1998 was the second year in a row in which these types of vehicles have made the top 10 stolen vehicles category.

FIGURE 11.2 Motor vehicle theft. Juvenile arrest rates for motor vehicle theft soared between 1984 and 1989, then decreased through the 1990s.

Arrests per 100,000 juveniles ages 10–17

The juvenile arrest rate for motor vehicle theft increased 130 percent between 1983 and 1989. The decline in the 1990s resulted in a 1999 arrest rate that was about the same as the 1983 low point and equal to the 1980 rate.

Source: *Juvenile Offenders and Victims: 1999 National Report.* ©55DP, National Report Series Bulletin, Dec. 2001

A variety of strategies are used to steal vehicles for financial gain. The "strip and run" occurs when a thief steals a car, strips it for its parts, and then abandons the vehicle. The frame of the car is all that is left. The "scissors job" occurs when scissors are jammed into certain ignition locks in mostly American-made cars, allowing the thief to easily start the car. A "valet theft" takes place when a thief dresses and poses as a valet attendant, opens the car door for the driver, takes the keys, and quickly drives away. Another strategy for vehicle theft is simply the "insurance fraud" scheme, in which a car owner reports his or her car stolen and hides the car for approximately 30 days. Once 30 days have passed without the car's being recovered, insurance claims are often paid without question. After the claim is paid, the cars are often miraculously "found," but are in very poor condition. The owner will then use the money from the insurance claim to purchase a newer car.[35]

Carjacking is considered a combination of motor vehicle theft and robbery. Not only is a car stolen, but it is stolen by use of force or threat of force. Carjacking has become quite a widespread occurrence over the past few years. During each year between 1992 and 1996, there was an average of about 49,000 completed or attempted nonfatal

TABLE 11.2 The Metropolitan Statistical Areas with the Ten Highest Vehicle Theft Rates

1. Phoenix, Arizona
2. Miami, Florida
3. Fresno, California
4. Detroit, Michigan
5. Sacramento, California
6. Tucson, Arizona
7. Tacoma, Washington
8. Stockton, California
9. Seattle, Washington
10. Jersey City, New Jersey

Source: NICB Vehicle Theft Study, 2001 (www.nicb.org/services/hotspotsrelease.html).

carjackings. In about half of the incidents, the offender was successful in taking the victim's automobile. Approximately 7 out of 10 completed carjackings involved the use of firearms, whereas about 2 out of 10 attempted carjackings involved the use of firearms. Surprisingly, most carjackings, whether they were completed or attempted, did not result in injury to the victim.[36]

The invention of the ignition key made it harder to steal cars. In recent years, manufacturers of automobiles have tried to make cars more theftproof. Steering-shaft locks, cutoff switches, better door locks, and alarm systems have increased the security of protected cars.

One of the most successful of the high-tech options for car protection may be electronic tracking systems, including the widely known and utilized Lo-Jack. A small electronic transmitter, installed in the car, is activated by police transmitters once a car is reported stolen. A homing signal allows tracking computers in police cruisers to determine the location of the stolen car. A direction finder and a signal-strength meter let the police know how close they are to the stolen car, thereby facilitating the search.[37] A newer type of antitheft device is called the "Unbrakeable Autolock." This particular device, when in place, locks one of the strongest parts of the car, the steel brake pedal. Once the Autolock is in place, the brake pedal cannot be depressed. Most cars built after 1990 feature a component called the "brake pedal shift interlock," which requires that the brake pedal be depressed before the vehicle can be put into gear. Since the Autolock locks the brake, it cannot be depressed, and therefore the car cannot be driven, making theft impossible.[38] One other recently developed antitheft device is the "Silent Scorpion." Unlike many car alarm systems, this device does not emit any sounds upon activation. Instead, it actually prevents the car thief from driving the car more than a quarter mile. The system is activated automatically whenever the driver's door is opened and then closed, while the engine is running. Once the Silent Scorpion is activated, the engine will run normally for about 4 seconds, at which time it will then begin to simulate engine failure. The engine will shudder and, after about 25 seconds, will shut off; the thief will be unable to restart the car.[39]

Philadelphia police officer John Logan carrying "chopped" parts of stolen cars from the city's East Frankford section.

PART III **Types of Crimes**

> **:// Crime Surfing**
>
> www.ncjrs.org/pdffiles1/bja/fs0002bl.pdf
>
> Check this website for more information on the Watch Your Car program.

A recent development by the U.S. attorney general's office in response to the Motor Vehicle Theft Prevention Act of 1994 is the national "Watch Your Car" program. A car owner can voluntarily display a decal or a special customized license plate on his or her vehicle signifying one of two things: that the car is normally not driven between the hours of 1:00 A.M. and 5:00 A.M. or that the vehicle is normally not driven in the proximity of international land borders or ports. As a member of this program, the car owner consents to vehicle stops if the car is being driven under the conditions described above.[40]

Such efforts (as we saw in Chapter 9) are examples of target hardening—that is, designing the target (the car) in such a way that it is harder to steal. Other means of providing for greater car protection include safer parking facilities. Ronald Clarke has demonstrated that parking lots with attendants experience far fewer motor vehicle thefts than unattended lots.[41]

Boat Theft

It is not our purpose to classify all larceny by the type of property stolen. We have singled out automobile theft and art theft to demonstrate the socioeconomic significance of these types of larceny, their dependence on the economic situation, and the challenge of changing the situational conditions that encourage people to commit them. Another type of larceny, the theft of working and pleasure boats, of little fishing skiffs and rowboats, is similarly tied to socioeconomic conditions.

No statistics were kept on boat theft in the United States before 1970. Obviously, boat thefts have occurred ever since there have been boats, but such thefts attained high proportions only in the 1970s and 1980s. The FBI's National Crime Information Center started a stolen-boat file in 1969. During the first few years this service was little known, and the number of boats listed as stolen was initially small. But by the mid-1970s,

U.S. Coast Guard law enforcement team boarding a vessel in American territorial waters.

law enforcement agencies all over the country had become familiar with this service and had begun reporting the number of stolen boats in their jurisdictions. Between 1975 and 1990 the number of boats stolen and not recovered tripled, from 11,000 to over 30,000, and that number did not include boats eliminated from the file after a given expiration period (of from 1 to 5 years). After 1990, the number of boats stolen declined.

Most boat thefts, both in the water and on land, are linked to the vast increase in the number of boats in the United States. Increased boat ownership among all population groups goes hand in hand with a proliferation of skills in handling boats and outboard motors. The number of automobile thefts rose during the days when automobile ownership and driving skills increased rapidly. Now we are witnessing the same phenomenon with boats. Some of the

Window to the World

Crime on the Oceans: Whose Problem?

While no accurate estimates of worldwide losses from modern-day piracy are possible, knowledgeable experts think the total is probably near $250 million a year. The thieves make off with tons of cement, coffee, sugar, tomato paste, ladies' undergarments, steel, and whatever other cargo they think they can fence on shore. Even more common is the direct attack on the safe in the captain's cabin—pirates may be able to collect $50,000 in cash during a 15-minute job. In 1991 more than 120 pirate attacks were reported worldwide, and it is likely that only 40 percent of the total are reported to authorities.(1)

A downturn of maritime commerce in Nigeria resulted in a decrease of piracies off Lagos. A sharp decrease also occurred in the Malacca Straits, a result of improved security measures. But piracies began to increase again in the mid-1990s, near ports in Cameroon and Angola, and particularly in the Brazilian ports of Santos and Rio de Janeiro. Most affected are vessels at anchor in the roadsteads.

THE LACK OF POLICING

Unfortunately, the world does not yet have an international marine enforcement agency to police the oceans. There is no one to spot a vessel dumping nuclear waste into the high seas or into an exclusive economic zone. Who can intercept arms or narcotics smugglers? Even powerful nations, like the United States, have trouble policing their own zones. The problems are much worse for small nations that cannot afford to maintain marine police forces of any size.(2) Most regions affected by piracy and terrorism are in areas of notoriously underpoliced territorial waters.

THE SCOPE OF CRIME ON THE OCEANS

All these problems are magnified when we realize that piracy is only one of many crimes committed on the oceans. Following are examples of other crimes:
- Frauds in the marine shipping industry have caused severe damage to international trade and threatened the collapse of entire national economies in Africa and Latin America.
- The international drug trade uses the oceans for about half its shipments from the points of origin or manufacture to the points of distribution.
- Currently about 30,000 American boats are listed in the FBI's Stolen Boat File as having been stolen and not recovered.

Sources

1. G. O. W. Mueller and Freda Adler, *Outlaws of the Ocean* (New York: Hearst Marine Books, 1985), p. 150; Alan Farnham, "Pirates," *Fortune,* July 15, 1991, pp. 113–118.
2. Roger Villar, *Piracy Today* (London: Conway Maritime Press, 1985), p. 59.

Questions for Discussion

1. What crimes against property are committed by those who engage in maritime fraud?
2. Propose a mechanism to control property crime on the high seas. Defend your proposal.

---

same crime-specific approaches developed to render cars more theftproof are currently being tried to protect boats and boating equipment—registration, secret and indelible identification numbers, locking devices, alarm systems, marina guards, protection campaigns for boat owners. Already we have some indication that the choices for boat thieves are becoming more limited and that the thieves are choosing their targets with increasing care.[42]

With the exception of some brazen pickpockets, people who commit larcenies tend to avoid personal contact with their victims. Other criminals seek such contact in order to deprive victims of their property by deception.

FRAUD

Fraud is the acquisition of the property of another person through cheating or deception. In England such crimes owed their existence to the interaction of five circumstances: the advancement of trade and commerce, the inventiveness of swindlers in exploiting these economic advances, the demand of merchants for better protection, the unwillingness of the royal courts to expand the old concept of larceny, and the willingness of Parliament to designate new crimes in order to protect mercantile interests. In brief, medieval England developed a market economy that required the transport of goods by wagon trains across the country, from producer or importer to consumer. Later on, when the Crown sought to encourage settlement of colonies overseas, stock companies were created to raise money for such ventures. People with money to invest acquired part ownership in these companies in the expectation of profit.

Just as some dishonest transporters withheld some of the property entrusted to them for transport, some dishonest investment clerks used funds entrusted to them for their own pur-

Darlene Gillespie, former Mouseketeer, was convicted of fraud in Los Angeles, California, federal court in 1999.

poses. Merchants suffered greatly from such losses, yet the royal courts refused to extend the definition of larceny to cover this new means of depriving owners of their property. But merchants demanded protection, and from time to time, as need arose, Parliament designated new, noncapital offenses so that the swindlers could be punished.

Obtaining Property by False Pretenses

The essence of the crime of **obtaining property by false pretenses** is that the victim is made to part with property voluntarily, as a result of the perpetrator's untrue statements regarding a supposed fact. Assume the doorbell rings. A gentleman greets you politely and identifies himself as a representative of a charitable organization, collecting money for disaster victims. On a typed list are the names of all the households in your building, with a dollar amount next to each name. Each household has supposedly contributed an average of $20. Not wanting to be considered cheap, you hand the gentleman a $20 bill. He promptly writes "$20" next to your name and thanks you.

Of course, the gentleman does not represent the charitable organization, there may not even be such a charity, there may not have been a disaster, and you may have been the first victim on his list. The man has obtained property from you by false pretenses. He has not committed a common law larceny because he did not engage in any "trespassory taking" of property.

Cheating was made a crime relatively late in history (in 1757 in England). Until that time the attitude was that people should look out for their own interests. Today obtaining property by false pretenses is a crime in all 50 states, and some states have included it in their general larceny statutes.

Confidence Games and Frauds

In an attempt to protect people from their own greed, a few fraud statutes have included a statutory offense called **confidence game.** In an effort to cover the enormous variety of confidence swindles, legislators have worded the statutory definitions somewhat vaguely. The essence of the offense is that the offender gains the confidence of the victim, induces in the victim the expectation of a future gain, and—by abusing the trust thus created—makes the victim part with some property. In a sense, confidence games are an aggravated form of obtaining property by false pretenses.

To illustrate: A woman (A) sees a shiny object lying on the sidewalk. As she stoops to pick it up, a man (B) grabs it. A dispute ensues over who should have the "lost diamond ring." A third person (C) comes by and offers to mediate. He happens to be a jeweler, he says. C takes a jeweler's loupe out of his pocket, examines the diamond ring, and pronounces it worth $500. At this point, B generously offers his share in the ring to A for a mere $100. A pays—and gets what turns out to be a worthless object. By the time she discovers this fact, B and C are long gone.

Frauds of this sort have been with us for centuries. But frauds change with commercial developments. Some of the more prevalent fraud schemes of today would have been unimaginable a few decades ago, simply because the commercial opportunities for their occurrence had not yet been invented.

Check Forgery

Those motivated to deprive others of their property have always exploited new opportunities to do so. The invention of "instant cash," or credit, by means of a check issued by a creditable, trustworthy person provided just such new opportunities. Ever since checks were invented, they have been abused. All jurisdictions make it a criminal offense to use a counterfeit or stolen check or to pass a check on a nonexistent account, or even on one with insufficient funds, with intent to defraud. The intent may be demonstrated by the defendant's inability or unwillingness to reimburse the payee within a specified time period.

Another fraud, called **check forging,** consists of altering a check with intent to defraud. The criminologist Edwin Lemert found that most check forgers—or "hot-check artists," as they are frequently called—are amateurs who act in times of financial need or stress, do not consider themselves criminals, and often believe that nobody really gets hurt.[43] With the increase in check forgeries over the past few decades, the primary means of dealing with the problem has been the introduction of identification requirements needed when either cashing a check at a financial institution or presenting a check for payment. The downside of this approach is the annoyance to check users of having to put up with increased restrictions.[44] Some retailers have begun using Telecheck, where a check presented for payment is run through a machine that verifies whether or not the funds presented as payment on the check are in fact available at the time of sale.

Credit Card Crimes

Just as the introduction of checks for payment for goods and services opened up opportunities for thieves to gain illegitimate financial advantage, so did the introduction of "plastic money." Many believe that the widespread use of credit cards, debit cards, and charge cards is quickly making ours a cashless society.[45] There were 7 billion credit card transactions worldwide in 1991; of these, 3 billion took place in the United States. Now, the number of annual credit card transactions is over 21 billion.[46] Visa and MasterCard reported losses from credit card fraud of half a billion dollars in the United States in 1991. This amount has been increasing as the volume of cards in circulation goes up. Losses from credit card crime are expected to surpass all other retailer-reported losses, such as those from bad checks, counterfeit currency, and shoplifting.

Credit card fraud during the 1980s was associated primarily with counterfeiting and lost or stolen cards. Now many cards are stolen while in transit from the issuer to the cardholder. In other instances an offender may simply use false information about a real person to obtain a genuine card. Or a person may make a purchase by mail order or telephone using a genuine card number, but have the goods delivered to an address other than the address of the card owner.[47] Traffickers in stolen cards sell them for cash, with the amount based on the credit limit of the account—a $2,000 credit line might bring $250.[48] The availability of new and relatively inexpensive technological equipment, however, keeps transforming the nature of the fraud. Stolen, lost, or expired credit cards are now modified with computers and encoding devices so that they appear to be valid. Totally counterfeit credit cards are also fabricated with the help of laser copiers or other duplicating techniques. And, more recently, credit card account numbers are being stolen from the Internet.

The economic rewards of credit card fraud are quick and relatively easy. The risks are low. Usually merchants do not ask for personal identification; cards are issued in banks that are often in other states or countries; and authorization procedures are weak. Originally, the users of stolen credit cards had the inconvenience of selling the merchandise they obtained with the cards. But when banks introduced the practice of cashing the checks of strangers as long as the transactions were guaranteed by a credit card,

Attorney General Ben Chandler holds a device during a news conference Monday, February 3, 2003 in Frankfort, Kentucky, which he said can be used to steal credit card information. Authorities used the occasion to announce the arrest of 22 people for various crimes connceted to identity theft after a four month investigation.

perpetrators gained direct access to cash and no longer had to resort to dealers in stolen goods.[49]

The banking industry has studied credit card schemes and has improved the electronic system with target-hardening responses. In 1971 Congress enacted legislation that limited the financial liability of owners of stolen credit cards to $50. Many states have enacted legislation making it a distinct offense to obtain property or services by means of a stolen or forged credit card, while others include this type of fraud under their larceny statutes.

Several fraud-prevention initiatives have been developed in response to the prevalence of credit card fraud. The use of laser-engraved photography and signatures on credit cards makes impersonation more difficult. Other initiatives are the use of increased authorization levels on credit card transactions, as well as reduced floor limits above which transactions must be authorized to be guaranteed. Better technology has been developed to quickly transmit data on cards that have been reported lost and stolen to retailers worldwide. Further with the ever increasing "card not present" situations, such as when a person is purchasing items over the Internet, additional methods are being developed to verify the identity of the cardholder.[50]

Insurance Fraud

Insurance fraud is a major problem in the United States. Auto insurance, in particular, has been the target of many dishonest schemes. About $60 billion is paid in auto insurance claims annually. It is estimated that 10 percent of those claims are fraudulent.[51] The National Automobile Theft Bureau holds manufacturers' records on 188 million vehicles (about 95 percent of U.S. cars); its theft and loss data indicate that 15 percent of all reported thefts are fraudulent.[52] Auto insurance schemes include:

- *Staged claims.* Parts of a car are removed, reported stolen, and later replaced by the owner.

- *Owner dumping.* The car is reported stolen; it is stripped by the owner, and the parts are sold.

- *Abandoned vehicles.* The car is left in a vulnerable spot for theft; then it is reported stolen.[53]

- *Staged accidents.* No collision occurs, but an "accident scene" is prepared with glass, blood, and so forth.

- *Intended accidents.* All parties to the "accident" are part of the scheme.

- *Caused accidents.* The perpetrator deliberately causes an innocent victim in a targeted car to crash into his or her car (often in the presence of "friendly" witnesses).[54]

There are many types of insurance fraud besides that involving automobiles. One rapidly growing type involves filing fraudulent health insurance claims. Various terms have been created to describe the schemes that are used in medical fraud. "Overutilization" involves billing for superfluous and unnecessary tests and other services.[55] "Ping-Ponging" occurs when physicians refer patients to several practitioners when symptoms do not warrant such referrals. "Family ganging" takes place when a doctor extends several unnecessary services to all members of a patient's family. "Steering" is a practice in which doctors direct patients to the clinic's pharmacy to fill unneeded prescriptions. Finally, "upgrading" occurs when a patient is billed for services more extensive than those that were actually performed.[56]

Credit card crimes and insurance schemes are comparatively recent types of fraud, but they are not the last opportunities for swindlers to deprive others of their property. Computer crime, for example, is a growing concern, and technological advances continue to offer new possibilities for theft. Opportunities will always challenge the imagination of entrepreneurs—illegitimate as well as legitimate. In regard to the illegitimate entrepreneurs, the problem invariably is whether they are in violation of existing criminal laws or whether new legislation will have to be drawn up to cover their schemes.

HIGH-TECH CRIMES: CONCERNS FOR TODAY AND TOMORROW

Orange County, California (September 15, 1999). Six Southern California telemarketers have been charged in connection with an Internet gaming scam. Federal prosecutors say the scam took in almost $5 million from more than 500 investors. The six worked for Gecko Holdings. They offered investors stock in Gecko, telling them it was an online gambling business about to go public. Investors were promised that their shares, priced at two dollars, would double or triple the value in a few months. But the stock never went public. Instead, prosecutors say, the owners took off with the money. The six are charged with 26 counts each of mail and wire fraud.[57]

Crimes evolve with the environments we live in. The rise of computers and other high-technology equipment has paved the way for the genesis of new crime types. These present yet another set of challenges for potential victims, law enforcement personnel, criminologists, and other criminal justice professionals.

What exactly is high-technology crime? While there may be debates over the definition of this phenomenon, it is generally agreed that **high-tech crime** involves an attempt to pursue illegal activities through the use of advanced electronic media. We shall define "high technology" as "a form of sophisticated electronic device—computer, cellular telephone, and other digital communication—that is in common use today."[58] The new waves of computer crime are perhaps the most illustrative examples of high-technology crime, although sophisticated credit card fraud schemes and cellular telephone scams are also modern problems. In this section, we will refer to crimes relying on modern electronic technology as "high-tech crimes."

> **:// Crime Surfing**
> www.nipc.gov
>
> The National Infrastructure Protection Center, located at FBI headquarters, tracks computer crimes like the famous **Love Bug** virus.

Characteristics of High-Tech Crimes

High-tech crimes have affected the nature of property crimes by taking on the following few distinct characteristics.

Role of Victims, Type of Property Criminals engaging in high-tech crimes no longer need actual direct contact with their victims; computers equipped with modems have unlimited range, enabling offenders to victimize

Insurance Fraud on the Rise: New Jersey's Experience

Consider the case of Ernest Woodson, who fell and broke his eyeglasses on his way out of a supermarket in Cumberland County, New Jersey, and received $250 as compensation for the damage. Was this settlement fair to both parties? One might think so, unless you know that Mr. Woodson executed nearly two dozen similar falls on the premises of various New Jersey merchants in less than a year, filing insurance claims that added up to more than $30,000. When state authorities caught up with him in September 1999, Woodson entered a guilty plea and was eligible to be sentenced to up to 12 months behind bars.

Ernest Woodson is just one example of insurance fraud in action. Now offenders face not only civil monetary penalties but jail time as well, depending on the extent and type of fraud. With insurance fraud on the rise, particularly health care claims fraud, New Jersey has taken steps to expand its resources and has become one of the few states in this country that has waged such a concentrated effort to combat insurance fraud at all levels. Other states maintain antifraud bureaus, but New Jersey is the first and only state to have a fraud-prevention program headed by a special prosecutor.(1) The handling of suspicious insurance claims and fraud cases was handled formerly by the Insurance Fraud Division (IFD) of the Department of Banking and Insurance. However, with New Jersey's Automobile Insurance Cost Reduction Act of 1998, the Office of the Insurance Fraud Prosecutor (OIFP) was created in the Division of Criminal Justice to "investigate all types of insurance fraud and serve as the focal point for all criminal, civil, and administrative prosecutions of insurance fraud."(2)

After being in business for only 14 months, the Office of the Insurance Fraud Prosecutor is making an impressive name for itself. During 1998, 66 convictions were won, $2.5 million in fines were imposed, and $1.6 million in restitution was obtained. In the first 8 months of 1999, the OIFP filed charges against 104 people, obtained convictions against 49 people, imposed more than $3.7 million in civil fines, and won nearly $5 million in restitution. As of September 1999, OIFP investigators had sent 11 defendants to jail for a total of 39 years.(1) In addition, as part of its antifraud efforts, a toll-free fraud hotline was instituted so that anyone, including ordinary citizens, who suspects incidents of insurance fraud can report to the OIFP and remain anonymous if he or she so chooses. Advertisements about the OIFP and this hot-line were heard and seen on radio and television during the fall of 1999.

The following are results of some of the groundbreaking OIFP investigations:
- Karen Lawder, a licensed clinical social worker, received a three-year prison sentence for committing health care claims fraud. She was the first person prosecuted under the state's new Health Care Claims Fraud Act in December 1998. Lawder had submitted at least five fictitious bills for health care services for which she received over $4,000 from health insurers.
- Dr. Jayen Shah was sentenced to five years in prison for second-degree attempted theft and third-degree theft. Shah pretended to be wheelchair-bound in order to collect insurance money. After he was caught on tape walking into a restaurant, a sting operation led to his arrest. His medical license was revoked, he paid a $45,000 civil penalty, and he repaid over $70,000 in undeserved disability payments to the Social Security Administration.
- Former psychologist Carl Lichtman received a 5½ year prison sentence for his role in a scheme that involved more than 200 "patients" and cost 35 insurance carriers and the state of New Jersey more than $3.5 million. North Jersey private-sector employees and school district employees (including a vice principal, 27 teachers, and 6 custodians) were among 65 people indicted for allegedly receiving kickbacks for being "no-show" patients or for receiving "referral fees" for participating in Lichtman's insurance fraud scheme.(2)

These are just a few examples of how insurance fraud offenders are punished. Other offenders who sell phony insurance cards and file false claims face similar fates. Insurance fraud is no laughing matter. It is estimated that this particular type of fraud may increase insurance bills and premiums as much as 15 percent.(1) Insurance fraud in New Jersey costs over $1 billion a year. Although in its early stages, New Jersey's experiment in fraud-busting is well on its way to success. Other states will likely follow in its footsteps.

Sources

1. Joe Donahue, "Slip and Fall? Better Be Prepared to Prove It," *Star Ledger* (Newark, N.J.), Sept. 12, 1999, pp. 33–34.
2. Department of Law and Public Safety, Office of the Insurance Fraud Prosecutor, "Initial Report of the Office of the Insurance Fraud Prosecutor: Pursuant to N.J.S.A. 17:33A-24d," Mar. 1, 1999 (http://www.njinsurancefraud.org).

Questions for Discussion

1. What type of punishment is appropriate for an insurance fraud offender?
2. What other types of laws and policies can be created in an attempt to prevent insurance fraud?

people thousands of miles away. The reach of motivated offenders has been considerably extended. Physical movement has been replaced by electronic travel, especially with the recognition that computers are global networks.

The type of property that is stolen or affected is also very different in nature. While other property crimes (arson, vandalism, theft, larceny, burglary) victimize concrete targets, high-tech crimes involve less-visible and tangible kinds of property such as information, data, and computer networks. In addition, many victims of high-tech crime realize they have been victimized only long after the crime has taken place. In most other property crimes there is often little time between the actual crime and the realization that a crime has taken place (as in cases of burglary or arson, for example).

Profits of Crime The profits from high-tech crimes are vast. The rise in the incidence of computer crime, for example, is a testament to its efficacy and the profit to be made. The British Banking Association in London estimates the cost of computer fraud worldwide at about $8 billion a year.[59] With the increasing sophistication of equipment, computer hackers are able to steal greater amounts with greater ease, and sometimes a single act can victimize multiple people or places at once.

Detection High-tech crime is also attractive to some individuals because they find evading detection and prosecution relatively easy. Few law enforcement agencies are equipped to detect the high-tech crimes occurring within their jurisdictions. Furthermore, since the nature of high-tech crime allows perpetrators to carry out their illegal activities without any geographic limitations, tracing high-tech criminal activity to the responsible individual is very difficult. Identifying the crime location becomes harder to do since street corners and physical space have been replaced by airwaves, cyberspace, and other electronic media. Often, by the time illegal activity has been detected, the criminals have already moved on to a new target.

Degree of Criminal Complexity Another important aspect of high-technology crimes involves the complicated nature of the crimes being committed. Every day, new crimes are being developed and refined by highly skilled computer users. Traditional law enforcement techniques are not designed to deal with such novel and complex crimes. High-tech criminals are, in a sense, sophisticated criminals. Stealing credit card numbers from the Internet for illicit purposes requires a certain degree of proficiency in Internet navigation, knowledge of how to break into the system to commit the thefts, and, finally, experience in using the stolen credit card numbers for criminal gain—all the while avoiding detection.

International Component Phone companies and computer network systems often advertise that using their services will allow individuals to communicate with people located at the other end of the globe. Such ease of electronic travel is appealing to high-tech criminals, who now participate in a modern phenomenon: global criminality. High-tech crimes can easily go beyond national boundaries, making them transnational crimes, a criminal activity of serious concern for targeted countries. Using a computer, a high-tech criminal can make illegal international money transfers, steal information from a computer located in another country, or diffuse illicit information (such as child pornography or terrorist propaganda) worldwide. The ability to detect and successfully deal with such criminal activities is a major challenge for law enforcement agencies around the world.

Computers and the Internet: Types of Crime[60]

High-tech criminals have also created their own crime types. While some seek the same ends as more traditional property offenders (financial gain), modern technology allows for novel and totally new crimes.

There are three main categories of computer crimes. First, the computer can be used as a storage or communication device whereby information can be created, stored, manipulated,

In 2003, officer Mike Casida of the Clovis, California police helped track down child pornographers as part of an investigation that spread over four continents. Eighteen people have been arrested in the United States.

and communicated electronically. In this instance, the computer is incidental, since it is not required for the crime itself, but is used in some way that is connected to the criminal activity. An example is financial records kept on a drug dealer's computer.

Second, the computer can be used as an instrument or a tool of crime. In this case, the computer is used to commit traditional offenses, such as the creation of counterfeit money or official documents, or newer computer crime offenses, such as the distribution of child pornography, confidence schemes, and illegal gambling networks on the Internet.

Finally, a computer can be used as a weapon to commit attacks on the confidentiality, integrity, and availability of information, including theft of information, theft of services, and damage to computer systems.[61] This type of computer crime involves the widespread problem of viruses and other forms of siege attacks, such as those referred to as "denial of service" attacks. The purpose of a denial of service attack is to prevent the normal operation of a digital system. It is often committed by "cyber vandals." An increasing number of electronic siege attacks employing some form of denial of service have been initiated against organizations worldwide in recent years.[62] In 1999 alone, 1154 computer intrusion calls were reported to the FBI.

Computer Network Break-Ins There are two types of computer network break-ins. The first is commonly known as "hacking." It is not practiced for criminal gain and can therefore be considered more mischievous than malicious. Nevertheless, network intrusions have been made illegal by the U.S. federal government. A hacker's reward is being able to tell peers that he or she has managed to break into a network, demonstrating superior computing ability, especially the ability to bypass security measures. Hackers, for the most part, seek entry into a computer system and "snoop around," often leaving no sign of entry. It can be likened to an individual's stealthily gaining entry into another person's house, going through a few personal belongings, and carefully leaving without taking anything.

The second type of break-in is the one done for illegal purposes. A criminal might break into a large credit card company to steal card numbers or into a network to steal data or sensitive

> **Did You Know?**
>
> ...that online auctions were named the number-one Internet fraud problem for 1998?

information. Other criminal acts include computer vandalism, whereby individuals break into a system, alter its operating structure, delete important files, change passwords, or plant viruses that can destroy operating systems, software programs, and data.

Industrial Espionage In an age where information can create power, it should not be surprising that competing industries are very curious to know what the others are doing. "Cyber spies" can be hired to break into a competitor's computer system and gather secret information, often leaving no trace of the intrusion. Once again, these spies have such powerful technology at their disposal that they are able to target computers and information that may be thousands of miles away, making detection even more difficult.

Software Piracy It is estimated by the U.S. Software-Publisher's Association that approximately $7.5 billion worth of American software is illegally copied and distributed annually worldwide. Software piracy ranges from friends sharing and occasionally copying software, to international fraudulent schemes whereby software is replicated and passed on as the original product, sometimes at a lower price. Recent research indicates that employees contribute significantly to the presence of illegal software in the workplace, either by bringing software from home (40 percent), downloading unauthorized copies from the Internet (24 percent), or sharing programs with other employees (24 percent).[63] The duplication process is relatively simple, and once mastered, any software can be pirated and copies sold worldwide. Software developers are constantly trying to stay ahead of the pirates by attempting to render their software resistant to such duplication. The advent of the compact disc and digital video disc unfortunately makes casual software piracy relatively easy.

Pornography Online The Internet provides a forum for the display of information. Some individuals, however, see this venue as a means to distribute or seek illegal information such as child pornography. Finding and downloading such material from the Internet is a simple task, even for amateur computer users. While law enforcement agencies occasionally intercept child pornography and those who engage in its dissemination over the airwaves, most offenders are never caught. Also, such material can be strategically hidden or altered to appear to be something else. "Morphing" is a practice that involves using computers to digitally alter pictures. Using such a method, an individual can superimpose two images or cut and paste parts of one image onto another. This technique has become a tool for child pornographers to evade prosecution. They simply attach the head of an adult to a child's body, and claim the image indeed portrays an adult.

Many cases of online pedophilia have been reported as well. A former employee of Infoseek, Patrick Naughton was a successful computer guru, who in 1990 helped develop the popular Java programming language at Sun Microsystems. However, his career ended in October 1999 when Naughton faced charges of online pedophilia after he arranged to meet a 13-year-old girl with whom he initiated contact in an online chat room. On arrival at a Santa Monica pier for a rendezvous with his online buddy, Naughton was met by FBI agents. The "13-year-old girl" turned out to be a male FBI agent.[64]

Pornography is finding itself online in other ways as well. In fact, Web pages are being "page-jacked." A recent scheme involved two hackers who cloned legitimate Web pages, including sites such as Audi and Paine Webber. When computer users attempted to reach the legitimate sites, they were "page-jacked" to pornographic websites. When attempting to escape the pornographic sites by clicking on the "Back" or "Home" buttons on their browsers, users were then "mouse-trapped" and sent to additional pornographic websites.[65]

The New York Times

Whose Identity Is It Anyway?

Kim Bradbury thought she was speaking to another annoying telemarketer when she heard it was First USA calling. It turned out the credit card company was calling to warn her. "Someone has applied for a credit card in your name," said the caller, "and it doesn't match other addresses we have for you."

It was later discovered that a lab assistant at Ms. Bradbury's former place of employment had stolen a box of personnel records. More than three dozen of these records were used to obtain about 75 credit cards, buy at least $100,000 in merchandise, open 20 cellular telephone accounts, and rent three apartments.

"People take this situation lightly, but once it happens to you it's a nightmare," said Ms. Bradbury, a biologist and the mother of two children. "I feel so violated, and I'm very, very angry."

Law enforcement authorities are becoming increasingly worried about the rise in identity theft, the pilfering of people's personal information for use in obtaining credit cards, loans, and other goods. Law-enforcement officials and consumer advocates say the Internet is making identity theft one of the signature crimes of the digital era. The Social Security Administration attributes the rise in identity theft to the ease with which social security data can be collected on the Internet.

Even a cursory tour through cyberspace turns up a host of vendors peddling personal information. One online company, Net Detective 8.0, promotes itself as "an amazing new tool that allows you to find out *everything* you ever wanted to know about your friends, family, neighbors, employees, and even your boss!"

If an identity thief needs to know someone's social security number, for example, it is easy enough to buy it on the Internet. One website, docusearch.com, will retrieve a person's social security number in one day for a $49 fee. Dan Cohn, the director of docusearch.com, said he got the numbers from "various sources" but that none of his company's services have contributed to identity theft. "Social security numbers are pretty much public numbers anyway," Mr. Cohn observed.

Social security numbers matched with other personal information enable identity thieves to apply for credit cards on the Internet, often with minimal scrutiny from issuers. And if an identity thief uses a credit card to briefly build up a solid credit history by paying off monthly bills, he or she then has the credibility to apply for big-ticket items like loans for cars and rental property.

Consumers rarely face monetary losses related to identity theft because merchants or banks are typically the ones stuck with bogus credit card charges. In addition, credit card issuers are generally vigilant about monitoring customers' buying patterns and flagging questionable transactions very quickly.

The real damage felt by consumers like Ms. Bradbury and other victims of identity theft is not monetary—it is emotional. Victims say they not only must face the reality that their financial privacy has been compromised by an anonymous thief, but also they often endure lengthy, painstaking struggles to clean up credit records that have been tarnished by identity thieves. In some of the worst cases, when identity thieves commit crimes and use their false identities to mislead police, victims of identity theft find themselves saddled with false criminal records.

To prevent identity theft, consumers should check their credit reports at least once a year by calling Equifax (1-800-525-6285), Trans Union (1-800-680-7289), or Experian (1-800-301-7195). If identity theft is suspected, consumers can call the Social Security Administration's Fraud Hot Line (1-800-269-0271) or the Federal Trade Commission's ID Theft Hot Line (1-877-IDTHEFT).

Source

Adapted from Timothy L. O'Brien, "Officials Worried over a Sharp Rise in Identity Theft," *New York Times,* Apr. 3, 2002. Reprinted with permission.

Questions for Discussion

1. Some lawmakers have suggested that it should be made more difficult—if not illegal—to purchase information like social security numbers from the Internet. Do you agree? Do you think, given the global reach of cyberspace, that this would be an enforceable law?
2. Do the owners of the information websites have any responsibility to monitor the dissemination of this type of information? Or are they just supplying information that the public can find elsewhere anyway?

Child pornography is easy to find on the Internet if you know where to go, for example, newsgroups, chatrooms, and bulletin boards. Popular search engines are highly suggestive, but rarely bring you to illegal images. Most "legal" sites are self-regulated, requiring an adult content alert and some form of registration.
©The Excite Network, Inc. All rights reserved. Reprinted with permisson.

Going after such offenders becomes difficult if different countries are involved in the illegal act. Let us suppose an individual in country A posts pornographic material on the Internet, and in country A, such material is legal. If the same material is retrieved in country B (although the source is country A), where the material is considered illegal, who is to blame, and where has the crime occurred? Jurisdictional questions about information found on the Internet remain largely unresolved. They will surely become more complex with the increasing traffic of illicit information and images.

Mail Bombings Computers can be used to steal money and information. They can also be used for more aggressive purposes. Like the bully told to rough up the new kid in the school yard, computers can be instructed to attack other machines. A common method is that of mail bombings. Mail bombs are the products of computer programs that instruct a computer to literally bombard another computer with information, often irrelevant electronic mail (email). Mail bombs are capable of shutting down computers, and even entire networks, if the amount of information is too large for the receiving computer to digest.

Password Sniffers Entry into a computer system often requires a password or some other form of user identification to protect the information it contains. Password sniffers are programs that carefully record the names and passwords of network users as they log in. With such confidential information, unauthorized users are able to gain unlawful access to the computer and the information it contains. Passwords can also be sold to other users for illegal purposes.

Credit Card Fraud Computers and the Internet are used more and more to conduct business. It has become commonplace to order merchandise, make payments, and conduct personal banking online. This use of credit cards is very appealing to people involved in credit card fraud. Computers can facilitate credit card fraud in two ways. First, a conventionally stolen credit card can be used to order merchandise online and, because no time is wasted going from store to store, a perpetrator can maximize his or her gain before the card is inactivated. Detection is also reduced since there is no physical contact with sales staff who might alert authorities should they suspect fraud. Second, credit card numbers can be stolen from the Internet as customers are making legitimate purchases. Programs similar to those that are designed to steal passwords from unsuspecting users are often used for this purpose. Another way of stealing credit card numbers is for offenders to access computers located in credit bureaus or financial institutions.

Currently, no one really knows the actual cost of computer crime. Estimates, however, suggest that the costs range from $500 million to $5 billion per year. Computer crime is underdetected and underreported. Furthermore, computer crime is not considered a major priority for many police departments. Greater attention and resources are focused on violent-crime-reduction efforts and, more recently, on community policing. Combating computer crime is not a priority for several reasons: It is difficult to police the Internet, and the necessary resources are not available to adequately handle this type of crime. There is no public outcry against computer crime, since the public is more interested in violent crime. Finally, many police officers feel that they did not choose their profession to police computer crime, but rather to help people and arrest the criminals.[66] Despite these problems, training programs on combating computer crime are being designed and implemented in some police departments.

> :// **Crime Surfing**
>
> https://www.ifccfbi.gov/
>
> Go to this website to report a potential online fraud.

Characteristics of the High-Tech Criminal

While all the crimes and deviant acts discussed so far rely heavily on technology, there are still human offenders behind them. Do these people, however, resemble other property criminals, or do they have distinct characteristics? It is true that modern technology is so widespread that virtually anyone is capable of high-tech crime, but it also remains a fact that most high-tech offenders, especially computer hackers, fit a rather unique profile. These individuals are usually young (14 to 19 years old) white males from middle-class backgrounds. They often possess superior levels of intelligence (IQ over 120), but on a social level they tend to be withdrawn and associate mainly with peers who share their fascination for electronic gadgets and computer-related activities. Some youths also believe that they are part of a counterculture, fighting censorship, liberating information, and challenging big business and major

David L. Smith, the 30-year-old computer programmer from New Jersey, who created the "Melissa" virus.

corporations.[67] In a way, they perceive themselves as modern-day Robin Hoods.

The Criminal Justice Problem

High-tech crimes pose a special problem to law enforcement agencies for two reasons. First, these crimes are not easily detected since the offenders can quietly commit them from any computer terminal, usually in the comfort of their own homes. Second, while a few organizations have mobilized to attack high-tech crime, most law enforcement agencies are not equipped to deal with the phenomenon: "Technology changes at an astounding rate while law enforcement techniques, which traditionally are reactionary, do not."[68] It is clear that the police forces of the future need to address this problem by concentrating on detection and by arming themselves with the technological tools necessary to deal with it. By necessity, computer and/or Internet classes should soon find their way into police academies.

BURGLARY

A "burg," in Anglo-Saxon terminology, was a secure place for the protection of oneself, one's family, and one's property. If the burg protects a person from larceny and assault, what protects the burg? The burghers, perhaps. But there had to be a law behind the burghers. And that was the law of burglary, which made it a crime to break and enter the dwelling of another person at night with the intention of committing a crime therein. (Of course it had to be at night, for during the day the inhabitants could defend themselves, or so it was thought.) The common law defined **burglary** as:

The breaking
And entering
Of the dwelling house
Of another person
At night
With the intention to commit a felony or larceny inside

By "breaking," the law meant any trespass (unauthorized entry), but usually one accompanied by a forceful act, such as cracking the lock, breaking a windowpane, or scaling the roof and entering through the chimney. The "entering" was complete as soon as the perpetrator extended any part of his or her body into the house in pursuit of the objective of committing a crime in the house. The house had to be a "dwelling," but that definition was extended to cover the "curtilage," the attached servants' quarters, carriage houses, and barns. The dwelling also had to be that of "another." And as we mentioned, the event had to occur at "night," between sundown and sunup.

The most troublesome element has always been the "intention to commit a felony or larceny" (even a petty or misdemeanor larceny) inside the premises. How can we know what a burglar intends to do? The best evidence of intent is what the burglar actually does inside the premises: Steal jewelry? Commit a rape? Set the house afire? Any crime the burglar commits inside is considered evidence of criminal intention at the moment the burglar broke and entered the dwelling.[69]

Today burglary is no longer limited to night attacks, although by statute the crime may be considered more serious if it is committed at night. Statutes have also added buildings other than dwellings to the definition. The UCR defines burglary simply as the unlawful entry into a structure (criminal trespass) to commit a felony or theft. The use of force to gain entry is not a required element of burglary under the UCR.

> **Theory Connects**
>
> **Burglary**
>
> Rational choice theories, when first imported to criminology, were used to explain residential burglary. What insights can you bring from rational choice theory to the practical effort of crime prevention?

Burglary rates have consistently declined over the past decade. Even so, in 2001, almost 2.1 million burglaries were reported to the police, with an overall loss of $3.3 billion. These crimes account for nearly a fifth of all Index offenses. Most burglaries (87 percent) are not cleared by arrests.[70]

Criminologists ask questions about the characteristics of offenders who commit burglaries and of the places that are burglarized. Neal Shover described the "good burglar" as one having competence, personal integrity, a specialty in burglary, financial success, and an ability to avoid prison.[71] Another study demonstrated that burglars are versatile, committing a wide range of offenses, but that they do specialize in burglary for short periods of time. Compared with male burglars, female burglars begin offending at a later age, more often commit burglaries with others, and have fewer contacts with the criminal justice system.[72]

Recent research on burglary asks questions not only about who is likely to commit a burglary or what distinguishes one burglar from another. In addition, as we notice in Chapter 9, criminologists are looking, for instance, at the process that leads to the burglary of a particular house in a specific neighborhood—that is, how a burglar discriminates between individual areas and targets when there are so many alternatives—and ways to make the process of burglary more difficult for any burglar.

FENCING: RECEIVING STOLEN PROPERTY

We are treating burglary as a property crime. An occasional burglar enters with the intention of committing rape, arson, or some other felony inside the building. But most burglars are thieves; they are looking for cash and for other property that can be turned into cash. Burglars and thieves depend on a network of fences to turn stolen property into cash.

Jonathan Wild controlled the London underworld from about 1714 until his hanging in 1725. For over 2½ centuries he has captured the imagination of historians, social scientists, and writers. Henry Fielding wrote *The Life of Mr. Jonathan Wild, the Great,* and Mack the Knife in John Gay's *Beggar's Opera* was modeled on Wild. Wild was known as a "thief-taker." Thief-takers made an occupation of capturing thieves and claiming the rewards offered for their arrest. By law, thief-takers were allowed to keep the possessions of the thieves they caught, except objects that had been stolen, which were returned to their owners.

Wild added a devious twist to his trade: He bought stolen goods from thieves and sold them back to their rightful owners. The owners paid much more than the thief could get from the usual fences, so both Wild and the thief made a considerable profit. To thieves, he was a fellow thief; to honest people, he was a legitimate citizen helping them get back their property. Playing both roles well, he ran competing fencing operations out of business, employed about 7,000 thieves, and became the most famous fence of all time.[73]

A **fence** is a person who buys stolen property, on a regular basis, for resale. Fences, or dealers in stolen property, operate much like legitimate businesses: They buy and sell for profit. Their activity thrives on an understanding of the law governing the receiving of stolen property, on cooperation with the law when necessary, and on networking. The difference between a legitimate business and a fencing operation is that the channeling of stolen goods takes place in a clandestine environment (created by law enforcement and deviant associates) with high risks and with a need to justify one's activities in the eyes of conventional society.

Carl Klockars's *Professional Fence* and Darrell Steffensmeier's *Fence*, each focusing on the life of a particular fence, present us with fascinating accounts of this criminal business. The proprietors of such businesses deal in almost any commodity. "Oh, I done lots of business with him," said Klockars's fence, Vincent Swazzi. "One time I got teeth, maybe five thousand teeth in one action. You know, the kind they use for making false teeth—you see, you never know what a thief's gonna come up with." And many fences are quite proud of their positions in the community. Said Swazzi, "The way I look at it, this is actually my street. I mean I am the mayor. I walk down the street an' people come out the doors to say hello."[74]

Until recently it was believed that professional thieves and fences were totally interdependent and that their respective illegal activities were mutually reinforcing. Recent research, however, demonstrates a change in the market for stolen goods. D'Aunn Webster Avery, Paul F. Cromwell, and James N. Olson conducted extensive interviews with 38 active burglars, shoplifters, and their fences and concluded that it is no longer the professional fence who takes care of stolen goods but, rather, occasional receivers—otherwise honest citizens—who buy from thieves directly or at flea markets.[75] This willingness to buy merchandise that the buyers must at least suspect has been stolen may indicate that the general public is more tolerant of stealing than previous generations were.

ARSON

The crimes against property that we have discussed so far involve the illegitimate transfer of possession. The property in question is "personal property" rather than real property, or real estate. Only two types of property crime are concerned with real property. Burglary is one; the other is arson.

The common law defined **arson** as the malicious burning of or setting fire to the dwelling of another person. Modern statutes have distinguished degrees of severity of the offense and have increased its scope to include other structures and even personal property, such as automobiles. The most severe punishments are reserved for arson of dwellings, because of the likelihood that persons in the building may be injured or die.

Arson always has been viewed as a more violent crime than burglary. In comparison with burglary, however, arson is a fairly infrequent offense. A total of 76,760 arson offenses were reported in 2001.[76] A national survey of fire departments, however, indicates that the actual number of arson incidents is likely to be far higher than the reported figure.[77]

Buildings were the most frequent targets (42.2 percent); 32.5 percent of the targets were mobile property (motor vehicles, trailers, and the like); and crops and timber constituted 25.4 percent.[78] The annual estimated property loss is over $2 billion. In 1993, 560 civilian lives were lost as a result of suspicious fires.[79]

The seriousness of this crime is demonstrated by a series of spectacular fires set in resort hotels in such cities as San Juan, Puerto Rico (in conjunction with a labor dispute), and Las Vegas, Nevada. Although these fires were not set with the intent to kill any of the people in the buildings, many lives were lost. The inferno created by arsonists in the Du Pont Plaza Hotel in San Juan in 1987 killed 97 people. The arson at the Las Vegas Hilton caused no deaths but did result in $14 million in damages, not including the loss of business.

While insurance fraudsters and organized-crime figures may be responsible for some of the more spectacular arsons, it is juveniles who account for the single most significant share. Consider the following statistics:

- In 2001 juveniles under age 18 accounted for about 50 percent of the arson arrests nationwide.[80]

- Juveniles under age 15 accounted for about 32 percent of arson arrests.

- Of children in grades 1 to 8 in Rochester, New York, 38 percent admitted playing with fire.[81]

- Of the 18,749 arrests (adult and juvenile) for arson in 2001, 84 percent were males, 77 percent were white, and 21 percent were black.[82]

- There was a 1 percent increase arson offenses nationwide between 2000 and 2001, with a 7 percent increase in cities with populations between 50,000 and 99,999.[83]

Why do children set fires?[84] Recent research suggests that the motive may be psychological pain, anger, revenge, need for attention, malicious mischief, or excitement.[85] Juvenile fire setters have been classified in three groups: the playing-with-matches fire setter, the crying-for-help fire setter, and the severely disturbed fire setter.[86] Many juvenile fire setters are in urgent need of help. In response to their needs, juvenile arson intervention programs have been established in recent years.[87]

An interesting English study found that while arsonists were in many respects comparable to offenders classified as violent, they had a lower incidence of interpersonal aggression and rated themselves as less assertive than did violent offenders—perhaps because, as the study showed, arsonists were taken into care at an earlier age.[88] The motives of adult arsonists are somewhat different from those of juveniles. Though here, too, we find disturbed offenders (pyromaniacs) and people who set fires out of spite. We are also much more likely to encounter insurance fraudsters, as well as organized-crime figures who force compliance or impose revenge by burning establishments (the "torches").[89] One classification of fire setters by motive includes:

- Revenge, jealousy, and hatred
- Financial gain (mostly insurance fraud)
- Intimidation and/or extortion (often involving organized crime)
- Need for attention
- Social protest
- Arson to conceal other crimes
- Arson to facilitate other crimes
- Vandalism and accidental fire setting[90]

As arson continues to be a serious national problem, policy makers have been developing two distinct approaches for dealing with it. The offender-specific approach focuses on educational outreach in schools and the early identification of troubled children, for purposes of counseling and other assistance.[91] The offense-specific (geographic) approach focuses on places. It seeks to identify areas with a high potential for arson. The aim is to deploy arson specialists to correct problems and to stabilize endangered buildings and neighborhoods.[92]

COMPARATIVE CRIME RATES

The rates of property crime are much higher than those of the violent crime we discuss in Chapter 10. It is interesting to compare these rates for various regions of the world. If we compare the property-owning, consumer-oriented countries of the industrialized Western world with the still largely agricultural but rapidly urbanizing countries of the Third World, we note a significant discrepancy: The rate of theft per 100,000 in the developed countries was 4,200, while the rate in developing countries was 600.[93]

Recall the Coca-Cola bottle that disrupted the lives of the aborigines in *The Gods Must Be Crazy*. We just may have discovered the secret of that bottle: If there is no Coke bottle, no one is going to steal it. The more property people have, especially portable property, the more opportunity other people have to make off with it. Europeans have an old saying: "Opportunity makes thieves." The foremost opportunity for theft may simply be an abundance of property.

REVIEW

Not all crimes against property are aimed at acquiring such property. A burglar invades a dwelling or other structure usually—but not necessarily—to commit a larceny inside. An arsonist endangers the existence of the structure and its occupants. Both amateurs and professionals commit property crimes of all sorts. Each new form of legitimate trade, such as the development of credit cards and computers, offers criminals new opportunities to exploit the situation for gain. It is evident that most high-tech offenders are quite sophisticated and, given the vastness of such technological wonders as the Internet, a new challenge lies ahead for social scientists and criminal justice professionals alike.

Some property-oriented crimes, as we will see in Chapter 12, depend not only on the cunning and daring of the perpetrator who targets a lone victim, but on the normal business operations of legitimate enterprises.

CRIMINOLOGY & PUBLIC POLICY

In the mid 1990s, fear of violent crime hit Californian voters with vengeance. Reeling from the vicious crimes of repeat offenders, like Richard Allen Davis, Californians lobbied their state representatives for legislative change. Davis, a twice convicted kidnapper, abducted 12 year old Polly Klass, murdering her soon thereafter. In 1994, the year following Klass's killing, the state legislature passed a "Three Strikes" law, requiring prison terms of 25 years to life for any offender convicted of a third felony after two prior ones. The United States

Supreme Court reviewed the California law this term, considering whether or not the law should be applied if the third strike is for a lesser offense—a misdemeanor. (Source: Adapted from: http://www.sentencingproject.org/pubs/3strikes.pdf)

Questions for Discussion Do you think it is fair to sentence a person to prison for life for petty theft or shoplifting-after they two prior felony convictions? Would it change your mind if the intent of three strikes laws is to deter felonies (serious crimes)?

YOU BE THE CRIMINOLOGIST

Computers are now part of our everyday lives at work, or in school, or at home as vehicles to pay bills, shop online, or simply surf the Internet. With the growing use of computers in all facets of our lives, the potential for misuse increases as well. This chapter has discussed some of the most pressing issues at the heart of computer crimes, including online credit card fraud, the use of the Internet in promoting child pornography, viruses and worms that invade the hard drives of computers, and software piracy. Select at least two forms of computer crime. What, in your opinion, are the causes of and the motivations for committing such crimes? What specifically does the offender stand to gain? Describe ways to counteract the problem. What can be done to prevent this emerging type of property crime?

KEY TERMS

The numbers next to the terms refer to the pages on which the terms are defined.

arson (312)
burglary (310)
check forging (299)
confidence game (298)
false pretenses, obtaining property by (299)
fence (311)
fraud (298)
high-tech crime (302)
larceny (290)
shoplifting (292)

CHAPTER 12
White-Collar and Corporate Crime

Defining White-Collar Crime
Crimes Committed by Individuals
Types of White-Collar Crimes

Corporate Crime
Frequency and Problems of Definition
Phases of Corporate Criminal Law
Theories of Corporate Liability
Models of Corporate Culpability
Governmental Control of Corporations
Investigating Corporate Crime
Environmental Crimes
Curbing Corporate Crimes
The Future of White Collar and Corporate Crime

REVIEW

CRIMINOLOGY & PUBLIC POLICY

YOU BE THE CRIMINOLOGIST

KEY TERMS

Boxes
Window to the World: Tracking Progress in the Fight against Corruption: The Emergence of a National Integrity System
From the Pages of The New York Times: *Rare Reviews or Questionable Quotes? Deceptive Advertising Goes to the Movies*
Of Immediate Concern: Dangerous Ground: The World of Hazardous Waste Crime

Special Features
Crime Surfing
Did You Know?
Theory Connects

KEY TERMS
bankruptcy fraud
boiler rooms
churning
consumer fraud
corporate compliance programs
corporate crime
corporate due diligence
corporate ethos
corporate policy
disgorgement
embezzlement
insider trading
occupational crimes
proactive corporate faults
reactive corporate faults
Sherman Antitrust Act
stock manipulation
vicarious liability
whistle-blower
white-collar crime

Once the nation's seventh largest company, Enron filed for bankruptcy after multiple disclosures of fraud. Enron's collapse in December 2001 shocked Wall Street.

David Duncan, a fired Arthur Andersen LLP partner, took the witness stand a week into the criminal trial of Andersen in May 2002, and admitted that he intentionally obstructed justice when he asked his employees to shred documents relating to the Enron Corporation. "Yes, I obstructed justice. I instructed people on the [Enron audit] team to follow the document retention policy, which I knew would result in the destruction of documents." Duncan's statements all but sealed the fate of the Arthur Andersen partnership—one of the largest and most highly respected accounting firms in the world. Andersen (as a partnership) was convicted of obstruction of justice nearly a month later and is now in bankruptcy—one more casualty in the latest round of corporate scandals.

Add Tyco International CEO Kozlowski to this list of scandals for possible tax evasion. Next, add CEO Rigas of Adelphia for securities fraud charges. We cannot help but mention Enron for securities, insider trading, and perjury charges against senior management and fraud charges against the company. Daily, the list of casualties appears never ending, with recent allegations of insider trading and securities fraud in Global Crossing; and high profile civil investigations of Worldcom, Qwest, Martha Stewart, Dynegy, CMS Energy, El Paso Corp., Halliburton, and Williams Cos.

* * *

"This is not our proudest day," said Donald J. Carty, chairman of AMR Corporation, the parent company of American Airlines. Prosecutors in Miami, Florida, felt otherwise. On December 16, 1999, one of the nation's largest airlines pleaded guilty to transporting hazardous and poisonous materials on its passenger jets for more than five years. The passengers and employees of American Airlines were placed at risk by the dangerous handling of hazardous materials, according to Assistant

317

Attorney General Lois Schiffer. The airline was fined $8 million and placed on probation for three years. It agreed to place a full-page advertisement in the *Miami Herald* apologizing for its actions.

The potential for harm from illegally transporting hazardous materials is a matter of great public concern. This case comes on the heels of the conviction of Sabre Tech, Inc. in federal court on eight counts of recklessly mishandling hazardous materials, leading to the crash of ValuJet Flight 592, in May 1996. The DC-9, on route to Atlanta, plunged into the Everglades after catching on fire. Experts trace the cause of the fire to improperly packaged oxygen canisters in the cargo hold. All 110 people aboard were killed. Sabre Tech, Inc. still faces felony murder charges in state court.[1]

What do all of these crimes have in common? White-collar, corporate, and organized crimes all involve business enterprises.[2] It is the use of a legitimate or illegitimate business enterprise for illegal profit that distinguishes organizational crimes from other types of offenses. Organizational offenses are also different in another important respect. Unlike violent crimes and property offenses, which the Model Penal Code classifies quite neatly, organizational offenses are a heterogeneous mix of crimes, from homicide, fraud, and conspiracy to racketeering and the violation of a host of federal environmental statutes.

DEFINING WHITE-COLLAR CRIME

With a daily barrage of media reports on the latest corporate scandal—from allegations of insider trading by Martha Stewart to reports of ex–General Electric's CEO Jack Welch's outlandish compensation—it is only natural to think that we are in the midst of an unprecedented wave of white-collar and corporate crime. Anecdotal evidence aside, there is no empirical evidence that much, if anything, has changed.

Not surprisingly, politicians seized the opportunity to call for corporate reforms in light of almost daily accusations of illegalities. With little reflection, President Bush signed the Sarbanes-Oxley Act of 2002 to quell public concerns over the legitimacy and integrity of the markets. This act adopts tough provisions to deter and punish corporate and accounting fraud and corruption.

According to a press release from the White House, the act "ensures justice for wrongdoers, and protects the interests of workers and shareholders. This bill improves the quality and transparency of financial reporting, independent audits, and accounting services for public companies."

To its credit, the Sarbanes-Oxley Act of 2002 does the following:

- Creates a public company accounting oversight board to enforce professional standards, ethics, and competence for the accounting profession
- Acts to strengthen the independence of firms that audit public companies
- Increases corporate responsibility and the usefulness of corporate financial disclosure
- Increases penalties for corporate wrongdoing
- Protects the objectivity and independence of securities analysts
- Increases Securities and Exchange Commission resources

Perhaps most noteworthy, CEOs and chief financial officers must personally vouch for

Martha Stewart, an icon of good homemaking, is accused of selling thousands of share of ImClone Systems, Inc., stock just prior to the company's announcement that it failed to receive Food and Drug Administration approval for an anti-cancer drug. Was this insider trading? Did she trade on material, nonpublic information?

the truth and fairness of their company's disclosures.

For those who think that the problem of white-collar and corporate crime is young, consider that in ancient Greece public officials reportedly violated the law by purchasing land slated for government acquisition. Much of what we today define as white-collar crime, however, is the result of laws passed within the last century. For example, the Sherman Antitrust Act, passed by Congress in 1890, authorized the criminal prosecution of corporations engaged in monopolistic practices.[3] Federal laws regulating the issuance and sale of stocks and other securities were passed in 1933 and 1934. In 1940 Edwin H. Sutherland provided criminologists with the first scholarly account of white-collar crime. He defined it as crime "committed by a person of respectability and high social status in the course of his occupation."[4]

The conviction of Arthur Andersen, LLP, demonstrates that Sutherland's definition is not entirely satisfactory: White-collar crime can be committed by a corporation as well as by an individual. As Gilbert Geis has noted, Sutherland's work is limited by his own definition. He has a "striking inability to differentiate between the corporations themselves and their executive management personnel."[5] Other criminologists have suggested that the term "white-collar crime" not be used at all; we should speak instead of "corporate crime" and "occupational crime."[6] Generally, however, **white-collar crime** is defined as a violation of the law committed by a person or group of persons in the course of an otherwise respected and legitimate occupation or business enterprise[7] (see Table 12.1).

Just as white-collar and corporate offenses include a heterogeneous mix of corporate and individual crimes, from fraud, deception, and corruption (as in the S&L case) to pollution of the environment, victims of white-collar crime range from the savvy investor to the unsuspecting consumer. No one person or group is immune[8] (see Table 12.2). The Vatican lost millions of dollars in a fraudulent stock scheme; fraudulent charities have swindled fortunes from unsuspecting investors; and many banks have been forced into bankruptcy by losses due to deception and fraud.[9] Perhaps as important, public perceptions of the legitimacy of financial institutions and markets have been undermined, at least in part, by allegations of corporate abuses.

> **Theory Connects**
>
> **Crimes Committed by Individuals (White-Collar Crime)**
>
> To what extent does Robert Merton's strain theory (page 215) offer an explanation for such white-collar crimes as embezzlement and tax fraud?

Crimes Committed by Individuals

As we have noted, white-collar crime occurs during the course of a legitimate occupation or business enterprise. Over time socioeconomic developments have increasingly changed the

TABLE 12.1 The NIBRS Classifications of White-Collar Offenses

Criminal Behavior	
Academic crime	Insider trading
Adulterated food, drugs, or cosmetics	Insufficient funds checks
Antitrust violations	Insurance fraud
ATM fraud	Investment scams
Bad checks	Jury tampering
Bribery	Kickback
Check kiting	Land sale frauds
Combinations in restraint of trade	Mail fraud
Computer crime	Managerial fraud
Confidence game	Misappropriation
Contract fraud	Monopoly in restraint of trade
Corrupt conduct by juror	Ponzi schemes
Counterfeiting	Procurement fraud
Defense contract fraud	Racketeering Influenced and Corrupt Organizations (RICO)
Ecology law violations	Religious fraud
Election law violations	Sports bribery
Embezzlement	Strategic bankruptcy
Employment agency and education-related scams	Subornation or perjury
Environmental law violations	Swindle
False advertising and misrepresentation of products	Tax law violations
False and fraudulent actions on loans, debts, and credits	Telemarketing or boiler room scams
False pretenses	Telephone fraud
False report/statement	Travel scams
Forgery	Unauthorized use of a motor vehicle [lawful access but the entrusted vehicle is misappropriated]
Fraudulent checks	
Health and safety laws	Uttering
Health care providers fraud	Uttering bad checks
Home improvement frauds	Welfare fraud
Impersonation	Wire fraud
Influence peddling	

Source: Cynthia Barnett, *The Measurement of White-Collar Crime Using Uniform Crime Reporting (UCR) Data* (Washington, D.C.: Department of Justice, 2000).

dimensions of such crimes.[10] Once, people needed only a few business relationships to make their way through life. They dealt with an employer or with employees. They dealt on a basis of trust and confidence with the local shoemaker and grocer. They had virtually no dealings with government.

This way of life has changed significantly and very rapidly during the past few decades. People have become dependent on large bureaucratic structures; they are manipulated by agents and officials with whom they have no personal relationship. This situation creates a basis for potential abuses in four sets of relations:

TABLE 12.2 Victims of White-Collar Crime (NIBRS)

	Total	Property	Fraud	Bribery	Counterfeiting	Embezzlement
Total victims	5,886,566	4,069,324	103,993	198	110,545	21,356
Individual	3,998,310	2,621,843	47,826	143	45,270	3,006
Business	934,469	934,469	47,907	16	55,676	17,627
Financial Institution	11,378	11,378	2,989	0	5,310	182
Government	73,623	73,623	3,844	36	2,949	260
Religious Organization	10,794	10,794	70	0	104	35
Society or Other	857,992	417,217	1,357	3	1,236	246

Source: Cynthia Barnett, The *Measurement of White-Collar Crime Using Uniform Crime Reporting (UCR) Data* (Washington, D.C.: Department of Justice, 2000).

- Employees of large entities may abuse their authority for private gain by making their services to members of the public contingent on a bribe, a kickback, or some other favor. A corrupt employee of an insurance company, for example, may write a favorable claim assessment in exchange for half of the insurance payment.

- Taking advantage of the complexity and anonymity of a large organization, such as a corporation, employees may abuse the systems available to them or the power they hold within the structure for purposes of unlawful gain, as by embezzlement.

- Members of the public who have to deal with a large organization do not have the faith and trust they had when they dealt with individual merchants. If they see an opportunity to defraud a large organization, they may seize it in the belief that the organization can easily absorb the loss and nobody will be hurt.

- Since the relation of buyer to seller (or of service provider to client) has become increasingly less personal in an age of medical group practice, HMOs, large law firms, and drugstore chains, opportunities for **occupational crimes**—crimes committed by individuals for themselves in the course of rendering a service—have correspondingly increased. Medicare fraud, misuse of clients' funds by lawyers and brokers, substitution of inferior goods—all such offenses are occupational crimes.[11]

Ricky Churchwell, former chancery clerk from Lucedale, Mississippi, was indicted on 15 counts of embezzlement in July 2002. Churchwell is the fourth clerk in four years to be indicted in Mississippi.

Types of White-Collar Crimes

White-collar crimes are as difficult to detect as they are easy to commit.[12] The detection mechanisms on which police and government traditionally rely seem singularly inadequate for this vast new body of crimes. Moreover, though people have learned through the ages to be wary of strangers on the street, they have not yet learned to protect themselves against vast enterprises. Much more scientific study has to be undertaken on the causes, extent, and characteristics of white-collar crimes before we can develop workable prevention strategies.[13]

Eight categories of white-collar offenses committed by individuals can be identified:

- Securities-related crimes
- Bankruptcy fraud
- Fraud against the government
- Consumer fraud
- Insurance fraud
- Tax fraud
- Bribery, corruption, and political fraud
- Insider-related fraud[14]

Let us briefly examine each type of crime.

Securities-Related Crimes State and federal securities laws seek to regulate both the registration and issuance of a security and the employment practices of personnel in the securities industries. After the stock market crash on October 26, 1929, the federal government enacted a series of regulatory laws, including the Securities Act of 1933 and the Securities Exchange Act of 1934, aimed at prohibiting manipulation and deceptive practices. The 1934 act provided for the establishment of the Securities and Exchange Commission (SEC), an organization with broad regulatory and enforcement powers. The SEC is empowered to initiate civil suits and administrative actions and to refer criminal cases to the U.S. Department of Justice.

> **Theory Connects**
>
> Rational Choice theory (Chapter 9) predicts that crimes are committed by rational persons who carefully weigh the costs and benefits of their actions. To what extent does Rational Choice theory offer explanations for the wide range of white collar crimes?

Crime in the securities field remains common. The problem of securities fraud was made more apparent in recent years with some notable cases. The significance of the problem, however, is highlighted by the sheer size of the equities market.

Four kinds of offenses are prevalent: churning, trading on insider information, stock manipulation, and boiler-room operations.

Churning is the practice of trading a client's shares of stock frequently in order to generate large commissions. A broker earns a commission on every trade, so whether or not the stock traded increases or decreases in value, the broker makes money. Churning is difficult to prove, because brokers typically are allowed some discretion. Therefore, unless the client has given the broker specific instructions in writing, a claim of churning often amounts to no more than the client's word against the broker's.

Insider trading is the use of material, nonpublic, financial information to obtain an unfair advantage in trading securities.[15] A person who has access to confidential corporate information may make significant profits by buying or selling stock on the strength of that information. The prototype case of insider trading was against Dennis Levine. Levine, a 34-year-old managing director of the securities firm formerly known as Drexel Burnham Lambert, used insider information to purchase stock for himself and others in such corporations as International Telephone and Telegraph, Sperry Corporation, Coastal Corporation, American National Resources, and McGraw Edison. After the SEC found out, Levine implicated other Wall Street executives—including Ivan Boesky, who had made millions of dollars in illegal profits.

Stock manipulation is common in the "pink sheets" over-the-counter market, in which some stocks are traded at very low prices, but it is by no means limited to such stocks. Brokers who have a stake in a particular security may make misleading or even false statements to clients to give the impression that the price of the stock is about to rise and thus to create an artificial demand for it.

Boiler rooms are operations run by stock manipulators who, through deception and misleading sales techniques, seduce unsuspecting and uninformed individuals into buying stocks in obscure and often poorly financed corporations. Significant federal and state legislation has been passed (Penny Stock Reform Act of 1990) to curtail these operations, but the manipulation continues. The problem is particularly significant in Florida where the state has warned the public.

Bankruptcy Fraud The filing of a bankruptcy petition results in proceedings in which the property and financial obligations of an insolvent person or corporation are disposed of. Bankruptcy proceedings are governed by laws enacted to protect insolvent debtors. Unscrupulous persons have devised numerous means to commit **bankruptcy fraud**—any scam designed to take advantage of loopholes in the bankruptcy laws. The most common are the "similar-name" scam,

Dr. Samuel Waksal, former chief executive officer, ImClone Systems, Inc., testifies before the U.S. House Energy and Commerce Subcommittee on Oversight and Investigations hearing on "An Inquiry into the ImClone Cancer-Drug Story" in Washington on June 13, 2002. On June 10, 2003, he was sentenced to over seven years in jail and ordered to pay $4 million in back taxes and fines.

Fired Arthur Andersen auditor David Duncan, right, listens to his attorney Robert Giuffra on Capitol Hill Thursday, January 24, 2002, before a House Energy subcommittee hearing on the destruction of Enron-related documents. Duncan cited his Fifth Amendment rights, declining to testify to Congress about anything he knows or anything he did in the destruction of Enron documents.

the "old-company" scam, the "new-company" technique, and the "successful-business" scam.

The similar-name scam involves the creation of a corporation that has a name similar to that of an established firm. The objective is to create the impression that this new company is actually the older one. If the trick is successful, the swindlers place large orders with established suppliers and quickly resell any merchandise they receive, often to fences. At the same time the swindlers remove all money and assets of the corporation and either file for bankruptcy or wait until creditors sue. Then they leave the jurisdiction or adeptly erase their tracks.

The old-company scam involves employees of an already established firm who, motivated by a desire for quick profits, bilk the company of its money and assets and file for bankruptcy. Such a scam is typically used when the company is losing money or has lost its hold on a market.

The new-company scam is much like the similar-name scam: A new corporation is formed, credit is obtained, and orders are placed. Once merchandise is received, it is converted into cash with the assistance of a fence. By the time the company is forced into bankruptcy, the architects of this scheme have liquidated the corporation's assets.

The successful-business scam involves a profitable corporation that is well positioned in a market but experiences a change in ownership. After the new owners have bilked the corporation of all its money and assets, the firm is forced into bankruptcy.

The Federal Bureau of Investigation estimates that 10 percent of all bankruptcy filings involve fraud. On average, in recent years, this suggests that approximately 250 fraudulent bankruptcies were filed every day. Two-thirds of these cases involve some form of hidden assets.

The FBI launched a series of joint undercover investigations with multiple field offices, for example, Remington Raider and Total Disclosure. Operation Total Disclosure alone resulted in the arrest of 110 bankruptcy fraud subjects.

> **:// Crime Surfing**
>
> www.ojp.usdoj.gov/ovc/ncvrw/1999/cost.htm
>
> How much does crime cost society? Consider the estimates of street crimes from a host of different sources. Then determine how you would go about assessing the costs associated with white-collar and corporate crime.

Window to the World

Tracking Progress in the Fight against Corruption: The Emergence of a National Integrity System

Over the years, Transparency International (TI) has been leading the fight against global corruption. Most recently, TI has engaged in an audit of the "national integrity system" (NIS) of more than 20 countries. NIS is a comprehensive method—a holistic approach—to fighting corruption comprised of interdependent pillars (e.g., public awareness, public anticorruption strategies, public participation, "watchdog" agencies, the judiciary, the media, the private sector, and international cooperation) (see table). The core objectives are simple but exceedingly difficult to achieve: first, combat corruption as part of the larger struggle against misconduct and misappropriation. Second, create an efficient and effective government working in the public interest. Honesty, integrity, and good governance must go hand in hand to achieve democracy.

Combating corruption, the scourge of democracy, requires vigilant monitoring. "Monitoring corruption cannot be left only to public prosecutors and to the forces of law and order,"[1] according to TI. Investigatory and prosecutorial resources are insufficient. But there is some hope. As one of the founders of TI concludes, "Although corruption can never be completely monitored, it can be controlled through a combination of ethical codes, decisive legal prosecutions against offenders, organizational changes, and institutional reform."[1]

To make this effort real, countries have to engage in corruption proofing—to use existing laws against corruption, to fight countervailing political influences, lack of commitment, and greed and self-interest. They also have to ensure both vertical and horizontal accountability. The former requires accountability that originates at the top of the political system and filters down. The latter concerns accountability between and among agencies and organizations charged with combating corruption.

Countries must rely on the NIS pillars, from a firm political will to fight corruption; the rule of law; a strong, independent, and informed judiciary; independent anticorruption agencies; to a law-abiding private sector.

Recent audits of NIS countries reveal the obvious—corruption and social development are inextricably connected. As the table reveals, many countries have a long way to go. According to the most recent TI report on NIS, "The nature, levels and impact of corruption are very much reflective of a country's development and current political and institutional configuration although there may also be degrees of similarity between countries with similar development trajectories or similar types (for example, the specific issues of micro-states are reflected in both Fiji and Trinidad and Tobago). On the other hand, while both Argentina and Brazil reflect similar concerns and issues that may be linked to wide social disparities, the impact of economic growth and authoritarian political traditions, they also have very different backgrounds, traditions, and directions that might also indicate that the former has been experiencing economic shrinkage for many years—which the latter has not—and has a healthier and more intense political participation than the latter."[2]

Jeremy Pope, one of the founders of TI, has written that "It is exceptionally difficult to measure the progress being made in countering corruption in any given country, yet without knowing whether progress is being made, it is impossible to know if efforts are succeeding. Perceptions are not enough. We need to know much more about underlying realities."[1] The NIS is a significant step forward toward understanding the realities of corruption.

Sources

1. J. Pope, ed, *The TI Source Book*. (Berlin, Germany: Transparency International, 1997), p. 19.
2. Transparency International, National Integrity System, 2001, at http://www.transparency.org/activities/nat_integ_systems/dnld/overviewreport.pdf.

Questions for Discussion

1. Which of the NIS pillars do you suppose are most effective?
2. How do these pillars differentiate the progress made in the United States from countries with perceived "high" rates of corruption?

Fraud against the Government Governments at all levels are victims of a vast amount of fraud, which includes collusion in bidding, payoffs and kickbacks to government officials, expenditures by a government official that exceed the budget, the filing of false claims, the hiring of friends or associates formerly employed by the government, and offers of inducements to government officials.

Consider, for example, the fall of Wedtech—a military contractor with annual sales in excess of $100 million. At one time the Wedtech Corporation was hailed as the first major employer of blacks and Hispanics in New York City's blighted

THE OBJECTIVES, ELEMENTS, AND PILLARS OF A NATIONAL INTEGRITY SYSTEM

NIS Objectives

- Mechanisms supporting accountability and transparency in the democratic process, such as parliamentary and electoral processes
- Building a creative partnership between government and civil society organizations
- Administrative reform and countering conflict of interest in the public service
- Administrative law as a common element in any system of probity and accountability of decision-makers
- Appropriate mechanisms which provide public officials with channels for reporting acts of alleged corruption and also ensure independent monitoring of procedures and systems
- Independence of judiciary and ensuring that legal procedures and remedies provide an effective deterrent to corruption
- An open, genuinely competitive and transparent system of public procurement
- Private sector self-regulation and the role of legal deterrence against corrupt practice
- An alert press, free to discharge its role as public watchdog and increase public awareness of right and responsibilities
- Independent anti-corruption agencies and cooperation with other countries to assist in combating international corruption

Elements of the NIS

- Clear commitment by leaders
- Emphasis on preventing corruption and changing systems, not witch hunts
- Comprehensive anticorruption legislation implemented by agencies of manifest integrity
- Identification of government activities that are most prone to corruption and a review of both substantive law and administrative procedures
- A program to ensure adequate salaries of civil servants and political leaders
- A study of legal and administrative remedies to ensure they provide adequate deterrence
- The creation of a partnership between government and all elements of civil society
- Making corruption a "high-risk, low-profit" undertaking

NIS Pillars

- Political will
- Civil society, public awareness, public participation
- Parliament
- Public service
- "Watchdog" agencies
- Rule of law and the judiciary
- Ombudsman
- Attorney-general
- Auditor-general
- Public procurement and good financial arrangements
- The media
- The private sector
- International context

Source: Transparency International, National Integrity System International, 2001, p. 9 at: http: www.transparency.org/activities/nat_integ_systems/dnld/overviewreport.pdf.

South Bronx. Before its fall from grace, Wedtech was a high flier on the New York Stock Exchange. What fueled the company? As a minority-controlled business, it won defense contracts without the need to bid. But in early 1986 Wedtech lost its status as a minority business, and by the end of that year the company was in ruins.

Wedtech officials had used fraudulent accounting methods, issued false financial reports, and counted profits before they were received. Caught in the cross fire of charges was Congressman Mario Biaggi, who was later convicted of soliciting bribes in order to obtain special government support for Wedtech. Other company and government officials either pleaded guilty or were convicted.[16]

Is the Wedtech scandal an isolated case? Clearly not. From 1986 through 1994, the Department of Defense reported that 138 defense contractors made 325 voluntary disclosures of potential procurement fraud. Recoveries from these disclosures amounted to $290 million.[17]

An important step to curb government contract fraud was taken with the passage of the Major Fraud Act (1988), creating a separate offense of government contract fraud in excess of $1 million. What kinds of activities does this act cover? Federal prosecutors seek indictments against contractors who engage in deceptive pricing or overcharging by submitting inaccurate cost and pricing data; mischarging by billing the government for improper or nonallowable charges; collusion in bidding (a conspiracy between presumed competitors to inflate bids); product substitution or the delivery of inferior, nonconforming, or untested goods; or the use of bribes, gratuities, conflicts of interest, and a whole range of other techniques designed to influence procurement officials.

Clearly there is more to government-related fraud than the manipulation of contractors and consultants.[18] The Inspector General's Office in the Department of Health and Human Services reported that an estimated $20 billion may be lost annually to fraud in the Medicare program alone.[19]

Consumer Fraud Consumer fraud is the act of causing a consumer to surrender money through deceit or a misrepresentation of a material fact. These offenses range from home repair fraud to mail order fraud (see Figure 12.1). Consumer frauds often appear as confidence games and may take some of the following forms:

- *Home-improvement fraud.* Consumers have been defrauded through the promise of low-cost home renovation. The home owners give sizable down payments to the contractors, who have no plans to complete the job. In fact, contractors often leave the jurisdiction or declare bankruptcy.

- *Deceptive advertising.* Consumers are often lured into a store by an announcement that

FIGURE 12.1 The Range of Consumer Fraud Complaints (2001)

- Furniture/Appliances (1315)
- Utilities/Energy (1567)
- Mortgage (2116)
- Home Repairs (2425)
- Retail Sales (2362)
- Telecommunications (2484)
- Landlord/Tennant (2694)
- Mail Order (3678)
- Credit (5384)
- Automobiles (5904)

a product is priced low for a limited period of time. Once in the store, the customer is told that the product is sold out, and he or she is offered a substitute, typically of inferior quality or at a much higher price. Such schemes are known as "bait-and-switch advertising."

- *Telemarketing fraud.* You are no doubt familiar with the old adage "If a deal sounds too good to be true, if probably is!" Each day, countless phone calls are made to homes around the United States with a very familiar opening script: "Congratulations! You are a grand prize winner." "Please donate money to _____ fund or _____ charity." Telemarketers lure consumers by making attractive offers (e.g., vacations, prizes, discounts on household items) that are nothing more than scams. Once you pay, you name is often added to a "sucker list" that may be sold to other scam telemarketers.

Of course, not all telemarketing is fraudulent. The New York State Attorney General, for example, estimates that approximately 10 percent of over 140,000 New York businesses using telemarketing to sell their products are frauds. (See Figure 12.2.)

- *Land fraud.* Consumers are easy prey for land fraud swindlers. Here the pitch is that a

FIGURE 12.2 Common Telemarketing Scams.

ADVANCE-FEE LOAN OR CREDIT SCHEMES
Telemarketers seek out people with bad credit and offer them loans or credit cards in exchange for fees. Victims offered loans never receive them. Victims offered credit cards usually only get a standard application form or generic information on how to apply.

FOREIGN LOTTERY SCHEMES
Telemarketers offer victims the opportunity to "invest" in tickets in well-known foreign lotteries (e.g., Canada or Australia), or give them a "one in six" chance of winning a substantial prize. This is a common cross-border offense since it plays upon the ignorance of victims of the rules (or even the existence) of foreign lotteries. If offenders purport to sell real lottery chances but deceive victims about their chances of winning, it may be both a gambling offense and fraud. If real chances are sold without deception, it may still be a gambling offense.

INVESTMENT SCHEMES
Victims are sold "investments" in a wide range of merchandise or securities that appear to offer high profit margins. The fraud lies in misrepresenting the true value (or actual existence) of what is being sold, and/or the true extent of the risk in buying it. Common "opportunities" have involved stocks or securities, investment-grade gemstones, precious or strategic metals or minerals, and business opportunities such as oil and gas ventures, pizza ovens, and ostrich farms. These schemes commonly defraud victims more than once (see "reloading" schemes). Once funds have been committed, the victim can be induced to make additional payments to increase the value of the "investment" or avoid its loss (e.g., "margin calls"). Since legitimate investments normally tie up assets for extended periods, victims often do not realize for some time that they have been defrauded.

PRIZE PROMOTION
Telemarketers "guarantee" that the victims have won valuable prizes or gifts, such as vacations or automobiles, but require victims to submit one or more payments for non-existent shipping, taxes, customs or bonding fees, or anything else the offender thinks plausible. Some schemes never provide their victims with any prize or gift, while others provide inexpensive items, often called "gimme gifts" by U.S. telemarketers and "cheap gifts" by Canadian telemarketers.

TELEFUNDING SCHEMES
These prey on the charity of victims by soliciting donations for worthy causes such as antidrug programs or victims of natural disasters. The pitch may simply ask for donations or it may include other inducements, such as donor eligibility for valuable prizes, which never materialize (see "prize promotion" schemes). Charitable donors do not usually expect something in return for their contribution, and may thus never become aware that they have been defrauded.

TRAVEL-RELATED SCHEMES
Fraudulent telemarketers purporting to be travel agencies offer substantial travel packages at comparatively low cost. The use of travel as a commodity makes the long-distance nature of the transaction plausible. The fraud usually involves lies, misrepresentations, or non-disclosure of information about the true value of travel and accommodations, limitations or restrictions on when or where purchasers may go, or what awaits them at the destination. In some cases, the travel proves to be a complete fabrication or has so many terms and conditions as to be completely unusable.

RELOADING AND RECOVERY ROOM SCHEMES
These target the same victims again and again. Persons victimized once are most likely to be deceived repeatedly. Unfortunately, victims' understandable desires to recover their original losses make them more vulnerable to further schemes. This is known as "reloading" or "loading." Those who "invest" money are "reloaded" for more to protect or increase their investment, those asked for customs or shipping fees are "reloaded" for additional charges, and those who give to a spurious "worthy cause" are often "reloaded" for further donations.

Recovery room schemes exploit the victim's desire to recover losses from previous frauds. Offenders, often from the same organization which defrauded the victim in the first place, call with inside knowledge of the fraud and a promise to recover the losses if "taxes" or "fees" are paid. A common tactic of callers is to represent themselves as law enforcement or other government or professional employees (e.g., bank or stock-exchange officials), using inside knowledge of the victim and the fraud to establish credibility. Recovery room operations frequently deprive victims of their last remaining funds.

Source: http://www.fbi.gov/majcases/db/comscams.htm.

---

certain piece of vacation or retirement property is a worthy investment, many improvements to the property will be made, and many facilities will be made available in the area. Consumers often make purchases of worthless or overvalued land.

- *Business opportunity fraud.* The objective of business opportunity fraud is to persuade a consumer to invest money in a business concern through misrepresentation of its actual worth. Work-at-home frauds are common: Victims are told they can make big money by addressing envelopes at home or performing some other simple task. Consumers lose large sums of money investing in such ventures.

Insurance Fraud There are many varieties of insurance fraud: Policyholders defraud insurers, insurers defraud the public, management defrauds the public, and third parties defraud insurers. Policyholder fraud is most often accomplished by the filing of false claims for life, fire, marine, or casualty insurance. Sometimes an employee of the insurance company is part of the fraud and assists in the preparation of the claim. The fraud may be simple—a false death claim—or it may become complex when multiple policies are involved.

From the Pages of The New York Times

Rave Reviews or Questionable Quotes? Deceptive Advertising Goes to the Movies

Can every movie be as much of a "rollicking good time" or "the feel-good" film of the season as the advertisements would like to make you believe?

In January of 2003, the Federal Trade Commission announced that it had its doubts, and was reviewing its guidelines on endorsements and testimonials, including the blurbs of movie reviews that studios use to publicize their films. Not that deceptive ads are anything new. In newspaper ads for the 1978 Chevy Chase/Goldie Hawn movie *Foul Play*, critic David Ansen was quoted as describing the film as "good fun." The problem was that Ansen's full quote read, "Though it is all intended as good fun, it's about as much fun as getting hit by a bus."

And in 2001, Sony Pictures Entertainment was discovered to be using quotes from a movie reviewer who didn't even exist. They used quotes from a "critic" named David Manning, who turned out to be a medical equipment salesman. Several other studios, including 20th Century Fox and Universal Pictures, admitted that they had hired actors or paid employees to appear in "man-in-the-street" commercials and praise the films they had just seen as if they were unpaid moviegoers.

Unfortunately, even an FTC "crackdown" doesn't hold much clout. The agency that exposed the earlier deceptive advertising didn't really do anything about it. "We haven't taken any action," said Mary Engle, associate director for advertising practices, citing the commission's limited budget and competing causes. "We get many, many complaints about many issues, including serious health and safety issues, or significant monetary loss to consumers."

Others in the entertainment industry, like Roger Ebert, film critic at the *Chicago Sun-Times* and co-host of "Ebert & Roeper" feel that the bad publicity these practices engender help correct any wayward marketing practices and curtail abuses. The Motion Picture Association of America, on the other hand, plans to track the FTC's assessments of the industry's marketing practices, according to spokeswoman Marta Grutka, but has no position on the guidelines or their application.

Source
Adapted from: Nat. Ives, "The U.S. Plans to See if There Is Misleading Marketing of Movies," *New York Times*, Jan. 14, 2003. Reprinted with permission.

Questions for Discussion
1. Some people might say that it doesn't really matter that much if advertisers use hype to sell their movies. Who really cares, after all, what David Ansen did or did not say about *Foul Play*? Others, however, see movie studios practicing deceptive advertising, making false claims as to the worth of their product. How do you judge the severity of such a crime?
2. The FTC claims, in essence, that they don't have the time or resources to do anything except expose the hype. Do you think they should be paying more attention? If so, what type of punishment do you think is just—and who should be held accountable?

A different type of insurance fraud is committed when a small group of people create a "shell" insurance firm without true assets. Policies are sold with no intent to pay legitimate claims. In fact, when large claims are presented to shell insurance companies, the firms disband, leaving a trail of policyholder victims. In yet another form of insurance fraud, middle- and upper-level managers of an insurance company loot the firm's assets by removing funds and debiting them as payments of claims to legitimate or bogus policyholders.[20]

Criminologists Paul Tracy and James Fox conducted a field experiment to find out how many auto-body repair shops in Massachusetts inflate repair estimates to insurance companies, and by how much. These researchers rented two Buick Skylarks with moderate damage, a Volvo 740 GLE with superficial damage, and a Ford Tempo with substantial damage. They then obtained 191 repair estimates, some with a clear understanding that the car was insured, others with the understanding that there was no insurance coverage. The results were unequivocal: Repair estimates for insured vehicles were significantly higher than those for noncovered cars. This finding is highly suggestive of fraud.[21]

Tax Fraud The Internal Revenue Code makes willful failure to file a tax return a misdemeanor. An attempt to evade or defeat a tax, nonpayment of a tax, or willful filing of a fraudulent tax return is a felony. What must the government prove? In order to sustain a conviction, the government must present evidence of income tax due and owing, willful avoidance of payment, and an affirmative act toward tax evasion.[22] How are tax frauds accomplished? Consider the following techniques:

- *Keeping two sets of books.* A person may keep one set of books reflecting actual profits and losses and another set for the purpose of misleading the Internal Revenue Service.
- *Shifting funds.* In order to avoid detection, tax evaders often shift funds continually from account to account, from bank to bank.
- *Faking forms.* Tax evaders often use faked invoices, create fictitious expenses, conceal assets, and destroy books and records.

The IRS lacks the resources to investigate all suspicious tax forms. When the difficulty of distinguishing between careless mistakes and willful evasion is taken into account, the taxes that go uncollected each year are estimated to exceed $100 billion.[23]

Bribery, Corruption, and Political Fraud
Judges who fix traffic tickets in exchange for political favors, municipal employees who speculate with city funds, businesspeople who bribe local politicians to obtain favorable treatment—all are part of the corruption in our municipal, state, and federal governments. The objectives of such offenses vary—favors, special privileges, services, business. The actors include officers of corporations as well as of government; indeed, they may belong to the police or the courts.

Bribery and other forms of corruption are ingrained in the political machinery of local and state governments. Examples abound: Mayors of large cities attempt to obtain favors through bribes; manufacturers pay off political figures for favors; municipal officials demand kickbacks from contractors.[24] In response to the seriousness of political corruption and bribery, Congress established two crimes: It is now a felony to accept a bribe or to provide a bribe.[25] Of course, political bribery and other forms of corruption do not stop at the nation's borders. Kickbacks to foreign officials are common practice and countries develop reputations for facilitating corruption (Table 12.3) and tolerating corruption (Table 12.4).[26] Business sectors develop reputations for corruption as well (Table 12.5).

Corruption can be found in private industry as well. One firm pays another to induce it to use a product or service; a firm pays its own

TABLE 12.3 The Transparency International Bribe Payers Index 2002

A total of 835 business experts in 15 leading emerging market countries were asked: In the business sectors with which you are most familiar, please indicate how likely companies from the following countries are to pay or offer bribes to win or retain business in this country?

Rank		Score	Rank		Score
1	Australia	8.5	12	France	5.5
2	Sweden	8.4	13	United States	5.3
	Switzerland	8.4		Japan	5.3
4	Austria	8.2	15	Malaysia	4.3
5	Canada	8.1		Hong Kong	4.3
6	Netherlands	7.8	17	Italy	4.1
	Belgium	7.8	18	South Korea	3.9
8	United Kingdom	6.9	19	Taiwan	3.8
9	Singapore	6.3	20	People's Republic of China	3.5
	Germany	6.3	21	Russia	3.2
11	Spain	5.8		*Domestic companies*	1.9

Note: A perfect score, indicating a zero-perceived propensity to pay bribes, is 10.0, and thus the ranking starts with companies from countries that are seen to have a low propensity for foreign bribe paying. All the survey data indicated that domestically owned companies in the 15 countries surveyed have a very high propensity to pay bribes—higher than that of foreign firms.

Source: Transparency International, New Bribe Payers Index, press release, May 14, 2002.

TABLE 12.4 Transparency International Corruption Perceptions Index 2002

Rank	Country	CPI 2002 score	Rank	Country	CPI 2002 score	Rank	Country	CPI 2002 score	Rank	Country	CPI 2002 score
1	Finland	9.7	27	Slovenia	6.0	52	Czech Republic	3.7	77	Pakistan	2.6
2	Denmark	9.5	28	Namibia	5.7		Latvia	3.7		Philippines	2.6
	New Zealand	9.5	29	Estonia	5.6		Morocco	3.7		Romania	2.6
4	Iceland	9.4		Taiwan	5.6		Slovak Republic	3.7		Zambia	2.6
5	Singapore	9.3	31	Italy	5.2		Sri Lanka	3.7	81	Albania	2.5
	Sweden	9.3	32	Uruguay	5.1	57	Colombia	3.6		Guatemala	2.5
7	Canada	9.0	33	Hungary	4.9		Mexico	3.6		Nicaragua	2.5
	Luxembourg	9.0		Malaysia	4.9	59	China	3.5		Venezuela	2.5
	Netherlands	9.0		Trinidad & Tobago	4.9		Dominican Rep.	3.5	85	Georgia	2.4
10	United Kingdom	8.7	36	Belarus	4.8		Ethiopia	3.5		Ukraine	2.4
11	Australia	8.6		Lithuania	4.8	62	Egypt	3.4		Vietnam	2.4
12	Norway	8.5		South Africa	4.8		El Salvador	3.4	88	Kazakhstan	2.3
	Switzerland	8.5		Tunisia	4.8	64	Thailand	3.2	89	Bolivia	2.2
14	Hong Kong	8.2	40	Costa Rica	4.5		Turkey	3.2		Cameroon	2.2
15	Austria	7.8		Jordan	4.5	66	Senegal	3.1		Ecuador	2.2
16	USA	7.7		Mauritius	4.5	67	Panama	3.0		Haiti	2.2
17	Chile	7.5		South Korea	4.5	68	Malawi	2.9	93	Moldova	2.1
18	Germany	7.3	44	Greece	4.2		Uzbekistan	2.9		Uganda	2.1
	Israel	7.3	45	Brazil	4.0	70	Argentina	2.8	95	Azerbaijan	2.0
20	Belgium	7.1		Bulgaria	4.0	71	Cote d'Ivoire	2.7	96	Indonesia	1.9
	Japan	7.1		Jamaica	4.0		Honduras	2.7		Kenya	1.9
	Spain	7.1		Peru	4.0		India	2.7	98	Angola	1.7
23	Ireland	6.9		Poland	4.0		Russia	2.7		Madagascar	1.7
24	Botswana	6.4	50	Ghana	3.9		Tanzania	2.7		Paraguay	1.7
25	France	6.3	51	Croatia	3.8		Zimbabwe	2.7	101	Nigeria	1.6
	Portugal	6.3							102	Bangladesh	1.2

Explanatory notes: A more detailed description of the CPI 2002 methodology is available at http://www.transparency.org/cpi/index.html#cpi or at www.gwdg.de/~uwvw/2002.html.

CPI 2002 Score

relates to perceptions of the degree of corruption as seen by businesspeople and risk analysts, and ranges between 10 (highly clean) and 0 (highly corrupt).

Source: Transparency International, Corruption Perception Index, August 28, 2002.

board of directors or officers to dispense special favors; two or more firms, presumably competitors, secretly agree to charge the same prices for their products or services.

Insider-Related Fraud Insider-related fraud involves the use and misuse of one's position for pecuniary gain or privilege. This category of offenses includes embezzlement, employee-related thefts, and sale of confidential information.

Embezzlement is the conversion (misappropriation) of property or money with which one is entrusted or for which one has a fiduciary responsibility. Yearly losses attributable to embezzlement are estimated at over $1 billion.[27]

Employee-related thefts of company property are responsible for a significant share of industry losses. Estimates place such losses between $4 billion and $13 billion each year. Criminologists John Clark and Richard Hollinger have estimated that the 35 percent rate of employee pilferage in some corporations results primarily from vocational dissatisfaction and a perception of exploitation.[28] And not only goods and services are taken; time and money are at risk as well. Phony payrolls, fictitious overtime charges, false claims for business-related travel, and the like, are common.

Finally, in a free marketplace where a premium is placed on competition, corporations

TABLE 12.5 Bribery in Business Sectors

How likely is it that senior public officials in this country would demand or accept bribes, for example, for public tenders, regulations, or licensing in the following business sectors?

Business Sector	Score
Public works/construction	1.3
Arms and defence	1.9
Oil and gas	2.7
Real estate/property	3.5
Telecoms	3.7
Power generation/transmission	3.7
Mining	4.0
Transportation/storage	4.3
Pharmaceuticals/medical care	4.3
Heavy manufacturing	4.5
Banking and finance	4.7
Civilian aerospace	4.9
Forestry	5.1
Information technology	5.1
Fishery	5.9
Light manufacturing	5.9
Agriculture	5.9

Note: The score is the mean of all the responses on a 0 to 10 basis where 0 represents very high perceived levels of corruption, and 10 represents extremely low perceived levels of corruption.

Source: Transparency International, New Bribe Payers Index, press release, May 14, 2002.

must guard against the *sale of confidential information* and trade secrets. The best insurance policy is employee loyalty. Where there is no loyalty, or where loyalty is compromised, abuse of confidential information is possible. The purchase of confidential information from employees willing to commit industrial espionage is estimated to be a multimillion-dollar business.[29]

CORPORATE CRIME

The idea of white-collar crime is straightforward. Employees in a business step over the line by pocketing corporate funds. Tax avoiders become tax evaders. Home owners file fraudulent insurance claims. The crimes of white-collar criminals make fascinating television and movie scripts, from complex insider trading scandals to smoke-filled, boiler room stock frauds. There are, however, other kinds of crimes that take place in the course of a respected and legitimate business enterprise. For the balance of this chapter, we will consider crimes by one or more employees of a corporation that are attributed to the organization itself—corporate crimes. The concept of **corporate crime** may be familiar if you have heard or read about the fall of Arthur Andersen and other companies that were convicted—as corporations—of a host of criminal law violations. In fact, the concept of a "corporate" crime is more than a century old.

Frequency and Problems of Definition

There is no central repository for data on the number of cases of corporate crime either in state or federal courts. The best source of data, the United States Sentencing Commission, is less than ideal. The commission compiles information on cases of corporations that have been convicted of a federal crime.

On average, between 200 and 350 corporations are convicted each year in federal courts for offenses ranging from tax law violations to environmental crimes. The vast majority of these companies are small- to medium-size privately held corporations. In fact, between November 1, 1987, and June 30, 2001, nearly 80 percent of all corporations convicted had fewer than 100 employees. Only 5 percent of all convicted corporations had more than 500 employees.

One problem with corporate crime is defining it. In 1989 the supertanker *Exxon Valdez* ran aground in Prince William Sound, Alaska, spilling 250,000 barrels of oil. The spill became North America's largest ecological disaster. Prosecutors were interested in determining the liability of the captain, his officers, and his crew. But there were additional and far-reaching questions. Was the Exxon Corporation liable? If so, was this a corporate crime? The same problem presented itself with the filing of criminal charges against Arthur Andersen. Should the firm bear the brunt of the crimes of its employees?

In Mexia, Texas, Jim and Kathy Taylor hold a photo of their daughter Jessica, a cheerleader who died in a tire blowout crash on her way to a game. Their lawyer, Randell Roberts, holds a Firestone tire from the SUV. Subsequently, Firestone recalled 6.5 million of its most widely used product.

During the Great Depression thousands of unemployed people heard that there was work to be had in the little West Virginia town of Hawk's Nest, where a huge tunnel was to be dug. Thousands of people came to work for a pittance. The company set the men up in crude camps and put them to work drilling rock for the tunnel project—without masks or other safety equipment. The workers breathed in the silicon dust that filled the air. Many contracted silicosis, a chronic lung disease that leads to certain death. They died by the dozens. Security guards dragged the bodies away and buried them secretly. No one was to know. The work went on. The deaths multiplied. Who was to blame? The corporation?[30]

Phases of Corporate Criminal Law

Corporate criminal law has moved through five distinct phases over the past century (see Figure 12.3). In the first phase, courts wrestled with the idea that a corporation may be a "person" who is criminally liable. But can a corporation have a soul? Judges concluded that the idea that a corporation, without a soul, intended harm was too much of a fiction. Between 1850 and 1910, however, rising concerns over the possibility of corporate abuses captured the public's attention. Corporate criminal liability, no matter how illusory or illogical, became increasingly appealing as a hedge against the abuses considered inevitable with the rise of corporate power.

In the second phase, initiated by the decision of *New York Central Railroad*, (1909) courts reviewed a wide variety of criminal cases against corporations.[31] Corporate regulation in this new world of interstate commerce required a more powerful and formal social control. This was all the more true as the first wave of mergers ended and large corporations increasingly spun-off divisions—decentralizing. Centralized functions were now specialized and complex. In the years leading up to *New York Central Railroad*, concerns emerged that as corporations grew large,

> ▶ **Theory Connects**
>
> What would Social Control theorists (p. 169) say about the power of fines against corporations? Would they propose other sanctions that might be more effective? If so, what would those punishments look like?

FIGURE 12.3 The Five Phases of the Corporate Criminal Law 1850–present

PHASE ONE
Concerns with importance and meaning of corporate personhood

PHASE TWO
The rise and immediate fall of vicarious liability: Strategic risk shifting by employers and employees

PHASE THREE
New era of regulatory law

PHASE FOUR
Post Guidelines Partnership

PHASE FIVE
Selective use of existing law

PHASE ONE: Without a soul, corporations cannot have a "wicked" intent. Only human beings can be charged with perjury, treason, and violent crimes. Most crimes go beyond the purposes and powers of a corporation. Corporations, however, may be charged with nonfeasance and some affirmative acts. *State v. Morris & Essex Railroad*, (1852); *Commonwealth v. Proprietors of New Bedford Bridge* (1854)

PHASE TWO: The emergence of large-scale multidivisional organizations, the move from horizontal to vertical integration, the separation of corporate ownership and control, and the rising prominence of railroad conglomerates in interstate commerce led Congress and then federal courts to implement the power of the criminal law as a regulatory weapon

The nonfeasance-misfeasance distinction in abandoned for reasons of practicality. Immunizing corporations from the criminal law would deprive the law of a powerful form of social control

The emergence of a due diligence defense *John Gund Brewing Co. v. U.S.* (1913)

"Golden Age" of white-collar crime prosecution

Sentencing Guidelines for Organizations (1991)

Prosecutorial Guidelines for Organizations (1999)

Reliance on vicarious liability in a select number of high-profile prosecutions

---

Timeline markers:

- Corporations increasingly subjected to criminal liability for types of nuisances
- Sherman Act
- Corporate criminal liability extended to crimes of intent
- *New York Central & Hudson River Railroad v. U.S.* (1909)
- Securities Act of 1993 and Securities Exchange Act of 1934
- Model Penal Code provisions on corporate criminal liability
- Standard Oil Company of Texas v. U.S. (1962)
- *U.S. v. Hilton Hotels Corp.* (1973)
- *U.S. v. Bank of New England* (1987)
- *In re Caremark Int'l Inc.* (1996)
- Andersen Conviction/Enron
- Tyco/Global Crossing

Years: 1850 | 1860 | 1870 | 1880 | 1890 | 1900 | 1910 | 1920 | 1930 | 1940 | 1950 | 1960 | 1970 | 1980 | 1990 | 2000 | 2002

Between 1850 and 1910, courts acceded to the realities of rising monopolistic powers and rapid market integration by expanding the fiction of corporate criminal liability. Criminal liability as well as the rise of civil liability regimes, provided needed relief from the risks associated with the rise of the modern corporation.

By the culmination of the first merger wave, which ended in 1904, traditionally centralized functions in many large corporations had become increasingly decentralized. Departments, managerial oversight, as well as employee functions and roles, were highly specialized. With decentralized, specialization, and an increasing organizational complexity came concerns over loss of corporate control across the managerial hierarchy.

Of central concern was the increasing separation in status and role of shareholders and management. Managers with an insignificant ownership interest assumed prominent decision-making roles as shareholders forfeited active control over corporate operations.

Increased power given to OSHA, EPA, and other federal agencies with the passage of a host of regulatory statutes

Post-guidelines enforcement and prosecution determined by compliance with guidelines and regulatory statements.

Symbolic prosecutions follow in the wake of Enron and Andersen. Prosecutions follow the strictures of existing law—reliance on vicarious liability.

333

managerial oversight and control of employees would diminish.[32] Holding management responsible, through vicarious corporate criminal liability, soon became the rule of law in all federal courts.

Perceptions that this rule was unduly harsh prompted pleas by firms that they should be given a break for attempting compliance with laws.[33] No fewer than four years after *New York Central Railroad*, corporations were telling courts that they were doing everything possible to comply with the law—even if sometimes they failed.

In the third phase of the corporate criminal law there was a significant rise in the power of government regulators and, not surprisingly, the reach of regulatory law. Getting companies to comply with laws replaced punishment as the preferred sanction. Literally hundreds of thousands of criminal provisions were found in a wide range of federal statutory law.[34] Marshall Clinard and his colleagues captured a glimpse of the effects of this new regulatory state on large corporations in their influential work *Illegal Corporate Behavior*.[35]

In the fourth phase, defined by the passage of the Sentencing Guidelines for Organizations, corporations joined with the government in routing out crime (see Figure 12.4). Following significant lobbying from business associations, a congressionally appointed body—the United States Sentencing Commission—announced guidelines that govern the sentencing of corporations in federal courts. Drafters of the sentencing guidelines wanted corporations to face the threat of significant punishment and, at the same time, the possibility of mitigation, leniency, and amnesty (see Table 12.6). This was the incentive for corporations to help ferret out crime.

The sentencing guidelines require judges to consider a fine multiplied by a score reflecting factors that make the corporation more or less blameworthy. A corporation's willingness to accept responsibility, cooperate with authorities, and implement a compliance reveal corporate due diligence and mitigates a sanction. To help companies understand how to best position themselves relative to prosecutors and regulators, consultants for a new and emerging industry—the corporate compliance industry—offered their skills.

Attendees at the Committee on Financial Services hearing on WorldCom, (L-R) Melvin Dick, former Arthur Andersen Senior Global Managing Partner, Technology, Media and Communications Practice; former WorldCom CEO Bernard Ebbers; and former WorldCom Chief Financial Officer Scott Sullivan listen to Jack Grubman, telecommunications analyst for Salomon Smith Barney, testifying before the U.S. House Financial Services Committee hearing on Capitol Hill on July 8, 2002. The house committee is investigating the improper accounting method used by the No. 2 U.S. long-distance company, WorldCom, in expensing almost $4 billion.

The compliance industry markets the story that evidence of organizational due diligence (cooperating with authorities, creating an ethics code, hiring ethics officers, etc.) likely forestalls a criminal investigation, minimizes the likelihood of a criminal indictment, and regularly leads to a grant of governmental leniency, if not amnesty. Regulators and prosecutors decline cases involving corporations that demonstrate a commitment to compliance and actively cooperative with authorities. Declinations reward firms for their proactive, reactive, and cooperative efforts, reserving resources for the most abusive firms.

The result is a new enforcement landscape—one of substantial assistance, mitigation credits, and voluntary disclosure. In theory, the substantive corporate criminal law is unchanged since *New York Central & Hudson River Railroad*. In practice, negotiated compliance has all but replaced the substantive law. Corporate cooperation that facilitates the flow of evidence to authorities is the critical feature of this regulatory strategy.

FIGURE 12.4 The Development of the Corporate Criminal Law Pre-guidelines–present

Pre-Guidelines

Post-Guidelines I: "A practical partnership" between government and business. New age of government-corporate cooperation characterized by a shift away from command and control strategies of corporate regulation to negotiated compliance, coerced cooperation, and regulatory persuasion. Concerns: gaming, moral hazards, and flipping

Rise of "reverse whistleblowing"

Post-Guidelines
A period of "Corporate Accountability" emerged with the appearance of widespread corporate deviance. Strategic call for corporate investigation, prosecution, and law reform are designed to calm investor fears and return confidence to the markets.

| 1988 | 1989 | 1990 | 1991 | 1992 | 1993 | 1994 | 1995 | 1996 | 1997 | 1998 | 1999 | 2000 | 2001 | 2002 |

- U.S. Sentencing Commission, Sentencing of Organizations (Discussion Draft 1988)
- United States Sentencing Commission, Sentencing of Organizations (Preliminary Draft 1989)
- United States Sentencing Commission, Sentencing of Organizations (Proposed Guidelines 1990)
- U.S. Sentencing Commission, Guidelines for Organizations (1991)
- Antitrust Division, Corporate Amesty Policy, Antitrust Division, DOJ, 1993
- DOJ, Factors in Decisions on criminal Prosecutions for Environmental Violations in the Context of Significant Voluntary Compliance or Disclosure Efforts by the Violator (1994); Memorandum Regarding Exercise of Investigative Discretion, Office of Criminal Enforcement, EPS (1994)
- Sequa Corp. plea agreement
- Prudential plea agreement
- Voluntary Disclosure Program Guidelines, Office of the Inspector General, Department of Health and Human Services (1995); Incentives for Self-Policing: Discovery, Disclosure, Correction and Prevention of Violations, United States Environmental Protection Agency (EPA) (1995)
- *In re* Caremark Int'l Inc. (1996)
- Reputation management and compliance risk management practices join the business ethics cottage industry in counseling corporations
- Prosecutorial Guidelines for Organizations (1999)
- Enron & Andersen
- Tyco/Global Crossing

Debate over optimal penalty theory and the possible role, in any, of mitigating circumstances in the drafts of the sentencing guidelines for organizations. Heavy lobbying from industry groups and big business to include some recognition of organizational due diligence.

In this phase of "post-Guidelines" cases, corporate compliance for large, decentralized multinationals in bought and sold as cost-effective risk management in a marketplace of experts from "businnee integrity" consulting, insurance, and accounting firms. Evidence of organizational due diligence may forestall an investigation, minimize the chance of a criminal indictment, and possibly lead to a grant of governmental amnesty.

Prosecutors are increasingly likely to decline cases involving organizations with compliance programs modeled after Guidelines' prescriptive steps. This is especially true in complex white-collar and corporate crime cases (e.g., antitrust and securities fraud) that require significant investigative and prosecutorial resources. Declinations reward firms for their proactive and reactive efforts, focusing scarce resources on the most-abusive firms.

The Prosecutorial and Sentencing Guidelines provide reciprocal promises—organizational cooperation and acceptance of responsibility in exchange for mitigation, exculpation, or absolution.

Symbolic prosecution follows in the wake of Enron and Andersen. Prosecution follow the strictures of existing reliance on vaicarious liability.

TABLE 12.6 United States Sentencing Guidelines for Organizational Defendants (1991)

Factors to Be Considered in Sentencing Organizations	Organizational Factors to Be Considered in Sentencing
1. The organization must have established compliance standards and procedures to be followed by its employees and other agents that are reasonably capable of reducing the prospect of criminal conduct.	Firm size is considered in the assessment of organizational culpability.
2. Specific individual(s) within high-level personnel of the organization must have been assigned overall responsibility to oversee compliance with such standards and procedures.	If by custom or convention it is more likely that deviance will occur in a particular business, business sector, or market, an organization is more culpable if it failed to put in place and enforce policies to prevent such deviance from occurring.
3. The organization must have used due care not to delegate substantial discretionary authority to individuals whom the organization knew, or should have known through the exercise of due diligence, had a propensity to engage in illegal activities.	The criminal history of an organization will affect the assessment of culpability.
4. The organization must have taken steps to communicate effectively its standards and procedures to all employees and other agents.	Corporate compliance programs that are perceived to be effective decrease culpability.
5. The organization must have taken reasonable steps to achieve compliance with its standards, e.g., by utilizing monitoring and auditing systems reasonably.	Organizational obstruction of justice increases culpability.
6. The standards must have been consistently enforced through appropriate disciplinary mechanisms, including, as appropriate, discipline of individuals responsible for the failure to detect an offense.	Organizational cooperation, admission of guilt, and acceptance of responsibility reduce culpability.
7. After an offense has been detected, the organization must have taken all reasonable steps to respond appropriately to the offense and to prevent further similar offenses—including any necessary modifications to its program to prevent and detect violations of law.	Closely held organizations may be alter egos of management.

In the final and most recent phase, characterized by the high-profile criminal cases against Arthur Andersen and Sotheby's; settlements with Merrill Lynch, Piper Jaffray, and Xerox; and pending investigations against Enron, WorldCom, Qwest, Tyco, ImClone, Martha Stewart, Global Crossing, Dynegy, CMS Energy, El Paso Corp., Halliburton, and Williams Cos., calls for reforms—with a focus on greater individual accountability—have changed little in this landscape.

Theories of Corporate Liability

A "corporation" is an artificial person created by state charter. The charter provides such an entity with the right to engage in certain activities—to buy and sell certain goods or to run a railroad, for instance. The charter limits the liability of the persons who own the corporation (the shareholders) to the extent of the value of their investment (their shares). The corporation thus is an entity separate from the people who own or manage it. This convenient form of pooling resources for commercial purposes, with a view toward profiting from one's investment, has had a significant impact on the development of the United States as a commercial and industrial power. Moreover, millions of wage earners whose savings or union funds are invested in corporate stocks and bonds reap dividends from such investments in the form of income or retirement benefits.

But what if a senior official of a corporation engages in unlawful activity? Can we say that the corporation committed the crime? If so, what can be done about it?[36] Initially corporations were considered incapable of committing crimes. After all, crimes require mens rea, an awareness of wrongdoing. Since corporations are bodies without souls, they were deemed to be incapable of forming the requisite sense of wrongdoing. Nor could a corporation be imprisoned for its crimes. Further, corporations were not authorized to commit crimes; they were authorized only to engage in the business for which they had been chartered. So, how should the "blameworthiness" or "culpability" of a corporation be conceived?

Models of Corporate Culpability

Over the past several decades, scholars have revisited the allegiance of courts to **vicarious liability.** Should courts consider the reactions of a corporation to the discovery of illegal behavior? Should courts focus on corporate cultures that encourage crime commission or corporate policies that tolerate, if not promote, law violation? Nearly a century after the criminal law was first applied to the corporations, there is increasing interest in proactive, reactive, culture-based, and corporate policy models of culpability.

Proactive corporate fault (PCF) assumes that a corporation is to blame where practices and procedures are inadequate to prevent the commission of a crime. Corporations are culpable when they fail to take reasonable steps to implement policies and practices that reduce the likelihood of crime commission.

Reactive corporate fault (RCF) considers the corporate reaction to the discovery of a criminal act. Evidence of a how well a company reacts to the discovery of an offense is the basis of finding blame. Failure to undertake reasonable corrective or remedial measures in reaction to an offense is evidence of fault.

Where an organization's ethos or personality encourages agents to commit criminal acts there is liability under a theory of **corporate ethos.** Such a corporate ethos is determined by the corporate hierarchy, corporate goals and policies, efforts to ensure compliance with ethics codes and legal regulations, and the indemnification of guilty employees. Questions relating to the role of the board of directors, and how the corporation has reacted to past violations, if any, will be asked as well.

Finally, commentators have argued that corporate actions and intention may be found in decisions and choices that are communicated through **corporate policy** (CP). It has been argued, for example, that the components of the corporation's internal decision structure, consisting of the corporation's flow-chart and procedures, define corporate intentionality. A summary of all four models appears in Table 12.7.

Sotheby's auction house head Alfred Taubman leaves federal court April 22, 2002, in New York City. A federal judge sentenced Taubman to a year in prison and ordered him to pay a $7.5 million fine for price-fixing.

> **:// Crime Surfing**
>
> www.herring.com/mag/issue22/crime.html
>
> Corporate crime poses serious law enforcement investigatory problems. How much more difficult is the investigation of corporate crime in high-tech industries?

An additional model of corporate blame has been proposed—constructive corporate culpability. Here the concern is with whether corporations may be said to have a culpable "mental state." Of course, corporations do not actually have mental states. That is precisely why this is a "constructive" theory. Constructive corporate culpability asks such questions as: Did the corporation act "purposely"? Did the corporation act "knowingly"? Did the corporation act "recklessly"? Did the corporation act "negligently"?

TABLE 12.7 Summary of Models

Models	Postulates	Constructs	Hypotheses
PCF	Culpability is a function of the reasonableness of steps taken to prevent an offense	Proactive corporate fault; Proactive due diligence; Proactive duty	An entity is more or less blameworthy if it engages or fails to engage in proactive efforts. Proactive safeguards (e.g., internal audits) are effective in inhibiting law violation.
RCF	Culpability is a function of the reasonableness of steps taken in reaction to the discovery of an offense	Reactive corporate fault; Reactive due diligence; Reactive duty	An entity is more or less blameworthy if it engages or fails to engage in reactive or remedial efforts. Reactive programs and remedial efforts are effective in controlling corporate deviance.
CE	Culpability derives from the corporate ethos, culture, or personality	Corporate ethos; Corporate personality; Corporate culture	Corporate ethos is strongly associated with, or causes, corporate deviance. A distinct corporate culture and personality may be determined from organizational attributes.
CP	Corporate intentionality is found in decisions and choices that are communicated through corporate policy	Corporate internal decision structure (CID); Corporate policy	Corporate policies, goals, and objectives reflect corporate rather than individual intentionality.

Evidence of corporate mental states may be gleaned from asking these questions in relation to what an average corporation would have intended. Courts would, therefore, ask whether a corporation, given the circumstances, exhibits an awareness of the illegality. Did it appear to disregard risks that are associated with the crimes alleged? Should the company have known of the illegalities?

Governmental Control of Corporations

Corporate misconduct is covered by a broad range of federal and state statutes, including the federal conspiracy laws; the Racketeer Influenced and Corrupt Organizations (RICO) Act; federal securities laws; mail-fraud statutes; the Federal Corrupt Practices Act; the Federal Election Campaign Act; legislation on lobbying, bribery, and corruption; the Internal Revenue Code (especially regarding major tax crimes, slush funds, and improper payments); the Bank Secrecy Act; and federal provisions on obstruction of justice, perjury, and false statements.

The underlying theory is that if the brain of the artificial person (usually the board of directors of the corporation) authorizes or condones the act in question, the body (the corporation) must suffer criminal penalty. That seems fair enough, except for the fact that if the corporation gets punished—usually by a substantial fine—the penalty falls on the shareholders, most of whom had no say in the corporate decision. And the financial loss resulting from the fine may be passed on to the consumer. The counterargument, of course, is that shareholders often benefit from the illegal actions of the corporation. Thus, in fairness, they should suffer some detriment or loss when and if the corporation is apprehended and convicted.

> **Theory Connects**
>
> **Corporate Crime**
>
> In what ways may subcultural theories of crime (p. 161) help explain white-collar and organizational offenses?

Reliance on Civil Penalties Beginning in the nineteenth century, corporations were suspected of wielding monopolistic power to the detriment of consumers. The theory behind monopoly is simple: If you buy out all your competitors or drive them out of business, then you are the only one from whom people can buy the product you sell. So you can set the price, and you set it very high, for your profit and to the detriment of the consumers. The Sugar Trust was one such monopoly. A few powerful businessmen eliminated all competitors and then drove the price of sugar up, to the detriment of the public. Theodore Roosevelt fought and broke up the Sugar Trust.

In 1890 Congress passed the **Sherman Antitrust Act,** which effectively limited the exercise of monopolies.[37] The act prohibited any contract, conspiracy, or combination of business interests in restraint of foreign or interstate trade. This legislation was followed by the Clayton Antitrust Act (1914), which further curbed the ability of corporations to enrich their shareholders at the expense of the public, by prohibiting such acts as price-fixing.[38] But the remedies this act provided consisted largely of splitting up monopolistic enterprises or imposing damages, sometimes triple damages, for the harm caused. In a strict sense, this was not a use of the criminal law to govern corporate misconduct.

Criminal Liability A movement away from exclusive reliance on civil remedies was apparent in the 1960s, when it was discovered that corporate mismanagement or negligence on the part of officers or employees could inflict vast harm on identifiable groups of victims. Negligent management at a nuclear power plant can result in the release of radiation and injury to thousands or millions of people. The marketing of an unsafe drug can cause crippling deformities in tens of thousands of bodies.[39] Violation of environmental standards can cause injury and suffering to generations of people who will be exposed to unsafe drinking water, harmful air, or eroded soil. The manufacture of hazardous products can result in multiple deaths.[40]

The problem of corporate criminal liability since the 1960s, then, goes far beyond an individual death or injury. Ultimately, it concerns the health and even the survival of humankind. Nor is the problem confined to the United States. It is a global problem. It thus becomes necessary to look at the variety of activities attributable to corporations which in recent years have been recognized as particularly harmful to society.

When it comes to proving corporate criminal liability, prosecutors face formidable problems: Day-to-day corporate activity has a low level of visibility. Regulatory agencies that monitor corporate conduct have different and uncoordinated recording systems. Offending corporations operate in a multitude of jurisdictions, some of which regard a given activity as criminal, while others do not. Frequently, the facts of a case are not adjudicated at a trial; the parties may simply agree on a settlement approved by the court. Those corporations that are convicted tend to be first offenders without effective compliance programs (see Table 12.8).

In recent years, New York Attorney General Elliot Spitzer has championed the efforts of regulators to bring needed reforms to Wall Street. In April 2003, Spitzer and Stephen Cutler (U.S. Securities and Exchange Commission) announced a settlement of $1.4 billion in penalties against securities firms to settle charges of investor abuses.

> **Did You Know?**
>
> . . . that more than 95 percent of all corporations convicted of crimes each year in federal courts are small, privately held entities? Why do you suppose that this is a consistent finding over time?

Investigating Corporate Crime

We know very little about the extent of economic criminality in the United States. There is no national database for the assessment of corporate criminality, and corporations are not likely to release information about their own wrongdoing. The situation is worse in other countries, especially in the developing countries of Africa south of the Sahara, where few national crime statistics are kept and where corporations are least subject to governmental

TABLE 12.8 Corporations Sentenced under Guidelines (2001)[1]

Fiscal Year 2001

Involvement in or Tolerance of Criminal Activity by Authority—§8C2.5(b)	Number	Percent
Involvement/tolerance in an organization/unit of 5,000+ employees	0	0.0
Involvement/tolerance in an organization/unit of 1,000+ employees	4	4.3
Involvement/tolerance in an organization/unit of 200+ employees	5	5.3
Involvement/tolerance in an organization of 50+ employees	16	17.0
Involvement/tolerance in an organization of 10 or more employees	41	43.6
No involvement/tolerance or fewer than 10 employees	28	29.8
TOTAL	94	100.0

Prior History—§8C2.5(c)	Number	Percent
One similar criminal/two similar administrative violations within 10 years	1	1.1
One similar criminal/two similar administrative violations within 5 years	1	1.1
Organization had no prior record	91	97.8
TOTAL	93	100.0

Violation of an Order—§8C2.5(d)	Number	Percent
Organization did violate an order	0	0.0
Organization did not violate an order	94	100.0
TOTAL	94	100.0

Obstruction of Justice—§8C2.5(e)	Number	Percent
Organization obstructed justice	3	3.2
Organization did not obstruct justice	91	96.8
TOTAL	94	100.0

Effective Program to Prevent and Detect Violations of Law—§8C2.5(f)	Number	Percent
Organization did have an effective compliance program	0	0.0
Organization had a compliance program, but it was not effective	2	2.2
Organization had no compliance program	90	97.8
TOTAL	92	100.0

Self-Reporting, Cooperation, and Acceptance of Responsibility—§8C2.5(g)	Number	Percent
Reported offense to governmental authorities	0	0.0
Cooperated with investigation	47	50.0
Accepted responsibility	34	36.2
Organization did not self-report, cooperate, or accept responsibility	13	13.8
TOTAL	94	100.0

Note:[1] Of the 238 cases sentenced pursuant to Chapter Eight of the Sentencing Guidelines in FY01, 150 cases involved offenses covered by the list of applicable guidelines in §8C2.1. For 44 of these cases, the fine guidelines application data are missing or inapplicable due to guideline provisions such as a "preliminary determination of inability to pay fine" (§8C2.2). The total for each factor may add up to less than the overall total due to missing information for that variable. Descriptions of variables used in this table are provided in Appendix A. A description of Chapter Eight culpability factors can be found in USSG §8C2.5.

Source: U.S. Sentencing Commission, Organizational Datafile, FY2001.

control. Yet the evidence in regard to corporate crime is gradually coming in.[41]

As we noted earlier, the first American criminologist who was alert to the potential for harm in corporate conduct was Edwin Sutherland, who described the criminal behavior of 70 of the 200 largest production corporations in his 1946 book *White Collar Crime*.[42] An even more ambitious study was completed by Marshall B. Clinard and Peter C. Yeager, who investigated corporations within the jurisdiction of 25 federal agencies during 1975 and 1976. Of 477 major American corporations whose conduct was regulated by these agencies, 60 percent had violated the law. Of the 300 violating corporations, 38 (or 13 percent) accounted for 52 percent of all violations charged in 1975 and 1976, an average of 23.5 violations per firm.[43] Large corporations were found to be the chief violators, and a few particular industries (pharmaceutical, automotive) were the most likely to violate the law.

According to Clinard and Yeager, what makes it so difficult to curb corporate crime is the enormous political power corporations wield in the shaping and administration of the laws that govern their conduct. This is particularly the case in regard to multinational corporations that wish to operate in developing countries. The promise of jobs and development by a giant corporation is a temptation too great for the governments of many such countries to resist. They would rather have employment opportunities that pollute air and water than unemployment in a clean environment. Government officials in some Third World countries can be bribed to create or maintain a legal climate favorable to the business interests of the corporation, even though it may be detrimental to the people of the host country.

The work of Sutherland, Clinard and Yeager, and other traditional scholars, as well as that of a group of radical criminologists;[44] hearings on white-collar and corporate crime held by the Subcommittee on Crime of the House Judiciary Committee, under the leadership of Congressman John Conyers Jr. in 1978; the consumer protection movement, spearheaded by Ralph Nader; and investigative reporting by the press have all contributed to public awareness of large corporations' power to inflict harm on large population groups.

In 1975 James Q. Wilson still considered such crime to be insignificant,[45] but more recent studies show that the public considers corporate criminality at least as serious as, if not more serious than, street crime. Marvin Wolfgang and his associates found in a national survey that Americans regard illegal retail price-fixing (the artificial setting of prices at a high level, without regard for the demand for the product) as a more serious crime than robbery committed with a lead pipe.[46] Within the sphere of corporate criminality perhaps no other group of offenses has had so great an impact on public consciousness as crimes against the environment. As we shall see, however, enforcement of major environmental statutes has been weak in the past. There is some evidence that this is changing.

Environmental Crimes

The world's legal systems also include few effective laws and mechanisms to curb destruction of the environment. The emission of noxious fumes into the air and the discharge of pollutants into the water have until recently been regarded as common law nuisances at the level of misdemeanors, commanding usually no more than a small fine. Industrial polluters could easily absorb such a fine and regard it as a kind of business tax. Only in 1969 did Congress pass the National Environmental Policy Act (NEPA). Among other things, the act created the Environmental Protection Agency (EPA). It requires environmental impact studies so that any new development that would significantly affect the environment can be prevented or controlled.

The EPA is charged with enforcing federal statutes and assisting in the enforcement of state laws enacted to protect the environment. The agency monitors plant discharges all over the country and may take action against private industry or municipal governments. Yet during the first five years of its existence, the EPA referred only 130 cases to the U.S. Department of Justice for criminal prosecution, and only 6 of those involved major corporate offenders.[47] The government actually charged only one of the corporations, Allied Chemical, which admitted responsibility for 940 misdemeanor counts of discharging toxic chemicals into the Charles River in Virginia, thereby causing 80 people to become ill.[48]

A 1979 report of the General Accounting Office stated that the EPA inadequately monitored, inaccurately reported, and ineffectively enforced the nation's basic law on air pollution, although the agency's chief at that time contended that corrective action had been taken during the previous year.[49] The situation improved during the 1990s, but the environment is far from safe. Catastrophic releases of toxic and even nuclear substances, usually attributable to inadequate safeguards and human negligence, pose a particularly grave hazard, as the disasters at Bhopal in India and at Chernobyl in the former Soviet Union have demonstrated.

The effects of environmental crimes touch more than the environment. Employees in "culpable" companies may be victims as well. Consider, for example, the criminal investigation and prosecution of Darling International, Inc., a meat and meat-processing company located in Minnesota, for violations of the Clean Water Act.[50] The case of *United States v. Darling* is often thought of as representing a trend of management to exchange or trade culpable employees for corporate leniency.[51]

In 1989, Darling International bought a rendering plant in Blue Earth, Minnesota. Under significant pressure to increase production to meet sales objectives, their waste water system soon became overloaded. Beginning in 1991, employees sought to remedy this situation by illegally dumping millions of gallons of ammonia and blood-contaminated water into the Blue Earth River, causing significant environmental damage. Soon thereafter, on orders of the plant manager and with the knowledge of the vice president of environmental affairs, employees attempted to hide the illegal dumping by diluting and tampering with at least nine watewater samples sent to state pollution control authorities. The government had evidence that employees also fabricated and submitted discharge-monitoring reports and related documents that were later sent to state regulators.

The federal government's investigation into these environmental crimes stalled until Darling's board required retained counsel to cooperate with authorities and provide evidence of any criminal acts by its employees. With newly offered evidence, prosecutors obtained criminal convictions of four employees, all of whom had been fired by Darling after fully cooperating with counsel retained by the company and federal prosecutors. Darling entered into a plea agreement, and prosecutors recognized the company's cooperation by recommending a significantly mitigated fine—one quarter of the originally recommended fine. The company promptly implemented an environmental compliance program, adopted a code of business conduct, and created a corporate ombudsman's position to "encourage employees to report suspected problems even when they are reluctant to go directly to their supervisors, legal counsel, or someone else in management."[52]

Darling is notable for many reasons: the complicity and knowledge of management, the distance between the employees held responsible and those cooperating with authorities, the absence of compliance initiatives or programs, and a culture that permits scapegoating and the deception that can and often does accompany it. Simply put, existing principles and practices of corporate criminal law offer a less than optimal solution and remedy.

Enforcing Legislation The difficulties of enforcing legislation designed to protect the environment are enormous. Consider the 250,000 barrels of oil spilled by the *Exxon Valdez* in 1989. What legislation could have prevented the disaster? Developing effective laws to protect the environment is a complex problem. It is far easier to define the crimes of murder and theft than to define acts of pollution, which are infinitely varied. A particular challenge is the separation of harmful activities from socially useful ones. Moreover, pollution is hard to quantify. How much of a chemical must be discharged into water before the discharge is considered noxious and subjects the polluter to punishment? Discharge of a gallon by one polluter may not warrant punishment, and a small quantity may not even be detectable. But what do we do with a hundred polluters, each of whom discharges a gallon?

Many other issues must be addressed as well. For instance, should accidental pollution warrant the same punishment as intentional or negligent pollution? Since many polluters are corporations, what are the implications of penalties that force a company to install costly antipollution devices? To cover the costs, the corporation may have to increase the price of its product, and so the consumer pays. Should the company be allowed to lower plant workers' wages instead? Should the plant be forced or permitted to shut down, thereby increasing unemployment in the community? The company may choose to move its plant to another state or country that is more hospitable.

Addressing Sensitive Issues Fines imposed on intentional polluters have been increased so that they can no longer be shrugged off as an ordinary cost of doing business. The

A catastrophic explosion at the Union Carbide plant in Bhopal, India, on December 2, 1984, spewed clouds of deadly gas, causing nearly 6,500 fatalities and more than 20,000 injuries.

General Electric Company was fined $7 million and the Allied Chemical Corporation $13.2 million for pollution offenses. Fines of such magnitude are powerful incentives to corporations to limit pollution. But since many of the enterprises that are likely to pollute are in the public sector, or produce for the public sector, the public ultimately will have to pay the fine in the form of increased gas or electricity bills.[53]

In the Third World, problems of punishing and preventing pollution are enormous. Industries preparing to locate there have the power to influence governments and officials, surreptitiously and officially, into passing legislation favorable to the industry. The desire to industrialize outweighs the desire to preserve the environment. Some countries find ways to address the problem, only to relinquish controls when they prove irksome. While Japan was trying to establish its industrial dominance, for example, it observed a constitutional provision stating: "The conservation of life environment shall be balanced against the needs of economic development."[54] This provision was deleted in 1970, when Japan had achieved economic strength.

Developing Effective Legislation U.S. legislators have several options in developing legislation to protect the environment:

- *The independent use of the criminal sanction: direct prohibition of polluting activities.* This is the way American legislators have typically tried to cope with the problem in the past. They simply made it a criminal offense to maintain a "nuisance," that is, an ongoing activity that pollutes the water, the soil, or the air.

- *The dependent-direct use of the criminal sanction: prohibition of certain polluting activities that exceed specified limits.* This is a more sophisticated legislative method. If pollution is to be kept at a low level, no one person or company can be allowed to emit more than an insignificant amount of noxious waste into the environment. This amount is fixed by administrative regulation. Anyone who exceeds the limit commits a criminal offense.

- *The dependent-indirect approach: criminal sanction reserved for firms that fail to comply with specific rulings rendered by administrative organs against violators of standards.* Under this option, polluters have already been identified by regulatory agencies, and they are now under order to comply with the agencies' requirements. If they violate these orders, a criminal punishment can be imposed.

- *The preventive use of the criminal sanction: penalties imposed for failure to install or maintain prescribed antipollution equipment.* This is the newest and most sophisticated means of regulating polluting industries. The law determines what preventive and protective measures must be taken (to filter industrial waste water, to put chemical screens on smokestacks, and so on). Any firm that fails to take the prescribed measures is guilty of a violation.[55]

In the past, legal systems relied primarily on the independent use of the criminal sanction. More recent legislation has concentrated on administrative orders and technological prevention.

Curbing Corporate Crime

Laws and regulations prescribing criminal sanctions have been passed and continue to be passed to guard the public against the dangers rooted in the power of corporate enterprise. As we noted, Congress passed sentencing guidelines that significantly increased corporate sanctions, but at the same time allowed for reductions in fines where there was evidence of organizational due diligence—that is, implementation of effective ethics **corporate compliance programs**.[56] While such laws, regulations, and guidelines may provide some disincentives for illegal acts, many governments recognize that criminal justice systems are not well prepared to deal with economic crimes, in terms of both strategy and resources.[57] They also recognize the importance of attacking this problem at the international level, perhaps by designing strategies, standards, and guidelines that may be helpful to all governments.[58]

A disturbing thought remains: Is imposing of criminal liability on the corporations themselves for their conduct really the best way to curb corporate misconduct? If corporations act on the decisions of their principal officers or agents, might it not be appropriate to restrict the reach of the law to these corporate actors rather than to subject the innocent and uninformed shareholders to financial loss? Why not rely more on administrative and civil proceedings? Both can and often do contain penalties that exceed those of the criminal law.

The recent spate of corporate scandals has brought about new legislation to combat corporate crime. Of particular note, is the Sarbanes-Oxley Act of 2002. At the center of this act are provisions that mandate auditor independence and increased penalties for securities fraud.

Specifically, the act:

1. Creates a full-time oversight board with broad authorities to regulate auditors of public companies, set auditing standards, and investigate violations of accounting practices. The board can enforce rules and prosecute violators without having to vet its decisions elsewhere. The new board will be funded by mandatory fees paid by all public companies.

2. Restricts the nonaudit services a public accounting firm may provide to its clients that are public companies.

3. Strengthens existing criminal penalties for corporate crime by expanding wire and mail fraud to 20-year crimes; creates a securities fraud felony punishable by up to 20 years in prison; and creates a new crime for schemes to defraud shareholders.

4. Raises the statute of limitations for financial fraud from three years to five years and to two years from the date of discovery.

5. Requires audit documents to be preserved for five years.

6. Protects victims' rights to recoup their losses by preventing fraud artists from hiding in bankruptcy or concealing their crime and using an unfair statute of limitations to hide.

7. Improves corporate whistleblower protections in cases of securities fraud by delineating remedies, including reinstatement, back pay, and compensatory damages, if the claimant prevails.

8. Requires that CEOs and CFOs forfeit bonuses, incentive-based compensation, and profits from stock sales if accounting

U.S. President Geoge W. Bush swears in William H. Donaldson as the new chairman of the Securities and Exchange Commission while White House Counsel Alberto R. Gonzales (L) and Donaldson's wife Jane (R) look on during the ceremony February 18, 2003, at the White House in Washington, DC. Donaldson replaced Harvey Pitt to head the Commission.

restatements result from material noncompliance with SEC financial reporting requirements.

9. Requires the SEC to adopt rules designed to protect the independence and integrity of securities analysts.

10. Bans companies from making personal loans to top executives.

11. Requires that the SEC conduct a study of corporations' use of off-balance-sheet transactions.

12. Prohibits corporate decision-makers from selling company stock at a time when their employees are prohibited from doing so.

13. Authorizes additional annual funding for the SEC—$776 million, up from $467 million.

14. Forces Wall Street investment research analysts to disclose any conflicts of interest that they or their financial institution might have in the investment recommendations that they make.

15. Requires the General Accounting Office, GAO, to conduct a study of the factors that have led to consolidation in the accounting industry and the impact that this has had on the securities markets.

16. Calls for an SEC study with respect to aider and abettor violations of the federal securities law.

17. Requires lawyers to notify company directors of any management misconduct that top officers refuse to rectify.

18. Requires corporate insiders, such as CEOs, when they trade the stock of the companies they manage, to take reasonable steps to disclose those transactions to their shareholders, including electronically disclosing those sales within two days.

19. Calls on the SEC to issue rules of professional conduct for corporate lawyers.

20. Requires members of a corporation's board of directors audit committee to be "independent" (not tied to company management).

21. Requires CEOs to certify the financial books of their company.[59]

Critics of the bill and other law reforms following the debacle of Enron and Andersen say this is a step in the right direction. Not surprisingly, however, they share a perception that not enough has been done to curb corporate abuses. One citizen watch group, Citizenworks, has detailed what was left out of the Sarbanes-Oxley Act of 2002 and what additional reforms are now necessary.

What Was Left Out? The bill does not deal with the biggest accounting loophole of all—the ability for companies to avoid expensing stock

Of Immediate Concern

Dangerous Ground: The World of Hazardous Waste Crime

What kind of person would illegally dump hazardous waste into the waterways and landscapes of America? Many would guess it might be a sinister organized crime operator. Some past published works on hazardous waste crime have, in fact, described this area of crime as being synonymous with syndicate crime.

This is the introduction to criminologist Donald J. Rebovich's controversial book *Dangerous Ground: The World of Hazardous Waste Crime*, in which he reports the results of an empirical study of hazardous waste offenders in four states. He continues:

> Surprisingly enough, the study has found that, most commonly, the criminal dumper is an ordinary, profit-motivated businessman who operates in a business where syndicate crime activity may be present but by no means pervasive. The research uncovers a criminal world of the hazardous waste offender unlike any theorized in the past. It is a world where the intensity, duration, and methods of the criminal act will be more likely determined by the criminal opportunities available in the legitimate marketplace than by the orders of a controlling criminal syndicate.

Rebovich's portrait of hazardous waste crime replaces our ideas about midnight dumping and masked dumpers with straightforward descriptions of hazardous waste treatment/storage/disposal (TSD) facilities failing to comply with state and federal regulations:

> The mark of a successful hazardous waste criminal—one who can maintain his criminal lifestyle for a lengthy duration—is his skill in effectively analyzing the potential threats to his livelihood and his versatility in adapting to those threats. For many TSD-facility operators, the serious game of working the system was played out by eluding the regulatory inspectors by capitalizing on either the inspectors' unfamiliarity with treatment apparatus or their lack of diligence in inspecting thoroughly.
>
> TSD-facility offenders did have to contend with monitoring devices, installed by regulators, that were used to gauge volume and properties of effluents released into local sewer systems to determine compliance with existing discharge standards. The mechanisms were intended to sample effluents randomly but, in reality, offenders found the system seriously flawed and did not hesitate to seize their opportunities to work the system in a new way.... The tests were simply rigged to elicit a false impression of the toxicity of the substances discharged into the sewer.

Rebovich makes this prediction:

> The characteristics of future hazardous waste offenders, and the crimes that they commit, will more than likely be determined by developments in several areas external to the criminal act: (1) pressure from the general public and public interest groups for stricter enforcement, (2) legislative expansion of the scope of legal coverage, (3) redesigned enforcement, and (4) future availability of affordable disposal outlets. These areas can be seen as the components of an equation that could lead to a reduction in hazardous waste crime.

Source

Donald J. Rebovich, *Dangerous Ground: The World of Hazardous Waste Crime* (New Brunswick, N.J.: Transaction, 1992).

Questions for Discussion

1. Illegal hazardous waste practices may be punished by fining the company or industry. Should individuals be punished as well?
2. Some TSD-facility operators have claimed that they were forced to use illegal practices because it is economically impossible to take care of hazardous wastes under current regulations. What is your reaction to such a defense?

---

options, even as they get a tax write-off. Relevant amendments by Senators John McCain (R-AZ) and Carl Levin (D-MI) were blocked. The bill does not extend responsibility for corporate fraud to accountants, lawyers, and banks, all of whom make fraud possible. A relevant amendment by Senator Richard Shelby (R-AL) was blocked.

The bill is limited in its **disgorgement.** The bill requires CEOs and CFOs to give back money they made from financial fraud. But two amendments that would have strengthened disgorgement were blocked. One, introduced by Senator Max Cleland (D-GA), would have expanded the disgorgement to all officers and directors who knew about the misconduct in filing the financial report. The other, introduced by Senator Byron Dorgan (D-ND), would have extended executives' disgorgement to 12 months prior to the filing of bankruptcy.

What Should Happen? Deeper reforms need to happen. Here are a few ideas:

1. *Deepen whistle-blower protection.* The accounting reform bill gives meaningful protection to corporate whistle-blowers who report information related to SEC violations or to the defrauding of shareholders. Similar protection must be afforded to those whistle-blowers who provide information on violations of consumer, environmental, and workplace safety laws and regulations.

2. *Repeal the 1995 Private Securities Litigation Reform Act.* This act facilitated the present scandals, protecting the enablers and internal watchdogs—the accountants and lawyers—from suit. It must be repealed.
3. *Debar lawbreakers.* The government shouldn't do business with crooks. Companies that are repeat lawbreakers should be ineligible for government contracts. Certainly a society that tolerates three-strikes-and-you're-out laws for individuals should apply a modest debarment sanction against corporate wrongdoers.
4. *Create a corporate crime database.* The FBI should maintain a corporate crime database, and produce an annual report, Corporate Crime in America, as an analog to its current Crime in America report (focused on street crime only).
5. *Outlaw the use of offshore tax havens.*[60] Offshore banks handled literally hundreds of billions of dollars, most for individuals and "businesses" dodging U.S. tax authorities. In the 400 or more banks in the Bahamas, for example, approximately $300 billion dollars are on deposit.

Curbing corporate crime is as much a matter of politics as careful law reform. As the effects of new legislation take place, we will see if critics are right that these first few steps are not enough.

The Future of White-Collar and Corporate Crime

Some of the most respected names on Wall Street are under investigation or indictment. Others have been criminally convicted and are bankrupt—desperately reinventing themselves or out of business entirely. From WorldCom to Merrill Lynch, the very companies that made billions for investors in the 1990s are both perpetrators and victims of fraud, mismanagement, and conflicts of interest (Table 12.9). And repercussions from the scandals continue. In April 2003, 10 Wall Street firms were forced to pay $1.4 billion to resolve charges that each firm issued biased research reports and hyped stocks. The firms represent the cream of the crop on the "Street"—Credit Suisse First Boston, Citigroup/Salomon Smith Barney, Bear Stearns, J. P. Morgan Chase, Lehman Brothers, UBS Warburg, Merrill Lynch, Morgan Stanley, Piper Jaffray, and Goldman Sachs.

The icon of this wave of corporate scandals is a company that now lays in ruin, bankrupt. Its property is up for auction. Its employees are desperately searching for jobs. If you are ever on eBay, you can buy a copy of the company's ethics code put up for sale by former employees looking to make a couple of dollars and prove the point that what companies say they are doing—and what they actually do—are often two very different things. In 2000 this company had worldwide assets of more than $65 billion and revenue of $101 billion. If you have guessed that this company was the pride of Houston, Texas, you are right! As of 2000, *Fortune* magazine called it "The Most Innovative Company in America." That year, the same magazine ranked it 22nd of the "100 Best Companies to Work for in America."

One can not imagine working for a more ethical and socially minded company. In its 2000 Corporate Responsibility Annual Report, the chairman and CEO of this company, Kenneth Lay, articulated four of its guiding principles:

Respect: We will work to foster mutual respect with communities and stakeholders who are affected by our operations; we will treat others as we would like to be treated ourselves.

Integrity: We will examine the impacts, positive and negative, of our business on the environment and on society, and will integrate human health, social, and environmental considerations into our internal management and value system.

Communication: We will strive to foster understanding and support with our stakeholders and communities, as well as measure and communicate our performance.

Excellence: We will continue to improve our performance and will encourage our business partners and suppliers to adhere to the same standards.

TABLE 12.9

WorldCom
• WorldCom has admitted orchestrating one of the largest accounting frauds in history.
• The company admitted that it had inflated its profits by $3.8 billion between January 2001 and March 2002. The firm was already shrouded in scandal after the departure of its founder and chief executive, Bernie Ebbers, in April. Mr. Ebbers borrowed hundreds of millions from the firm to underwrite the inflated prices he had paid for the company's own shares.
Enron
• When energy giant Enron reported its third quarter results on October 2001, it revealed a large, mysterious black hole that sent its share price tumbling.
• The U.S. financial regulator—the Securities and Exchange Commission—launched an investigation into the firm and its results. Enron then admitted it had inflated its profits, sending shares even lower. Enron is now bankrupt.
• Once it became clear that the firm's success was in effect an elaborate scam, a chorus of outraged investors, employees, pension holders, and politicians wanted to know why Enron's failings were not spotted earlier. The U.S. government is now thought to be studying the best way of bringing criminal charges against the company.
Andersen
• Attention quickly turned to Enron's auditors—Arthur Andersen. The obvious question was why did the auditors—charged with verifying the true state of the company's books—not know what was going on?
• Andersen reacted by destroying Enron documents, and on June 15, 2002, a guilty verdict was reached in an obstruction of justice case. The verdict signaled an end to the already mortally wounded accountancy firm. This wasn't the first time Andersen's practices had come under scrutiny—it had previously been fined by the SEC for auditing work for waste-disposal firm Waste Management in the mid-1990s.
• The Andersen case raises a wider question about accounting in the United States and how it might restore its reputation as the guarantor of the honest presentation of accounts.
Adelphia
• Telecom company Adelphia Communications filed for bankruptcy on June 25, 2002.
• The sixth largest American cable television operator is facing regulatory and criminal investigations into its accounting. The company has restated its profits for the past two years and admitted that it didn't have as many cable television subscribers as it claimed. The firm has dismissed its accountants, Deloitte & Touche.
Xerox
• In April, the SEC filed a civil suit against photocopy giant Xerox for misstating four years' worth of profits, resulting in an overstatement of close to $3 billion. Xerox negotiated a settlement with the SEC with regard to the suit.
• As part of that agreement, Xerox agreed to pay a $10 million fine and restate four years' worth of trading statements, while neither admitting, nor denying, any wrongdoing. The penalty is the largest ever imposed by the SEC against a publicly traded firm in relation to accounting misdeeds.
Tyco
• In early June, the U.S. District Attorney extended a criminal investigation of the firm's former chief executive, Dennis Kozlowski.
• Dennis Kozlowski—the man behind the creation of the Tyco conglomerate—is charged with avoiding $1 million in New York state sales taxes on purchases of artwork worth $13 million. The SEC enquiry into Tyco is understood to relate solely to Mr. Kozlowski—but there are investor fears the probe could reveal accounting irregularities. Tyco said it has filed a lawsuit against one of its former directors, Frank Walsh, for taking an unauthorized fee of $20 million.
Global Crossing
• Global Crossing was briefly one of the shiniest stars of the hi-tech firmament.
• The telecom network firm filed for Chapter 11 bankruptcy on January 28, 2001. The peculiar economics of bandwidth meant that firms could drum up the appearance of lively business by trading network access with each other. They could effectively book revenues when in many cases no money at all changed hands.
• U.S. regulators are now looking closely at the collapse, questioning whether it is another case of a company flattering its figures.
Merrill Lynch
• In this atmosphere of corporate distrust, the role of investment banks has also faced increased scrutiny.
• Analysts were suspected of advising investors to buy stocks they secretly thought were worthless. The rationale for this "false advice" was that they might then be able to secure investment banking business from the companies concerned. Merrill Lynch reached a settlement with New York attorney general Eliot Spitzer. The settlement imposed a $100 million fine upon Merrill but demanded no admission of guilt.
• Under the deal, Merrill Lynch has agreed to sever all links between analysts' pay and investment banking revenues.

The name of this company, in case you have not yet guessed it, is Enron Corporation. Enron was created in 1985 following a merger of Houston Natural Gas and InterNorth, a natural gas company with headquarters in Omaha, Nebraska. Both companies were in the business of transporting and selling natural gas and their merger created a network of more than 37,000 miles of gas pipeline. Soon after the merger, however, deregulation of the nation's energy markets, including the natural gas market, posed a significant challenge for Enron's business model. With the help of the large and prestigious consulting firm of McKinsey & Co., Enron diversified, going into the business of creating its own natural gas market, that is, buying and selling gas through contracts while controlling costs and prices.

Jeff Skilling, the young McKinsey consultant who brought the idea of Enron creating its own energy market, was hired as chairman and CEO of Enron Finance Corporation, later becoming president and chief operating officer of Enron. And the rest is history, a very sad page of business history. The history of Enron is marked by a single employee corporate **whistle-blower,** Sherron Watkins, who sent a one-page anonymous letter to Ken Lay (then chief executive officer) immediately after Jeff Skilling resigned, unexpectedly. Portions of it read:

> Has Enron become a risky place to work? For those of us who didn't get rich over the last few years, can we afford to stay? . . . The spotlight will be on us, the market just can't accept that Skilling is leaving his dream job. I think that the valuation issues can be fixed and reported with other good will write-downs to occur in 2002. How do we fix the Raptor and Condor deals? They unwind in 2002 and 2003, we will have to pony up Enron stock and that won't go unnoticed.
>
> To the layman on the street, it will look like we recognized funds flow of $800 million from merchant asset sales in 1999 by selling to a vehicle (Condor) that we capitalized with a promise of Enron stock in later years. Is that really funds flow or is it cash from equity issuance?
>
> We have recognized over $550 million of fair value gains on stocks via our swaps with Raptor. Much of that stock has declined significantly—Avici by 98 percent from $178 million, to $5 million; the New Power Company by 80 percent from $40 a share, to $6 a share. The value in the swaps won't be there for Raptor, so once again Enron will issue stock to offset these losses. Raptor is an LJM entity. It sure looks to the layman on the street that we are hiding losses in a related company and will compensate that company with Enron stock in the future.
>
> I am incredibly nervous that we will implode in a wave of accounting scandals. My eight years of Enron work history will be worth nothing on my résumé, the business world will consider the past successes as nothing but an elaborate accounting hoax. Skilling is resigning now for "personal reasons" but I would think he wasn't having fun, looked down the road and knew this stuff was unfixable and would rather abandon ship now than resign in shame in two years.

You need not understand the accounting alchemy that Enron used to defraud investors, for example, special purpose entities like Raptor or Condor and "related party transactions and disclosures." Many accountants still find these technicalities difficult to explain. Suffice it to say, Enron was built on an accounting house of cards. When that house tumbled down, a host of victims emerged, from the thousands of loyal and hardworking Enron employees to countless investors whose pensions and retirement plans dramatically lost value. Once nearly a $90 per share stock, Enron stock certificates trade on eBay as collectors' items. The accounting firm that offered advice and counsel to Enron, Arthur Andersen, LLP, was indicted and convicted of obstruction of justice for shredding thousands of documents relating to Enron audits. They, too, suffered corporate death. Tens of thousands of Andersen employees sought employment elsewhere as the accounting world watched in horror. It was common to refer to Andersen as one of the top five accounting firms. Now there are four.

Most important, Enron and the fall of Arthur Andersen sent a strong signal that Wall Street had a problem with corporate governance, that is, the way in which a corporation is managed and overseen. Principles of corporate governance require that both senior management and the board of directors participate in the affairs of the company. But they do so differently. Senior managers run the day-to-day operations of the company. The board of directors has the special function of providing an independent oversight of senior manager—an independent check on managers. This is accomplished through audit committees, finance committees, and compensation committees that tirelessly review the health of the company. In recent years, boards were called upon to see that systems of internal controls are implemented and monitored.

What happened to the systems of control and governance structures of Enron? Why did they fail? Answers are difficult to find, particularly because Enron followed many of the "best practices" of corporate governance, including an independent board of directors of competent outsiders. Enron had all of the trappings of an ethical, Fortune 500 company with a bright future. Until answers to the many questions of Enron emerge, it is only fair to ask: How significant is the problem of corporate misgovernance in the United States? To this the only answer is that the future of Wall Street and its perceived legitimacy hang in the balance.

REVIEW

Organizational crimes are characterized by the use of a legitimate or illegitimate business enterprise for illegal profit. As American corporations grew in the nineteenth and twentieth centuries, they amassed much of the nation's wealth. Many corporations abused their economic power. Government stepped in to curb such abuses by legislation.

Edwin Sutherland, who provided the first scholarly insight into the wrongdoing of corporations, originated the concept of white-collar crime. Subsequent scholars have distinguished white-collar crime, committed by individuals, from corporate crime, committed by business organizations. Corporate or individual white-collar offenses include securities-related crimes, such as misrepresentation and churning; bankruptcy fraud of various kinds; fraud against the government, in particular contract and procurement fraud; consumer fraud; insurance fraud; tax fraud; bribery and political fraud; and insider-related fraud. In the twentieth century, corporations have been subjected to criminal liability for an increasing number of offenses, including common law crimes and environmental as well as other statutory offenses.

The phases of the corporate criminal law include a transition from a period when concerns over personhood predominated to a time when corporations used creative strategies to avoid criminal liability. In recent years the United States Sentencing Guidelines for Organizations serve as an inspiration for the ethical behavior of corporations. Models of corporate culpability that focus on proactive fault, reactive fault, corporate culture, constructive concepts of organizations, and corporate policy extend current law. With a recent history of corporate scandals, it seems clear that the future of organizational criminality and the legitimacy of Wall Street, are inextricably connected.

CRIMINOLOGY & PUBLIC POLICY

"Sutherland challenged the traditional image of criminals and the predominant etiological theories of crime of his day. The white-collar criminals he identified were middle-aged men of respectability and high-social status. They lived in affluent neighborhoods, and they were well respected in the community. Sutherland was not the first to draw attention to such criminals. In earlier decades, scholars such as W. A. Bonger (1916) and E. A. Ross (1907) and popular writers such as Upton Sinclair (1906) and Lincoln Steffens (1903) pointed out a variety of misdeeds by businessmen and elites. However, such people were seldom considered by those who wrote about or studied crime and were not a major concern of the public or policy makers when addressing the crime problem."[1]

(Source: David Weisburd and Elin Waring, *White-Collar Crime and Criminal Careers* p. 8 (2001).)

Questions for Discussion Professors Weisburd and Waring make the point, in the introduction to their book White-Collar Crime and Criminal Careers, that much of the conventional wisdom of white-collar offenders is untrue. These researchers previously established that white-collar offenders are not "elite" offenders as Sutherland conceived. White-collar criminals generally come from the middle class and have multiple contacts with the criminal justice system. White-collar offenders have criminal careers, as well! What can you conclude from the similarity between and among white-collar and street criminals? Should criminologists expect meaningful differences in the life course of their offender? Should policy makers ensure different or similar treatmen in the criminal process?

YOU BE THE CRIMINOLOGIST

For obvious reasons the extent of corporate crime is difficult to assess and measure. But criminologists do not shy away from significant challenges. How would you approach the problem of assessing and measuring crimes committed by corporations?

KEY TERMS

The numbers next to the terms refer to the pages on which the terms are defined.

bankruptcy fraud (322)
boiler rooms (322)
churning (322)
consumer fraud (326)
corporate compliance programs (344)
corporate crime (331)
corporate due diligence (344)
corporate ethos (337)
corporate policy (337)
disgorgement (346)
embezzlement (330)
insider trading (322)
occupational crimes (321)
proactive corporate fault (337)
reactive corporate fault (337)
Sherman Antitrust Act (339)
stock manipulation (322)
vicarious liability (337)
whistle-blower (348)
white-collar crime (319)

CHAPTER 13
Public Order Crimes

Drug Abuse and Crime
    The History of Drug Abuse
    The Extent of Drug Abuse
    Patterns of Drug Abuse
    Crime-Related Activities
    The International Drug Economy
    Drug Control

Alcohol and Crime
    The History of Legalization
    Crime-Related Activities

Sexual Morality Offenses
    Deviate Sexual Intercourse by Force or Imposition
    Prostitution
    Pornography

REVIEW

CRIMINOLOGY & PUBLIC POLICY

YOU BE THE CRIMINOLOGIST

KEY TERMS

Boxes
    From the Pages of *The New York Times*: *One City Wonders: Can We Win the War on Drugs?*
    Of Immediate Concern: *Cyberporn: Problems and Controversies*
    Window to the World: *Global Sexual Slavery: Women and Children*

Special Features
    Crime Surfing
    Did You Know?
    Theory Connects

KEY TERMS
money laundering
pimp
pornography
prostitution
sodomy
statutory rape

Strip club and x-rated shops tend to be concentrated in the seedier parts of town.

In cities across the country and around the world, people buying and selling illicit goods and services congregate in certain areas that are easily identifiable by theater marquees advertising live sex shows. Shops feature everything from child pornography to sadomasochistic slide shows; prostitutes openly solicit clients; drunks propped up in doorways clutch brown bags; drug addicts deal small amounts of whatever they can get to sell to support their habits. The friendly locals will deliver virtually any service to visitors, for a price.

The activities involved—prostitution, drunkenness, sex acts between consenting adults for money, drug use—were commonly called "victimless" crimes. Perhaps that is because it was assumed that people who engaged in them rationally chose to do so and did not view themselves as victims. Often no one complains to the police about being victimized by such consensual activity.

But contemporary forms of such activities and their ramifications may entail massive victimizations: How many murders are committed during drug gang wars? How many thefts are committed by addicts seeking to support their habits? How much damage is done to persons and property by drunken drivers? Does pornography encourage physical abuse? And what of the future of children sold for prostitution?

DRUG ABUSE AND CRIME

A woman arrives at the airport in Los Angeles with very few belongings, no hotel reservations, no family or friends in the United States, and a passport showing eight recent trips from Bogotá, Colombia. A pat-down and strip search reveal a firm, distended abdomen, which is discovered to hold 88 balloons filled with cocaine.[1] In New York City, a heroin addict admits that "the only livin' thing that counts is the fix . . . : Like I would steal off anybody—anybody, at all, my own mother gladly included."[2] In Chicago, crack cocaine has transformed some of the country's toughest gangs into ghetto-based drug-trafficking organizations that guard their turf with automatic weapons and assault rifles.[3]

On a college campus in the northeast a crowd sits in the basement of a fraternity house drinking beer and smoking pot through the night. At a beachfront house in Miami three young professional couples gather for a barbecue. After dinner they sit down at a card table in the playroom. On a mirror, someone lines up a white powdery substance into rows about 1/8 inch wide and 1 inch long. Through rolled-up paper they breathe the powder into their nostrils and await the "rush" of the coke. In a quiet suburban home two middle school students inhale paint thinner after school.

These incidents demonstrate that when we speak of the "drug problem," we are talking about a wide variety of conditions that stretch beyond our borders, that involve all social classes, that in one way or another touch most people's lives, and that cost society significant sums of money (Figure 13.1). The drug scene includes manufacturers, importers, primary distributors (for large geographical areas), smugglers (who transport large quantities of drugs from their place of origin), dealers (who sell drugs on the street and in crack houses), corrupt criminal justice officials, users who endanger other people's lives through negligence (train engineers, pilots, physicians), and even unborn children (Table 13.1).

The drug problem is further complicated by the wide diversity of substances abused, their varying effects on the mind and body, and the kinds of dependencies users develop. There is also the much-debated issue of the connection between drug use and crime—an issue infinitely more complex than the stereotype of maddened addicts committing heinous acts because they either were under the influence of drugs or needed to get the money to support a habit. Many of the crimes we have discussed in earlier chapters are part of what has been called the nation's (or the world's) drug problem. Let us examine this problem in detail.

> **:// Crime Surfing**
>
> www.whitehousedrugpolicy.gov/
>
> Find out more about the national drug control policy.

The History of Drug Abuse

The use of chemical substances that alter physiological and psychological functioning dates back to the Old Stone Age.[4] Egyptian relics from 3500 B.C. depict the use of opium in religious rituals. By 1600 B.C. an Egyptian reference work listed opium as an analgesic, or painkiller. The Incas of South America are known to have used cocaine at least 5,000 years ago. Cannabis, the hemp plant from which marijuana and hashish are derived, also has a 5,000-year history.[5]

Since antiquity, people have cultivated a variety of drugs for religious, medicinal, and social purposes. The modern era of drug abuse in the United States began with the use of drugs for medicinal purposes. By the nineteenth century the two components of opium, which is derived from the sap of the opium poppy, were identified and given the names "morphine" and "codeine." Ignorant of the addictive properties of these drugs, physicians used them to treat a wide variety of human illnesses. So great was their popularity that they found their way into almost all patent medicines used for pain relief and were even incorporated in soothing syrups for babies (Mother Barley's Quieting Syrup and Mumm's Elixir were very popular).

During the Civil War the use of injectable morphine to ease the pain of battle casualties was so extensive that morphine addiction among veterans came to be known as the "soldier's disease."[6] By the time the medical profession and the public recognized just how addic-

FIGURE 13.1 National Spending for Drug Control.

FY 2003 President's Request, by Function (Total Resources: $11.5 Billion)

- Prevention w/Research $1,988.6 — 17%
- $2,859.5 Domestic Law Enforcement — 25%
- Interdiction $2,155.8 — 19%
- International $1,113.2 — 10%
- Treatment w/Research $3,377.6 — 29%

Dollars in Millions

Demand Reduction and Domestic Law Enforcement Account for the Bulk of Federal Drug Control Spending (Fiscal Year 1986–2001)

FY2000 and 2001 include U.S. support for Plan Colombia and the Andean Region.

$2.9 B … $12.0 B … $13.1 B … $19.2 B

— Demand Reduction
— Domestic Law Enforcement
— International
— Interdiction

*enacted

Source: Office of National Drug Control Policy, *Fact Sheet: Drug Data Summary* (Washington, D.C.: U.S. Government Printing Office, April 1999), updated to 2002.

tive morphine was, its use had reached epidemic proportions. Then in 1898 the Bayer Company in Germany introduced a new opiate, supposedly a nonaddictive substitute for morphine and codeine. It came out under the trade name Heroin; yet it proved to be even more addictive than morphine.[7]

When cocaine, which was isolated from the coca leaf in 1860, appeared on the national drug scene, it too was used for medicinal purposes. (Its use to unblock the sinuses initiated the "snorting" of cocaine into the nostrils.) Its popularity spread, and soon it was used in other products: Peruvian Wine of Coca ($1 a bottle in

TABLE 13.1 Roles and Functions in the Drug Distribution Business Compared with those in Legitimate Industry

Approximate Role Equivalents in Legal Markets	Roles by Common Names at Various Stages of the Drug Distribution Business	Major Functions Accomplished at This Level
Grower producer	Coca farmer, opium farmer, marijuana grower	Grow coca, opium, marijuana: the raw materials
Manufacturer	Collector, transporter, elaborator, chemist, drug lord	All stages for preparation of heroin, cocaine, marijuana as commonly sold
Traffickers		
Importer	Multikilo importer, mule, airplane pilot, smuggler, trafficker, money launderer	Smuggling of large quantities of substances into the United States
Wholesale distributor	Major distributor, investor, "kilo connection"	Transportation and redistribution of multikilograms and single kilograms
Dealers		
Regional distributor	Pound and ounce men, weight dealers	Adulteration and sale of moderately expensive products
Retail store owner	House connections, suppliers, crack-house supplier	Adulteration and production of retail-level dosage units (bags, vials, grams) in very large numbers
Assistant manager, security chief, or accountant	"Lieutenant," "muscle men," transporter, crew boss, crack-house manager/proprietor	Supervises three or more sellers, enforces informal contracts, collects money, distributes multiple dosage units to actual sellers
Sellers		
Store clerk, salesmen (door-to-door and phone)	Street drug seller, runner, juggler	Makes actual direct sales to consumer; private seller responsible for both money and drugs
Low-Level Distributors		
Advertiser, security guards, leaflet distributor	Steerer, tout, cop man, lookout, holder runner, help friend, guard, go-between	Assists in making sales, advertises, protects seller from police and criminals, solicits customers; handles drugs or money but not both
Servant, temporary employee	Run shooting gallery, injector (of drugs), freebaser, taster, apartment cleaner, drug bagger, fence, money launderer	Provides short-term services to drug users or sellers for money or drugs; not responsible for money or drugs

Source: Bruce D. Johnson, Terry Williams, Kojo A. Dir, and Harry Sanabria, "Drug Abuse in the Inner City: Impact on Hard-Drug Users and the Community," in *Drugs and Crime*, vol. 13: *Crime and Justice*, eds. Michael Tonry and James Q. Wilson (Chicago: University of Chicago Press, 1990), p. 19. © 1990 by the University of Chicago Press. All rights reserved. From U.S. Department of Justice, *Drugs, Crime and the Justice System* (Washington, D.C.: U.S. Government Printing Office, 1992).

the Sears, Roebuck catalog), a variety of tonics, and, the most famous of all, Coca-Cola, which was made with coca until 1903.[8]

As the consumption of opium products (narcotics) and cocaine spread, states passed a variety of laws to restrict the sale of these substances. Federal authorities estimated that there were 200,000 addicts in the early 1900s. Growing concern over the increase in addiction led in 1914 to the passage of the Harrison Act, designed to regulate the domestic use, sale, and transfer of opium and coca products. Though this legislation decreased the number of addicts, it was a double-edged sword: By restricting the importation and distribution of drugs, it paved the way for the drug smuggling and black-market operations that are so deeply entrenched today.

It was not until the 1930s that the abuse of marijuana began to arouse public concern. Because marijuana use was associated with groups outside the social mainstream—petty criminals, jazz musicians, bohemians, and, in the Southwest, Mexicans—a public outcry for its regulation arose.[9] Congress responded with the Marijuana

Tax Act of 1937, which placed a prohibitive tax of $100 an ounce on the drug. With the passage of the Boggs Act in 1951, penalties for possession of and trafficking in marijuana (and other controlled substances) increased. Despite all the legislation, the popularity of marijuana continued.

As the drugs being used proliferated to include glue, tranquilizers (such as Valium and Librium), LSD, and many others, the public became increasingly aware of the dangers of drug abuse. In 1970 another major drug law, the Comprehensive Drug Abuse Prevention and Control Act (the Controlled Substances Act), updated all federal drug laws since the Harrison Act.[10] This act placed marijuana in the category of the most serious substances. The 1970 federal legislation made it necessary to bring state legislation into conformity with federal law. The Uniform Controlled Substances Act was drafted and now is the law in 48 states, the District of Columbia, Puerto Rico, the Virgin Islands, and Guam.

Most of the basic federal antidrug legislation has been drawn together in Title 21 of the United States Code, the collection of all federal laws. It includes many amendments passed since 1970, especially the Anti-Drug Abuse Act of 1988, which states: "It is the declared policy of the United States Government to create a drug-free America by 1995."[11]

Title 21, as amended, has elaborate provisions for the funding of national and international drug programs; establishes the Office of National Drug Control Policy, headed by a so-called drug czar; and provides stiff penalties for drug offenses. The manufacture, distribution, and dispensing of listed substances in stated (large) quantities are each subject to a prison sentence of 10 years to life and a fine (for individuals) of $4 million to $10 million. Even simple possession now carries a punishment of up to 1 year in prison and a $100,000 fine. Title 21, along with other recent crime-control legislation, defines many other drug crimes as well and provides for the forfeiture of any property constituting or derived from the proceeds of drug trading.

The Extent of Drug Abuse

Historically, the substance (other than alcohol) most frequently abused in the United States has been marijuana. In annual surveys, high school seniors were asked whether they ever used marijuana. Between 1975 and 1991, the percentage answering yes ranged from a high of 51 percent in 1979 to a low of 37 percent in 1991. The survey also found that in 1991, 24 percent had used marijuana in the past year, and 14 percent in the past month.[12]

The most recent national household survey shows a slight decrease in drug use among youths between the ages of 12 and 17 after almost a decade of rising rates. Almost 10 percent of America's youths report the recent use of illegal drugs, and an estimated 13.6 million Americans, or 6.2 percent of the population over age 12, reported recent drug use. After dramatic increases in the use of marijuana, cocaine, LSD, and other hallucinogens between 1992 and 1995, the rate of use for all these drugs has stabilized.[13]

In the 1980s cocaine constituted the country's major drug problem. An estimated 22 million people had tried the substance, and another 4 million were using it regularly. In 1998 the number of regular users had dropped to 1.5 million.[14] The use of heroin is much less pervasive; the number of users is estimated to be about 600,000.[15] Other drugs on the market are crack (a derivative of cocaine) and the so-called designer drugs—substances that have been chemically altered in such a way that they no longer fall within the legal definition of controlled substances.[16]

It is difficult to measure how many people abuse drugs in any given period. The national household survey has shown a decline in the use of illicit drugs between 1979 and 1991, followed by an increase. The most recent data demonstrate a leveling off of drug use by high school students (Table 13.2 and Figure 13.2).[17]

Patterns of Drug Abuse

New and more potent varieties of illicit substances, as well as increasing levels of violent crime associated with drug abuse, have led researchers to ask many questions about the phenomenon. Is drug abuse a symptom of an underlying mental or psychological disorder that makes some people more vulnerable than others? Some investigators argue that the addict is

TABLE 13.2 Highlights of the 2001 National Household Survey

Illicit Drug Use

- In 2001, an estimated 15.9 million Americans were current illicit drug users, meaning they had used an illicit drug in the month prior to the interview. This number represents a slight decrease from 2000. The number of illicit drug users was at its highest level in 1979, when there were 25 million.
- Between 1997 and 1998, the rate of past-month illicit drug use among youths decreased from 11.4 percent to 9.9 percent. The rate is still twice what it was in 1992.
- In 1998, youth marijuana use decreased slightly from its 1997 level, from 9.4 percent to 8.3 percent.
- The overall number of current cocaine users did not change significantly between 1997 and 1998 (1.8 million in 1998 and 1.5 million in 1997). However, use is down from a peak of 5.7 million in 1985.
- There were an estimated 1.1 million new hallucinogen users in 1997. The rate of initiation among youths ages 12 to 17 increased between 1991 and 1995, from 11.1 to 25.0 per thousand potential new users, and was constant from 1995 to 1997 (23.9 percent).
- In 1997, an estimated 81,000 people used heroin for the first time. The rate of initiation for youths between 1994 and 1997 was at the highest level since the early 1970s.
- An estimated 2.1 million persons first used marijuana in 1997. This number represents a significant decrease since 1996.
- In 1997 and 1998 an estimated 4.1 million people met diagnostic criteria for dependence on illicit drugs, including 1.1 million youths ages 12 to 17.

Alcohol Use

- In 2001, 109 million Americans age 12 and older had used alcohol in the past month. About 33 million engaged in binge drinking (five or more drinks on at least one occasion in the past month), and about 12 million were heavy drinkers (drinking five or more drinks per occasion on 5 or more days in the past 30 days).
- About 10.1 million drinkers were under age 21 in 2001. Of these, 6.8 million were binge drinkers, including 2.1 million heavy drinkers.

Cigarette Use

- In 2001 an estimated 66.5 million Americans were current smokers. This number represents a smoking rate of 29.5 percent.
- Among youths ages 12 to 17, there were no significant changes in rates of use of the different forms of tobacco products.
- Current smokers are more likely to be heavy drinkers and illicit drug users than are nonsmokers. Youths ages 12 to 17 who currently smoked cigarettes were 11.4 times more likely to use illicit drugs and 16 times more likely to drink heavily than nonsmoking youths.
- In 1997, an estimated 2.1 million people became daily smokers. More than half of these new smokers were under age 18 (3,000 new youth smokers per day).

characterized by strong dependency needs, feelings of inadequacy, a need for immediate gratification, and lack of internal controls.[18] Or is it possible that addicts lack certain body chemicals and that drugs make them feel better by compensating for that deficit?

Perhaps the causes are environmental. Is drug abuse a norm in deteriorated inner cities, where youngsters are learning how to behave from older addicted role models? Do people escape from the realities of slum life by retreating into drug abuse?[19] If so, how do we explain drug abuse among the upper classes?

Just as there are many causes of drug abuse, there are many addict lifestyles—and the lifestyles may be linked to the use of particular substances. During the 1950s, heroin abuse began to increase markedly in the inner cities, particularly among young black and Hispanic males.[20] In fact, it was their drug of choice throughout the 1960s and early 1970s. Heroin addicts spend their days buying heroin, finding a safe place to shoot the substance into a vein with a needle attached to a hypodermic syringe, waiting for the euphoric feeling, or rush, that follows the injection, and ultimately reaching a feeling of overall well-being known as a high, which lasts about four hours.[21] The heroin abuser's lifestyle is typically characterized by poor health, crime, arrest, imprisonment, and

The counter-cultural Woodstock Music and Art Fair in 1969 drew over 450,000 people to open fields in New York state. The rock concert, where drugs and "free" love flowed, lasted for four days.

temporary stays in drug treatment programs.[22] Today AIDS, which is spread, among other ways, by the shared use of needles, has become the most serious health problem among heroin addicts.

During the 1960s marijuana became one of the major drugs of choice in the United States, particularly among white, middle-class young people who identified themselves as antiestablishment. Their lifestyles were distinct from those of the inner-city heroin addicts. What began as a hippie drug culture in the Haight-Ashbury area of San Francisco spread quickly through the country's college campuses.[23] In fact, a Harvard psychologist, Timothy Leary, traveled across the country in the 1960s telling students to "turn on, tune in, and drop out."

Young marijuana users tended to live for the moment. Disillusioned by what they perceived as a rigid and hypocritical society, they challenged its norms through deviant behavior. Drugs—first marijuana, then hallucinogens (principally LSD), amphetamines, and barbiturates—came to symbolize the counterculture.[24]

In the 1960s and 1970s, attitudes toward recreational drug use became quite lax, perhaps as a result of the wide acceptance of marijuana.[25] By the 1980s, cocaine, once associated only with deviants, had become the drug of choice among the privileged, who watched (and copied) the well-publicized drug-oriented lifestyles of some celebrities and athletes. Typical cocaine users were well-educated, prosperous, upwardly mobile professionals in their twenties and thirties. They were lawyers and architects, editors and stockbrokers. They earned enough money to spend at least $100 an evening on their illegal recreational activities. By and large they were otherwise law-abiding, even though they knew their behavior was against the law.

The popularity of cocaine waned toward the end of the 1980s. The same is not true for crack, however, which spread to the inner-city population that had abused heroin in the latter part of the 1980s.[26] Crack is cheaper than powdered cocaine, fast-acting, and powerful. Though individual doses are inexpensive, once a person is hooked on crack, a daily supply can run between $100 and $250.

FIGURE 13.2 Past month drug use by high school seniors, by drug type: 1975 to 2001

Source: From Office of National Drug Control Policy, Drug Use Trends: October 2002 (www.whitehousedrugpolicy.gov/publications/factsht/druguse/).

Actor Robert Downey Jr. in a Malibu, California, courtroom just prior to being sentenced to six months in jail for violating parole on a prior drug conviction. Subsequently, in 2002, he was once again in trouble when authorities allegedly found drugs in his Palm Springs hotel room.

Drug addicts continually search for new ways to extend their highs. In 1989 a mixture of crack and heroin, called "crank," began to be used. Crank is smoked in a pipe.[27] It is potentially very dangerous, first, because it prolongs the brief high of crack alone and, second, because it appeals to younger drug addicts who are concerned about the link between AIDS and the sharing of hypodermic needles. The history of drug abuse is evolutionary. "Crank" is now the name of methamphetamine—also known as "ice," "crystal," "chalk," and "speed."

Crime-Related Activities

Many researchers have examined the criminal implications of addiction to heroin and, more recently, cocaine. James Inciardi found that 356 addicts in Miami, according to self-reports, committed 118,134 offenses (27,464 Index crimes) over a one-year period.[28] A national program, Drug Use Forecasting, found that in 1996, 49 to 82 percent of arrestees in 24 major U.S. cities had used drugs.[29] Official statistics on drug-related offenses make it quite clear that street crime is significantly related to drug abuse.

The nature of the drug-crime relationship, however, is less clear. Is the addict typically an adolescent who never committed a crime before he or she became hooked, but who thereafter was forced to commit crimes to get money to support the drug habit? In other words, does drug abuse lead to crime?[30] Or does criminal behavior precede drug abuse? Another possibility is that both drug abuse and criminal behavior stem from the same factors (biological, psychological, or sociological).[31] The debate continues, and many questions are still unanswered. But on one point most researchers agree: Whatever the temporal or causal sequence of drug abuse and crime, the frequency and seriousness of criminality increase as addiction increases. Drug abuse may not "cause" criminal behavior, but it does enhance it.[32]

Until the late 1970s most investigators of the drug-crime relationship reported that drug abusers were arrested primarily for property offenses. Recent scholarly literature, however, presents a different perspective. There appears to be an increasing amount of violence associated with drugs, and it may be attributable largely to the appearance of crack. Beginning in the 1980s and continuing to today, drug wars became more frequent. Cities across the country have been divided into distinct turfs. Rival drug dealers settle disputes with guns, power struggles within a single drug enterprise lead to assaults and homicides, one dealer robs another, informers are killed, their associates retaliate, and bystanders, some of them children, get caught in the cross fire.[33]

The International Drug Economy

The drug problem is a worldwide phenomenon, beyond the power of any one government to deal with.[34] Nor are drugs a concern simply of law enforcement agencies. Drugs influence politics, international relations, peace and war, and the economies of individual countries and of the world. Let us take a look at the political and economic impact of the international drug trade, specifically as it concerns cocaine, heroin, and marijuana. Figure 13.3 shows the sources of these drugs and some shipping routes.

FIGURE 13.3 Worldwide drug smuggling routes, 1993.

A Lahu hill tribe girl in Myanmar holds opium poppies as she assists her tribe in eradicating illegal poppies.

Cocaine Today the largest cocaine producer is Peru, although harvests have been decreasing since 1995. Annual harvests of 95,600 to 130,200 metric tons of coca leaves yield from 178 to 242 tons of pure cocaine. Cocaine production in Colombia has increased in recent years, with a cocaine base production of 580 tons in 2000.[35] Colombia also exports more than any other country—over half the world's supply—because much of the raw coca of Peru and other coca producers, such as Bolivia, is refined into cocaine in Colombia. The "cocaine cartel," which controls production and distribution, is said to be composed of no more than 12 families, located principally in Colombia and Bolivia. However, organized-crime interests in other South American countries are establishing themselves in the market.

Each year nearly half of all cocaine seized was shipped to the United States on private planes. Small planes evade controls and land on little-used airstrips or drop their cargos offshore to waiting speedboats.[36] Boats carrying drugs then mingle with local pleasure craft and bring the cargo to shore. Wholesalers who work for the Colombian cartels take care of the nationwide distribution. Some of the estimated 100,000 Colombians living illegally in the United States are thought to belong to the distribution apparatus.

Heroin "Just five years ago, almost all of the heroin seized came from Asia. Today, 32 percent of heroin seized can be traced to South America, with an estimated 20,000 hectares of opium poppies being cultivated in Colombia alone." This statement, made by the former head of the Justice Department's Drug Enforcement Administration, Thomas Constantine, sheds light on the recent expansion in scope of Colombia's cash crop. This diversification is a direct result of simple economics—while 1 kilogram of cocaine sells for $10,000 to $40,000 on the streets, an equal amount of South American heroin fetches anywhere from $85,000 to $180,000.

Production of heroin in all countries is organized by local warlords, illegitimate traders, and corrupt administrators; it is tending to come increasingly under the control of *triads*—organized-crime families of Chinese origin based in Hong Kong and Taiwan. More and more, heroin in the United States comes from

> **Did You Know?**
>
> . . . that white intravenous drug users outnumber black users 5 to 1? However, for every 100 white addicts there are 5 arrests, compared with 20 arrests for every 100 black addicts.

Mexico. Most of the heroin from the Golden Crescent and Golden Triangle enters the United States on commercial aircraft, whereas Mexican heroin comes overland. In Europe and in the United States the traditional Sicilian Mafia families have assumed significant roles in the refining and distribution of heroin.

Marijuana Because marijuana is bulky, smugglers initially transported it on oceangoing vessels. From January through October 1986, 87 percent of the total volume of marijuana seized was taken from privately owned pleasure craft or charter vessels not engaged in commercial trade. Today, most of the Colombian marijuana—about one-third of all marijuana imported into the United States—is shipped by sea. Mexican marijuana, trucked overland, makes up another third, and the remainder comes in by private plane from such countries as Belize and Jamaica. Hashish, a concentrated form of marijuana that comes predominantly from Pakistan (60 to 65 percent) and Lebanon (25 to 30 percent), is brought in by noncommercial ships.

Money Laundering The illegal drug economy is vast. Annual sales are estimated to be between $300 billion and $500 billion. The American drug economy alone generates $40 billion to $50 billion in sales. Profits are enormous, and no taxes are paid on them. Because the profits are "dirty money," they must undergo **money laundering**. Typically, the cash obtained from drug sales in the United States is physically smuggled out of the country because it cannot be legally exported without disclosure (Table 13.3).

Smuggling cash is not easy—$1 million in $20 bills weighs 100 pounds—yet billions of dollars are exported, in false-bottomed suitcases and smugglers' vests, to countries that allow numbered bank accounts without identification of names (the Cayman Islands, Panama, Switzerland, Austria, and Liechtenstein, among others).

New methods of laundering drug profits, not involving physical transfer of cash, have recently been devised, such as fake real estate transactions; purchase of gold, antiques, and art; and cybercurrency (microchip-based electronic money), which utilizes the Internet. Such transactions permit electronic transfer of drug funds worldwide with minimum chance of detection. Once deposited in foreign accounts, the funds are "clean" and can be returned to legitimate businesses and investments. They may also be used for illegal purposes, such as the purchase of arms for export to terrorist groups.

The Political Impact The political impact of the drug trade on producer countries is devastating. In the late 1970s and early 1980s, the government of Bolivia became completely corrupt. The minister of justice was referred to as the "minister of cocaine." In Colombia, drug lords and terrorists combined their resources to wrest power from the democratically elected government. Thirteen supreme court judges and 167 police officers were killed; the minister

TABLE 13.3 A Typical Money-Laundering Scheme

La Mina, The Mine, reportedly laundered $1.2 billion for the Colombian cartels over a 2-year period.

Currency from selling cocaine was packed in boxes labeled "jewelry" and sent by armored car to Ropex, a jewelry maker in Los Angeles.

↓

The cash was counted and deposited in banks but few suspicions were raised because the gold business is based on cash.

↓

Ropex then wire-transferred the money to New York banks in payment for fictitious gold purchased from Ronel, allegedly a gold bullion business.

↓

Ronel shipped Ropex bars of lead painted gold to complete the fake transaction. Ropex used the alleged sale of this gold to other jewelry businesses to cover further currency conversions.

↓

Ronel then transferred the funds from American banks to South American banks where the Colombian cartel could gain access to them.

Source: Adapted from "Getting Banks to Just Say 'No,'" *Business Week*, Apr. 17, 1989, p. 17; and Maggie Mahar, "Dirty Money: It Triggers a Bold New Attack in the War on Drugs," *Barron's*, **69** (June 1989): 6–38, at p. 7. From the U.S. Department of Justice, *Drugs, Crime and the Justice System* (Washington, D.C.: U.S. Government Printing Office, 1992).

of justice and the ambassador to Hungary were assassinated.

The message was that death was the price for refusal to succumb to drug corruption. In 1989 a highly respected Colombian presidential candidate who had come out against the cocaine cartel was assassinated. The government remained fragile and the situation precarious. Over the years, the scandal aroused by liaisons between notorious drug lords and high-ranking government officials has endured. One of the scandals, perhaps most injurious to diplomatic relations with the United States, was that involving Colombia's former president Ernesto Samper. Samper received $6 million toward his 1994 campaign fund from the renowned Cali cartel—the leader in cocaine trafficking. Despite his exoneration by Colombia's House of Representatives, the United States government sent an unequivocal message to President Samper by revoking his U.S. visa and decertifying Colombia (the United States "certifies" countries considered an ally in the drug war).

Nor is Colombia alone in its efforts to cope with the drug problem. Before General Manuel Noriega was arrested in a U.S. invasion of Panama to face charges of drug smuggling, he had made himself military dictator of Panama. By 1996 (seven years later), however, little had really changed:

> President Ernesto Perez Balladares has admitted that his 1994 campaign received $51,000 from a Colombian businessman later jailed on drug charges. Other donations to the President are also under scrutiny. . . . Seven years after the military intervention, Panama's banking system once again is a conduit for drug traffickers laundering their profits. Secret numbered accounts, legal in Panama, prevent prosecutors from putting a name to a number. Lawyers create shell corporations with little more than a stroke of a pen and about $1,000. Those behind the companies remain a mystery. The collapse earlier this year of a Panamanian bank, under investigation in the US for money laundering, with links to two senior aides of the president underscored, for many, the pervasiveness of the problem.[37]

Corruption and crime rule in all drug-producing countries. Government instability is the necessary consequence. Coups replace elections. The populations of these countries are not immune to addiction themselves. Several South American countries, including Colombia, Bolivia, and Peru, are now experiencing major addiction problems; Peru alone has some 60,000 addicts. The Asian narcotics-producing countries, which thought themselves immune to the addiction problem, also became victims of their own production. Pakistan now counts about 200,000 addicts.[38]

One of the more remarkable aspects of the expansion of the drug trade has been the spread of addiction and the drug economy to the Third World and to the newly democratic, formerly socialist countries. Of all political problems, however, the most vicious is the alliance that drug dealers have forged with terrorist groups in the Near East, in Latin America, and in Europe.[39]

Drug Control

In September 1989 former President George Bush unveiled his antidrug strategy. On the international level, the president sought modest funding for the United Nations effort to combat the international narcotics drug traffic. He also called for far greater expenditures for bilateral cooperation with other countries to deal with producers and traffickers. This effort extends to crop eradication programs.[40] He singled out Colombia, Bolivia, and Peru for such efforts and immediately sent U.S. Army assistance, including helicopters and crews, to Colombia for use in that country's very difficult battle with the Medellín cartel.

On the national level, the strategy focused on federal aid to state and local police for street-level attacks on drug users and small dealers, for whom alternative punishments such as house arrest (confinement in one's home rather than in a jail cell) and boot camps (short but harsh incarceration with military drill) were started. It also called for rigorous enforcement of forfeiture laws, under which money is confiscated from offenders if it can be established that it came from the drug trade; property purchased with such money is also forfeited.[41] The Bush war on drugs followed a host of federal drug-control initiatives. All of them, like the Bush administration initiatives, have been at best only slightly effective.[42]

The New York Times

From the Pages of

One City Wonders: Can We Win the War on Drugs?

In this city where 60,000 people, about 1 in 10 residents, are addicted to narcotics, a simple message appears on billboards, police cruisers, city buses, T-shirts, brochures, and in television advertisements: "Believe."

That slogan, from a $2 million antidrug campaign Baltimore began in 2002, is part exhortation, part call to action, part desperate plea to take back the neighborhoods, to report drug dealers, to seek drug treatment, to become a police officer or a mentor to a troubled youngster.

But what's good in theory turned out to be fatal for one Baltimore family. Angela Dawson grew up in the poorest section of northeast Baltimore, dropped out of high school in the 10th grade, and had her first baby at the age of 18. In 1990 she married Carnell Dawson, and together they had five more children. By all accounts, Angela was a great mother. She was also a neighborhood crusader who constantly shooed drug dealers away from her house. She called the police for help many times, but in her case, the drug dealers won.

Baltimore is the most violent of the country's 20 largest cities, with 39 homicides and 2,272 violent crimes per 100,000 residents. The city, which has made some strides in fighting crime, still has one of the highest per capita rates of intravenous drug use.

"In Baltimore, we learned long ago what I guess a lot of people are learning just now: the war on drugs was lost," said David Simon, who wrote the police dramas "Homicide" and "The Corner," both set in Baltimore. "All's that left are a few battles raging in the muck."

Mrs. Dawson was not intimidated by this. She would often hold fiery pep talks on her porch. On Oct. 2, she testified against a neighbor, John L. Henry, whom she accused of assault. The next day, a Molotov cocktail was thrown through her front window but Mr. Dawson smelled the smoke, ran downstairs and put the fire out.

Two weeks later, someone again set fire to the Dawson's house. This time, Angela Dawson, 36, and five of her children, ages 9 to 14, were killed.

Police swiftly arrested Darrell Brooks, 21, who lived just a few houses down from the Dawsons. Neighbors said he was friends with a John Henry, the man Angela Dawson testified against. Neighbors also blamed the police for not doing more to protect the family after the first fire incident.

Meetings were held immediately after the incident attended by the police commissioner and city and state lawmakers, where there were heated exchanges and criticism of what many view as inadequate police protection and a criminal justice system that routinely returns drug dealers and violent offenders to the streets quickly.

Even so, residents vowed not to be intimidated by what happened. But reality is different.

"Who's going to squeal now?" said Lucretia Coates, the principal of the Dr. Bernard Harris Elementary School, which four of the Dawson children attended. "I got four little desks empty in my school. Why wouldn't that intimidate you?"

Source

Adapted from Jeffrey Gettleman, "Ashes and Tears in Lost Battle of Drug War," *New York Times,* Oct. 18, 2002; and National Desk, "Fire Fatal to 6 Leads a City to Scrutinize Its Drug War," *New York Times,* Oct. 19, 2002. Reprinted with permission.

Questions for Discussion

1. In response to the accusation that police had not protected the family, the commissioner, Edward Norris, said his office recommended that the family move, but he said, "they said they wouldn't be driven out of the neighborhood by drug dealers." He also said that he had increased patrols of the neighborhood after the first firebombing. Obviously, neither of these responses were effective. What else might the police have done to protect the family?
2. What do you think of Baltimore's antidrug billboards with the word "Believe"? Do you think this might be an effective tactic? If you had to come up with an antidrug advertisement campaign for the city, what would you do?

The Bush plan continued the American emphasis on law enforcement options for drug control. Treatment and prevention received only a fraction of the money allocated to traditional law enforcement efforts throughout the 1980s and early 1990s. The Clinton administration's approach, unveiled on February 9, 1994, earmarked $13 billion for a national strategy that emphasized antidrug education as well as treatment programs. His 1995 strategy, which targeted four major initiatives, was advanced by the drug czar, Barry McCaffrey. McCaffrey placed a decided emphasis on treatment, prevention, domestic law enforcement, interdiction, and international control. The White House established a budget of almost $18 billion for the

1999 drug-control strategy, which continued to focus on law enforcement, education, and treatment, as well as on reducing the supply of drugs coming into the country.

Treatment The treatment approach to drug control is not new. During the late 1960s and into the 1970s, hope for the country's drug problem centered on treatment programs. These programs took a variety of forms, depending on the setting and modality, for example, self-help groups (Narcotics Anonymous, Cocaine Anonymous), psychotherapy, detoxification ("drying out" in a hospital), "rap" houses (neighborhood centers where addicts can come for group therapy sessions), various community social-action efforts (addicts clean up neighborhoods, plant trees, and so on), and—the two most popular—residential therapeutic communities and methadone maintenance programs.[43]

The therapeutic community is a 24-hour, total-care facility where former addicts and professionals work together to help addicts become drug-free. In methadone maintenance programs, addicts are given a synthetic narcotic, methadone, which prevents withdrawal symptoms (physical and psychological pain associated with giving up drugs), while addicts reduce their drug intake slowly over a period of time. Throughout the program addicts receive counseling designed to help them return to a normal life.

It is difficult to assess the success of most treatment programs. Even if individuals appear to be drug-free within a program, it is hard to find out what happens to them once they leave it (or even during a week when they do not show up). In addition, it may well be that the addicts who succeed in drug treatment programs are those who have already resolved to stop abusing drugs before they voluntarily come in for treatment; the real hard-core users may not even make an effort to become drug-free.

A program to divert drug offenders (users and purchasers) from criminal careers is the drug court, in which the judge has the option to divert nonviolent drug offenders to a counseling program in lieu of incarceration. Since the first drug court was established in Dade County, Florida, in 1989, 400 similar courts have been established in counties throughout the country. The S.T.O.P. program in Portland, Oregon, diverted 944 cases within an 18-month period and has a rearrest rate of 6 percent for the first year following completion of the program. Other drug courts enjoy similar success rates. The most recent diversion program is in Arizona, where all nonviolent drug offenders were diverted to treatment and probation in 1998. The program has not only had a high success rate in keeping people drug-free, but also saved the state an estimated $2.5 million during the first year of operation.[44]

> **:// Crime Surfing**
>
> www.betterworldfund.org/factsheets/o_21520.shtml
>
> Find out what the United Nations has been doing to combat drugs and violence.

Education While drug treatment deals with the problem of addiction after the fact, education tries to prevent people from taking illegal drugs in the first place. The idea behind educational programs is straightforward: People who have information about the harmful effects of illegal drugs are likely to stay away from them. Sometimes the presentation of the facts has been coupled with scare techniques. Some well-known athletes and entertainers have joined the crusade with public-service messages ("a questionable approach," says Howard Abadinsky, "given the level of substance abuse reported in these groups").[45]

The educational approach has several drawbacks. Critics maintain that most addicts are quite knowledgeable about the potential consequences of taking drugs but think of them as just a part of the "game."[46] Most people who begin to use drugs believe they will never become addicted, even when they have information about addiction.[47] Inner-city youngsters do not lack information about the harmful effects of drugs. They learn about the dangers from daily exposure to addicts desperately searching for drugs, sleeping on the

> **Did You Know?**
>
> ... that under federal law a cocaine user with 100 grams of cocaine receives the same sentence as someone caught with 1 gram of crack, a cocaine derivative?

Alcohol and driving don't mix. A drunk driver (there are almost 1.5 million arrests per year for driving under the influence) caused this fatal accident in Austin, Texas.

streets, going through withdrawal, and stealing family belongings to get money.[48]

Legalization   Despite increases in government funding for an expanded war on drugs, the goal of a drug-free society in the 1990s was not achieved and is hardly likely to be achieved within the next decade. There is much evidence that all the approaches, even the "new" ones, have been tried before with little or no effect. Some experts are beginning to advocate a very different approach—legalization. Their reasoning is that since the drug problem seems to elude all control efforts, why not deal with heroin and cocaine the same way we deal with alcohol and tobacco? In other words, why not subject these drugs to some government control and restrictions, but make them freely available to all adults?[49]

They argue that current drug-control policies impose tremendous costs on taxpayers without demonstrating effective results. In addition to spending less money on crime control, the government would make money on tax revenue from the sale of legalized drugs. This is, of course, a hotly debated issue. Given the dangers of drug abuse and the moral issues at stake, legalization surely offers no easy solution and has had little public support. However, the surgeon general of the United States, in 1994, mentioned the option of legalization—only to be rebuffed by the president.

ALCOHOL AND CRIME

Alcohol is another substance that contributes to social problems. One of the major differences between alcohol and the other drugs we have been discussing is that the sale and purchase of alcohol are legal in most jurisdictions of the United States. The average annual consumption of alcoholic beverages by each individual 14 years of age and over is equivalent to 591 cans of beer, or 115 bottles of wine, or 35 fifths of liquor; this is more than the average individual consumption of coffee and milk.[50] Alcohol is consumed at recreational events, business meetings, lunches and dinners at home, and celebrations; in short, drinking alcohol has become the expected behavior in many social situations.

Drinking is widespread among young people. While the rate of use has been fairly steady since 1994, the number of current drinkers increased by 5 million between 2000 and 2001. Recent research demonstrates that 10.1 million current drinkers (9.2 percent of current drinkers) were 12 to 20 years old. Of this group, more than 50 percent (6.8 million) engaged in binge drinking and over 20 percent (2.1 million) were classified as heavy drinkers. Individuals between the ages of 18 and 20 are the heaviest users; 53 percent reported using alcohol in the past 30 days. This amount is equivalent to the rate of use reported by those age 35 and older.[51] (See Table 13.2.)

The History of Legalization

Alcohol consumption is not new to our culture; in colonial days alcohol was considered safer and healthier than water. Still, the history of alcohol consumption is filled with controversy. Many people through the centuries have viewed it as wicked and degenerate. By the turn of the twentieth century, social reformers linked liquor to prostitution, poverty, the immigrant culture, and corrupt politics.

Various lobbying groups, such as the Women's Christian Temperance Union and the American Anti-Saloon League, bombarded politicians with demands for the prohibition of alcohol.[52] On January 16, 1920, the Eighteenth Amendment to the Constitution went into force, prohibiting the manufacture, sale, and transportation of alcoholic beverages. The Volstead Act of 1919 had already defined as "intoxicating liquor" any beverage that contained more than ½ of 1 percent alcohol.

Historians generally agree that no law in America has ever been more widely violated or more unpopular. Vast numbers of people continued to consume alcohol. It was easy to manufacture and to import. The illegal business brought tremendous profits to suppliers, and it could not be controlled by enforcement officers, who were too inefficient, too few, or too corrupt. The unlawful sale of alcohol was called "bootlegging." The term originated in the early practice of concealing liquor in one's boot to avoid payment of liquor taxes.

Bootlegging created empires for such gangsters as Al Capone and Dutch Schultz, as we saw in Chapter 10. Private saloons, or "speakeasies," prospered. Unpopular and unenforceable, the Eighteenth Amendment was repealed 13 years after its birth—on December 5, 1933. Except for a few places, the manufacture and sale of alcohol have been legal in the United States since that time.

Crime-Related Activities

The alcohol-related activities that have become serious social problems are violent crime, drunk driving, and public intoxication.

Violence National surveys of inmates in jails and prisons show the following:

- About 40 percent of the convicted offenders incarcerated for violent crimes used alcohol immediately before the crimes.
- About 40 percent of prison inmates engaged in binge drinking in the past.
- Over one-third of prison inmates have gotten into a physical fight while drinking or directly afterwards.
- About one-third of state inmates convicted of violent crimes described themselves as daily drinkers.[53]

For many decades criminologists have probed the relationship between alcohol and violence. Marvin Wolfgang, in a study of 588 homicides in Philadelphia, found that alcohol was present in two-thirds of all homicide cases (both victim and offender, 44 percent; victim only, 9 percent; offender only, 11 percent).[54] Similar findings were reported from northern Sweden: Two-thirds of the offenders who committed homicide between 1970 and 1981 and almost half of their victims were intoxicated when the crime was committed.[55]

Many other offenses show a significant relationship between alcohol and violence. In the United States, 58 percent of those convicted for assault and 64 percent of offenders who assaulted police officers had been drinking.[56] In about one-third of rapes, the offender, the victim, or both had been drinking immediately before the attack.[57] The role of alcohol in violent family disputes has been increasingly recognized. Among 2413 American couples, the rate of severe violence by the husband was 2.10 per 100 couples in homes where the husbands were never drunk and 30.89 per 100 couples in homes where the husbands were drunk "very often."[58]

Many explanations have been offered for the relationship between alcohol and violence.[59] Some studies focus on the individual. When people are provoked, for example, alcohol can reduce restraints on aggression.[60] Alcohol also escalates aggression by reducing awareness of consequences.[61] Other studies analyze the social situation in which drinking takes place. Experts argue that in some situations aggressive behavior is considered appropriate or is even expected when people drink together.[62]

Drunk Driving

The effect of alcohol on driving is causing continuing concern. The incidence of drunk driving, referred to in statutes as "driving under the influence" and "driving while intoxicated" (depending on the level of alcohol found in the blood), has been steadily rising. Statistics indicate the extent of the problem:

- Between 1990 and 1997 the number of arrests for driving under the influence decreased 19 percent, while the number of licensed drivers increased nearly 15 percent.
- Before arrest for driving while intoxicated (DWI), the majority of convicted offenders drink at least 4 ounces of pure alcohol within four hours.
- About 45 percent of prison inmates have driven while intoxicated.
- In 1996 there were an estimated 17,126 alcohol-related traffic fatalities (40.9 percent of all traffic fatalities for that year).
- The annual cost of drunk driving (property damage, medical bills, and so on) is estimated at $24 billion.
- There were 1,434,852 arrests for driving under the influence in 2001.[63]

Cari Lightner, age 13, was killed in May 1980 by a drunk driver while she was walking on a sidewalk.[64] The driver had been arrested only a few days before on a DUI charge. The victim's mother, Candy, took action almost immediately to push for new legislation that would mandate much stiffer penalties for drunk driving. It was difficult at first to get government to respond, but she did get the attention of journalists. By the end of the year in which Cari died, Mrs. Lightner had organized the Governor's Task Force on Drinking and Driving in California.

And her own advocacy group, Mothers Against Drunk Driving (MADD), was in the national spotlight. MADD's members were people who themselves had been injured or whose family members had been injured or killed in an accident involving an intoxicated driver. The organization has grown to more than 300 chapters.[65] Remove Intoxicated Drivers (RID) and Students Against Drunk Drivers (SADD) have joined the campaign.

The citizens' groups called public attention to a major health and social problem, demanded action, and got it. Congress proclaimed one week each December to be Drunk and Drugged Awareness Week, and the Presidential Commission on Drunk Driving was formed. Candy Lightner was appointed a commissioner. The federal government attached the distribution of state highway funds to various anti-drunk-driving measures, thereby pressuring the states into putting recommendations into action. Old laws have been changed, and new laws have been passed.

After the ratification in 1971 of the Twenty-Sixth Amendment to the U.S. Constitution, which lowered the voting age to 18 years, many states lowered their minimum-age requirement for the purchase and sale of alcoholic beverages. By 1983, 33 states had done so; but by 1987, all but one state had raised the minimum drinking age back to 21. Under New York's Civil Forfeiture Law, the government can take any car involved in a felony drunk-driving case, sell it, and give the money to the victims. Texas has a similar law.[66] Tuscarawas County in Ohio places brightly colored orange plates on cars of drivers whose licenses have been suspended for drunk driving.[67]

Other objectives of legislation have been to limit the "happy hours" during which bars serve drinks at reduced prices, to shorten hours when alcoholic beverages can be sold, to make hosts and bartenders liable for damages if their guests or patrons drink too much and become

---

Theory Connects

Criminologists have identified many associations between illegal drug/alcohol use and strain (Chapter 5), cultural deviance (Chapter 5), and social control theories (Chapter 7). But these casual influences are both contingent and probabilistic, i.e., drugs and alcohol may contribute to crime and crime may contribute to drug and alcohol use. Criminologists are still uncovering all of the variables that contribute to the substance abuse-crime connection. What do you think?

involved in an accident, to limit advertisements, and to put health warnings on bottles. Most states have increased their penalties for drunk driving to include automatic license suspension, higher minimum fines, and even mandatory jail sentences.

Thus far the results of such legislation are mixed. A study carried out in Seattle, Minneapolis, and Cincinnati found that such measures did indeed lower the number of traffic deaths, while other investigations did not show positive results.[68] Nevertheless, drunk driving has achieved national attention, and even modern technology is being used in the effort to find solutions: Japanese and American technicians have come up with a device that locks the ignition system and can be unlocked only when the attached Breathalyzer (which registers alcohol in the blood) indicates that the driver is sober.[69] California, Washington, Texas, Michigan, and Oregon have passed legislation authorizing its use.

SEXUAL MORALITY OFFENSES

All societies endeavor to regulate sexual behavior, although what specifically is considered not permissible has varied from society to society and from time to time. The legal regulation of sexual conduct in Anglo-American law has been greatly influenced by both the Old and the New Testaments. In the Middle Ages the enforcement of laws pertaining to sexual morality was the province of church courts. Today, to the extent that immorality is still illegal, it is the regular criminal courts that enforce such laws.

Morality laws have always been controversial, whether they seek to prevent alcohol abuse or to prohibit certain forms of sexual behavior or its public display or depiction. Sexual activity other than intercourse between spouses for the purpose of procreation has been severely penalized in many societies and until only recently in the United States. Sexual intercourse between unmarried persons ("lewd cohabitation"), seduction of a female by promise of marriage, and all forms of "unnatural" sexual relations were serious crimes, some carrying capital sentences, as late as the nineteenth century. In 1962 the Model Penal Code proposed some important changes. Fornication and lewd cohabitation were dropped from the list of offenses, as was homosexual intercourse between consenting adults.

Gay rights advocates protest existing sex laws.

The idea behind these changes is that the sexual relations of consenting adults should be beyond the control of the law, not only because throughout history such legal efforts have proved ineffective but also because the harm to society, if any, is too slight to warrant the condemnation of law. "The state's power to regulate sexual conduct ought to stop at the bedroom door or at the barn door," said sex researcher Alfred Kinsey four decades ago.[70]

Although the Model Penal Code (MPC) has removed or limited sanctions for conduct among consenting adults, the code retains strong prohibitions against sexual activities involving children. Penalties are severe for **statutory rape** (intercourse by an adult male with an underage female regardless of consent), deviate sexual intercourse with a child, corruption of a minor, sexual assault, and endangering the welfare of a child. Of course, the recommendations of the American Law Institute are not always accepted by state legislatures.

Let us take a close look at three existing offenses involving sexual morality: "deviate sexual intercourse by force or imposition," prostitution, and pornography.

Deviate Sexual Intercourse by Force or Imposition

The Model Penal Code defines "deviate sexual intercourse" as "sexual intercourse per os or per anum [by mouth or by anus] between human beings who are not husband and wife, and any form of sexual intercourse with an animal" [sec. 213.2(1)]. The common law called such sexual acts **sodomy,** after the biblical city of Sodom, which the Lord destroyed for its wickedness, presumably because its citizens had engaged in such acts. The common law dealt harshly with sodomy, making it a capital offense and referring to it as *crimen innominatum*—a crime not to be mentioned by name.

Yet other cultures, including ancient Greece, did not frown on homosexual activities. And Alfred Kinsey reminded us that homosexual (from the Greek word *homos,* meaning "same") relations are common among all mammals, of which humans are but one species.[71] The MPC subjects "deviate sexual intercourse" between two human beings to punishment only if it is accomplished by severe compulsion or if the other person is incapable of granting consent or is a child less than 10 years old. To conservative lawmakers, this model legislation is far too liberal; to liberals, it does not go far enough. Generally, liberal thinkers prefer the law not to interfere with the sexual practices of consenting adults at all.

The gay and lesbian rights movements have done much to destigmatize consensual, private adult sexual relationships. Yet legislatures have been slow to respond, and the U.S. Supreme Court has taken a conservative stance as well. In 1986 the Court sustained a Georgia statute that criminalizes consensual sexual acts between adults of the same gender, even if they are performed in the privacy of one's home.[72]

Prostitution

Not so long ago it was a crime to be a prostitute.[73] The law punished women for a status acquired on the basis of sexual intercourse with more than one man. Under some statutes it was not even necessary to prove that money was paid for the sexual act. The Supreme Court ruled in 1962—in a case involving the status of being a drug addict—that criminal liability can be based only on conduct, that is, on doing something in violation of law.[74] This decision would seem to apply to prostitution as well. Therefore, one can no longer be penalized for being a prostitute. But soliciting for sex is an act, not a status, and nearly all states make solicitation of sex for money the misdemeanor of **prostitution.**

The Uniform Crime Reports recorded 80,854 arrests for prostitution and commercialized vice during 2001 (see Figure 13.4).[75]

The number would be extremely high if we were to include all acts of sexual favor granted in return for some gratuity. Even if the number were limited to straightforward cash transactions (including, nowadays, credit card transactions), there is no way of arriving at a figure. Many persons may act as prostitutes for a while and then return to legitimate lifestyles. There are part-time and full-time prostitutes, male and female prostitutes, itinerant and resident prostitutes, street hookers and high-priced escorts who do not consider themselves prostitutes.[76]

Many law enforcement agencies do not relish the task of suppressing prostitution. In some jurisdictions the police have little time to spend on vice control, given the extent of violent and property crimes. Thus, when prostitutes are arrested, it is likely to be in response to demands by community groups, business establishments, or church leaders to "clean up the neighborhood." Occasionally, the police find it expedient to arrest prostitutes because they may divulge information about unsolved crimes, such as narcotics distribution, theft, receiving stolen property, or organized crime.

Prostitution encompasses a variety of both acts and actors. The prostitute, female or male, is not alone in the business of prostitution. A **pimp** provides access to prostitutes and protects and exploits them, living off their proceeds.

FIGURE 13.4 Estimated number of prostitution arrests in United States, 1970–2001.

Source: Uniform Crime Reports, 1994–2002.

There are still madams who maintain houses of prostitution. And finally, there are the patrons of prostitutes, popularly called "johns." Ordinarily, it is not a criminal offense to patronize a prostitute; yet the framers of the MPC proposed to criminalize this act. The section was hotly debated before the American Law Institute. A final vote of the members rejected criminalization.

Researchers have found that many prostitutes come from broken homes and poor neighborhoods and are school dropouts. Yet all social classes contribute to the prostitution hierarchy. High-priced call girls, many of them well-educated women, may operate singly or out of agencies. The television "blue channels" that broadcast after midnight in most metropolitan areas carry commercials advertising the availability of call girls, their phone numbers, and sometimes their specialties. At the next lower level of the prostitution hierarchy are the massage parlor prostitutes. When Shirley, a masseuse, was asked, "Do you consider yourself a prostitute?" she answered: "Yes, as well as a masseuse, and a healer, and a couple of other things."[77] One rung lower on the prostitution ladder are the "inmates" (a term used by the MPC) of the houses of prostitution, locally called bordellos, whorehouses, cathouses, or red-light houses.

According to people "in the life" (prostitution), the streetwalkers are the least-respected class in the hierarchy. They are the "working girls" or "hookers." They are found clustered on their accustomed street corners, on thoroughfares, or in truck and bus depots, dressed in bright attire, ready to negotiate a price with any passerby. Sexual services are performed in vehicles or in nearby "hot-sheet" hotel rooms. Life for these prostitutes—some of whom are transvestite males—is dangerous and grim. Self-reports suggest that many are drug addicts and have been exposed to HIV.[78] Other varieties of prostitution range from the legal houses that a few counties permit to operate in Nevada to troupes of prostitutes who travel from one place of opportunity to another (work projects, farm labor camps, construction sites) and bar ("B") girls who entertain customers in cocktail lounges and make themselves available for sexual activities for a price.

For years, the Mustang Ranch was one of many legal brothels in Las Vegas, Nevada. The Ranch property was forfeited to the federal government in 1999 after guilty verdicts were obtained against the ranch's owner in a fraud and racketeering trial. The 104-room brothel is being demolished but as of 2003 officials had not yet decided what to do with the property.

Popular, political, and scientific opinions on prostitution have changed, no doubt largely because prostitution has changed. Around the turn of the century it probably was true that a large number of prostitutes had been forced into the occupation by unscrupulous men. Indeed, it was this pattern that led to the enactment of the White Slave Traffic Act (called the Mann Act, after the senator who proposed the bill), prohibiting the interstate transportation of females for purposes of prostitution. There is some evidence that today the need for money, together with few legitimate opportunities to obtain it, prompts many young women and men to become prostitutes.

Sex researcher Paul Gebhard found in 1969 that only 4 percent of U.S. prostitutes were forced into prostitution. More recently Jennifer James found that the majority entered the life because of its financial rewards.[79] Whatever view we take of adult prostitutes as victims of a supposedly victimless criminal activity, one subgroup clearly is a victimized class: children, female and male, who are enticed and sometimes forced into prostitution, especially in large cities. Some are runaways, picked up by procurers at bus depots; some are simply "street children"; and others have been abused and molested by the adults in their lives.[80]

Pornography

Physical sexual contact is a basic component of both sodomy and prostitution. **Pornography** requires no contact at all; it simply portrays sexually explicit material. Statutes in all states make it a criminal offense to produce, offer for sale, sell, distribute, or exhibit pornographic (sometimes called obscene, lewd, or lascivious) material. Federal law prohibits the transportation of such material in interstate commerce and outlaws the use of the mails, the telephone, radio, and television for the dissemination of pornographic material.[81]

The Problem of Definition The term "pornographic" is derived from the Greek *pornographos* ("writing of harlots," or descriptions of the acts of harlots). The term "obscene" comes from the Latin *ob* ("against," "before") plus *caenum* ("filth"), or possibly from *obscena* ("offstage"). In Roman theatrical performances, disgusting and offensive parts of plays took place offstage, out of sight but not out of hearing of the audience.[82] Courts and legislators have used the two terms interchangeably, but nearly all statutes and decisions deal with pornography (with the implication of sexual arousal) rather than with obscenity (with its implication of filth).[83]

Scholars generally agree that the statutes in existence appear to be addressed primarily to

Of Immediate Concern

Cyberporn: Problems and Controversies

- The dean of the Harvard Divinity School recently resigned his post after a computer tech discovered an extensive collection of hard-core pornography on his Harvard-owned computer. This Lutheran minister, divinity school dean, scholar, and father of two committed no crime, but his actions violated the school's ban on having materials that are "inappropriate, obscene, bigoted or abusive" on school computers.(1) The case received widespread media coverage.

- A deputy sheriff from Palmdale, California, was indicted on federal charges for child pornography. The evidence was found on his hard drive. Also, he allegedly tried to solicit sex via the Internet from a person he thought was a 13-year-old girl. The deputy sheriff faces up to 15 years in prison if convicted.(2)

- A Cub Scout leader from Long Island was arrested for having child pornography on his computer, which he downloaded from the Internet and reportedly swapped with other porn peddlers.(3)

- A 23-year-old woman started her own porn website two years ago as a hobby. She expects to make about $50,000 a week on the site in the next year. This money will allow her to cut back on making movies and dancing at clubs. She is one of many women in the porn industry who have set up their own websites as alternative businesses.(4)

- Some men find themselves "addicted" to cyberporn, spending as much as 80 hours per week online. Their real sex lives and relationships are damaged as online sex becomes more important and fulfilling than the real thing, leading some marriages to end in divorce.(5)

The Internet provides an ever-increasing number of avenues for the distribution of pornography. For entrepreneurs setting up porn sites, the Internet is proving quite lucrative. However, some of those who use it find themselves in legal trouble when they go beyond legal pornography to child pornography or use sex chat rooms to solicit sex with children. Even those who stick to legal porn may face problems related to their jobs or their personal relationships. It is unlikely that pornography—both legal and illegal—on the Internet will decrease in the years to come.

Of all the issues regarding pornography on the Internet, one of the most hotly debated is censorship. While some programs exist that limit access to porn sites, they do not prevent the exploitation of children or keep those who wish to access the sites from doing so. Child pornographers are creative and adaptable, shying away from explicit child pornography. Many frequent preteen and teen nudism news groups and sites, where thousands of photographs of nude children await them in an apparently "constitutionally protected" cyberspace. The question remains as to what can be done to limit children's access to pornographic sites as well as to prevent their exploitation on the Internet.

Sources

1. Trent Gegax, "An Odd Fall from Grace: Computer Porn Undoes a Divinity-School Dean," *Newsweek*, May 31, 1999, p. 70.
2. "Deputy in Custody Allegedly Tried to Solicit Sex in Internet Chat Room," *City News Service*, Oct. 22, 1999.
3. "Scout Leader Accused of Child Pornography," *New York Times*, Oct. 22, 1999, p. B14.
4. John Leland, "More Bang for the Buck: How Sex on the Internet Has Transformed the Business of Pornography," *Newsweek*, Oct. 11, 1999, p. 73.
5. Greg Gutfield, "The Sex Drive: Web Pornography Has Turned Computers into Sex Objects, and Men, by the Millions, Are Hooking Up, Should You?" *Men's Health*, Oct. 1, 1999, p. 116.

Questions for Discussion

1. Why do you think seemingly normal individuals procure child pornography on the Internet or become "addicted" to cyberporn?
2. What can society do to limit the damage to children by child pornographers who use the Internet as a means of distribution? What should be done with those who are caught?

---

pornographic materials.[84] What, then, is the contemporary meaning of "pornography"? The Model Penal Code (1962) says that a publication is pornographic (obscene or indecent) "if, considered as a whole, its predominant appeal is to prurient interests," and if, "in addition, it goes substantially beyond customary limits in describing or representing such matters" (sec. 251.4). This definition, which is full of ambiguities, was to play a major role in several Supreme Court decisions.

Two presidential commissions were no more successful in defining the term. The Commission on Obscenity and Pornography (1970) avoided a definition and used instead the term "explicit sexual material."[85] The Attorney General's Commission on Pornography (1986) gave no definition.[86] The definition created by a

British parliamentary committee in 1979 seems to describe pornography best:

> A pornographic representation combines two features: It has a certain function or intention, to arouse its audience sexually, and also a certain content, explicit representation of sexual materials (organs, postures, activity, etc.).[87]

This definition indicates nothing about any danger inherent in pornography. The law will step in only when pornography is exhibited or distributed in a manner calculated to produce harm.

Historically, that harm has been seen as a negative effect on public morals, especially those of children. That was the stance taken by many national and local societies devoted to the preservation of public morality in the nineteenth century. More recently, the emphasis has shifted to the question of whether the availability and use of pornography produce actual, especially violent, victimization of women, children, or, for that matter, men.

> **Theory Connects**
>
> Psychologists have long studied the deleterious effect on children of violence on television (Chapter Four). Does cyber pornography pose similar threats to children? To what extent does violent pornography, freely available on the Internet, legitimize violence against girls and women?

Pornography and Violence The National Commission on Obscenity and Pornography in 1970 and the Attorney General's Commission on Pornography in 1986 reviewed the evidence of an association between pornography, on the one hand, and violence and crime, on the other. The National Commission provided funding for more than 80 studies to examine public attitudes toward pornography, experiences with pornography, the association between the availability of pornography and crime rates, the experience of sex offenders with pornography, and the relation between pornography and behavior. The commission concluded:

> [E]mpirical research designed to clarify the question has found no evidence to date that exposure to explicit sexual materials plays a significant role in the causations of delinquent or criminal behavior among youth or adults. The Commission cannot conclude that exposure to erotic materials is a factor in the causation of sex crimes or sex delinquency.[88]

Between 1970 (when the National Commission reported its findings) and 1986 (when the Attorney General's Commission issued its report), hundreds of studies have been conducted on this question. For example:

- Researchers reported in 1977 that when male students were exposed to erotic stimuli, those stimuli neither inhibited nor had any effect on levels of aggression. When the same research team worked with female students, they found that mild erotic stimuli inhibited aggression and that stronger erotic stimuli increased it.[89]

- Researchers who exposed students to sexually explicit films during six consecutive weekly sessions in 1984 concluded that exposure to increasingly explicit erotic stimuli led to a decrease in both arousal responses and aggressive behavior. In short, these subjects became habituated to the pornography.[90]

After analyzing such studies, the Attorney General's Commission concluded that nonviolent and nondegrading pornography is not significantly associated with crime and aggression. It did conclude, however, that exposure to pornographic materials:

> (1) leads to a greater acceptance of rape myths and violence against women; (2) results in pronounced effects when the victim is shown enjoying the use of force or violence; (3) is arousing for rapists and for some males in the general population; and (4) has resulted in sexual aggression against women in the laboratory.[91]

The Feminist View: Victimization To feminists, these conclusions supported the call for greater restrictions on the manufacture and dissemination of pornographic material. The historian Joan Hoff has coined the term "pornerotic," meaning:

> any representation of persons that sexually objectifies them and is accompanied by actual or implied violence in ways designed to encourage readers or

Window to the World

Global Sexual Slavery: Women and Children

"I thought I was going to work as a waitress," a young Dominican, transported to Greece, told BBC television, her eyes welling with tears. "Then they said if I didn't have sex, I'd be sent back to Santo Domingo without a penny. I was beaten, burned with cigarettes. I knew nobody. I was a virgin. I held out for five days, crying, with no food. [Eventually] I lost my honor and my virginity for $25."(1)

This woman's story is a common one. While some women become prostitutes by choice, many are forced into it. The growing sex trade around the world needs a constant supply of bodies, and it is getting them however it can. The statistics are horrifying: For the brothels of Bombay, some 7,000 adolescents from Nepal's Himalayan hill villages are sold to slave traders each year. In Brazil the number of girls forced into prostitution in mining camps is estimated at 25,000. Japan's bars feature approximately 70,000 Thai "hostesses" working as sex slaves. Some 200,000 Bangladeshi women have been kidnapped into prostitution in Pakistan.(1)

The numbers of underage prostitutes are equally shocking, whether the children were sold into slavery or are trying to survive in a harsh world by selling their bodies: 800,000 in Thailand; 400,000 in India; 250,000 in Brazil; and 60,000 in the Philippines. Child prostitution recently has increased in Russian and East European cities, with an estimated 1,000 youngsters working in Moscow alone.(2) In Vietnam, fathers may act as pimps for their daughters to get money for the family to survive:

> Dr. Hoa, [a] pediatrician from Vietnam, said she asked the fathers of her young patients why they sold their daughters' services. "One father came with his 12-year-old daughter," Dr. Hoa recalled. "She was bleeding from her wounds and as torn as if she had given birth. He told me, 'We've earned $300, so it's enough. She can stop now.'"(3)

The physical wounds suffered by underage prostitutes are part of the terrible irony of the growing market for sex with children. Customers request children under the mistaken belief that they are less likely to be infected with the virus that causes AIDS. In fact, because children are so likely to incur injuries in intercourse, they are more vulnerable to infection.(2)

Experts at a 1993 conference on the sex trade and human rights cited the global AIDS epidemic, pornography, peep shows, and "sex tours" as factors responsible for the increasing demand for child prostitutes.(3) Organized sex tours form a large part of the market for bodies of any age; Taiwan, South Korea, the Philippines, and Thailand have been favorite destinations for sex tourists, and many other places are gaining in popularity.

A UNICEF report from January 2002 estimates that one million children are brought into the multi-billion dollar global trade every year. (4)

Sources

1. Margot Hornblower, "The Skin Trade," *Time,* June 21, 1993, pp. 45–51.
2. Michael S. Serrill, "Defiling the Children," *Time,* June 21, 1993, pp. 53–55.
3. Marlise Simons, "The Sex Market: Scourge on the World's Children," *New York Times,* Apr. 9, 1993, p. A3.
4. UNICEF Press Release, Jan. 18, 2002, UNICEF Media, Geneva, Switzerland.

Questions for Discussion

1. How would you begin to fight the exploitation of women and children in the sex market?
2. What are some of the forces at work that would make such a fight difficult?

The Child Sex Trade

The sexual exploitation of children is on the rise. Sex rings around the world buy and sell kids for prostitution, pornography and other forms of abuse.

Eastern Europe: It has become a low-cost alternative to the Far East for Westerners looking for child sex. Children from Eastern Europe are sent to Western countries.

Thailand: Long a center for the sex-tourism business. Underage sex is readily available. The area serves as a hub for worldwide child trafficking.

Latin America: Sex tourism is increasing, especially in Brazil and the Dominican Republic. Children are shipped to Europe and the Middle East.

West Africa: An export center for young girls.

Subcontinent: Children from Nepal, and Bangladesh are shipped into India and then farther abroad. Increasingly, boys serve as prostitutes for male tourists in Sri Lanka.

Asia: UNICEF estimates that there are 1 million children working as prostitutes.

viewers that such sexual subordination of women (or children or men) is acceptable behavior or an innocuous form of sex education.[92]

Hoff's definition also suggests that pornography, obscenity, and erotica may do far more than offend sensitivities. Such material may victimize not only the people who are depicted but all women (or men or children, if they are the people shown). Pornographers have been accused of promoting the exploitation, objectification, and degradation of women. Many people who call for the abolition of violent pornography argue that it also promotes violence toward women. Future state and federal legislation is likely to focus on violent and violence-producing pornography, not on pornography in general.

The Legal View: Supreme Court Rulings
Ultimately, defining pornographic acts subject to legal prohibition is a task for the U.S. Supreme Court. The First Amendment to the Constitution guarantees freedom of the press. In a series of decisions culminating in *Miller v. California* (1973), however, the Supreme Court articulated the view that obscenity, really meaning pornography, is outside the protection of the Constitution. Following the lead of the Model Penal Code and reinterpreting its own earlier decisions, the Court announced the following standard for judging a representation as obscene or pornographic:

- The average person, applying contemporary community standards, would find that the work, taken as a whole, appeals to prurient interests.
- The work depicts or describes, in a patently offensive way, sexual conduct specifically defined by the applicable state law.
- The work, taken as a whole, lacks serious literary, artistic, political, or scientific value.[93]

While this proposed standard is flexible enough to be expanded or contracted as standards change over time and from place to place, its terms are so vague that they give little guidance to local law enforcement officers or to federal and state courts. In 1987 the Supreme Court addressed this problem and modified the Miller decision. In *Pope v. Illinois* the Court ruled that the third aspect of Miller (that the work has "no value") may be judged by an objective test rather than by local community standards. Justice Byron White wrote for the majority:

> The proper inquiry is not whether an ordinary person of any given community will find serious literary, artistic, political, or scientific value in the allegedly obscene material, but whether a reasonable person would find such value in the material, taken as a whole.[94]

Whether this test will make juries' tasks easier when they must decide whether a film or magazine is pornographic or obscene is still not clear.

> **:// Crime Surfing**
> www.ecommerce.vanderbilt.edu/research/topics/cyberporn
>
> Check out the debate on cyberporn.

Pornography and the Internet Any child with basic knowledge of a computer and a minimal amount of curiosity can, with a few clicks of a mouse, open a doorway to the world of cyberporn: pictures of adults having sexual intercourse, adults having intercourse with animals, video clips of adults having sex with children, and guides to bordellos, massage parlors, and various pleasure districts—both local and international.[95]

Censorship of the Internet has been a heavily debated issue in recent times. Almost everyone agrees that access of minors to pornographic material over the Internet should be restricted, but the primary point of contention remains: Who should be responsible for policing access to such material? Parents? Educators? The government? Responding to a nationwide outcry, Congress passed the Communications Decency Act (CDA) on February 8, 1996. This portion of the Telecommunications Decency Act of 1996 made it a felony to "knowingly use a telecommunications device or interactive computer to send an indecent communication to a child or to use a computer to display indecent material in a manner

Anyone with a computer and a modem can access cyber pornography. Pornography of all sorts—from child pornography to bondage and S & M—is available on binary files in newsgroups, chat rooms, bulletin boards, and individual websites. The FBI, U.S. Customs Service, Department of Justice, and U.S. Postal Service have committed significant resources to investigate and prosecute distributors and consumers of child pornography.

accessible to a child." Violations of this act are punishable by up to 2 years' imprisonment and a fine of $250,000.

Four months after the passage of this law, however, a federal court in Philadelphia ruled that it is in conflict with the constitutional right to free speech. According to the court, blocking enforcement of the CDA was justified because (1) the term "indecent" was found to be impermissibly vague; and (2) while the CDA could restrict Americans from disseminating "indecent" material, it had no jurisdiction over communications originating outside the United States and would thus be ineffective. Existing federal and state laws, however, still ban the sale and possession of child pornography.

One of the biggest issues surrounding government regulation of pornography on the Internet is the lack of global cooperation. The recent conviction of the head of the German division of the American online service CompuServe for the spread of child pornography on the Internet highlights this fact. Legislation on pornography varies around the world, and thus means that pornography can be easily sent across borders. Strategies are currently being developed by several international agencies to increase communication, provide hot lines for users to report illegal material, make laws more unified, and prevent the exploitation of children on a global scale.

Another significant issue is the fine line between what some call eroticism and others call child pornography. Perhaps the most famous photographer of young girls—David Hamilton—prides himself on belonging to an elite group of art photographers. His books—which no doubt appeal to child pornographers—are carried by most large chain bookstores and are "on" the Internet. But is this art or child pornography? Is it constitutionally protected or should it be criminally prosecuted? These two questions will be at the forefront of a debate about pornography on and off the Web.

In the wake of the continued controversy over "cybersmut," several computer programs have been developed to assist parents and educators in regulating children's access to the Internet. Programs such as Net Nanny, Cyber Patrol, and Surf Watch are designed to block access to sites deemed inappropriate for children.

These programs, however, are far from effective. The software must be continually updated to keep up with the new sites added on a daily basis. If activated by certain keywords, access may also be limited to potentially educational sites (such as those related to sexual harassment). Also, the cost of implementing such programs in a particular school district could run into tens of thousands of dollars.

The Gap between Behavior and Law
When we examine sexual morality offenses, we note an enormous gap between the goals of law and actual behavior. As long ago as the late 1940s and early 1950s the pioneering Kinsey reports brought us evidence about this gap. According to these studies, of the total white male population in the United States:

- 69 percent had had some experience with prostitutes
- Between 23 and 37 percent had had extramarital intercourse
- 37 percent had had at least one homosexual experience[96]

Among women:

- 26 percent could be expected to have extramarital intercourse by age 40
- 19 percent had had some physical contact with other females which was deliberately and consciously, at least on the part of one of the partners, intended to be sexual[97]

Morton Hunt noted that the frequency with which Americans were breaking legally imposed moral standards had increased significantly by the 1970s, yet far fewer American men were buying sex from prostitutes than had done so in the 1940s.[98] This finding raised the question of whether the sexual revolution of the 1960s and 1970s made access to sexual partners more freely available.

REVIEW

Intoxicating substances have been used for religious, medicinal, and recreational purposes throughout history. Lifestyles of people who use them are as varied as the drugs they favor.

Governments have repeatedly tried to prevent the abuse of these substances. The drug problem today is massive, and it grows more serious every year. Heroin and cocaine in particular are associated with many crimes. A vast international criminal empire has been organized to promote the production and distribution of drugs. Efforts of law enforcement and health agencies to control the drug problem take the forms of international cooperation in stemming drug trafficking, treatment of addicts, education of the public, and arrest and incarceration of offenders. Some observers, comparing the drug problem with the wide evasion of the Prohibition amendment and the consequent rise in crime, believe that drugs should be legalized.

Legalization of alcoholic beverages, however, has not solved all problems related to alcohol. The abuse of alcohol has been reliably linked to violence, and the incidence of drunk driving has increased so alarmingly that citizen groups have formed to combat the problem.

The legal regulation of sexual conduct has undergone striking changes in recent decades. Many sexual "offenses" once categorized as capital crimes no longer concern society or government. In this sphere, research has done much to influence public opinion and, consequently, legislation. Pornography, however, remains a hotly debated issue.

CRIMINOLOGY & PUBLIC POLICY

"Child pornography law presents the opportunity for a case study of how censorship law responds to and shapes a cultural crisis. We have two corresponding events. On the one hand, we have the 'discovery' in the late 1970s of the twin problems of child sexual abuse and child pornography, and the continuation of the problems to the point where they have reached the level of an ongoing, 'ever-widening' crisis. On the other hand, we have child pornography law. Born in the same period, created to solve the problem of child sexual abuse, child pornography law too has grown dramatically in the past two decades, expanding and proliferating along with the underlying problem that it targets. Yet, curiously, the law's expansion has not solved the problem, but only presided over its escalation. As child pornography law has expanded since the late 1970s,

so has a 'culture of child abuse,' a growing 'panic' about the threat to children.

"What, if any, is the relationship between these two concurrent phenomena—the expansion of child pornography law and the growing problem of child sexual abuse, including child pornography? Does their correlative temporal connection allow us to draw any conclusions about a possible causal relationship?

"There is a standard, conventional explanation for this correlation. This account casts law in a reactive stance: As the sexual exploitation of children, or at least our awareness of the problem, has risen, legislatures and courts have responded by passing and upholding tougher child pornography laws. As the crisis has surged, so has the law. In this view, cultural horror drives law to play a game of catch-up. Law is always a step behind the problem, racing to keep pace with a burgeoning social crisis.

"I am sure that is at least part of what is going on. But in this Article, I propose two alternative readings—readings that do not exclude the conventional account described above, but supplement it. In the first reading, I explore the possibility that certain sexual prohibitions invite their own violation by increasing the sexual allure of what they forbid. I suggest that child pornography law and the eroticization of children exist in a dialectic of transgression and taboo: The dramatic expansion of child pornography law may have unwittingly heightened pedophilic desire.

"I then turn to a second reading, which reveals the previous one to be an only partially satisfactory account. In the second reading, I view law and the culture it regulates not as dialectical opposites, but as intermingled. Child pornography law may represent only another symptom of and not a solution to the problem of child abuse or the cultural fascination with sexual children. The cross purposes of law and culture that I describe above (law as prohibition, which both halts and incites desire) may mask a deeper harmony between them: The legal discourse on prohibiting child pornography may represent yet another way in which our culture drenches itself in sexualized children.

"Child pornography law explicitly requires us to take on the gaze of the pedophile in order to root out pictures of children that harbor secret pedophilic appeal. The growth of child pornography law has opened up a whole arena for the elaborate exploration of children as sexual creatures. Cases require courts to engage in long, detailed analyses of the 'sexual coyness' or playfulness of children, and of their potential to arouse. Courts have undertaken Talmudic discussions of the meaning of 'pubic area' and 'discernibility' of a child's genitals in a picture at issue. But even when a child is pictured as a sexual victim rather than a sexual siren, the child is still pictured as sexual. Child pornography law becomes in this view a vast realm of discourse in which the image of the child as sexual is preserved and multiplied.

"The point of this Article is that laws regulating child pornography may produce perverse, unintended consequences and that the legal battle we are waging may have unrecognized costs. I do not doubt, however, that child pornography law has substantial social benefits. In fact, I do not doubt that these benefits might outweigh the costs detailed. I nonetheless focus on these costs as a means to unsettle the confident assumption of most courts, legislators, and academics that the current approach to child pornography law is unequivocally sound. I question their conviction that the more regulation we impose the more harm we avert. Ultimately, I raise questions about the nature of censorship itself." (*Source:* Amy Adler, "The Perverse Law of Child Pornography" *Columbia Law Review*, **101** (2001): 209.)

Questions for Discussion What do you think of Prof. Adler's thesis? Is it possible that child pornography laws further the very victimization that they are designed to inhibit?

YOU BE THE CRIMINOLOGIST

Significant debate continues over how to reduce drug use and what to do with users and dealers. If you were to make a recommendation to the president on how to design the next drug-control strategy, what would you recommend? On what evidence would you base your recommendations?

KEY TERMS

The numbers next to the terms refer to the pages on which the terms are defined.

money laundering (371)

pimp (372)

pornography (373)

prostitution (371)

sodomy (371)

statutory rape (370)

CHAPTER 14 International and Comparative Criminology

What Is Comparative Criminology?
- The Definition of Comparative Criminology
- The History of Comparative Criminology
- The Goals of Comparative Research

Engaging in Comparative Criminological Research
- Preparatory Work
- Comparative Research
- Comparative Research Tools and Resources
- The Special Problems of Empirical Research

Theory Testing
- Validation of Major Theories
- The Socioeconomic Development Perspective

Practical Goals
- Learning from Others' Experiences
- Developing International Strategies

Globalization versus Ethnic Fragmentation

REVIEW

CRIMINOLOGY & PUBLIC POLICY

YOU BE THE CRIMINOLOGIST

KEY TERMS

Boxes
- Of Immediate Concern: *Cross-Cultural Research: Smoking One's Way into Cheyenne Culture*
- From the Pages of *The New York Times*: *The Youngest Victims of International Crime*
- Window to the World: *BCCI: International Fraud*

Special Features
- Crime Surfing
- Did You Know?
- Theory Connects

KEY TERMS
comparative criminology
international crimes
international criminal court
transnational crime

Neo-Nazi groups march in Germany on the anniversary of the death of Rudolf Hess, one of Hitler's best-known associates and one of the few Nazis to serve a long prison term.

In June 1993 the FBI arrested eight "skinheads" who had been plotting to bomb the First African Methodist Episcopal Church in Los Angeles and shoot worshipers. American skinheads have become notorious for their random assaults on blacks, Jews, gays, immigrants, minority groups—anybody they perceive as different and whom they therefore dislike. They revere Hitler and his terror, delight in overt racist music, display swastikas and Nazi flags, and serve as shock troops for more established racist organizations. Between 3,300 and 3,500 skinheads are scattered in 160 or so groups in 40 states. They have become so dangerous that the FBI had to withdraw some undercover agents who had infiltrated their ranks.[1]

Few people had heard of skinheads prior to May 1985, when groups from Britain, Belgium, Denmark, and France staged a riot at a soccer game in Belgium, which left 38 people of color dead and another 200 wounded. Since then, skinheads have become a daily news item in many countries. During the first Gulf War, 1990 to 1991, skinheads burned 20 mosques to the ground in the London area.

Recently, an estimated 70,000 youths, in 33 countries, on six continents, adhered to the neo-Nazi skinhead movement, with the largest concentrations in Germany, Hungary, the Czech Republic, the United States, Poland, the United Kingdom, Brazil, Italy, and Sweden (listed in descending order).[2]

Hardest hit has been Germany, the birthplace of Nazism, where the homes of Jewish families have been firebombed and hundreds of foreign workers and asylum seekers have been attacked or killed. The skinheads attack with screams of "Heil Hitler," waving their favorite symbol, the old German imperial flag.

> Their ideology, if that is the word, is primitive . . . they know nothing about Hitler, or the war, beyond the fact that Hitler exterminated people who were "different" which is what they like to do themselves. They do not even know about the "ethnic cleansing" perpetrated recently in Bosnia. They do not read newspapers. They read killer comic books and listen to Oi music, which is a kind of heavy-metal rock about the pleasures of "genocide."[3]

In 1990–1991 it had been the mosques of the London region. By 1994–1995 the torch was turned on some 70 African American churches in the American South, nearly all with the hallmark of hate crime. In France hate has now reversed. The new "enemy," born of the suburban ghettos, is of mostly African origin, a ragtag subcultural group. Their common language is "hip-hop." Their roots are "in the Bronx and Kingston, Jamaica; in South-Central Los Angeles and Brixton, London; in Dakar and Algiers, in Islam and the N.B.A."[4] Its hallmarks are rage, graffiti, drug dealing, and firearms. For the time being, this movement has been dubbed the "guerrilla renaissance." What has caused the rise of neo-Nazism and the formation of skinhead groups, of torchers of houses of worship, and of "guerrilla renaissance," almost simultaneously, in so many different parts of the world? Who defines the often bizarre ideology of such groups? Do adherents communicate with each other across borders?

To answer these questions, criminologists must engage in comparative research. But so far, there are few answers. For the skinheads, criminologist Mark Hamm has begun this process with his work *American Skinheads—The Criminology and Control of Hate Crime*, which presents the phenomenon in an international perspective. He traces American developments to earlier occurrences in England and to the ideological background of Nazism in Germany.[5] Yet much more comparative research remains to be done to explain the almost simultaneous occurrence of identical crime problems in many parts of the world.

We begin this chapter on comparative criminology with an attempt to define it. We look next at the history of comparative criminology in order to identify its purpose and goals. Later in the chapter we focus on the prerequisites for comparative criminological research, the process itself, and the challenges globalization is posing to comparative criminology.

WHAT IS COMPARATIVE CRIMINOLOGY?

Comparison is something all human beings do every day. In choosing a home, for example, you compare such elements as number of rooms and price; location; access to transportation, shopping, and recreation; age of the structure; beauty of the surroundings; and so on. This comparison can become a science if it is done in a systematic manner. And so it is with comparative criminology.[6]

The Definition of Comparative Criminology

What is **comparative criminology?** Simply put, it is the cross-cultural or cross-national study of crime and crime control applying the comparative method in the science of criminology.[7]

Many criminologists use comparisons. Just think of a study comparing one group with another group, a control group. But this is not what we mean by comparative criminology; it requires comparison across cultures or nations. A comparative study of victimization rates between Montana and Mississippi is not comparative criminology, because the two states are part of one nation and of one basic culture. But if we were to compare the role of alcohol in the escalation of violence among the Cheyenne nation, in Montana or Wyoming, with that among the people of the rest of the state, we might well

Luther and Johnny Htoo, 12-year-old twin Myanamar messianic guerrilla leaders. Luther prepares to fire an M-16 rifle.

have a cross-cultural comparison, because the Cheyenne have a distinct legal system and a culture of their own.

The History of Comparative Criminology

Comparative criminology is not new. When the Romans had a crime problem in the fifth century B.C., they sent a delegation to the more advanced nation of Greece to learn better techniques for dealing with crime, such as the publication of laws. In the late Middle Ages and during the Renaissance (fourteenth to sixteenth centuries), all of continental Europe became a vast comparative laboratory as laws that had developed in the various principalities and cities were compared against the rediscovered laws of the old Roman Empire.

It was also during this era that crime-control methods became ever more brutal. The situation did not change until the eighteenth century, when—again through comparison, cooperation, and transfer—the work of the classical school (see Chapter 3) began to introduce rationality and humanitarian principles into crime control in Europe and America. In the nineteenth century, as communications improved, policy makers and scholars of criminology compared approaches and introduced into one another's systems what seemed to work. Such ideas as the juvenile court, the penitentiary, the reformatory, probation, and parole gained worldwide acceptance as a result of comparison. Yet the comparisons of the nineteenth and early twentieth centuries lacked scientific rigor; they were impressionistic and often emotional. For example, the juvenile court, first established in Chicago in 1899, seemed such a good idea that it gained acceptance in many parts of the world. But as later experience showed, it did not necessarily work everywhere.

The founders of criminology, including those of American criminology, were, for the most part, comparatists. They would gather at international meetings and trade ideas; they would visit each other and stimulate criminological thought. But truly comparative studies, measuring up to scholarly standards, could not be done until criminology itself became a science. Throughout the first half of the twentieth century internationalism met resistance from isolationism. Comparatists were regarded as dreamers, and the comparative approach was seen as not very practical.

The Global Village: Advantages Now circumstances have changed drastically. Comparative criminologists have become a necessity, simply because the world has become a "global village." Consider these figures from the U.S. Department of Commerce: In 1960 U.S. exports amounted to $19,659 million. By 2000 that figure had increased to $1.3 trillion. Similarly, in 1960 imports amounted to $15,073 million. By 2000 that figure had increased to 1,532.3 trillion. And that is only part of the global trade picture.

World economies have become totally integrated and interdependent. The Japanese car you own was probably manufactured in the United States, and your American car may have parts made in more than 30 countries. Your shirt may come from Hong Kong, your shoes from Italy, and your Swiss watch from the American Virgin Islands. The situation is no different abroad, where Coke and Pepsi and American fast-food chains are only the most visible aspects of economic globalization.

Communications likewise have become global. Sitting in your living room before a TV, you participate in world events as they happen. Phone and fax and computer networking have made instant personal and business communications possible. Transportation advances, especially since the introduction of jumbo jets, together with the opening of frontiers, have made it possible for millions of people to move across oceans within hours. Air-traffic volume increased from 26 billion passenger miles in 1960 to close to 2 trillion by the end of 2000.

Europe is feeling the effects of globalization even more intensely than the rest of the world. The collapse of Communist dictatorships in central and eastern Europe[8] and the virtual abolition of frontiers within Europe[9] have brought crime problems until now unheard of in Europe. Consequently, national criminology had to become international criminology. Criminology has in fact been globalized.[10]

The Global Village: Disadvantages While many aspects of the global village are beneficial, others have brought great problems. Instant communication promotes not only the spread of benefits, in goods, lifestyles, and useful knowledge, but also the dissemination of dysfunctional ideas and values—like the skinhead phenomenon. Economic globalization, as much as it promotes useful commerce, also aids organized crime and fosters the global spread of frauds that were once confined to smaller localities or single countries.

Jet planes transport not just legitimate travelers but also illegal aliens, criminal entrepreneurs, drug dealers, money launderers, and terrorists. Airlines themselves have become the targets and tools of international criminals. Moreover, the industrialization of the world brings not just economic benefits but threats to the world ecology so severe that, unless checked, they could compromise the food, water, and clean air supply for all people. It is little wonder, then, that criminologists too must look across borders to study crime and crime-control efforts, and to search for internationally acceptable solutions to common problems.

The Goals of Comparative Research

Before the 1970s there was very little literature on comparative research in criminology. Since then, however, it has been growing rapidly. That is attributable to (1) a realization that we will learn more about crime if we test our theories under diverse cultural conditions and (2) renewed interest in trying to discover what we can learn from the experience of other nations.[11]

Comparative criminology, then, has both theoretical and practical goals. It helps us better understand crime causation and find successful means of crime control, so that no nation need repeat costly mistakes made elsewhere. Presently, a large number of UN and affiliated organizations are engaged in the task of establishing international measures to deal with dangers that threaten people of all cultures. (See Table 14.1.)

Before we discuss the implementation of comparative research, we must look at the methods used by comparative criminologists.

ENGAGING IN COMPARATIVE CRIMINOLOGICAL RESEARCH

Comparative research requires special preparatory work to ensure that research data and information are in fact comparable. Empirical research presents additional obstacles.

Preparatory Work

Studying Foreign Law Before beginning a comparative study, the researcher must become familiar with the laws of the country or culture to which the comparison extends. Every country belongs to one or more of the world's great families of law, or legal systems (Table 14.2):

- *The civil law system.* This system grew out of the Roman legal tradition, was refined

TABLE 14.1 United Nations Organizations and Affiliates: Solving Worldwide Crime Problems

Center for International Crime Prevention, in the Office for Drug Control and Crime Prevention (of the UN Secretariat at Vienna, Austria): Reports to the UN Commission on Crime Prevention and Criminal Justice and conducts the quinquennial UN Congress on the Prevention of Crime and the Treatment of Offenders; provides extensive reports, research, documentation, and technical assistance; is responsible for UN standards and guidelines in criminal justice; conducts worldwide statistical surveys.

UNICRI—United Nations Interregional Crime and Justice Research Institute (located in Turin, Italy): Research arm of the UN Secretariat in crime prevention and criminal justice; is responsible for extensive research and publications.

UNAFEI—United Nations Asia and Far East Institute for the Prevention of Crime and the Treatment of Offenders (Fuchu, Japan): Services the region with training, technical assistance, research, and publications.

ILANUD—United Nations Latin American Institute for the Prevention of Crime and the Treatment of Offenders (San José, Costa Rica): Services the region with training, technical assistance, research, and publications.

UNAFRI—United Nations African Regional Institute for the Prevention of Crime and the Treatment of Offenders (Kampala, Uganda): Services the region with training and technical assistance.

HEUNI—Helsinki European Institute for Crime Prevention and Control; affiliated with the United Nations (Helsinki, Finland): Provides extensive research, training, research publications, and technical assistance services on behalf of European countries for both developed and developing countries.

AIC—Australian Institute of Criminology (Canberra, Australia): Under agreement with the UN, provides research, publication, training, and technical assistance services for Oceania, including Australia and New Zealand.

Arab Security Studies and Training Centre (Riyadh, Saudi Arabia): In close cooperation with the UN, provides extensive educational and training services, research, publications, and development and technical assistance to Arab countries.

International Centre for Criminal Law Reform and Criminal Justice Policy (Vancouver, B.C., Canada): Newly established, by agreement with the UN, to provide services within its sphere of expertise.

ISPAC—International Scientific and Professional Advisory Council of the United Nations Crime Prevention and Criminal Justice Programme (Milan, Italy): By agreement with the UN, provides advisory services to the UN with respect to data and information, both in general and on specific subjects falling within the mandate of the UN.

UNCJIN—United Nations Crime and Justice Information Network (Albany, N.Y.): In close cooperation with *WCJLN*—World Criminal Justice Library Network (Newark, N.J.)—assembles, integrates, and disseminates criminal justice information and data worldwide, with a view to complete electronic accessibility.

NIJ—The National Institute of Justice, of the U.S. Department of Justice: By an agreement with the United Nations signed in 1995, joined the Network of UN-affiliated institutes to make the services of the National Criminal Justice Reference Service—especially its UNOJUST computer services—available to the UN community, through its International Center.

NGOs—Nongovernmental organizations in consultative status with the United Nations Economic and Social Council: International organizations whose expertise is made available to the UN. They include many major scientific, professional, and advocacy groups, such as:

- International Association of Penal Law
- International Penal and Penitentiary Foundation (special status)
- International Society of Criminology
- International Society of Social Defense
- Institute of Higher Studies in Criminal Sciences
- Centro Nazionale di Prevenzione e Difesa Sociale
- International Association of Chiefs of Police
- International Prisoners Aid Association
- Amnesty International

NGO Alliances in Crime Prevention and Criminal Justice (New York, N.Y., and Vienna, Austria): Made up of the headquarters' representatives of NGOs; provide coordination and research services to the UN.

UN agencies: Concerned with various aspects of crime and justice. The agencies include:

- Centre for Human Rights (Geneva, Switzerland)
- UNICEF—United Nations Children's Fund (New York, N.Y.)

The United Nations Centre for International Drug Control: Concerned with various aspects of international drug control and drug abuse prevention. The programs include:

- Division on Narcotic Drugs
- International Narcotic Drug Control Board
- UN Fund for Drug Abuse Control

Regional intergovernmental organizations: Have organizational units and/or conduct programs concerned with crime prevention and criminal justice. Examples include:

- Council of Europe
- European Union (EU)
- Organization of American States
- Organization of African Unity
- North Atlantic Treaty Organization

Group of seated Afghani men gathers for Shura (or elders) meeting near Kandahar, Afganistan.

by scholars, and was codified under Napoleon in the early nineteenth century. Today it is found in systematic codes of law. The countries of continental Europe belong to this family of law, as do their former colonies in Africa, Latin America, and Asia, including Japan and China (now socialist), which chose the civil law system when they modernized.

- *The common law system.* Common law originated in England and then spread to the various English colonies. Today it is the legal system not only of the United Kingdom but also of the United States, Canada (except Quebec), Australia, New Zealand, India, many of the Caribbean islands, and African and Asian countries that were once English colonies. Although common law is now found in written form, it originated from case law, and case precedents still play a determining role.
- *Other legal systems.* (See Table 14.2.)

Having identified the legal system to which the country under study belongs, the comparatist studies the applicable law and its precise interpretation. Foreign legal systems, just like that of the United States, contain penal codes, codes of criminal procedure, constitutions, and case reports. But they also include special legislation on such topics as environmental protection and money laundering. In federal countries both federal and state legislation may have to be studied.

Then there is the problem of finding the country's laws. For the English-speaking researcher this need not be an insurmountable task. The laws, court decisions, and textbooks of English-speaking countries, for the most part, are accessible in libraries. The constitutions,[12] criminal codes,[13] and codes of criminal procedure[14] of many other countries are available in English. For a number of non-English-speaking countries there are English-language texts about their criminal law or procedure.[15] But since there is always a gap between the law on the books and the law in action, the comparatist must also consult the criminal justice research literature.

Understanding Foreign Criminal Justice Systems Laws function within a country's criminal justice system. It is the practitioners of the system who make the laws function. There are reports from around the world based on their experience.[16] There is also a considerable amount of periodical literature and statistical information in English describing the function-

TABLE 14.2 Dominant Criminal Justice Systems

Roman (Civil) Law	Common Law	Other Legal Systems
Law and procedure governed by separate, comprehensive, systematized codes, which are forward-looking, wishing to anticipate new problems.	Law and procedure governed by laws and precedents, which, if codified at all, simply organize past experiences.	*Islamic Law.* Called the Sharia; based in part on the Koran; of divine origin; covers all aspects of a Muslim's life; interpreted by judges and legal scholars; reasoning by analogy.
Codes based on scholarly analysis and conceptualizations.	Laws reflect experience of practitioners, on a case-by-case basis.	*Customary Law.* Also called tribal law; administered by elders; often exists side by side with civil or common law.
Supreme courts interpret nuances of law.	Supreme courts develop law.	
Legal proceedings must establish entire truth.	Truth finding strictly limited by pleadings and rules of evidence.	*Socialist Law.* Basically civil law; legal propositions subject to social/political policy.
Judges free to find and interpret facts.	Rules of evidence limit fact-finding process. Parties produce evidence.	*Mixed Systems.* A mix of civil and common law; may exist within a province or in a nation as a whole.
Very little lay participation.	Grand and petit juries play strong role.	
Originally, no presumption of guilt or innocence. Now presumption of innocence recognized.	Presumption of innocence.	

ing of criminal justice systems in a variety of countries (Table 14.3).[17]

Contemporary cross-cultural texts and treatises contain descriptions of the developments in criminology and criminal justice for over 50 countries.[18] In addition to the descriptions of entire criminal justice systems, there are accounts of the functioning of subsystems. For example, a five-volume series examines the area of delinquency and juvenile justice in more than two dozen countries and regions throughout the world.[19] Other aspects of criminal justice have been investigated by specialists in such areas as policing,[20] corrections,[21] and the incidence of female criminality.[22]

Learning about a Foreign Culture Comparatists may have an understanding of their own culture. To do comparative work, they must study a foreign culture: They must become familiar with its history, politics, economy, and social structure. Scholars of comparative criminology—such as Marshall B. Clinard, working in Switzerland as well as India and other developing countries,[23] Louise I. Shelley, working in eastern European socialist countries and elsewhere,[24] and William Clifford, having worked in several African countries as well as Japan[25]—have successfully demonstrated that the immersion in the cultures under study that comparative research requires can be accomplished without losing the objectivity of the detached scientific researcher.

Collecting Data Research, as we emphasized in Chapter 2, requires factual information. Although some countries do not yet have the resources for systematically collecting information on their crime problems,[26] the great majority send statistics to the International Criminal Police Organization (Interpol), which publishes the data biannually,[27] or participate in the United Nations Surveys of Crime Trends, Operation of Criminal Justice Systems and Crime Prevention Strategies. The UN surveys, published periodically, began with data for the year 1970 and by now include statistics from well over 100 countries on prevalence of crime and the operation of criminal systems.[28]

Several other international databases are available to the researcher, including the homicide statistics of the World Health Organization;[29]

TABLE 14.3 English-Language Periodical Literature for Comparative Criminology

Abstracting Services

Criminal Justice Abstracts
Criminology, Penology, and Police Science Abstracts

Periodicals

Advances in Criminological Theory
Crime Prevention and Criminal Justice Newsletter (UN)
Criminal Justice International
Criminal Justice—The International Journal of Policy and Practice (2001)
Criminal Law Forum: An International Journal
Dutch Penal Law and Policy
EuroCriminology
European Journal of Crime, Criminal Law and Criminal Justice
European Journal on Criminal Policy and Research
Forensic Science International
Forum on Crime and Society
Home Office Research and Planning Unit Research Bulletin
International Annals of Criminology
International Criminal Justice Review
International Criminal Police Review
International Journal of Comparative and Applied Criminal Justice
International Journal of Law and Psychiatry
International Journal of Offender Therapy and Comparative Criminology
International Journal of the Addictions
International Journal on Drug Policy
International Review of Victimology
Japanese Journal of Sociological Criminology
Police Practice and Research: An International Journal
Revue de Science Criminelle et de Droit Penal Comparée
Revue Internationale de Criminologie et de Police Technique
Revue Internationale de Droit Penal
Studies in Conflict and Terrorism
Studies on Crime and Crime Prevention (Norway)
Terrorism
UNAFEI Resource Material Series
Violence, Aggression and Terrorism
Violence and Victims

the private-initiative Comparative Crime Data File, which covers 110 sovereignties (published 1984);[30] and the Correlates of Crime (published 1989).[31]

International (or nation-by-nation) crime statistics suffer from the same problems as American UCR statistics, only magnified several times.[32]

Consequently, to obtain a more accurate picture of the crime situation in various countries, researchers have devised two additional statistical instruments:

1. The International Crime Victim Survey (ICVS). Beginning in 1989 and working through 1997, a group of researchers from various countries and research centers has conducted three victimization surveys in numerous developed (industrialized) and developing countries; 130,000 people were interviewed around the world, in 40 languages.[33]

2. A self-report study has measured delinquency among 14- to 21-year-old subjects in 12 countries, extending to property, violence, and drug criminality. This 1992 survey did not include developing countries.[34]

A comparison between the "official" crime rates of the UN surveys and the victimization rates shows that the two are reasonably related, although victimization studies usually show higher crime rates and tend to fluctuate over the years more than the UN survey rates. (See Figure 14.1.) One may cautiously conclude that the UN survey rates provide a fairly reasonable account of crime rates for most countries.

Comparative Research

Up to this point we have reviewed the general approach to doing comparative criminological research: studying foreign law, criminal justice systems, cultures, and available data. Comparative criminological research begins only after these requirements have been met. It is at this point that the comparatist sets sail for uncharted seas. The comparatist meets two problems right at the outset: the interdependence of all crime and criminal justice phenomena, and culture specificity.

Interdependent Phenomena Think of an elaborately assembled mobile hanging from the ceiling. All the parts are in perfect balance. If you remove a single part, the whole mobile will shift out of balance. It is the same with problems of crime and justice in any society: The existence of each is related to all the others and is explainable by reference to the others. Bicycle thefts may exist in countries like China, Den-

FIGURE 14.1 Police and victim survey data. Comparison between police data of UN Crime and Justice Survey (UNCJS) and victim survey data (ICVS), percent change in reported crime 1988–1995.

Source: Global Report on Crime and Justice (New York: United Nations, 1999), p. 69.

mark, and the Netherlands—all of which rely heavily on bicycle transportation—as well as in the United States or Mexico. But such theft plays a different role in the various countries, generates different responses, and leads to different consequences.

Is the bicycle theft problem comparable around the world? What could be learned from a comparison, and what factors must be considered? Would it be more useful to compare the Chinese bicycle theft problem with the Italian automobile theft problem? How do these problems fit in their countries' respective crime and justice mobiles?

Culture-Specific Phenomena The task of a comparative criminologist is like that of a surgeon about to transplant a heart or a liver. The surgeon studies a great variety of factors to be sure the donor's organ is compatible with the recipient's body. If we want to compare Japan's low crime rates with the high crime rates in the United States, we must consider many factors, such as the role of shame in Japanese society. Misconduct brings shame not only on individual Japanese wrongdoers, but also on their families, schools, and companies: Could shaming, as a sanction, play a role in American criminal justice, or is it too culture-specific? It is easier to ask such questions than it is to answer them, since research experience in comparative criminology is still limited.

Comparative Research Tools and Resources

The first book entitled *Comparative Criminology* appeared as recently as 1965. Its author, the late German-English scholar Hermann Mannheim, relied on his vast cross-cultural experience in criminology but offered no guide to the comparative method.[35] Researchers and

:// **Crime Surfing**

www.ncjrs.org

For the most extensive references to the field of international and comparative criminology and criminal justice, check the website of the National Criminal Justice Reference Service. The international section provides four options, including the all-important UNOJUST and UNCJIN.

The preferred means of transportation during rush hour in the streets of Beijing, China.

teachers of the field now have at their disposal a variety of reference works,[36] textbooks,[37] scholarly books,[38] and book-length informative coverage of United Nations activities in the field, of which the *Global Report on Crime and Justice* is the most significant.[39]

The Special Problems of Empirical Research

Criminologists who cannot find or rely upon comparative data must generate their own, usually by parallel field investigations proceeding more or less simultaneously. They confront three problems: first, the identification of comparable problems; second, the identification of sources of information; and third, the selection of a research method compatible in the countries under comparison.

Identification of Comparable Problems Researchers of New York University's Comparative Criminal Law Project, in the 1960s, compared the prevalence of delinquency in several cultures. To their surprise, they learned that Egypt had a high rate of delinquency for railroad offenses. Only local assistance could provide a plausible answer: The long railroad line running parallel to the Nile River is a favored haunt for local youths. Their delinquent acts were recorded as railroad offenses, rather than as delinquency.[40] These "railroad offenses" had to be made comparable to nonrailroad delinquencies in both Egypt and the other countries under comparison.

Identification of Sources of Information The social groups of one society may not be comparable to those of another. American junior high school students may represent American youngsters of that age range as a whole, but Haitian junior high school students would not. What groups are comparable to such favorite research subjects as American college students, blue-collar workers, and self-employed small-business-people? What is a fair cross section of any country's population?

Police records may be highly reliable in Belgium, but are they in Mali and

> **Theory Connects**
>
> Social control theorists study beliefs in law, with the hypothesis that holding conventional, law-abiding values promotes law abidance (Chapter 7). What would these theorists say about comparable beliefs in transitional economies, where the rule of law is compromised and governments are in a chaotic transition?

Cross-Cultural Research: Smoking One's Way into Cheyenne Culture

It was in the summer of 1935 that Karl N. Llewellyn, renowned legal philosopher, and his friend E. Adamson Hoebel, noted anthropologist, visited the northern Cheyennes on the Tongue River Reservation at Lame Deer, Montana. High Forehead of the Cheyennes served as their interpreter. Sitting in a circle with several Cheyennes, a chief filled the pipe and held it to the five directions. After the pipe had been passed around, he asked why the two white men had come.(1)

"To learn of your laws," answered the visitors. There was silence and more pipe puffing. Obviously the term "laws" meant nothing. Llewellyn went on, "For example, your rules on homicide . . . ?" More silence, more puffing. "Well," said Llewellyn, making another attempt, "what happens when there is trouble because one of your warriors has killed another man of the tribe?"

At this there was a smile of recognition, and Calf Woman spoke:

> Cries Yia Eya had been gone from the camp for three years because he had killed Chief Eagle in a whiskey brawl. The chiefs had ordered him away for his murder, so we did not see anything of him for that time. Then one day he came back, leading a horse packed with bundles of old-time tobacco. He stopped outside the camp and sent a messenger in with the horse and tobacco who was to say to the chiefs for him, "I am begging to come home."

> The chiefs all got together for a meeting, and the soldier societies were told to convene. The tobacco was divided up and chiefs' messengers were sent out to invite the soldier chiefs to come to the lodge of the tribal council. "Here is the tobacco that that man sent in," [the big chiefs] told the soldier chiefs. "Now we want you soldiers to decide if you think we should accept his request. If you decide that we should let him return, then it is up to you to convince his family that it is all right." (The relatives of Chief Eagle had told everybody that they would kill Cries Yia Eya on sight if they ever found him.) The soldier chiefs took the tobacco and went out to gather their troops. Each society met in its own separate lodge to talk among themselves.

> At last one man said, "I think it is all right. I believe the stink has blown from him. Let him return!" This view was passed around, and this is the view that won out among the soldiers. Then the father of Chief Eagle was sent for and asked whether he would accept the decision. "Soldiers," he replied, "I shall listen to you. Let him return! But if that man comes back, I want never to hear his voice raised against another person. If he does, we come together."

> Cries Yia Eya had always been a mean man, disliked by everyone, but he had been a fierce fighter against the enemies. After he came back to the camp, however, he was always good to the people.(2)

Llewellyn and Hoebel went on to collect hundreds of anecdotes of Cheyenne "conflict and case law." While they knew that the Cheyennes had structured institutions, they were surprised at the "juristic beauty" that the research revealed. In the introduction to their work on the subject, *The Cheyenne Way,* the authors comment:

> Three years of puzzlement went into the analysis of the material before order emerged; and this happened (as it does in modern case law) when the data of sixty or eighty years were arranged not on a flat time-plane, but against the moving time-perspective of the culture and the individual life.(2)

Sources

1. As told in class, ca. 1950, by Karl N. Llewellyn, University of Chicago.
2. Calf Woman's story is excerpted from K. N. Llewellyn and E. Adamson Hoebel, *The Cheyenne Way* (Norman: University of Oklahoma Press, 1941), pp. 12–13.

Questions for Discussion

1. What are some of the problems of doing criminological research in other cultures?
2. What are the best ways of ensuring that those problems are overcome?

Of Immediate Concern

Malawi or in Armenia? And if they are not, what comparable substitutes can the comparatist find? Such problems challenge the researcher's ingenuity.

Selection of Compatible Research Methods Criminologist James Finckenauer, studying attitudes toward legal and other values among American and Russian youngsters, was at first confronted with the reluctance of Russian administrators to ask youngsters to report (even anonymously) their own delinquencies. The Soviet culture had blocked any such initiative. The problem was overcome only by indirect questions to the youngsters, such as: "How wrong would it be (to do this, that, or the other)?" This was followed by further semidirect questions, such as: "Do your peers (parents, and so on) view you as a good kid, bad kid, or something in between?" It was only after the end of communism in 1992 that Finckenauer could administer a self-report delinquency questionnaire.

Certain research methods simply are unknown in many other countries or, if known, are frowned upon. In a study of perceptions of police power in four cultures, for example, the commanding officer of a foreign police department was asked to have some questionnaires distributed to his officers. At first the officer responded: "You don't seem to understand our police! It is we who ask the questions!" Finally, he agreed and distributed the questionnaires.

After the results were analyzed, the researchers were astonished to find that all the answers were identical. Apparently, all the questionnaires had been reviewed and "corrected" by an attorney to make sure they were "accurate."[41]

THEORY TESTING

As we noted earlier, the cross-cultural testing of criminological theories has become one of the major goals of comparative criminology. Recent studies have extended to several of the crime-causation theories discussed in this book. Yet cross-cultural theory testing requires utmost caution.[42]

Validation of Major Theories

After Sheldon and Eleanor Glueck had completed *Unraveling Juvenile Delinquency* (1950),[43] their work was criticized as too culture-specific because it was based on a sample of American children. In response, scholars replicated the Glueck research in different cultural settings—Puerto Rico, Germany, and Japan. As the Gluecks themselves put it, "All these [studies] ... have provided the most definite of all proofs, that of applicability to other samples by other researchers."[44] These cross-cultural validations of the Gluecks' delinquency-prediction system are some of the earliest empirical, comparative criminological studies.

More recently, criminologist Obi Ebbe has reviewed the Gluecks' studies and found their theories applicable to juvenile delinquents in Nigeria.[45] He has also examined the cross-cultural validity of other American theories, such as differential association, social control, and culture conflict. During the last few years other scholars have tested opportunity theory,[46] situational characteristics of crime,[47] routine-activity theory,[48] differen-

The proliferation of supermarkets, like this one in Moscow, Russia, is a phenomenon of socio-economic development which brings about an increase in crime.

> **Theory Connects**
>
> Some strain theorists focus on the "American Dream" and the frustration that sets in when achievement is limited by opportunities (Chapter 5). To what extent is the American Dream a cross-culturally valid explanation of crime? Would it explain crime in China? Switzerland? Cameroon?

tial opportunity theory,[49] social control and strain theory,[50] the synnomie explanation of low crime rates,[51] and Durkheim's anomie theory.[52] Most of these studies have shown the theories to have moderate to significant validity.[53]

The Socioeconomic Development Perspective

Cross-cultural researchers have devoted particular attention to the recently developed hypothesis that modernization and urbanization lead to increases in crime[54] as well as to the general question of whether socioeconomic development necessarily brings an increase in crime.[55] Several have noted a connection between rapid development and an increase in certain types of crime, especially property crime.[56] Other research has demonstrated that sudden urbanization and industrialization have not led to increased crime in some countries,[57] but that unguided socioeconomic and political changes, such as the current transformation from a socialist to a market economy in central and eastern Europe, do produce an increase in crime.[58] The complexity of the relation between development and crime has prompted some comparative criminologists to warn that, as yet, there is no universal theoretical framework linking crime and development.[59]

PRACTICAL GOALS

Learning from Others' Experiences

With increasing globalization, the similarity of crime problems increases as well. It is natural that criminologists would look at the experiences of other countries in their search for solutions, especially the experiences of countries that seem to have found workable solutions.[60] For the worldwide drunk-driving problem, for example, comparative research has been done in Australia, Norway, and the United States.[61] As for gun-control one study investigated the situation in 7 nations;[62] another, in 26.[63] Insurance fraud researchers have looked at the situation in 8 countries;[64] insider-trading researchers, in 3.[65]

A recent symposium compared differential methods of dealing with ecological crime in the United States, Germany, Austria, Japan, and Taiwan.[66] Comparative criminological research has also been done on violent crime, such as homicides of children,[67] spousal homicides,[68] homicides among young males,[69] and urban violence.[70] For the past 25 years, much attention has been devoted to the comparative study of the problem of juvenile delinquency.[71]

By now there is also a considerable body of cross-cultural research on various aspects of crime-control policy. One of the earliest studies in this area examined the perception of police power among divergent population groups in four countries.[72] The perception of law was studied in six cultures,[73] and teenagers' perception of crime and criminal justice was the subject of a more recent two-country study.[74]

Issues in policing[75] as well as sanctions[76] occupy the attention of comparatists in their search for "what works." Victimologists have been particularly active in cross-cultural study.[77]

Developing International Strategies

Comparative criminology reveals that most crime problems are not unique to a single country. So we are challenged to develop strategies jointly with other countries in order to establish crime-prevention and crime-control programs to benefit all. This is particularly necessary for those crime problems that have international implications. For the sake of convenience, we can group crime problems reaching beyond national borders into three categories:

- Internationally induced local crime problems
- Transnational crime
- International crime

Internationally Induced Local Crime Problems The skinhead phenomenon is a prime example of the simultaneous appearance of a similar type of crime in various parts of the world.[78] As yet, little is known about what causes such simultaneous appearances, although instantaneous reporting in the mass media may aid the process,[79] and some international organizational connections also may play a role. Recently, the Internet has come to play a role in connecting people pursuing common

From the Pages of The New York Times

The Youngest Victims of International Crime

"Each year, millions of children—boys as well as girls—are bought and sold like fresh produce, commodities in a global sex industry steeped in greed and unspeakable cruelty," said Carol Bellamy, executive director of Unicef, which sponsored a four-day conference with the Japanese government and two private groups in December 2001. Unicef estimated that every year, one million children around the world under the age of 18 are forced into the sex trade.

The conference drew 3,000 delegates, three times the number that took part in the first such gathering five years earlier in Stockholm. Subjects covered ranged from pedophiles who prey online, to gangs who lure young girls out of their homes from Burmese villages, to Bangkok bordellos.

The problem of teenage prostitution has a constantly shifting geography. When social groups brought the problem in Thailand to worldwide attention, girls from Cambodia, Laos, Myanmar—formerly Burma—and southern China began appearing in Bangkok brothels.

"In Korea, Japan and Taiwan, there is a new awareness of child sex tourism because men have gotten caught," said Samuel Koo, director of the Unicef office in Japan. Japan is one of 21 countries, including the United States, that have adopted laws that allow the police to arrest people for paying for sex with children while overseas.

In developed nations, the Internet and cellular telephone explosion has been a boon to adults who prey on young people for sex, conference participants said.

"We have this image of pedophiles lurking around playgrounds, looking for victims," said Nigel Williams, chief executive of Childnet International, a British-based group working to reduce the vulnerabilities of children on the Internet. "Now they don't even have to leave their own homes. They can reach children playing online. From a pedophile's perception, this is a wonderful playground."

In Europe, Japan, and the United States, about 20 police teams have been trained with the technological skills to track down pedophiles through the Internet, estimated John Carr, a technology expert with End Child Prostitution in Asian Tourism, one of the meeting's private sponsoring groups.

He cited the case of Manchester, England, where the police in 1996 seized 12 child pornographic images, all photographs or videos. In 1999, the same police department seized 41,000 child pornography images, with almost all originating from the Internet.

In the United States, the FBI has estimated that online offenses against minors appear to be growing about 10 percent a year. To help identify victims, Interpol has developed a huge database of images culled from the Internet and available to the group's 179 member countries, said Hamish McCullough, an officer with Interpol's Trafficking in Human Beings Branch.

Conference participants urged the police to stop looking at young people in prostitution as criminals. They said that travel agents, hotel clerks, and parents monitoring their children's Internet and cell phone usage were the first lines of community defense against youth prostitution and sexual abuse.

"In the middle of the night, 4 o'clock in the morning, I would go to a store and grab a package of cigarettes and a package of condoms and the guy at the counter never asked me if I was O.K.," said Cherry Kingsley, a Shuswap Indian woman from British Columbia who fell into prostitution at age 12.

Hotel clerks, she added, never questioned her when she checked into Vancouver hotel rooms at age 14 with an older man.

Source

Adapted from James Brooke, "Sex Web Spun Worldwide Traps Children," *New York Times,* Dec. 23, 2001. Reprinted with permission.

Questions for Discussion

1. Some conference participants felt that people who knew what was going on in the teenage sex trade—travel agents and hotel clerks, for instance—should take more social responsibility against this type of sexual abuse. What about legal responsibility? Should a travel agent who knows an adult is traveling to Thailand for sex with underage girls be held legally liable in some way? What about the hotel clerk who rents a room to an adult and a teenager? What about the parent who doesn't monitor a child's use of the Internet? Should any of these people be held accountable? And if so, how?

2. Some conference participants wanted law enforcement to stop looking at young prostitutes as criminals. Should there be different laws for prostitutes of different ages? Should there be different laws for people who were "forced" into prostitution as opposed to those who "volunteered"? How would these laws be enforced?

criminal goals. (Yet none of these factors was present in another simultaneous occurrence of a crime problem, namely, piracy in several widely separated waterways of the world in the mid-1970s, perpetrated in large part by rootless young offenders.[80]) The skinheads are part of the broader problem of crimes of discrimination against minorities, which itself is fueled by vastly increased intracontinental and intercontinental migrations. The appearance of new ethnic minorities within heretofore mono-ethnic communities often results in the victimization of minorities. These population migrations have also resulted in the migration of crime perpetrated by migrants—often against their fellow migrants, but also against the indigenous population. Consequently, criminologists have had to look for new ways to deal with these new forms and dimensions of crime.[81]

Internationally induced local crime problems can be far greater than hate crimes or other forms of crime associated with culture conflict and migration. Consider that drugs produced abroad and distributed locally create a vast problem of crime: Not only is drug dealing illegal, but a considerable portion of street crime is associated with narcotics. Ultimately, it could be said that there are very few crime problems that are not associated with persons and events abroad over which we have no direct control. Although the problem is a vast, yet largely uncharted territory, a number of criminal activities with foreign connections have recently been identified and given the title "transnational crime."

Transnational Crime Criminologists use the term **transnational crime** to refer to criminal activities, transactions, or schemes that violate the laws of more than one country or have a direct impact on a foreign country. Neither individually, nor by type, nor collectively by category do transnational crimes conform to the definitions and categorizations found in penal codes.

In a recent questionnaire sent to all the world's national governments, and in a subsequent report on the results, the United Nations, for the first time in history, demonstrated the existence and prevalence of transnational crime.[82] Eighteen categories of transnational criminality emerged. While it is conceivable that all these activities could be committed within a single jurisdiction, and/or by individual perpetrators, it is the hallmark of all that they are typically perpetrated by means of transnational activities and by organized groups of perpetrators.[83]

1. *Money laundering.* This category ranks number 1 on the list because of its massive impact on the economy of the entire world. Money laundering is an activity aimed at making illegally obtained funds seem legitimate, so that such funds can be spent or invested in the legitimate economy without arousing suspicion. Consider that a substantial part of the financial gain of the world's citizens is ill-gotten, for example, by bribery, by corruption, by black-market activities and transactions outside the tax laws, and especially by dealing in contraband.

The drug barons and others who have illegitimate income have devised many schemes to launder dirty money, including bogus real estate transactions, purchases of gold (many times consisting of lead bars with a coating of gold), and sales (real or fictitious) of art and antiques. But the standard method remains the physical transfer of cash out of the country (by planes or ships or by trucks and trailers with false bottoms), deposit of such cash abroad, followed by a series of international (electronic) transfers, at the end of which the source is untraceable, and the money seems clean and legitimately invested in the economy (Figure 14.2).

The true dimensions of money laundering are largely unknown. Estimates are as high as $500 billion annually.[84] Nevertheless, policy research (especially the Financial Transactions Task Force of the Group of Seven [highly industrialized countries]) has resulted in some remedies.

2. *Terrorist activities.* Americans had been largely unaware of the international scope of terrorist activities, primarily because their homeland had remained unaffected. This naiveté changed with the growing awareness that Americans, and American interests and

Pandemonium in a Moscow theater where 41 Chechen terrorists held 800 people hostage for 57 hours.

installations abroad, have become targets of international terrorists. But only the bombing of the World Trade Center in New York City in February 1993 by an organized group of Middle Eastern terrorists alerted Americans to the vulnerability of their own country. Similarly, Russians were shocked when Chechen rebels took 800 people hostage in a Moscow theater in October 2002. Rescue efforts killed 41 terrorists and 123 hostages. Of course, the victimization of air transport to and from America is a continuing reminder of terrorists' capability to harm American interests. The most horrific demonstration of air terrorism was the use of four hijacked jets by Al Queda terrorists to completely destroy the World Trade Center towers and damage the Pentagon on September 11, 2001, with a loss of nearly 3,000 lives (see Chapter 10).[85]

Much scholarly inquiry has been directed at understanding and explaining international terrorism.[86] And there have been legislative responses. As a matter of fact, a network of international conventions is in place to deal with international terrorism. International judicial and police cooperation have been vastly improved. Yet there is no international machinery in operation to ensure the arrest or adjudication of international terrorists, and criminologists have yet to arrive at theoretically sound explanations that would help deal with a problem that knows no boundaries.

3. *Theft of art and cultural objects.* This category obtained a number 3 ranking because of its potential for robbing entire cultures and nations of their cultural heritage. Tombs and monuments have been plundered since the time of the pharaohs. But with the development of modern tools and the high demand for cultural objects, as well as the ease of transport, international thieves have developed systems that can strip an entire region or country of its heritage—as well as the work of contemporary artists. There is no country that has not been victimized. An estimated $4.5 billion worth of fine art is stolen every year for sale on the international market. A database lists 45,000 stolen art objects, with an increase of 2,000 items a month.[87] With few exceptions,[88] criminologists have paid scant attention to this phenomenon, though the art industry has endeavored to come up with some practical solutions.[89]

4. *Theft of intellectual property.* Theft of intellectual property includes the unauthorized use of the rights of authors and performers, and

FIGURE 14.2 The operational principles of money laundering are as follows: First, move the funds from direct association with the crime; second, disguise the trail to foil pursuit; and third, make the money available to the criminal once again with its origins hidden.

A TYPICAL MONEY LAUNDERING SCHEME

PLACEMENT: Collection of Dirty Money → BANK Dirty Money Integrates into the Financial System

LAYERING: Transfer on the Bank Account of Company "X" → Wire Transfer → Offshore Bank → Loan to Company "Y" → Payment by "Y" of False Invoice to Company "X"

INTEGRATION: Purchase of Luxury Assets, Financial Investments, Commercial/Industrial Investments

Source: United Nations Office for Drug Control and Crime Prevention, *United Nations Global Programme against Money Laundering* (New York: United Nations, 1998), pp. 18, 19.

of copyrights and trademarks. There is obviously a high temptation to reproduce works of protected originators at a fraction of franchise (or similar) costs, especially in countries with relatively unregulated economies. Yet the destructive impact on the economies of producing or originating countries is immediately apparent—though hard to assess in monetary terms. One type of theft of intellectual property, namely the illegal copying of software, has been quantified by the U.S. Software Publishers Association: It amounts to an astounding loss of $7.5 billion annually.[90] Despite international agreements, this transnational crime category is a problem without a solution.

5. *Illicit traffic in arms.* Local, regional, or national armed conflicts, which plague us today in every part of the globe, would not be imaginable without an international network of weapons producers and suppliers. This is a shadowy world beyond the reach of statistical assessment. Criminological information on the illegal arms trade is also lacking. Yet the largest portion of the world's homicides is potentially traceable to the illegal trade in arms.

The most lethal part of the world's illegal arms trade centers on the transfer of nuclear materials. It is clear now that during the past few years several relatively small quantities of nuclear material, including pure plutonium, have been diverted from nuclear facilities in former Soviet republics and offered for sale in Germany and other countries west of Russia.

First indications are that the diversions of nuclear material that have occurred so far were carried out by small groups of individuals, rather than organized crime, for motives of individual gain (or possibly to assist in financing totally underfunded former Soviet laboratories and scientists). Most of the efforts were amateurish, and none of the material apparently reached a viable buyer. Indeed, most ended up in sting operations. However, quantities of nuclear material seized by authorities are not insubstantial. In September 1999, Georgian authorities seized 2.2 pounds of uranium 235 at the Georgian-Turkish border.[91] In several cases the thieves, transporters, and the public have been exposed to radiation hazards—in itself a not insubstantial danger.[92] Criminologists have been caught by surprise. As yet, there have been few criminological responses.[93] At this point, governments have cooperated to control nuclear materials at the source.

6. *Aircraft hijacking.* The system for curbing and responding to the illegal interception of aircraft is in place and has proved somewhat effective. The number of hijackings has declined significantly, yet incidents still occur with regularity, as the events of September 11, 2001, have horribly demonstrated.

The airline industry had been plagued by aircraft hijackings in the 1970s and into the 1980s. While a few such incidents were attributable to individuals who demanded ransom, most were political statements with typical terrorist characteristics, seeking to demonstrate the ability of the terrorist organization to strike at vulnerable targets almost anywhere in the world.

Since the entire world community was affected, especially diplomats and politicians, whose mobility depends on air travel, the reaction to the flood of hijackings was swift. The industry itself reacted by increasing security measures.

The criminological literature on this phenomenon is considerable, centering on the profiles of hijackers, causes, regions, carriers involved, and the like, all of which has led to the improvement of controls.

7. *Sea piracy.* Virtually forgotten until the mid-1970s, sea piracy has resurfaced on two fronts since then:

- The illegal narcotics drug smuggling from South and Central America into the United States initially relied heavily on yachts and fishing vessels captured at sea or in port, after owners and crews were killed. Several thousand vessels were victimized. As the drug trade became prosperous, smugglers began to rely on purchased or illegally chartered vessels.

- At the roadstead of Lagos, Nigeria, and the narrow shipping channel of the Malacca Straits—as well as in several other comparable sea lanes—the opportunity of deriving some benefit by attacking commercial vessels at anchor or slow speed attracted thousands of marginalized young men in Africa, Southeast Asia, and Latin America. Such piracies (often not piracies in the international law sense, since they occurred in the territorial waters of states) reached a high level of frequency (one a day in the 1980s), but are on the decline now, thanks largely to the research and policy activities of the International Maritime Bureau (London) of the International Chamber of Commerce (Paris), the International Maritime Organization (UN), and research by a number of criminologists.[94] (See "Window to the World," Chapter 11.)

While the problem has been ameliorated, it has by no means ended. Prudent shipping lines order "piracy watches" on their vessels in affected waters. National and regional maritime law enforcement agencies maintain closer watch, and the International Maritime Bureau maintains a special branch office in Kuala Lumpur, Malasia, to monitor developments.

8. *Land hijacking.* The inclusion of land hijacking in the list of transnational crimes was a surprise. At the national level, hijacking of trucks had been well documented as a form of robbery or theft. But the world economy has changed. Long-distance trucking from eastern to western Europe, or from the central Asian republics to the Baltic States, now is a reality, and involves a high percentage of goods transported transnationally. The opportunity to divert such cargos has increased proportionately.

It is telling that only four countries responded to this item on the UN questionnaire. At this point the evidence is entirely episodic but seems to point to the involvement of organized groups. Predictably, the problem will increase as a result of the openness of borders, the growth of organized crime (especially in eastern Europe), and the lack of data and criminological analysis.

9. *Insurance fraud.* The insurance industry is internationally linked, especially through reinsurance and other methods of spreading risks and benefits. Thus, local insurance fraud ultimately affects all insurers, and all insured, worldwide. The global dimensions of the problem have not been calculated, but for the United States alone the loss likely amounts to $100 billion annually.[95]

10. *Computer crime.* Just as computers serve legitimate commerce, governments, and researchers, the global Internet is also accessible for criminal schemes, exploitation, and use by organized crime. Current estimates of losses through computer crime range up to $8 billion annually.[96] Unfortunately, on this issue we lack information, though criminologists take an increasing interest in the development of legal and other protections.

11. *Environmental crime.* Well into the middle of the twentieth century, harming the environment was regarded as a matter to be controlled by local authorities. It was not until the United Nations Congress on the Environment (Stockholm, 1972) that the global dimensions of environmental destruction, and thus the need for its control, were recognized. In the three decades since Stockholm, much has been achieved in recognizing environmental dangers, quantifying them, and devising control mechanisms (by treaties, legislation, and ultimately, technology) in order to avert these dangers. Criminological research has contributed a great deal in this regard.[97]

12. *Trafficking in persons.* Original forms of trafficking in persons included the slave trade and the white slave trade (traffic in women). While the slave trade may be a matter of the past, the traffic in persons is on the increase, including:

- The transport of illegal immigrants, often resulting in involuntary servitude
- The transport of women and young children for purposes of prostitution
- The transport of migratory laborers to work under slavelike conditions
- The transport of household workers from developing countries
- The transfer of children for adoptions not sanctioned by law

For the most part, laws are in place to prevent the illegal trafficking in persons. Their enforcement is another matter. The problem is bound to increase as the populations of a stagnant Third World press to emigrate to the relatively prosperous countries.

Much of the illegal population flow is controlled by organized crime.[98] The newcomers in the industrialized countries, being largely unemployable, are forming a new marginalized class, likely to be exploited, but also contributing to crime and unrest.

13. *Trade in human body parts.* The first kidney transplant was performed in 1954, the first lung transplant in 1963, and the first heart transplant in 1967. By now close to half a million kidneys have been transplanted. Transplant surgery has become a highly specialized branch of medicine, and the supply of transplantable organs has spawned a very large industry. In the United States, 69 transplant agencies have been established, and federal and state laws seek to control their activities.

Yet, at any given moment, 35,000 people are waiting for a transplant (and the number increases by 14 percent annually); thus, the demand far outstrips the supply. (The number of potential donors in the United States is estimated at about 12,000.) An illegitimate industry has sprung up to provide a service. Recipients are flown to a country where organs can be procured virtually on demand. "Donors" may in fact have been murdered for their organs, or they are children of poor parents sold for their organs, at extremely low prices.

14. *Illicit drug trafficking.* Illicit traffic in narcotic drugs is entirely controlled by organized-crime networks, loosely related with each other geographically, as well as at the various levels of production and marketing and by type of narcotic drugs.[99] The criminological literature exploring this phenomenon from every angle is vast but by no means clear in terms of policy implications.[100] With the Single Convention on Narcotic Drugs

(1961), the Convention on Psychotropic Substances (1971), and the United Nations Convention against Illicit Traffic in Narcotic Drugs and Psychotropic Substances (1988), a theoretically perfect international legal structure to control this traffic is in place. Yet its application and enforcement suffer from the following shortcomings:

- The UN structure to oversee this treaty scheme is inadequate, primarily due to underfunding.
- Similarly underfunded are comparable national and regional programs.
- Nations differ vastly in their emphases (interdiction versus repression and control versus tolerance versus treatment approaches).
- Some of the most important countries of origin suffer from corruption at all levels—due to the vast income base of the trade—thus affecting enforcement.
- Corruption similarly affects law enforcement in many countries.
- Most developing and newly democratic countries lack the legal and technical infrastructure necessary to implement the treaties.

No other form of transnational and organized crime is as costly in terms of human and national financial suffering as the illicit trade in narcotic drugs.

15. *Fraudulent bankruptcy.* The internationalization of commerce has turned fraudulent bankruptcy from a local to a transnational crime. The dimensions of the phenomenon are largely unknown. Evidence is anecdotal but includes information that organized crime, after acquiring an enterprise, may subject it to bankruptcy when the gains from bankruptcy exceed the expectations of profit. There is a need to strengthen national enforcement efforts and to coordinate these efforts internationally.

16. *Infiltration of legal business.* This is the logical and temporal sequence of money laundering, the principal objective of which is seemingly legitimate investment. At this point the existing information permits no quantitative or qualitative assessment of the phenomenon, but it must be considered that the drug trade alone has between $200 billion and $500 billion to invest in the market. At this rate one could theoretically predict a time at which the world's economy would be controlled by organized crime.[101]

17. *Corruption and bribery of public officials, party officials, and elected representatives.* While bribery of party officials is not punishable in several countries, all other forms of bribery encompassed by this title are prohibited by penal codes. The problem lies with the enforceability of such laws, in both developed and developing countries, particularly with respect to international investments and trade. Disguised as "commissions," "consultancies," and agency or attorneys' fees, bribes have become a necessary cost of doing business worldwide. Nor is the practice universally condemned. Traders and investors have often proclaimed that it cannot be their business to improve the business or political ethics in countries with which they have commercial relations.[102] A recently established international organization, Transparency International (Berlin), has undertaken the formidable task of investigating international business ethics. Among its accomplishments are:

- Publishing a country-by-country bribery index
- Pressing for national legislation abolishing the tax deductibility of bribes
- Seeking international governmental cooperation in criminalizing the bribing of officials
- Strengthening international cooperation among nongovernmental organizations, such as the International Chamber of Commerce

> **:// Crime Surfing**
>
> www.uncjin.org/Statistics/WCTS/wcts.html
>
> How does the United States crime rate compare with that of the world as a whole? You will find this information in the UN Survey of Crime Trends and Operations of Criminal Justice Systems.

- Creating independent watchdog mechanisms

18. *Other offenses committed by organized criminal groups.* This catchall category permitted governments to report problems that could not be easily included in the 17 other categories. For example, both North America and western Europe are experiencing large-scale automobile theft, with the stolen vehicles being transported abroad. These activities are controlled by international organized criminal groups. They affect not just individual owners, but the insurance industry of each country.

> **:// Crime Surfing**
> www.interpol.com
>
> ... If you want to find out how the International Criminal Police Organization (ICPO—Interpol) helps in the fight against transnational crime (or anything else you ever wanted to know about Interpol), access the organization's website.

This review of the 18 categories of transnational criminality demonstrates the vast impact these criminal activities have on individuals, various branches of the economy, and the world economy itself. Individuals and individual commercial enterprises can do relatively little to protect themselves from these dangers, and increased international cooperation among nations has been recognized as absolutely necessary. But international action must be preceded by research. Thus, comparative criminological research will increasingly focus on transnational crime.[103]

International Crime International crimes are the major criminal offenses so designated by the community of nations for the protection of interests common to all humankind. They may be found in precedent (much like the Anglo-American common law of crimes) or in written form in international conventions. They can be tried in the courts of countries that recognize them, or they can be tried by international courts. The war crimes tribunals that tried German and Japanese war criminals after World War II were such courts. In 1993, the UN Security Council ordered the establishment of an international tribunal, to sit in the Netherlands, for war crimes committed on the territory of the former Yugoslavia; a court for the trial of persons charged with genocide in Rwanda was added. These courts have issued several hundred indictments—the exact number is unknown because they are sealed. Several trials have been held, leading to convictions as well as acquittals. Those in custody pending trial include General Momir Talic, the chief of staff of the Bosnian Serb

Investigators excavate one of many mass grave sites in the former Yugoslavia, October 1995.

army, who was arrested in Austria, on August 24, 1999. Some other powerful indicted war criminals are still in hiding, but they cannot leave the small territories under their control, for fear of likewise being taken into custody under outstanding international arrest warrants. Indeed, the former President of Yugoslavia, Slobodan Milosevic, is currently on trial for war crimes, at the Amsterdam Tibunal of the United Nations.

In May 2002, a long-standing dream of establishing a permanent **international criminal court** became a reality, after more than 60 nations ratified the treaty. The court, which will try only cases involving the most heinous crimes, became effective on July 1. The ICC will be a court of last resort—it will only try future cases that other countries cannot or will not handle. The jurisdiction of the new court extends only to the most serious international crimes, such as crimes against humanity, genocide, and war crimes. While such an agreement was impossible during the era of the cold war, the governments of the world, meeting in Rome in 1998, agreed by a vast majority vote to establish the Permanent International Court. Under the Clinton Administration, the United States signed the treaty in 2000. However, in a decision that has provoked outrage among human rights organizations around the world, in May 2002, the Bush administration withdrew from the treaty, declaring it to be against American interests. The handful of other nations that have not yet approved of the treaty are Pakistan, China, India, and a few small—so-called rogue—countries. Many fear that the power of the court will be greatly weakened without the support of these countries. Except for the few major international crimes over which the international court has jurisdiction, all others are triable only before national criminal courts.

> **:// Crime Surfing**
>
> www.iccnow.org
>
> For the latest developments on the establishment of the permanent International Criminal Court, check their website.

Which crimes are listed as international crimes? The Draft Code of Crimes lists the following as crimes against the peace and security of humanity:

- Crimes against humanity
- Aggression (by one state against another)
- Threat of aggression
- Intervention (in the internal or external affairs of another state)
- Colonial domination and other forms of alien domination
- Genocide (destroying a national, ethnic, racial, or religious group)
- Apartheid (suppression of a racial or an ethnic group)
- Systematic or mass violations of human rights
- Exceptionally serious war crimes
- Recruitment, use, financing, and training of mercenaries (soldiers of fortune)
- International terrorism
- Illicit traffic in narcotic drugs
- Willful and severe damage to the environment[104]

These crimes occur in many forms. For example, "systematic or mass violations of human rights" may be organized, large-scale rapes of women in occupied territories, as in Bosnia in 1992 and 1993.[105]

In addition to the listed international crimes, many others are recognized by convention; these include the cutting of undersea cables, the transportation of women for purposes of prostitution ("white slavery"), and fisheries offenses. There is now a

> **Did You Know?**
>
> ...that the United Nations started in 1945 with 51 Member States? By fall 1999, there were 188 Member States, united "to achieve international cooperation in solving economic, social, cultural and humanitarian problems," including the prevention of crime. By 2003, the number of Member States stood at 191.

BCCI: International Fraud

"Massive fraud." "World's biggest banking crash." "Financial deception of 'epic proportions.'" Journalists had a field day characterizing the magnitude of the collapse of the Bank of Credit & Commerce International (BCCI), which failed in July 1991. But let's talk numbers instead of adjectives:

- Founded in Pakistan, the international financial institution owed some $2 billion when it folded.
- A senior official admitted to playing a major role in frauds totaling $1.242 billion.
- Thousands of creditors, both businesses and individuals, lost every penny of the money they had deposited.
- In 1991, BCCI agreed to forfeit $550 million to begin compensating depositors worldwide and to salvage institutions the corporation owned secretly in the United States.
- The U.S. investigation that preceded the prosecution of a single person accused of participating in the scandal cost a whopping $20 million.
- In England alone, BCCI had a staff of 1,200 and 45,000 customers—personnel who lost their jobs and customers who lost their life savings when the bank failed.

Big numbers! What are the crimes that led to this scandal of "epic proportions"? In the United States, BCCI pleaded guilty to federal and state charges of racketeering, fraud, and money laundering. Individuals have been charged with withholding information in a scheme to defraud federal and state bank regulators and depositors. In Britain, charges against bank officials include false accounting, the furnishing of false information, and conspiracy to defraud.

HOW IT WORKED

A picture of the corporation's operations has unfolded since the crash:

> BCCI's reported profits had been "falsely inflated" by $614 million between January 1983 and December 1985. The misuse of clients' funds by the bank amounted to another $627 million by the end of 1985.... By the early 1980s the bank needed to demonstrate its profitability and a healthy balance sheet to maintain the confidence of banking regulators and current and potential investors. In desperation, the bank's founder and his senior officers turned to the trading of commodities as a likely source of funds and began a series of high-risk speculations trading in futures. Most of these were in options on large-scale purchases of silver, which went badly wrong when the price of the metal turned sharply downwards. As money was lost upon money, the frauds became more widespread. The methods involved to maintain the pretense of solidity included filing accounts in which commissions on silver-trading deals that had never taken place were recorded as profits.... Accounts were falsified and large sums of customers' money diverted using a financial labyrinth to fool auditors into thinking the bank was solvent when it was actually hugely in deficit.(1)

A HARD LESSON

While the settlement in the United States provided funds for the compensation of some depositors, many more will never see their money again. Some consider this a "school of hard knocks" lesson about the inability of the criminal justice system to deal effectively with international fraud. Gathering the documents needed to provide evidence ranges from difficult to impossible. After one trial in the United States, a *Chicago Tribune* editorial commented: "International financial transactions can be made so complex as to effectively conceal what is really going on; key officials can always flee the jurisdiction and take vital evidence with them."(2) One lawyer summed up his observation of the outcomes of big international cases very succinctly: "No one gets caught but huge sums of money disappear."(3)

Sources

1. Ben Fenton and Sonia Purnell, "Bank Official Admits $750m Fraud, 'Financial Juggler' Was at the Heart of BCCI Scandal," *Daily Telegraph,* Sept. 28, 1993, p. 1.
2. "BCCI Still a Mystery," *Chicago Tribune,* Aug. 27, 1993, p. 23.
3. Peter Blackman, "The BCCI Problem; System's Flaws Stymie Probes of Foreign Banks," *New York Law Journal,* Aug. 26, 1993, p. 5.

Questions for Discussion

1. How could depositors be protected from losing their money in international scams like BCCI's?
2. Would an international criminal court be better able to deal with massive international fraud?

Window to the World

considerable body of research and scholarship on international crimes.[106]

Globalization versus Ethnic Fragmentation

We have entered the twenty-first century. Comparative criminologists view the new millennium with some uneasiness. Globalization raises great hopes for a better future for all human beings. Yet it brings with it grave dangers in terms of the internationalization of crime. Comparative criminology has a significant role to play in the investigation of new forms of transnational crime. Researchers can apply the methods used when such crimes were strictly local or national but using the sophistication of the science of comparative criminology.

The new millennium presents additional hazards arising from the trend toward balkanization. "Balkanization," the opposite of globalization, is the breakup of nation-states into ethnic entities. Many ethnic groups are striving for the independence and sovereignty denied to them when they were incorporated in larger nation-states, as in the former Soviet Union or Yugoslavia; or when they were joined arbitrarily with other groups in colonial times, as in Africa; or when other accidents of history included them within empires, as in western Europe. Frequently, such ethnic groups had to abide by laws and customs that were not of their own choosing and had to suppress their own languages and cultures. Now they are searching for identities, territories, and criminal justice systems of their own. Unfortunately, the struggle has brought with it human rights violations, war crimes, and genocide on a massive scale. This is the latest challenge for criminologists and criminal justice specialists working on the international level.

REVIEW

Comparative criminology, despite its historical antecedents, is a young science, a subspecialty of criminology. In view of the globalization of the world—brought about by recent technological advances and the enormous increase in international commerce, both legal and illegal—comparative studies in criminology have become a necessity. Comparatists are called upon to assist governments in devising strategies to deal with a wide variety of international and transnational crimes.

In this chapter we traced the history of comparative criminology, sought to define it, and attempted to identify its goals. These goals may be theoretical, like the cross-cultural testing of prominent theories of crime. They can also be very practical, like the search for transplantable crime-fighting strategies or for techniques to deal with specific transnational and international crimes.

There are a number of requirements for successful comparative research: studying foreign law, understanding foreign criminal justice systems, learning about a foreign culture, collecting reliable data, engaging in comparative research, and, when needed, doing cross-cultural empirical research.

We paid special attention to three dimensions that pose special challenges to comparative criminology: internationally induced local crime, transnational crime, and international crime. There is much research to be conducted before progress can be expected in these three areas.

The accomplishments of criminologists who have engaged in comparative studies form the foundation for further research. The tools of comparative criminology should prove useful in helping both individual nations and the United Nations solve some of their common crime problems. The United Nations and its agencies continue to do very practical work to help nations deal with crime on a worldwide basis.

CRIMINOLOGY & PUBLIC POLICY

Why is it that criminologists rarely if ever study genocide? Have we forgotten the systematic decimation of 1½ million Armenians by the Young Turks during World War I, the planned killing of 6 million Jews, and the extermination of another 5 million untermenschen, *including Gypsies, political opponents, mentally ill, retarded, and other "inferior" peoples between 1941 and 1945. How could criminology have neglected an examination of the crimes against humanity that resulted in an estimated*

7 to 16 million deaths over the past 50 years since World War II?

Some of the more obvious and yet unacceptable reasons are offered below.

1. Genocide is a political act reflecting the will of sovereignty.
2. Genocide is a breach of international norms and international law.
3. Genocide is committed by the state.
4. The magnitude of victimization in genocide defies belief.
5. Criminology has little to offer the study of genocide.
6. There are problems in denying or in admitting atrocity.

"Consider how the criminology of genocide would add to our knowledge of victimization, homicide, aggression, and violence. Consider, as well, how research on genocide might support the theoretical work of critical and Marxist scholars in their efforts to explain a different conception of the state in relation to crime. Most important, reflect on the contribution that criminologists could make to further our understanding as to how genocide may be prevented. Nowhere are matters of prevention more important than with the crime of genocide.

"It is all too easy to say that criminology's neglect of genocide suggests a disciplinary denial; that our failure to recognize genocide implicitly contributes to the evil of revisionism; and that we should know better than to have the boundaries of our field permanently fixed by the criminal law—especially where extant law is so frail and uncertain. It is all too easy to say these things, because they are true."

(Source: William S. Laufer, "The Forgotten Criminology of Genocide," *The Criminology of Criminal Law: Advances in Criminological Theory*, 8, 1999)

Questions for Discussion Why do you suppose that the field of criminology neglects the study of genocide? Is it justifiable if genocide is the most serious form of homicide?

YOU BE THE CRIMINOLOGIST

What advice would you give to the U.S. Congress regarding how to alleviate the global crime problem as it affects U.S. citizens? Should the United States go it alone? Enter into bilateral arrangements? Attempt to find global solutions? Explain your recommendations.

KEY TERMS

The numbers next to the terms refer to the pages on which the terms are defined.

comparative criminology (384)

international crimes (403)

international criminal court (404)

transnational crime (397)

Notes

CHAPTER 1

1. Paul W. Tappan, *Crime, Justice and Correction* (New York: McGraw-Hill, 1960).
2. G:\WORK\CRIME\111401\76122.000.
3. *Patterns of Global Terrorism 1999* (Washington, D.C.: U.S. State Department, April 2000).
4. www.transform-drugs.org.uk/drug&terrorism.htm.
5. Robert Spear and Philip Shenou, "Customs Switches Priority from Drugs to Terrorism," *New York Times,* Oct. 10, 2001, www.crimelynx.com/custswitch.html; Jerry Seper, "Mexicans, Russian Mob New Partners in Crime," *Washington Times,* Sept. 14, 2002, www.rusnet.nl/info/cis-today/archive/01-05/28wnl.shtm.
6. Secret bank account transfers are not the only method of laundering money. Other methods are Market Peso Exchange, cash smuggling, gold transfers, and many others.
7. Steven Erlanger, "Hamburg Police Raid 2 Import-Export Firms," www.nytimes.com/2002/09/11/international/11GERM.html; "3 Former Executives Indicted in Fraud," *New York Times,* Sept. 6, 2002, Sec. C, p. 4.; Leif Pagrotsky and Joseph Stiglitz, "Blocking the Terrorists' Funds: The Global Financial System Provides Hiding Places for Dirty Money," *Financial Times,* Dec. 7, 2001; Daniel Williams, "Swiss Probe Illustrates Difficulties in Tracking Al Qaeda's Cash," *Washington Post,* Nov. 12, 2001.
8. P. K. Semler, "Rich Linked to Money Laundering," *Washington Times,* June 21, 2002, www.washtimes.com/world/20020621-417508.htm. The reference to the American fugitive financier, Mark Rich, who defrauded clients of millions of dollars, found safe haven (and business opportunities), in Zug, Switzerland, and was ultimately pardoned by President Clinton.
9. R. Mark Bortner, "Cyberlaundering; Anonymous Digital Cash and Money Laundering," (1996), www.law.miami.edu/~fro@mkin/seminar/papers/bortner.htm.
10. Jim Wolf, "Cyber Attack Fears Stir Security Offices," http://story.news.yahoo.com/news?tmplstory2@cid-ncid-564@e-11@u-lnm/2002.
11. Barton Gellman "Cyber-Attacks by Al Qaeda Feared," www.crime-research.org/eng/library/Barton.htm (2002).
12. For example, Associated Press, International News, "Italian Police Arrest 15 Alleged Islamic Extremists," Sept. 16, 2002, famulus.msnbc.com/Famulus Intl/ap09-12-150217.asp?reg=Europe.
13. For example, see Ross Sorkin, "2 Top Tyco Executives Charged with $600 Million Fraud Scheme," *New York Times,* Sept. 13, 2002, pp. 1, C3.
14. "The Mariner Group—Oil Spill History," www.marinergroup.com/oil-spill-history.htm; CNN.com/world, "Chinese Oil Tanker Explodes at Sea," www.cnn.com/2002/WORLD/asia pcf/east/09/11/china.tanker.reut/index.html; Toby Reynolds, "South Africa Blocks Oil Spill from Wetlands," www.swissinfo.org/sen/Swissinfo.html.Environmental; Timeline, www.mapreport.com/subtopics/d/l.html; Incident News, www.incidentnews.gov/, National Ocean Service, National Oceanic and Atmospheric Administration, Apr. 11, 2002.
15. Raffaele Garofalo, *Criminologia* (Naples, 1885), published in English as *Criminology,* trans. Robert W. Millar (Boston: Little, Brown, 1914; rpt., Montclair, N.J.: Patterson Smith, 1968).
16. Paul Topinard, "L'Anthropologie criminelle," *Revue d'anthropologie,* **2** (1887).
17. Edwin H. Sutherland, *Principles of Criminology,* 2d ed. (Philadelphia: Lippincott, 1934), originally published as *Criminology,* 1924.
18. Some legal scholars argue that criminologists should study only law-breaking. See Note 1.
19. Jack D. Douglas and Frances C. Waksler, *The Sociology of Deviance* (Boston: Little, Brown, 1982).
20. Garofalo, *Criminologia,* p. 5.
21. Émile Durkheim, *Rules of Sociological Method,* trans. S. A. Solaway and J. H. Mueller (Glencoe, Ill.: Free Press, 1958), p. 64.
22. Freda Adler, "Our American Society of Criminology, the World, and the State of the Art—The American Society of Criminology 1995 Presidential Address," *Criminology,* **34** (1995): 1–9.
23. *Critical Criminal Justice Issues: Task Force Reports to Attorney General Janet Reno* (Washington, D.C.: National Institute of Justice/American Society of Criminology, 1995).

CHAPTER 2

1. The Anglo-American concept of crime was developed by a long line of distinguished legal scholars, as discussed in G. O. W. Mueller, *Crime, Law, and the Scholars* (London: Heinemann; Seattle: University of Washington Press, 1969).

2. Jerome Hall, *General Principles of Criminal Law,* 2d ed. (Indianapolis: Bobbs-Merrill, 1960).
3. American Law Institute, Model Penal Code, sec. 2.01(1). The American Law Institute, dedicated to law reform, is an association of some of the most prestigious American lawyers. Between 1954 and 1962 this group sought to codify the best features of the penal codes of the various states. The resultant Model Penal Code (MPC) has had considerable influence on law reform in many states, and has been adopted nearly in full by New Jersey and Pennsylvania. We shall have frequent occasion to refer to the MPC as "typical" American criminal law. See also Gerhard O. W. Mueller, "The Public Law of Wrongs—Its Concepts in the World of Reality," *Journal of Public Law,* **10** (1961): 203–260; Michael Moore, *Act and Crime—The Philosophy of Action and Its Implications for Criminal Law* (Oxford: Clarendon Press, 1993).
4. Nanci Adler, *The Gulag Survivor: Beyond the Soviet System* (New Brunswick, N.J.: Transaction Publishers, 2002).
5. *Robinson v. California,* 370 U.S. 660 (1962).
6. *State v. Palendrano,* 120 N.J. Super 336, 293 A. 2d 747 (1972).
7. G. O. W. Mueller, "Causing Criminal Harm," in *Essays in Criminal Science,* ed. Mueller (South Hackensack, N.J.: Fred B. Rothman, 1961), pp. 167–214.
8. *Lambert v. California,* 355 U.S. 225 (1957). This decision must be approached with care. It does not stand for the proposition that ignorance of the law is an excuse. The Supreme Court was very careful to limit the scope of its decision to offenses by omission of adherence to regulations not commonly known, when the defendant in fact did not know—and had no means of knowing—of the prohibition.
9. G. O. W. Mueller, "On Common Law Mens Rea," *Minnesota Law Review,* **42** (1958): 1043–1104, at p. 1060.
10. For a recent look at the insanity defense, and its many challenges, see Richard Moran, *Knowing Right from Wrong: The Insanity Defense of Daniel McNaughtan* (New York: Free Press, 2000).
11. James O. Finckenauer and Patricia W. Gavin, *Scared Straight: The Panacea Phenomenon Revisited* (Prospect Heights, Ill.: Waveland, 1999).
12. Personal communication from Anne Campbell. Based on Campbell, *The Girls in the Gang: A Report from New York City* (New York: Basil Blackwell, 1984).
13. Edwin H. Sutherland, *The Professional Thief* (Chicago: University of Chicago Press, 1937).
14. Marvin E. Wolfgang, "Ethics and Research," in *Ethics, Public Policy, and Criminal Justice,* ed. A. F. Ellison and N. Bowie (Cambridge, Mass.: Oelgeschlager, Gunn & Hain, 1982).
15. "Draft of ASC Code of Ethics," *Criminologist,* **24** (July–August 1999): 13–21.
16. Seth A. Bloomberg and Leslie Wilkins, "Ethics of Research Involving Human Subjects in Criminal Justice," *Crime and Delinquency,* **23** (1977): 435–444.
17. Lawrence Sherman and Barry Glick, "The Quality of Arrest Statistics," *Police Foundation Reports,* **2** (1984): 1–8.
18. Michael Couzens, "Getting the Crime Rate Down: Political Pressure and Crime Reporting," *Law and Society Review,* **8** (1974): 457–493.
19. President's Commission on Law Enforcement and Administration of Justice, *The Challenge of Crime in a Free Society* (Washington, D.C.: U.S. Government Printing Office, 1967), p. 25.
20. Patrick Jackson, "Assessing the Validity of Official Data on Arson," *Criminology,* **26** (1988): 181–195.
21. Patrick G. Jackson, "Sources of Data," in *Measurement Issues in Criminology,* ed. Kimberly L. Kempf (New York: Springer-Verlag, 1990), p. 42. For a comparison of the NCVS, UCR, and NIBRS, with a particular emphasis on what can be learned from incident-based police data that cannot be learned from other sources, see Michael G. Maxfield, "The National Incident-Based Reporting System: Research and Policy Applications," *Journal of Quantitative Criminology,* **15** (1999): 119–149.
22. For a comparison of victimization data with official police data, see Alfred Blumstein, Jacqueline Cohen, and Richard Rosenfeld, "Trend and Deviation in Crime Rates: A Comparison of UCR and NCS Data for Burglary and Robbery," *Criminology,* **29** (1991): 237–263.
23. James Levine, "The Potential for Crime Over-reporting in Criminal Victimization Surveys," *Criminology,* **14** (1976): 307–330.
24. James S. Wallerstein and Clement J. Wyle, "Our Law-Abiding Law-Breakers," *Probation,* **25** (March–April 1947): 107–112.
25. Martin Gold, "Undetected Delinquent Behavior," *Journal of Research in Crime and Delinquency,* **3** (1966): 27–46.
26. D. Wayne Osgood, Lloyd Johnston, Patrick O'Malley, and Jerald Bachman, "The Generality of Deviance in Late Adolescence and Early Adulthood," *American Sociological Review,* **53** (1988): 81–93.
27. Franklin Dunford and Delbert Elliott, "Identifying Career Offenders Using Self-Reported Data," *Journal of Research in Crime and Delinquency,* **21** (1983): 57–86.
28. Josine Junger-Tas, Gert-Jan Terlouw, and Malcolm W. Klein, eds., *Delinquent Behavior among Young*

NOTES

29. Michael Hindelang, Travis Hirschi, and Joseph Weis, *Measuring Delinquency* (Beverly Hills, Calif.: Sage, 1981).
30. Tom Squitieri, "Soaring Murder Rate 'Tears Apart' Charlotte," *USA Today,* Jan. 31, 1992, p. 6A.
31. U.S. Department of Justice, Federal Bureau of Investigation, *Crime in the United States, 1992* (hereafter cited as Uniform Crime Reports) (Washington, D.C.: U.S. Government Printing Office, 1993), p. 140; Uniform Crime Reports, 1986, p. 94; Uniform Crime Reports, 1997, p. 147; Uniform Crime Reports, 2001, p. 142.
32. Uniform Crime Reports, 2001, p. 67.
33. U.S. Department of Justice, Bureau of Justice Statistics, *Criminal Victimization, 2000* (Washington, D.C.: U.S. Government Printing Office, December 2001), p. 3.
34. Uniform Crime Reports, 2001, p. 6.
35. *Criminal Victimization,* 2001, p. 11.
36. Bureau of Justice Statistics, *Crime and Victim Statistics,* found at http://www.ojp.usdoj.gov/bjs/cvict_c.htm#place, Sept. 17, 2002.
37. FBI's National Incidence-Based Reporting System master files for years 1991–1996; as cited in *Juvenile Offenders and Victims: 1999 National Report.*
38. Derral Cheatwood, "The Effects of Weather on Homicide," *Journal of Quantitative Criminology,* **11** (1995): 51–70.
39. U.S. Department of Justice, "The Severity of Crime, Bureau of Justice Statistics Bulletin" (Washington, D.C.: U.S. Government Printing Office, Jan. 1984).
40. Uniform Crime Reports, 2001, p. 216.
41. James C. McKinley Jr., "Six Armed Men, Aged 40–72, Held in Bungled Robbery of a Club," *New York Times,* Apr. 20, 1989, p. D6.
42. *New York Times,* Nov. 6, 1994, p. 24.
43. Uniform Crime Reports, 2001, pp. 226–227.
44. U.S. Bureau of the Census, *Statistical Abstract of the United States: 1998* (Washington, D.C.: U.S. Government Printing Office, 1998), p. 15.
45. Michael Gottfredson and Travis Hirschi, "The True Value of Lambda Would Appear to Be Zero: An Essay on Career Criminals, Criminal Careers, Selective Incapacitation, Cohort Studies, and Related Topics," *Criminology,* **24** (1986): 213–234.
46. Michael Gottfredson and Travis Hirschi, "Science, Public Policy, and the Career Paradigm," *Criminology,* **26** (1988): 37–55. For a test of those contentions, see Sung Joon Jang and Marvin D. Krohn, "Developmental Patterns of Sex Differences in Delinquency among African American Adolescents: A Test of the Sex-Invariance Hypothesis," *Journal of Quantitative Criminology,* **11** (1995): 195–222.
47. James Q. Wilson and Richard Herrnstein, *Crime and Human Nature* (New York: Simon & Schuster, 1985), pp. 126–147.
48. Alfred Blumstein, Jacqueline Cohen, and David Farrington, "Criminal Career Research: Its Value for Criminology," *Criminology,* **26** (1988): 1–35.
49. Dawn R. Jeglum Bartusch, Donald R. Lynum, Terrie E. Moffitt, and Phil A. Silva, "Is Age Important? Testing a General versus a Developmental Theory of Antisocial Behavior," *Criminology,* **35** (1997): 13–48.
50. Alfred Blumstein, Jacqueline Cohen, Jeffrey Roth, and Christy Visher, *Criminal Careers and "Career Criminals"* (Washington, D.C.: National Academy Press, 1986). On the relationship between crime and age, see Robert J. Sampson and John H. Laub, *Crime in the Making: Pathways and Turning Points through Life* (Cambridge, Mass.: Harvard University Press, 1993); Neal Shover and Carol Y. Thompson, "Age, Differential Expectations, and Crime Desistance," *Criminology,* **30** (1992): 89–104; David F. Greenberg, "The Historical Variability of the Age-Crime Relationship," *Journal of Quantitative Criminology,* **10** (1994): 361–373; Daniel S. Nagin, David P. Farrington, and Terrie E. Moffitt, "Life-Course Trajectories of Different Types of Offenders," *Criminology,* **33** (1995): 111–139; and Julie Horney, Wayne Osgood, and Ineke Haen Marshall, "Criminal Careers in the Short-Term: Intra-individual Variability in Crime and Its Relation to Local Life Circumstances," *American Sociological Review,* **60** (1995): 655–673.
51. Marvin Wolfgang, Robert Figlio, and Thorsten Sellin, *Delinquency in a Birth Cohort* (Chicago: University of Chicago Press, 1972). For a discussion of how each delinquent act was weighted for seriousness, see Thorsten Sellin and Marvin Wolfgang, *The Measurement of Delinquency* (New York: Wiley, 1964). See also Douglas A. Smith, Christy A. Visher, and G. Roger Jarjoura, "Dimensions of Delinquency: Exploring the Correlates of Participation, Frequency, and Persistence of Delinquent Behavior," *Journal of Research in Crime and Delinquency,* **28** (1990): 6–32.
52. Marvin E. Wolfgang, Terence Thornberry, and Robert Figlio, *From Boy to Man, from Delinquency to Crime* (Chicago: University of Chicago Press, 1987).
53. Paul E. Tracy, Marvin E. Wolfgang, and Robert M. Figlio, *Delinquency Careers in Two Birth Cohorts* (New York: Plenum, 1990), pp. 275–280.
54. Terence P. Thornberry, "What's Working and What's Not Working in Safeguarding Our Children and

54. ...Preventing Violence," Safeguarding Our Youth: Violence Prevention for Our Nation's Children, speech presented at Department of Education, Washington, D.C., July 20, 1993.
55. Uniform Crime Reports, 2001, p. 233.
56. *Criminal Victimization in the United States,* 2000, p. 51.
57. Uniform Crime Reports, 1997, p. 229.
58. Delbert Elliott and Suzanne Ageton, "Reconciling Race and Class Differences in Self-Reported and Official Estimates of Delinquency," *American Sociological Review,* **45** (1980): 95–110; and Roy L. Austin, "Recent Trends in Official Male and Female Crime Rates: The Convergence Controversy," *Journal of Criminal Justice,* **21** (1993): 447–466.
59. John Hagan, John Simpson, and A. R. Gillis, "Class in the Household: A Power Control Theory of Gender and Delinquency," *American Journal of Sociology,* **92** (1987): 788–816. See also Gary F. Jensen, John Hagan, and A. R. Gillis, "Power-Control vs. Social Control Theories of Common Delinquency: A Comparative Analysis," in *New Directions in Criminological Theory,* eds. Freda Adler and William S. Laufer (New Brunswick, N.J.: Transaction, 1993), pp. 363–398.
60. Merry Morash and Meda Chesney-Lind, "A Reformulation and Partial Test of the Power Control Theory of Delinquency," *Justice Quarterly,* **8** (1991): 347–377. For an examination of sexual abuse of girls and how it leads to later delinquency, as well as a discussion of how the double standard influences female criminality, see Meda Chesney-Lind, *The Female Offender: Girls, Women, and Crime* (Thousand Oaks, Calif.: Sage, 1997). For a discussion about the role family controls have on female delinquency, see Karen Keimer and Stacy De Coster, "The Gendering of Violent Delinquency," *Criminology,* **37** (1999): 277–318. For an application of strain theory to female crime, see Lisa Broidy and Robert Agnew, "Gender and Crime: A General Strain Theory Perspective," *Journal of Research in Crime and Delinquency,* **34** (1997): 275–306. For a discussion of the implications of the feminization of poverty and welfare on property crime and assault, see Anne Campbell, Steven Muncer, and Daniel Bibel, "Female–Female Criminal Assault: An Evolutionary Perspective," *Journal of Research in Crime and Delinquency,* **35** (1998): 413–428; and Lance Hannon and James DeFronzo, "Welfare and Property Crime," *Justice Quarterly,* **15** (1998): 273–288.
61. Cesare Lombroso and William Ferrero, *The Female Offender* (London: T. Fisher Unwin, 1895).
62. Sheldon Glueck and Eleanor T. Glueck, *Five Hundred Delinquent Women* (New York: Knopf, 1934).
63. Otto Pollack, *The Criminality of Women* (Philadelphia: University of Pennsylvania Press, 1950).
64. Freda Adler, *Sisters in Crime* (New York: McGraw-Hill, 1975), pp. 6–7.
65. Rita Simon, *The Contemporary Woman and Crime* (Rockville, Md.: National Institute of Mental Health, 1975).
66. Meda Chesney-Lind, "Female Offenders: Paternalism Reexamined," in *Women, the Courts, and Equality,* eds. Laura Crites and Winifred Hepperle (Newbury Park, Calif.: Sage, 1987).
67. Darrell J. Steffensmeier, "Crime and the Contemporary Woman: An Analysis of Changing Levels of Female Property Crimes, 1960–1975," *Social Forces,* **57** (1978): 566–584; Lee H. Bowker, *Women, Crime, and the Criminal Justice System* (Lexington, Mass.: Heath, 1978). For a description of the typical female offender, see Nancy T. Wolfe, Francis T. Cullen, and John B. Cullen, "Describing the Female Offender: A Note on the Demographics of Arrests," *Journal of Criminal Justice,* **12** (1984): 483–492.
68. Mary E. Gilfus, "From Victims to Survivors to Offenders: Women's Routes of Entry and Immersion into Street Crime," *Women and Criminal Justice,* **4** (1992): 63–89; and Sally S. Simpson and Lori Ellis, "Doing Gender: Sorting Out the Caste and Crime Conundrum," *Criminology,* **33** (1995): 47–81. For a discussion of the internalization of gender roles by female prisoners, see Edna Erez, "The Myth of the New Female Offender: Some Evidence from Attitudes toward Law and Justice," *Journal of Criminal Justice,* **16** (1988): 499–509.
69. Nanci Koser Wilson, "The Masculinity of Violent Crime—Some Second Thoughts," *Journal of Criminal Justice,* **9** (1981): 111–123; Ronald L. Simons, Martin G. Miller, and Stephen M. Aigner, "Contemporary Theories of Deviance and Female Delinquency: An Empirical Test," *Journal of Research in Crime and Delinquency,* **17** (1980): 42–57.
70. For a discussion of a unisex theory of crime, see Coramae Richey Mann, *Female Crime and Delinquency* (Tuscaloosa: University of Alabama Press, 1984). For an analysis of the relation of both gender and race to crime, see Vernetta D. Young, "Women, Race, and Crime," *Criminology,* **18** (1980): 26–34; Gary D. Hill and Elizabeth M. Crawford, "Women, Race, and Crime," *Criminology,* **28** (1990): 601–626; and Sally S. Simpson, "Caste, Class, and Violent Crime: Explaining Differences in Female Offending," *Criminology,* **29** (1991): 115–136. For a discussion of female crime in countries around the world, see

Freda Adler, ed., *The Incidence of Female Criminality in the Contemporary World* (New York: New York University Press, 1984). See also Freda Adler and Rita James Simon, eds., *The Criminology of Deviant Women* (Boston: Houghton Mifflin, 1979). For other sources on the subject of female crime, see Victoria E. Brewster and M. Dwayne Smith, "Gender Inequality and Rates of Female Homicide Victimization across U.S. Cities," *Journal of Research in Crime and Delinquency,* **32** (1995): 175–190; R. Barri Flowers, *Female Crime, Criminals and Cellmates: An Exploration of Female Criminality and Delinquency* (Jefferson, N.C.: McFarland & Company, 1995); R. Emerson Dobash, Russell P. Dobash, and Lesley Noaks, eds., *Gender and Crime* (Cardiff: University of Wales Press, 1995); and Ruth Triplett and Laura B. Myers, "Evaluating Contextual Patterns of Delinquency: Gender-Based Differences," *Justice Quarterly,* **12** (1995): 59–84. For an examination of women who commit murder, see Coramae Richey Mann, *When Women Kill* (Albany, N.Y.: SUNY Press, 1996).
71. Charles Tittle, Wayne Villemez, and Douglas Smith, "The Myth of Social Class and Criminality: An Empirical Assessment of the Empirical Evidence," *American Sociological Review,* **43** (1978): 643–656; Charles R. Tittle and Robert F. Meier, "Specifying the SES/Delinquency Relationship," *Criminology,* **28** (1990): 271–299. For a discussion of the relationship between crime and aspects of social class that influence juveniles' personality and behavior, see G. Roger Jarjoura and Ruth A. Triplett, "Delinquency and Class: A Test of the Proximity Principle," *Justice Quarterly,* **14** (1997): 763–792. For an elaboration on the relationship between socioeconomic status (SES) and delinquency, see Bradley R. Entner Wright, Avshalom Caspi, Terrie E. Moffitt, Richard A. Miech, and Phil A. Silva, "Reconsidering the Relationship between SES and Delinquency: Causation but Not Correlation," *Criminology,* **37** (1999): 175–194.
72. Elliott and Ageton, "Reconciling Race and Class Differences."
73. Delbert Elliott and David Huizinga, "Social Class and Delinquent Behavior in a National Youth Panel: 1976–1980," *Criminology,* **21** (1983): 149–177.
74. The data on socioeconomic factors come from U.S. Department of Justice, *Report to the Nation on Crime and Justice,* pp. 48–49.
75. U.S. Department of Justice, Bureau of Justice Statistics, *Annual Report, Fiscal 1986* (Washington, D.C.: U.S. Government Printing Office, April 1987), p. 39.
76. Uniform Crime Reports, 1997, p. 240. See also Gary LaFree, Kriss A. Drass, and Patrick O'Day, "Race and Crime in Postwar America: Determinants of African-American and White Rates, 1957–1988," *Criminology,* **30** (1992): 157–188.
77. Joan Petersilia, "Racial Disparities in the Criminal Justice System: A Summary," *Crime and Delinquency,* **31** (1985): 15–34.
78. *Criminal Victimization in the United States,* 1993, p. 44.
79. Delbert Elliott and Harwin Voss, *Delinquency and Dropout* (Lexington, Mass.: Lexington Books, 1974).

CHAPTER 3

1. Quote: attributed to Socrates by Plato, wording unconfirmed by researchers; see *Respectfully Quoted,* ed. Suzy Platt (Washington, D.C.: Library of Congress, 1989), p. 42.
2. Leon Radzinowicz, *Ideology and Crime* (New York: Columbia University Press, 1966), p. 2; Marc Ancel, *Introduction to the French Penal Code,* ed. G. O. W. Mueller (South Hackensack, N.J.: Fred B. Rothman, 1960), pp. 1–2.
3. Thorsten Sellin, *Slavery and the Penal System* (New York: Elsevier, 1976); Thorsten Eriksson, *The Reformers: An Historical Survey of Pioneer Experiments in the Treatment of Criminals* (New York: Elsevier, 1976).
4. Marcello T. Maestro, *Cesare Beccaria and the Origins of Penal Reform* (Philadelphia: Temple University Press, 1973), p. 16.
5. George Rude, *The Crowd in the French Revolution* (New York: Oxford University Press, 1959), appendix.
6. Harry Elmer Barnes, *The Story of Punishment: A Record of Man's Inhumanity to Man,* 2d ed. (Montclair, N.J.: Patterson Smith, 1972), p. 99.
7. Cesare Beccaria, *On Crimes and Punishment,* 2d ed., trans. Edward D. Ingraham (Philadelphia: Philip H. Nicklin, 1819), pp. 15, 20, 22–23, 30–32, 60, 74–75, 80, 97–98, 149, 156. For a debate on the contribution of Beccaria to modern criminology, see G. O. W. Mueller, "Whose Prophet Is Cesare Beccaria? An Essay on the Origins of Criminological Theory," *Advances in Criminological Theory,* **2** (1990): 1–14; Graeme Newman and Pietro Marongiu, "Penological Reform and the Myth of Beccaria," *Criminology,* **28** (1990): 325–346; and Piers Beirne, "Inventing Criminology: The 'Science of Man,' in Cesare Beccaria's *Dei delitti e delle pene,*" *Criminology,* **29** (1991): 777–820.

8. Marcello T. Maestro, *Voltaire and Beccaria as Reformers of Criminal Law* (New York: Columbia University Press, 1942), p. 73.
9. Jeremy Bentham, *A Fragment on Government and an Introduction to the Principles of Morals and Legislation,* ed. Wilfred Harrison (Oxford: Basil Blackwell, 1967), p. 21.
10. Barnes, *The Story of Punishment,* p. 102.
11. Quoted in Leon Radzinowicz, *A History of English Criminal Law and Its Administration from 1750,* vol. 1 (New York: Macmillan, 1948), p. 330.
12. Charles Darwin, *Origin of Species* (1854; Cambridge, Mass.: Harvard University Press, 1859); Charles Darwin, *The Descent of Man and Selection in Relation to Sex* (1871; New York: A. L. Burt, 1874).
13. Havelock Ellis, *The Criminal,* 2d ed. (New York: Scribner, 1900), p. 27.
14. Christopher Hibbert, *The Roots of Evil* (Boston: Little, Brown, 1963), p. 187.
15. Arthur E. Fink, *The Causes of Crime: Biological Theories in the United States, 1800–1915* (Philadelphia: University of Pennsylvania Press, 1938), p. 1.
16. Hermann Mannheim, *Comparative Criminology* (Boston: Houghton Mifflin, 1965), p. 213.
17. George B. Vold, *Theoretical Criminology* (New York: Oxford University Press, 1958), pp. 44–49.
18. Gina Lombroso Ferrero, *Criminal Man: According to the Classification of Cesare Lombroso,* with an Introduction by Cesare Lombroso (1911; Montclair, N.J.: Patterson Smith, 1972), pp. xxiv–xxv.
19. Cesare Lombroso and William Ferrero, *The Female Offender* (New York: Appleton, 1895), pp. 151–152.
20. Cesare Lombroso, *Crime, Its Causes and Remedies* (Boston: Little, Brown, 1918).
21. Marvin Wolfgang, "Cesare Lombroso," in *Pioneers in Criminology,* ed. Hermann Mannheim (London: Stevens, 1960), p. 168.
22. Thorsten Sellin, "The Lombrosian Myth in Criminology," *American Journal of Sociology,* **42** (1937): 898–899. For Lombroso's impact on American anthropological criminology, see Nicole Hahn Rafter, "Criminal Anthropology in the United States," *Criminology,* **30** (1992): 525–545.
23. Wolfgang, "Cesare Lombroso."
24. Thorsten Sellin, "Enrico Ferri: Pioneer in Criminology, 1856–1929," in *The Positive School of Criminology: Three Lectures by Enrico Ferri,* ed. Stanley E. Grupp (Pittsburgh: University of Pittsburgh Press, 1968), p. 13.
25. Raffaele Garofalo, *Criminology,* trans. Robert Wyness Millar (Montclair, N.J.: Patterson Smith, 1968), pp. 4–5.
26. Marc Ancel, *Social Defense: The Future of Penal Reform* (Littleton, Colo.: Fred B. Rothman, 1987).
27. Charles B. Goring, *The English Convict: A Statistical Study* (London: His Majesty's Stationery Office, 1913), p. 145. For a critique of Goring's work, see Piers Beirne, "Heredity versus Environment," *British Journal of Criminology,* **28** (1988): 315–339.
28. E. A. Hooten, *The American Criminal* (Cambridge, Mass.: Harvard University Press, 1939), p. 308.
29. E. A. Hooten, *Crime and the Man* (Cambridge, Mass.: Harvard University Press, 1939), p. 13.
30. Ernst Kretschmer, *Physique and Character* (New York: Harcourt Brace, 1926).
31. William H. Sheldon, *Varieties of Delinquent Youth: An Introduction to Constitutional Psychiatry* (New York: Harper, 1949). See also Emil M. Hartl, Edward P. Monnelly, and Ronald D. Elderkin, *Physique and Delinquent Behavior: A Thirty-Year Follow-Up of William H. Sheldon's Varieties of Delinquent Youth* (New York: Academic Press, 1982).
32. Eleanor Glueck and Sheldon Glueck, *Unraveling Juvenile Delinquency* (Cambridge, Mass.: Harvard University Press, 1950). See also Sheldon Glueck and Eleanor Glueck, *Of Delinquency and Crime* (Springfield, Ill.: Charles C. Thomas, 1974), p. 2. For a recent reanalysis of the Gluecks' data, see John H. Laub and Robert J. Sampson, "Unravelling Families and Delinquency: A Reanalysis of the Gluecks' Data," *Criminology,* **26** (1988): 355–380. For the life and work of Eleanor Touroff Glueck, see John H. Laub and Jinney S. Smith, "Eleanor Touroff Glueck: An Unsung Pioneer in Criminology," *Women in Criminal Justice,* **6** (1995): 1–22.
33. S. L. Washburn, book review, "Varieties of Delinquent Youth, An Introduction to Constitutional Psychiatry," *American Anthropologist,* **53** (1951): 561–563.
34. Richard L. Dugdale, *The Jukes: A Study in Crime, Pauperism, Disease, and Heredity,* 5th ed. (New York: Putnam, 1895), p. 8.
35. Henry H. Goddard, *The Kallikak Family: A Study in the Heredity of Feeble-Mindedness* (New York: Macmillan, 1912), p. 50.
36. *Buck v. Bell,* 274 U.S. 200, 207 (1927).
37. Isaac Ray, *The Medical Jurisprudence of Insanity* (Boston: Little, Brown, 1838).
38. Philippe Pinel, *A Treatise on Insanity* (1806; New York: Hafner, 1962).
39. Peter Scott, "Henry Maudsley," *Journal of Criminal Law, Criminology, and Police Science,* **46** (March–April 1956): 753–769.
40. Henry H. Goddard, *The Criminal Imbecile* (New York: Macmillan, 1915), pp. 106–107.
41. Adolphe Quételet, *A Treatise on Man,* facs. ed. of 1842 ed., trans. Salomon Diamond (1835;

Gainesville, Fla.: Scholars Facsimiles and Reprints, 1969), p. 97.
42. Quételet, *A Treatise on Man,* p. 103. For Quételet's influence on modern scholars, see Derral Cheatwood, "Is There a Season for Homicide?" *Criminology,* **26** (1988): 287–306.
43. Gabriel Tarde, *Penal Philosophy,* trans. R. Howell (Boston: Little, Brown, 1912), p. 252.
44. Gabriel Tarde, *Social Laws: An Outline of Sociology* (New York: Macmillan, 1907).
45. Émile Durkheim, *The Rules of Sociological Method,* ed. George E. G. Catlin (Chicago: University of Chicago Press, 1938), p. 71.

CHAPTER 4

1. FBI Press Release, October 25, 2002 (found at http://www.fbi.gov/pressrel/pressrel02/directorl02502.htm).
2. http://www.cnn.com/2002/US/10/28/sproject.sniper.muhammad.profile/index.html.
3. See Ronald Blackburn, *The Psychology of Criminal Conduct: Theory, Research, and Practice* (Chichester, England: Wiley, 1993); and Hans Toch, *Violent Men: An Inquiry into the Psychology of Violence,* rev. ed. (Washington, D.C.: American Psychological Association, 1992).
4. See, e.g., Cathy Spatz Widom, "Cycle of Violence," *Science,* **244** (1989): 160–165; and Nathaniel J. Pallone and J. J. Hennessey, *Criminal Behavior: A Process Psychology Analysis* (New Brunswick, N.J.: Transaction, 1992).
5. See, e.g., Sigmund Freud, *A General Introduction to Psychoanalysis* (New York: Liveright, 1920); and Sigmund Freud, *The Ego and the Id* (London: Hogarth, 1927).
6. August Aichhorn, *Wayward Youth* (New York: Viking, 1935).
7. Kate Friedlander, *The Psycho-Analytic Approach to Juvenile Delinquency* (New York: International Universities Press, 1947).
8. See Hans Eysenck, *The Rise and Fall of the Freudian Empire* (New York: Plenum, 1987).
9. Lawrence Kohlberg, "The Development of Modes of Moral Thinking and Choice in the Years Ten to Sixteen," Ph.D. dissertation, University of Chicago, 1958.
10. Lawrence Kohlberg, "Stage and Sequence: The Cognitive-Developmental Approach to Socialization," in *Handbook of Socialization Theory and Research,* ed. David A. Goslin (Chicago: Rand McNally, 1969).
11. Carol Gilligan has studied moral development in women—extending Kohlberg's role-taking theory of moral development. She found that moral reasoning differed in women. Women, according to Gilligan, see morality as the responsibility to take the view of others and to ensure their well-being. See Carol Gilligan, *In a Different Voice: Psychological Theory and Women's Development* (Cambridge, Mass.: Harvard University Press, 1982).
12. William S. Jennings, Robert Kilkenny, and Lawrence Kohlberg, "Moral Development Theory and Practice for Youthful Offenders," in *Personality Theory, Moral Development, and Criminal Behavior,* eds. William S. Laufer and James M. Day (Lexington, Mass.: Lexington Books, 1983). See also Daniel D. Macphail, "The Moral Education Approach in Treating Adult Inmates," *Criminal Justice and Behavior,* **15** (1989): 81–97; Jack Arbuthnot and Donald A. Gordon, "Crime and Cognition: Community Applications of Sociomoral Reasoning Development," *Criminal Justice and Behavior,* **15** (1988): 379–393; and J. E. LeCapitaine, "The Relationships between Emotional Development and Moral Development and the Differential Impact of Three Psychological Interventions on Children," *Psychology in the Schools,* **15** (1987): 379–393.
13. John Bowlby, *Attachment and Loss,* 2 vols. (New York: Basic Books, 1969, 1973). See also Bowlby's "Forty-Four Juvenile Thieves: Their Characteristics and Home Life," *International Journal of Psychoanalysis,* **25** (1944): 19–52.
14. John Bowlby, *The Making and Breaking of Affectional Bonds* (London: Tavistock, 1979). See also Michael Rutter, *Maternal Deprivation Reassessed* (Harmondsworth, Engl.: Penguin, 1971).
15. Michael Lewis, Candice Feiring, Carolyn McGuffog, and John Jaskir, "Predicting Psychopathology in Six-Year-Olds from Early Social Relations," *Child Development,* **55** (1984): 123–136.
16. L. Sroufe, "Infant Caregiver Attachment and Patterns of Adaptation in Preschool: The Roots of Maladaption and Competence," in *Minnesota Symposium on Child Psychology,* vol. 16, ed. Marion Perlmutter (Hillsdale, N.J.: Erlbaum, 1982).
17. Alicia F. Lieberman, "Preschoolers' Competence with a Peer: Influence of Attachment and Social Experience," *Child Development,* **48** (1977): 1277–1287.
18. Joan McCord, "Some Child-Rearing Antecedents of Criminal Behavior," *Journal of Personality and Social Psychology,* **37** (1979): 1477–1486; Joan McCord, "A Longitudinal View of the Relationship between Paternal Absence and Crime," in *Abnormal Offenders, Delinquency, and the Criminal Justice System,* eds. John Gunn and David P. Farrington (London: Wiley, 1982). See also Scott W. Henggeler, Cindy L. Hanson, Charles M. Borduin,

Sylvia M. Watson, and Molly A. Brunk, "Mother-Son Relationships of Juvenile Felons," *Journal of Consulting and Clinical Psychology,* **53** (1985): 942–943; and Francis I. Nye, *Family Relationships and Delinquent Behavior* (New York: Wiley, 1958).

19. Sheldon Glueck and Eleanor T. Glueck, *Unraveling Juvenile Delinquency* (New York: Commonwealth Fund, 1950); Lee N. Robins, "Aetiological Implications in Studies of Childhood Histories Relating to Antisocial Personality," in *Psychopathic Behaviour,* eds. Robert D. Hare and Daisy Schalling (Chichester, Engl.: Wiley, 1970); Lee N. Robins, *Deviant Children Grow Up* (Baltimore: Williams & Wilkins, 1966).
20. Joan McCord, "Instigation and Insulation: How Families Affect Antisocial Aggression," in *Development of Antisocial and Prosocial Behavior: Research Theories and Issues,* eds. Dan Olweus, Jack Block, and M. Radke-Yarrow (London: Academic Press, 1986).
21. Albert Bandura, *Aggression: A Social Learning Analysis* (Englewood Cliffs, N.J.: Prentice-Hall, 1973); Albert Bandura, "The Social Learning Perspective: Mechanism of Aggression," in *Psychology of Crime and Criminal Justice,* ed. Hans Toch (New York: Holt, Rinehart & Winston, 1979).
22. Leonard D. Eron and L. Rowell Huesmann, "Parent-Child Interaction, Television Violence, and Aggression of Children," *American Psychologist,* **37** (1982): 197–211; Russell G. Geen, "Aggression and Television Violence," in *Aggression: Theoretical and Empirical Reviews,* vol. 2, eds. Russell G. Geen and Edward I. Donnerstein (New York: Academic Press, 1983).
23. Leonard D. Eron and L. Rowell Huesmann, "The Control of Aggressive Behavior by Changes in Attitudes, Values, and the Conditions of Learning," in *Advances in the Study of Aggression,* vol. 1, eds. Robert J. Blanchard and D. Caroline Blanchard (Orlando, Fla.: Academic Press, 1984).
24. *National Television Violence Study: Executive Summary* 1994–1995 (Studio City, Calif.: Mediascope, 1996); O. Wiegman, M. Kuttschreuter, and B. Baarda, "A Longitudinal Study of the Effects of Television Viewing on Aggressive and Prosocial Behaviors," *British Journal of Social Psychology,* **31** (1992): 147–164; B. S. Centerwall, "Television and Violence: The Scale of the Problem and Where to Go from Here," *Journal of the American Medical Association,* **267** (1992): 3059–3063; J. E. Ledingham, C. A. Ledingham, and John E. Richardson, *The Effects of Media Violence on Children* (Ottawa, Canada: National Clearinghouse on Family Violence, Health and Welfare, 1993); M. I. Tulloch, M. L. Prendergast, and M. D. Anglin, "Evaluating Aggression: School Students' Responses to Television Portrayals of Institutionalized Violence," *Journal of Youth and Adolescence,* **24** (1995): 95–115.
25. See Gerald R. Patterson, R. A. Littman, and W. Brickler, *Assertive Behavior in Children: A Step toward a Theory of Aggression,* monograph of the Society for Research in Child Development, no. 32 (1976).
26. Bandura, *Aggression.*
27. C. Ray Jeffery, "Criminal Behavior and Learning Theory," *Journal of Criminal Law, Criminology and Police Science,* **56** (1965): 294–300.
28. Ernest L. Burgess and Ronald L. Akers, "A Differential Association-Reinforcement Theory of Criminal Behavior," *Social Problems,* **14** (1966): 128–147. See also Reed Adams, "Differential Association and Learning Principles Revisited," *Social Problems,* **20** (1973): 458–470.
29. See D. W. Andrews and J. Stephen Wormith, "Personality and Crime: Knowledge Destruction and Construction in Criminology," *Justice Quarterly,* **6** (1989): 149–160.
30. William S. Laufer, Dagna K. Skoog, and James M. Day, "Personality and Criminality: A Review of the California Psychological Inventory," *Journal of Clinical Psychology,* **38** (1982): 562–573.
31. Richard E. Tremblay, "The Prediction of Delinquent Behavior from Childhood Behavior: Personality Theory Revisited," in *Facts, Frameworks, and Forecasts: Advances in Criminological Theory,* vol. 3, ed. J. McCord (New Brunswick, N.J.: Transaction, 1992).
32. Michael L. Gearing, "The MMPI as a Primary Differentiator and Predictor of Behavior in Prison: A Methodological Critique and Review of the Recent Literature," *Psychological Bulletin,* **36** (1979): 929–963.
33. Edwin I. Megargee and Martin J. Bohn, *Classifying Criminal Offenders* (Beverly Hills, Calif.: Sage, 1979); William S. Laufer, John A. Johnson, and Robert Hogan, "Ego Control and Criminal Behavior," *Journal of Personality and Social Psychology,* **41** (1981): 179–184; Edwin I. Megargee, "Psychological Determinants and Correlates of Criminal Violence," in *Criminal Violence,* eds. Marvin E. Wolfgang and Neil A. Weiner (Beverly Hills, Calif.: Sage, 1982); Edwin I. Megargee, "The Role of Inhibition in the Assessment and Understanding of Violence," in *Current Topics in Clinical and Community Psychology,* ed. Charles Donald Spielberger (New York: Academic Press, 1971); Edwin I. Megargee, "Undercontrol and Overcontrol

in Assaultive and Homicidal Adolescents," Ph.D. dissertation, University of California, Berkeley, 1964; Edwin I. Megargee, "Undercontrolled and Overcontrolled Personality Types in Extreme Antisocial Aggression," *Psychological Monographs,* **80** (1966); and Edwin I. Megargee and Gerald A. Mendelsohn, "A Cross-Validation of Twelve MMPI Indices of Hostility and Control," *Journal of Abnormal and Social Psychology,* **65** (1962): 431–438.
34. See, e.g., William S. Laufer and James M. Day, eds., *Personality Theory, Moral Development, and Criminal Behavior* (Lexington, Mass.: Lexington Books, 1983).
35. Milton Metfessel and Constance Lovell, "Recent Literature on Individual Correlates of Crime," *Psychological Bulletin,* **39** (1942): 133–164.
36. Karl E. Schuessler and Donald R. Cressey, "Personality Characteristics of Criminals," *American Journal of Sociology,* **55** (1950): 476–484.
37. Daniel J. Tennenbaum, "Personality and Criminality: A Summary and Implications of the Literature," *Journal of Criminal Justice,* **5** (1977): 225–235. See also G. P. Waldo and Simon Dinitz, "Personality Attributes of the Criminal: An Analysis of Research Studies, 1950–1965," *Journal of Research in Crime and Delinquency,* **4** (1967): 185–202; and R. D. Martin and D. G. Fischer, "Personality Factors in Juvenile Delinquency: A Review of the Literature," *Catalog of Selected Documents in Psychology,* vol. 8 (1978), ms. 1759.
38. Samuel Yochelson and Stanton Samenow, *The Criminal Personality* (New York: Jason Aronson, 1976).
39. Laufer et al., "Personality and Criminality"; Harrison G. Gough and Pamela Bradley, "Delinquent and Criminal Behavior as Assessed by the Revised California Psychological Inventory," *Journal of Clinical Psychology,* **48** (1991): 298–308.
40. See Anne Campbell and John J. Gibbs, eds., *Violent Transactions: The Limits of Personality* (Oxford: Basil Blackwell, 1986); Lawrence A. Pervin, "Personality: Current Controversies, Issues, and Direction," *Annual Review of Psychology,* **36** (1985): 83–114; and Lawrence A. Pervin, "Persons, Situations, Interactions: Perspectives on a Recurrent Issue," in Campbell and Gibbs, *Violent Transactions.*
41. See Hans J. Eysenck, *Crime and Personality* (London: Routledge & Kegan Paul, 1977); H. J. Eysenck, "Personality and Crime: Where Do We Stand?" *Psychology, Crime and Law,* **2** (1996): 143–152; Hans J. Eysenck, "Personality, Conditioning, and Antisocial Behavior," in Laufer and Day, *Personality Theory;* Hans J. Eysenck, "Personality and Criminality: A Dispositional Analysis," in *Advances in Criminological Theory,* vol. 1, eds. William S. Laufer and Freda Adler (New Brunswick, N.J.: Transaction, 1989); and Hans J. Eysenck and Gisli H. Gudjonsson, *The Causes and Cures of Crime* (New York: Plenum, 1990).
42. Seymour L. Halleck, *Psychiatry and the Dilemmas of Crime* (New York: Harper & Row, 1967); Nicholas N. Kittrie, *The Right to Be Different: Deviance and Enforced Therapy* (Baltimore, Md.: Johns Hopkins Press, 1971).
43. Karl Menninger, *The Crime of Punishment* (New York: Viking, 1968).
44. See Daniel L. Davis et al., "Prevalence of Emotional Disorders in a Juvenile Justice Institutional Population," *American Journal of Forensic Psychology,* **9** (1991): 5–17.
45. Hervey Cleckley, *The Mask of Sanity,* 5th ed. (St. Louis: Mosby, 1976), pp. 271–272.
46. Ibid., p. 57; Robert D. Hare, *Psychopathy: Theory and Research* (New York: Wiley, 1970); M. Philip Feldman, *Criminal Behavior: A Psychological Analysis* (New York: Wiley, 1978); William McCord and Joan McCord, *Psychopathy and Delinquency* (New York: Wiley, 1956).
47. *The American Psychiatric Association's Diagnostic and Statistical Manual of Mental Disorders,* 3d rev. ed. (DSM III-R) (Washington, D.C., 1987), classifies psychopathy as "antisocial personality." See Benjamin Karpman, "On the Need of Separating Psychopathy into Two Distinct Clinical Types: The Symptomatic and the Idiopathic," *Journal of Criminal Psychopathology,* **3** (1941): 112–137.
48. Eysenck and Gudjonsson, *The Causes and Cures of Crime.* See also Robert D. Hare, "Research Scale for the Assessment of Psychopathology in Criminal Populations," *Personality and Individual Differences,* **1** (1980): 111–119.
49. Anastasia Toufexis, "Dancing with Devils: Forensic Psychiatrist Park Dietz Tracks America's Serial Killers, Bombers and Mass Murderers," *Psychology Today,* **32**(3) (May 1999): 54.
50. See, generally, A. J. Reiss, Jr., K. A. Klaus, and J. A. Roth, eds., *Biobehavioral Influences:* vol. 2, *Understanding and Preventing Violence* (Washington, D.C.: National Academy Press, 1994); M. Hillbrand and N. J. Pallone, "The Psychobiology of Aggression: Engines, Measurement, Control," *Journal of Offender Rehabilitation,* **21** (1994): 1–243; J. T. Tedeschi and R. B. Felson, *Violence, Aggression, and Coercive Actions* (Washington, D.C.: American Psychological Association, 1994).

51. J. Puig-Antich, "Biological Factors in Prepubertal Major Depression," *Pediatric Annals,* **12** (1986): 867–878.
52. See, e.g., Guenther Knoblich and Roy King, "Biological Correlates of Criminal Behavior," in McCord, *Facts, Frameworks, and Forecasts;* Diana H. Fishbein, "Biological Perspectives in Criminology," *Criminology,* **28** (1990): 17–40; David Magnusson, Britt af Klinteberg, and Hakan Stattin, "Autonomic Activity/Reactivity, Behavior, and Crime in a Longitudinal Perspective," in McCord, *Facts, Frameworks, and Forecasts;* Frank A. Elliott, "Violence: The Neurologic Contribution: An Overview," *Archives of Neurology,* **49** (1992): 595–603; L. French, "Neuropsychology of Violence," *Corrective and Social Psychiatry and Journal of Behavior Technology Methods and Therapy,* **37** (1991): 12–17; and Elizabeth Kandel and Sarnoff A. Mednick, "Perinatal Complications Predict Violent Offending," *Criminology,* **29** (1991): 519–530.
53. Edward O. Wilson, *Sociobiology: The New Synthesis* (Cambridge, Mass.: Harvard University Press, 1975).
54. C. Ray Jeffery, *Biology and Crime* (Beverly Hills, Calif.: Sage, 1979).
55. P. A. Brennan and S. A. Mednick, "Genetic Perspectives on Crime," *Acta Psychiatria Scandinavia,* **370** (1993): 19–26.
56. See Sarnoff A. Mednick, Terrie E. Moffitt, and Susan A. Stack, *The Causes of Crime: New Biological Approaches* (New York: Cambridge University Press, 1987).
57. A. A. Sandberg, G. F. Koepf, and T. Ishihara, "An XYY Human Male," *Lancet* (August 1961): 488–489.
58. Herman A. Witkin, et al., "Criminality, Aggression, and Intelligence among XYY and XXY Men," in *Biosocial Bases of Criminal Behavior,* eds. Sarnoff A. Mednick and Karl O. Christiansen (New York: Wiley, 1977).
59. Johannes Lange, *Verbrechen als Schicksal* (Leipzig: Georg Thieme, 1929).
60. Cf. Gregory Carey, "Twin Imitation for Antisocial Behavior: Implications for Genetic Environment Research," *Journal of Abnormal Psychology,* **101** (1992): 18–25.
61. See Karl O. Christiansen, "A Preliminary Study of Criminality among Twins," in Mednick and Christiansen, *Biosocial Bases of Criminal Behavior.*
62. David C. Rowe and D. Wayne Osgood, "Heredity and Sociological Theories of Delinquency: A Reconsideration," *American Sociological Review,* **49** (1986): 526–540; David C. Rowe, "Genetic and Environmental Components of Antisocial Behavior: A Study of 256 Twin Pairs," *Criminology,* **24** (1986): 513–532.
63. Sarnoff A. Mednick, William Gabrielli, and Barry Hutchings, "Genetic Influences in Criminal Behavior: Evidence from an Adoption Court," in *Prospective Studies of Crime and Delinquency,* ed. K. Teilmann et al. (Boston: Kluwer-Nijhoff, 1983).
64. These and other studies are reviewed in Mednick et al., *The Causes of Crime.*
65. Hannah Bloch and Dick Thompson, "Seeking the Roots of Violence," *Time,* Apr. 19, 1993, pp. 52–53.
66. Daniel Goleman, "New Storm Brews on Whether Crime Has Roots in Genes," *New York Times,* Sept. 15, 1992, p. C1.
67. Hannah Bloch and Dick Thompson, "Seeking the Roots of Violence."
68. Fox Butterfield, "Study Cites Biology's Role in Violent Behavior," *New York Times,* Nov. 13, 1992, p. A7.
69. Goleman, "New Storm Brews on Whether Crime Has Roots in Genes."
70. Ibid.
71. Hugo Munsterberg, *On the Witness Stand* (New York: Doubleday, 1908); and Henry H. Goddard, *Feeble-Mindedness: Its Causes and Consequences* (New York: Macmillan, 1914).
72. Edwin H. Sutherland, "Mental Deficiency and Crime," in *Social Attitudes,* ed. K. Young (New York: Henry Holt, 1931).
73. Robert H. Gault, "Highlights of Forty Years in the Correctional Field—and Looking Ahead," *Federal Probation,* **17** (1953): 3–4.
74. Arthur Jensen, *Bias in Mental Testing* (New York: Free Press, 1979).
75. Ibid.; Richard J. Herrnstein, *IQ in the Meritocracy* (Boston: Atlantic–Little, Brown, 1973).
76. Travis Hirschi and Michael J. Hindelang, "Intelligence and Delinquency: A Revisionist Review," *American Sociological Review,* **42** (1977): 571–586.
77. Travis Hirschi, *Causes of Delinquency* (Berkeley: University of California Press, 1969).
78. Marvin E. Wolfgang, Robert F. Figlio, and Thorsten Sellin, *Delinquency in a Birth Cohort* (Chicago: University of Chicago Press, 1972).
79. Albert J. Reiss and Albert L. Rhodes, "The Distribution of Juvenile Delinquency in the Social Class Structure," *American Sociological Review,* **26** (1961): 720–732.
80. James Q. Wilson and Richard Herrnstein, *Crime and Human Nature* (New York: Simon & Schuster, 1985); Deborah W. Denno, "Sociological and Human Developmental Explanations of Crime: Conflict or Consensus?" *Criminology,* **23** (1985):

NOTES

711–740. See also Deborah W. Denno, "Victim, Offender, and Situational Characteristics of Violent Crime," *Journal of Criminal Law and Criminology,* **77** (1986): 1142–1158.
81. "Taking the Chitling Test," *Newsweek,* July 15, 1968.
82. Sandra Scarr and Richard Weinberg, "I.Q. Test Performance of Black Children Adopted by White Families," *American Psychologist,* **31** (1976): 726–739.
83. See Doris J. Rapp, *Allergies and the Hyperactive Child* (New York: Simon & Schuster, 1981).
84. Diana H. Fishbein and Susan Pease, "The Effects of Diet on Behavior: Implications for Criminology and Corrections," *Research on Corrections,* **1** (1988): 1–45.
85. Stephen Schoenthaler, "Diet and Crime: An Empirical Examination of the Value of Nutrition in the Control and Treatment of Incarcerated Juvenile Offenders," *International Journal of Biosocial Research,* **4** (1982): 25–39.
86. Heather M. Little, "Food May Be Causing Kids' Problems," *Chicago Tribune,* Oct. 29, 1995, p. 1; Abram Hoffer, "The Relation of Crime to Nutrition," *Humanist in Canada,* **8** (1975): 2–9.
87. Benjamin F. Feingold, *Why Is Your Child Hyperactive?* (New York: Random House, 1975).
88. James W. Swanson and Marcel Kinsbourne, "Food Dyes Impair Performance of Hyperactive Children on a Laboratory Test," *Science,* **207** (1980): 1485–1487.
89. Anthony R. Mawson and K. W. Jacobs, "Corn Consumption, Tryptophan, and Cross-National Homicide Rates," *Journal of Orthomolecular Psychiatry,* **7** (1978): 227–230.
90. "Toddler Dies after Being Thrown in Lake by Dad in Diabetic Seizure," *Chicago Tribune,* July 10, 1995, p. 9.
91. Matti Virkkunen, "Insulin Secretion during the Glucose Tolerance Test among Habitually Violent and Impulsive Offenders," *Aggressive Behavior,* **12** (1986): 303–310.
92. E. A. Beeman, "The Effect of Male Hormones on Aggressive Behavior in Mice," *Physiological Zoology,* **20** (1947): 373–405.
93. D. A. Hamburg and D. T. Lunde, "Sex Hormones in the Development of Sex Differences," in *The Development of Sex Differences,* ed. Eleanor E. Maccoby (Stanford, Calif.: Stanford University Press, 1966).
94. A. Booth and D. W. Osgood, "The Influence of Testosterone on Deviance in Adulthood: Assessing and Explaining the Relationship," *Criminology,* **31** (1993): 93–117; L. E. Kreuz and R. M. Rose, "Assessment of Aggressive Behavior and Plasma Testosterone of a Young Criminal Population," *Psychosomatic Medicine,* **34** (1972): 321–332; R. T. Rada, D. R. Laws, and R. Kellner, "Plasma Testosterone Levels in the Rapist," *Psychosomatic Medicine,* **38** (1976): 257–268.
95. Katharina Dalton, *The Premenstrual Syndrome* (Springfield, Ill.: Charles C. Thomas, 1971).
96. Julie Horney, "Menstrual Cycles and Criminal Responsibility," *Law and Human Behavior,* **2** (1978): 25–36.
97. *Regina v. Charlson,* 1 A11. E.R. 859 (1955).
98. L. P. Chesterman et al., "Multiple Measures of Cerebral State in Dangerous Mentally Disordered Inpatients," *Criminal Behavior and Mental Health,* **4** (1994): 228–239; Lee Ellis, "Monoamine Oxidase and Criminality: Identifying an Apparent Biological Marker for Antisocial Behavior," *Journal of Research in Crime and Delinquency,* **28** (1991): 227–251.
99. H. Forssman and T. S. Frey, "Electroencephalograms of Boys with Behavior Disorders," *Acta Psychologica et Neurologia Scandinavica,* **28** (1953): 61–73; H. de Baudouin et al., "Study of a Population of 97 Confined Murderers," *Annales Medico-Psychologique,* **119** (1961): 625–686.
100. Sarnoff A. Mednick, Jan Volavka, William F. Gabrielli, and Turan M. Itil, "EEG as a Predictor of Antisocial Behavior," *Criminology,* **19** (1981): 219–229.
101. Jan Volavka, "Electroencephalogram among Criminals," in Mednick et al., *The Causes of Crime.* See also J. Volavka, *Neurobiology of Violence* (Washington, D.C.: American Psychiatric Press, 1995).
102. DSM III-R, 314.01. See also Michael Rutter, "Syndromes Attributed to 'Minimal Brain Dysfunction' in Children," *American Journal of Psychiatry,* **139** (1980): 21–33.
103. Lorne T. Yeudall, D. Fromm-Auch, and P. Davies, "Neuropsychological Impairment of Persistent Delinquency," *Journal of Nervous and Mental Disorders,* **170** (1982): 257–265; R. D. Robin et al., "Adolescents Who Attempt Suicide," *Journal of Pediatrics,* **90** (1977): 636–638.
104. Edward Sagarin, "Taboo Subjects and Taboo Viewpoints in Criminology," in *Taboos in Criminology,* ed. Sagarin (Beverly Hills, Calif.: Sage, 1980), pp. 8–9.
105. Diana H. Fishbein, "Biological Perspectives in Criminology," *Criminology,* **28** (1990): 27–40.
106. Wilson and Herrnstein, *Crime and Human Nature.* Infants develop attachment to mothers, or mother substitutes, for comfort, security, and warmth.

CHAPTER 5

1. Ysabel Rennie, *The Search for Criminal Man* (Lexington, Mass.: Lexington Books, 1978), p. 125.
2. James T. Carey, *Sociology and Public Affairs: The Chicago School* (Beverly Hills, Calif.: Sage, 1975), pp. 19–20.
3. See the discussion of sociological theory in Frank P. Williams III and Marilyn D. McShane, *Criminological Theory* (Englewood Cliffs, N.J.: Prentice-Hall, 1988).
4. Émile Durkheim, *The Division of Labor in Society* (New York: Free Press, 1964).
5. Émile Durkheim, *Rules of Sociological Method* (New York: Free Press, 1966).
6. Émile Durkheim, *Suicide* (Glencoe, Ill.: Free Press, 1951), pp. 241–276.
7. Ibid., p. 247.
8. Robert K. Merton, "Social Structure and Anomie," *American Sociological Review,* **3** (1938): 672–682. For a complete history of the social structure and anomie paradigm, see recent reflections of Merton in Robert K. Merton, "Opportunity Structure: The Emergence, Diffusion, and Differentiation of a Sociological Concept, 1930s–1950s," in *Advances in Criminological Theory: The Legacy of Anomie,* vol. 6, eds. Freda Adler and William S. Laufer (New Brunswick, N.J.: Transaction, 1994), pp. 3–78. Several measures of anomie have been developed. Probably the best-known indicator of anomie at the social level was formulated by Bernard Lander in a study of 8,464 cases of juvenile delinquency in Baltimore between 1939 and 1942. Lander devised a measure that included the rate of delinquency, the percentage of nonwhite population in a given area, and the percentage of owner-occupied homes. According to Lander, those factors were indicative of the amount of normlessness (anomie) in a community. See Bernard Lander, *Towards an Understanding of Juvenile Delinquency* (New York: Columbia University Press, 1954), p. 65.
9. Joseph Dalaker, "Poverty in the United States: 2000," United States Census Bureau.
10. Oscar Lewis, "The Culture of Poverty," *Scientific American,* **215** (1966): 19–25.
11. Gunnar Myrdal, *The Challenge of World Poverty* (New York: Vintage, 1990).
12. William Julius Wilson, *The Truly Disadvantaged* (Chicago: University of Chicago Press, 1987).
13. Robert K. Merton, *Social Theory and the Social Structure* (New York: Free Press, 1957), p. 187.
14. Albert J. Reiss Jr. and Albert L. Rhodes, "The Distribution of Juvenile Delinquency in the Social Class Structure," *American Sociological Review,* **26** (1961): 720–732. For the relationship between economic changes and crime, see Pamela Irving Jackson, "Crime, Youth Gangs, and Urban Transition: The Social Dislocations of Postindustrial Economic Development," *Justice Quarterly,* **8** (1991): 380–397.
15. F. Ivan Nye, James F. Short, and Virgil J. Olson, "Socioeconomic Status and Delinquent Behavior," *American Journal of Sociology,* **63** (1958): 381–389.
16. Charles R. Tittle, Wayne J. Villemez, and Douglas A. Smith, "The Myth of Social Class and Criminality: An Empirical Assessment of the Empirical Evidence," *American Sociological Review,* **43** (1978): 652; and Charles R. Tittle and Robert F. Meier, "Specifying the SES/Delinquency Relationship by Social Characteristics of Contexts," *Journal of Research in Crime and Delinquency,* **28** (1991): 430–455.
17. Gary F. Jensen and Kevin Thompson, "What's Class Got to Do with It? A Further Examination of Power-Control Theory," *American Journal of Sociology,* **95** (1990): 1009–1023.
18. John Braithwaite, "The Myth of Social Class and Criminality Reconsidered," *American Sociological Review,* **46** (1981): 41. See also Delbert S. Elliott and Suzanne S. Ageton, "Reconciling Race and Class Differences in Self-Reported and Official Estimates of Delinquency," *American Sociological Review,* **45** (1980): 95–110; Michael W. Neustrom and William M. Norton, "Economic Dislocation and Property Crime," *Journal of Criminal Justice,* **23** (1995): 29–39; and James De Frongo, "Welfare and Homicide," *Journal of Research in Crime and Delinquency,* **34** (1997): 395–406.
19. Nikos Passas, "Anomie, Reference Groups, and Relative Deprivation," in *The Future of Anomie Theory,* eds. Nikos Passas and Robert Ignew (Boston: Northeastern Press, 1997), pp. 64–65.
20. Terence P. Thornberry and Margaret Farnsworth, "Social Correlates of Criminal Involvement: Further Evidence on the Relationship between Social Status and Criminal Behavior," *American Sociological Review,* **47** (1982): 505–518; Thomas J. Bernard, "Control Criticisms of Strain Theories: An Assessment of Theoretical and Empirical Adequacy," *Journal of Research in Crime and Delinquency,* **21** (1984): 353–372; and Delbert S. Elliott and David Huizinga, "Social Class and Delinquent Behavior in a National Youth Panel," *Criminology,* **21** (1983): 149–177.
21. Bradley R. Entner Wright, Avshalom Caski, Terrie E. Moffitt, Richard A. Miech, and Phil A. Silva, "Reconsidering the Relationship between SES and

Delinquency Causation but Not Correlation," *Criminology,* **37** (1999): 175–194.
22. Tomislav V. Kovandzic, Lynne M. Vieraitis, and Mark R. Yeisley, "The Structural Covariates of Urban Homicide: Reassessing the Impact of Income Inequality and Poverty in the Post-Reagan Era," *Criminology,* **36** (1998): 569–600.
23. William R. Avison and Pamela L. Loring, "Population Diversity and Cross-National Homicide: The Effects of Inequality and Heterogeneity," *Criminology,* **24** (1986): 733–749; Harvey Krahn, Timothy F. Hartnagel, and John W. Gartrell, "Income Inequality and Homicide Rates: Cross-National Data and Criminological Theories," *Criminology,* **24** (1986): 269–295; and Richard Fowles and Mary Merva, "Wage Inequity and Criminal Activity: An Extreme Bounds Analysis for the United States, 1975–1990," *Criminology,* **34** (1996): 163–182.
24. Krahn et al., "Income Inequality," p. 288.
25. David Brownfield, "Social Class and Violent Behavior," *Criminology,* **24** (1986): 421–438.
26. David Matza, "The Disreputable Poor," in *Class, Status, and Power,* eds. Reinhard Bendix and Seymour M. Lipset (New York: Free Press, 1966). See also William S. Laufer, "Vocational Interests of Homeless, Unemployed Men," *Journal of Vocational Behavior,* **18** (1981): 196–201; and Chris Hale, "Unemployment and Crime: Differencing Is No Substitute for Modeling," *Journal of Research in Crime and Delinquency,* **28** (1991): 426–429.
27. John Hagan, "The Social Embeddedness of Crime and Unemployment," *Criminology,* **31** (1993): 465–492.
28. Judith R. Blau and Peter M. Blau, "The Cost of Inequality: Metropolitan Structure and Violent Crime," *American Sociological Review,* **47** (1982): 114–129. For a discussion of the relationship of job accessibility and racial inequality to crime rates within racial groups, see Karen F. Parker and Patricia L. McCall, "Structural Conditions and Racial Homicide Patterns: A Look at the Multiple Disadvantages in Urban Areas," *Criminology,* **37** (1999): 447–478. See also Steven F. Messner and Reid M. Golden, "Racial Inequality and Racially Disaggregated Homicide Rates: An Assessment of Alternative Theoretical Explanations," *Criminology,* **30** (1992): 421–446; and James A. Chambers, *Blacks and Crime: A Function of Class* (Westport, Conn.: Praeger, 1995).
29. John Braithwaite, *Inequality, Crime, and Public Policy* (London: Routledge & Kegan Paul, 1979), p. 219.
30. Thomas J. Bernard, "Merton versus Hirschi: Who Is Faithful to Durkheim's Heritage?" in *Advances in Criminological Theory,* vol. 4, pp. 81–91; Nikos Passas, "Continuities in the Anomie Tradition," in *Advances in Criminological Theory,* vol. 4, pp. 91–112; Scott Menard, "A Developmental Test of Mertonian Anomie Theory," *Journal of Research in Crime and Delinquency,* **32** (1995): 136–174.
31. Gary F. Jensen, "Salvaging Structure through Strain: A Theoretical and Empirical Critique," in *Advances in Criminological Theory,* vol. 4, pp. 139–158; Velmer S. Burton Jr., Francis T. Cullen, T. David Evans, and R. Gregory Dunaway, "Reconsidering Strain Theory: Operationalization, Rival Theories, and Adult Criminality," *Journal of Quantitative Criminology,* **10** (1994): 213–239.
32. Ian Taylor, Paul Walton, and Jock Young, *The New Criminology* (New York: Harper & Row, 1973), p. 107.
33. Freda Adler, *Nations Not Obsessed with Crime* (Littleton, Colo.: Fred B. Rothman, 1983).
34. Steven F. Messner and Richard Rosenfeld, *Crime and the American Dream* (Belmont, Calif.: Wadsworth, 1994).
35. Mitchell B. Chamlin and John K. Cochran, "Assessing Messner and Rosenfeld's Institutional Anomie Theory: A Partial Test," *Criminology,* **33** (1995): 411–429.
36. Freda Adler, "Synnomie to Anomie: A Macrosociological Formulation," in *Advances in Criminological Theory,* vol. 4, pp. 271–283.
37. Robert Agnew, "Foundations for a General Strain Theory of Crime and Delinquency," *Criminology,* **30** (1992): 47–87.
38. Robert Agnew, "The Contribution of Social-Psychological Strain Theory to the Explanation of Crime and Delinquency," in *Advances in Criminological Theory,* pp. 113–137. See also John P. Hoffman and Alan S. Miller, "A Latent Variable Analysis of General Strain Theory," *Journal of Quantitative Criminology,* **14** (1998): 83–110.
39. Raymond Paternoster and Paul Mazerolle, "General Strain Theory and Delinquency: A Replication and Extension," *Journal of Research in Crime and Delinquency,* **31** (1994): 235–263; see also Robert Agnew, Timothy Brezina, John Paul Wright, and Francis T. Cullen, "Strain, Personality Traits, and Delinquency: Extending General Strain Theory," *Criminology,* **40** (2002): 43–71; Paul Mazerolle and Jeff Maahs, "General Strain and Delinquency: An Alternative Examination of Conditioning Influences," *Justice Quarterly,* **17** (2000): 753–773; Timothy Brezina, "Adapting to Strain: An Examination of Delinquent Coping Responses," *Criminology,* **34** (1996): 39–60; and Robert Agnew and Helene Raskin White, "An Empirical Test of General Strain

Theory," *Criminology,* **30** (1992): 475–499. For an examination of gender and delinquent behavior from a general strain theory perspective, see Paul Mazerolle, "Gender, General Strain and Delinquency: An Emperical Examination," *Justice Quarterly,* **15** (1998): 65–91.
40. David Phinney, "Community News Focus: To Head Start Sanchez Serves as 'Model of Success,' " *Los Angeles Times,* Jan. 11, 1997, p. 83.
41. John R. Berrueta-Clement, Lawrence J. Schweinhart, W. Steven Barnett, Ann S. Epstein, and David P. Weekart, *Changed Lives: The Effects of the Perry Preschool Program on Youths through Age 19* (Ypsilanti, Mich.: High/Scope, 1984).
42. Jane Gross, "Remnants of the War on Poverty, Job Corps Is Still a Quiet Success," *New York Times,* Feb. 17, 1992, pp. 1, 14.
43. Tammy Joyner, "Atlanta Job Corps Exec Wins Award," *Atlanta Journal and Constitution,* June 8, 1999, p. 2F.
44. Lawrence W. Sherman, Denise Gottfredson, Doris McKenzie, John Eck, Peter Reuter, and Sharon Bushway, *Preventing Crime: What Works, What Doesn't, What's Promising,* U.S. Department of Justice, Office of Justice Programs, February 1997, chap. 6, p. 40.
45. W. I. Thomas and Florian Znaniecki, *The Polish Peasant in Europe and America* (Boston: Gorham, 1920).
46. Robert E. Park, "Human Ecology," *American Journal of Sociology,* **42** (1936): 1–15.
47. Clifford R. Shaw, Frederick M. Forbaugh, Henry D. McKay, and Leonard S. Cottrell, *Delinquency Areas* (Chicago: University of Chicago Press, 1929).
48. Clifford R. Shaw and Henry D. McKay, *Juvenile Delinquency and Urban Areas* (Chicago: University of Chicago Press, 1942); see also the revised and updated edition: Clifford R. Shaw and Henry D. McKay, *Juvenile Delinquency and Urban Areas: A Study of Delinquency in Relation to Differential Characteristics of Local Communities in American Cities* (Chicago: University of Chicago Press, 1969); and Frederick M. Thrasher, *The Gang* (Chicago: University of Chicago Press, 1927).
49. Ralph B. Taylor, "The Impact of Crime on Communities," *The Annals of the American Academy,* **539** (1995): 28–45.
50. Ralph B. Taylor, Steve D. Gottfredson, and Sidney Brower, "Attachments to Place: Discriminant Validity and Impacts of Disorder and Diversity," *American Journal of Community Psychology,* **13** (1985): 525–542.
51. Michael Marriott, "Living in 'Lockdown,' " *Newsweek,* Jan. 23, 1995, p. 57.
52. Lynn Newhart Smith and Gary D. Hill, "Victimization and Fear of Crime," *Criminal Justice and Behavior,* **18** (1991): 217–239; see also Fred E. Markowitz, Paul E. Bellair, Allen E. Liska, and Jianhong Liu, "Extending Social Disorganization Theory: Modeling the Relationships between Cohesion, Disorder, and Fear," *Criminology,* **39** (2001): 293–319; and Randy L. LaGrange, Kenneth F. Ferraro, and Michael Supancic, "Perceived Risk of Fear of Crime: Role of Social and Physical Incivilities," *Journal of Research in Crime and Delinquency,* **29** (1992): 311–334. For research that measures safety and perceived safety resources in the context of other environmental concerns (as an alternative to measuring fear of crime), see John J. Gibbs and Kathleen J. Hanrahan, "Safety Demand and Supply: An Alternative to Fear of Crime," *Justice Quarterly,* **10** (1993): 369–394.
53. Ralph Taylor and Jeanette Covington, "Community Structural Change and Fear of Crime," *Social Problems,* **40** (1993): 374–392.
54. Douglas A. Smith, "The Neighborhood Context of Police Behavior," in *Communities and Crime,* eds. Albert J. Reiss and Michael Tonry (Chicago: University of Chicago Press, 1986), pp. 313–341; Terance D. Miethe, Michael Hughes, and David McDowall, "Social Change in Crime Rates: An Evaluation of Alternative Theoretical Approaches," *Social Forces,* **70** (1991): 165–185; E. Britt Paterson, "Poverty, Income Inequality, and Community Crime Rates," *Criminology,* **29** (1991): 755–776; Josefina Figueira-McDonough, "Community Structure and Delinquency: A Typology," *Social Service Review,* **65** (1991): 65–91; and Denise C. Gottfredson, Richard J. McNeil, and Gary D. Gottfredson, "Social Area Influence on Delinquency: A Multilevel Analysis," *Journal of Research in Crime and Delinquency,* **28** (1991): 197–226.
55. Dina R. Rose and Todd R. Clear, "Incarceration, Social Capital, and Crime: Implications for Social Disorganization Theory," *Criminology,* **36** (1998): 441–479.
56. Robert J. Sampson and Dawn Jeglum Bartusch, *Attitudes toward Crime, Police, and the Law: Individual and Neighborhood Differences,* National Institute of Justice Research Preview, June 1999.
57. Steve J. South and Gary D. Deane, "Race and Residential Mobility: Individual Determinants and Structural Constraints," *Social Forces,* **72** (1993): 147–167.
58. See Faith Peeples and Rolf Loeber, "Do Individual Factors and Neighborhood Context Explain Ethnic Differences in Juvenile Delinquency?" *Journal of*

Quantitative Criminology, **10** (1994): 141–157; and Thomas A. Petee, Gregory S. Kowlaski, and Don W. Duffield, "Crime, Social Disorganization, and Social Structure: A Research Note on the Use of Interurban Ecological Models," *American Journal of Criminal Justice,* **19** (1994): 117–132; for generalizability of social disorganization theory to nonurban areas, see D. Wayne Osgood and Jeff M. Chambers, "Social Disorganization Outside the Metropolis: An Analysis of Rural Youth Violence," *Criminology,* **38** (2000): 81–115.

59. Taylor, "The Impact of Crime on Communities," p. 36.
60. Andrew J. Buck, Simon Hakim, and Ulrich Spiegel, "Casinos, Crime, and Real Estate Values: Do They Relate?" *Journal of Research in Crime and Delinquency,* **28** (1991): 288–303.
61. Robert J. Bursik and Harold G. Grosmick, *Neighborhoods and Crime* (New York: Lexington Books, 1993).
62. Anthony Sorrentino and David Whittaker, "The Chicago Area Project—Addressing the Gang Problem," *FBI Law Enforcement Bulletin,* **63** (1994): 8–12; "Philadelphia Settles with Estates of MOVE Members," *Jet,* Feb. 17, 1997, p. 40; Steven Schlossman, Goul Zellman, and Richard Shavelson, "Delinquency Prevention in South Chicago: A Fifty-Year Assessment of the Chicago Area Project," report prepared for the National Institute of Education by the Rand Corporation, May 1984, p. 1; Solomon Kobrin, "The Chicago Area Project: 25 Years of Assessment," *Annals of the American Academy of Political and Social Science,* **332** (1959): 20–29.
63. Terence Dunworth and Gregory Mills, *National Evaluation of Weed and Seed,* NIJ Research in Brief, June 1999.
64. M. Isolina Ferre, "Prevention and Control of Violence through Community Revitalization, Individual Dignity, and Personal Self-Confidence," *Annals of the American Academy of Political and Social Science,* **494** (1987): 27–36.
65. Edwin H. Sutherland, *Principles of Criminology,* 3d ed. (Philadelphia: Lippincott, 1939).
66. William Chambliss, *Boxmen* (New York: Harper & Row, 1972).
67. James S. Short, "Differential Association as a Hypothesis: Problems of Empirical Testing," *Social Problems,* **8** (1960): 14–15.
68. Travis Hirschi, *Causes of Delinquency* (Berkeley: University of California Press, 1969), p. 95.
69. Beth Bjerregaard and Carolyn Smith, "Patterns of Male and Female Gang Membership," working paper no. 13, Rochester Youth Development Study (Albany, N.Y.: Hindelang Criminal Justice Research Center, 1992), p. 20. For contradictory findings, see Mark D. Reed and Pamela Wilcox Roundtree, "Peer Pressure and Adolescent Substance Abuse," *Journal of Quantitative Criminology,* **13** (1997), 143–180. For the relationship of delinquents to their delinquent siblings, see Janet L. Lauritsen, "Sibling Resemblance in Juvenile Delinquency: Findings from the National Youth Survey," *Criminology,* **31** (1993): 387–409.
70. Mark Warr, "Age, Peers, and Delinquency," *Criminology,* **31** (1993): 17–40.
71. Charles Tittle, *Sanctions and Social Deviance* (New York: Praeger, 1980).
72. Clayton A. Hartjen, *Crime and Criminalization* (New York: Praeger, 1974), p. 51.
73. Ross L. Matsueda, "The Current State of Differential Association," *Crime and Delinquency,* **34** (1988): 277–306; and Craig Reinarman and Jeffrey Fagan, "Social Organization and Differential Association: A Research Note from a Longitudinal Study of Violent Juvenile Offenders," *Crime and Delinquency,* **34** (1988): 307–327.
74. Susan Chira, "A Program That Works for Teen-Age Mothers," *New York Times,* Apr. 28, 1993, p. A12.
75. Fox Butterfield, "Programs Seek to Stop Trouble before It Starts," *New York Times,* Dec. 30, 1994, A25.
76. Thorsten Sellin, *Culture Conflict and Crime,* Bulletin 41 (New York: Social Science Research Council, 1938); Avison and Loring, "Population Diversity and Cross-National Homicide"; Mark R. Pogrebin and Eric D. Poole, "Culture Conflict and Crime in the Korean-American Community," *Criminal Justice Policy Review,* **4** (1990): 69–78; and Ira Sommers, Jeffrey Fagan, and Deborah Baskin, "The Influences of Acculturation and Familism on Puerto Rican Delinquency," *Justice Quarterly,* **11** (1994): 207–228.

CHAPTER 6

1. Carla Crowder, "Hmong Pipeline Leads to Colorado Authorities Uncovering Trail of Southeast Asian Gangs Who Are Fleeing California," *(Denver) Rocky Mountain News,* Sept. 12, 1999, p. A4; R. Robin McDonald, "Human Contraband: Asian Women Expected Jobs, Not Prostitution," *Atlanta Constitution,* Aug. 31, 1999, p. C1.
2. Arlen Egley Jr., "Highlights of the 1999 National Youth Gang Survey," National Youth Gang Center (http://www.ncjrs.org/txtfiles1/ojjdp/fs200020.txt). For how gangs spread, see John A. Laskey, "Gang Migration: The Familial Gang Transplant

Phenomenon," *Journal of Gang Research,* **3** (1996): 1–15; and Cheryl L. Maxon, "Investigating Gang Migration: Contextual Issues for Intervention," *Gang Journal,* **1** (1993): 1–8.

3. Albert K. Cohen, *Delinquent Boys: The Culture of the Gang* (Glencoe, Ill.: Free Press, 1955).
4. For example, James F. Short Jr. and Fred L. Strodtbeck, *Group Process and Gang Delinquency* (Chicago: University of Chicago Press, 1965).
5. Kenneth Polk and Walter B. Schafer, eds., *School and Delinquency* (Englewood Cliffs, N.J.: Prentice-Hall, 1972); Alexander Liazos, "School, Alienation, and Delinquency," *Crime and Delinquency,* **24** (1978): 355–370.
6. Travis Hirschi, *Causes of Delinquency* (Berkeley: University of California Press, 1969).
7. Delbert S. Elliott and Harwin L. Voss, *Delinquency and Dropout* (Lexington, Mass.: Lexington Books, 1974).
8. G. Roger Jarjoura, "Dropping Out of School Enhances Delinquent Involvement? Results from a Large-Scale National Probability Sample," *Criminology,* **31** (1993): 149–172.
9. Albert J. Reiss and Albert L. Rhodes, "Deprivation and Delinquent Behavior," *Sociological Quarterly,* **4** (1963): 135–149.
10. Marvin Krohn, R. L. Akers, M. J. Radosevich, and L. Lanza-Kaduce, "Social Status and Deviance," *Criminology,* **18** (1980): 303–318.
11. Mark Warr, "Organization and Instigation in Delinquent Groups," *Criminology,* **34** (1996): 11–37.
12. David F. Greenberg, "Delinquency and the Age Structure of Society," *Contemporary Crisis,* **1** (1977): 189–223.
13. John I. Kitsuse and David C. Dietrick, "Delinquent Boys: A Critique," *American Sociological Review,* **24** (1959): 208–215.
14. David J. Bordua, "Delinquent Subcultures: Sociological Interpretations of Gang Delinquency," *Annals of the American Academy of Political and Social Science,* **338** (1961): 119–136.
15. Albert K. Cohen and James F. Short Jr., "Research in Delinquent Subcultures," *Journal of Social Issues,* **14** (1958): 20–37.
16. Richard A. Cloward and Lloyd E. Ohlin, *Delinquency and Opportunity* (Glencoe, Ill.: Free Press, 1960).
17. Clifford R. Shaw, *The Jack-Roller* (Chicago: University of Chicago Press, 1930), p. 54.
18. James R. David, *Street Gangs* (Dubuque, Iowa: Kendall/Hunt, 1982).
19. Hirschi, *Causes of Delinquency,* p. 227.
20. John M. Hagedorn, "Homeboys, Dope Fiends, Legits, and New Jacks," *Criminology,* **32** (1994): 197–219.
21. James Short, Ramon Rivera, and Ray Tennyson, "Perceived Opportunities, Gang Membership, and Delinquency," *American Sociological Review,* **30** (1965): 56–57.
22. Lecture by Ko-lin Chin, Rutgers University, Nov. 22, 1993. See also K. Chin, *Chinese Subculture and Criminality: Nontraditional Crime Groups in America,* Criminology and Penology Series, vol. 29 (Westport, Conn.: Greenwood, 1990); Mark Warr, "Organization and Instigation in Delinquent Groups," *Criminology,* **34** (1996): 11–37; Kevin M. Thompson, David Brownfield, and Ann Marie Sorenson, "Specialization Patterns of Gang and Nongang Offending: A Latent Structure Analysis," *Journal of Gang Research,* **3** (1996): 25–35.
23. Finn-Aage Esbensen and David Huizinga, "Gangs, Drugs, and Delinquency in a Survey of Urban Youth," *Criminology,* **31** (1993): 565–587; Terence P. Thornberry, Marvin D. Krohn, Alan J. Lizotte, and Deborah Chard-Wierschem, "The Role of Juvenile Gangs in Facilitating Delinquent Behavior," *Journal of Research in Crime and Delinquency,* **30** (1993): 55–87; Malcolm Klein, Cheryl L. Maxson, and Lea C. Cunningham, " 'Crack,' Street Gangs, and Violence," *Criminology,* **29** (1991): 623–650.
24. K. Chin and J. Fagan, "Social Order and Gang Formation in Chinatown," in *Advances in Criminological Theory,* vol. 6, eds. Freda Adler and William S. Laufer (New Brunswick, N.J.: Transaction, 1994).
25. George W. Knop, Edward D. Tromanhauser, James G. Houston, et al., *The Economics of Gang Life: A Task Force Report of the National Gang Crime Research Center* (Chicago: National Crime Research Center, 1995).
26. Ibid., p. ii.
27. John P. Hoffman and Timothy Ireland, "Cloward and Ohlin's Strain Theory Reexamined: An Elaborated Theoretical Model," in *Advances in Criminological Theory,* vol. 6.
28. Marvin E. Wolfgang and Franco Ferracuti, *The Subculture of Violence* (London: Tavistock, 1967).
29. Howard S. Erlanger, "The Empirical Status of the Subcultures of Violence Thesis," *Social Problems,* **22** (1974): 280–292. For the relationship of the thesis to routine activities, see Leslie W. Kennedy and Stephen W. Baron, "Routine Activities and a Subculture of Violence: A Study on the Street," *Journal of Research in Crime and Delinquency,* **30** (1993): 88–112. For an examination of differences between blacks and whites, see Liqun Cao, Anthony Adams, and Vickie J. Jensen, "A Test of the Black Subculture of Violence Thesis: A Research Note," *Criminology,* **35** (1997): 367–379. For a look at regional differences in punitiveness, see Marian

J. Borg, "The Southern Subculture of Punitiveness? Regional Variation in Support for Capital Punishment," *Journal of Research in Crime and Delinquency,* **34** (1997): 25–45.
30. William G. Doerner, "A Regional Analysis of Homicide Rates in the United States," *Criminology,* **13** (1975): 90–101.
31. Jo Dixon and Alan J. Lizotte, "Gun Ownership and the Southern Subculture of Violence," *American Journal of Sociology,* **93** (1987): 383–405.
32. Colin Loftin and Robert Hill, "Regional Subculture of Violence: An Examination of the Gastril-Hackney Thesis," *American Sociological Review,* **39** (1974): 714–724.
33. Judith Blau and Peter Blau, "Metropolitan Structure and Violent Crime," *American Sociological Review,* **47** (1982): 114–129. For a study that examines the subculture of violence thesis as it relates to three groups—blacks, Hispanics, and American Indians—see Donald J. Shoemaker and J. Sherwood Williams, "The Subculture of Violence and Ethnicity," *Journal of Criminal Justice,* **15** (1987): 461–472.
34. Wolfgang and Ferracuti, *The Subculture of Violence,* pp. 258–265. See also Marvin E. Wolfgang, *Patterns in Criminal Homicide* (Philadelphia: University of Pennsylvania Press, 1958).
35. Marvin E. Wolfgang, Robert M. Figlio, and Thorsten Sellin, *Delinquency in a Birth Cohort* (Chicago: University of Chicago Press, 1972); Simon I. Singer, "Victims of Serious Violence and Their Criminal Behavior: Subcultural Theory and Beyond," *Violence and Victims,* **1** (1986): 61–70. See also Neil Alan Weiner and Marvin E. Wolfgang, "The Extent and Character of Violent Crime in America, 1969–1982," in *American Violence and Public Policy,* ed. Lynn Curtis (New Haven, Conn.: Yale University Press, 1985), pp. 17–39.
36. Steven Messner, "Regional and Racial Effects on the Urban Homicide Rate: The Subculture of Violence Revisited," *American Journal of Sociology,* **88** (1983): 997–1007.
37. Scott H. Decker, "Collective and Normative Features of Gang Violence," *Justice Quarterly,* **13** (1996): 243–264.
38. Jeffrey Fagan, "The Social Organization of Drug Use and Drug Dealing among Urban Gangs," *Criminology,* **27** (1989): 633–666.
39. Joseph B. Treaster, "Jamaica's Gangs Take Root in U.S.," *New York Times,* Nov. 13, 1988, p. 15.
40. Walter B. Miller, "Lower-Class Culture as a Generating Milieu of Gang Delinquency," *Journal of Social Issues,* **14** (1958): 5–19.
41. Claude Brown, *Manchild in the Promised Land: A Modern Classic of the Black Experience* (New York: New American Library, 1965), p. 22.
42. Ibid., p. 129.
43. Miller, "Lower-Class Culture."
44. Stephen A. Cernovich, "Value Orientations and Delinquency Involvement," *Criminology,* **15** (1978): 443–458.
45. Gresham Sykes and David Matza, "Techniques of Neutralization: A Theory of Delinquency," *American Sociological Review,* **22** (1957): 664–673.
46. Barbara Kantrowitz, "Wild in the Streets," *Newsweek,* Aug. 2, 1993, p. 46.
47. Eugene O'Neill, *Long Day's Journey into Night,* in *Great Scenes from the World Theater,* ed. James L. Steffenson Jr. (New York: Avon, 1965), p. 199.
48. Peter T. Kilborn, "Finding a Way: The Quest of Derrick, 19," *New York Times,* Apr. 22, 1993, p. 1.
49. Jean Merl, "Sentencing and Elegy for Slain Boy Court: Emotional Statements by Victim's Family Have Many in Tears. Three Gang Members Receive Lengthy Terms," *Los Angeles Times,* Sept. 16, 1999, p. B1.
50. Michael Cooper, "17-Year-Old Is Arrested in Boy's Death: Slaying of Bystander Is Linked to Gangs," *New York Times,* Aug. 22, 1999, p. 37.
51. Bill Miller, "Guilty Plea in Slaying of D.C. Boy, 12; Teen Was Triggerman in Gang-Related Case," *Washington Post,* Feb. 21, 1998, p. D01.
52. Rene Sanchez, "Placid Santa Monica Roiled by 5 Gang War Deaths in 2 Weeks," *Washington Post,* Oct. 31, 1998, p. A02.
53. Jeffrey Fagan, "The Political Economy of Drug Dealing among Urban Gangs," in *Drugs and the Community,* eds. Robert Davis, Arthur Lurigio, and Dennis Rosenbaum (Springfield, Ill.: Charles C. Thomas, 1993), pp. 19–54.
54. John Bonfante, "Entrepreneurs of Crack," *Time,* Feb. 27, 1995, p. 22.
55. Beth Bjerregaard and Alan J. Lizotte, "Gun Ownership and Gang Membership," *The Journal of Criminal Law and Criminology,* **86** (1995): 37–58; Alan J. Lizotte, James M. Tesoriero, Terence P. Thornberry, and Marvin D. Krohn, "Patterns of Adolescent Firearms Ownership and Use," *Justice Quarterly,* **11** (1994): 51–74. On the extent of gang organizations, see Scott H. Decker, Tim Bynum, and Deborah Weisel, "A Tale of Two Cities: Gangs as Organized Crime Groups," *Justice Quarterly,* **15** (1998): 395–425.
56. Office of Juvenile Justice and Delinquency Prevention, *Juvenile Offenders and Victims: 1999 National Report* (Washington, D.C.: Office of Juvenile Justice and Delinquency Prevention, 1999), pp. 19, 20, 117; U.S. Department of Justice, Federal Bureau of Investigation, *Uniform Crime Report 1985–1995* (Washington, D.C.: Federal Bureau of Investigation, 1999). See also Alfred

Blumstein, "Youth, Violence, Guns and the Illicit Gun Industry," *Journal of Criminal Law and Criminology,* **86** (1995): 10–36.
57. John P. Sullivan and Martin E. Silverstein, "The Disaster within Us: Urban Conflict and Street Gang Violence in Los Angeles," *Journal of Gang Research,* **2** (1995): 11–30 (p. 28).
58. Cohen and Short, "Research in Delinquent Subcultures."
59. Anne Campbell, *The Girls in the Gang* (New York: Basil Blackwell, 1984), p. 267.
60. Jill Leslie Rosenbaum, "A Violent Few: Gang Girls in the California Youth Authority," *Journal of Gang Research,* **3** (1996): 17–23. For reasons girls join gangs, see Finn-Aage Eshensen and Elizabeth Piper Deschenes, "A Multisite Examination of Youth Gang Membership: Does Gender Matter?" *Criminology,* **36** (1998): 799–828.
61. *New Mexico Street Gangs, 1994: Update* (Albuquerque: New Mexico Department of Public Safety, 1994).
62. Seth Mydans, "Life in Girls' Gang: Colors and Bloody Noses," *New York Times,* Jan. 29, 1990, pp. 1, 20.
63. David Lauderback, Joy Hansen, and Dan Waldorf, "'Sisters Are Doin' It for Themselves': A Black Female Gang in San Francisco," *Gang Journal,* **1** (1992): 57–72.
64. Ibid., p. 67.
65. Beth Bjerregaard and Carolyn Smith, *Rochester Youth Development Study: Patterns of Male and Female Gang Membership,* working paper no. 13 (Albany, N.Y.: Hindelang Criminal Justice Research Center, 1992).
66. Seth Mydans, "Not Just the Inner City: Well-to-Do Join Gangs," *New York Times,* Apr. 10, 1990, p. A10.
67. C. Ronald Huff, ed., *Gangs in America* (Newbury Park, Calif.: Sage, 1990).
68. Mydans, "Not Just the Inner City."
69. Dan Korem, *Suburban Gangs: Affluent Rebels* (Richardson, Tex.: International Focus, 1994).
70. As quoted in Mydans, "Not Just the Inner City."
71. Korem, *Suburban Gangs.*
72. U.S. Dept of Justice "Hate Crime.", Fact sheet, November 25, 2002.
73. Wayne S. Wooden, *Renegade Kids, Suburban Outlaws: From Youth Culture to Delinquency* (Belmont, Calif.: Wadsworth, 1995), p. 190.
74. "L.A. Style: A Street Gang Manual of the Los Angeles County Sheriff's Department," in *The Modern Gang Reader,* eds. Malcolm W. Klein, Cheryl L. Maxson, and Jody Miller (Los Angeles: Roxbury, 1995).
75. Albert K. Cohen, "Middle-Class Delinquency and the Social Structure," in *Middle-Class Delinquency,* ed. E. W. Vaz (New York: Harper & Row, 1967), pp. 207–221.
76. Korem, *Suburban Gangs,* p. 50.
77. Jim Burch and Candice Kane, "Implementing the OJJDP Comprehensive Gang Model," *OJJDP Fact Sheet,* **112** (July 1999).
78. Lynn A. Curtis, Preface to "Policies to Prevent Crime: Neighborhood, Family, and Employment Strategies," *Annals of the American Academy of Political and Social Science,* **494** (1987).
79. Robert Reinhold, "In the Middle of L.A.'s Gang Warfare," *New York Times Magazine,* May 22, 1988, p. 31.
80. Ibid., p. 70.
81. Jon D. Hull, "No Way Out," *Time,* Aug. 17, 1992, p. 40.
82. *Time,* June 15, 1992, p. 37.

CHAPTER 7

1. William Golding, *Lord of the Flies* (New York: Coward-McCann, 1954), p. 31.
2. Jack P. Gibbs, "Social Control, Deterrence, and Perspectives on Social Order," *Social Forces,* **56** (1977): 408–423. See also Freda Adler, *Nations Not Obsessed with Crime* (Littleton, Colo.: Fred B. Rothman, 1983).
3. Travis Hirschi, *Causes of Delinquency* (Berkeley: University of California Press, 1969).
4. Donald J. Black, *The Behavior of Law* (New York: Academic Press, 1976), p. 105. See Allan V. Horwitz, *The Logic of Social Control* (New York: Plenum, 1990), for an exceptional evaluation of Black's work.
5. Joseph Perkins, "Smoke Signals Taxes, Harsh Rules Go Too Far in Crusade to Snuff Out Habit," *San Diego Union-Tribune,* Mar. 12, 1993, p. B7; editorial, "Smoke Clouds the Political Air in California's City of Angels," *Washington Times,* July 17, 1993, p. C2.
6. Nanette J. Davis and Bo Anderson, *Social Control: The Production of Deviance in the Modern State* (New York: Irvington, 1983); S. Cohen and A. Scull, eds., *Social Control and the State* (New York: St. Martin's Press, 1983).
7. Jackson Toby, "Social Disorganization and Stake in Conformity: Complementary Factors in the Predatory Behavior of Hoodlums," *Journal of Criminal Law, Criminology, and Police Science,* **48** (1957): 12–17.
8. Scott Briar and Irving Piliavin, "Delinquency, Situational Inducements, and Commitment to Conformity," *Social Problems,* **13** (1965): 41.
9. Ibid, p. 36.

NOTES

10. Hirschi, *Causes of Delinquency*.
11. See John Bowlby, *Attachment and Loss*, 2 vols. (New York: Basic Books, 1969, 1973); John Bowlby, "Forty-Four Juvenile Thieves: Their Characteristics and Home Life," *International Journal of Psychoanalysis*, **25** (1944): 19–25; and John Bowlby, *The Making and Breaking of Affectional Bonds* (London: Tavistock, 1979).
12. Hirschi, *Causes of Delinquency*.
13. Ibid., p. 145.
14. June Gross, "Successful Program Shows Difficulty of Job Training," *Los Angeles Times*, Apr. 22, 1996, p. 1.
15. Hirschi, *Causes of Delinquency*.
16. Teresa D. Brown, "School Adds After-School Fun," *St. Petersburg Times*, Jan. 12, 1995, p. 3.
17. Jeff Lofvers, "I Don't Understand Why Teens Get Such a Bad Rap," *Orlando Sentinel*, June 5, 1996, p. A13.
18. Michael J. Hindelang, "Causes of Delinquency: A Partial Replication and Extension," *Social Problems*, **20** (1973): 471–487.
19. Marvin D. Krohn and James L. Massey, "Social Control and Delinquent Behavior: An Examination of the Elements of the Social Bond," *Sociological Quarterly*, **21** (1980): 529–544.
20. Michael D. Wiatrowski, David Griswold, and Mary K. Roberts, "Social Control Theory and Delinquency," *American Sociological Review*, **46** (1985): 525–541.
21. Robert Agnew, "Social Control Theory and Delinquency: A Longitudinal Test," *Criminology*, **23** (1985): 47–61. See also Scott Menard, "Demographic and Theoretical Variables in the Age-Period-Cohort Analysis of Illegal Behavior," *Journal of Research in Crime and Delinquency*, **29** (1992): 178–199; Stephen A. Cernovich and Peggy C. Giordano, "School Bonding, Age, Race, and Delinquency," *Criminology*, **30** (1992): 261–291; Kimberly L. Kempf, "The Empirical Status of Social Control Theory," in *New Directions in Criminological Theory*, eds. Freda Adler and William S. Laufer (New Brunswick, N.J.: Transaction, 1993), pp. 143–185; Marc LeBlanc and Aaron Caplan, "Theoretical Formalization, a Necessity: The Example of Hirschi's Bonding Theory," in *New Directions in Criminological Theory*, pp. 237–336; and Orlando Rodriguez and David Weisburd, "The Integrated Social Control Model and Ethnicity: The Case of Puerto Rican American Delinquency," *Criminal Justice and Behavior*, **18** (1991): 464–479.
22. David F. Greenberg, "The Weak Strength of Social Control Theory," *Crime and Delinquency*, **45** (1999): 66–81.
23. Kimberly K. Leonard and S. H. Decker, "The Theory of Social Control: Does It Apply to the Very Young?" *Journal of Criminal Justice*, **22** (1994): 89–105; Karen S. Rook, "Promoting Social Bonding: Strategies for Helping the Lonely and Socially Isolated," *American Psychologist*, **39** (1984): 1389–1407.
24. Milton Rokeach, *The Nature of Human Values* (New York: Free Press, 1973).
25. See Donald J. Shoemaker, *Theories of Delinquency: An Examination of Explanations of Delinquent Behavior*, 2d ed. (New York: Oxford University Press, 1990), pp. 172–207, for an evaluation of social control theory.
26. Terence P. Thornberry, "Toward an Interactional Theory of Delinquency," *Criminology*, **25** (1987): 863–891.
27. David Matza, *Delinquency and Drift* (New York: Wiley, 1964), p. 21.
28. Gresham Sykes and David Matza, "Techniques of Neutralization: A Theory of Delinquency," *American Sociological Review*, **22** (1957): 664–670. For a more recent look at techniques of neutralization, see John Hamlin, "The Misplaced Role of Rational Choice in Neutralization Theory," *Criminology*, **26** (1988): 425–438.
29. Richard A. Ball, "An Empirical Exploration of Neutralization Theory," *Criminologica*, **4** (1966): 103–120. See also N. William Minor, "The Neutralization of Criminal Offense," *Criminology*, **18** (1980): 103–120.
30. Robert Gordon, James F. Short Jr., D. Cartwright, and Fred L. Strodtbeck, "Values and Gang Delinquency: A Study of Street Corner Groups," *American Journal of Sociology*, **69** (1963): 109–128.
31. Albert J. Reiss, "Delinquency as the Failure of Personal and Social Controls," *American Sociological Review*, **16** (1951): 206.
32. Toby, "Social Disorganization," p. 137.
33. Walter C. Reckless, "A New Theory of Delinquency and Crime," *Federal Probation*, **25** (1961): 42–46; Walter C. Reckless, Simon Dinitz, and E. Murray, "Self-Concept as an Insulator against Delinquency," *American Sociological Review*, **21** (1956): 744–746; Frank R. Scarpitti, Ellen Murray, Simon Dinitz, and Walter C. Reckless, "The Good Boy in a High Delinquency Area: Four Years Later," *American Sociological Review*, **25** (1960): 555–558. See also K. Heimer and R. L. Matsueda, "Role-Taking, Role Commitment, and Delinquency: A Theory of Differential Social Control," *American Sociological Review*, **59** (1994): 365–390.
34. Walter C. Reckless, "A Non-causal Explanation: Containment Theory," *Excerpta Criminologia*, **2** (1962): 131–132.

35. Francis Ivan Nye, *Family Relationships and Delinquent Behavior* (New York: Wiley, 1958).
36. L. Edward Wells and Joseph H. Rankin, "Broken Homes and Juvenile Delinquency: An Empirical Review," *Criminal Justice Abstracts,* **17** (1985): 249–272.
37. Mary Reige, "Parental Affection and Juvenile Delinquency in Girls," *British Journal of Criminology,* **12** (1972): 55–73; Lawrence Rosen, "Family and Delinquency: Structure or Function?" *Criminology,* **23** (1985): 553–573.
38. L. Edward Wells and Joseph H. Rankin, "Direct Parental Controls and Delinquency," *Criminology,* **26** (1988): 263–285. See also Douglas Smith and Raymond Paternoster, "The Gender Gap in Theories of Deviance: Issues and Evidence," *Journal of Research in Crime and Delinquency,* **24** (1987): 140–172; and John Hagan, A. R. Gillis, and John Simpson, "The Class Structure of Gender and Delinquency: Toward a Power-Control Theory of Common Delinquent Behavior," *American Journal of Sociology,* **90** (1985): 1151–1178. See Joan McCord, "Some Child-Rearing Antecedents of Criminal Behavior in Adult Men," *Journal of Personality and Social Psychology,* **36** (1979): 1477–1486. For an examination of the family backgrounds of female offenders, see Jill Leslie Rosenbaum, "Family Dysfunction and Female Delinquency," *Crime and Delinquency,* **35** (1989): 31–44.
39. Betti Jane Levine, "Tender Mercies: They Traded Their Humanity for a Life in Crime," *Los Angeles Times,* June 21, 1996, p. 1.
40. Reckless et al., "Self-Concept as an Insulator"; Scarpitti et al., "The Good Boy in a High Delinquency Area."
41. Gary F. Jensen, "Delinquency and Adolescent Self-Conceptions: A Study of the Personal Relevance of Infraction," *Social Problems,* **20** (1972): 84–103.
42. Clarence Schrag, *Crime and Justice American Style* (Washington, D.C.: U.S. Government Printing Office, 1971), pp. 82–89.
43. Alan Liska, Marvin D. Krohn, and Steven F. Messner, "Strategies and Requisites for Theoretical Integration in the Study of Crime and Deviance," in *Theoretical Integration in the Study of Deviance and Crime: Problems and Prospects,* eds. S. F. Lessner, M. D. Krohn, and A. Liska (New York: SUNYA, 1989), p. 4. See also R. J. Hepburn, "Testing Alternative Models of Delinquency Causation," *Journal of Criminal Law and Criminology,* **67** (1977): 450–460; T. Ross Matsueda, "Testing Control Theory and Differential Association: A Causal Modeling Approach," *American Sociological Review,* **47** (1982): 489–497; Frank S. Pearson and Neil A. Weiner, "Toward an Integration of Criminological Theories," *Journal of Criminal Law and Criminology,* **76** (1985): 116–150; Terrie E. Moffitt, "Adolescence-Limited and Life-Course-Persistent Antisocial Behavior: A Developmental Taxonomy," *Psychological Review,* **100** (1993): 674–701; Terrie E. Moffitt et al., "Childhood-Onset versus Adolescent-Onset Antisocial Conduct Problems in Males: Natural History from Ages 3 to 18 Years," *Development and Psychopathology,* **8** (1996): 399–424; and Terrie E. Moffitt, "Adolescence-Limited and Life-Course-Persistent Offending: A Complementary Pair of Developmental Theories," in ed. T. P. Thornberry, *Developmental Theories of Crime and Delinquency: Advances in Criminological Theory,* **7** (1997).
44. Robert J. Sampson and John H. Laub, *Crime in the Making: Pathways and Turning Points through Life* (Cambridge, Mass.: Harvard University Press, 1993); R. J. Sampson and J. H. Laub, "Understanding Variability in Lives through Time: Contributions of Life-Course Criminology," *Studies on Crime and Crime Prevention,* **4** (1995): 143–158.
45. Terence P. Thornberry, A. J. Lizotte, and M. D. Krohn, "Delinquent Peers, Beliefs, and Delinquent Behavior: A Longitudinal Test of Interactional Theory," *Criminology,* **32** (1994): 47–83; Terence P. Thornberry, Alan J. Lizotte, Marvin D. Krohn, Margaret Farnsworth, and Sung Juon Jung, "Testing Interactional Theory: An Examination of Reciprocal Causal Relationships among Family, School, and Delinquency," *Journal of Criminal Law and Criminology,* **82** (1991): 3–35; see also Madeline G. Aultman and Charles F. Wellford, "Toward an Integrated Model of Delinquency Causation: An Empirical Analysis," *Sociology and Social Research,* **63** (1979): 316–317; and Thornberry, *Developmental Theories of Crime and Delinquency.*
46. D. S. Nagin and D. P. Farrington, "The Onset and Persistence of Offending," *Criminology,* **30** (1992): 501–524; D. S. Nagin and D. P. Farrington, "The Stability of Criminal Potential from Childhood to Adulthood," *Criminology,* **30** (1992): 235–260; D. P. Farrington, "Explaining the Beginning, Progress, and Ending of Antisocial Behavior from Birth to Adulthood," *Advances in Criminological Theory,* **3** (1992): 253–286.
47. Delbert S. Elliott, Suzanne S. Ageton, and R. J. Canter, "An Integrated Theoretical Perspective on Delinquent Behavior," *Journal of Research in Crime and Delinquency,* **16** (1979): 3–27;

S. Menard and Delbert S. Elliott, "Delinquent Bonding, Moral Beliefs, and Illegal Behavior: A Three Wave Panel Model," *Justice Quarterly,* **11** (1994): 173–188.

48. David J. Hawkins and Joseph G. Weis, "The Social Development Model: An Integrated Approach to Delinquency Prevention," *Journal of Primary Prevention,* **6** (1985): 73–97.

49. Michael R. Gottfredson and Travis Hirschi, *A General Theory of Crime* (Stanford, Calif.: Stanford University Press, 1990); Michael Gottfredson and Travis Hirschi, "A Propensity-Event Theory of Crime," in *Advances in Criminological Theory,* vol. 1, eds. W. Laufer and F. Adler (New Brunswick, N.J.: Transaction, 1989); B. J. Arneklev, H. G. Grasmick, and C. R. Tittle, "Low Self-Control and Imprudent Behavior," *Journal of Quantitative Criminology,* **9** (1993): 225–247; D. Brownfield and A. M. Sorenson, "Self Control and Juvenile Delinquency: Theoretical Issues and an Empirical Assessment of Selected Elements of a General Theory of Crime," *Deviant Behavior,* **14** (1993): 243–264; T. Hirschi and M. Gottfredson, "Commentary: Testing the General Theory of Crime," *Journal of Research in Crime and Delinquency,* **30** (1993): 47–54.

50. Travis Hirschi and Michael Gottfredson, "The Significance of White-Collar Crime for a General Theory of Crime," *Criminology,* **27** (1989): 359–371; Darrell Steffensmeier, "On the Causes of 'White Collar' Crime: An Assessment of Hirschi and Gottfredson's Claim," *Criminology,* **27** (1989): 345–358.

51. Carl Keane, Paul S. Maxim, and James J. Teevan, "Drinking and Driving, Self-Control, and Gender: Testing a General Theory of Crime," *Journal of Research in Crime and Delinquency,* **30** (1993): 30–46.

52. See, e.g., A. Sorenson and D. Brownfield, "Adolescent Drug Use and a General Theory of Crime: An Analysis of a Theoretical Integration," *Canadian Journal of Criminology,* **37** (1995): 19–37; J. J. Gibbs and D. Giever, "Self-Control and Its Manifestations among University Students: An Empirical Test of Gottfredson and Hirschi's General Theory," *Justice Quarterly,* **12** (1995): 231–255; Harold G. Grasmick, Charles R. Tittle, and Robert J. Bursik Jr., "Testing the Core Empirical Implications of Gottfredson and Hirschi's General Theory of Crime," *Journal of Research in Crime and Delinquency,* **30** (1993): 5–29; Hirschi and Gottfredson, "Commentary: Testing the General Theory of Crime"; S. L. Miller and C. Burack, "A Critique of Gottfredson and Hirschi's General Theory of Crime: Selective (In)Attention to Gender and Power Positions," *Women and Criminal Justice,* **4** (1993); M. L. Benson and E. Moore, "Are White-Collar and Common Offenders the Same? An Empirical and Theoretical Critique of a Recently Proposed General Theory of Crime," *Journal of Research in Crime and Delinquency,* **29** (1992): 251–272; and Robert Agnew, "Testing the Leading Crime Theories: An Alternative Strategy Focusing on Motivational Processes," *Journal of Research in Crime and Delinquency,* **32** (1995): 363–398.

53. Don Weatherburn, "On the Quest for a General Theory of Crime," *Australian and New Zealand Journal of Criminology,* **26** (1993): 35–46.

54. See W. Timothy Austin, "Crime and Custom in an Orderly Society: The Singapore Prototype," *Criminology,* **25** (1987): 279–294; J. M. Day and William S. Laufer, eds., *Crime, Values, and Religion* (Norwood, N.J.: Ablex, 1987); and Freda Adler and William S. Laufer, "Social Control and the Workplace," in *US-USSR Approaches to Urban Crime Prevention,* ed. James Finckenauer and Alexander Yakovlev (Moscow: Soviet Academy of State and Law, 1987).

55. David J. Hawkins, Richard F. Catalano, Gwen Jones, and David Fine, "Delinquency Prevention through Parent-Training: Results and Issues from Work in Progress," in *From Children to Citizens:* vol. 3, *Families, Schools, and Delinquency Prevention,* eds. James Q. Wilson and Glenn C. Loury (New York: Springer Verlag, 1987), pp. 186–204.

56. Denise C. Gottfredson, "An Empirical Test of School-Based Environmental and Individual Interventions to Reduce the Risk of Delinquent Behavior," *Criminology,* **24** (1986): 705–731.

57. Jeffrey Fagan, "Neighborhood Education, Mobilization, and Organization for Juvenile Crime Prevention," *Annals of the American Academy for the Advancement of Political and Social Sciences,* **494** (1987): 54–70.

58. For an examination of community social control, see David Weisburd, "Vigilantism as Community Social Control: Developing a Quantitative Criminological Model," *Journal of Quantitative Criminology,* **4** (1988): 137–153.

59. "Fostering the Family: An Intensive Effort to Keep Kids with Parents," *Newsweek,* June 22, 1992, p. 64.

60. Ibid.

61. George Judson, "Fighting Temptations of Summer: Bridgeport Puts Teenagers to Work Helping Other Youths," *New York Times,* Aug. 22, 1992, p. B1.

62. Susan Chirn, "A 'Learnfare' Program Offers No Easy Lessons," *New York Times,* Apr. 28, 1993, p. A12.

CHAPTER 8

1. Howard S. Becker, *Outsiders: Studies in the Sociology of Deviance* (New York: Macmillan, 1963), p. 9.
2. For an excellent discussion of how society controls deviance, see Nicholas N. Kittrie, *The Right to Be Different* (Baltimore: Johns Hopkins University Press, 1972).
3. William I. Thomas, *The Unadjusted Girl* (1923; New York: Harper & Row, 1967).
4. George Herbert Mead, "The Psychology of Punitive Justice," *American Journal of Sociology,* **23** (1918): 577–602. See also Charles Horton Cooley, "The Roots of Social Knowledge," *American Journal of Sociology,* **32** (1926): 59–79.
5. Herbert Blumer, "Sociological Implications of the Thought of George Herbert Mead," in *Symbolic Interactionism,* ed. Blumer (Englewood Cliffs, N.J.: Prentice-Hall, 1969), pp. 62, 65, 66.
6. Frank Tannenbaum, *Crime and the Community* (Boston: Ginn, 1938), p. 27.
7. Edwin M. Lemert, *Social Pathology* (New York: McGraw-Hill, 1951).
8. Edwin M. Lemert, *Human Deviance, Social Problems, and Social Control* (Englewood Cliffs, N.J.: Prentice-Hall, 1967), chap. 3.
9. Lemert, *Social Pathology,* pp. 75–76.
10. Lemert, *Human Deviance,* p. 46. See also Albert K. Cohen, *Deviance and Control* (Englewood Cliffs, N.J.: Prentice-Hall, 1966), pp. 24–25.
11. Erving Goffman, *Stigma: Notes on the Management of Spoiled Identity* (Englewood Cliffs, N.J.: Prentice-Hall, 1963).
12. Gerhard O. W. Mueller, "Resocialization of the Young Adult Offender in Switzerland," *Journal of Criminal Law and Criminology,* **43** (1953): 578–591, at p. 584.
13. Kai T. Erickson, "Notes on the Sociology of Deviance," in *The Other Side: Perspectives on Deviance,* ed. Howard S. Becker (New York: Free Press, 1964), p. 11.
14. Edwin Schur, *Labeling Deviant Behavior* (New York: Harper & Row, 1971), p. 21.
15. Edwin M. Schur, *Crimes without Victims* (Englewood Cliffs, N.J.: Prentice-Hall, 1965).
16. M. Ray, "The Cycle of Abstinence and Relapse among Heroin Addicts," *Social Problems,* **9** (1961): 132–140.
17. David Matza, *Becoming Deviant* (Englewood Cliffs, N.J.: Prentice-Hall, 1969), pp. 44–53.
18. Becker, *Outsiders,* pp. 18, 20.
19. D. L. Rosenhan, "On Being Sane in Insane Places," *Science,* **179** (1973): 250–258. See also Bruce G. Link, "Understanding Labeling Effects in the Area of Mental Disorders: An Assessment of the Effects of Expectations of Rejection," *American Sociological Review,* **52** (1987): 96–112; and Anthony Walsh, "Twice Labeled: The Effect of Psychiatric Labeling on the Sentencing of Sex Offenders," *Social Problems,* **37** (1990): 375–389.
20. Carol Warren and John Johnson, "A Critique of Labeling Theory from the Phenomenological Perspective," in *Theoretical Perspectives on Deviance,* eds. J. D. Douglas and R. Scott (New York: Basic Books, 1973), p. 77; James P. Spradley, *You Owe Yourself a Drunk: An Ethnography of Urban Nomads* (Boston: Little, Brown, 1979), p. 254.
21. Richard D. Schwartz and Jerome H. Skolnick, "Two Studies of Legal Stigma," *Social Problems,* **10** (1962): 133–138.
22. Anthony Platt, *The Child Savers* (Chicago: University of Chicago Press, 1969). For a further discussion of the effects of stigmatization by the criminal justice system, see Charles W. Thomas and Donna M. Bishop, "The Effect of Formal and Informal Sanctions on Delinquency: A Longitudinal Comparison of Labeling and Deterrence Theories," *Journal of Criminal Law and Criminology,* **75** (1984): 1222–1245.
23. William J. Chambliss, "The Saints and the Roughnecks," *Society,* **11** (1973): 24–31.
24. Walter R. Gove, "Deviant Behavior, Social Intervention, and Labeling Theory," in *The Uses of Controversy in Sociology,* eds. Lewis A. Coser and Otto N. Larsen (New York: Free Press, 1976), pp. 219–227; Ross L. Matsueda, "Reflected Appraisals, Parental Labeling, and Delinquency: Specifying a Symbolic Interactionist Theory," *American Journal of Sociology,* **97** (1992): 1577–1611.
25. Ronald L. Akers, "Problems in the Sociology of Deviance," *Social Forces,* **46** (1968): 455–465.
26. Ronald L. Akers, *Deviant Behavior: A Social Learning Approach,* 2d ed. (Belmont, Calif.: Wadsworth, 1977); David Ward and Charles R. Tittle, "Deterrence or Labeling: The Effects of Informal Sanctions," *Deviant Behavior,* **14** (1993): 43–64.
27. Jack P. Gibbs, "Conceptions of Deviant Behavior: The Old and the New," *Pacific Sociological Review,* **9** (Spring 1966): 9–14.
28. Charles Wellford, "Labelling Theory and Criminology: An Assessment," *Social Problems,* **22** (1975): 343; Charles F. Wellford and Ruth A. Triplett, "The Future of Labeling Theory: Foundations and Promises," in *Advances in*

Criminological Theory, vol. 4, eds. Freda Adler and William S. Laufer (New Brunswick, N.J.: Transaction, 1993).
29. Alexander Liazos, "The Poverty of the Sociology of Deviance: Nuts, Sluts, and Perverts," *Social Problems,* **20** (1972): 103–120.
30. Howard S. Becker, "Labelling Theory Reconsidered," in *Outsiders: Studies in the Sociology of Deviance,* rev. ed., ed. Becker (New York: Free Press, 1973), pp. 177–208. See also Schur, *Labeling Deviant Behavior,* for an excellent review of labeling theory.
31. Robert J. Sampson and John H. Laub, "A Life-Course Theory of Cumulative Disadvantage and Stability of Delinquency," in T. Thornberry, ed., *Developmental Theories of Crime and Delinquency: Advances in Criminology Theory,* **7** (1997).
32. Compare this perspective with the emerging notion of criminology as peacemaking; see Harold E. Pepinsky and Richard Quinney, eds., *Criminology as Peace-Making* (Bloomington: Indiana University Press, 1991).
33. Émile Durkheim, *The Division of Labor in Society* (New York: Free Press, 1947), p. 80.
34. Ibid., p. 102.
35. Roscoe Pound, *An Introduction to the Philosophy of Law* (Boston: Little, Brown, 1922), p. 98.
36. Richard Quinney, *Crime and Justice in Society* (Boston: Little, Brown, 1969), pp. 26–30.
37. William Chambliss, "The State, the Law, and the Definition of Behavior as Criminal or Delinquent," in *Handbook of Criminology,* ed. Daniel Glaser (Chicago: Rand McNally, 1974), pp. 7–44.
38. Austin Turk, "Law as a Weapon in Social Conflict," *Social Problems,* **23** (1976): 276–291.
39. George Vold, *Theoretical Criminology* (New York: Oxford University Press, 1958), pp. 204, 209.
40. Ralf Dahrendorf, *Class and Class Conflict in Industrial Society* (Stanford, Calif.: Stanford University Press, 1959). See also Ralf Dahrendorf, "Out of Utopia: Toward a Reorientation of Sociological Analysis," *American Journal of Sociology,* **64** (1958): 127.
41. Austin Turk, *Criminality and Legal Order* (Chicago: Rand McNally, 1969), pp. 25, 33, 41–42, 48. See also Thomas O'Reilly-Fleming et al., "Issues in Social Order and Social Control," *Journal of Human Justice,* **2** (1990): 55–74.
42. Austin Turk, *Political Criminality: The Defiance and Defense of Authority* (Beverly Hills, Calif.: Sage, 1982), p. 15.
43. Turk, "Law as a Weapon."
44. William J. Chambliss, "A Sociological Analysis of the Law of Vagrancy," *Social Problems,* **12** (1966): 67–77. For an opposing view on the historical development of criminal law, see Jeffrey S. Adler, "A Historical Analysis of the Law of Vagrancy," *Criminology,* **27** (1989): 209–229; and a rejoinder to Adler: William J. Chambliss, "On Trashing Criminology," ibid., pp. 231–238.
45. Alan Lizotte, "Extra-Legal Factors in Chicago's Criminal Courts: Testing the Conflict Model of Criminal Justice," *Social Problems,* **25** (1978): 564–580. See also Kathleen Daly, "Neither Conflict nor Labeling nor Paternalism Will Suffice: Intersections of Race, Ethnicity, Gender, and Family in Criminal Court Decisions," *Crime and Delinquency,* **35** (1989): 136–168; and Elizabeth Comack, ed., "Race, Class, Gender and Justice," *Journal of Human Justice,* **2** (1990): 1–124.
46. Freda Adler, "Socioeconomic Variables Influencing Jury Verdicts," *New York University Review of Law on Social Change,* **3** (1973): 16–36. See also Martha A. Myers, "Social Background and the Sentencing Behavior of Judges," *Criminology,* **26** (1988): 649–675.
47. Celesta A. Albonetti, Robert M. Hauser, John Hagan, and Ilene H. Nagel, "Criminal Justice Decision-Making as a Stratification Process: The Role of Race and Stratification Resources in Pretrial Release," *Journal of Quantitative Criminology,* **5** (1989): 57–82.
48. Austin Turk, "Law, Conflict, and Order: From Theorizing toward Theories," *Canadian Review of Sociology and Anthropology,* **13** (1976): 282–294.
49. Georg Rusche and Otto Kirchheimer, *Punishment and Social Structure* (New York: Columbia University Press, 1939), p. 93.
50. Friedrich Engels, "To the Working Class of Great Britain," Introduction to *The Condition of the Working Class in England (1845),* in Karl Marx and Friedrich Engels, *Collected Works,* vol. 4 (New York: International Publishers, 1974), pp. 213–214, 298.
51. Karl Marx and Friedrich Engels, *The Communist Manifesto* (1848; New York: International Publishers, 1979), p. 9.
52. Willem Adriaan Bonger, *Criminality and Economic Conditions,* trans. Henry P. Horton (Boston: Little, Brown, 1916).
53. Ibid., p. 669.
54. J. M. Van Bemmelen, "Willem Adriaan Bonger," in *Pioneers in Criminology,* ed. Hermann Mannheim (London: Stevens, 1960), p. 361.
55. Ian Taylor, Paul Walton, and Jock Young, *The New Criminology: For a Social Theory of Deviance* (London: Routledge & Kegan Paul, 1973), pp. 264, 281. See also Jock Young, "Radical Criminology in Britain: The Emergence of a Competing Paradigm,"

British Journal of Criminology, **28** (1988): 159–183.

56. Gresham Sykes, "The Rise of Critical Criminology," *Journal of Criminal Law and Criminology,* **65** (1974): 206–213.
57. Richard Quinney, "Crime Control in Capitalist Society: A Critical Philosophy of Legal Order," *Issues in Criminology,* **8** (1973): 75–95; Richard Quinney, "There's a Lot of Us Folks Grateful to the Lone Ranger: Some Notes on the Rise and Fall of American Criminology," *Insurgent Sociologist,* **4** (1973): 56–64.
58. Richard Quinney, "Crime Control in Capitalist Society," in *Critical Criminology,* ed. Ian Taylor, Paul Walton, and Jock Young (London: Routledge & Kegan Paul, 1975), p. 199.
59. Richard Quinney, *Class, State, and Crime: On the Theory and Practice of Criminal Justice,* 2d ed. (New York: David McKay, 1977), p. 10.
60. Richard Quinney, *Critique of Legal Order: Crime Control in a Capitalist Society* (Boston: Little, Brown, 1974), pp. 11–13.
61. William Chambliss and Robert Seidman, *Law, Order, and Power* (Reading, Mass.: Addison-Wesley, 1971), p. 503.
62. Ibid., p. 504.
63. Barry Krisberg, *Crime and Privilege: Toward a New Criminology* (Englewood Cliffs, N.J.: Prentice-Hall, 1975).
64. Herman Schwendinger and Julia Schwendinger, "Delinquency and Social Reform: A Radical Perspective," in *Juvenile Justice,* ed. Lamar Empey (Charlottesville: University of Virginia Press, 1979), pp. 246–290.
65. Elliot Currie, "A Dialogue with Anthony M. Platt," *Issues in Criminology,* **8** (1973): 28.
66. Steven F. Messner and Marvin D. Krohn, "Class, Compliance Structures, and Delinquency: Assessing Integrated Structural-Marxist Theory," *American Journal of Sociology,* **96** (1990): 300–328.
67. Lance H. Selva and Robert M. Bohm, "A Critical Examination of the Informalism Experiment in the Administration of Justice," *Crime and Social Justice,* **29** (1987): 43–57; Timothy Carter and Donald Clelland, "A Neo-Marxian Critique, Formulation, and Test of Juvenile Dispositions as a Function of Social Class," *Social Problems,* **27** (1979): 96–108; David Greenberg and Drew Humphries, "The Co-optation of Fixed Sentencing Reform," *Crime and Delinquency,* **26** (1980): 216–225.
68. Jackson Toby, "The New Criminology Is the Old Sentimentality," *Criminology,* **16** (1979): 516–526; Jim Thomas and Aogan O'Maolchatha, "Reassessing the Critical Metaphor: An Optimistic Revisionist View," *Justice Quarterly,* **6** (1989): 143–171; David Brown and Russell Hogg, "Essentialism, Radical Criminology and Left Realism," *Australian and New Zealand Journal of Criminology,* **25** (1992): 195–230.
69. Carl B. Klockars, "The Contemporary Crises of Marxist Criminology," *Criminology,* **16** (1979): 477–515.
70. Ibid.
71. Richard F. Sparks, "A Critique of Marxist Criminology," in *Crime and Justice: An Annual Review of Research,* ed. Norval Morris and Michael Tonry (Chicago: University of Chicago Press, 1980), p. 159.
72. Milton Mankoff, "On the Responsibility of Marxist Criminology: A Reply to Quinney," *Contemporary Crisis,* **2** (1978): 293–301.
73. Austin T. Turk, "Analyzing Official Deviance: For Nonpartisan Conflict Analysis in Criminology," in *Radical Criminology: The Coming Crisis,* ed. James A. Inciardi (Beverly Hills, Calif.: Sage, 1980), pp. 78–91. See also Sykes, "The Rise of Critical Criminology," p. 212.
74. Philip L. Reichel and Andrzej Rzeplinski, "Student Views of Crime and Criminal Justice in Poland and the United States," *International Journal of Comparative and Applied Criminal Justice,* **13** (1989): 65–81.
75. Quinney, *Class, State, and Crime,* p. 40.
76. Meda Chesney-Lind, "Feminism and Criminology," *Justice Quarterly,* **5** (1988): 497–538; Pat Carlen, "Women, Crime, Feminism, and Realism," *Social Justice,* **17** (1990): 106–123.
77. Sally Simpson, "Feminist Theory, Crime and Justice," *Criminology,* **27** (1989): 605–632; Meda Chesney-Lind, "Judicial Enforcement of the Female Sex Role: The Family Court and the Female Delinquent," *Issues in Criminology,* **8** (1973): 51–69.
78. Martin D. Schwartz and Walter S. DeKeseredy, "Left Realist Criminology: Strengths, Weaknesses and the Feminist Critique," *Crime, Law and Social Change,* **15** (1991): 51–72; John Lowman and Brian D. MacLean, eds., *Realist Criminology: Crime Control and Policing in the 1990s* (Ontario: University of Toronto Press, 1990); Walter S. DeKeseredy and Martin D. Schwartz, "British and U.S. Left Realism: A Critical Comparison," *International Journal of Offender Therapy and Comparative Criminology,* **35** (1991): 248–262.
79. Pepinsky and Quinney, eds., *Criminology as Peace-Making;* Richard Quinney, "Socialist Humanism and the Problem of Crime," *Crime, Law and Social Change,* **23** (1995): 147–156; Robert Elias et al.,

Special Issue, "Declaring Peace on Crime," *Peace Review: A Transnational Quarterly,* **6** (1994): 131–254.

CHAPTER 9

1. Marlowe Churchill, "Jury Finds Man Guilty of One-Hour Sex Attack," *The Press-Enterprise,* Riverside, CA., July 26, 1996, p. B3.
2. "Suburban Digest," *Denver Post,* Apr. 10, 1996, p. B-2.
3. Daniel Sforza, "Thieves Favor Giant Malls When Shopping for Cars," *The Record,* Bergen County, New Jersey, June 26, 1996, pp. A1, A20.
4. Paul J. Brantingham and Patricia L. Brantingham, "Introduction: The Dimensions of Crime," in *Environmental Criminology,* ed. Brantingham and Brantingham (Prospect Heights, Ill.: Waveland, 1991), p. 8. For a discussion on the application of environmental criminology to urban planning, see Paul J. Brantingham and Patricia L. Brantingham, "Environmental Criminology: From Theory to Urban Planning Practice," *Studies on Crime and Crime Prevention,* **7** (1998): 31–60.
5. André M. Guerry, *Essai sur la Statistique Morale de la France* (Paris: Crochard, 1833).
6. Adolphe Quételet, *A Treatise on Man* (Edinburgh: Chambers, 1842), reprinted excerpt Adolphe Quételet, "Of the development of the propensity to crime," in *Criminological Perspectives: A Reader,* ed. John Muncie, Eugene McLaughlin, and Mary Langan (Thousand Oaks, Calif.: Sage, 1996), p. 19.
7. Ronald Clarke and Derek Cornish, "Modeling Offenders' Decisions: A Framework for Research and Policy," in *Crime and Justice,* vol. 6, ed. Michael Tonry and Norval Morris (Chicago: University of Chicago Press, 1985), pp. 147–185; Derek B. Cornish and Ronald V. Clarke, eds., *The Reasoning Criminal* (New York: Springer Verlag, 1986).
8. Jeremy Bentham, *On the Principles and Morals of Legislation* (New York: Kegan Paul, 1789) [reprinted 1948]; Gary S. Becker, "Crime and Punishment: An Economic Approach," *Journal of Political Economy,* **76** (1968): 169–217.
9. Lawrence E. Cohen and Marcus Felson, "Social Change and Crime Rate Trends: A Routine Activity Approach," *American Sociological Review,* **44** (1979): 588–608; Marcus Felson, "Linking Criminal Choices, Routine Activities, Informal Control, and Criminal Outcomes," in *The Reasoning Criminal: Rational Choice Perspectives on Offending,* ed. Derek B. Cornish and Ronald V. Clarke (New York: Springer-Verlag, 1986), pp. 119–128.
10. Marcus Felson, *Crime and Everyday Life: Insights and Implications for Society* (Thousand Oaks, Calif.: Pine Forge Press, 1994), pp. 20–21, 35.
11. Mangai Natarajan, "Telephones as Facilitators of Drug Dealing," paper presented at the Fourth International Seminar on Environmental Criminology and Crime Analysis, July 1995, Cambridge, England; Mangai Natarajan, Ronald V. Clarke and Mathieu Belanger, "Drug Dealing and Pay Phones: The Scope for Intervention," *Security Journal,* **7** (1996): pp. 245–251.
12. Lawrence W. Sherman, Patrick R. Gartin, and Michael E. Buerger, "Hot Spots of Predatory Crime: Routine Activities and the Criminology of Place," *Criminology,* **27** (1989): 27–55; Ronald V. Clarke and Patricia M. Harris, "A Rational Choice Perspective on the Targets of Automobile Theft," *Criminal Behaviour and Mental Health,* **2** (1992): 25–42. See also the following articles in Ronald V. Clarke and Marcus Felson, eds., *Routine Activity and Rational Choice, Advances in Criminological Theory,* vol. 5 (New Brunswick, N.J.: Transaction, 1993): Raymond Paternoster and Sally Simpson, "A Rational Choice Theory of Corporate Crime," pp. 37–58; Richard W. Harding, "Gun Use in Crime, Rational Choice, and Social Learning Theory," pp. 85–102; Richard B. Felson, "Predatory and Dispute-Related Violence: A Social Interactionist Approach," pp. 103–125; Nathaniel J. Pallone and James J. Hennessy, "Tinderbox Criminal Violence: Neurogenic Impulsivity, Risk-Taking, and the Phenomenology of Rational Choice," pp. 127–157; Max Taylor, "Rational Choice, Behavior Analysis, and Political Violence," pp. 159–178; Pietro Marongiu and Ronald V. Clarke, "Ransom Kidnapping in Sardinia, Subcultural Theory and Rational Choice," pp. 179–199; Bruce D. Johnson, Mangai Natarajan, and Harry Sanabria, "'Successful' Criminal Careers: Toward an Ethnography within the Rational Choice Perspective," pp. 201–221.
13. George Rengert and John Wasilchick, *Suburban Burglary: A Time and a Place for Everything* (Springfield, Ill.: Charles C Thomas, 1985).
14. Paul F. Cromwell, James N. Olson, and D'Aunn Webster Avary, *Breaking and Entering: An Ethnographic Analysis of Burglary* (Newbury Park, Calif.: Sage, 1991), pp. 45–46.
15. Richard T. Wright and Scott H. Decker, *Burglars on the Job: Streetlife and Residential Break-Ins* (Boston: Northeastern University Press, 1994), pp. 63–68. See also Alex Piquero and George F. Rengert, "Studying Deterrence with Active Residential Burglars: A Research Note," *Justice Quarterly,* **16** (1999): 451–472.

16. Richard T. Wright and Scott Decker, *Armed Robbers in Action: Stickups and Street Culture* (Boston: Northeastern University Press, 1994). For a feminist analysis of Wright and Decker's ethnographic work on street robbers, see Jody Miller, "Up It Up: Gender and the Accomplishment of Street Robbery," *Criminology,* **36** (1998): 37–66.
17. Philip J. Cook, *Robbery in the United States: An Analysis of Recent Trends and Patterns,* U.S. Department of Justice (Washington, D.C.: U.S. Government Printing Office, 1983).
18. Wayland Clifton Jr., *Convenience Store Robbery in Gainesville, Florida* (Gainesville, Fla.: Gainesville Police Department, 1987), p. 15.
19. Lawrence E. Cohen and Marcus Felson, "Social Change and Crime Rate Trends: A Routine Activity Approach," *American Sociological Review,* **44** (1979): 588–608.
20. Ronald V. Clarke, *Hot Products: Understanding, Anticipating and Reducing Demand for Stolen Goods,* Policing and Reducing Crime Unit, Police Research Series Paper 112 (London: Home Office, 1999). For discussions of what drives shoplifters, see Read Hayes, "Shop Theft: An Analysis of Shoplifter Perceptions and Situational Factors," *Security Journal,* **12** (1999): 7–18; and David P. Farrington, "Measuring, Explaining, and Preventing Shoplifting: A Review of British Research," *Security Journal,* **12** (1999): 9–28. For details on measuring and preventing crime against retail business, see a special issue of *Security Journal,* **7** (1996): 1–75.
21. Bonnie S. Fisher, John J. Sloan, Francis T. Cullen, and Chunmeng Lu, "Crime in the Ivory Tower: The Level and Sources of Student Victimization," *Criminology,* **36** (1998): 671–710. For additional research supporting the routine-activity approach, see also Verna A. Henson and William E. Stone, "Campus Crime: A Victimization Study," *Journal of Criminal Justice,* **27** (1999): 295–308.
22. Hans von Hentig, "Remarks on the Interaction of Perpetrator and Victim," *Journal of Criminal Law and Criminology,* **31** (1941): 303–309.
23. Hans von Hentig, *The Criminal and His Victim* (New Haven, Conn.: Yale University, 1948).
24. See Benjamin Mendelsohn, "The Origin of the Doctrine of Victimology," in *Victimology,* ed. Israel Drapkin and Emilio Viano (Lexington, Mass.: Lexington Books, 1974), pp. 3–4.
25. Frederic Wertham, *The Show of Violence* (Garden City, N.Y.: Country Life Press, 1948), p. 259.
26. Ezzat A. Fattah, "Victims and Victimology: The Facts and the Rhetoric," *International Review of Victimology,* **1** (1989): 44–66, at p. 44.
27. Ezzat A. Fattah, "The Rational Choice/Opportunity Perspective as a Vehicle for Integrating Criminological and Victimological Theories," in Clarke and Felson, *Routine Activity and Rational Choice,* pp. 230–231. For an examination of the relationship between lifestyle factors and the victimization of prostitutes, see Charisse Coston and Lee Ross, "Criminal Victimization of Prostitutes: Empirical Support for the Lifestyle/Exposure Model," *Journal of Crime and Justice,* **21** (1998): 53–70.
28. Fattah, "Victims and Victimology," p. 54.
29. Michael J. Hindelang, Michael R. Gottfredson, and James Garofalo, *Victims of Personal Crime: An Empirical Foundation for a Theory of Personal Victimization* (Cambridge, Mass.: Ballinger, 1978), p. 245.
30. Ibid., pp. 251–265.
31. Marvin E. Wolfgang, *Patterns in Criminal Homicide* (Philadelphia: University of Pennsylvania Press, 1958), p. 253.
32. James T. Tedeschi and Richard B. Felson, *Violence, Aggression, and Coercive Actions* (Washington, D.C.: American Psychological Association, 1994).
33. Richard B. Felson, "Big People Hit Little People: Sex Differences in Physical Power and Interpersonal Violence," *Criminology,* **34** (1996): 433–452.
34. Dan Olweus, "Aggressors and Their Victims: Bullying at School," in *Disruptive Behaviors in Schools,* ed. N. Frude and H. Gault (New York: Wiley, 1984), pp. 57–76.
35. Alan Trickett, Dan Ellingworth, Tim Hope, and Ken Pease, "Crime Victimization in the Eighties: Changes in Area and Regional Inequality," *British Journal of Criminology,* **35** (1995): 343–359; Graham Farrell, "Preventing Repeat Victimization," in *Building a Safer Society: Strategic Approaches to Crime Prevention, Crime and Justice,* vol. 19, ed. Michael Tonry and David P. Farrington (Chicago: University of Chicago Press, 1995), pp. 469–534.
36. Dan Ellingworth, Graham Farrell, and Ken Pease, "A Victim Is a Victim Is a Victim? Chronic Victimization in Four Sweeps of the British Crime Survey," *British Journal of Criminology,* **35** (1995): 360–365.
37. William Spelman, "Once Bitten, Then What? Cross-Sectional and Time-Course Explanations of Repeat Victimization," *British Journal of Criminology,* **35** (1995): 366–383.
38. Natalie Polvi, Terah Looman, Charlie Humphries, and Ken Pease, "The Time-Course of Repeat Burglary Victimization," *British Journal of Criminology,* **31** (1991): 411–414.
39. Graham Farrell, Coretta Phillips, and Ken Pease, "Like Taking Candy: Why Does Repeat Victimization Occur?" *British Journal of Criminology,* **35** (1995): 384–399.

40. Lawrence W. Sherman, Patrick R. Gartin, and Michael E. Buerger, "Hot Spots of Predatory Crime: Routine Activities and the Criminology of Place," *Criminology,* **27** (1989): 27–55.
41. Robert J. Sampson, "The Community," in *Crime,* ed. James Q. Wilson and Joan Petersilia (San Francisco: ICS Press, 1995), pp. 193–216.
42. Dennis W. Roncek and Donald Faggiani, "High Schools and Crime: A Replication," *Sociological Quarterly,* **26** (1985): 491–505.
43. Dennis W. Roncek and Pamela A. Maier, "Bars, Blocks, and Crimes Revisited: Linking the Theory of Routine Activities to the Empiricism of 'Hot Spots,' " *Criminology,* **29** (1991): 725–753.
44. Richard L. Block and Carolyn R. Block, "Space, Place and Crime: Hot Spot Areas and Hot Places of Liquor-Related Crime," in *Crime and Place: Crime Prevention Studies,* vol. 4, ed. John E. Eck and David Weisburd (Monsey, N.Y.: Criminal Justice Press; Washington, D.C.: The Police Executive Research Forum, 1995), pp. 145–183.
45. Per-Olof Wikström, "Preventing City-Center Street Crimes," in Tonry and Farrington, *Building a Safer Society,* vol. 19, pp. 429–468.
46. William Spelman, "Abandoned Buildings: Magnets for Crime?" *Journal of Criminal Justice,* **21** (1993): 481–495.
47. Dennis W. Roncek and Ralph Bell, "Bars, Blocks, and Crimes," *Journal of Environmental Systems,* **11** (1981): 35–47; Roncek and Faggiani, "High Schools and Crime."
48. Jeffrey Peck, G. O. W. Mueller, and Freda Adler, "The Vulnerability of Ports and Marinas to Vessel and Equipment Theft," *Security Journal,* **5** (1994): 146–153.
49. David Weisburd and Lorraine Green with Frank Gajewski and Charles Bellucci, Jersey City Police Department, "Defining the Street Level Drug Market," in *Drugs and Crime: Evaluating Public Policy Initiatives,* ed. Doris Layton MacKenzie and Craig Uchida (Newbury Park, Calif.: Sage, 1994), pp. 61–76. For a discussion of the role of place managers in controlling drug and disorder problems, see Lorraine Green Mazerolle, Colleen Kadleck, and Jan Roehl, "Controlling Drug and Disorder Problems: The Role of Place Managers," *Criminology,* **36** (1998): 371–404. For an analysis of problem-oriented policing in troubled areas, see Anthony A. Braga, David L. Weisburd, Elin J. Waring, Lorraine Green Mazerolle, William Spelman, and Francis Gajewski, "Problem-Oriented Policing in Violent Crime Places: A Randomized Controlled Experiment," *Criminology,* **37** (1999): 541–580.
50. Lawrence W. Sherman, "Hot Spots of Crime and Criminal Careers of Places," in Eck and Weisburd, *Crime and Place,* vol. 4, pp. 35–52.
51. See Fattah, "The Rational Choice/Opportunity Perspective," in Clark and Felson, *Routine Activity and Rational Choice,* pp. 225–258.
52. James R. Lasley, "Drinking Routines/Lifestyles and Predatory Victimization: A Causal Analysis," *Justice Quarterly,* **6** (1989): 529–542.
53. Martin D. Schwartz and Victoria L. Pitts, "Exploring a Feminist Routine Activities Approach to Explaining Sexual Assault," *Justice Quarterly,* **12** (1995): 9–31.
54. Robert F. Meier and Terance D. Miethe, "Understanding Theories of Criminal Victimization," in *Crime and Justice: A Review of Research,* vol. 17, ed. Michael Tonry (Chicago: University of Chicago Press, 1993), pp. 459–499; Richard Titus, "Bringing Crime Victims Back into Routine Activities Theory/Research," paper presented at Fourth International Seminar on Environmental Criminology and Crime Analysis, July 1995, Cambridge, England.
55. C. Ray Jeffery, *Crime Prevention through Environmental Design* (Beverly Hills, Calif.: Sage, 1971).
56. Oscar Newman, *Defensible Space: Crime Prevention through Urban Design* (New York: Macmillan, 1972).
57. Ronald V. Clarke, "Introduction," in *Situational Crime Prevention: Successful Case Studies,* ed. Ronald V. Clarke (New York: Harrow and Heston, 1992), pp. 3–36.
58. Ronald V. Clarke and Ross Homel, "A Revised Classification of Situational Crime Prevention Techniques," in *Crime Prevention at a Crossroads,* ed. Steven P. Lab (Cincinnati: Anderson, 1997). For a discussion of precipitating factors and opportunity, see Richard Wortley, "A Two-Stage Model of Situational Crime Prevention," *Studies on Crime and Crime Prevention,* **7** (1998): 173–188.
59. See Gresham M. Sykes and David Matza, "Techniques of Neutralization: A Theory of Delinquency," *American Sociological Review,* **22** (1957): 664–670; Harold G. Grasmick and Robert J. Bursik, "Conscience, Significant Others, and Rational Choice," *Law and Society Review,* **34** (1990): 837–861; John Braithwaite, *Crime, Shame and Reintegration* (Cambridge: Cambridge University, 1989).
60. Clifford D. Shearing and Phillip C. Stenning, "From the Panopticon to Disney World: The Development of Discipline," in *Perspectives in Criminal Law: Essays in Honour of John L. J. Edwards,* ed.

Anthony N. Doob and Edward L. Greenspan (Aurora: Canada Law Book, 1984), pp. 335–349.
61. See Clarke, "Introduction," in Clarke, *Situational Crime Prevention,* p. 5.
62. Kim Hazelbaker, "Insurance Industry Analyses and the Prevention of Motor Vehicle Theft," paper presented at the Business and Crime Prevention Conference, an International Seminar Sponsored by the National Institute of Justice and Rutgers, State University of New Jersey, New Brunswick, N.J., 1996.
63. Ronald D. Hunter and C. Ray Jeffery, "Preventing Convenience Store Robbery through Environmental Design," in Clarke, *Situational Crime Prevention,* pp. 194–204. See also Lisa C. Bellamy, "Situational Crime Prevention and Convenience Store Robbery," *Security Journal,* **7** (1996): 41–52.
64. All information for this section abstracted from Mary S. Smith, *Crime Prevention through Environmental Design in Parking Facilities,* Research in Brief, for National Institute of Justice (Washington, D.C.: U.S. Government Printing Office, 1996).
65. Patricia Mayhew, Ronald V. Clarke, and David Elliott, "Motorcycle Theft, Helmet Legislation and Displacement," *Howard Journal of Criminal Justice,* **28** (1989): 1–8. For an examination of how preventing repeat victimization can reduce displacement, see Adam C. Bouloukos and Graham Farrell, "On the Displacement of Repeat Victimization," in *Rational Choice and Situational Crime Prevention,* ed. Graeme Newman, Ronald V. Clarke, and S. Giora Shoham (Aldershot, U.K.: Dartmouth, 1997), pp. 219–232.

CHAPTER 10

1. *Crimes of Violence: A Staff Report Submitted to the National Commission on the Causes and Prevention of Violence* (Washington, D.C.: U.S. Government Printing Office, December 1969), vol. 12, p. xxvii; vol. 11, p. 4.
2. G. O. W. Mueller, "Where Murder Begins," *New Hampshire Bar Journal,* **2** (1960): 214–224; G. O. W. Mueller, "On Common Law Mens Rea," *Minnesota Law Review,* **42** (1958): 1043–1104.
3. Wayne R. LaFave and Austin W. Scott, *Handbook on Criminal Law* (St. Paul, Minn.: West, 1972), pp. 572–577.
4. *Commonwealth v. Welansky,* 316 Mass. 383, N.E. 2d 902 (1944), at pp. 906–907. See G. O. W. Mueller, "The Devil May Care—Or Should We? A Reexamination of Criminal Negligence," *Kentucky Law Journal,* **55** (1966–1967): 29–49.
5. Uniform Crime Reports, 2001, p. 19.
6. Ibid., pp. 19–20.
7. Ibid., pp. 22–23.
8. Ibid., p. 22.
9. Roland Chilton, "Twenty Years of Homicide and Robbery in Chicago: The Impact of the City's Changing Racial and Age Composition," *Journal of Quantitative Criminology,* **3** (1987): 195–213. See also Carolyn Rebecca Block, *Homicide in Chicago* (Chicago: Loyola University of Chicago, 1986), p. 7; and William Wilbanks, *Murder in Miami* (Lanham, Md.: University Press of America, 1984).
10. William Julius Wilson, "Work," *New York Times Magazine,* Aug. 18, 1996, pp. 27, 28.
11. William B. Harvey, "Homicide among Young Black Adults: Life in the Subculture of Exasperation," in *Homicide among Black Americans,* ed. Darnell F. Hawkins (Lanham, Md.: University Press of America, 1986), pp. 153–171. See also Robert L. Hampton, "Family Violence and Homicide in the Black Community: Are They Linked?" in *Violence in the Black Family,* ed. Hampton (Lexington, Mass.: Lexington Books, 1987), pp. 135–156.
12. Coramae Richey Mann, "Black Women Who Kill," in *Homicide among Black Americans,* pp. 157–186.
13. Hans von Hentig, *The Criminal and His Victim* (New Haven, Conn.: Yale University Press, 1948).
14. Marvin E. Wolfgang, *Patterns in Criminal Homicide* (Philadelphia: University of Pennsylvania Press, 1958), p. 253. See also Marvin E. Wolfgang, "A Sociological Analysis of Criminal Homicide," in *Studies in Homicide,* ed. Wolfgang (New York: Harper & Row, 1967), pp. 15–28.
15. Richard B. Felson and Steven F. Messner, "Disentangling the Effects of Gender and Intimacy on Victim Precipitation in Homicide," *Criminology,* **36** (1998): 405–423.
16. Robert A. Silverman and Leslie W. Kennedy, "Relational Distance and Homicide: The Role of the Stranger," *Journal of Criminal Law and Criminology,* **78** (1987): 272–308. See also Nanci Koser Wilson, "Gendered Interaction in Criminal Homicide," in *Homicide: The Victim/Offender Connection,* ed. Anna Victoria Wilson (Cincinnati: Anderson, 1993), pp. 43–62.
17. Margaret A. Zahn and Philip C. Sagi, "Stranger Homicides in Nine American Cities," *Journal of Criminal Law and Criminology,* **78** (1987): 377–397.
18. Uniform Crime Reports, 2001, p. 22.
19. Marc Riedel, "Stranger Violence: Perspectives, Issues, and Problems," *Journal of Criminal Law and Criminology,* **78** (1987): 223–258.
20. Kenneth Polk, "Observations on Stranger Homicide," *Journal of Criminal Justice,* **21** (1993): 573–582.

NOTES

21. Coramae Richey Mann, *When Women Kill* (Albany: State University of New York Press, 1996).
22. See, e.g., Colin Loftin, Karen Kindley, Sandra L. Norris, and Brian Wiersema, "An Attribute Approach to Relationships between Offenders and Victims in Homicide," *Journal of Criminal Law and Criminology*, **78** (1987): 259–271.
23. Angela Browne, "Assault and Homicide at Home: When Battered Women Kill," *Advances in Applied Social Psychology*, **3** (1986): 57–79.
24. Martin Daly and Margo Wilson, *Homicide* (New York: Aldine–De Gruyter, 1988), pp. 294–295.
25. Coramae Richey Mann, "Getting Even?: Women Who Kill in Domestic Encounters," *Justice Quarterly*, **5** (1988): 33–51.
26. Martha Smithey, "Infant Homicide: Victim/Offender Relationship and Causes of Death," *Journal of Family Violence*, **13** (1998): 285–297.
27. Ibid.
28. Lawrence A. Greenfeld, *Child Victimizers: Violent Offenders and Their Victims* (Washington, D.C.: Bureau of Justice Statistics, 1996), p. 3.
29. Etienne G. Krug, James A. Mercy, Linda Dahlberg, and Kenneth Powell, "Firearm- and Non-Firearm-Related Homicide among Children: An International Comparison," *Homicide Studies*, **2** (1998): 83–95.
30. Uniform Crime Reports, 2001, p. 24.
31. William R. Holcomb and Anasseril E. Daniel, "Homicide without an Apparent Motive," *Behavioral Sciences and the Law*, **6** (1988): 429–439.
32. See Michael Newton, *Mass Murder: An Annotated Bibliography* (New York: Garland, 1988).
33. N. R. Kleinfield, "Cruelty of Strangers: 3 Men Evoke a Fearsome Trend," *New York Times*, June 23, 1996, p. 27.
34. See http://www.mayhem.net/crime/serial.html.
35. Daniel Klaidman, "The End of the Line," *Newsweek*, July 26, 1999, p. 71.
36. Michael D. Kelleher and C. L. Kelleher, *Murder Most Rare: The Female Serial Killer* (Westport, Conn.: Praeger, 1998).
37. Daniel Pedersen, "Death in Dunblane," *Newsweek*, Mar. 25, 1996, pp. 24–29.
38. U.S. Department of Justice, Bureau of Justice Statistics, *Workplace Violence, 1992–1996* (Washington, D.C.: U.S. Government Printing Office, 1998).
39. Susan Faludi, "Rage of the American Male," *Newsweek*, Aug. 16, 1999, p. 31. See also http://www.cnn.com/US/9908/31/atlanta.shooting.03/.
40. See Dawn N. Castillo and E. Lynn Jenkins, "Industries and Occupations at High Risk for Work-Related Homicide," *Journal of Occupational Medicine*, **36** (1994): 125–132.
41. David Abrahamsen, *The Murdering Mind* (New York: Harper & Row, 1973).
42. Mel Heimer, *The Cannibal: The Case of Albert Fish* (New York: Lyle Stuart, 1971).
43. Margaret Cheney, *The Co-ed Killer* (New York: Walker, 1976).
44. Jack Levin and James Alan Fox, *Mass Murder: America's Growing Menace* (New York: Plenum, 1985). See also Ronald M. Holmes and Stephen T. Holmes, "Understanding Mass Murder: A Starting Point," *Federal Probation*, **56** (1992): 53–61.
45. James Fox and Jack Levin, "Multiple Homicide: Patterns of Serial and Mass Murder," in *Crime and Justice: A Review of Research*, ed. Michael Tonry (Chicago: University of Chicago Press, 1998), pp. 407–455.
46. James Alan Fox and Jack Levin, *Overkill: Mass Murder and Serial Killing Exposed* (New York: Plenum, 1994); and Philip Jenkins, "African-Americans and Serial Homicide," *American Journal of Criminal Justice*, **17** (1993): 47–60.
47. Ronald M. Holmes and James de Burger, *Serial Murder* (Newbury Park, Calif.: Sage, 1988), p. 155.
48. Cheryl L. Maxson, Margaret A. Gordon, and Malcolm W. Klein, "Differences between Gang and Nongang Homicides," *Criminology*, **23** (1985): 209–222.
49. G. David Curry and Irving A. Spergel, "Gang Homicide, Delinquency, and Community," *Criminology*, **26** (1988): 381–405.
50. Range Hutson, Deirdre Anglin, and Marc Eckstein, "Drive-by-Shootings by Violent Street Gangs in Los Angeles: A Five-Year Review from 1989 to 1993," *Academic Emergency Medicine*, **3** (1996): 300–303.
51. Sam Howe Verhovek, "Houston Knows Murder, but This . . . ," *New York Times*, July 9, 1993, p. A8.
52. Groeme Newman, ed., *Global Report on Crime and Justice* (New York: United Nations; Oxford University Press, 1999), p. 50.
53. Uniform Crime Reports, 2001.
54. U.S. Department of Justice, Office of Juvenile Justice and Delinquency Prevention, *Juvenile Offenders and Victims, 1999 National Report* (Washington, D.C.: U.S. Department of Justice, OJJDP, 1999), p. 17. See also Krug et al., "Firearm- and Non-Firearm-Related Homicide among Children."
55. Harvey Krahn, Timothy F. Hartnagel, and John W. Gartrell, "Income Inequality and Homicide Rates: Cross-National Data and Criminological Theories," *Criminology*, **24** (1986): 269–295.
56. Glenn D. Deane, "Cross-National Comparison of Homicide: Age/Sex-Adjusted Rates Using the 1980

57. Dane Archer and Rosemary Gartner, *Violence and Crime in Cross-National Perspective* (New Haven, Conn.: Yale University Press, 1984).
58. Candice Nelsen, Jay Corzine, and Lin Corzine-Huff, "The Violent West Reexamined; A Research Note on Regional Homicide Rates," *Criminology,* **32** (1994): 149–161.
59. See Scott H. Decker, "Exploring Victim-Offender Relationships in Homicide: The Role of Individual and Event Characteristics," *Justice Quarterly,* **10** (1993): 585–612. See also Scott H. Decker, "Reconstructing Homicide Events: The Role of Witnesses in Fatal Encounters," *Journal of Criminal Justice,* **23** (1995): 439–450.
60. David F. Luckenbill, "Criminal Homicide as a Situated Transaction," *Social Problems,* **25** (1977): 176–186. Although Luckenbill focused on homicides, the stages he identified are identical in assaults.
61. For a comprehensive, multidisciplinary review of the literature on violence, see James T. Tedeschi and Richard B. Felson, *Violence, Aggression, and Coercive Actions* (Washington, D.C.: American Psychological Association, 1994). See also Barry R. Ruback and Neil Alan Weiner, eds., *Interpersonal Violent Behaviors: Social and Cultural Aspects* (New York: Springer, 1994).
62. U.S. Department of Justice, Bureau of Justice Statistics, *Criminal Victimization,* 2001 (Washington, D.C.: U.S. Government Printing Office, 2002), p. 3.
63. C. H. Kempe, F. N. Silverman, B. F. Steele, W. Droegemueller, and H. K. Silver, "The Battered-Child Syndrome," *Journal of the American Medical Association,* **181** (1962): 17–24.
64. Elizabeth Pleck, "Criminal Approaches to Family Violence, 1640–1980," in *Family Violence,* ed. Lloyd Ohlin and Michael Tonry, vol. 2 (Chicago: University of Chicago Press, 1989), pp. 19–57.
65. For a special journal issue on the subject of family violence, see Richard J. Gelles, ed., "Family Violence," *Journal of Comparative Family Studies,* **25** (1994): 1–142.
66. Lyn Nell Hancock, "Why Batterers So Often Go Free," *Newsweek,* Oct. 16, 1995, pp. 61–62.
67. Murray A. Straus and Richard J. Gelles, "How Violent Are American Families?: Estimates from the National Family Violence Resurvey and Other Studies," in *Family Abuse and Its Consequences,* ed. Gerald T. Hotaling, David Finkelhor, John T. Kirkpatrick, and Murray A. Straus (Newbury Park, Calif.: Sage, 1988). See also Ann Goetting, *Homicide in Families and Other Special Populations* (New York: Springer, 1995); and Ronet Bachman, *Violence against Women: A National Crime Victimization Survey Report* (Washington, D.C.: U.S. Bureau of Justice Statistics, 1994).
68. Richard B. Felson, "Big People Hit Little People: Sex Differences in Physical Power and Interpersonal Violence," *Criminology,* **34** (1996): 433–452.
69. Straus and Gelles, "How Violent Are American Families?" p. 17.
70. Terrie E. Moffitt and Avshalom Caspi, *National Institute of Justice, Research in Brief, Findings about Partner Violence from the Dunedin Multidisciplinary Health and Development Study* (Washington, D.C.: U.S. Department of Justice, Office of Justice Programs, National Institute of Justice, July 1999).
71. Patrick A. Langan and Christopher A. Innes, *Preventing Domestic Violence against Women,* for U.S. Department of Justice, Bureau of Justice Statistics (Washington, D.C.: U.S. Government Printing Office, 1986).
72. Marvin E. Wolfgang and Franco Ferracuti, *The Subculture of Violence: Toward an Integrated Theory in Criminology* (London: Tavistock, 1967).
73. Joan McCord, "Parental Aggressiveness and Physical Punishment in Long-Term Perspective," in *Family Abuse and Its Consequences,* pp. 91–98.
74. Margery A. Cassidy, "Power-Control Theory: Its Potential Application to Woman Battering," *Journal of Crime and Justice,* **18** (1995): 1–15.
75. Donald G. Dutton, *The Domestic Assault of Women* (Boston: Allyn and Bacon, 1988), p. 15.
76. Lenore E. Walker, *The Battered Woman Syndrome* (New York: Springer Verlag, 1984); Brenda A. Miller, Thomas H. Nochajski, Kenneth E. Leonard, Howard T. Blane, Dawn M. Gondoli, and Patricia M. Bowers, "Spousal Violence and Alcohol/Drug Problems among Parolees and Their Spouses," *Women and Criminal Justice,* **1** (1990): 55–72.
77. Study conducted by Mohammed Ayat, Atiqui Abdelaziz, Najat Kfita, and El Khazouni Zineb, at the request of UNESCO and the Union of Arab Lawyers, Fez, Morocco, 1989.
78. David Levinson, *Family Violence in Cross-Cultural Perspective* (Newbury Park, Calif.: Sage, 1989).
79. Carolyn F. Swift, "Surviving: Women's Strength through Connections," in *Abuse and Victimization across the Life Span,* ed. Martha Straus (Baltimore: Johns Hopkins University Press, 1988), pp. 153–169.
80. See Christine Rasche, "Early Models for Contemporary Thought on Domestic Violence and Women Who Kill Their Mates: A Review of the Literature from 1895 to 1970," *Women and Criminal Justice,* **1** (1990): 31–53.
81. *Thurman v. Torrington,* 596 F. Supp. 1521 (1985).

82. Jeffrey Fagan, *The Criminalization of Domestic Violence: Promises and Limits* (Washington, D.C.: U.S. National Institute of Justice, 1996).
83. Lawrence W. Sherman and Richard A. Berk, "The Minneapolis Domestic Violence Experiment," *Police Foundation Reports,* **1** (1984): 1–8. See also J. David Hirschel, Ira W. Hutchinson, Charles W. Dean, and Anne-Marie Mills, "Review Essay on the Law Enforcement Response to Spouse Abuse: Past, Present and Future," *Justice Quarterly,* **9** (1992): 247–283; Cynthia Grant Bowman, "The Arrest Experiments: A Feminist Critique," *Journal of Criminal Law and Criminology,* **83** (1992): 201–208; Albert R. Roberts, "Psychosocial Characteristics of Batterers: A Study of 234 Men Charged with Domestic Violence Offenses," *Journal of Family Violence,* **2** (1987): 81–93; Donald G. Dutton and Susan K. Golant, *The Batterer: A Psychological Profile* (New York: Basic Books, 1995); Lisa A. Frisch, "Research That Succeeds, Policies That Fail," *Journal of Criminal Law and Criminology,* **83** (1992): 209–216; David B. Mitchell, "Contemporary Police Practices in Domestic Violence Cases: Arresting the Abuser: Is It Enough?" *Journal of Criminal Law and Criminology,* **83** (1992): 241–249; and Lawrence W. Sherman, Janell D. Schmidt, Dennis P. Rogan, Patrick R. Gartlin, Ellen G. Cohn, Dean J. Collins, and Anthony R. Bacich, "From Initial Deterrence to Long-Term Escalation: Short Custody Arrest for Poverty Ghetto Domestic Violence," *Criminology,* **29** (1991): 821–850.
84. Lawrence W. Sherman, Janell D. Schmidt, Dennis P. Rogan, Douglas A. Smith, Patrick R. Gartlin, Ellen G. Cohn, Dean J. Collins, and Anthony R. Bacich, "The Variable Effects of Arrest on Criminal Careers: The Milwaukee Domestic Violence Experiment," *Journal of Criminal Law and Criminology,* **83** (1992): 137–169. See also J. David Hirschel and Ira W. Hutchinson III, "Female Spouse Abuse and the Police Response: The Charlotte, North Carolina, Experiment," *Journal of Criminal Law and Criminology,* **83** (1992): 73–119.
85. Joan Zorza, "The Criminal Law of Misdemeanor Domestic Violence, 1970–1990," *Journal of Criminal Law and Criminology,* **83** (1992): 46–72. See also Candace Kruttschnitt and Maude Dornfeld, "Will They Tell? Assessing Preadolescents' Reports of Family Violence," *Journal of Research in Crime and Delinquency,* **29** (1992): 136–147.
86. National Child Abuse and Neglect Data System (NCANDS) Children's Bureau, Administration on Children, Youth, and Families, U.S. Department of Human Services, Summary Findings, 2002.
87. Ibid.
88. Edna Erez and Pamela Tontodonato, "Patterns of Reported Parent-Child Abuse and Police Response," *Journal of Family Violence,* **4** (1989): 143–159.
89. Cathy Spatz Widom and M. Ashley Ames, "Criminal Consequences of Childhood Sexual Victimization," *Child Abuse and Neglect,* **18** (1994): 303–318; Carolyn Smith and Terence P. Thornberry, "The Relationship between Childhood Maltreatment and Adolescent Involvement in Delinquency," *Criminology,* **33** (1995): 451–481.
90. U.S. Department of Justice, OJJDP, *Juvenile Offenders and Victims, 1999 National Report,* p. 41.
91. Ibid.
92. Kathleen Brewer, Daryl Rowe, and Devon Brewer, "Factors Related to Prosecution of Child Sexual Abuse Cases," *Journal of Child Sexual Abuse,* **6** (1997): 91–111.
93. Deborah Daro, "Half Full and Half Empty: The Evaluation of Results of Nineteen Clinical Research and Demonstration Projects," *Summary of Nineteen Clinical Demonstration Projects Funded by the National Center on Child Abuse and Neglect, 1978–81* (Berkeley: University of California, School of Social Welfare, 1986).
94. See Candace Kruttschnitt and Maude Dornfeld, "Childhood Victimization, Race, and Violent Crime," *Criminal Justice and Behavior,* **18** (1991): 448–463.
95. See "The Basics: What Is Elder Abuse?" at www.gwjapan.com/NCEA/basic/index.html (accessed online Sept. 19, 1999).
96. *U.S. Bureau of the Census, Statistical Abstract of the United States: 1994* (Washington, D.C.: U.S. Government Printing Office, 1994).
97. Craig J. Forsyth and Robert Gramling, "Elderly Crime: Fact and Artifact," in *Older Offenders,* ed. Belinda McCarthy and Robert Langworthy (New York: Praeger, 1988), pp. 3–13.
98. Mildred Daley Pagelow, "The Incidence and Prevalence of Criminal Abuse of Other Family Members," in Ohlin and Tonry, *Family Violence,* p. 267.
99. Jordan I. Kosberg and Juanita L. Garcia, eds., "Elder Abuse: International and Cross-Cultural Perspectives," *Journal of Elder Abuse and Neglect,* **6** (1995): 1–197.
100. See Mark Whatley, "For Better or Worse: The Case of Marital Rape," *Violence and Victims,* **8** (1993): 29–39.
101. Susan Brownmiller, *Against Our Will: Men, Women, and Rape* (New York: Simon & Schuster, 1975), pp. 1–9.
102. Duncan Chappell, "Sexual Criminal Violence," in *Pathways to Criminal Violence,* ed. Neil Alan Weiner and Marvin E. Wolfgang (Newbury Park, Calif.: Sage, 1989), pp. 68–108.
103. Uniform Crime Reports, 2001, pp. 14, 29. For a special issue devoted to an overview of adult sexual assault, see *Journal of Social Issues,* **48** (1992):

1–195, with an Introduction by Susan B. Sorenson and Jacqueline W. White.
104. Ibid., p. 31.
105. Menachem Amir, *Patterns in Forcible Rape* (Chicago: University of Chicago Press, 1977), pp. 233–234.
106. U.S. Department of Justice, Bureau of Justice Statistics, *Highlights from 20 Years of Surveying Crime Victims* (Washington, D.C.: U.S. Government Printing Office, 1993), p. 24.
107. Whatley, "For Better or Worse."
108. Ida Johnson and Robert Sigler, *Forced Sexual Intercourse in Intimate Relationships* (Brookfield, Vt.: Ashgate, 1997).
109. Clark Staten, "Roofies, The New Date Rape Drug of Choice," Jan. 6, 1996 (see http://www.emergency.com/roofies.htm).
110. M. P. Koss, C. A. Gidycz, and N. Wisniewski, "The Scope of Rape: Incidence and Prevalence of Sexual Aggression and Victimization in a National Sample of Higher Education Students," *Journal of Consulting and Clinical Psychology,* **55** (1987): 162–170.
111. Uniform Crime Reports 1998, p. 199.
112. James L. LeBeau, "Patterns of Stranger and Serial Rape Offending: Factors Distinguishing Apprehended and At Large Offenders," *Journal of Criminal Law and Criminology,* **78** (1987): 309–326.
113. J. Marolla and D. Scully, *Attitudes toward Women, Violence, and Rape: A Comparison of Convicted Rapists and Other Felons* (Rockville, Md.: National Institute of Mental Health, 1982).
114. Christine Alder, "An Exploration of Self-Reported Sexually Aggressive Behavior," *Crime and Delinquency,* **31** (1985): 306–331; P. R. Sanday, "The Socio-Cultural Context of Rape: A Cross-Cultural Study," *Journal of Social Issues,* **37** (1981): 5–27.
115. Julia R. Schwendinger and Herman Schwendinger, *Rape and Inequality* (Beverly Hills, Calif.: Sage, 1983), p. 220.
116. M. Dwayne Smith and Nathan Bennett, "Poverty, Inequality, and Theories of Forcible Rape," *Crime and Delinquency,* **31** (1985): 295–305.
117. Ruth D. Peterson and William C. Bailey, "Forcible Rape, Poverty, and Economic Inequality in U.S. Metropolitan Communities," *Journal of Quantitative Criminology,* **4** (1988): 99–119.
118. Matthew Hale, *History of the Pleas of the Crown,* vol. 1 (London, 1736), p. 635.
119. Martin D. Schwartz and Todd R. Clear, "Toward a New Law on Rape," *Crime and Delinquency,* **26** (1980): 129–151.
120. Patricia Frazier and Beth Haney, "Sexual Assault Cases in the Legal System: Police, Prosecutor, and Victim Perspectives," *Law and Human Behavior,* **20** (1996): 607–628.
121. Christian Berthelsen, "Women Are Speaking Out to Heal Trauma of Rape," *New York Times,* Apr. 4, 1999, p. 19, Section 1.
122. Cassia C. Spohn and Julie Horney, "The Impact of Rape Law Reform on the Processing of Simple and Aggravated Cases," *Journal of Criminal Law and Criminology,* **86** (1996): 861–884; Gilbert Geis, "Rape-in-Marriage: Law and Law Reform in England, the United States, and Sweden," *Adelaide Law Review,* **6** (1978): 284–303; Joel Epstein and Stacia Langenbahn, *The Criminal Justice and Community Response to Rape* (Washington, D.C.: U.S. National Institute of Justice, 1994).
123. Janet Gornick, Martha R. Burt, and Karen J. Pittman, "Structures and Activities of Rape Crisis Centers in the Early 1980's," *Crime and Delinquency,* **31** (1985): 247–268.
124. Alexis Chiu, "Dad Pleads Guilty to Kidnapping," May 28, 1999 (see http://more.abcnews.go.com/sections/us/DailyNews/father990527.html).
125. John Cloud, "Most Likely to Succeed," *Time,* Apr. 26, 1999, p. 72.
126. U.S. Department of Justice, *Report to the Nation on Crime and Justice,* 2d ed. (Washington, D.C.: U.S. Government Printing Office, 1988), p. 97.
127. Uniform Crime Reports, 1998.
128. U.S. Department of Justice, Bureau of Justice Statistics, *Criminal Victimization in the United States,* 1991 (Washington, D.C.: U.S. Government Printing Office, 1992), p. 76.
129. John Conklin, *Robbery and the Criminal Justice System* (Philadelphia: Lippincott, 1972), pp. 59–78.
130. Uniform Crime Reports, 1998, p. 31.
131. Terry L. Baumer and Michael D. Carrington, *The Robbery of Financial Institutions,* for U.S. Department of Justice (Washington, D.C.: U.S. Government Printing Office, 1986).
132. Uniform Crime Reports, 1994, p. 27.
133. Philip J. Cook, "Is Robbery Becoming More Violent?: An Analysis of Robbery Murder Trends since 1968," *Journal of Criminal Law and Criminology,* **76** (1985): 480–489.
134. John Lehmann and Al Guart, "Ciao: Gotti Gang Gone," *New York Post,* June 21, 2002, p. 5.
135. William Balsamo and George Carpozi Jr., *Under the Clock: The Inside Story of the Mafia's First 100 Years* (Far Hills, N.J.: New Horizon Press, 1988). Some legal historians trace the appearance of organized crime in the United States to the early 1860s; see Humbert S. Nelli, "A Brief History of

American Syndicate Crime," in *Organized Crime in America: Concepts and Controversies,* ed. Timothy S. Bynum (Monsey, N.Y.: Criminal Justice Press, 1987). See also Richard Gambino, *Blood of My Blood: The Dilemma of the Italian American* (Garden City, N.Y.: Doubleday, 1974), p. 3; Luigi Barzini, "Italians in New York: The Way We Were in 1929," *New York Magazine,* Apr. 4, 1977, p. 36; Howard Abadinsky, *Organized Crime,* 2d ed. (Chicago: Nelson Hall, 1985).

136. Abadinsky, *Organized Crime,* pp. 43–53.
137. Ibid., p. 91. For a description of some of the more colorful characters of the Prohibition era, see David E. Ruth, *Inventing the Public Enemy* (Chicago: University of Chicago Press, 1996); Joseph McNamara, "Dapper Bootlegger," *New York Daily News,* Oct. 15, 1995, p. 42; Charles Rappleye and Ed Becker, *All American Mafioso: The Johnny Roselli Story* (New York: Barricade Books, 1995); Mary M. Stolberg, *Fighting Organized Crime: Politics, Justice, and the Legacy of Thomas E. Dewey* (Boston: Northeastern University Press, 1995); Colin Wilson, Ian Schott, Ed Shedd, et al., *World Famous Crimes* (New York: Carroll & Graf, 1995); Jay Robert Nash, *World Encyclopedia of Organized Crime* (New York: Paragon House, 1992); Robert J. Schoenberg, *Mr. Capone: The Real and Complete Story of Al Capone* (New York: William Morrow, 1992); Robert Lacey, *Little Man: Meyer Lansky and the Gangster Life* (Boston: Little, Brown, 1991).
138. James Inciardi, *Careers in Crime* (Chicago: Rand McNally, 1975), p. 113; Norman Lewis, *The Honored Society: A Searching Look at the Mafia* (New York: Putnam, 1964), p. 25.
139. For a European perspective on the harms generated by the Sicilian Mafia, see John Follain, *A Dishonoured Society: Sicilian Mafia's Threat to Europe* (London: Little, Brown, 1995); Brian Freemantle, *The Octopus: Europe in the Grip of Organized Crime* (London: Orion Books, 1995). For a description of the Sicilian Mafia's reach into the former Soviet Union, see Werner Raith, *Das Neue Mafia-Kartell: Wie de Syndikate den Osten Erober* (The New Mafia Cartel: How the Syndicates Conquer the East) (Berlin: Rowohlt, 1994). For a global perspective, see Phil Williams and Ernesto U. Savona, "Problems and Dangers Posed by Organized Transnational Crime in the Various Regions of the World," *Transnational Organized Crime,* **1** (1995): 1–42; Louise I. Shelley, "Transnational Organized Crime: An Imminent Threat to the Nation-State?" *Journal of International Affairs,* **48** (1995): 463–489; Raimondo Catanzaro, *Men of Respect: A Social History of the Sicilian Mafia* (New York: Free Press, 1992); Pino Arlacchi, *Men of Dishonor: Inside the Sicilian Mafia* (New York: William Morrow, 1992). For a description of how the Sicilian Mafia attempted to join forces with the Colombian cocaine cartels, see William Gately and Yvette Fernandez, *Dead Ringer: An Insider's Account of the Mob's Colombian Connection* (New York: Donald I. Fine, 1994); Abadinsky, *Organized Crime,* pp. 56–62.
140. Ronald Goldfarb, *Perfect Villains, Imperfect Heros: Robert F. Kennedy's War against Organized Crime* (New York: Random House, 1995); Annelise Graebner Anderson, *The Business of Organized Crime: A Cosa Nostra Family* (Stanford, Calif.: Hoover Institution Press, 1979); Peter Maas, *The Valachi Papers* (New York: Putnam, 1968); U.S. Senate Committee on Governmental Affairs, Subcommittee on Investigations, *Organized Crime: 25 Years after Valachi* (Washington, D.C.: U.S. Government Printing Office, 1990).
141. Jay Albanese, *Organized Crime in America* (Cincinnati: Anderson, 1985), p. 25. See also Francis A. J. Ianni, *A Family Business: Kinship and Social Control in Organized Crime* (New York: Russell Sage, 1972); Joseph Albini, *The American Mafia: Genesis of a Legend* (New York: Irvington, 1971); Merry Morash, "Organized Crime," in *Major Forms of Crime,* ed. Robert F. Meier (Beverly Hills, Calif.: Sage, 1984), pp. 191–220. For a response, see Claire Sterling, *Octopus: The Long Reach of the International Sicilian Mafia* (New York: W. W. Norton, 1990); Ralph Blumenthal, *Last Days of the Sicilians: At War with the Mafia* (New York: Pocket Books, 1994). See also Shana Alexander, *The Pizza Connection* (New York: Weidenfeld & Nicolson, 1988).
142. For a perceptive analysis of the changing focus of the two most recent commission reports, see Jay S. Albanese, "Government Perceptions of Organized Crime: The Presidential Commissions, 1967 and 1987," *Federal Probation,* **52** (1988): 58–63.
143. For a popular account of how a Sicilian Mafia associate infiltrated and almost destroyed one of the largest movie studios in Hollywood, see "The Predator: How an Italian Thug Looted MGM, Brought Credit Lyonnais to Its Knees, and Made the Pope Cry," *Fortune,* July 8, 1996, p. 128. Despite the denial of generations of Italian and Sicilian organized-crime figures concerning the trafficking of illegal narcotics, criminologists have discussed the involvement of all major American syndicates; see Peter A. Lupsha, "La Cosa Nostra in Drug Trafficking," in Bynum, *Organized Crime in America.*

See also Dwight Smith, *The Mafia Mystique* (New York: Basic Books, 1975).

144. P. Beseler, Wayne Brewer, and Julienne Salzano, "Focus on Environmental Crimes," *FBI Law Enforcement Bulletin,* **64** (1995): 1–26; Joel Epstein, Theodore M. Hammett, and Laura Collins, *Law Enforcement Response to Environmental Crime* (Washington, D.C.: U.S. National Institute of Justice, 1995). For a global perspective on environmental stability, see Norman Myers, *Ultimate Security: The Environmental Basis of Political Stability* (New York: W. W. Norton & Company, 1993). For a uniquely Italian organized-crime perspective on the illegal disposal of toxic wastes throughout the United States, see Frank R. Scarpitti and Alan A. Block, "America's Toxic Waste Racket: Dimensions of the Environmental Crisis," in Bynum, *Organized Crime in America*. For a discussion of predicting which legitimate businesses will be infiltrated by organized crime, see Jay S. Albanese, "Predicting the Incidence of Organized Crime: A Preliminary Model," in Bynum, *Organized Crime in America,* pp. 103–114.

145. Past efforts to develop civil and criminal causes of action against corporations are found in RICO legislation. See Racketeer Influenced and Corrupt Organizations (RICO) Provisions of the Organized Crime Control Act of 1970 [Act of Oct. 15, 1970, Public Law 91-452, Section 901(a), 84 Stat. 941, 18 U.S.C. §§ 1961 through 1968, effective Oct. 15, 1970, as amended Nov. 2, 1978, Public Law 95-575, Sec. 3 (c), 92 Stat. 2465, and Nov. 6, 1978, Public Law 95-598, Sec. 314(g), 92 Stat. 2677]. For a discussion of the pros and cons of RICO, see Donald J. Rebovich, "Use and Avoidance of RICO at the Local Level: The Implementation of Organized Crime Laws," in *Contemporary Issues in Organized Crime,* ed. Jay Albanese (Monsey, N.Y.: Criminal Justice Press, 1995).

146. Fred Montanino, "Protecting Organized Crime Witnesses in the United States," *International Journal of Comparative and Applied Criminal Justice,* **14** (1990): 123–131.

147. For a description of the contemporary leadership of New York's five Italian-American organized-crime families, see Jeffrey Goldberg, "The Mafia's Morality Crisis," *New York Magazine,* Jan. 9, 1995, p. 22. See also Donald Cressey, *Theft of the Nation* (New York: Harper & Row, 1969).

148. Abadinsky, *Organized Crime,* pp. 8–23; Donald Cressey, in President's Commission, *Task Force Report,* pp. 7–8; Gay Talese, *Honor Thy Father* (New York: World, 1971).

149. For a discussion of "Commission" membership, mores, and dispute resolution, see William F. Roemer Jr., *Accardo: The Genuine Godfather* (New York: Donald I. Fine, 1995); Sidney Zion, *Loyalty and Betrayal: The Story of the American Mob* (San Francisco: Collins, 1994); John H. Davis, *Mafia Dynasty: The Rise and Fall of the Gambino Crime Family* (New York: HarperCollins, 1993); Sam Giancana and Chuck Giancana, *Double Cross: The Explosive, Inside Story of the Mobster Who Controlled America* (New York: Warner Books, 1992); John Cummings and Ernest Volkman, *Goombata: The Improbable Rise and Fall of John Gotti and His Gang* (Boston: Little, Brown, 1990).

150. *United States v. Bonanno,* 180 F. Supp. 71 (S.D.N.Y. 1960), upholding the Apalachin roundup as constitutional; *United States v. Bonanno,* 177 F. Supp. 106 (S.D.N.Y. 1959), sustaining the validity of the conspiracy indictment; *United States v. Bufalino,* 285 F. 2d 408 (2d Cir. 1960), reversing the conspiracy conviction.

151. James Walston, "Mafia in the Eighties," *Violence, Aggression, and Terrorism,* **1** (1987): 13–39. For a look into organized crime's once mighty and still lingering hand on gambling in the United States, see Jay Albanese, "Casino Gambling and Organized Crime: More Than Reshuffling the Deck," in Albanese, *Contemporary Issues in Organized Crime;* Ronald A. Farrelland and Carole Case, *The Black Book and the Mob: The Untold Story of the Control of Nevada's Casinos* (Madison: University of Wisconsin Press, 1995); Nicholas Pileggi, *Casino: Love and Honor in Las Vegas* (New York: Simon & Schuster, 1995); David Johnston, *Temples of Chance: How America Inc. Bought Out Murder Inc. to Win Control of the Casino Business* (New York: Doubleday, 1992).

152. Organized-crime activities are certainly not limited to local communities. Rather, an ever-evolving organized-crime syndicate feeds off ever-increasing global opportunities; see Petrus van Duyne and Alan A. Block, "Organized Cross-Atlantic Crime: Racketeering in Fuels," *Crime, Law and Social Change,* **22** (1995): 127–147; Umberto Santino, "The Financial Mafia: The Illegal Accumulation of Wealth and the Financial-Industrial Complex," *Contemporary Crises,* **12** (1988): 203–243.

153. For a description of the damage inflicted on society by contemporary Russian organized-crime figures, see New York State Organized Crime Task Force, New York State Commission of Investigation, New Jersey State Commission of Investigation, *An Analysis of Russian-Émigré Crime in the Tri-State Region* (White Plains, N.Y.: New York State

NOTES

Organized Crime Task Force, June 1996); Dennis J. Kenny and James O. Finckenauer, *Organized Crime in America* (Belmont, Calif.: Wadsworth, 1995).

154. Robert J. Kelly and Rufus Schatzberg, "Galvanizing Indiscriminate Political Violence: Mind-Sets and Some Ideological Constructs in Terrorism," *International Journal of Comparative and Applied Criminal Justice,* **16** (1992): 15–41; Jeffrey D. Simon, *The Terrorist Trap: America's Experience with Terrorism* (Bloomington: Indiana University Press, 1993); Brent L. Smith and Gregory P. Orvis, "America's Response to Terrorism: An Empirical Analysis of Federal Intervention Strategies during the 1980s," *Justice Quarterly,* **10** (1993): 661–681.

155. Cindy Combs, *Terrorism in the Twenty-First Century* (Upper Saddle River, N.J.: Prentice-Hall, 1997).

156. See "Bin-Laden Still Sought a Year after Embassy Bombings in Africa," Aug. 6, 1999 (http://cnn.com/US/9908/06/embassy.bombings).

157. See "Blast in Moscow Mall Wounds 33," Aug. 31, 1999 (http://www.cnn.com/wysiwgy://partner/55/http://cnn...europe/9908/31/moscow.blast.08/).

158. Dennis Pluchinsky, "Terrorism in the Former Soviet Union: A Primer, a Puzzle, a Prognosis," *Studies in Conflict and Terrorism,* **21** (1998): 119–147.

159. Harvey J. Iglarsh, "Terrorism and Corporate Costs," *Terrorism,* **10** (1987): 227–230.

160. Ariel Merari, Tamar Prat, Sophia Kotzer, Anat Kurz, and Yoram Schweitzer, *Inter 85: A Review of International Terrorism in 1985* (Boulder, Colo.: Westview, 1986), p. 106.

161. Noemi Gal-Or, *International Cooperation to Suppress Terrorism* (New York: St. Martin's Press, 1985), pp. 90–96.

162. "A Cloud of Terror and Suspicion," *Newsweek,* Apr. 3, 1995, pp. 36–41. See also Stewart A. Wright, ed., *Armageddon in Waco: Critical Perspectives on the Branch Davidian Conflict* (Chicago: University of Illinois Press, 1995).

163. James Brooke, "Wyoming City Braces for Gay Murder Trial," *New York Times,* Apr. 4, 1999, p. 14.

164. Sylvester Monroe, "A Burning in Alabama," *Time,* Mar. 15, 1999, p. 47.

165. Frank Gibney, Jr., "The Kids Got in the Way," *Time,* Aug. 23, 1999, p. 22.

166. Federal Bureau of Investigation, *Hate Crime Statistics 1998* www.fbi.gov/vcr/98hate.pdf.

167. Matt Bai and Vern E. Smith, "Evil to the End," *Newsweek,* Mar. 8, 1999, p. 22.

168. Rebecca Leung, "Hate Crimes in America: Texas Killing Spotlights Nation's Racial Divide," June 17, 1999 (see http://abcnews.go.com/sections/us/DailyNews/hatecrimes980611.html).

169. For discussions of recent events that have shaped the philosophy of militias, see Alan W. Bock, *Ambush at Ruby Ridge: How Government Agents Set Randy Weaver Up and Took His Family Down* (Irvine, Calif.: Dickens Press, 1995).

170. Morris Dees and James Corcoran, *Gathering Storm: America's Militia Threat* (New York: Harper Collins, 1996).

171. Michael Winerip, "Ohio Case Typifies the Tensions between Militia Groups and the Law," *New York Times,* June 23, 1996, p. 1.

172. "The View from the Far Right," *Newsweek,* May 1, 1995, pp. 36–39.

173. Ibid.

174. Gordon Crew and Reid Countes, *The Evolution of School Disturbance in America: Colonial Times to Modern Day* (Westport, Conn.: Praeger, 1997).

175. T. Trent Gepax, Jerry Adler, and Daniel Pedarion, "The Boys behind the Ambush," *Newsweek,* Apr. 6, 1998, pp. 20–24; Geoffrey Cowley, "Why Children Turn Violent," *Newsweek,* Apr. 6, 1998, pp. 24–26; Nadya Lobi, "The Hunter and the Choirboy," *Time,* Apr. 6, 1998, pp. 28–37; Richard Lacayo, "Toward the Root of the Evil," *Time,* Apr. 6, 1998, pp. 38–39.

176. Sam Howe Verhovek, "Sounds from a Massacre: 'Oh God, Kids, Stay Down,' " *New York Times,* Apr. 24, 1999, p. 1.

177. Tammerlin Drummond, "Battling the Columbine Copycats," *Time,* May 10, 1999, p. 29.

178. Vincent Schiraldi, "Hype Aside, School Violence Is Declining." This report appeared in *Newsday, The Washington Post,* and other media, Sept. 30, 1998.

179. U.S. Departments of Education and Justice, *1998 Annual Report on School Safety* (Washington, D.C.: U.S. Department of Education and Justice, 1999), p. 9.

180. Mary Jo Nolin, Elizabeth Davies, and Kathryn Chandler, "Student Victimization at School," *Journal of School Health,* **66** (1996): 216.

181. Samuel Walker, *Sense and Nonsense about Crime and Drugs: A Policy Guide,* 4th ed. (Belmont, Calif.: West/Wadsworth, 1998).

182. Richard Woodbury, "Taking Back the School," *Time,* Aug. 16, 1999, pp. 32–33.

183. Claudia Kalb, "Schools on the Alert," *Newsweek,* Aug. 23, 1999, pp. 42–44.

184. John Cloud, "What Can the Schools Do?" *Time,* May 3, 1999, pp. 38–40.

185. U.S. Department of Justice, Office of Justice Programs, *Promising Strategies to Reduce Gun Violence* (Washington, D.C.: Office of Juvenile

186. Matt Bai, "Caught in the Cross-Fire," *Newsweek,* June 28, 1999, pp. 31–32.
187. Sam Howe Verhovek, "2 Youths Wanted to 'Destroy the School,' Sheriff Says," *New York Times,* Apr. 23, 1999, p. 1.
188. Roger Rosenblatt, "Get Rid of the Damned Things," *Time,* Aug. 9, 1999, pp. 38–39.
189. Marianne W. Zawitz, *Guns Used in Crime* (Washington, D.C.: Bureau of Justice Statistics, 1995), p. 2.
190. Walker, *Sense and Nonsense about Crime and Drugs.*
191. Ibid.
192. See Martin Killias, "International Correlations between Gun Ownership and Rates of Homicide and Suicide," *Canadian Medical Association Journal,* **148** (1993): 1721–1776; Peter J. Carrington and Sharon Moyer, "Gun Availability and Suicide in Canada: Testing the Displacement Hypothesis," *Studies on Crime and Crime Prevention,* **3** (1994): 168–178.
193. Marianne W. Zawitz, *Firearm Injury from Crime* (Washington, D.C.: Bureau of Justice Statistics, 1996), p. 4.
194. Robert D. McFadden, "On a Bus in Queens, Three Bandits Stage a Frontier Robbery," *New York Times,* July 31, 1993, p. 1.
195. Alan J. Lizotte, James M. Tesoriero, Terence P. Thornberry, et al., "Patterns of Adolescent Firearms Ownership and Use," *Justice Quarterly,* **11** (1994): 51–74.
196. *Juvenile Offenders and Victims, 1999 National Report,* p. 69.
197. Joseph F. Sheley, "Drugs and Guns among Inner-City High School Students," *Journal of Drug Education,* **24** (1994): 303–321.
198. M. Dwayne Smith and Joseph F. Sheley, "The Possession and Carrying of Firearms among a Sample of Inner-City High School Females," *Journal of Crime and Justice,* **18** (1995): 109–128.
199. Jon D. Hull, "A Boy and His Gun," *Time,* Aug. 2, 1993.
200. Alan J. Lizotte, James M. Tesoriero, Terence P. Thornberry, et al., "Patterns of Adolescent Firearms Ownership and Use." See also Joseph F. Sheley and James D. Wright, *In the Line of Fire: Youth, Guns, and Violence in Urban America* (Hawthorne, N.Y.: Aldine de Gruyter, 1995); Joseph F. Sheley and Victoria E. Brewer, "Possession and Carrying of Firearms among Suburban Youth," *Public Health Reports,* **110** (1995): 18–26.
201. James B. Jacobs and Kimberly A. Potter, "Comprehensive Handgun Licensing and Registration: An Analysis and Critique of Brady II, Gun Control's Next (and Last?) Step," *Journal of Criminal Law and Criminology,* **89** (1998): 81–110.
202. U.S. Department of Justice, OJJDP, *Juvenile Offenders and Victims, 1999 National Report,* p. 69.
203. Glenn L. Pierce and William J. Bowers, "The Bartley-Fox Gun Law's Short-Term Impact on Crime in Boston," *Annals of the American Academy of Political and Social Science,* **455** (1981): 120–137.
204. Patrick W. O'Carroll, Colin Loftin, John B. Waller Jr., David McDowall, Allen Bukoff, Richard O. Scott, James A. Mercy, and Brian Wiersema, "Preventing Homicide: An Evaluation of the Efficacy of a Detroit Gun Ordinance," *American Journal of Public Health,* **81** (1991): 576–581.
205. Lawrence W. Sherman, James W. Shaw, and Dennis P. Rogan, *The Kansas City Gun Experiment* (Washington, D.C.: U.S. National Institute of Justice, 1995).
206. James A. Beha II, "And Nobody Can Get You Out: The Impact of a Mandatory Prison Sentence for the Illegal Carrying of a Firearm on the Administration of Criminal Justice in Boston," *Boston University Law Review,* **57** (1977): 96–146, 289–333.
207. Colin Loftin, Milton Heumann, and David McDowall, "Mandatory Sentencing and Firearms Violence: Evaluating an Alternative to Gun Control," *Law and Society Review,* **17** (1983): 288–318.
208. Michael Janofsky, "Fighting Crime by Making Federal Case about Guns," *New York Times,* Feb. 10, 1999, p. A12.
209. Elaine Shannon, "Have Gun? Will Travel," *Time,* Aug. 16, 1999, p. 30.
210. Janofsky, "Fighting Crime by Making Federal Case about Guns."
211. Colin Loftin, David McDowall, Brian Wiersema, and Talbert J. Cottey, "Effects of Restrictive Licensing of Handguns on Homicide and Suicide in the District of Columbia," *New England Journal of Medicine,* **325** (1991): 1615–1620.
212. U.S. Department of the Treasury, Bureau of Alcohol, Tobacco and Firearms, *Implementation of the Brady Law,* (Washington, D.C.: U.S. Government Printing Office September 1999).
213. U.S. Department of Justice, Bureau of Justice Statistics, *Presale Handgun Checks, the Brady Interim Period, 1994–1998* (Washington, D.C.: U.S. Government Printing Office, June 1999).
214. David McDowall and Alan Lizotte, "Gun Control," in *Introduction to Social Problems,* ed. Craig Calhoun and George Ritzer (New York: Primis Database, McGraw-Hill, 1993).
215. Marjolijn Bijlefeld, ed., *The Gun Control Debate: A Documentary History* (Westport, Conn.: Greenwood Press, 1997).

216. John A. Arthur, "Criminal Victimization, Fear of Crime, and Handgun Ownership among Blacks: Evidence from National Survey Data," *American Journal of Criminal Justice,* **16** (1992): 121–141; Gary S. Green, "Citizen Gun Ownership and Criminal Deterrence: Theory, Research, and Policy," *Criminology,* **25** (1987): 63–81; John A. Arthur, "Gun Ownership among Women Living in One-Adult Households," *International Journal of Comparative and Applied Criminal Justice,* **18** (1994): 249–263; and Wilbur Edel, *Gun Control: Threat to Liberty or Defense against Anarchy?* (Westport, Conn.: Praeger, 1995).
217. *Concealed Carry: The Criminal's Companion. Florida's Concealed Weapons Law—A Model for the Nation?* (Washington, D.C.: Violence Policy Center, 1995).
218. Fox Butterfield, "America under the Gun," *New York Times,* Sept. 16, 1999 (see http://www.nytimes.com/library/national/091699guns-overview.html).

CHAPTER 11

1. J. W. Cecil Turner, *Kenny's Outlines of Criminal Law,* 2d ed. (Cambridge, Mass.: Cambridge University Press, 1958), p. 238.
2. Jerome Hall, *Theft, Law, and Society* (Indianapolis: Bobbs-Merrill, 1935).
3. Uniform Crime Reports, 2001, p. 48.
4. U.S. Department of Justice, Bureau of Justice Statistics, *Criminal Victimization* 2001 (Washington, D.C.: U.S. Government Printing Office, 2001), p. 3.
5. Uniform Crime Reports, 2001, p. 51.
6. See Abraham S. Blumberg, "Typologies of Criminal Behavior," in *Current Perspectives on Criminal Behavior,* 2d ed., ed. Blumberg (New York: Knopf, 1981).
7. See John Hepburn, "Occasional Criminals," in *Major Forms of Crime,* ed. Robert Meier (Beverly Hills, Calif.: Sage, 1984), pp. 73–94; and John Gibbs and Peggy Shelly, "Life in the Fast Lane: A Retrospective View by Commercial Thieves," *Journal of Research in Crime and Delinquency,* **19** (1982): 299–330, at p. 327.
8. James Inciardi, "Professional Thief," in Meier, *Major Forms of Crime,* p. 224. See also Harry King and William Chambliss, *Box Man—A Professional Thief's Journal* (New York: Harper & Row, 1972).
9. *The Professional Thief,* annotated and interpreted by Edwin H. Sutherland (Chicago: University of Chicago Press, 1937).
10. Jo-Ann Ray, "Every Twelfth Shopper: Who Shoplifts and Why?" *Social Casework,* **68** (1987): 234–239. For a discussion of who gets caught and what kinds of treatment programs exist, see Gail A. Caputo, "A Program of Treatment for Adult Shoplifters," *Journal of Offender Rehabilitation* **27** (1998): 123–137.
11. Abigail Buckle and David P. Farrington, "An Observational Study of Shoplifting," *British Journal of Criminology,* **24** (1984): 63–73.
12. Donald Hartmann, Donna Gelfand, Brent Page, and Patrice Walder, "Rates of Bystander Observation and Reporting of Contrived Shoplifting Incidents," *Criminology,* **10** (1972): 247–267.
13. *1998–1999 Retail Theft Trends Report: Executive Summary* (Winter Park, Fla.: Loss Prevention Specialists, 1999).
14. P. James Carolin Jr., "Survey of Shoplifters," *Security Management,* **36** (1992): 11–12.
15. Pia Salmelainen, *The Correlates of Offending Frequency: A Study of Juvenile Theft Offenders in Detention* (Sydney, Australia: New South Wales Bureau of Crime Statistics and Research, 1995).
16. Mary Owen Cameron, *The Booster and the Snitch* (New York: Free Press, 1964). See also John Rosecrance, "The Stooper: A Professional Thief in the Sutherland Manner," *Criminology,* **24** (1986): 29–40.
17. Richard Moore, "Shoplifting in Middle America: Patterns and Motivational Correlates," *International Journal of Offender Therapy and Comparative Criminology,* **28** (1984): 53–64. See also Charles A. Sennewald and John H. Christman, *Shoplifting* (Boston: Butterworth-Heinemann, 1992).
18. Trevor N. Gibbens, C. Palmer, and Joyce Prince, "Mental Health Aspects of Shoplifting," *British Medical Journal,* **3** (1971): 612–615.
19. Hayes, *1998–1999 Retail Theft Trends Report.*
20. Ibid.
21. Barry Poyner and Ruth Woodall, *Preventing Shoplifting: A Study in Oxford Street* (London: Police Foundation, 1987).
22. John Carroll and Frances Weaver, "Shoplifters' Perceptions of Crime Opportunities: A Process-Tracing Study," in *The Reasoning Criminal,* ed. Derek Cornish and Ronald V. Clarke (New York: Springer Verlag, 1986), pp. 19–38.
23. Joshua Bamfield, "Retail Civil Recovery: Filling a Deficit in the Criminal Justice System?" *International Journal of Risk Security and Crime Prevention,* **3** (1998): 257–267.
24. Truc-Nho Ho, "Prevention of Art Theft at Commercial Art Galleries," *Studies on Crime and Crime Prevention,* **7** (1998): 213–219. See also "FBI—Major Investigations—National Stolen Art File" (http://www.fbi.gov/majcases/arttheft/art.htm).
25. See Truc-Nhu Ho, *Art Theft in New York City: An Exploratory Study in Crime Specificity,* Ph.D. dissertation, Rutgers University, 1992; Christopher

Dickey, "Missing Masterpieces," *Newsweek*, May 29, 1989, pp. 65–68.
26. Truc-Nhu Ho, "Prevention of Art Theft at Commercial Galleries."
27. Winnie Hu, "11 Arrested in Video Piracy Crackdown," *New York Times*, Aug. 21, 1999, p. B3.
28. Truc-Nho Ho, "Prevention of Art Theft at Commercial Art Galleries."
29. Uniform Crime Reports, 2001.
30. Ibid., p. 53.
31. Ibid., p. 238.
32. See Charles McCaghy, Peggy Giordano, and Trudy Knicely Henson, "Auto Theft," *Criminology*, **15** (1977): 367–385.
33. See http://www.lojack.com/theft.htm.
34. National Insurance Crime Bureau, "Vehicle Theft Booming in Port and Border Communities; People Should Be More Vigilant Than Ever, Warns NICB," press release, Apr. 30, 2002 (http://www.nicb.org/services/notspotsrelease.html).
35. Kevin Blake, "What You Should Know about Car Theft," *Consumer's Research* (October 1995): 26–28.
36. U.S. Department of Justice, Bureau of Justice Statistics, *Carjackings in the United States, 1992–1996* (Washington, D.C.: U.S. Government Printing Office, 1999), p. 1.
37. Eric Peters, "Anti–Car Theft System Starts in Virginia: D.C., Maryland Next," *Washington Times*, Aug. 13, 1993, p. G2.
38. Lawman Armor Corporation, *New BRAKEthrough Anti-Theft Device from Lawman Armor Corporation Puts the Brakes on Auto Theft*, press release, Sept. 16, 1999 (http://www.biz.yahoo.com/prnews/990917/pa_lawman_1.html).
39. See "The Silent Scorpion" (http://www.carjacking.com).
40. See "The Watch Your Car Program" (http://www.ojp.usdoj.gov/BJA/html/wycfaq.htm).
41. Ronald V. Clarke, "Situational Crime Prevention: Theoretical Basis and Practical Scope," in *Crime and Justice: An Annual Review of Research*, vol. 4, ed. Michael Tonry and Norval Morris (Chicago: University of Chicago Press, 1983).
42. Jeffrey Peck, G. O. W. Mueller, and Freda Adler, "The Vulnerability of Ports and Marinas to Vessel and Equipment Theft," *Security Journal*, **5** (1994): 146–153.
43. Edwin Lemert, "An Isolation and Closure Theory of Naive Check Forgery," *Journal of Criminal Law, Criminology, and Police Science*, **44** (1953–1954): 296–307.
44. Johannes Knutsson and Eckart Kuhlhorn, "Macro Measures against Crime: The Example of Check Forgeries," in *Situational Crime Prevention: Successful Case Studies*, 2d ed., ed. Ronald V. Clarke (Albany, N.Y.: Harrow and Heston, 1997).
45. W. A. Watts, "Credit Card Fraud: Policing Plastic," *Journal of Financial Crime*, **7** (1999): 67–69.
46. Richard Greer, "The Georgia 100," *Atlanta Constitution*, May 19, 1996, p. 13G.
47. Michael Levi and Jim Handley, *A Research and Statistics Directorate Report: The Prevention of Plastic and Cheque Fraud Revisited* (London: Home Office, 1998).
48. Barry Masuda, "Card Fraud: Discover the Possibilities," *Security Management*, **36** (1992): 71–74.
49. Pierre Tremblay, "Designing Crime," *British Journal of Criminology*, **26** (1986): 234–253.
50. Levi and Handley, *A Research and Statistics Directorate Report*.
51. Leonard Sloane, "Rising Fraud Worrying Car Insurers," *New York Times*, Nov. 16, 1991, p. 48.
52. Michael Clarke, "The Control of Insurance Fraud," *British Journal of Criminology*, **30** (1990): 1–23.
53. Sloane, "Rising Fraud Worrying Car Insurers."
54. Edmund J. Pankan and Frank E. Krzeszowski, "Putting a Claim on Insurance Fraud," *Security Management*, **37** (1993): 91–94.
55. P. Jesilow, H. N. Pontell, and G. Geis, "Physician Immunity from Prosecution and Punishment for Medical Program Fraud," in *Punishment and Privilege*, ed. W. B. Groves and G. R. Newman (New York: N.Y. Harrow and Heston, 1987), p. 8.
56. H. N. Pontell, P. Jesilow, and G. Geis, "Policing Physicians: Practitioner Fraud and Abuse in a Government Medical Program," *Social Problems*, **30** (1982): 117–125.
57. See Yahoo! News, Sept. 15, 1999 (http://www.dailynews.yahoo.com).
58. Larry E. Coutorie, "The Future of High-Technology Crime: A Parallel Delphi Study," *Journal of Criminal Justice*, **23** (1995): 13–27.
59. "Survey Finds Computer Crime Widespread in Corporate America," *The News and Observer*, Raleigh, N.C., Oct. 25, 1995.
60. Natalie D. Voss, "Crime on the Internet," *Jones Telecommunications and Multimedia Encyclopedia*, Drive D: \ Studios, Jones Digital Century (1996). (Found on the Internet at http://www.digitalcentury.com/encyclo/update/crime.html)
61. Marc Goodman, "Why the Police Don't Care about Computer Crime," *Harvard Journal of Law and Technology*, **10** (1997): 465–494.
62. Richard Overill, "Denial of Service Attacks: Threats and Methodologies," *Journal of Financial Crime*, **6** (1999): 351–353.

63. See Yahoo! News, "Employer Beware . . . National Survey Cites Employees as Significant Contributors to Software Piracy in the Workplace," Sept. 16, 1999 (http://www.biz.yahoo.com/bw/990916/dc_bsa_1.html).
64. Brad Stone, "A High Technology Crash," *Newsweek,* Oct. 4, 1999, p. 54.
65. Stephen Labaton, "Net Sites Co-Opted by Pornographers," *New York Times,* Sept. 23, 1999, p. 1.
66. Goodman, "Why the Police Don't Care about Computer Crime."
67. Robert W. Taylor, "Computer Crime," in *Criminal Investigation,* ed. C. R. Swanson, N. C. Chamelin, and L. Tersito (New York: Random House, 1991).
68. Coutorie, "The Future of High-Technology Crime."
69. Kenneth C. Sears and Henry Weihofen, *May's Law of Crimes,* 4th ed. (Boston: Little, Brown, 1948), pp. 307–317.
70. Uniform Crime Reports, 2001.
71. Neal Shover, "Structures and Careers in Burglary," *Journal of Criminal Law and Criminology,* **63** (1972): 540–549.
72. Scott Decker, Richard Wright, Allison Redfern, and Dietrich Smith, "A Woman's Place Is in the Home: Females and Residential Burglary," *Justice Quarterly,* **10** (1993): 143–162.
73. Darrell Steffensmeier, *The Fence: In the Shadow of Two Worlds* (Totowa, N.J.: Rowman & Littlefield, 1986), p. 7.
74. Carl Klockars, *The Professional Fence* (New York: Free Press, 1976), pp. 110, 113.
75. D'Aunn Webster Avery, Paul F. Cromwell, and James N. Olson, "Marketing Stolen Property: Burglars and Their Fences," paper presented at the 1988 Annual Meeting of the American Society of Criminology, Reno, Nev.
76. Uniform Crime Reports, 2001, p. 56.
77. Patrick G. Jackson, "Assessing the Validity of Official Data on Arson," *Criminology,* **26** (1988): 181–195.
78. Uniform Crime Reports, 2001, p. 56.
79. Michael J. Karter, Jr., "Fire Loss in the United States in 1993," *NFPA Journal,* **88** (1994): 59, 62, 64.
80. Uniform Crime Reports, 2001.
81. See Rebecca K. Hersch, *A Look at Juvenile Firesetter Programs,* for U.S. Department of Justice, Office of Justice Programs, Office of Juvenile Justice and Delinquency Prevention (Washington, D.C.: U.S. Government Printing Office, May 1989), p. 1.
82. Uniform Crime Reports, 2001.
83. Ibid.
84. Irving Kaufman and Lora W. Heims, "A Reevaluation of the Dynamics of Firesetting," *American Journal of Orthopsychiatry,* **31** (1961): 123–136.
85. Hersch, *A Look at Juvenile Firesetter Programs.*
86. Wayne S. Wooden and Martha Lou Berkey, *Children and Arson* (New York: Plenum, 1984), p. 3.
87. See Jessica Gaynor and Chris Hatcher, *The Psychology of Child Firesetting* (New York: Brunner/Mazel, 1987).
88. Howard F. Jackson, Susan Hope, and Clive Glass, "Why Are Arsonists Not Violent Offenders?" *International Journal of Offender Therapy and Comparative Criminology,* **31** (1987): 143–151.
89. See Wayne W. Bennett and Karen Matison Hess, *Investigating Arson* (Springfield, Ill.: Charles C Thomas, 1984), pp. 34–38.
90. John M. Macdonald, *Bombers and Firesetters* (Springfield, Ill.: Charles C Thomas, 1977), pp. 198–204.
91. See Federal Emergency Management Agency, U.S. Fire Administration, *Interviewing and Counseling Juvenile Firesetters* (Washington, D.C.: U.S. Government Printing Office, 1979).
92. Clifford L. Karchmer, *Preventing Arson Epidemics: The Role of Early Warning Strategies,* Aetna Arson Prevention Series (Hartford, Conn.: Aetna Life & Casualty, 1981).
93. "Third United Nations Survey of Crime Trends, Operations of Criminal Justice Systems and Crime Prevention Strategies," A/CONF. 144/6, July 27, 1990.

CHAPTER 12

1. Matthew L. Wald, "Airline Pleads Guilty to Illegal Storage of Hazardous Waste," *New York Times,* Dec. 17, 1999, p. 27; "ValuJet Jury Got It Right," *Chicago Tribune,* Dec. 17, 1999, p. 16.
2. Marshall B. Clinard and Peter C. Yeager, *Corporate Crime* (New York: Free Press, 1980), pp. 59–60.
3. Sally S. Simpson, "Strategy, Structure, and Corporate Crime: The Historical Context of Anticompetitive Behavior," in *Advances in Criminological Theory,* vol. 4, ed. Freda Adler and William S. Laufer (New Brunswick, N.J.: Transaction, 1993), pp. 71–93. See also Melissa Baucus and Terry Moorehead-Dworkin, "What Is Corporate Crime? It Is Not Illegal Corporate Behavior," *Law and Policy,* **13** (1991): 231–244; Ron Boostrom, *Enduring Issues in Criminology* (San Diego, Calif.: Greenhaven Press, 1995).
4. Edwin H. Sutherland, "White Collar Criminality," *American Sociological Review,* **5** (1940): 1–20.
5. Gilbert Geis, *On White Collar Crime* (Lexington, Mass.: Lexington Books, 1982), p. 9.

6. Marshall B. Clinard and Richard Quinney, *Criminal Behavior Systems,* 2d ed. (New York: Holt, Rinehart & Winston, 1982); Marshall B. Clinard, *Corporate Corruption: The Abuse of Power* (Westport, Conn.: Praeger, 1990); Gilbert Geis and Paul Jesilow, eds., "White-Collar Crime," *Annals of the American Academy of Political and Social Science,* **525** (1993): 8–169; David Weisburd, Stanton Wheeler, and Elin Waring, *Crimes of the Middle Classes: White-Collar Offenders in the Federal Courts* (New Haven, Conn.: Yale University Press, 1991); John Braithwaite, "Poverty, Power, White-Collar Crime and the Paradoxes of Criminological Theory," *Australian and New Zealand Journal of Criminology,* **24** (1991): 40–48; Frank Pearce and Laureen Snider, eds., "Crimes of the Powerful," *Journal of Human Justice,* **3** (1992): 1–124; Hazel Croall, *White Collar Crime: Criminal Justice and Criminology* (Buckingham, England: Open University Press, 1991); Stephen J. Rackmill, "Understanding and Sanctioning the White Collar Offender," *Federal Probation,* **56** (1992): 26–33; Brent Fisse, Michael Bersten, and Peter Grabosky, "White Collar and Corporate Crime," *University of New South Wales Law Journal,* **13** (1990): 1–171; Susan P. Shapiro, "Collaring the Crime Not the Criminal: Reconsidering the Concept of White-Collar Crime," *American Sociological Review,* **55** (1990): 346–365; Kip Schlegel and David Weisburd, eds., *White-Collar Crime Reconsidered* (Boston: Northeastern University Press, 1992); David Weisburd, Stanton Wheeler, Elin Waring, et al., *Crimes of the Middle Classes: White-Collar Offenders in the Federal Courts* (New Haven, Conn.: Yale University Press, 1991); David Weisburd, Ellen F. Chayet, and Elin J. Waring, "White-Collar Crime and Criminal Careers: Some Preliminary Findings," *Crime and Delinquency,* **36** (1990): 342–355; David Weisburd, Elin Waring, and Stanton Wheeler, "Class, Status, and the Punishment of White-Collar Criminals," *Law and Social Inquiry,* **15** (1990): 223–243; Lisa Maher and Elin J. Waring, "Beyond Simple Differences: White Collar Crime, Gender and Workforce Position," *Phoebe,* **2** (1990): 44–54; John Hagan and Fiona Kay, "Gender and Delinquency in White-Collar Families: A Power-Control Perspective," *Crime and Delinquency,* **36** (1990): 391–407.

7. See James W. Coleman, *The Criminal Elite: The Sociological White-Collar Crime,* 2d ed. (New York: St. Martin's Press, 1989); and Michael L. Benson and Elizabeth Moore, "Are White-Collar and Common Offenders the Same? An Empirical and Theoretical Critique of a Recently Proposed General Theory of Crime," *Journal of Research in Crime and Delinquency,* **29** (1992): 251–272. See also Lori A. Elis and Sally S. Simpson, "Informal Sanction Threats and Corporate Crime: Additive versus Multiplicative Models," *Journal of Research in Crime and Delinquency,* **32** (1995): 399–424. For a view of white-collar offending in which the risks and rewards are considered by potential offenders, see David Weisburd, Elin Waring, and Ellen Chayet, "Specific Deterrence in a Sample of Offenders Convicted of White-Collar Crimes," *Criminology,* **33** (1995): 587–605.

8. Not only are governments at all levels victimized by corporate crimes, governments of all nations are also victimized; see Karlhans Liebl, "Developing Trends in Economic Crime in the Federal Republic of Germany," *Police Studies,* **8** (1985): 149–162. See also Jurg Gerber and Susan L. Weeks, "Women as Victims of Corporate Crime: A Call for Research on a Neglected Topic," *Deviant Behavior,* **13** (1992): 325–347; Elizabeth Moore and Michael Mills, "The Neglected Victims and Unexamined Costs of White-Collar Crime," *Crime and Delinquency,* **36** (1990): 408–418.

9. August Bequai, *White Collar Crime: A 20th-Century Crisis* (Lexington, Mass.: Lexington Books, 1978), p. 3; Linda Ganzini, Bentson McFarland, and Joseph Bloom, "Victims of Fraud: Comparing Victims of White Collar and Violent Crime," *Bulletin of the American Academy of Psychiatry and the Law,* **18** (1990): 55–63.

10. For the relationship between patterns of crimes in the savings and loan industry and those in organized crime, see Kitty Calavita and Henry N. Pontell, "Savings and Loan Fraud as Organized Crime: Toward a Conceptual Typology of Corporate Illegality," *Criminology,* **31** (1993): 519–548.

11. For an international perspective on consumer fraud, see U.S. Senate Committee on Governmental Affairs, *International Consumer Fraud: Can Consumers Be Protected?* (Washington, D.C.: U.S. Government Printing Office, 1994); Gilbert Geis, Henry N. Pontell, and Paul Jesilow, "Medicaid Fraud," in *Controversial Issues in Criminology and Criminal Justice,* ed. Joseph E. Scott and Travis Hirschi (Beverly Hills, Calif.: Sage, 1987); Maria S. Boss and Barbara Crutchfield George, "Challenging Conventional Views of White Collar Crime: Should the Criminal Justice System Be Refocused?" *Criminal Law Bulletin,* **28** (1992): 32–58. See also Richard M. Titus, Fred Heinzelmann, and John M. Boyle, "Victimization of Persons by Fraud," *Crime and Delinquency,* **41** (1995): 54–72. For a description of fraud in an organizational setting presented from

the perspective of the perpetrator, fellow employees, and the organization itself, see Steve W. Albrecht, Gerald W. Wernz, and Timothy L. Williams, *Fraud: Bringing Light to the Dark Side of Business* (Burr Ridge, Ill.: Irwin Professional Publishing, 1995).
12. For an outline of a general theory of crime causation applicable to both street crime and white-collar crime, see Travis Hirschi and Michael Gottfredson, "Causes of White-Collar Crime," *Criminology,* **25** (1987): 949–974; James W. Coleman, "Toward an Integrated Theory of White Collar Crime," *American Journal of Sociology,* **93** (1987): 406–439; and James R. Lasley, "Toward a Control Theory of White Collar Offending," *Journal of Quantitative Criminology,* **4** (1988): 347–362.
13. Donald R. Cressey, "The Poverty of Theory in Corporate Crime Research," in *Advances in Criminological Theory,* vol. 1, ed. William Laufer and Freda Adler (New Brunswick, N.J.: Transaction, 1989); for a response, see John Braithwaite and Brent Fisse, "On the Plausibility of Corporate Crime Theory," in *Advances in Criminological Theory,* vol. 2, ed. William Laufer and Freda Adler (New Brunswick, N.J.: Transaction, 1990). See also Travis Hirschi and Michael Gottfredson, "The Significance of White-Collar Crime for a General Theory of Crime," *Criminology,* **27** (1989): 359–371; and Darrell Steffensmeier, "On the Causes of 'White Collar' Crime: An Assessment of Hirschi and Gottfredson's Claims," *Criminology,* **27** (1989): 345–358.
14. Bequai, *White Collar Crime.* Bequai also includes antitrust and environmental offenses, which are corporate crimes, discussed in the next section.
15. Kenneth Polk and William Weston, "Insider Trading as an Aspect of White Collar Crime," *Australian and New Zealand Journal of Criminology,* **23** (1990): 24–38. In a report before Congress, insider trading scandals were said to have cost the securities industry nearly half a billion dollars in the early 1970s; see U.S. Congress House Select Committee on Crime, *Conversion of Worthless Securities into Cash* (Washington, D.C.: U.S. Government Printing Office, 1973). For a review of the insider trading that persists on Wall Street, see Gene G. Marcial, *Secrets of the Street: The Dark Side of Making Money* (New York: McGraw-Hill, 1995); Martin Mayer, *Nightmare on Wall Street: Salomon Brothers and the Corruption of the Marketplace* (New York: Simon & Schuster, 1993); Nancy Reichman, "Insider Trading," in Michael Tonry and Albert J. Reiss Jr., eds., *Beyond the Law: Crime in Complex Organizations* (Chicago: University of Chicago Press, 1993).
16. For a more extensive review of the Wedtech debacle, see Mark S. Hamm, "From Wedtech and Iran-Contra to the Riots at Oakdale and Atlanta: On the Ethics and Public Performance of Edwin Meese III," *Journal of Crime and Justice,* **14** (1991): 123–147; Marilyn W. Thompson, *Feeding the Beast: How WedTech Became the Most Corrupt Little Company in America* (New York: Charles Scribner's Sons, 1990); William Power, "New York Rep. Biaggi and Six Others Indicted as Wedtech Scandal Greatly Expands," *The Wall Street Journal,* June 4, 1987, p. 9.
17. See http://www.fas.org/man/gao/gao9621.htm.
18. For a discussion of the many ways in which a person may be defrauded, see Phil Berger and Craig Jacob, *Twisted Genius: Confessions of a $10 Million Scam Man* (New York: Four Walls Eight Windows, 1995). For an Australian perspective of fraud, see M. Kapardis and A. Kapardis, "Co-regulation of Fraud Detection and Reporting by Auditors in Australia: Criminology's Lessons for Non-compliance," *Australian and New Zealand Journal of Criminology,* **28** (1995): 193–212.
19. Bequai, *White Collar Crime,* pp. 70–71.
20. For a European perspective on insurance fraud, with a particular focus on the enforcement activities in France and Belgium, see Andre Lemaitre, Rolf Lemaitre, Rolf Arnold, and Roger Litton, "Insurance and Crime," *European Journal on Criminal Policy,* **3** (1995): 7–92. For a description of insurance fraud prevalent in the American insurance industry, see Kenneth D. Myers, *False Security: Greed & Deception in America's Multibillion-Dollar Insurance Industry* (Amherst, N.Y.: Prometheus Books, 1995); Andrew Tobias, *The Invisible Banker* (New York: Washington Square Press, 1982).
21. Paul E. Tracy and James A. Fox, "A Field Experiment on Insurance Fraud in Auto Body Repair," *Criminology,* **27** (1989): 589–603.
22. Kathleen F. Brickey, *Corporate Criminal Liability,* 2 vols. (Wilmette, Ill.: Callaghan, 1984). See also Thomas Gabor, *Everybody Does It! Crime by the Public* (Toronto: University of Toronto Press, 1994). For a uniquely British perspective, see Doreen McBarnet, "Whiter Than White Collar Crime: Tax, Fraud, Insurance and the Management of Stigma," *British Journal of Sociology,* **42** (1991): 323–344.
23. Alan Murray, "IRS Is Losing Battle against Tax Evaders Despite Its New Gain," *The Wall Street Journal,* Apr. 10, 1984, p. 1.
24. Ralph Salerno and John S. Tompkins, "Protecting Organized Crime," in *Theft of the City,* ed. John A. Gardiner and David Olson (Bloomington: Indiana University Press, 1984); Edwin Sutherland, *The*

Professional Thief (Chicago: University of Chicago Press, 1937).
25. 18 U.S.C. § 166(b) and (c).
26. Bequai, *White Collar Crime*, p. 45.
27. Ibid., p. 87. See Virginia Department of Social Services, *Report of the Financial Exploitation of Older Adults and Disabled Younger Adults in the Commonwealth* (Richmond, Va.: Senate Document no. 37, 1994). For steps to take to avoid being a victim of embezzlement, see Russell B. Bintliff, *Complete Manual of White Collar Crime Detection and Prevention* (Englewood Cliffs, N.J.: Prentice Hall, 1993). For a historic account of embezzlement in the United Kingdom from 1845 to 1929, see George Robb, *White Collar Crime in Modern England: Financial Fraud and Business Morality, 1845–1929* (Cambridge: Cambridge University Press, 1992).
28. John Clark and Richard Hollinger, *Theft by Employees in Work Organization* (Washington, D.C.: U.S. Government Printing Office, 1983).
29. Bequai, *White Collar Crime*, p. 89.
30. M. David Ermann and Richard J. Lundman, "Corporate and Governmental Deviance: Origins, Patterns, and Reactions," in *Corporate and Governmental Deviance: Problems of Organizational Behavior in Contemporary Society*, 3d ed., ed. M. David Ermann and Richard J. Lundman (New York: Oxford University Press, 1996). A school of thought holds that, unlike people, corporations have no personality, no conscience, and no shame. See, for example, Thomas Donaldson, *Corporations and Morality* (Englewood Cliffs, N.J.: Prentice-Hall, 1982); Donald R. Cressey, "The Poverty of Theory in Corporate Crime Research," in *Advances in Criminological Theory*, vol 1. Over 100 years ago a New York court in *Darlington v. The Mayor,* 31 N.Y. 164 (1865), observed: "A corporation, as such, has no human wants to be supplied. It cannot eat, drink, or wear clothing, or live in houses." Steven Walt and William S. Laufer, "Corporate Criminal Liability and the Comparative Mix of Sanctions," in *White-Collar Crime Reconsidered,* ed. Kip Schlegel and David Weisburd (Boston: Northeastern University Press, 1992), describe corporations as being given a life and a moral personhood that clouds the distinction between crimes attributable to individuals (hourly employees, line managers, corporate officers, etc.) and those attributable to the corporate entity. John Braithwaite and Brent Fisse, "On the Plausibility of Corporate Crime Theory," in *Advances in Criminological Theory*, vol. 2.
31. William S. Laufer, *Corporate Bodies and Guilty Minds, Emory Law Journal,* **43** (1994): 647, 651–58 (discusses origins of corporate criminal liability).
32. See generally Richard S. Gruner, *Corporate Crime and Sentencing* (1994).
33. William S. Laufer, *Corporate Liability, Risk Shifting, and the Paradox of Compliance, Vanderbilt Law Review,* **52** (1999): 1343.
34. William S. Laufer, *Culpability and the Sentencing of Corporations, Nebraska Law Review,* 71 (1992): 1049.
35. Marshall Clinard, Peter C. Yeager, Jeanne Brissette, David Petrashek, and Elizabeth Harries, *Illegal Corporate Behavior* (1979).
36. Nearly a century ago D. R. Richberg asked the question, "Should it not be the effort of all legislation dealing with corporations, to place them as nearly as possible on a plane of equal responsibility with individuals?" D. R. Richberg, "The Imprisonment of the Corporation," *Case and Comment,* **18** (1912): 512–529. Saul M. Pilchen discovered that although notions of corporate criminal culpability have been broadened over the years, initial prosecutions under the federal sentencing guidelines for organizations generally have been limited in scope. Saul M. Pilchen, "When Corporations Commit Crimes: Sentencing under the Federal Organizational Guidelines," *Judicature,* **78** (1995): 202–206. Daniel R. Fischel and Alan O. Sykes, "Corporate Crime," *The Journal of Legal Studies,* **xxv** (1996): 319–349. Ronald L. Dixon believes, "No corporation should be unaware of these statutes or of the theories upon which criminal liability can be established. Corporations must realize that no one is immune from criminal liability, and corporate practices must reflect this fact." Ronald L. Dixon, "Corporate Criminal Liability," in *Corporate Misconduct: The Legal, Societal, and Management Issues,* ed. Margaret P. Spencer and Ronald R. Sims (Westport, Conn.: Quorum Books, 1995). For a British perspective on corporate liability, see "Great Britain, The Law Commission," in *Criminal Law: Involuntary Manslaughter: A Consultation Paper,* no. 135 (London: Her Majesty's Stationery Office, 1994). For a general overview of the corporate crime problem, see Francis T. Cullen, William J. Maakestad, and Gray Cavender, *Corporate Crime under Attack: The Ford Pinto Case and Beyond* (Cincinnati: Anderson, 1987), pp. 37–99.
37. Sherman Antitrust Act, Act of July 2, 1890, c. 647, 26 Stat. 209, 15 U.S.C. §§ 1–7 (1976).
38. Clayton Antitrust Act, Act of Oct. 15, 1914, c. 322, 38 Stat. 730, 15 U.S.C. §§ 12–27 (1976);

NOTES

Robinson-Patman Act, Act of June 19, 1936, c. 592, § 1, 49 Stat. 1526, 15 U.S.C. § 13(a) (1973). See also Brickey, *Corporate Criminal Liability*.

39. Phillip Knightly, Harold Evans, Elaine Potter, and Marjorie Wallace, *Suffer the Children: The Story of Thalidomide* (New York: Viking, 1979).

40. The Ford Pinto case is fully described in Cullen et al., *Corporate Crime under Attack*. For more information on crimes against consumer safety, see Raymond J. Michalowski, *Order, Law, and Crime* (New York: Random House, 1985), pp. 334–340. For a description of corporate greed in its most vile form, see James S. Kunen, *Reckless Disregard: Corporate Greed, Government Indifference, and the Kentucky School Bus Crash* (New York: Simon & Schuster, 1994).

41. For an examination of corporate criminality in the United States and the response of the criminal justice system of America, see Spencer and Sims, *Corporate Misconduct*. See also Russell Mokhiber, *Corporate Crime and Violence: Big Business Power and the Abuse of the Public Trust* (San Francisco: Sierra Club, 1988); Susan P. Shapiro, *Wayward Capitalists: Target of the Securities and Exchange Commission* (New Haven, Conn.: Yale University Press, 1984); M. David Ermann and Richard J. Lundman, *Corporate and Governmental Deviance: Problems of Organizational Behavior in Contemporary Society*, 2d ed. (New York: Oxford University Press, 1982); Cullen et al., *Corporate Crime under Attack*; Knightly et al., *Suffer the Children*; and W. Byron Groves and Graeme Newman, *Punishment and Privilege* (New York: Harrow & Heston, 1986).

42. See Edwin Sutherland, *White Collar Crime* (1946). Sutherland had earlier published articles on the topic, including "White Collar Criminality," *American Sociological Review*, **5** (1940): 1–12, and "Is White Collar Crime 'Crime'?" *American Sociological Review*, **10** (1945): 132–139.

43. See Gary E. Reed and Peter Cleary Yeager, "Organizational Offending and Neoclassical Criminology: Challenging the Reach of a General Theory of Crime," *Criminology*, **34** (1996): 357–382; Clinard and Yeager, *Corporate Crime*, p. 116. See also Peter C. Yeager, "Analysing Corporate Offences: Progress and Prospects," *Research in Corporate Social Performance and Policy*, **8** (1986): 93–120. For similar findings in Canada, see Colin H. Goff and Charles E. Reasons, *Corporate Crime in Canada* (Scarborough, Ontario: Prentice-Hall, 1978).

44. Richard Quinney, *Critique of Legal Order: Crime Control in Capitalist Society* (Boston: Little, Brown, 1974); Richard Quinney, *Class, State, and Crime: On the Theory and Practice of Criminal Justice* (New York: David McKay, 1977); Ian Taylor, Paul Walton, and Jock Young, *The New Criminology: For a Social Theory of Deviance* (London: Routledge & Kegan Paul, 1973); William Chambliss and Robert Seidman, *Law, Order, and Power,* 2d ed. (Reading, Mass.: Addison-Wesley, 1982).

45. James Q. Wilson, *Thinking about Crime* (New York: Basic Books, 1975). For a competing school of thought, see Gilbert Geis, "Criminal Penalties for Corporate Criminals," *Criminal Law Bulletin,* **8** (1972): 377–392; Chamber of Commerce of the United States, *White Collar Crime* (Washington, D.C.: U.S. Government Printing Office, 1974); John Collins Coffee Jr., "Beyond the Shut-Eyed Sentry: Toward a Theoretical View of Corporate Misconduct and an Effective Legal Response," *Virginia Law Review,* **63** (1977): 1099–1278; Gilbert Geis and Robert F. Meier, *White-Collar Crime: Offenses in Business, Politics, and the Professions* (New York: Free Press, 1977); Marshall B. Clinard, *Illegal Corporate Behavior* (Washington, D.C.: U.S. Government Printing Office, 1979); Miriam S. Saxon, *White-Collar Crime: The Problem and the Federal Response* (Report no. 80-84 EPW, Library of Congress, Congressional Research Service, Washington, D.C., Apr. 14, 1980); Laura S. Schrager and James F. Short Jr., "How Serious a Crime? Perceptions of Organizational and Common Crimes," in *White-Collar Crime: Theory and Research,* ed. Gilbert Geis and Ezra Stotland (Beverly Hills, Calif.: Sage, 1980). Contemporary works include James W. Coleman, *The Criminal Elite: The Sociology of White-Collar Crime* (New York: St. Martin's Press, 1989); Laureen Snider, "The Regulatory Dance: Understanding Reform Processes in Corporate Crime," *International Journal of the Sociology of Law,* **19** (1991): 209–236; Kip Schlegel and David Weisburd, *White-Collar Crime: The Parallax View* (Boston: Northeastern University Press, 1993); Michael Tonry and Albert J. Reiss, *Beyond the Law: Crime in Complex Organizations* (Chicago: University of Chicago Press, 1993); Robert Tillman and Henry Pontell, "Organizations and Fraud in the Savings and Loan Industry," *Social Forces,* **73** (1995): 1439–1463.

46. Patsy Klaus and Carol Kalish, *The Severity of Crime,* Bureau of Justice Statistics Bulletin NCJ-92326 (Washington, D.C.: U.S. Government Printing Office, 1984). See also Schrager and Short, "How Serious a Crime?" Francis Cullen, B. Link, and C. Polanzi, "The Seriousness of Crime Revisited," *Criminology,* **20**

(1982): 83–102; Francis Cullen, R. Mathers, G. Clark, and J. Cullen, "Public Support for Punishing White Collar Crime: Blaming the Victim Revisited," *Journal of Criminal Justice,* **11** (1983): 481–493; Richard Sparks, Hazel G. Genn, and David Dodd, *Surveying Victims* (New York: Wiley, 1977).

47. Mark A. Cohen, "Environmental Crime and Punishment: Legal/Economic Theory and Empirical Evidence on Enforcement of Federal Environmental Statutes," *Journal of Criminal Law and Criminology,* **82** (1992): 1054–1108. See, for an early treatment, Timothy R. Young, "Criminal Liability under the Refuse Act of 1899 and the Refuse Act Permit Program," *Journal of Criminal Law, Criminology and Police Science,* **63** (1972): 366–376. For a global perspective on the prevention of environmental crimes, see Boon Khoo Hui, Prathan Watanavanich, Edgar Aglipay, et al., *Effective Countermeasures against Crimes Related to Urbanization and Industrialization: Urban Crime, Juvenile Delinquency and Environmental Crime* (Tokyo: Report for 1993 and Resource Material Series no. 45, UNAFEI, 1994).

48. Clinard and Yeager, *Corporate Crime,* p. 92, citing *New York Times* survey of July 15, 1979.

49. Gerhard O. W. Mueller, "Offenses against the Environment and Their Prevention: An International Appraisal," *Annals of the American Academy of Political and Social Science,* **444** (1979): 56–66.

50. 33 U.S.C. § 1251 (2001).

51. *United States v. Darling Int'l Inc.,* No. CR 4-96-162 (D. Minn. July 10, 1997) (factual basis statement, plea agreement, and sentencing stipulations on file with author); see also Barry Shanoff, "Company Incriminates Employees: Darling International." *World Wastes* **40** (1997): 64,65 ("The Darling case is part of a pattern throughout the country. Companies under scrutiny are winning leniency for themselves by 'giving up' their employees."); Tom Meersman, "Company Fined $4 Million for Polluting," *Star Tribune,* Dec. 17, 1996, p. 1B ("[S]ome of the most serious charges resulted from the company 'blowing the whistle on itself.'"); Dean Starkman, "Pollution Case Highlights Tend to Let Employees Take the Rap," *The Wall Street Journal,* Oct. 9, 1997, p. B10 ("What happened in the Darling case is being repeated across the country. Corporations under government investigation are increasingly turning on their employees to win leniency for themselves.")

52. Defendent's Sentencing Memorandum, at 8–9 (on file with author).

53. Mueller, "Offenses against the Environment," p. 60.

54. Ryuichi Hirano, "The Criminal Law Protection of Environment: General Report," Tenth International Congress of Comparative Law, Budapest, 1978. For a discussion of the problems of multinational corporations operating in developing countries, see Richard Schaffer, Beverly Earle, and Filiberto Agusti, *International Business Law and Its Environment,* 2d ed. (St. Paul, Minn.: West, 1993). For a discussion of corporate crime in Japan, see Harold R. Kerbo and Mariko Inoue, "Japanese Social Structure and White Collar Crime: Recruit Cosmos and Beyond," *Deviant Behavior,* **11** (1990): 139–154.

55. Kerbo and Inoue, "Japanese Social Structure and White Collar Crime."

56. John Braithwaite, "Challenging Just Deserts: Punishing White-Collar Criminals," *Journal of Criminal Law and Criminology,* **73** (1982): 723–763; Stanton Wheeler, David Weisburd, and Nancy Boden, "Sentencing the White-Collar Offender," *American Sociological Review,* **47** (1982): 641–659. For a thoughtful analysis of corporate illegality, see Nancy Frank and Michael Lombness, *Corporate Illegality and Regulatory Justice* (Cincinnati: Anderson, 1988); Kip Schlegel, *Just Deserts for Corporate Criminals* (Boston: Northeastern University Press, 1990); and John C. Coffee Jr., Mark A. Cohen, Jonathan R. Macey, et al., "A National Conference on Sentencing of the Corporation," *Boston University Law Review,* **71** (1991): 189–453.

57. Sally S. Simpson and Christopher S. Koper, "Deterring Corporate Crime," *Criminology,* **30** (1992): 347–375; Genevra Richardson, *Policing Pollution: A Study of Regulation and Enforcement* (Oxford: Clarendon, 1982); Albert J. Reiss and Albert D. Biderman, *Data Sources on White-Collar Law-Breaking* (Washington, D.C.: National Institute of Justice, 1980); Susan Shapiro, "Detecting Illegalities: A Perspective on the Control of Securities Violations," Ph.D. dissertation, Yale University (University Microfilms), 1980. See also Brian Widlake, *Serious Fraud Office* (London: Little, Brown, 1995).

58. Dan Magnuson, ed., *Economic Crime: Programs for Future Research* (Stockholm: National Council for Crime Prevention, 1985); Michael L. Benson, Francis T. Cullen, and William A. Maakestad, *Local Prosecutors and Corporate Crime: Final Report* (Washington, D.C.: National Institute of Justice, 1991); Michael L. Benson, Francis T. Cullen, and William J. Maakestad, "Local Prosecutors and Corporate Crime," *Crime and Delinquency,* **36** (1990): 356–372.

59. For how the SEC is implementing this rule, visit http://www.sec.gov/rules/proposal/34-46300.htm.

60. Excerpted from Citizenworks (http://citizenworks.org/enron/accountinglaw.php).

CHAPTER 13

1. Christopher S. Wren, "A Pipeline of the Poor Feeds the Flow of Heroin," *New York Times,* Feb. 21, 1999, p. 37.
2. Arthur Santana, "For Liz, a Heroin User, Time Is Running Out—Health Officials Estimate 15,000 Addicts in King County," *Seattle Times,* July 12, 1999, p. B1.
3. David Heinzmann, "Violence No Stranger Where Boy Shot; 4-Year-Old Victim of Gun Battle in Good Condition," *Chicago Tribune,* Oct. 9, 1999, p. 5. See also Robert C. Davis and Arthur J. Lurigio, *Fighting Back: Neighborhood Antidrug Strategies* (Thousand Oaks, Calif.: Sage, 1996); Bureau of Justice Statistics, *Guns Used in Crime* (Washington, D.C.: U.S. Department of Justice, 1995); Susan J. Popkin, Lynn M. Olson, Arthur J. Lurigio, et al., "Sweeping Out Drugs and Crime: Residents' Views of the Chicago Housing Authority's Public Housing Drug Elimination Program," *Journal of Research in Crime and Delinquency,* **41** (1995): 73–99.
4. Mark D. Merlin, *On the Trail of the Ancient Opium Poppy* (Rutherford, N.J.: Fairleigh Dickinson University Press, 1984). For a historic account of alcohol consumption, see Harvey A. Siegal and James A. Inciardi, "A Brief History of Alcohol," in *The American Drug Scene: An Anthology,* ed. James A. Inciardi and Karen McElrath (Los Angeles: Roxbury, 1995).
5. Howard Abadinsky, *Drug Abuse: An Introduction* (Chicago: Nelson Hall, 1989), pp. 30–31, 54. For the medicinal benefits of marijuana, see Lester Grinspoon and James Bakalar, "Marijuana: The Forbidden Medicine," in Inciardi and McElrath, *The American Drug Scene.*
6. Michael D. Lyman, *Narcotics and Crime Control* (Springfield, Ill.: Charles C Thomas, 1987), p. 8. See also F. E. Oliver, "The Use and Abuse of Opium," in *Yesterday's Addicts: American Society and Drug Abuse, 1865–1920,* ed. H. Wayne Morgan (Norman: University of Oklahoma Press, 1974).
7. W. Z. Guggenheim, "Heroin: History and Pharmacology," *International Journal of the Addictions,* **2** (1967): 328. For a history of heroin use in New York City, from just after the turn of the twentieth century into the late 1960s, see Edward Preble and John J. Casey, "Taking Care of Business: The Heroin Addict's Life on the Street," *International Journal of the Addictions,* **4** (1969): 1–24.
8. Abadinsky, *Drug Abuse,* p. 52.
9. Ibid., p. 56.
10. Lyman, *Narcotics and Crime Control,* p. 10.
11. Public Law 100-690, of Nov. 18, 1988, 102 Stat. 4187.
12. Lloyd D. Johnston, Patrick M. O'Malley, and Jerald G. Bachman, *Drug Use among American High School Seniors, College Students, and Young Adults, 1975–1990,* vols. 1–2, for U.S. Department of Health and Human Services, National Institute on Drug Abuse (Washington, D.C.: U.S. Government Printing Office, 1991). For an early treatment, see James D. Preston and Patricia A. Fry, "Marijuana Use among Houston High School Students," *Social Science Quarterly,* **52** (1971): 170–178. For a look into how teen drug use can influence presidential elections, see Stewart Ugelow, "Drug Use Is Surging among Teenagers, and Dole Makes It a Campaign Issue," *The Wall Street Journal,* Aug. 21, 1996, p. A4.
13. Office of National Drug Control Policy, *Fact Sheet: Drug Use Trends* (Washington, D.C.: U.S. Government Printing Office, June 1999); Department of Health and Human Services, *Annual Drug Survey Results Released: Youth Drug Use Decreases; Overall Rates Remain Level,* Aug. 18, 1999 (http://www.health.org/pubs/nhsda/98hhs/nhs98rel.htm). For an early treatment of the extent of illegal drug use in Britain, see Pierce I. James, "Drug Abuse in Britain," *Medicine, Science and the Law,* **13** (1973): 246–251.
14. See Lyman, *Narcotics and Crime Control,* p. 21, for 1980 data. See Substance Abuse and Mental Health Services Administration, *1998 National Household Survey on Drug Abuse,* August 1999 (http://www.health.org/pubs/nhsda/98hhs/facts/factsheet.htm), for 1998 data.
15. National Institute on Drug Abuse, *National Household Survey* (Washington, D.C.: U.S. Government Printing Office, 1996), p. 9; see Robert J. Michaels, "The Market for Heroin before and after Legalization," in *Dealing with Drugs,* ed. Ronald Hamowy (Lexington, Mass.: Lexington Books, 1987), pp. 311–318.
16. Mark A. de Bernardo and Marci M. DeLancey, *Guide to Dangerous Drugs: Everything You Should Know about Marijuana, Cocaine, Alcohol, Depressants, Amphetamines, Heroin and Other Opiates, Inhalants and Hallucinogens* (Washington, D.C.: Institute for a Drug-Free Workplace, 1994); Abadinsky, *Drug Abuse,* p. 107; Lyman, *Narcotics and Crime Control,* pp. 33–34. For a description of emerging new drugs and availability, see Dana Hunt, *Pulse Check: National Trends in Drug Abuse*

(Washington, D.C.: Office of National Drug Control Policy, 1996).

17. Lloyd D. Johnston, Patrick M. O'Malley, and Jerald G. Bachman, *The National Survey Results on Drug Use from the Monitoring the Future Study, 1975–1993,* vol. 1, National Institutes of Health (Washington, D.C.: U.S. Government Printing Office, 1994). Office of National Drug Control Policy, *Fact Sheet;* Department of Health and Human Services, *Annual Drug Survey Results Released.* See also Allan L. McCutcheon and George Thomas, "Patterns of Drug Use among White Institutionalized Delinquents in Georgia: Evidence from a Latent Class Analysis," *Journal of Drug Education,* **25** (1995): 61–71; Bruce A. Jacobs, "Anticipatory Undercover Targeting in High Schools," *Journal of Criminal Justice,* **22** (1994): 445–457; Joseph F. Sheley, "Drugs and Guns among Inner-City High School Students," *Journal of Drug Education,* **24** (1994): 303–321; Ken C. Winters, Christine L. Weller, and James A. Meland, "Extent of Drug Abuse among Juvenile Offenders," *Journal of Drug Issues,* **23** (1993): 515–524. For a perspective on drug use among 12- and 19-year-olds living in England and Wales, see Joy Mott and Catriona Black Mirrlees, *Self-Reported Drug Misuse in England and Wales: Findings from the 1992 British Crime Survey* (London: Home Office, Research and Planning Unit, 1995). See, as an early treatment, Lloyd Johnson and Jerald G. Bachman, *Drug Use among American High School Students, 1975–1977* (Washington, D.C.: U.S. Government Printing Office, 1978); Henry Wechsler, "Alcohol Intoxication and Drug Use among Teen-Agers," *Journal of Studies on Alcohol,* **37** (1976): 1672–1677; U.S. House of Representatives, Select Committee on Crime, *Drugs in Our Schools. Hearings, September 21–23, 1972, Chicago, Illinois* (Washington, D.C.: U.S. Government Printing Office, 1972).

18. Lisa Maher, Eloise Dunlap, Bruce D. Johnson, and Ansley Hamid, "Gender, Power, and Alternative Living Arrangements in the Inner-City Crack Culture," *Journal of Research in Crime and Delinquency,* **33** (1996): 181–205; H. Virginia McCoy, Christine Miles, and James A. Inciardi, "Survival Sex: Inner-City Women and Crack-Cocaine," in Inciardi and McElrath, *The American Drug Scene;* Jody Miller, "Gender and Power on the Streets: Street Prostitution in the Era of Crack Cocaine," *Journal of Contemporary Ethnography,* **23** (1995): 427–452; Ann Sorenson and David Brownfield, "Adolescent Drug Use and a General Theory of Crime: An Analysis of a Theoretical Integration," *Canadian Journal of Criminology,* **37** (1995): 19–37. For a summary of psychiatric approaches, see Marie Nyswander, *The Drug Addict as a Patient* (New York: Grune & Stratton, 1956), chap. 4.

19. Richard Cloward and Lloyd Ohlin, *Delinquency and Opportunity* (New York: Free Press, 1960), pp. 178–186. See also Jeffrey A. Fagan, "The Social Organization of Drug Use and Drug Dealing among Urban Gangs," *Criminology,* **27** (1989): 633–669. See also Marcia R. Chaiken, *Identifying and Responding to New Forms of Drug Abuse: Lessons Learned from "Crack" and "Ice"* (Washington, D.C.: National Institute of Justice, 1993).

20. D. F. Musto, "The History of Legislative Control over Opium, Cocaine, and Their Derivatives," in Hamowy, *Dealing with Drugs.*

21. Marsha Rosenbaum, *Women on Heroin* (New Brunswick, N.J.: Rutgers University Press, 1981), pp. 14–15; Jeannette Covington, "Theoretical Explanations of Race Differences in Heroin Use," in *Advances in Criminological Theory,* vol. 2, ed. William S. Laufer and Freda Adler (New Brunswick, N.J.: Transaction). See also U.S. Senate Judiciary Committee, Subcommittee to Investigate Juvenile Delinquency, *The Global Connection: Heroin Entrepreneurs. Hearings, July 28 and August 5, 1976* (Washington, D.C.: U.S. Government Printing Office, 1976).

22. Freda Adler, Arthur D. Moffett, Frederick G. Glaser, John C. Ball, and Diana Horwitz, *A Systems Approach to Drug Treatment* (Philadelphia: Dorrance, 1974).

23. Erich Goode, *Drugs in American Society* (New York: Basic Books, 1972). See also Ned Polsky, *Hustlers, Beats, and Others* (Chicago: Aldine, 1967).

24. Norman E. Zinberg, "The Use and Misuse of Intoxicants: Factors in the Development of Controlled Abuse," in Hamowy, *Dealing with Drugs,* p. 262.

25. Abadinsky, *Drug Abuse,* p. 53. See also, as an early treatment, Hope R. Victor, Jan Carl Grossman, and Russell Eisenman, "Openness to Experience and Marijuana Use in High School Students," *Journal of Consulting and Clinical Psychology,* **41** (1973): 78–85; U.S. Narcotics and Dangerous Drugs Bureau, *Marijuana: An Analysis of Use, Distribution and Control* (Washington, D.C.: U.S. Government Printing Office, 1971); California Department of Public Health and Welfare, Research and Statistics Section, *Five Mind-Altering Drugs: The Use of Alcoholic Beverages, Amphetamines, LSD,*

Marijuana, and Tobacco, Reported by High School and Junior High School Students, San Mateo County, California, Two Comparable Surveys, 1968 and 1969* (San Mateo: California Department of Public Health, 1969); Erich Goode, "Multiple Drug Use among Marijuana Smokers," *Social Problems,* **17** (1969): 48–64.

26. Bruce A. Jacobs, "Crack Dealers' Apprehension Avoidance Techniques: A Case of Restrictive Deterrence," *Justice Quarterly,* 13 (1996): 359–381; Bruce A. Jacobs, "Crack Dealers and Restrictive Deterrences: Identifying Narcs," *Criminology,* **34** (1996): 409–431; Bruce D. Johnson, Andrew Golub, and Jeffrey Fagan, "Careers in Crack, Drug Use, Drug Distribution, and Nondrug Criminality," *Journal of Crime and Delinquency,* **41** (1995): 275–295; Abadinsky, *Drug Abuse,* p. 83. See also Jeffrey A. Fagan, "Initiation into Crack and Powdered Cocaine: A Tale of Two Epidemics," *Contemporary Drug Problems,* **16** (1989): 579–618; Jeffrey A. Fagan, Joseph G. Weis, and Y. T. Cheng, "Drug Use and Delinquency among Inner City Youth," *Journal of Drug Issues,* **20** (1990): 349–400; and James A. Inciardi et al., "The Crack Epidemic Revisited," *Journal of Psychoactive Drugs,* **24** (1992): 305–416. See also B. D. Johnson, M. Natarajan, E. Dunlap, and E. Elmoghazy, "Crack Abusers and Noncrack Abusers: A Comparison of Drug Use, Drug Sales, and Nondrug Criminality," *Journal of Drug Issues,* **24** (1994): 117–141. Smoking crack is certainly not limited to the inner cities of America. For a description of crack use in the tropical paradise of Hawaii, see Gordon James Knowles, "Dealing Crack Cocaine: A View from the Streets of Honolulu," *The FBI Law Enforcement Bulletin,* July 1996: 1–7.

27. Michael Marriott, "Potent Crack Blend on the Streets Lures a New Generation to Heroin," *New York Times,* July 13, 1989, pp. A1, B3.

28. James Inciardi, "Heroin Use and Street Crime," *Crime and Delinquency,* **25** (1979): 335–346; Bruce D. Johnson, Paul J. Goldstein, Edward Preble, James Schmeidler, Douglas S. Lyston, Barry Spunt, and Thomas Miller, *Taking Care of Business: The Economics of Crime by Heroin Abusers* (Lexington, Mass.: Heath, 1985); James Inciardi, *The War on Drugs: Heroin, Cocaine, Crime, and Public Policy* (Palo Alto, Calif.: Mayfield, 1986); Eric Wish and Bruce Johnson, "The Impact of Substance Abuse on Criminal Careers," in *Criminal Careers and Career Criminals,* ed. Alfred Blumstein, Jacqueline Cohen, Jeffrey A. Roth, and Christy A. Visher (Washington, D.C.: National Academy Press, 1986), pp. 52–58.

29. Office of National Drug Control Policy, Drug Facts. Marijuana, 2002 (www.whitehousedrugpolicy.gov/drugfact/marijuana/index.html).

30. For a determination of the causal link between drug use and crime, see Bruce L. Benson and David W. Rasmussen, *Illicit Drugs and Crimes* (Oakland, Calif.: The Independent Institute, 1996); James A. Inciardi, Duane C. McBride, and James E. Rivers, *Drug Control and the Courts* (Thousand Oaks, Calif.: Sage, 1996); Inciardi and McElrath, *The American Drug Scene;* Sybille M. Guy, Gene M. Smith, and P. M. Bentler, "The Influence of Adolescent Substance Use and Socialization on Deviant Behavior in Young Adulthood," *Criminal Justice and Behavior,* **21** (1994): 236–255.

31. George Speckart and M. Douglas Anglin found that criminal records preceded drug use; see their "Narcotics Use and Crime: An Overview of Recent Research Advances," *Contemporary Drug Problems,* **13** (1986): 741–769, and "Narcotics and Crime: A Causal Modeling Approach," *Journal of Quantitative Criminology,* **2** (1986): 3–28. See also Cheryl Carpenter, Barry Glassner, Bruce D. Johnson, and Julia Loughlin, *Kids, Drugs, and Crime* (Lexington, Mass.: Heath, 1988). See also Louise L. Biron, Serge Brochu, and Lyne Desjardins, "The Issue of Drugs and Crime among a Sample of Incarcerated Women," *Deviant Behavior,* **16** (1995): 25–43.

32. James A. Inciardi and Anne E. Pottieger, "Kids, Crack, and Crime," *Journal of Drug Issues,* **21** (1991): 257–270; David N. Nurco, Thomas E. Hanlon, Timothy W. Kinlock, and Karen R. Duszynski, "Differential Criminal Patterns of Narcotics Addicts over an Addiction Career," *Criminology,* **26** (1988): 407–423; M. Douglas Anglin and George Speckart, "Narcotics Use and Crime: A Multisample, Multimethod Analysis," *Criminology,* **26** (1988): 197–233; M. Douglas Anglin and Yining Hser, "Addicted Women and Crime," *Criminology,* **25** (1987): 359–397.

33. Paul Goldstein, "Drugs and Violent Crime," in *Pathways to Criminal Violence,* ed. Neil Alan Weiner and Marvin E. Wolfgang (Newbury Park, Calif.: Sage, 1989), pp. 16–48.

34. This section is based on Inciardi, *The War on Drugs.* See also Fernando Cepeda Ulloa, "International Cooperation and the War on Drugs," in *Drug Trafficking in the Americas,* ed. Bruce M. Bagley and William O. Walker III (Coral Gables, Fla.: North-South Center Press, University of Miami, 1996); Ronald Kessler, *The FBI* (New York: Pocket Books, 1993); *United States v. Celio,* 945 F.2d 180 (7th Cir. 1991), where the U.S. Court of Appeals for the

Seventh Circuit acknowledged the need for a concerted effort on behalf of various law enforcement agencies to combat international drug-trafficking cartels.
35. Office of National Drug Control Policy, *Source Countries and Drug Transit Zones: Colombia* (Washington, D.C.: U.S. Government Printing Office, 2002).
36. *The Illicit Drug Situation in the United States and Canada* (Ottawa: Royal Canadian Mounted Police, 1984–1986), p. 19. See also William Gately and Yvette Fernandez, *Dead Ringer: An Insider's Account of the Mob's Colombian Connection* (New York: Donald I. Fine, 1994).
37. Colin McMahon, "Panama's Future Uncertain as Ever; Corruption Persists in Post-Noriega Era," *Chicago Tribune*, Aug. 25, 1996, p. 17.
38. United Nations, "Commission on Narcotic Drugs, Comprehensive Review of the Activities of the United Nations Fund for Drug Abuse Control in 1985," E/CN.7/1986/ CRP.4, Feb. 4, 1986. See also Elaine Sciolino, "U.N. Report Links Drugs, Arms, and Terror," *New York Times*, Jan. 12, 1987.
39. John Warner, "Terrorism and Drug Trafficking: A Lethal Partnership," *Security Management*, **28** (1984): 44–46. See, as an early treatment, U.S. Congress, House Public Health and Environment Subcommittee, *Production and Abuse of Opiates in the Far East* (Washington, D.C.: U.S. Government Printing Office, 1971).
40. For a review of drug enforcement policies aimed directly at the users of illicit narcotics, see Richard Lawrence Miller, *Drug Warriors and Their Prey: From Police Power to Police State* (Westport, Conn.: Praeger, 1996). For a comprehensive guide to state agencies that address drug abuse concerns, see Bureau of Justice Statistics, *State Drug Resources: 1994 National Directory* (Washington, D.C.: U.S. Department of Justice, 1994).
41. James A. Inciardi, *The War on Drugs II: The Continuing Epidemic of Heroin, Cocaine, Crack, Crime, AIDS, and Public Policy* (Mountain View, Calif.: Mayfield, 1992).
42. Even before President Bush's drug initiatives, government agencies recognized the ineffectiveness of narcotic countermeasures during the 1970s; see U.S. Comptroller General, *Gains Made in Controlling Illegal Drugs, Yet the Drug Trade Flourishes* (Washington, D.C.: U.S. Government Printing Office, 1979).
43. See Rae Sibbitt, *The Ilps Methadone Prescribing Project* (London: Home Office, 1996); Paul J. Turnbull, Russell Webster, and Gary Stillwell, *Get It While You Can: An Evaluation of an Early Intervention Project for Arrestees with Alcohol and Drug Problems* (London: Home Office, 1996); Ira Sommers, Deborah R. Baskin, and Jeffrey Fagan, "Getting out of the Life: Crime Desistance by Female Street Offenders," *Deviant Behavior*, **15** (1994): 125–149; Sandra L. Tunis, *The State of the Art in Jail Drug Treatment Programs* (San Francisco: National Council on Crime and Delinquency, 1994).
44. See Peter Finn and Andrea K. Newlyn, *Miami's "Drug Court,"* National Institute of Justice (Washington, D.C.: U.S. Government Printing Office, 1993), for Dade County; see Christopher S. Wren, "Arizona Finds Cost Savings in Treating Drug Offenders," *New York Times*, Apr. 21, 1999, for Arizona; see also Bureau of Justice Assistance, *Two Special Drug Court Models: Dedicated Drug Treatment vs. Speedy Trial and Differentiated Case Management (DCM)—The Program Concept* (Washington, D.C.: U.S. Government Printing Office, 1998); Jonathan Alter, "The Buzz on Drugs," *Newsweek*, September 6, 1999, pp. 25–28.
45. Abadinsky, *Drug Abuse*, p. 171.
46. David N. Nurco, Norma Wegner, Philip Stephenson, Abraham Makofsky, and John W. Shaffer, *Ex-Addicts' Self-Help Groups: Potentials and Pitfalls* (New York: Praeger, 1983); Harold I. Hendler and Richard C. Stephens, "The Addict Odyssey: From Experimentation to Addiction," *International Journal of the Addictions*, **12** (1977): pp. 25–42.
47. For a perspective on how corporate America educates employees on the risks of drug abuse, see Mark A. de Bernardo, *What Every Employee Should Know about Drug Abuse* (Washington, D.C.: Institute for a Drug-Free Workplace, 1993); Troy Duster, *The Legislation of Morality: Law, Drugs, and Moral Judgment* (New York: Free Press, 1970), p. 192.
48. Dan Waldorf, "Natural Recovery from Opiate Addiction," *Journal of Drug Issues*, **13** (1983): 237–280.
49. See James A. Inciardi, Duane C. McBride, Clyde B. McCoy, et al., "Violence, Street Crime and the Drug Legalization Debate: A Perspective and Commentary on the U.S. Experience," *Studies on Crime and Crime Prevention*, **4** (1995): 105–118; Steven Foy Luper, Curtis Brown, et al., *Drugs, Morality, and the Law* (New York: Garland, 1994); Robert J. MacCoun, James P. Kahan, and James Gillespie, "A Content Analysis of the Drug Legalization Debate," *Journal of Drug Issues*, **23** (1993): 615–629; Arnold S. Trebach and James A. Inciardi, *Legalize It? Debating American Drug Policy* (Washington, D.C.: American University Press, 1993).
50. James B. Jacobs, *Drunk Driving: An American Dilemma* (Chicago: University of Chicago Press, 1989), p. xiii.

51. Substance Abuse and Mental Health Services Administration, *2001 National Household Survey on Drug Abuse.*
52. James Inciardi, *Reflections on Crime* (New York: Holt, Rinehart & Winston, 1978), pp. 8–10. For an even earlier perspective, see Herbert Berger and Andrew A. Eggston, "Should We Legalize Narcotics?" *Coronet,* **38** (June 1995): 30–34.
53. Lawrence A. Greenfield, *Alcohol and Crime: An Analysis of National Data on the Prevalence of Alcohol Involvement in Crime* (Washington, D.C.: U.S. Government Printing Office, 1998); Christopher J. Mumola, *Substance Abuse and Treatment, State and Federal Prisoners, 1997* (Washington, D.C.: U.S. Government Printing Office, January 1999).
54. Marvin E. Wolfgang, *Patterns in Criminal Homicide* (New York: Wiley, 1966).
55. P. Linquist, "Criminal Homicides in Northern Sweden, 1970–81: Alcohol Intoxication, Alcohol Abuse, and Mental Disease," *International Journal of Law and Psychiatry,* **8** (1986): 19–37. See also Roland Gustafson, "Is It Possible to Link Alcohol Intoxication Causally to Aggression and Violence? A Summary of the Swedish Experimental Approach," *Studies on Crime and Crime Prevention,* **4** (1995): 22–42.
56. D. Mayfield, "Alcoholism, Alcohol Intoxification, and Assaultive Behavior," *Diseases of the Nervous System,* **37** (1976): 288–291; C. K. Meyer, T. Magendanz, B. C. Kieselhorst, and S. G. Chapman, *A Social-Psychological Analysis of Police Assaults* (Norman: Bureau of Government Research, University of Oklahoma, April 1978).
57. For the role of alcohol consumption in violent episodes against intimates and women, see Christine A. Scronce and Kevin J. Corcoran, "The Influence of the Victim's Consumption of Alcohol on Perceptions of Stranger and Acquaintance Rape," *Violence against Women,* **1** (1995): 241–253; Bureau of Justice Statistics, *Violence between Intimates* (Washington, D.C.: U.S. Department of Justice, 1994); Bureau of Justice Statistics, *Violence against Women: A National Crime Victimization Survey Report* (Washington, D.C.: U.S. Department of Justice, 1994); S. D. Johnson, L. Gibson, and R. Linden, "Alcohol and Rape in Winnipeg, 1966–1975," *Journal of Studies on Alcohol,* **39** (1987): 1877–1894; Menachem Amir, *Patterns of Forcible Rape* (Chicago: University of Chicago Press, 1971), p. 99.
58. D. H. Coleman and M. A. Straus, "Alcohol Abuse and Family Violence," in *Alcohol, Drug Abuse, and Aggression,* ed. E. Gottheil, K. A. Druley, T. E. Skoloda, and H. M. Waxman (Springfield, Ill.: Charles C Thomas, 1983).
59. See Maggie Sumner and Howard Parker, *Law in Alcohol: A Review of International Research into Alcohol's Role in Crime Causation* (Manchester, U.K.: Department of Social Policy and Social Work, University of Manchester, 1995); Klaus A. Miczek et al., "Alcohol, Drugs of Abuse, Aggression, and Violence," in *Understanding and Preventing Violence,* ed. Albert J. Reiss Jr. and Jeffrey A. Roth (Washington, D.C.: National Academy Press, 1993).
60. K. E. Leonard, "Alcohol and Human Physical Aggression," *Aggression,* **2** (1983): 77–101. See also Matthew W. Lewis, Jon F. Merz, Ron D. Hays, et al., "Perceptions of Intoxication and Impairment at Arrest among Adults Convicted of Driving under the Influence of Alcohol," *Journal of Drug Issues,* **25** (1995): 141–160.
61. C. M. Steele and L. Southwick, "Alcohol and Social Behavior: I. The Psychology of Drunken Excess," *Journal of Personality and Social Psychology,* **48** (1985): 18–34. See also Peter B. Wood, John K. Cochran, Betty Pfefferbaum, et al., "Sensation-Seeking and Delinquent Substance Use: An Extension of Learning Theory," *Journal of Drug Issues,* **25** (1995): 173–193.
62. S. Ahlstrom-Laakso, "European Drinking Habits: A Review of Research and Time Suggestions for Conceptual Integration of Findings," in *Cross-Cultural Approaches to the Study of Alcohol,* ed. M. W. Everett, J. O. Waddell, and D. Heath (The Hague: Mouton, 1976).
63. Uniform Crime Reports, 2001, p. 233; Lawrence A. Greenfield, *Drunk Driving,* for Bureau of Justice Statistics (Washington, D.C.: U.S. Government Printing Office, February 1988), p. 1; William K. Stevens, "Deaths from Drunken Driving Increase," *New York Times,* Oct. 29, 1987, p. 12. See also Gwen W. Bramlet, "DUI Offenders, Drug Users, and Criminals: A Comparison," *Journal of Crime and Justice,* **18** (1995): 59–78; Greenfield, *Alcohol and Crime;* and Mumola, *Substance Abuse and Treatment.*
64. Joseph R. Gusfield, "The Control of Drinking-Driving in the United States: A Period of Transition," in *Social Control of the Drinking Driver,* ed. Michael D. Lawrence, John R. Snortum, and Franklin E. Zimring (Chicago: University of Chicago Press, 1988).
65. Jacobs, *Drunk Driving,* p. xvi.
66. Faye Silas, "Gimme the Keys," *American Bar Association Journal,* **71** (1985): 36.
67. Atic Press, "The Menace on the Roads," *Newsweek,* Dec. 21, 1987, p. 42.
68. Brandon K. Applegate, Francis T. Cullen, Bruce G. Link, Pamela J. Richards, and Lonn Lanza-Kaduce, "Determinants of Public Punitiveness toward Drunk Driving: A Factorial Survey Approach," *Justice Quarterly,* **13** (1996): 57–79; Stephen D. Mastrofski

and R. Richard Ritti, "Police Training and the Effects of Organization on Drunk Driving Enforcement," *Justice Quarterly,* **13** (1996): 291–320.

69. *The Effectiveness of the Ignition Interlock Device in Reducing Recidivism among Driving under the Influence Cases* (Honolulu: Criminal Justice Commission, 1987).

70. Personal communication, 1951. See, as additional early treatments, Dr. Eustace Chesser, *Strange Loves: The Human Aspects of Sexual Deviation* (New York: William Morrow, 1971); David Reuben, *Everything You Always Wanted to Know about Sex: But Were Afraid to Ask* (New York: David McKay, 1969). Contemporary works include Samuel S. Janus and Cynthia L. Janus, *The Janus Report on Sexual Behavior: The First Broad-Scale Scientific National Survey since Kinsey* (New York: Wiley, 1993).

71. Alfred C. Kinsey, Wardel B. Pomeroy, and Clyde E. Martin, *Sexual Behavior in the Human Male* (Philadelphia: Saunders, 1948), p. 613. See also Judith A. Reisman and Edward W. Eichel, *Kinsey, Sex and Fraud: The Indoctrination of a People* (Lafayette, La.: Huntington House, 1990).

72. *Bowers v. Hardwick,* 478 U.S. 186; reh. denied, 478 U.S. 1039 (1986).

73. Nickie Roberts, *Whores in History: Prostitution in Western Society* (London: HarperCollins, 1992).

74. *Robinson v. California,* 370 U.S. 660 (1962).

75. Uniform Crime Reports, 2001, p. 233.

76. See Cudore L. Snell, *Young Men in the Street: Help-Seeking Behavior of Young Male Prostitutes* (Westport, Conn.: Praeger, 1995); Sari van der Poel, "Solidarity as Boomerang: The Fiasco of the Prostitutes' Rights Movement in the Netherlands," *Crime, Law and Social Change,* **23** (1995): 41–65; Barbara Sherman Heyl, "The Madam as Teacher: The Training of House Prostitutes," in *Deviant Behavior,* ed. Delos H. Kelly (New York: St. Martin's Press, 1993); Sari van der Poel, "Professional Male Prostitution: A Neglected Phenomenon," *Crime, Law, and Social Change,* **18** (1992): 259–275; David F. Luckenbill, "Deviant Career Mobility: The Case of Male Prostitutes," *Social Problems,* **33** (1986): 283–296.

77. Jeremiah Lowney, Robert W. Winslow, and Virginia Winslow, *Deviant Reality—Alternative World Views,* 2d ed. (Boston: Allyn and Bacon, 1981), p. 156. For a law enforcement perspective on countering prostitution in New York City, where female undercover police officers are used to seek out the patrons of prostitutes, see Dean Chang, "Dear John, It's a Bust: Cops Target Sex Clients," *New York Daily News,* June 26, 1994, p. 10.

78. Bureau of Justice Statistics, *HIV in Prisons 1994* (Washington, D.C.: U.S. Department of Justice, 1996); Bureau of Justice Statistics, *HIV in Prisons and Jails, 1993* (Washington, D.C.: U.S. Department of Justice, 1995); James A. Inciardi, Anne E. Pottieger, Mary Ann Forney, et al., "Prostitution, IV Drug Use, and Sex-for-Crack Exchanges among Serious Delinquents: Risks for HIV Infection," *Criminology,* **29** (1991): 221–236; Joseph B. Kuhns III and Kathleen M. Heide, "AIDS-Related Issues among Female Prostitutes and Female Arrestees," *International Journal of Offender Therapy and Comparative Criminology,* **36** (1992): 231–245; David J. Bellis, "Reduction of AIDS Risk among 41 Heroin Addicted Female Street Prostitutes: Effects of Free Methadone Maintenance," *Journal of Addictive Diseases,* **12** (1993): 7–23; L. Maher and R. Curtis, "Women on the Edge of Crime: Crack Cocaine and the Changing Contexts of Street-Level Sex Work in New York City," *Crime, Law, and Social Change,* **18** (1992): 221–258; Edward V. Morse, Patricia M. Simon, Stephanie A. Baus, et al., "Cofactors of Substance Use among Male Street Prostitutes," *Journal of Drug Issues,* **22** (1992): 977–994.

79. Paul Gebhard, "Misconceptions about Female Prostitution," *Medical Aspects of Human Sexuality,* **3** (1969): 28–30; Jennifer James, "Prostitutes and Prostitution," in *Deviants: Voluntary Action in a Hostile World,* ed. Edward Sagarin and F. Montamino (Glenview, Ill.: Scott, Foresman, 1977), p. 384.

80. R. Karl Hanson, Heather Scott, and Richard A. Steffy, "A Comparison of Child Molesters and Nonsexual Criminals: Risk Predictors and Long-Term Recidivism," *Journal of Research in Crime and Delinquency,* **32** (1995): 325–337; Dennis Howitt, *Paedophiles and Sexual Offences against Children* (Chichester, U.K.: Wiley, 1995); Human Rights Watch: Asia, *Rape for Profit: Trafficking of Nepali Girls and Women to India's Brothels* (New York: Human Rights Watch, 1995).

81. See Gerhard O. W. Mueller, *Legal Regulation of Sexual Conduct* (New York: Oceana, 1961), pp. 139–147, tables 9A, 9B. Note, however, that some states have amended their statutes since these data were collected.

82. Edward Donnerstein et al., *The Question of Pornography: Final Report of the Attorney General's Commission on Pornography* (Nashville, Tenn.: Rutledge Hill Press, 1986), p. 147.

83. For the now famous Justice Potter Stewart comment on pornography, where he couldn't truly define obscenity, but stated he knew it when he saw it, see *Jacobellis v. Ohio,* 378 U.S. 184 (1964). Joel Feinberg, "Pornography and Criminal Law," in *Pornography and Censorship,* ed. D. Copp and S. Wendell (New York: Prometheus, 1979).

84. See Susan M. Easton, *The Problem of Pornography: Regulation and the Right to Free Speech* (London:

Routledge, 1994); Donald A. Downs, *The New Politics of Pornography* (Chicago: University of Chicago Press, 1989). See also Donnerstein et al., *The Question of Pornography,* chap. 7; and Gordon Hawkins and Franklin E. Zimring, *Pornography in a Free Society* (New York: Cambridge University Press, 1988), p. 26.
85. *The Report of the Commission on Obscenity and Pornography* (Washington, D.C.: U.S. Government Printing Office, 1970).
86. U.S. Department of Justice, *Attorney General's Commission on Pornography, Final Report,* vols. 1 and 2 (Washington, D.C.: U.S. Government Printing Office, 1986). For comments on the scientific underpinnings of this report, see Edward Donnerstein, "The Pornography Commission Report: Do Findings Fit Conclusions?" *Sexual Coercion and Assault Issues and Perspectives,* **1** (1986): 185–188.
87. Home Office, *Report of the Committee on Obscenity and Film Censorship* (London: Her Majesty's Stationery Office, 1979), p. 103. See also Dennis Howitt and Guy Cumberbatch, *Pornography: Impacts and Influences: A Review of Available Research Evidence on the Effects of Pornography* (London: Research and Planning Unit, U.K. Home Office, 1990).
88. *The Report of the Commission on Obscenity and Pornography.*
89. R. A. Barron and P. A. Bell, "Sexual Arousal and Aggression by Males: Effects of Type of Erotic Stimuli and Prior Provocation," *Journal of Personality and Social Psychology,* **35** (1977): 79–87. For a more current study, see Scot B. Boeringer, "Pornography and Sexual Aggression: Associations of Violent and Nonviolent Depictions with Rape and Rape Proclivity," *Deviant Behavior,* **15** (1994): 289–304.
90. Dolf Zillman and Jennings Bryant, "Pornography, Sexual Callousness, and the Trivialization of Rape," *Journal of Communication,* **32** (1984): 10–21. See also Berl Kutchinsky, "Evidence Proves That Pornography Does Not Promote Rape," in the Current Controversies series, *Violence against Women,* ed. Karin L. Swisher, Carol Wekesser, and William Barbour (San Diego: Greenhaven Press, 1994); Cynthia S. Gentry, "Pornography and Rape: An Empirical Analysis," *Deviant Behavior,* **12** (1991): 277–288.
91. Donnerstein et al., *The Question of Pornography,* esp. pp. 38–47. See also Swisher, Wekesser, and Barbour, *Violence Against Women;* Myriam Miedzian, "How Rape Is Encouraged in American Boys and What We Can Do to Stop It," in *Transforming a Rape Culture,* ed. Emilie Buchwald, Pamela R. Fletcher, and Martha Roth (Minneapolis: Milkweed Editions, 1993); Judith A. Reisman, *Images of Children, Crime and Violence in Playboy, Penthouse and Hustler* (Washington, D.C.: Office of Juvenile Justice and Delinquency Prevention, Office of Justice Assistance, Research and Statistics, U.S. Department of Justice, 1990).
92. Joan Hoff, "Why Is There No History of Pornography?" in *For Adult Users Only: The Dilemma of Violent Pornography,* ed. Susan Gubar and Joan Hoff (Bloomington: Indiana University Press, 1989), p. 18. See also Franklin Mark Osanka and Sara Lee Johann, "Pornography Contributes to Violence against Women," in Swisher, Wekesser, and Barbour, *Violence against Women.*
93. *Miller v. California,* 413 U.S. 15 (1973). See also Laura Lederer, Richard Delgado, et al., *The Price We Pay: The Case against Racist Speech, Hate Propaganda, and Pornography* (New York: Hill and Wang, 1995).
94. *Pope v. Illinois,* 481 U.S. 497 (1987). See also Adele M. Stan et al., *Debating Sexual Correctness: Pornography, Sexual Harassment, Date Rape, and the Politics of Sexual Equality* (New York: Dell, 1995); Bill Thompson, *Soft Core: Moral Crusades against Pornography in Britain and America* (London: Cassell, 1994); Catherine Itzen et al., *Pornography: Women, Violence and Civil Liberties* (Oxford: Oxford University Press, 1993).
95. Laura Davis, Marilyn D. McShane, and Frank P. Williams III, "Controlling Computer Access to Pornography: Special Conditions for Sex Offenders," *Federal Probation,* **59** (1995): 43–48; Marty Rimm, "Marketing Pornography on the Information Superhighway: A Survey of 917,410 Images, Descriptions, Short Stories and Animations Downloaded 8.5 Million Times by Consumers in Over 2,000 Cities in Forty Countries, Provinces, and Territories," *Georgetown Law Journal,* **83** (1995): 1849–2008; Great Britain House of Commons, *Computer Pornography* (London: Her Majesty's Stationery Office, 1994). For a perspective on the government's plan to police the Internet's superhighway, see James Aley, "How Not to Help High Tech," *Fortune Magazine,* May 16, 1994, p. 100.
96. Kinsey et al., *Sexual Behavior in the Human Male.*
97. Alfred C. Kinsey, Wardel B. Pomeroy, Clyde E. Martin, and Paul H. Gebhard, *Sexual Behavior in the Human Female* (Philadelphia: Saunders, 1953), p. 453.
98. See Jules Older, "Mother Nature's Dirty Trick: Our Bodies Design Bespeaks Promiscuous Urges," *Los Angeles Times,* March 12, 1988, p. 8.

CHAPTER 14

1. Peter Applebome, "Skinhead Violence Grows, Experts Say," *New York Times,* July 18, 1993, p. 25.

2. *The Skinhead International: A World-Wide Survey of Neo-Nazi Skinheads* (New York: Anti-Defamation League of B'nai B'rith, 1995).
3. Jane Kramer, "Neo-Nazis: A Chaos in the Head," *New Yorker,* July 14, 1993, pp. 52–70, at p. 53. See also Marie C. Douglas, "Ausländer Raus! Nazi Raus! An Observation of German Skins and Jugendgangen," *International Journal of Comparative and Applied Criminal Justice,* **16** (1992): 129–134.
4. John Leland and Marcus Mabry, "Toasting the 'Head,' " *Newsweek,* Feb. 26, 1996, pp. 42–43.
5. Mark S. Hamm, *American Skinheads—The Criminology and Control of Hate Crime* (Westport, Conn.: Praeger, 1993).
6. Piers Beirne and David Nelken, eds., *Issues in Comparative Criminology* (Aldershot, U.K.: Dartmouth, 1997), is a useful anthology of scientific issues in comparative criminology.
7. The term "comparative criminology" appears to have been coined by Sheldon Glueck. See Sheldon Glueck, "Wanted: A Comparative Criminology," in *Ventures in Criminology,* ed. Sheldon Glueck and Eleanor Glueck (London: Tavistock, 1964), pp. 304–322.
8. James O. Finckenauer, *Russian Youth: Law, Deviance and the Pursuit of Freedom* (New Brunswick, N.J.: Transaction, 1995); Nanci Adler, "Planned Economy and Unplanned Criminality: The Soviet Experience," *International Journal of Comparative and Applied Criminal Justice,* **17** (1993): 189–201; Wojciech Cebulak, "White-Collar Crime in Socialism: Myth or Reality?" *International Journal of Comparative and Applied Criminal Justice,* **15** (1991): 109–120; Klaus Sessar, "Crime Rate Trends before and after the End of the German Democratic Republic—Impressions and First Analyses," in *Fear of Crime and Criminal Victimization,* ed. Wolfgang Bilsky, Christian Pfeiffer, and Peter Wetzels (Stuttgart, Germany: Ferdinand Enke Verlag, 1993), pp. 231–244; Louise I. Shelley et al., "East Meets West in Crime," *European Journal on Criminal Policy and Research,* **3** (1995): 7–107. As China is undergoing a transformation, mostly economic, changes in that country are noteworthy. See Yue Ma, "Crime in China: Characteristics, Causes and Control Strategies," *Journal of Comparative and Applied Criminal Justice,* **34** (1994): 54–68.
9. Martin Kilias et al., "Cross-Border Crime," *European Journal on Criminal Policy and Research,* **1** (1993): 7–134.
10. William F. McDonald, "The Globalization of Criminology: The New Frontier Is the Frontier," *Transnational Organized Crime,* 1 (1995): 1–12.
11. Piers Beirne and Joan Hill, *Comparative Criminology—An Annotated Bibliography* (New York: Greenwood, 1991), pp. vii–viii.
12. See especially Albert P. Blaustein and G. H. Flenz, *Constitutions of the Countries of the World,* 21 vols. (updated) (Dobbs Ferry, N.Y.: Oceana, 1971 and continuing).
13. The Comparative Criminal Law Project at Wayne State University Law School (formerly at New York University School of Law) has published 21 criminal codes in *The American Series of Foreign Penal Codes,* ed. G. O. W. Mueller, cont. by Edward M. Wise (Littleton, Colo.: Fred B. Rothman, since 1960); G. O. W. Mueller and Fré Le Poole Griffiths, *Comparative Criminal Procedure* (New York: New York University Press, 1969); Albin Eser and George Fletcher, *Justification and Excuse—Comparative Perspectives,* 2 vols. (Freiburg, Germany: Max Planck Institut, 1987); Edward M. Wise and G. O. W. Mueller, eds., *Studies in Comparative Criminal Law,* Comparative Criminal Law Project Publications Series, vol. 9 (Littleton, Colo.: Fred B. Rothman, 1975); Marc Ancel, *Social Defense: The Future of Penal Reform,* Comparative Criminal Law Project Publications Series, vol. 16 (Littleton, Colo.: Fred B. Rothman, 1987). For a historical survey, see G. O. W. Mueller, *Comparative Criminal Law in the United States,* Comparative Criminal Law Project Monograph Series, vol. 4 (South Hackensack, N.J.: Fred B. Rothman, 1970).
14. Seven codes of criminal procedure have appeared in Mueller and Wise, *The American Series of Foreign Penal Codes.*
15. E.g., Shigemitsu Dando, *Japanese Criminal Procedure,* Comparative Criminal Law Project Publications Series, vol. 4 (Littleton, Colo.: Fred B. Rothman, 1965).
16. UNAFEI, 1–26 Harumicho, Fuchu, Tokyo, Japan. There are now 51 volumes.
17. Kristiina Kangaspunta, ed., *Profiles of Criminal Justice Systems in Europe and North America* (Helsinki: HEUNI, 1995); Matti Joutsen, *Criminal Justice Systems in Europe: Finland* (Helsinki: HEUNI, 1995).
18. Dae H. Chang, *Criminology: A Cross-Cultural Perspective,* 2 vols. (Durham, N.C.: Carolina Academic Press, 1976); George F. Cole, Stanislaw J. Frankowski, and Marc G. Gertz, *Major Criminal Justice Systems—A Comparative Survey,* 2d ed. (Newbury Park, Calif.: Sage, 1987); Richard J. Terrill, *World Criminal Justice Systems,* 2d ed. (Cincinnati: Anderson, 1985); Robert Heiner, ed., *Criminology—A Cross-Cultural Perspective* (Minneapolis/St. Paul: West, 1996); Obi N. I. Ebbe, ed., *Comparative and International Criminal Justice Systems* (Boston: Butterworth-Heinemann, 1996); Charles B. Fields and Richter H. Moore, eds., *Comparative Criminal Justice: Traditional and Non-*

NOTES

traditional Systems of Law and Control (Prospect Heights, Ill.: Waveland Press, 1996).

19. V. Lorne Stewart, *Justice and Troubled Children around the World*, vols. 1–5 (New York: New York University Press, 1980–1983).
20. David H. Bayley, *Patterns of Policing—A Comparative International Analysis* (New Brunswick, N.J.: Rutgers University Press, 1985).
21. Roy Walmsley, *Prison Systems in Central and Eastern Europe* (Helsinki: HEUNI, 1996).
22. Freda Adler, ed., *The Incidence of Female Criminality in the Contemporary World* (New York: New York University Press, 1984).
23. Marshall B. Clinard, *Cities with Little Crime: The Case of Switzerland* (London: Cambridge University Press, 1978).
24. Louise I. Shelley, *Crime and Modernization: The Impact of Industrialization and Urbanization on Crime* (Carbondale: Southern Illinois University Press, 1981).
25. William Clifford, *Crime Control in Japan* (Lexington, Mass.: Lexington Books, 1976).
26. G. O. W. Mueller, *World Survey on the Availability of Criminal Justice Statistics*, Internet-UNCJIN-ftp238.33.18WSAYL. See also G. O. W. Mueller, "International Criminal Justice: Harnessing the Information Explosion—Coasting Down the Electronic Superhighway," *Journal of Criminal Justice Education* **7**(2) (Fall 1996):253–261.
27. Interpol, located in Lyons, France, has published the crime statistics supplied to it by member states since 1951.
28. First survey: 1970–1975, A/32/199; second survey: 1975–1980, A/Conf. 121/18; third survey: 1980–1986, A/Conf. 144/6; fourth survey: 1986–1990, A/Conf. 169/15 and Add. 1; fifth survey (see United Nations, *Global Report on Crime and Justice*). See "Window to the World" in Chapter 2.
29. World Health Organization, "Homicide Statistics," in *World Health Statistics* (Geneva: World Health Organization, annually).
30. Dane Archer and Rosemary Gartner, *Violence and Crime in Cross-National Perspective* (New Haven, Conn.: Yale University Press, 1984).
31. Richard R. Bennett, *Correlates of Crime: A Study of Nations, 1960–1984* (Ann Arbor, Mich.: Inter-University Consortium for Political and Social Research, 1989).
32. Richard R. Bennett and James P. Lynch, "Does a Difference Make a Difference?" *Criminology*, **28** (1990): 155–182; Carol B. Kalish, *International Crime Rates* (Washington, D.C.: Bureau of Justice Statistics, 1988).
33. Jan J. M. Van Dijk, Pat Mayhew, and Martin Killias, *Experiences of Crime across the World: Key Findings from the 1989 International Crime Survey* (Deventer, Netherlands: Kluwer, 1990); Richard R. Bennett and R. Bruce Wiegand, "Observations on Crime Reporting in a Developing Nation," *Criminology*, **32** (1994): 135–148; Ugljesa Zvekic and Anna Albazzi del Frate, eds., *Criminal Victimization in the Developing World* (Rome: United Nations Interregional Crime and Justice Research Institute, 1995); Gail Travis et al., "The International Crime Surveys: Some Methodological Concerns," *Current Issues in Criminal Justice*, **6** (1995): 346–361; Van Dijk, Box 0.9 in *Global Report on Crime and Justice*, p. 9.
34. Josine Junger-Tas, Gert-Jan Terlouw, and Malcolm W. Klein, *Delinquent Behavior among People in the Western World* (Amsterdam: RDC Ministry of Justice, Kugler Publ., 1994); Junger-Tas, Box 0.10 in *Global Report on Crime and Justice*, p. 16.
35. Hermann Mannheim, *Comparative Criminology* (Boston: Houghton Mifflin, 1965).
36. See Jerome L. Neapolitan, *Cross-National Crime—A Research Review and Sourcebook* (Westport, Conn.: Greenwald Press, 1997); Dennis Benamati, Phyllis Schultze, Adam Bouloukos, and Graeme Newman, *Criminal Justice Information: How to Find It, How to Use It* (Phoenix, Ariz.: Onyx Press, 1997); Harry R. Dammer and Philip L. Reichel, eds., *Teaching about Comparative/International Criminal Justice—A Resource Manual* (Highland Heights, N.Y.: Academy of Criminal Justice Sciences, 1997).
37. Elmer H. Johnson, ed., *International Handbook of Contemporary Developments in Criminology*, 2 vols. (Westport, Conn.: Greenwood Press, 1983); George F. Cole, Stanislaw J. Frankowski, and Marc G. Gertz, *Major Criminal Justice Systems—A Comparative Survey*, 2d ed. (Newbury Park, Calif.: Sage, 1987); Richard J. Terrill, *World Criminal Justice Systems: A Survey* (Cincinnati: Anderson, 1984); Obi N. Ignatius Ebbe, *Comparative and International Criminal Justice Systems* (Boston: Butterworth, 1996); Philip L. Reichel, *Comparative Criminal Justice Systems: A Topical Approach* (Upper Saddle River, N.J.: Prentice Hall, 1994); Brunon Holyst, *Comparative Criminology* (Lexington, Mass.: Lexington Books, 1979); Louise I. Shelley, ed., *Readings in Comparative Criminology* (Carbondale: Southern Illinois University Press, 1981).
38. United Nations, *The United Nations Crime Prevention and Criminal Justice Program: Formulation of Standards and Efforts at Their Implementation* (Philadelphia: University of Pennsylvania, 1994); Benedict Alper and Jerry F. Boren, *Crime: International Agenda* (Lexington, Mass.: Lexington Books, 1972); Ethan N. Nadelman, *Cops across Borders* (University

Park: Penn State Press, 1993); André Bossard, *Transnational Crime and Criminal Law* (Chicago: Office of International Criminal Justice, 1990).

39. Graeme Newman, ed., *Global Report on Crime and Justice,* United Nations Office for Drug Control and Crime Prevention, Centre for International Crime Prevention (New York: Oxford University Press, 1999). See also, *The United Nations and Crime Prevention: Seeking Security and Justice for All* (New York: UNDPI, 1996); and *The United Nations and Criminal Justice, 1946–1996: Resolutions, Reports, Documents and Publications, International Review of Criminal Policy,* Issue 47–48 (Vienna: United Nations, 1996/97).
40. G. O. W. Mueller, Michael Gage, and Lenore R. Kupperstein, *The Legal Norms of Delinquency: A Comparative Study,* Criminal Law Education and Research Center Monograph Series, vol. 1 (South Hackensack, N.J.: Fred B. Rothman, 1969).
41. Anastassios Mylonas, *Perception of Police Power: A Study in Four Cities,* Comparative Criminal Law Project Monograph Series, vol. 8 (South Hackensack, N.J.: Fred B. Rothman, 1973).
42. Setsuo Miyazawa, "The Enigma of Japan as a Testing Ground for Cross-Cultural Criminological Studies," *Annales Internationales de Criminologie,* **32** (1994): 81–103; B. Hebenton and J. Spencer, "The Contribution and Limitations of Anglo-American Criminology to Understanding Crime in Central-Eastern Europe," *European Journal of Crime, Criminal Law and Criminal Justice,* **2** (1994): 50–61.
43. Sheldon Glueck and Eleanor Glueck, *Unraveling Juvenile Delinquency* (New York: The Commonwealth Fund; Cambridge, Mass.: Harvard University Press, 1950).
44. Sheldon Glueck and Eleanor Glueck, *Of Delinquency and Crime—A Panorama of Years of Search and Research,* Publications of the Criminal Law Education and Research Center, vol. 8 (Springfield, Ill.: Charles C Thomas, 1974), p. 332.
45. Obi N. I. Ebbe, "Juvenile Delinquency in Nigeria: The Problem of Application of Western Theories," *International Journal of Comparative and Applied Criminal Justice,* **16** (1992): 353–370.
46. Rosemary Gartner, "The Victims of Homicide: A Temporal and Cross-National Comparison," *American Sociological Review,* **55** (1990): 92–106.
47. Gary LaFree and Christopher Birkbeck, "The Neglected Situation: A Cross-National Study of the Situational Characteristics of Crime," *Criminology,* **29** (1991): 73–98.
48. Richard R. Bennett, "Routine Activities: A Cross-National Assessment of a Criminological Perspective," *Social Forces,* **70** (1991): 147–163.
49. Richard R. Bennett and P. Peter Basiotis, "Structural Correlates of Juvenile Property Crime: A Cross-National, Time-Series Analysis," *Journal of Research in Crime and Delinquency,* **28** (1991): 262–287.
50. Sam S. Souryal, "Juvenile Delinquency in the Cross-Cultural Context: The Egyptian Experience," *International Journal of Comparative and Applied Criminal Justice,* **16** (1992): 329–352.
51. Adel Helal and Charisse T. M. Coston, "Low Crime Rates in Bahrain: Islamic Social Control—Testing the Theory of Synnomie," *International Journal of Comparative and Applied Criminal Justice,* **15** (1991): 125–144.
52. Gregory C. Leavitt, "General Evaluation and Durkheim's Hypothesis of Crime Frequency: A Cross-Cultural Test," *Sociological Quarterly,* **33** (1992): 241–263; and Suzanne T. Ortega, Jay Corzine, and Cathleen Burnett, "Modernization, Age Structure, and Regional Context: A Cross-National Study of Crime," *Sociological Spectrum,* **12** (1992): 257–277.
53. Christopher Birkbeck, "Against Ethnocentrism: A Cross-Cultural Perspective on Criminal Justice Theories and Policies," *Journal of Criminal Justice Education,* **4** (1993): 307–323.
54. Shelley, *Crime and Modernization.*
55. David Shichor, "Crime Patterns and Socio-Economic Development: A Cross-National Analysis," *Criminal Justice Review,* **15** (1990): 64–78; and John Arthur, "Development and Crime in Africa: A Test of Modernization Theory," *Journal of Criminal Justice,* **19** (1991): 499–513.
56. "New Perspectives in Crime Prevention and Criminal Justice and Development: The Role of International Co-operation," working paper prepared by the Secretariat, United Nations, 1980, A/Conf. 87/10.
57. Freda Adler, *Nations Not Obsessed with Crime,* Comparative Criminal Law Project Publications Series, vol. 15 (Littleton, Colo.: Fred B. Rothman, 1983).
58. See Note 8.
59. See Ugljesa Zvekic, ed., *Essays on Crime and Development* (Rome: U.N. Interregional Crime and Justice Research Institute, 1990).
60. V. Lee Hamilton and Joseph Sanders, *Everyday Justice: Responsibility and the Individual in Japan and the United States* (New Haven, Conn.: Yale University Press, 1992); Hans Joachim Schneider, "Crime and Its Control in Japan and in the Federal Republic of Germany, a Comparative Study," *International Journal of Offender Therapy and Comparative Criminology,* **36** (1992): 47–63.
61. Dale E. Berger et al., "Deterrence and Prevention of Alcohol-Impaired Driving in Australia, the United States, and Norway," *Justice Quarterly,* **7** (1990): 453–465.

62. David B. Kopel, *The Samurai, the Mountie, and the Cowboy: Should America Adopt the Gun Controls of Other Democracies?* (Buffalo, N.Y.: Prometheus, 1992).
63. Robert L. Nay, *Firearms Regulations in Various Foreign Countries* (Washington, D.C.: Law Library of Congress, 1990).
64. Michael Clarke, "The Control of Insurance Fraud: A Comparative View," *British Journal of Criminology,* **30** (1990): 1–23.
65. Kenneth Polk and William Weston, "Insider Trading as an Aspect of White Collar Crime," *Australian and New Zealand Journal of Criminology,* **23** (1990): 24–38.
66. Yü-Hsiu Hsü, ed., *International Conference on Environmental Criminal Law* (Taipei: Taiwan/ROC Chapter of the International Association of Penal Law, 1992).
67. Rosemary Gartner, "Family Structure, Welfare Spending, and Child Homicide in Developed Democracies," *Journal of Marriage and the Family,* **53** (1991): 231–240.
68. Margo I. Wilson and Martin Daly, "Who Kills Whom in Spouse Killings? On the Exceptional Sex Ratio of Spousal Homicides in the United States," *Criminology,* **30** (1992): 189–215.
69. Lois A. Fingerhut and Joel C. Kleinman, "International and Interstate Comparisons of Homicide among Young Males," *Journal of the American Medical Association,* **263** (1990): 3292–3295.
70. F. H. McClintock and Per-Olof H. Wikstrom, "The Comparative Study of Urban Violence—Criminal Violence in Edinburgh and Stockholm," *British Journal of Criminology,* **32** (1992): 505–520.
71. Dae H. Chang and Galan M. Janeksela, eds., "Special Issue on Comparative Juvenile Delinquency," *International Journal of Comparative and Applied Criminal Justice,* **16** (1992): 135–170, with contributions by Gaban M. Janeksela, David P. Farrington, Alison Hatch and Curt T. Griffiths, Günther Kaiser, Josine Junger-Tas, Paul C. Friday, James O. Finckenauer and Linda Kelly, Hualing Fu, Michael S. Vaughn and Frank F. Y. Huang, Byung In Cho and Richard J. Chang, Clayton A. Hartjen and Sesharajani Kethineni, Sam S. Souryhal, and Obi N. I. Ebbe.
72. Mylonas, *Perception of Police Power.*
73. Graeme Newman, *Comparative Deviance: Perception and Law in Six Cultures* (New York: Elsevier Scientific, 1976).
74. Russel P. Dobash, R. Emerson Dobash, Scott Balliofyne, Karl Schuman, Reiner Kaulitzki, and Hans-Werner Guth, "Ignorance and Suspicion: Young People and Criminal Justice in Scotland and Germany," *British Journal of Criminology,* **30** (1990): 306–320.
75. Ronald D. Hunter, "Three Models of Policing," *Police Studies,* **13** (1990): 118–124; R. I. I. Mawby, *Comparable Policing Issues: The British and American Experience in International Perspective* (London: Unwin Hyman, 1990).
76. Leslie T. Wilkins, *Punishment, Crime and Market Forces* (Aldershot, England: Dartmouth, 1991); Dennis Wiechman, Jerry Kendall, and Ronald Bae, "International Use of the Death Penalty," *International Journal of Comparative and Applied Criminal Justice,* **14** (1990): 239–259.
77. See Gunther Kaiser, Helmut Kury, and Hans-Jorg Albrecht, eds., *Victims and Criminal Justice,* 3 vols. (Freiburg, Germany: Max Planck Institut, 1991); Emilio C. Viano, ed., *Critical Issues in Victimology—International Perspectives* (New York: Springer Verlag, 1992).
78. Jack Levin and Jack McDevitt, *Hate Crimes—The Rising Tide of Bigotry and Bloodshed* (New York: Plenum, 1993).
79. See Hans-Dieter Schwind et al., "Causes, Prevention and Control of Violence," *Revue Internationale de Criminologie et de Police Technique,* **43** (1990): 395–520.
80. Gerhard O. W. Mueller and Freda Adler, *Outlaws of the Ocean: The Complete Book of Contemporary Crime on the High Seas* (New York: Hearst Marine Books, 1985); Gerhard O. W. Mueller and Freda Adler, "A New Wave of Crime at Sea," *The World and I* (February 1986): 96–103.
81. Mike King, *Towards Federalism: Policing the Borders of a "New" Europe* (Leicester, United Kingdom: University of Leicester, 1993); H. Lensing, "The Federalization of Europe: Towards a Federal System of Criminal Justice," *European Journal of Crime, Criminal Law and Criminal Justice,* **1** (1993): 212–229; Ethan A. Nadelman, *Cops across Borders: The Internationalization of U.S. Criminal Law Enforcement* (University Park: Penn State University Press, 1994).
82. See fourth U.N. Survey, 1986–1990, A/Conf.169/15 and Add. 1.
83. See, for example, Jonathan Reuvid, ed., *The Regulation and Prevention of Economic Crime Internationally* (London: Kogan Page, 1995).
84. United Nations Office for Drug Control and Crime Prevention, *United Nations Global Programme against Money Laundering* (New York: United Nations, 1998), p. 19.
85. Laurence Zuckerman and John Sullivan, "An FAA Study Shows Few Gains in Improving Security at Airports," *New York Times,* Nov. 5, 1999, p. 30.

86. Several journals are devoted entirely to terrorism. See *Terrorism* (New York); *Studies in Conflict and Terrorism* (London); *Violence, Aggression, Terrorism* (Danbury, Conn.).
87. "High-Tech Art Sleuths Snare Thieves," *C.J. International,* **9** (1993): 4:6.
88. Truc-Nhu Ho, *Art Theft in New York City: An Explanatory Study in Crime Specificity,* Ph.D. dissertation, Rutgers University, 1992.
89. Ralph Blumenthal, "Museums Getting Together to Track Stolen Art," *New York Times,* July 16, 1996, pp. C13, C15.
90. Natalie D. Voss, "Crime on the Internet," *Jones Telecommunications and Multimedia Encyclopedia,* Drive D:\Studio, Jones Digital Century, 1996.
91. Michael R. Gordon, "Stolen Uranium Intercepted by Georgia in the Caucasus," *New York Times,* Sept. 24, 1999, p. 6.
92. "For Sale—Nukes: Deadly Plutonium from Russia's Vast Nuclear Network Is Turning Up on the European Market. Who Is Buying—and Can They Be Stopped?" *Newsweek,* Aug. 29, 1994, pp. 30–31; Bruce W. Nolan, "Formula for Terror," *Time,* Aug. 29, 1994.
93. Les Johnston, "Policing Plutonium: Issues in the Provision of Policing Services at Nuclear Facilities and for Related Materials in Transit," *Policing and Society,* **4** (1994): 53–72; Phil Williams and Paul H. Woessnar, *Nuclear Material Trafficking: An Interim Assessment* (Pittsburgh: Ridgway Center for International Security Studies, 1995).
94. Eric Ellen, "The Dimensions of International Maritime Crime," in *Issues in Maritime Crime: Mayhem at Sea,* ed. Martin Gill (Leicester, United Kingdom: Perpetuity Press, 1995), pp. 4–11; Martin Gill, *Crime at Sea: A Forgotten Issue in Police Co-operation* (Leicester, United Kingdom: Centre for the Study of Public Order, 1995); Gerhard O. W. Mueller and Freda Adler, "Piraterie: le 'Jolly Roger' flotte à nouveau les Corsaires des Caribes," *Revue Internationale de Criminologie et de Police Technique,* **4** (1992): 408–424.
95. National Insurance Crime Bureau, fax of July 29, 1996.
96. British Banking Association estimate. See Larry E. Coutoria, "The Future of High-Technology Crime: A Parallel Delphi Study," *Journal of Criminal Justice,* **23** (1995): 13–27.
97. E.g., Sally M. Edwards, Terry D. Edwards, and Charles B. Fields, eds., *Environmental Crime and Criminality* (New York: Garland, 1996).
98. Ko-lin Chin, *Chinese Subculture and Criminality: Non-traditional Crime Groups in America* (Westport, Conn.: Greenwood, 1990); Alex P. Schmid, ed., *Migration and Crime* (Milan, Italy: International Scientific and Professional Advisory Council of the United Nations Crime Prevention and Criminal Justice Programme, 1998).
99. Michael Woodiwiss, "Crime's Global Reach," in *Global Crime Connections,* ed. Frank Pearce and Michael Woodiwiss (Houndmills, United Kingdom: Macmillan, 1993), pp. 1–31.
100. Raphael F. Perl, ed., *Drugs and Foreign Policy: A Critical Review* (Boulder, Colo.: Westview Press, 1994); Günther Kaiser, "International Experiences with Different Strategies of Drug Policy," *EuroCriminology,* **7** (1994): 3–29.
101. See Frederick T. Martens, "Transnational Enterprise Crime and the Elimination of Frontiers," *International Journal of Comparative and Applied Criminal Justice,* **15** (1991): 99–107; Wojciech Cebulak, "The Antitrust Doctrine: How It Was Internationalized," *International Journal of Comparative and Applied Criminal Justice,* **14** (1990): 261–267.
102. See "Crime Prevention and Criminal Justice in the Context of Development: Realities and Perspectives of International Cooperation," *International Review of Criminal Policy,* **41/42** (1993): 1–19.
103. Gerhard O. W. Mueller, "Transnational Crime: An Experience in Uncertainties," in *Organized Crime: Uncertainties and Dilemmas,* ed. S. Einstein and M. Amir (Chicago: Office of International Criminal Justice, 1999), pp. 3–18.
104. Draft Articles of the Draft Code of Crimes against the Peace and Security of Mankind, adopted by the International Law Commission on First Reading, United Nations, New York, 1991. For a complete listing, see M. Cherif Bassiouni, *International Criminal Law—A Draft International Criminal Code* (Alphen an den Rijn, Netherlands: Sijthoff & Noordhoff, 1980).
105. Shana Swiss and Joan E. Giller, "Rape as a Crime of War," *Journal of the American Medical Association,* **270** (1993): 612–615.
106. For an analysis of all international crimes, see M. Cherif Bassiouni, ed., *International Criminal Law:* vol. 1, *Crimes,* 2d ed. (Ardsley, N.Y.: Transnational, 1999); M. Cherif Bassiouni, *A Draft International Criminal Code and Draft Statute for an International Criminal Tribunal* (Dordrecht, Netherlands: Martinus Nijhoff, 1987); Farhad Malekian, *International Criminal Law,* 2 vols. (Motala, Sweden: Borgstroms Trycker, 1991); Gerhard O. W. Mueller and Edward M. Wise, *International Criminal Law,* Comparative Criminal Law Project, Publications Series, vol. 2 (South Hackensack, N.J.: Fred B. Rothman, 1965).

Glossary

A

Accommodate In regard to achieving the American Dream, to adjust noneconomic needs so that they are secondary to and supportive of economic ones.

Accomplice A person who helps another commit a crime.

Aggravated assault An attack on another person in which the perpetrator inflicts serious harm on the victim or uses a deadly weapon.

Aging-out phenomenon A concept that holds that offenders commit less crime as they get older because they have less strength, initiative, stamina, and mobility.

Anomie A societal state marked by normlessness, in which disintegration and chaos have replaced social cohesion.

Arson At common law, the malicious burning of the dwelling house of another. This definition has been broadened by state statutes and criminal codes to cover the burning of other structures or even personal property.

Assault At common law, an unlawful offer or attempt with force or violence to do a corporal hurt to another or to frighten another.

Atavistic stigmata Physical features of a human being at an earlier stage of development, which—according to Cesare Lombroso—distinguish a born criminal from the general population.

Attachment The bond between a parent and child or between individuals and their family, friends, and school.

B

Bankruptcy fraud A scam in which an individual falsely attempts to claim bankruptcy (and thereby erase financial debts) by taking advantage of existing laws.

Battery A common law crime consisting of the intentional touching of or inflicting of hurt on another.

Behavioral modeling Learning how to behave by fashioning one's behavior after that of others.

Belief The extent to which an individual subscribes to society's values.

Biocriminology The subdiscipline of criminology that investigates biological and genetic factors and their relation to criminal behavior.

Birth cohort A group consisting of all individuals born in the same year.

Boiler room An operation run by one or more stock manipulators who, through deception and misleading sales techniques, seduce the unsuspecting and uninformed public into buying stocks in obscure and often poorly financed corporations.

Born criminal According to Lombroso, a person born with features resembling an earlier, more primitive form of human life, destined to become a criminal.

Burglary A common law felony; the nighttime breaking and entering of the dwelling house of another, with the intention to commit a crime (felony or larceny) therein.

C

Case study An analysis of all pertinent aspects of one unit of study.

Check forging The criminal offense of making or altering a check with intent to defraud.

Chromosomes Basic cellular structures containing genes, i.e., biological material that creates individuality.

Churning Frequent trading, by a broker, of a client's shares of stock for the sole purpose of generating large commissions.

Classical school of criminology A criminological perspective suggesting that (1) people have free will to choose criminal or conventional behavior; (2) people choose to commit crime for reasons of greed or personal need; and (3) crime can be controlled by criminal sanctions, which should be proportionate to the guilt of the perpetrator.

Commitment A person's support of and participation in a program, cause, or social activity, which ties the individual to the moral or ethical codes of society.

Comparative criminology The study of crime in two or more cultures in an effort to gain broader information for theory construction and crime-control modeling.

Conditioning The process of developing a behavior pattern through a series of repeated experiences.

Conduct norms Norms that regulate the daily lives of people and that reflect the attitudes of the groups to which they belong.

Confidence game A deceptive means of obtaining money or property from a victim who is led to trust the perpetrator.

Conflict model A model of crime in which the criminal justice system is seen as being used by the ruling class to control the lower class. Criminological investigation of the conflicts within society is emphasized.

Conformity Correspondence of an individual's behavior to society's patterns, norms, or standards.

Consensus model A model of criminal lawmaking that assumes that members of society agree on what is right and wrong and that law is the codification of agreed-upon social values.

Consumer fraud An act that causes a consumer to surrender money through deceit or a misrepresentation of a material fact.

Containment theory A theory positing that every person possesses a containing external structure and a protective internal structure, both of which provide defense, protection, or insulation against delinquency.

Corporate compliance program Corporate codes and training programs designed to prevent crimes and ethical violations.

Corporate due diligence Actions taken by a corporation to prevent or respond to criminal activity.

Corporate crime A crime attributed to a corporation, but perpetrated by or on the authority of an officer or high managerial agent.

Corporate ethos Corporate culture or character and its effect on the actions of an organization.

Corporate policy Standards and decisions of a corporation that produce policies resulting in law abidance or law violation.

Cortical arousal Activation of the cerebral cortex, a structure of the brain that is responsible for higher intellectual functioning, information processing, and decision making.

Crime An act in violation of law that causes harm, is identified by law, is committed with criminal intent, and is subject to punishment.

Crimes against property Crimes involving the illegal acquisition or destruction of property. *See* Crime.

Crimes against the person Crimes violative of life or physical integrity. *See* Crime.

Criminal attempt An act or omission constituting a substantial step in a course of conduct planned to culminate in the commission of a crime.

Criminal careers A concept that describes the onset of criminal activity, the types and amount of crime committed, and the termination of such activity.

Criminal justice system The interdependent and interactive components of police, courts, and corrections that form a unified whole (a system).

Criminologists Collect information on crime and criminals for study and analysis in accordance with the research methods of modern science.

Criminology The body of knowledge regarding crime as a social phenomenon. It includes within its scope the process of making laws, of breaking laws, and of reacting toward the breaking of laws (Sutherland). Thus, criminology is an empirical, social-behavioral science that investigates crime, criminals, and criminal justice.

Cultural deviance theories Theories positing that crime results from cultural values which permit, or even demand, behavior in violation of the law.

Cultural transmission A theory that views delinquency as a socially learned behavior transmitted from one generation to the next in disorganized urban areas.

Culture conflict theory A theory positing two groups may clash when their conduct norms differ, resulting in criminal activity.

D

Data Collected facts, observations, and other pertinent information from which conclusions can be drawn.

Deviance A broad concept encompassing both illegal behavior and behavior that departs from the social norm.

Differential association-reinforcement A theory of criminality based on the incorporation of psychological learning theory and differential association with social learning theory. Criminal behavior, the theory claims, is learned through associations and is contained or discontinued as a result of positive or negative reinforcements.

Differential association theory A theory of criminality based on the principle that an individual becomes delinquent because of an excess of definitions learned that are favorable to violation of law over definitions learned that are unfavorable to violation of law.

Differential opportunity theory A theory that attempts to join the concept of anomie and differential association by analyzing both legitimate and illegitimate opportunity structures available to individuals. It posits that illegitimate opportunities, like legitimate opportunities, are unequally distributed.

Direct control An external control that depends on rules, restrictions, and punishments.

Displacement In the event that a crime has been prevented, the commission of a quantitatively similar crime at a different time or place.

Dizygotic (DZ) twins Fraternal twins, who develop from two separate eggs fertilized at the same time. *See also* Monozygotic twins.

Drift According to David Matza, a state of limbo in which youths move in and out of delinquency and in which their lifestyles can embrace both conventional and deviant values.

Due process According to the Fourteenth Amendment of the U.S. Constitution, a fundamental mandate that a person should not be deprived of life, liberty, or property without reasonable and lawful procedures.

E

Ego The part of the psyche that, according to psychoanalytic theory, governs rational behavior; the moderator between the superego and the id.

Embezzlement The crime of withholding or withdrawing (conversion or misappropriation), without consent, funds entrusted to an agent (e.g., a bank teller or officer).

Equal protection A clause of the Fourteenth Amendment to the U.S. Constitution that guarantees equal protection of the law to everyone, without regard to race, origin, economic class, gender, or religion.

Eugenics A science, based on the principle of heredity, that has for its purpose the improvement of the race.

Experiment A research technique in which an investigator introduces a change into a process in order to make measurements or observations that evaluate the effects of the change.

Extroversion According to Hans Eysenck, a dimension of the human personality; describes individuals who are sensation-seeking, dominant, and assertive.

F

False pretenses, obtaining property by Leading a victim to part with property on a voluntary basis through trickery, deceit, or misrepresentation.

Federal Witness Protection Program A program, established under the Organized Crime Control Act of 1970, designed to protect witnesses who testify in court by relocating them and assigning to them new identities.

Felony A severe crime, subject to punishment of 1 year or more in prison or to capital punishment.

Felony murder The imposition of criminal liability for murder upon one who participates in the commission of a felony that is dangerous to life and that causes the death of another.

Fence A receiver of stolen property who resells the goods for profit.

Field experiment An experiment conducted in a real-world setting, as opposed to one conducted in a laboratory.

Fraud An act of trickery or deceit, especially involving misrepresentation.

G

General strain theory A criminological theory positing that criminal behavior can result from strain caused by failure to achieve positively valued goals, stress caused by the removal of positively valued stimuli from the individual, or strain caused by the presentation of negative stimuli.

H

High-tech crime The pursuit of illegal activities through the use of advanced electronic media.

Homicide The killing of one person by another.

Hypoglycemia A condition that may occur in susceptible individuals when the level of blood sugar falls below an acceptable range, causing anxiety, headaches, confusion, fatigue, and aggressive behavior.

Hypothesis A proposition set forth as an explanation for some specified phenomenon.

I

Id The part of the personality that, according to psychoanalytic theory, contains powerful urges and drives for gratification and satisfaction.

Index crimes The eight major crimes included in Part I of the Uniform Crime Reports: criminal homicide, forcible rape, robbery, aggravated assault, burglary, larceny-theft, auto theft, and arson.

Indirect control A behavioral influence that arises from an individual's identification with noncriminals and his or her desire to conform to societal norms.

Insider trading The use of material nonpublic financial information to obtain an unfair advantage in trading securities.

Internalized control Self-regulation of behavior and conformity to societal norms as a result of guilt feelings arising in the conscience.

International crimes The major criminal offenses so designated by the community of nations for the protection of interests common to all humankind.

International criminal court The United Nations court with jurisdiction over the most heinous international crimes.

Involuntary manslaughter Homicide in which the perpetrator unintentionally but recklessly causes the death of another person by consciously taking a grave risk that endangers the person's life.

Involvement An individual's participation in conventional activities.

J

Justifiable homicide A homicide, permitted by law, in defense of a legal right or mandate.

K

Kidnapping A felony consisting of the seizure and abduction of a person by force or threat of force and against the victim's will. Under federal law, the victim of a kidnapping is one who has been taken across state lines and held for ransom.

L

Labeling theory A theory that explains deviance in terms of the process by which a person acquires a negative identity, such as "addict" or "ex-con," and is forced to suffer the consequences of outcast status.

Larceny The trespassory (unconsented) taking and carrying away of personal property belonging to another with the intent to deprive the owner of the property permanently.

Laws of imitation An explanation of crime as learned behavior. Individuals are thought to emulate behavior patterns of others with whom they have contact.

GLOSSARY

Longitudinal study An analysis that focuses on studies of a particular group conducted repeatedly over a period of time.

M

Macrosociological study The study of overall social arrangements, their structures, and their long-term effects.

Mafia The entirety of those Sicilian families which, in both the United States and Sicily, are loosely associated with one another in operating organized crime.

Malice aforethought The mens rea requirement for murder, consisting of the intention to kill with the awareness that there is no right to kill. *See also* Mens rea.

Manslaughter Criminal homicide without malice, committed intentionally after provocation (voluntary manslaughter) or recklessly (involuntary manslaughter).

Mass murder The killing of several persons, in one act or transaction, by one perpetrator or a group of perpetrators.

Mens rea (Latin, "guilty mind") Awareness of wrongdoing; the intention to commit a criminal act or behave recklessly.

Microsociological study The study of everyday patterns of behavior and personal interactions.

Minimal brain dysfunction (MBD)
An attention-deficit disorder that may produce such asocial behavior as impulsivity, hyperactivity, and aggressiveness.

Misdemeanor A crime less serious than a felony and subject to a maximum sentence of 1 year in jail or a fine.

Money laundering The process by which money derived from illegal activities (especially drug sales) is unlawfully taken out of the country, placed in a numbered account abroad, and then transferred as funds no longer "dirty."

Monozygotic (MZ) twins Identical twins, who develop from a single fertilized egg that divides into two embryos. *See also* Dizygotic twins.

Murder The unlawful (usually intentional) killing of a human being with malice aforethought.

N

Neuroticism A personality disorder marked by low self-esteem, excessive anxiety, and wide mood swings (Eysenck).

Nonparticipant observation A study in which investigators observe closely but do not become participants.

O

Occupational crime A crime committed by an individual for his or her own benefit, in the course of performing a profession.

P

Participant observation Collection of information through involvement in the social life of the group a researcher is studying.

Penologist A social scientist who studies and applies the theory and methods of punishment for crime.

Phrenology A nineteenth-century theory based on the hypothesis that human behavior is localized in certain specific brain and skull areas. According to this theory, criminal behavior can be determined by the bumps on the head.

Physiognomy The study of facial features and their relation to human behavior.

Pimp A procurer or manager of prostitutes who provides access to prostitutes and protects and exploits them, living off their proceeds.

Population A large group of persons in a study.

Pornography The portrayal, by whatever means, of lewd or obscene (sexually explicit) material prohibited by law.

Positivist school of criminology A criminological perspective that uses the scientific methods of the natural sciences and suggests that human behavior is a product of social, biological, psychological, or economic forces.

Primary data Facts and observations that researchers gather by conducting their own measurements for a study.

Principals Perpetrators of a criminal act.

Proactive corporate fault The failure of a corporation to prevent ethical or legal violations.

Prostitution The practice of engaging in sexual activities for hire.

Psychoanalytic theory In criminology, a theory of criminality that attributes delinquent and criminal behavior to a conscience that is either so overbearing that it arouses excessive feelings of guilt or so weak that it cannot control the individual's impulses.

Psychopathy A condition in which a person appears to be psychologically normal but in reality has no sense of responsibility, shows disregard for truth, is insincere, and feels no sense of shame, guilt, or humiliation (also called sociopathy).

Psychosis A mental illness characterized by a loss of contact with reality.

Psychoticism A dimension of the human personality describing individuals who are aggressive, egocentric, and impulsive (Eysenck).

R

Racketeer Influenced and Corrupt Organizations (RICO) Act A federal statute that provides for forfeiture of assets derived from a criminal enterprise.

Radical criminology A criminological perspective that studies the relationships between economic disparity and crime, avers that crime is the result of a struggle between owners of capital and workers for the distribution of power and resources, and posits that crime will disappear only when capitalism is abolished.

Random sample A sample chosen in such a way as to ensure that each person in the population to be studied has an equal chance of being selected. *See also* Sample.

Rape At common law, a felony consisting of the carnal knowledge (intercourse), by force and violence, by a man of a woman (not his wife) against her will. The stipulation that the woman not be the man's wife is omitted in modern statutes. Many states now call rape "sexual assault."

Rational choice A theory stating that crime is the result of a decision-making process in which the offender weighs the potential penalties and rewards of committing a crime.

Reaction formation An individual response to anxiety in which the person reacts to a stimulus with abnormal intensity or inappropriate conduct.

Reactive corporate fault The failure of a corporation to respond reasonably to the discovery of an ethical or legal violation.

Robbery The taking of the property of another, or out of his or her presence, by means of force and violence or the threat thereof.

Routine activity A theory stating that an increase or decrease in crime rates can be explained by changes in the daily habits of potential victims; based on the expectation that crimes will occur where there is a suitable target unprotected by guardians.

S

Sample A selected subset of a population to be studied. *See also* Random sample.

Secondary data Facts and observations that were previously collected for a different study.

Self-report survey A survey in which respondents answer in a confidential interview or, most often, by completing an anonymous questionnaire.

Serial murder The killing of several victims over a period of time by the same perpetrator(s).

Sherman Antitrust Act An act (1890) of Congress prohibiting any contract, conspiracy, or combination of business interests in restraint of foreign or interstate trade.

Shoplifting Stealing goods from stores or markets.

Simple assault An attack that inflicts little or no physical harm on the victim.

Social control theory An explanation of criminal behavior that focuses on control mechanisms, techniques, and strategies for regulating human behavior, leading to conformity or obedience to society's rules, and which posits that deviance results when social controls are weakened or break down, so that individuals are not motivated to conform to them.

Social disorganization theory A theory of criminality in which the breakdown of effective social bonds, primary-group associations, and social controls in neighborhoods and communities is held to result in development of high-crime areas.

Social interactionists Scholars who view the human self as formed through a process of social interaction.

Social learning theory A theory of criminality that maintains that delinquent behavior is learned through the same psychological processes as nondelinquent behavior, e.g., through reinforcement.

Social norms Perceived standards of acceptable behavior prevalent among members of a society.

Sociopath A person who has no sense of responsibility; shows disregard for truth; is insincere; and feels no sense of shame, guilt, or humiliation.

Sodomy Sexual intercourse by mouth or anus; a felony at common law.

Somatotype school of criminology A criminological perspective that relates body build to behavioral tendencies, temperament, susceptibility to disease, and life expectancy.

Statutory rape Sexual intercourse with a person incapable of giving legally relevant consent, because of immaturity (below age), mental, or physical condition.

Stock manipulation An illegal practice of brokers in which clients are led to believe that the price of a particular stock will rise, thus creating an artificial demand for it.

Strain theory A criminological theory positing that a gap between culturally approved goals and legitimate means of achieving them causes frustration which leads to criminal behavior.

Stranger homicide Criminal homicide committed by a person unknown and unrelated to the victim.

Strict liability Liability for a crime or violation imposed without regard to the actor's guilt; criminal liability without mens rea. *See also* Mens rea.

Subculture A subdivision within the dominant culture that has its own norms, beliefs, and values.

Subculture of violence A subculture with values that demand the overt use of violence in certain social situations.

Superego In psychoanalytic theory, the conscience, or those aspects of the personality that threaten the person or impose a sense of guilt or psychic suffering and thus restrain the id.

Survey The systematic collection of information by asking questions in questionnaires or interviews.

Synnomie A societal state, opposite of anomie, marked by social cohesion achieved through the sharing of values.

T

Target hardening A crime-prevention technique that seeks to make it more difficult to commit a given offense, by better protecting the threatened object or person.

Terrorism The use of violence against a target to create fear, alarm, dread, or coercion for the purpose of obtaining concessions or rewards or commanding public attention for a political cause.

Theories of victimization Theories that explain the role that victims play in the crimes that happen to them.

Theory A coherent group of propositions used as principles in explaining or accounting for known facts or phenomena.

Tort An injury or wrong committed against another, subject to compensation; an infringement of the rights of an individual that is not founded on either contract or criminal law prohibition.

Transnational crime A criminal act or transaction violating the laws of more than one country, or having an impact on a foreign country.

U

Utilitarianism A criminological perspective positing that crime prevention and criminal justice must serve the end of providing the greatest good for the greatest number; based on the rationality of lawgivers, law enforcers, and the public at large.

V

Variables Changeable factors.

Vicarious liability The imputation of liability from an agent to a principal, e.g. from an employee to an employer.

Victim precipitation Opening oneself up, by either direct or subliminal means, to a criminal response.

Victimization survey A survey that measures the extent of crime by interviewing individuals about their experiences as victims.

Violation Minor criminal offense, usually under a city ordinance, commonly subject only to a fine.

Voluntary manslaughter Homicide in which the perpetrator intentionally, but without malice, causes the death of another person, as in the heat of passion, in response to strong provocation, or possibly under severe intoxication.

W

White-collar crime A sociological concept encompassing any violation of the law committed by a person or group of persons in the course of an otherwise respected and legitimate occupation or business enterprise.

Whistle-blower An employee, or interested party, who reports corporate illegalities to authorities.

"Did You Know..." Sources

14: T. F. T. Plucknett, *A Concise History of The Common Law,* 5th edition (London: Butterworth and Co., 1956), pp. 15, 156, 323, 355; **34:** *Juvenile Offenders and Victims: 1999 National Report,* Office of Juvenile Justice and Delinquency Prevention, September 1999; **42:** *Juvenile Offenders and Victims: 1999 National Report,* Office of Juvenile Justice and Delinquency Prevention, September 1999; **63:** http://www.utm.edu/research/rep/b/beccarea.htm; **70:** http://www.epub.orgbr/cm/m01/frenolog/frenmod.htm; **84:** Former FBI Agent Jack Douglas, quoted in Kevia Johnson, "Several Serial Killers Said to Be At Large," *USA Today,* July 1, 1999, p. 12A; **101:** "Cholesterol and Violence: Is There a Connection?" *Annals of Internal Medicine,* 128 (1998): 478–487; **119:** http://www.ssc.wisc.edu/irp/faqs/faq3dir/povtab01-one.htm; **138:** *Juvenile Offenders and Victims: 1999 National Report,* Office of Juvenile Justice and Delinquency Prevention, September, 1999; **152:** http://www.dailynews.com/Stories/0,1413,200%257E20954%257E1302698.00.html; **159:** http://www.clasp.org/Pubs/DMS/Documents/1012503181.48/teen_pregnancy_a_key_strategy.pdf; **180:** Anthony Walsh and Lee Ellis, "Political Ideology and American Criminologists' Explanations for Criminal Behavior," *Criminologist,* 24 (1999): 1; **185:** http://www.ifs.univie.ac.at/~pr2gq1/85275.html# funsoc; **217:** Marcus Felson and Ronald V. Clarke, "Routine Precautions, Criminology, and Crime Prevention," in *Crime and Public Policy: Putting Theory to Work,* ed. Hugh D. Barlow, Boulder, Colo.: Westview Press, 1995; **228:** Ronald V. Clarke, *Hot Products: Understanding, Anticipating and Reducing Demand for Stolen Goods,* Policing and Reducing Crime Unit, Police Research Series Paper 112 (London: Home Office, 1999); John Burrow and D. Cooper, *Theft and Loss from UK Libraries,* Police Research Group Crime Prevention Unit Series Paper 37 (London: Home Office, 1992); **242:** *Juvenile Offenders and Victims: 1999 National Report,* Office of Juvenile Justice and Delinquency Prevention, 1999, p. 16; **246:** *Juvenile Offenders and Victims: 1999 National Report,* Office of Juvenile Justice and Delinquency Prevention, 1999, p. 17; **308:** "1998 Internet Fraud Statistics" (http://www.fraud.org/internet/9923stat.htm); **363:** Editorial Observer, "Why Some Get Busted and Some Go Free," *New York Times,* May 10, 1999; **366:** Anti–Drug Abuse Act of 1986, 21 USC 801.

Photo Credits

3: Heather Hall/Agence France Presse/Corbis; **6:** PhotoDisc; **7:** Alfred/SIPA; **8:** EFE/SIPA; **9:** Paula Bronstein/Getty Images; **10:** Timothy Fadek/Gamma Presse; **11:** Laski Diffusion/Gamma Presse; **15:** Giraudon/Art Resource; **19:** A Ramey/Stock, Boston; **23:** Haviv/Corbis Saba; **26:** Robert Brenner/PhotoEdit; **30:** Al Grillo/AP/Wide World Photos; **31:** Mike Derer/AP/Wide World Photos; **42:** Andy Uzzle/Gamma Presse; **49:** The Image Works; **52:** Daniel Sheehan/Getty Images; **53:** Michael Probost/AP/Wide World Photos; **59:** Pushkin Museum of Fine Arts, Moscow, Scala/Art Resource; **60:** PhotoEdit; **61:** Gerhard Hinterleitner/Gamma Presse; **63:** Granger Collection; **65:** AP/Wide World Photos; **68:** The British Museum; **69:** *"How to Read Character: A New Illustrated Hand-Book of Physiology, Phrenology and Physiognomy for Students and Examiner ,"* by Samuel Wells, Fowler & Wells Co., NY, 1890 (Collection of B. Salz); **71:** Topham/The Image Works; **73:** Arthur Estabrook Papers, M.E. Grenander Department of Special Collections and Archives, University at Albany; **76:** Corbis Bettmann; **83:** Mark Richards/PhotoEdit; **84:** Joel Gordon; **85:** Corbis Bettmann; **89:** Martin Rodgers/ Stock, Boston; **94:** Steve Senne/Reuters/Landov; **96:** Gretchen Ertl/AP/Wide World Photos; **99:** George Wideman/AP/Wide World Photos; **101:** SIPA; **107:** Jose Azel/Aurora Photos; **110:** Richard Carson/Reuters/Landov; **115:** Joseph Sohm/Corbis; **118:** Paolo da Silva/Corbis Sygma; **120:** Elaine Thompson/AP/ Wide World Photos; **124:** Ramey/Stock, Boston; **129:** Gregg Smith/Corbis Saba; **133:** Sankei Shimbun/Corbis Sygma; **136:** Lisa Terry/Getty Images; **139:** Darrell Wong/The Fresno Bee/AP/Wide World Photos; **140:** Mary D' Anella/Corbis Sygma; **143:** A. Ramey/PhotoEdit; **146:** Bob Daemmrich/Stock, Boston; **147:** Mark Peterson/Corbis Saba; **150:** Rick Hunter/SA Express News/Corbis Sygma; **153:** Jim Cooper/AP/Wide World Photo; **157:** Greg Mellis; **160:** A. Ramey/PhotoEdit; **162:** Steven Rubin/The Image Works; **167:** Frederic J. Brown/Agence France Presse; **168:** Pat Little/AP/Wide World Photos; **172:** Joel Gordon; **176:** Morry Gash/AP/Wide World Photos; **179:** Joel Gordon; **181:** Richard Sheinwald/AP/Wide World Photos; **184:** Fujifotos/The Image Works; **189:** Jonathan Nourok/PhotoEdit; **193:** John Paul Filo; **197:** Rick Reinhard; **199:** Steve Lehman/Corbis Saba; **201:** James McCoy/Buffalo News/Corbis Sygma; **206:** Rick Reinhard; **207:** Stephen Ferry/Getty Images; **209:** Geuorgui Pinkhassov/Magnum; **213:** Mark Richards/PhotoEdit; **215:** Mark Peterson/Corbis Saba; **219:** Lon C. Diehl/PhotoEdit; **218:** Courtesy Gerhard O.W. Mueller; **220:** Oscar Abolafia/Getty Images; **222:** Mike Siluk/The Image Works; **225:** Rudi Von Briel/PhotoEdit; **230:** Joel Gordon; **229:** David Butow/Corbis Saba; **237:** Ceneta Manuel/Gamma Presse; **239:** Paul Sakuma/AP/Wide World Photos; **241:** Taylor/Montgomery Journal/Gamma Presse; **242:** Scott Dalton/AP/Wide World Photos; **244:** Norman Y. Lono/The New York Times; **247:** Dwayne Newton/PhotoEdit; **249:** Charles Drupa/AP/Wide World Photos; **252:** Joel Gordon; **256:** John Todd/AP/ Wide World Photos; **259:** Library of Congress; **260:** Alan Tannenbaum; **266:** Mark Cardwell/Reuters/Archive/Getty Images; **264:** Stephen Ferry/Getty Images; **269:** Shannon Stapleton/Reuters/Landov; **275:** Cynthia Howe/Corbis Sygma; **273:** Pam Francis/Getty Images; **277:** Christian Fischer/DDP /SIPA; **279:** Linda Spillers/The New York Times; **281:** Rick Reinhard; **282:** Amy Sancetta/AP/Wide World Photos; **289:** Douglas Burrows/Getty Images; **293:** Los Angeles County Courts/Getty Images; **296:** George Widman/AP/Wide World Photos; **297:** Courtesy Freda Adler; **299:** Mark Terrill/AP Wide World Photos; **301:** Ed Reinke/AP Wide World Photos; **305:** Gary Kazanjian; **308:** Bonnie Kamin/PhotoEdit; **309:** Daniel Hulshizer/AP/Wide World Photos; **317:** Thomas E. Witte/Gamma Presse; **319:** William Miller/SIPA; **321:** Jason Straziuso/AP/Wide World Photos; **322:** 8383/Gamma Presse; **323:** Kenneth Lambert/AP/Wide World Photos; **332:** Bob Shaw; **334:** Hyungwon Kang/Reuters/Landov; **337:** Getty Images; **339:** Kath Willens/AP/Wide World Photos; **343:** Baldev/Corbis Sygma; **345:** Alex Wong/Getty Images; **353:** Michael Schmelling/AP/Wide World Photos; **359:** Tom Miner/The Image Works; **360:** Nick Ut/AP/Wide World Photos; **362:** Apichart Weerawong/AP/Wide World Photos; **367:** Larry Kolvoord/The Image Works; **371:** Joel Gordon; **373:** Jim Wilson/Woodfin Camp & Associates; **378:** T. Crosby/Getty Images; **383:** Chip Hires/Gamma Presse; **385:** Apichart Weerawong/AP/Wide World Photos; **388:** Mia Foster/PhotoEdit; **393:** A. Ramey/Woodfin Camp & Associates; **395:** Peter Blakely/Corbis Saba; **398:** Vladimir Sichov/SIPA; **404.**

Illustration & Text Credits

Chapter 2

Figure 2.2 From Richard F. Sparks, H. G. Genn, and D. J. Dodd, *Surveying Victims: A Study of the Measurement of Criminal Victimization, Perceptions of Crime, and Attitudes to Criminal Justice*, p. 6. Copyright © 1977 John Wiley & Sons Limited. Reproduced with permission.

Chapter 4

Table 4.1 Adapted from Robert S. Feldman, *Understanding Psychology*, p. 378. Copyright © 1987 by The McGraw-Hill Companies, Inc. Reprinted by permission of The McGraw-Hill Companies, Inc.

Table 4.3 Adapted from *Criminal Law: Principles and Cases* by Thomas J. Gardner and Terry M. Anderson. Copyright © 2000 Wadsworth. Reprinted with permission of Wadsworth, a division of Thomson Learning: www.thomsonrights.com. Fax 800-730-2215.

Figure 4.1 From J. Federman, ed., *National Television Violence Study*, vol. 3, pp. 120–122. Copyright © 1998 by Sage Publications, Inc. Reprinted by permission of Sage Publications, Inc.

Chapter 5

Table 5.1 Reprinted with permission of The Free Press, a Division of Simon & Schuster Adult Publishing Group, from *Social Theory and Social Structure* by Robert K. Merton. Copyright © 1957 by The Free Press. Copyright © renewed 1985 by Robert K. Merton.

Figure 5.2 From Jane Gross, "Remnant of the War on Poverty: Job Corps Is Still a Quiet Success," *The New York Times*, February 17, 1992, p. A14. Copyright © 1992 by The New York Times Co. Reprinted with permission.

Figure 5.3 From *Theories of Delinquency*, Fourth Edition by Donald J. Shoemaker, p. 79. Copyright © 1984, 1990, 1996, 2000 by Oxford University Press, Inc. Used by permission of Oxford University Press, Inc.

Figure 5.4 From Robert E. Park, Ernest W. Burgess, and Roderick D. McKenzie, *The City*, p. 55. Copyright © 1925 by The University of Chicago. All rights reserved. Reprinted by permission of the University of Chicago Press.

Chapter 6

Figure 6.1 From *Theories of Delinquency*, Fourth Edition by Donald J. Shoemaker, p. 109. Copyright © 1984, 1990, 1996, 2000 by Oxford University Press, Inc. Used by permission of Oxford University Press, Inc.

Figure 6.2 From *Theories of Delinquency*, Fourth Edition by Donald J. Shoemaker, p. 117. Copyright © 1984, 1990, 1996, 2000 by Oxford University Press, Inc. Used by permission of Oxford University Press, Inc.

Figure 6.4 From *Theories of Delinquency*, Fourth Edition by Donald J. Shoemaker, p. 125. Copyright © 1984, 1990, 1996, 2000 by Oxford University Press, Inc. Used by permission of Oxford University Press, Inc.

Chapter 7

Table 7.1 Reprinted by permission of Transaction Publishers. From *Causes of Delinquency* by Travis Hirschi. Copyright © 2002 by Transaction Publishers.

Figure 7.1 Reprinted by permission of Transaction Publishers. From Marc LeBlanc, "A Generic Control Theory of the Criminal Phenomenon: The Structural and Dynamic Statements of an Integrative Multilayered Control Theory," in T. P. Thornberry, ed., *Developmental Theories of Crime and Delinquency*, Advances in Criminological Theory, Vol. 7, p. 238. Copyright © 1997 by Transaction Publishers.

Chapter 9

Table 9.1 From Marcus Felson and Ronald V. Clarke, *Opportunity Makes the Thief: Practical Theory for Crime Prevention*, Police Research Series Paper 98 (London: Home Office, 1998), p. 9. © Crown Copyright 1998. Reprinted by permission of Her Majesty's Stationery Office.

Table 9.2 From Ronald V. Clarke and Ross Homel, "A Revised Classification of Situational Crime Prevention Techniques," in *Crime Prevention at a Crossroads*, ed. Steven P. Lab. Reprinted by permission of Anderson Publishing Company.

Table 9.4 Reprinted by permission of the National Insurance Crime Bureau.

Table 9.5 From Zachary Fleming, Patricia Brantingham, and Paul Brantingham, "Exploring Auto Theft in British Colombia," in *Crime Prevention Studies*, vol. 3, ed. Ronald V. Clarke (Monsey, New York: Criminal Justice Press, 1994), p. 62. Reprinted by permission of the publisher.

Figure 9.1 Adapted from Ronald V. Clarke and Derek B. Cornish, "Modeling Offenders Decisions: A Framework for Research and Policy," *Crime and Justice*, vol. 6, ed. Michael Tonry and Norval Morris, p. 169. Copyright © 1985 by The University of Chicago. All rights reserved. Reprinted by permission of the University of Chicago Press.

Figure 9.3 From George Rengert and John Wasilchick, *Suburban Burglary: A Time and a Place for Everything*, 1985, p. 35. Courtesy of Charles C. Thomas, Publisher, Ltd., Springfield, Illinois.

Chapter 10

Figure 10.3 From *Chinese Subculture and Criminality: Nontraditional Crime Groups in America* by Ko-lin Chin, p. 76 (Contributions in Criminology and Penology, Number 29). Copyright © 1990 by Ko-lin Chin. Reproduced with permission of Greenwood Publishing Group, Inc., Westport, CT.

Figure 10.4 From Gregory L. Vistica "Extremism in the Ranks," *Newsweek,* March 25, 1996, p. 36. Copyright © 1996 Newsweek, Inc. All rights reserved. Reprinted by permission.

Figure 10.5 From Claudia Kalb, "Schools on the Alert," *Newsweek,* Aug. 23, 1999, p. 42. Copyright © 1999 Newsweek, Inc. All rights reserved. Reprinted by permission.

Figure 10.6 From "A National Backlash: State and Local Governments Are Taking Aim at the Gun Industry, Either by Enacting Legislation or by Filing Lawsuits," *Time,* August 9, 1999, p. 28. Copyright © 1999 Time Inc. Reprinted by permission.

Chapter 11

Table 11.1 From Read Hayes, *1996 Retail Theft Trends: An Analysis of Customer Theft in Stores,* Winter Park, FL: Loss Prevention Specialists, 1996. Reprinted by permission of the author.

Table 11.2 From NICB Vehicle Theft Study, 2001. www.nicb.org/services/hotspotsrelease.html. Reprinted by permission of the National Insurance Crime Bureau.

Chapter 12

Table 12.3 From Transparency International New Bribe Payers Index (BPI) 2002 (Berlin, 14 May 2002). Reprinted by permission of Transparency International.

Table 12.4 From Transparency International Corruption Perceptions Index 2002 (Berlin, 28 August 2002). Reprinted by permission of Transparency International.

Table 12.5 From Transparency International New Bribe Payers Index (BPI) 2002 (Berlin, 14 May 2002). Reprinted by permission of Transparency International.

Chapter 13

Table 13.1 From Bruce D. Johnson, Terry Williams, Kojo A. Dir, and Harry Sanabria, "Drug Abuse in the Inner City: Impact on Hard-Drug Users and the Community," in *Drugs and Crime,* ed. Michael Tonry and James Q. Wilson, (Crime and Justice, Vol. 13), p. 19. Copyright © 1990 by The University of Chicago. All rights reserved. Reprinted by permission of the University of Chicago Press.

Name Index

Abadinsky, Howard, 261, 366, N-33, N-45
Abdelaziz, Atiqui, N-30
Abraham, Nathaniel, 181
Abrahamsen, David, N-29
Adams, Anthony, N-16
Adams, Reed, N-8
Adele, Stan M., N-52
Adler, Amy, 380
Adler, Freda, 51, 61, 125, 141, 184, 185, 201, 298, N-1, N-4, N-5, N-9, N-12, N-13, N-16, N-18, N-19, N-21, N-23, N-27, N-38, N-40, N-41, N-46, N-47, N-53, N-56
Adler, Jeffrey S., N-23
Adler, Jerry, N-35
Adler, Jill, 198
Adler, Nanci, N-2
Africa, John, 140
Ageton, Suzanne S., 53, N-4, N-12, N-20
Aglipay, Edgar, N-44
Agnew, Robert, 126, 173, N-4, N-19, N-21
Agusti, Filiberto, N-44
Ahlstrom-Laakso, S., N-49
Aichhorn, August, N-7
Aigner, Stephen M., N-4
Akers, Ronald L., 196, N-8, N-16, N-22
Albanese, Jay S., 261, N-33, N-34
Albini, Joseph, N-33
Albonetti, Celesta A., N-23
Albrecht, Hans-Jorg, N-56
Albrecht, Steve W., N-41
Alder, Christine, N-32
Alexander, Shana, N-33
Aley, James, N-52
Almendarez, Armando, 125
Alper, Benedict, N-54
Ames, M. Ashley, N-31
Amir, Menachem, 254, N-32, N-49, N-57
Ancel, Marc, N-6, N-53
Anderson, Annelise Graebner, N-33
Anderson, Bo, N-18
Anderson, Pamela, 249
Andrews, D. W., N-8
Angew, Robert, N-13
Angier, Natalie, 178
Anglin, Deirdre, N-29
Anglin, Douglas M., N-47
Anglin, M. D., N-8
Ansen, David, 328
Applebome, Peter, N-52
Applegate, Brandon K., N-50
Archer, Dane, N-53
Arlacchi, Pino, N-33
Arneklev, B. J., N-21

Arnold, Rolf, N-41
Arthur, John A., N-37, N-55
Asahara, Shoko, 133, 272
Asbury, Herbert, 155
Atkins, Daryl, 74
Aultman, Madeline G., N-20
Austin, James, 187
Austin, Roy L., N-4
Austin, W. Timothy, N-21
Avery, D'Aunn Webster, 311, N-25, N-39
Avison, William R., N-13, N-15
Ayat, Mohammed, 250, N-30

Baarda, B., N-8
Bachman, Jerald G., N-2, N-45, N-46
Bachman, Ronet, N-30
Bacich, Anthony R., N-31
Bae, Ronald, N-56
Bagley, Bruce M., N-48
Bai, Matt, N-35, N-36
Bailey, William C., N-32
Bakalar, James, N-45
Ball, John C., N-47
Ball, Richard A., N-19
Balliofyne, Scott, N-55
Balsamo, William, N-32
Bamfield, Joshua, N-37
Bandura, Albert, 90, 94, N-8
Barbour, William, N-51
Barmlet, Gwen W., N-50
Barnes, Harry Elmer, 63, N-5
Barnett, Cynthia, 320
Barnett, W. Steven, N-14
Baron, Stephen W., N-16
Barovick, Harriet, 176
Barron, R. A., N-51
Barton, Mark O., 245
Bartusch, Dawn Jeglum, N-14
Barzini, Luigi, N-33
Basiotis, P. Peter, N-54
Baskin, Deborah R., N-15, N-48
Bassiouni, M. Cherif, N-57
Baumer, Terry L., N-32
Baus, Stephanie A., N-50
Bayley, David H., N-53
Beals, Gregory, 43
Beccaria, Cesare, 62–64
Beck, Allen J., 91
Becker, Gary S., N-25
Becker, Howard S., 190–191, 193, 196, N-22, N-23
Beeman, E. A., N-11
Beha, James A., II, N-36
Beirne, Piers, N-5, N-6, N-52
Belanger, Mathieu, N-25
Bell, Ralph, N-27

Bellair, Paul E., N-14
Bellamy, Carol, 396
Bellamy, Lisa C., N-28
Bellis, David J., N-50
Bellucci, Charles, N-27
Benamati, Dennis, N-54
Bendix, Reinhard, N-13
Bennett, Nathan, N-32
Bennett, Richard R., N-53, N-54
Bennett, Wayne W., N-39
Bennett, William, 55
Benson, Bruce L., N-47
Benson, M. L., N-21
Benson, Michael L., N-40, N-45
Bentham, Jeremy, N-6, N-25
Bentler, P. M., N-47
Bequai, August, N-40
Berger, Dale E., N-55
Berger, Herbert, N-49
Berger, Phil, N-41
Berk, Richard A., N-31
Berkey, Martha Lou, N-39
Berkowitz, David, 243
Bernard, Thomas J., N-12, N-13
Berrueta-Clement, John R., N-14
Bersten, Michael, N-40
Berthelsen, Christian, N-32
Beseler, P., N-34
Biaggi, Mario, 325
Bibel, Daniel, N-4
Biderman, Albert D., N-45
Bijlefeld, Marjolijn, N-36
Binstein, Michael, N-39
Bintliff, Russell B., N-42
Birkbeck, Christopher, N-54, N-55
Biron, Louis L., N-47
Bishop, Donna M., N-22
Bjerregaard, Beth, N-15, N-17, N-18
Black, Donald J., 169, N-18
Blackman, Peter, 405
Blackstone, Sir William, 257
Blair, Jayson, 164
Blair, Tony, 4
Blake, Kevin, N-38
Blanchard, Caroline D., N-8
Blanchard, Robert J., N-8
Blane, Howard T., N-30
Blau, Judith R., N-13, N-17
Blau, Peter M., 123, N-13, N-17
Blaustein, Albert P., N-52
Blick, Barry, 36
Bloch, Hannah, 92, N-10
Block, Alan A., N-34
Block, Carolyn Rebecca, N-27, N-28
Block, Jack, N-8
Block, Richard L., N-27

I-1

Bloom, Joseph, N-40
Bloomberg, Michael, 226
Bloomberg, Seth A., 33, N-2
Blumberg, Abraham S., N-37
Blumenthal, Ralph, N-33, N-56
Blumer, Herbert, N-22
Blumstein, Alfred, 35, 48, N-2, N-3, N-17–N-18, N-47
Bock, Alan W., N-35
Boden, Nancy, N-44
Boesky, Ivan, 322
Bohm, Robert M., N-24
Bohn, Martin J., N-8
Boleyn, Anne, 200
Bonfante, Dennis, N-17
Bonfante, John, N-17
Bonger, Willem Adriaan, 203, N-23
Bontham, Jeremy, 65, 66
Boostrom, Ron, N-40
Booth, A., N-11
Bordua, David J., N-16
Borduin, Charles M., N-7
Boren, Jerry F., N-54
Borg, Marian J., N-16–N-17
Boss, Maria S., N-41
Bossard, André, N-54
Bouloukos, Adam C., N-28, N-54
Bowden, Charles, N-39
Bowers, Patricia M., N-30
Bowers, William J., N-36
Bowie, N., N-2
Bowker, H., N-4
Bowlby, John, 87–88, N-7, N-19
Bowman, Cynthia Grant, N-31
Boyle, John M., N-41
Bradbury, Kim, 307
Bradley, Pamela, N-9
Brady, James, 284
Braga, Anthony A., N-27
Braithwaite, John, 123, 209, N-12, N-13, N-27, N-40, N-42, N-44
Brantingham, Patricia L., 232, N-25
Brantingham, Paul J., 232, N-25
Bratton, William J., 42, 43
Brennan, P. A., N-10
Brewer, Devon, N-31
Brewer, Kathleen, N-31
Brewer, Victoria E., N-36
Brewer, Wayne, N-34
Brewster, Victoria E., N-5
Brezina, Timothy, N-13
Briar, Scott, 169, N-18
Brickey, Kathleen F., N-42
Brickler, W., N-8
Brissette, Jeanne, N-43
Brochu, Serge, N-47
Broidy, Lisa, N-4
Brooke, James, 16, 396, N-35
Brower, Sidney, N-14
Brown, Claude, 154, N-17
Brown, Curtis, N-49
Brown, David, N-24
Brown, Teresa D., N-19

Browne, Angela, N-29
Brownfield, D., N-21
Brownfield, David, 123, N-13, N-16
Brownmiller, Susan, 253, N-31
Brunk, Molly A., N-8
Bryant, Jennings, N-51
Buchwald, Emilie, N-51
Buck, Andrew J., N-15
Buckle, Abigail, N-37
Buerger, Michael E., 224, N-25, N-27
Bukoff, Allen, N-36
Bundy, Theodore "Ted", 83, 243
Burack, C., N-21
Burch, Jim, N-18
Burgess, Ernest L., 130, 131, N-8
Burnett, Cathleen, N-55
Bursik, Robert J., N-15, N-27
Bursik, Robert J., Jr., N-21
Burt, Martha R., N-32
Burton, Velmer S., Jr., N-13
Bush, George W., 345, 364
Bushway, Sharon, N-14
Butler, Charles, 273
Butterfield, Fox, 35, 91, N-10, N-15, N-37
Bynum, Tim, N-17
Bynum, Timothy S., N-33
Byrd, James, 272, 273

Calavita, Kitty, N-39, N-40, N-41
Calaway, Nancy, 92
Calder, Paul, 245
Caldwell, Charles, 68
Calhoun, Craig, N-36
Cameron, Mary Owen, 292, N-37
Camp, Camille Graham, 43
Camp, George M., 43
Campbell, Anne, 32, 158–160, N-2, N-4, N-9, N-18
Canter, R. J., N-20
Cao, Liqun, N-16
Caplan, Aaron, N-19
Capone, Al, 259
Caputo, Gail A., N-37
Carey, Gregory, N-10
Carey, James T., N-12
Carlen, Pat, N-24
Carneiro, Robert L., 61, 118
Carolin, P. James, Jr., N-37
Caroll, John, N-37
Carpenter, Cheryl, N-47
Carpozi, George, Jr., N-32
Carr, John, 396
Carrington, Michael D., N-32
Carrington, Peter J., N-36
Carter, Timothy, N-24
Cartmill, Randi S., 43
Cartwright, D., N-19
Carty, Donald J., 317
Casida, Mike, 305
Caspi, Avshalom, N-5, N-12, N-30
Cassidy, Margery A., N-30
Castillo, Dawn N., N-29

Catalano, Richard F., N-21
Catanzaro, Raimondo, N-33
Catherine II, Empress, 64
Catherine of Aragon, 200
Catlin, George E.G., N-7
Cavender, Gray, N-43
Cebulak, Wojciech, N-52, N-57
Centerwall, B. S., N-8
Cernovich, Stephen A., 156, N-17, N-19
Chaiken, Marcia R., N-46
Chambers, James A., N-13
Chambers, Jeff M., N-15
Chambliss, William J., 194–195, 204, N-15, N-22, N-23, N-24, N-43
Chamlin, Mitchell B., N-13
Chandler, Ben, 301
Chandler, Kathryn, N-35
Chang, Dae H., N-53, N-55
Chang, Dean, N-50
Chang, Richard J., N-55
Chapman, S. G., N-49
Chappell, Duncan, N-31
Chard-Wierschem, Deborah, N-16
Charren, Peggy, 95
Chayet, Ellen F., N-40
Cheatwood, Derral, N-3
Cheney, Margaret, N-29
Cheng, Y. T., N-47
Chernoff, David, 118
Chesney-Lind, Meda, 50, N-4
Chesser, Eutace, N-50
Chesterman, L. P., N-11
Chilton, Roland, 241, N-28
Chin, Ko-lin, 149, N-16
Chira, Susan, N-15, N-21
Chiu, Alexis, N-32
Cho, Byung In, N-55
Christiansen, Karl O., 103, N-10
Christman, John H., N-37
Chunmeng Lu, N-26
Churchill, Marlowe, N-25
Churchwell, Ricky, 321
Clark, Douglas, 243
Clark, G., N-44
Clark, John, 187, 330, N-42
Clarke, Michael, N-38, N-55
Clarke, Ronald V., 215, 216, 221, 227, 297, N-25–N-28, N-37, N-38
Clear, Todd R., 132, 255, 256, N-14, N-32
Cleckley, Hervey, 98–99, N-9
Cleland, Max, 346
Clelland, Donald, N-24
Clifford, William, 389, N-53
Clifton, Wayland, Jr., N-26
Clinard, Marshall B., 185, 334, 340, 341, 389, N-39, N-40, N-43, N-44, N-53
Clinton, Bill, N-1
Cloud, John, N-32, N-35
Cloward, Richard A., 147–151, N-16, N-46
Cochran, John K., N-13, N-49
Coffee, John Collins, Jr., N-44
Cohen, Albert K., 144–147, 158, 162, N-16, N-18, N-22

NAME INDEX

Cohen, Jacqueline, N-2, N-3, N-47
Cohen, Lawrence E., 217, N-25, N-26
Cohen, Mark A., N-44
Cohen, S., N-18
Cohn, Ellen G., N-31
Colburn, James Blake, 74
Cole, George F., N-53, N-54
Coleman, D. H., N-49
Coleman, James W., N-40, N-41, N-44
Coler, Michelle, 256
Collins, Dean J., N-31
Collins, Thomas, 95
Comack, Elizabeth, N-23
Combs, Cindy, N-35
Comte, Auguste, 67
Conklin, John, 258, N-32
Conyers, John, Jr., 341
Cook, Philip J., N-26, N-32
Cooley, Charles Horton, 191, N-22
Cooper, Michael, N-17
Copp, D., N-51
Corcoran, James, N-35
Corcoran, Kevin J., N-49
Cordero, Wilfredo, 249
Cornish, Derek B., 215, 216, N-25, N-37
Corzine, Jay, N-30, N-55
Corzine-Huff, Lin, N-30
Coston, Charisse T. M., N-26, N-54
Cottey, Talbert J., N-36
Cottrell, Leonard S., N-14
Countes, Reid, N-35
Coutorie, Larry E., N-38, N-56
Covington, Jeannette, N-14, N-46
Crawford, Elizabeth M., N-4
Crawford, Yvonne, 83
Cressey, Donald R., 97, N-9, N-34, N-41, N-42
Crew, Gordon, N-35
Crites, Laura, N-4
Croall, Hazel, N-40
Cromwell, Paul F., 311, N-25, N-39
Crowder, Carla, N-15
Cullen, Francis T., N-4, N-13, N-26, N-43, N-44, N-45, N-50
Cullen, John B., N-4, N-44
Cummings, John, N-34
Cunningham, Lea C., N-16
Currie, Elliot, N-24
Curry, G. David, N-29
Curtis, Lynn A., N-17, N-18
Curtis, Marvin E., N-17
Curtis, Richard, 42, 43, N-50
Curtis, Thomas, 257
Cutler, Stephen, 339

Dahlberg, Linda, N-29
Dahmer, Jeffrey, 101, 243
Dahrendorf, Ralf, 200, N-23
Dalaker, Joseph, N-12
Dalton, Katharina, 109, N-11
Daly, Kathleen, N-23
Daly, Martin, N-29, N-55
Damiens, Robert-François, 62

Dammer, Harry R., N-54
Dando, Shigemistu, N-53
Daniel, Anasseril E., N-29
Daro, Deborah, N-31
D'Arpa-Calandra, Angela, 156
Darwin, Charles, 67, N-6
David, James R., N-16
Davidson, Bruce, 155
Davies, Elizabeth, N-35
Davies, P., N-11
Davis, Daniel L., N-9
Davis, John H., N-34
Davis, Laura, N-52
Davis, Nanette J., N-18
Davis, Richard Allen, 313
Davis, Robert C., N-17, N-45
Day, J. M., N-21
Day, James M., N-7–N-9
de Bernardo, Mark A., N-46, N-48
de Bracton, Henry, 290
de Burger, James, N-29
De Coster, Stacy, N-4
De Frongo, James, N-12
de Gruyter, Aldine, N-36
Dean, Charles W., N-31
Deane, Gary D., N-14
Deane, Glenn D., N-29
Decker, Scott H., 221, N-17, N-19, N-25, N-26, N-30, N-39
Dees, Morris, N-35
DeFronzo, James, N-4
DeKeseredy, Walter S., N-24
del Frate, Anna Albazzi, N-53
DeLancey, Marci M., N-46
Delbert, Elliott, N-4
Denno, Deborah W., 79, N-10, N-11, 106
Dershowitz, Alan M., 234
Desaigoudar, Chan, 54
Deschenes, Elizabeth Piper, N-18
Desjardins, Lyne, N-47
Dick, Melvin, 334
Dickey, Christopher, N-37–N-38
Dietrick, David C., N-16
Dietz, Park, 100
Dinitz, Simon, N-9, N-19, N-20
Dionne, E. J., 133
Dir, Kojo A., 356
Dixon, Jo, N-17
Dixon, Ronald L., N-43
Dobash, R. Emerson, N-5, N-55
Dobash, Russell P., N-5, N-55
Dodd, D. J., 34
Dodd, David, N-44
Doerner, William G., N-17
Donahue, Joe, 303
Donaldson, William H., 345
Donnerstein, Edward I., N-8, N-51
Donohue, John, III, 42
Doob, Anthony N., N-28
Dorgan, Byron, 346
Dornfeld, Maude, N-31
Douglas, Jack D., 13, 14, N-1, N-22
Douglas, M., N-48

Downey, Robert, Jr., 360
Downs, Donald A., N-51
Downs, R. E., 118
Drapkin, Israel, N-26
Drass, Kriss A, N-5
Droegemueller, W., N-30
Druley, K. A., N-49
Drummond, Tammerlin, N-35
Duffield, Don W., N-15
Dugdale, Richard, 72–73
Dunaway, R. Gregory, N-13
Duncan, David, 317, 323
Dunford, Franklin, N-2
Dunlap, Eloise, N-46, N-47
Dunworth, Terence, N-15
Dupont, John, 99
Durkheim, Émile, 15, 76–77, 116–117, 197, N-1, N-7, N-12, N-23
Duszynski, Karen R., N-48
Dutton, Donald G., N-30, N-31
Dzerzhinsky, Felix, 209

Earle, Beverly, N-44
Ebbe, Obi N. Ignatius, 395, N-53, N-54, N-55
Ebbers, Bernard, 334, 349
Eck, John E., 227, N-14, N-27
Eckstein, Marc, N-29
Edwards, John L. J., N-27
Edwards, Sally M., N-56
Edwards, Terry D., N-56
Egley, Arlen, Jr., N-15
Eichel, Edward W., N-50
Einstein, S., N-57
Eisenman, Russell, N-47
Elderkin, Ronald D., N-6
Elias, Robert, N-24
Elis, Lori A., N-40
Ellen, Eric, N-56
Ellingworth, Dan, N-26
Elliott, David, N-28
Elliott, Delbert S., 53, 146, 180, 182, N-2, N-5, N-12, N-16, N-20, N-21
Elliott, Frank A., N-10
Ellis, Havelock, N-6
Ellis, Lee, N-11
Ellis, Lori, N-4
Ellison, A. F., N-2
Elmoghazy, E., N-47
Empey, Lamar, N-24
Engels, Friedrich, 202, N-23
Entner Wright, Bradley R., N-5
Epstein, Ann S., N-14
Epstein, Joel, N-32
Erez, Edna, N-4, N-31
Erickson, Kai T., 192, N-22
Erikisson, Thorsten, N-5
Erlanger, Howard S., N-16, 152
Erlanger, Steven, N-1
Ermann, M. David, N-42, N-43
Eron, Leonard D., 91, N-8
Esbensen, Finn-Aage, N-16
Eser, Albin, N-53

Eshensen, Finn-Aage, N-18
Evans, Harold, N-43
Evans, T. David, N-13
Everett, M. W., N-49
Eysenck, Hans J., 97–98, N-7, N-9

Fagan, J., N-16
Fagan, Jeffrey A., 153, N-15, N-17, N-21, N-31, N-46, N-47, N-48
Fagan, Lisa, 257
Fagan, Rachael, 257
Fagan, Stephen, 257
Faggiani, Donald, N-27
Faludi, Susan, N-29
Farley, Christopher John, 16
Farnsworth, Margaret, 122, N-12, N-20
Farrell, Graham, N-26, N-28
Farrelland, Ronald A., N-34
Farrington, David P., 180, 181, 392, N-3, N-7, N-20, N-26, N-37, N-55
Fattah, Ezzat A., 222, N-26
Favre, Brett, 176
Federman, J., 93
Fehr, Ernst, 178
Feinblatt, John, 226
Feingold, Benjamin F., 108, N-11
Feiring, Candice, N-7
Feldman, M. Philip, N-9
Feldman, Robert S., 88
Felson, Marcus, 215, 217, N-25, N-26
Felson, Richard B., 224, 242, 248, N-9, N-25, N-26, N-28, N-30
Fenton, Ben, 405
Fernandez, Yvette, N-33, N-48
Ferracuti, Franco, 151, 152, N-16, N-17, N-30
Ferraro, Kenneth F., N-14
Ferre, M. Isolina, N-15, 135
Ferrero, Gina Lombroso, N-6
Ferrero, William, N-4
Ferri, Enrico, 70–71
Ferri, Gian Luigi, 245
Fields, Charles B., N-53, N-56
50 Cent, 153
Figlio, Robert M., 44, 45, 49, N-3, N-10, N-17
Figueira-McDonough, Josefina, N-14
Finckenauer, James O., 31, 393, N-2, N-21, N-35, N-55
Fine, David, N-21
Fingerhut, Lois A., N-55
Fink, Arthur E., N-6
Finkelhor, David, N-30
Finkenauer, James O., N-52
Finn, Peter, N-48
Fischel, Daniel R., N-43
Fischer, D. G., N-9
Fish, Albert, 245
Fishbein, Diana H., 111, N-10, N-11
Fisher, Bonnie S., N-26
Fisse, Brent, N-40, N-42
Fla, Geinesville, N-7
Fleming, Zachary, 232

Flenz, G. H., N-52
Fletcher, George, N-53
Fletcher, Pamela R., N-51
Flowers, R. Barri, N-5
Follain, John, N-33
Forbaugh, Frederick M., N-14
Forney, Mary Ann, N-50
Forssman, H., N-11
Forsyth, Craig J., N-31
Fowles, Richard, N-13
Fox, James Alan, 245, 328, N-29, N-42
Frank, Nancy, N-44
Frankel, Martin, 53
Frankowski, Stanislaw J., N-53, N-54
Frantz, Douglas, 6
Frazier, Patricia, N-32
Freemantle, Brian, N-33
French, L., N-10
Freud, Sigmund, 85, N-7
Frey, T. S., N-11
Friday, Paul C., N-55
Friedrich II, King, 64
Frisch, Lisa A., N-31
Fromm-Auch, D., N-11
Fry, Patricia A., N-45
Furrow, Buford O., 273

Gabrielli, William F., N-10, N-11
Gachter, Simon, 178
Gage, Michael, N-54
Gaither, Billy Jack, 273
Gajewski, Francis, N-27
Gal-Or, Noemi, N-35
Gall, Franz Joseph, 68
Ganzini, Linda, N-40
Garcia, Juanita L., N-31
Garofalo, James, 223, N-26
Garofalo, Raffaele, 12, 14, 71, N-1, N-6
Gartin, Patrick R., 224, N-25, N-27, N-31
Gartner, Rosemary, N-53, N-54, N-55
Gartrell, John W., N-13, N-29
Gately, William, N-33, N-48
Gault, Robert H., 105, N-10
Gavin, Patricia W., N-2
Gearing, Michael L., N-8
Gebhard, Paul H., 373, N-50, N-52
Gebhardt, Bruce, 16
Geen, Russell G., N-8
Gegax, Trent, 374
Geis, Gilbert, 319, N-38, N-40, N-41, N-42, N-44
Gelfand, Donna, N-37
Gelles, Richard J., 249, N-30
Gellman, Barton, N-1
Genn, Hazel G., 34, N-44
Gentle, Fay, 91
Gentry, Cynthia S., N-51
George, Barbara Crutchfield, N-41
Gepax, T. Trent, N-35
Gerber, Jurg, N-40
Gert-Jan, Terlouw, N-2
Gertz, Marc G., N-53, N-54
Gettleman, Jeffrey, 365

Giancana, Chuck, N-34
Giancana, Sam, N-34
Gibbens, Trevor N., N-37
Gibbs, Jack P., N-18, N-22
Gibbs, John J., N-9, N-14, N-21
Gibney, Frank, Jr., N-35
Gibson, Emory, 195
Gibson, L., N-49
Gidycz, C. A., N-32
Giever, D., N-21
Gilfus, Mary E., N-4
Gill, Martin, N-56
Giller, Joan E., N-57
Gillespie, Darlene, 299
Gillespie, James, N-49
Gilligan, Carol, N-7
Gillis, A. R., N-4, N-20
Giordano, Peggy C., N-19, N-38
Giuffra, Robert, 323
Giuliani, Rudolph, 226
Glaser, Daniel, N-23
Glaser, Fredrick G., N-47
Glass, Civil, N-39
Glassner, Barry, N-47
Glick, Barry, N-2
Glueck, Eleanor Touroff, 51, 72, 89, 395, N-6, N-8, N-54
Glueck, Sheldon, 51, 72, 89, 395, N-4, N-6, N-8, N-52, N-54
Goddard, Henry H., 73, 75, 105, N-6, N-10
Goff, Colin H., N-43
Goffman, Erving, N-22
Golant, Susan K., N-31
Gold, Martin, N-2
Goldberg, Jeffrey, N-34
Golden, Andrew, 276
Golden, Reid M., N-13
Goldfarb, Ronald, N-33
Golding, William, N-18
Goldman, Ronald, 249
Goldstein, Paul J., N-47
Goleman, Daniel, N-10
Golub, Andrew, N-47
Gondoli, Dawn M., N-30
Gonzales, Alberto R., 345
Good, Kenneth, 118
Goode, Eric, 43, N-47
Goodman, Marc, N-38
Gordon, Margaret A., N-29
Gordon, Michael R., N-56
Gordon, Robert, N-19
Goring, Charles Buckman, 71–72, N-6
Gornick, Janet, N-32
Goslin, David A., N-7
Gottfredson, Denise C., N-14, N-21
Gottfredson, Gary D., N-14
Gottfredson, Michael R., 48, 182–183, 223, N-3, N-21, N-26, N-41
Gottfredson, Steve D., N-14
Gottheil, E., N-49
Gotti, John, Jr., 260

NAME INDEX

Gough, Harrison G., N-9
Gove, Walter R., N-22
Grabosky, Peter, N-40
Gramling, Robert, N-31
Grasmick, Harold G., N-21, N-27
Green, Lorraine, N-27
Greenberg, David F., N-3, N-16, N-19, N-24
Greenfield, Lawrence A., N-29, N-49, N-50
Greenhouse, Linda, 74
Greenspan, Edward L., N-28
Griffiths, Curt T., N-55
Griffiths, Fré Le Poole, N-52
Grinspoon, Lester, N-45
Griswold, David, N-19
Grosmick, Harold G., N-15
Gross, Jane, 128, N-14, N-19
Grossman, Jan Carl, N-47
Groves, W. Byron, N-38, N-43
Grubman, Jack, 334
Grupp, Stanley E., N-6
Guart, Al, N-32
Gudjonnson, Gisli H., N-9
Guerry, André Michel, 75, 215, N-25
Guggenheim, W. Z., N-45
Gulleck, Eleanor T., N-4
Gunn, John, N-7
Gusfield, Joseph R., N-50
Gutfield, Greg, 374
Guth, Hans-Werner, N-55
Gwynne, S. C., 231

Hagan, John, 123, N-4, N-13, N-20, N-23, N-40
Hagedorn, John M., 149, 160, 165, N-16
Hakim, Simon, 228, N-15
Hale, Chris, N-13
Hale, Sir Matthew, 255, N-32
Hall, Jerome, 24, N-2, N-37
Halleck, Seymour L., 98, N-9
Hamburg, D. A., N-11
Hamilton, David, 378
Hamilton, Thomas, 244
Hamilton, V. Lee, N-55
Hamlin, John, N-19
Hamm, Mark S., 384, N-41, N-52
Hamowy, Ronald, N-46
Hampton, Robert L., N-28
Hancock, Lyn Nell, N-30
Handley, Jim, N-38
Haney, Beth, N-32
Hanlon, E., N-48
Hannon, Lance, N-4
Hanrahan, Kathleen J., N-14
Hansen, Joy, N-18
Hanson, Cindy L., N-7
Hanson, Karl R., N-51
Harden, Blaine, 155
Harding, Richard W., N-25
Hare, Robert D., N-8, N-9
Harries, Elizabeth, N-43
Harris, Eric, 277

Harris, Lee, 139
Harris, Patricia M., N-25
Harrison, Wilfred, N-6
Hartjen, Clayton A., N-15, N-55
Hartl, Emil M., N-6
Hartmann, Donald, N-37
Hartnagel, Timothy F., N-13, N-29
Harvey, William B., N-28
Hatch, Alison, N-55
Hatch, Orrin, 127
Hauser, Robert M., N-23
Hawkins, Darnell F., N-28
Hawkins, David J., N-21
Hawkins, Gordon, N-51
Hayes, Read, 294, N-26
Hazelbaker, Kim, N-28
Heath, D., N-49
Hebenton, B., N-54
Heide, Kathleen M., 92, N-50
Heimer, K., N-19
Heimer, Mel, N-29
Heims, Lora W., N-39
Heiner, Robert, N-53
Heinzelmann, Fred, N-41
Heinzmann, David, N-45
Helal, Adel, N-54
Henderson, Russell, 272–273
Hendler, Harold I., N-48
Henggeler, Scott W., N-7
Hennessy, James J., N-7, N-25
Henry, D. Alan, 187
Henry, Jessica S., 274
Henry VIII, 200
Henson, Trudy Knicely, N-38
Henson, Verna A., N-26
Hepburn, John, N-37
Hepburn, R. J., N-20
Hepperie, Winifred, N-4
Herrnstein, Richard J., 48, 105, 106, 111, N-3, N-10, N-11
Hersch, Rebecca K., N-39
Hess, Karen Matison, N-39
Heumann, Milton, N-36
Heymann, Philip, 233
Hibbert, Christopher, N-6
Hill, Gary D., N-4, N-14
Hill, James Brian, 92
Hill, Joan, N-52
Hill, Robert, 152, N-17
Hillbrand, M., N-9
Hinckley, John W., Jr., 25, 284
Hindelang, Michael J., 39, 106, 223, N-3, N-10, N-19, N-26
Hirano, Ryuichi, N-44
Hirschel, J. David, N-31
Hirschi, Travis, 39, 48, 106, 137, 146, 169–173, 182–183, N-3, N-10, N-15, N-16, N-18, N-19, N-21, N-41
Ho, Truc-Nho, N-37, N-38
Hobbs, Sylvester, III, 92
Hoebel, E. Adamson, 394
Hoff, Joan, 377, N-51
Hoffer, Abram, N-11

Hoffman, John P., N-13, N-16
Hogan, Robert, N-8
Hogg, Russell, N-24
Holcomb, William R., N-29
Hollinger, Richard, 330, N-42
Holmes, Oliver Wendell, Jr., 73
Holmes, Ronald M., N-29
Holmes, Stephen T., N-29
Holt, Joe, 109
Homel, Ross, 227, N-27
Honeywood, Wesley (Pop), 44, 45
Hood, Kevin, 282
Hooten, Ernest, 72
Hoover, Edgar, 34
Hope, Susan, N-39
Hope, Tim, N-26
Hornblower, Margot, 376
Horney, Julie, N-3, N-11, N-32
Horowitz, Irving Louis, 208
Horwitz, Allan V., N-18
Horwitz, Diana, N-47
Hotaling, Gerald T., N-30
Houston, James G., N-16
Howell, James C., 174
Howitt, Dennis, N-51
Htoo, Luther and Johnny, 385
Hu, Winnie, N-38
Hualing Fu, N-55
Huang, Frank F., N-55
Hubbard, Benjamin J., 274
Huberty, James, 244
Huesmann, Rowell, N-8
Huff, C. Ronald, N-18
Hughes, Michael, N-14
Hui, Boon Khoo, N-44
Huizinga, David, N-5, N-12, N-16
Hull, Jon D., N-18, N-33, N-36
Humphries, Charlie, N-26
Humphries, Drew, N-24
Hunt, Dana, N-46
Hunt, Morton, 379
Hunter, Ronald D., N-28, N-55
Hutchings, Barry, N-10
Hutchinson, Ira W., III, N-31
Hutson, Range, N-29

Ianni, Francis A. J., N-33
Iglarsh, Harvey J., N-35
Ignew, Robert, N-12
Ileto, Joseph, 273
Inciardi, James A., 360, N-24, N-33, N-37, N-45–N-50
Ingraham, Edward D., N-5
Innes, Christopher A., N-30
Inoue, Mariko, N-44
Ireland, Timothy, N-16
Ishihara, T., N-10
Itil, Turan M., N-11

Jackson, Howard F., N-39
Jackson, Pamela Irving, N-12
Jackson, Patrick G., N-2, N-39
Jacob, Craig, N-41

Jacobs, Bruce A., N-46, N-47
Jacobs, James B., 274, N-36, N-49
Jacobs, K. W., 108, N-11
James, Frank, 140
James, Jennifer, N-51
Janeksela, Galan M., N-55
Jang, Sung Joon, N-3, N-20
Janofsky, Michael, N-36
Janus, Cythnthia, L., N-50
Janus, Samuel S., N-50
Jarjoura, G. Roger, 146, N-3, N-5, N-16
Jaskir, John, N-7
Jeffery, C. Ray, 102, 226, N-8, N-10, N-27, N-28
Jeglum Bartusch, Dawn R., N-3
Jenkins, E. Lynn, N-29
Jennings, William S., N-7
Jensen, Arthur, 105, N-10
Jensen, Gary F., 122, N-4, N-12, N-13, N-20
Jensen, Vickie J., N-16
Jesilow, Paul, N-38, N-40, N-41
Johann, Sara Lee, N-51
Johnson, Bruce D., 356, N-25, N-46, N-47
Johnson, D., N-47
Johnson, Elmer H., N-54
Johnson, Harold, 30
Johnson, Ida, N-32
Johnson, John, N-8, N-22
Johnson, Lloyd, N-46
Johnson, Lyndon, 126, 162
Johnson, S. D., N-49
Johnston, David, N-34
Johnston, Les, N-56
Johnston, Lloyd D., N-2, N-45, N-46
Jones, Gwen, N-21
Jones, Jim, 133
Jones, Richard Lezin, 195
Jordan, James, 280
Jordan, Michael, 119
Joutsen, Matti, N-53
Joyner, Tammy, N-14
Judson, George, N-21
Junger-Tas, Josine, N-2, N-54, N-55

Kadleck, Colleen, N-27
Kagan, Jerome, 105
Kahan, James P., N-49
Kaiser, Günther, N-55, N-56, N-57
Kalb, Claudia, N-35
Kalish, Carol B., N-44, N-53
Kallikak, Martin, 73
Kandel, Elizabeth, N-10
Kane, Candice, N-18
Kangaspunta, Kristiina, N-53
Kantrowitz, Barbara, N-17
Kapardis, A., N-41
Kapardis, M., N-41
Karchmer, Clifford L., N-39
Karpman, Benjamin, N-9
Karter, Michael J, Jr., N-39
Kaufman, Irving, N-39

Kaulitzki, Reiner, N-55
Kay, Fiona, N-40
Keane, Carl, N-21
Keimer, Karen, N-4
Kelleher, C. L., N-29
Kelleher, Michael D., N-29
Kelling, George L., 42, 43
Kellner, R., N-11
Kelly, Delos H., N-50
Kelly, Linda, N-55
Kelly, Mary, 292
Kelly, Robert J., N-35
Kempe, C. H., N-30
Kemper, Edmund, 245
Kempf, Kimberly L., N-2, N-19
Kendall, Jerry, N-56
Kennedy, John F., 162
Kennedy, Leslie W., 242, N-16, N-28
Kenny, Dennis J., N-35
Kerbo, Harold R., N-44
Kethineni, Sesharajani, N-55
Kfita, Najat, N-30
Kieselhorst, B. C., N-49
Kilborn, Peter T., N-17
Kilias, Martin, N-52
Kilkenny, Robert, N-7
Killias, Martin, N-36, N-53
Kilmer, Beau, 369
Kindley, Karen, N-29
King, John William, 272
King, Mike, N-56
King, Roy, N-10
Kingsley, Cherry, 396
Kinlock, Timothy W., N-48
Kinsbourne, Marcel, N-11
Kinsey, Alfred C., 370, 371, N-50, N-52
Kirchheimer, Otto, 203, N-23
Kirkpatrick, John T., N-30
Kitsuse, John I., N-16
Kittrie, Nicholas N., N-9, N-22
Klaidman, Daniel, N-29
Klass, Polly, 313
Klaus, K. A., N-9
Klaus, Patsy, N-44
Klebold, Dylan, 277
Klein, Malcolm W., N-2, N-16, N-18, N-29, N-54
Kleinfield, N. R., N-29
Kleinman, Joel C., N-55
Klinteberg, Britt af, N-10
Klockars, Carl B., 205, N-24, N-39
Knightly, Phillip, N-43
Knoblich, Guenther, N-10
Knop, George W., N-16
Knowles, Gordon James, N-47
Knutsson, Johannes, N-38
Kobrin, Solomon, N-15
Koepf, G. F., N-10
Kohlberg, Lawrence, 86–88, N-7
Koo, Samuel, 396
Kopel, David B., N-55
Koper, Christopher S., N-44
Korem, Dan, N-18

Koresh, David, 133, 272
Kosberg, Jordan I., N-31
Koss, M. P., N-32
Kotzer, Sophia, N-35
Kovandzic, Tomislav V., N-13
Kowlaski, Gregory S., N-15
Kozlowski, Dennis, 349
Krahn, Harvey, N-13, N-29
Kramer, Jane, N-52
Krauss, Clifford, 43
Kretschmer, Ernest, 72, N-6
Kreuz, L. E., N-11
Krisberg, Barry, 205, N-24
Kroc, Ray, 119
Krohn, Marvin D., 146, N-3, N-16, N-19, N-20, N-24
Krug, Etienne G., N-29
Kruttschnitt, Candace, N-31
Krzeszowski, Frank E., N-38
Kuhlhorn, Eckart, N-38
Kuhns, Joseph, B., III, N-50
Kuklinski, Richard, 244
Kunen, James S., N-43
Kupperstein, Lenore R., N-54
Kurth, Barbara, 257
Kury, Helmut, N-56
Kurz, Anat, N-35
Kutchinsky, Berl, N-51
Kuttschreuter, M., N-8

Lab, Steven P., N-27
Labaton, Stephen, N-39
Lacayo, Richard, 133, N-35
Lacey, Robert, N-33
LaFave, Wayne R., N-28
LaFree, Gary, 42, N-5, N-54
LaGrange, Randy L., N-14
Lander, Bernard, N-12
Langam, Patrick, 392
Langan, Mary, N-25
Langan, Patrick A., N-30
Lange, Johannes, 103, N-10
Langenbahn, Stacia, N-32
Langer, Lawrence L., 208
Langworthy, Robert, N-31
Lanz-Kaduce, Lonn, N-16, N-50
Laskey, John A., N-15
Lasley, James R., N-27, N-41
Laub, John H., 180, 181, 196, N-3, N-6, N-20, N-23
Lauderback, David, N-18
Laufer, William S., 141, 208, 407, N-4, N-7–N-9, N-12, N-13, N-16, N-19, N-21, N-23, N-40, N-41, N-42, N-46
Lavater, Johann Kaspar, 68
Lawder, Karen, 303
Lawrence, D., N-50
Laws, D. R., N-11
Lay, Kenneth, 347, 348
Leary, Timothy, 359
Leavitt, Gregory C., N-55
LeBeau, James L., N-32
LeBlanc, Marc, 180, 182, N-19

NAME INDEX

LeCapitaine, J. E., N-7
Lederer, Laura, N-51
Ledingham, C. A., N-8
Ledingham, J. E., N-8
Lee, Tommy, 249
LeFree, Gary, 43
Lehmann, John, N-32
Leland, John, 374, N-52
Lemaitre, Andre, N-41
Lemaitre, Rolf, N-41
Lemert, Edwin M., 191–192, 300, N-22, N-38
Lensing, H., N-56
Leonard, Kenneth E., N-30, N-49
Leonard, Kimberly K., N-19
Lepse, Kerry and Sammy, 120
Lessner, S. F., N-20
Letourneau, Mary Kay, 52
Leung, Rebecca, N-35
Levi, Michael, N-38
Levin, Carl, 346
Levin, Jack, 245, N-29, N-56
Levine, Betti Jane, N-20
Levine, Dennis, 322
Levine, James, N-2
Levinson, David, N-30
Levitt, Steven, 42
Levung, Shirley, 133
Lewis, Matthew W., N-49
Lewis, Michael, N-7
Lewis, Oscar, 119, N-12
Liazos, Alexander, N-23
Lichtman, Carl, 303
Lieberman, Alicia F., N-7
Liebl, Karlhans, N-40
Lightner, Candy, 369, 370
Lightner, Cari, 369
Lindbergh, Charles, 257
Linden, R., N-49
Link, Bruce G., N-22, N-44, N-50
Linquist, P., N-49
Lipset, Seymour M., N-13
Lipstadt, Deborah, 208
Liska, Allen E., N-14, N-20
Little, Heather M., N-11
Littman, R. A., N-8
Liu, Jianhong, N-14
Lively, Sara, 256
Lizotte, Alan J., 201, 283, N-20, N-23, N-16–N-17, N-36
Llewellyn, Karl N., 394
Loeber, Rolf, N-14
Loftin, Colin, 152, N-17, N-29, N-36
Lofvers, Jeff, 171, N-19
Logan, John, 296
Lombness, Michael, N-44
Lombros, Gina, 98
Lombroso, Cesare, 12, 50, 68–70, 71, N-4, N-6
Looman, Terah, N-26
Lopez, Pedro Alonso, 244
Loring, Pamela L., N-13, N-15
Loughlin, Julia, N-47

Loury, Glenn C., N-21
Lovell, Constance, 97, N-9
Lowman, John, N-24
Lowney, Jeremiah, N-50
Lu, Chunmeng Lu, N-26
Luckernbill, David F., N-30, N-50
Lunde, D. T., N-11
Lundman, Richard J., N-42, N-43
Luper, Steven Foy, N-49
Lupsha, Peter A., N-33
Lurigio, Arthur J., N-17, N-45
Lyman, Michael D., N-45
Lynch, James P., N-53
Lynum, Donald R., N-3
Lyston, Douglas S., N-47

Ma, Yue, N-52
Maahs, Jeff, N-13
Maakestad, William J., N-43, N-45
Maas, Peter, N-33
Mabry, Marcus, N-52
Maccoby, Eleanor E., N-11
MacCoun, Robert J., 369, N-49
Macdonald, John M., N-39
Macey, Jonathan R., N-44
MacKenzie, Doris Layton, N-27
MacLean, Brian D., N-24
Macphail, Daniel D., N-7
Maestro, Marcello T., N-5, N-6
Magendanz, T., N-49
Magnuson, Dan, N-45
Magnusson, David, N-10
Mahar, Maggie, 363
Maher, Lisa, N-46, N-50
Maier, Pamela A., N-27
Makofsky, Abraham, N-48
Malekian, Farhad, N-57
Maltz, Michael D., 43
Malvo, John Lee, 83, 245
Mankoff, Milton, N-24
Mann, Coramae Richey, 241, N-4, N-5, N-28, N-29
Mannheim, Hermann, 391, N-6
Manuel, Yolanda, 239
Marcial, Gene G., N-41
Mark Bortner, R., N-1
Markowitz, Fred E., N-14
Marolla, J., N-32
Marongiu, Pietro, N-5, N-25
Marriott, Michael, N-14, N-47
Marshall, Ineke Haen, N-3
Martens, Frederick T., N-57
Martin, Clyde E., N-50, N-52
Martin, R. D., N-9
Martin, William, 257
Martone, Mark, 92
Marx, Karl, 202, N-23
Massey, James L., N-19
Mastrofski, Stephen D., N-50
Masuda, Barry, N-38
Mathers, R., N-44
Matsueda, Ross L., N-15, N-19, N-20, N-22

Matza, David, 123, 175, N-13, N-17, N-19, N-22, N-27
Maudsley, Henry, 74
Mawson, Anthony R., 108, N-11
Maxfield, Michael G., N-2
Maxim, Paul S., N-21
Maxson, Cheryl L., N-16, N-18, N-29
Mayer, Jim, N-44
Mayfield, D., N-49
Mayhew, Pat, N-53
Mayhew, Patricia, N-28
Mazerolle, Lorraine Green, N-27
Mazerolle, Paul, N-13, N-14
Mc Kay, David, N-50
McBarnet, Doreen, N-42
McBride, Duane C., N-47, N-49
McCaffrey, Barry, 365
McCaghy, Charles, N-38
McCain, John, 346
McCall, Patricia L., N-13
McCarthy, Belinda, N-31
McClelland, Kenneth J., 195
McClintock, F. H., N-55
McCord, Joan, 89, N-7, N-9, N-20, N-30
McCord, John, N-8
McCord, William, N-9
McCoy, Clyde B., N-49
McCullough, Hamish, 396
McCutcheon, Allan L., N-46
McDevitt, Jack, N-56
McDonald, R. Robin, N-15
McDonald, William F., N-52
McDowall, David, 283, N-14, N-36
McDowell, Jeanne, 92
McElrath, Karen, N-45
McFadden, Robert D., N-36
McFarland, Bentson, N-40
McGuffog, Carolyn, N-7
McKay, Henry D., 130–131, 134–135, N-14
McKenzie, Doris, N-14
McKenzie, R. D., 131
McKinley, James C., Jr., N-3
McKinney, Aaron, 272–273
McLaughlin, Eugene, N-25
McMahon, Colin, N-48
McNamara, Joseph, N-33
McNeil, Richard J., N-14
McShane, Marilyn D, N-12, N-52
McVeigh, Timothy, 275
Mead, George Herbert, 191, N-22
Mednick, Sarnoff A., 103, 104, 110, N-10, N-11
Meese, Edwin, III, N-41
Megargee, Edwin I., N-8, N-9
Meier, Robert F., N-5, N-12, N-27, N-33, N-44
Meland, James A., N-46
Menard, Scott, N-13, N-19, N-21
Mendelsohn, Benjamin, 222, N-26
Mendelsohn, Gerald A., N-9
Menninger, Karl, 98, N-9
Merari, Ariel, N-35

Mercy, James A., N-29, N-36
Merl, Jean, N-17
Merlin, Mark D., N-45
Merton, Robert K., 117–124, 144, N-12
Merva, Mary, N-13
Merz, Jon F., N-49
Messner, Robert F., 226
Messner, Steven F., 124, 125, 141, 242, N-13, N-17, N-20, N-24, N-28
Metfessel, Milton, 97, N-9
Meyer, C. K., N-49
Michaels, Robert J., N-46
Michalowski, Raymond J., N-43
Miczek, Klaus A., N-49
Miech, Richard A., N-5, N-12
Miethe, Terence D., N-14, N-27
Milk, Harvey, 108
Millar, Robert W., N-1
Miller, Alan S., N-13
Miller, Bill, N-17
Miller, Brenda A., N-30
Miller, Jody, N-18, N-26
Miller, Lawrence Richard, N-48
Miller, Martin G., N-4
Miller, S. L., N-21
Miller, Thomas, N-47
Miller, Walter B., 153–156, N-17
Mills, Anne-Marie, N-31
Mills, Gregory, N-15
Mills, Michael, N-40
Minor, N. William, N-19
Mirrlees, Catriona Black, N-46
Mitchell, David B., N-31
Miyazawa, Setsuo, N-54
MoCord, J., N-8
Moffett, Arthur D., N-47
Moffitt, Terrie E., N-3, N-5, N-10, N-12, N-20, N-30
Molosivich, Slovudon, 403
Monnelly, Edward P., N-6
Monroe, Sylvester, N-35
Montanino, Fred, N-34, N-51
Moore, Elizabeth, N-21, N-40
Moore, Joan, 165
Moore, Michael, N-2
Moore, Molly, 95
Moore, Richard, N-37
Moore, Richter H., N-53
Moorehead-Dworkin, Terry, N-40
Moran, Thomas Bartholomew, 292
Morash, Merry, 50, N-4, N-33
Morris, Norval, 216, N-24, N-25
Morse, Edward V., N-50
Morse, Stephen J., 100, 112
Moscone, George, 108
Mott, Joy, N-46
Moyer, Sharon, N-36
Mueller, Gerhard O. W., 61, 218, 298, N-1, N-2, N-5, N-22, N-27, N-28, N-38, N-44, N-51, N-52, N-53, N-54, N-56, N-57
Mueller, J. H., N-1

Muhammad, John Allen, 83, 245
Mullins, Steven, 273
Mumola, Christopher J., N-49
Muncer, Steven, N-4
Muncie, John, N-25
Munsterberg, Hugo, 105, N-10
Murray, Alan, N-42
Murray, E., N-19, N-20
Murray, Ellen, N-19, N-20
Musto, D. F., N-46
Mydans, Seth, N-18
Myers, Kenneth D., N-41
Myers, Laura B., N-5
Myers, Martha A., N-23
Myers, Norman, N-34
Mylonas, Anastassios, N-54
Myrdal, Gunnar, 119, N-12

Nadelman, Ethan A., N-56
Nadelman, N., N-54
Nader, Ralph, 341
Nagel, Ilene H., N-23
Nagin, D. S., N-20
Nash, Jay Robert, N-33
Nat, Ives, 328
Natarajan, Mangai, N-25, N-47
Naughton, Patrick, 306
Nay, Robert L., N-55
Neapolitan, Jerome L., N-54
Nelken, David, N-52
Nelsen, Candice, N-30
Nelson, Randy, 16
Nerep, Erik, 61
Nerep, Wiweka Warnling, 61
Neustrom, Michael W., N-12
Newlyn, Andrea K., N-48
Newman, Graeme, 47, N-5, N-29, N-38, N-43, N-54, N-55
Newman, Oscar, 226, N-27
Newton, Michael, N-29
Nichols, Terry, 275
Noaks, Lesley, N-5
Nochajski, Thomas H., N-30
Nolan, Brudce W., N-56
Nolin, Mary Jo, N-35
Noriega, Manuel, 364
Norris, Sandra L., N-29
Norton, William M., N-12
Nurco, David N., N-48
Nye, Francis Ivan, 179, N-12, N-20
Nyswander, Marie, N-46

O'Brien, Margaret, 160
O'Brien, Timothy L., 307
O'Carroll, Patrick W., N-36
O'Day, Patrick, N-5
Ohlin, Lloyd E., 147–151, N-16, N-46
Older, Jules, N-52
Oliver, F. E., N-45
Olson, James N., 311, N-25, N-39
Olson, Lynn M., N-45
Olson, Virgil J., N-12

Olson, Walter, 231
Olweus, Dan, N-8, N-26
O'Malley, Patrick M., N-2, N-45, N-46
O'Maolchatha, Aogan, N-24
O'Neill, Eugene, 156, N-17
Ong, Benny, 266
O'Reilly-Fleming, Thomas, N-23
Ortega, Suzanne T., N-55
Orvis, Gregory P., N-35
Osanka, Franklin Mark, N-51
Osgood, D. Wayne, 103, N-2, N-3, N-10, N-11, N-15
Overill, Richard, N-38
Owens, Terrell, 139

Page, Brent, N-37
Pagelow, Midlred Daley, N-31
Pagrotsky, Leif, N-1
Palendrano, Marion, 25
Pallone, Nathaniel J., N-7, N-9, N-25
Palmer, C., N-37
Pankan, Edmund J., N-38
Park, Robert E., 130, 131, N-14
Parker, Howard, N-49
Parker, Karen F., N-13
Parker, Robert Nash, 43
Passas, Nikos, 122, N-12, N-13
Paternoster, Raymond, N-13, N-20, N-25
Paterson, E. Britt, N-14
Patterson, Gerald R., 94, N-8
Pearce, Frank, N-40, N-56
Pearson, Frank S., N-20
Pearson, Karl, 71
Pease, Ken, N-26
Pease, Susan, N-11
Peck, Jeffrey, N-27, N-38
Pedarion, Daniel, N-35
Pedersen, Daniel, N-29
Peeples, Faith, N-14
Pepinsky, Harold E., N-23, N-24
Perkins, Joseph, N-18
Perl, Raphael F., N-56
Perlmutter, Marion, N-7
Pervin, Lawrence A., N-9
Petee, Thomas A., N-15
Peters, Eric, N-38
Petersilia, Joan, N-5
Peterson, Ruth D., N-32
Petrashek, David, N-43
Pfefferbaum, Betty, N-49
Pfeiffer, Christian, N-52
Philip, Diana, 231
Phillips, Coretta, N-26
Phinney, David, N-14
Pierce, Glenn L., N-36
Pileggi, Nicholas, N-34
Piliavin, Irving, 169, N-18
Pinel, Philippe, 74, 98, N-6
Piquero, Alex, N-25
Pittman, Karen J., N-32

NAME INDEX

Pitts, Victoria L., N-27
Platt, Anthony, 194, 205, N-22
Platt, Suzy, N-5
Pleasant, Dean, 16
Pleck, Elizabeth, N-30
Pluchinsky, Dennis, N-35
Pogrebin, Mark R., N-15
Poindexter, John, 286
Polanzi, C., N-44
Polk, Kenneth, N-16, N-28, N-41, N-55
Pollack, Otto, 51, N-4
Polvi, Natalie, N-26
Pomeroy, Wardel B., N-50, N-52
Pontell, Henry N., N-38, N-39, N-40, N-41
Poole, Eric D., N-15
Pope, Jeremy, 324
Popkin, Susan J., N-45
Porta, Giambattista della, 66–67
Potter, Elaine, N-43
Potter, Kimberly A., N-36
Pottieger, Anne E., N-47, N-50
Pound, Roscoe, N-23
Powell, Kenneth, N-29
Power, William, N-41
Poyner, Barry, N-37
Prat, Tamar, N-35
Preble, Edward, N-47
Prendergast, M. L., N-8
Preston, James D., N-45
Prichard, James C., 98
Prince, Joyce, N-37
Puig-Antich, J., N-10
Purnell, Sonia, 405

Quételet, Adolphe, 75, 215, N-6, N-25
Quinney, Richard, 204, 206, N-23, N-24, N-40, N-43

Rackmill, Stephen J., N-40
Rada, R. T., N-11
Radke-Yarrow, M., N-8
Radosevich, M. J., N-16
Radzinowicz, Leon, N-5
Rafter, Nicole Hahn, N-6
Raith, Werner, N-33
Rankin, Joseph H., N-20
Rapp, Doris J., N-11
Rasche, Christine, N-30
Rasmussen, David W., N-47
Ray, Issac, 74, N-6
Ray, Jo-Ann, N-37
Ray, M., N-22
Reagan, Ronald, 283, 284
Reasons, Charles E., N-43
Rebovich, Donald J., 346, N-34
Reckless, Walter C., 177–180, N-19, N-20
Redfern, Allison, N-39
Reed, Gary E., N-43
Reed, Mark D., N-15
Reichel, Philip L., N-24, N-54
Reige, Mary, N-20
Reinarman, Craig, N-15

Reinhold, Robert, N-18
Reisman, Judtih A., N-50, N-51
Reiss, Albert J., Jr., 106, 146, 175, N-9, N-10, N-12, N-14, N-16, N-19, N-41, N-44, N-45, N-49
Renfrew, P., N-40
Rengert, George F., 219–221, N-25
Rennie, Ysabel, N-12
Reno, Janet, N-1
Resendez, Angel Leonicio Reyes Maturino, 244
Reuben, David, N-50
Reuter, Peter, 369, N-14
Reyna, S. P., 118
Reynolds, Arthur J., 125
Reynolds, Toby, N-1
Rhodes, Albert L., 106, 146, N-10, N-12, N-16
Rich, Mark, N-1
Richards, Pamela J., N-50
Richardson, John E., N-8
Ricker, Robert A., 279
Riedel, Marc, 242, N-28
Rifkin, Joel, 243
Rimm, Marty, N-52
Ritti, Richard R., N-50
Ritzer, George, N-36
Rivera, Ramon, N-16
Robb, George, N-42
Roberts, Albert R., N-31
Roberts, Mary K., N-19
Roberts, Nickie, N-50
Roberts, Randell, 332
Robins, Lee N., 89
Rodriguez, Orlando, N-19
Roehl, Jan, N-27
Roemer, William F., Jr., N-34
Rogan, Dennis P., N-31, N-36
Rokeach, Milton, N-19
Romilly, Sir Samuel, 66
Roncek, Dennis W., N-27
Rook, Karen S., N-19
Roosevelt, Theodore, 339
Rose, Dina R., 132, N-14
Rose, R. M., N-11
Rosen, Lawrence, N-20
Rosenbaum, Dennis, N-17
Rosenbaum, Jill Leslie, N-18, N-20
Rosenbaum, Marsha, N-46
Rosenblatt, Roger, N-36
Rosenfeld, Richard, 124, 125, 141, N-2, N-13
Rosenhan, D. L., N-22
Ross, E. A., 168
Ross, Lee, N-26
Roth, J. A., N-9
Roth, Jeffrey A., N-3, N-47, N-49
Roth, Martha, N-51
Rothman, Fred B., N-53, N-55
Roundtree, Pamela Wilcox, N-15
Rowe, Daryl, N-31
Rowe, David C., 103, N-10

Ruback, Barry R., N-30
Rude, George, N-5
Rudovsky, David, 56
Rumsey, Spencer, 274
Rusche, Georg, 203, N-23
Ruth, David E., N-33
Rutter, Michael, N-7, N-11
Ryder, Winona, 293
Rzeplinski, Andrzej, N-24

Sachs, Andrea, 199
Sagarin, Edward, 110, N-11
Sagi, Philip C., 242, N-28
Saker, Anne, 92
Salerno, Ralph, N-42
Salim, Mamdouh Mahmud, 6
Salmelainen, Pia, N-37
Salzano, Julienne, N-34
Samenow, Stanton, 97, N-9
Samper, Ernesto, 364
Sampson, Robert J., 180, 181, 196, N-3, N-6, N-14, N-20, N-23, N-27
Sanabria, Harry, 356, N-25
Sanchez, Loretta, 127
Sanchez, Rene, N-17
Sand, Leonard, 198
Sandberg, A. A., N-10
Sanders, Joseph, N-55
Santana, Arthur, N-45
Santino, Umberto, N-34
Sargarin, Edward, N-51
Savona, Ernesto U., N-33
Saxon, Miraim S., N-44
Scarpitti, Frank R., N-19, N-20, N-34
Scarr, Sandra, 106, N-11
Scatchard, Dave, 96
Schafer, Walter B., N-16
Schaffer, Richard, N-44
Schalling, Daisy, N-8
Schatzberg, Rufus, N-35
Schichor, David, N-55
Schiffer, Lois, 317
Schiraldi, Vincent, N-35
Schlegel, Kip, N-40, N-42, N-44
Schlossman, Steven, N-15
Schmid, Alex P., N-56
Schmidt, Janell D., N-31
Schneidler, James, N-47
Schoenberg, Robert J., N-33
Schoenthaler, Stephen, 108, N-11
Schott, Ian, N-33
Schrag, Clarence, N-20
Schrager, Laura S., N-44
Schuessler, Karl E., 97, N-9
Schultze, Phyllis, N-54
Schuman, Karl, N-55
Schur, Edwin, 192, 193, N-22, N-23
Schwartz, Martin D., 255, 256, N-24, N-27, N-32
Schwartz, Richard D., 194, N-22
Schweinhart, Lawrence J., N-14
Schweitzer, Yoram, N-35

Schwendinger, Herman, 205, 255, N-24, N-32
Schwendinger, Julia R., 205, 255, N-24, N-32
Schwind, Hans-Dieter, N-56
Sciolino, Elaine, N-48
Scorcese, Martin, 155
Scott, Ann, 95
Scott, Austin W., N-28
Scott, Heather, N-51
Scott, Joseph E., N-41
Scott, Peter, N-6
Scott, R., N-22
Scott, Richard O., N-36
Scronce, Christine A., N-49
Scull, A., N-18
Scully, D., N-32
Sears, Kenneth C., N-39
Seda, Heriberto, 244
Seidman, Robert, 204, N-24, N-43
Sellin, Thorsten, 49, 70, 71, 139, 140, N-3, N-5, N-6, N-10, N-15, N-17
Selva, Lance H., N-24
Semier, P. K. , N-1
Sennewald, Charles A., N-37
Seper, Jerry, N-1
Serrill, Michael S., 376
Sessar, Klaus, N-52
Sforza, Daniel, N-25
Shachmurove, Yochanan, 228
Shaffer, John W., N-48
Shah, Jayen, 303
Shannon, Elaine, N-36
Shapiro, Susan P., N-40, N-43, N-45
Shavelson, Richard, N-15
Shaw, Bud, 176
Shaw, Clifford R., 130–131, 134–135, N-14, N-16
Shaw, James W., N-36
Shearing, Clifford D., N-27
Shedd, Ed, N-33
Shelby, Richard, 346
Sheldon, William H., 72, N-6
Sheley, Joseph F., N-36, N-46
Shelley, Louise I., 389, N-33, N-52, N-53, N-54
Shenou, Philip, N-1
Sherman, Lawrence W., 36, 224, N-2, N-14, N-25, N-27, N-31, N-36
Shoemaker, Donald J., 130, 145, 148, 154, N-17, N-19
Shoham, S. Giora, N-28
Short, James F., Jr., 137, 147, 158, N-12, N-16, N-18, N-19, N-44
Short, James S., N-15
Shover, Neal, 310, N-3, N-39
Sibbitt, Rae, N-48
Sigler, Robert, N-32
Silas, Faye, N-50
Silva, Phil A., N-3, N-5, N-12
Silver, H. K., N-30
Silverman, F. N., N-30

Silverman, Robert A., 242, N-28
Silverstein, Martin E., N-18
Simon, Jeffrey D., N-35
Simon, Patricia M., N-50
Simon, Rita James, 52, N-4, N-5
Simon, Ronald L., N-4
Simons, Marlise, 376
Simpson, John, N-4, N-20
Simpson, Nicole Brown, 249
Simpson, O. J., 249
Simpson, Sally S., N-4, N-24, N-25, N-40, N-44
Sims, Ronald R., N-43
Singer, Peter, 65
Singer, Simon I., 44, 45, N-17
Skilling, Jeff, 348
Skolnick, Jerome H., 194, N-22
Skoog, Dagna K., N-8, N-9
Sloan, John J., N-26
Sloane, Leonard, N-38
Smith, Brent L., N-35
Smith, Carolyn, N-15, N-18, N-31
Smith, David L., 309
Smith, Dietrich, N-39
Smith, Douglas, 53, 132, N-3, N-5, N-12, N-14, N-20
Smith, Dwight, N-39
Smith, Gene M., N-47
Smith, Jinney S., N-6
Smith, Lynn Newhart, N-14
Smith, M. Dwayne, N-5, N-32, N-36
Smith, Mary S., N-28
Smith, Vern E., N-35
Smithey, Martha, N-29
Snell, Cudore L., N-50
Snider, Laureen, N-40, N-44
Snortum, John R., N-50
Solaway, S. A., N-1
Sommers, Ira, N-48
Sorenson, Ann Marie, N-16, N-21
Sorenson, Susan B., N-32
Sorrentino, Anthony, N-15
Sosa, Sammy, 119
Souryhal, Sam S., N-54, N-55
South, Steve J., N-14
Sparks, Richard F., 34, 205, N-24, N-44
Spear, Robert, N-1
Speck, Richard, 102
Speckart, George, N-47
Spelman, William, N-26, N-27
Spencer, J., N-54
Spencer, Margaret P., N-43
Spergel, Irving A., N-29
Spiegel, Ulrich, N-15
Spielberger, Charles Donald, N-8
Spitzer, Elliot, 339
Spohn, Cassia C., N-32
Spradley, P., N-22
Spunt, Barry, N-47
Spurzheim, Johann Kaspar, 68
Squitieri, Tom, N-3
Sroufe, L., N-7

Stack, Susan A., N-10
Staten, Clark, N-32
Stattin, Hakan, N-10
Steele, B. F., N-30
Steffensmeier, Darrell, N-4, N-21, N-39
Steffenson, James L., N-17
Steffy, Richard A., N-51
Steinberg, Jacques, 231
Steinhauer, Jennifer, 226
Stenning, Phillip C., N-27
Stephens, Richard C., N-48
Stephenson, Philip, N-48
Stevens, Larry, 244
Stevens, William K., N-50
Stewart, Lorne V., N-53
Stewart, Martha, 319
Stewart, Potter, N-51
Stiglitz, Joseph, N-1
Stolberg, Mary M., N-33
Stone, Brad, N-39
Stone, William E., N-26
Straus, Martha, N-30
Straus, Murray A., 249, N-30, N-49
Strodtbeck, Fred L., N-16, N-19
Stuntz, William J., 21
Sullivan, John P., N-18, N-56
Sullivan, Scott, 334
Sumner, Maggie, N-49
Sung Joon Jang, N-3, N-20
Supancic, Michael, N-14
Sutherland, Edwin H., 12, 15, 32, 105, 136, 144, 292, 319, 340, N-2, N-10, N-15, N-37, N-40, N-42, N-43
Swanson, James W., N-11
Swift, Carolyn F., N-30
Swisher, Karin L., N-51
Swiss, Shana, N-57
Sykes, Alan O., N-43
Sykes, Gresham M., N-17, N-19, N-24, N-27

Takagi, Paul, 204
Talese, Gay, N-34
Talic, Momir, 403
Tannenbaum, Frank, N-22
Tappan, Paul W., N-1
Tarde, Gabriel, 75–76, N-7
Taubman, Alfred, 337
Taylor, Ian, 204, N-13, N-23, N-24
Taylor, Jim, 332
Taylor, Kathy, 332
Taylor, Ralph B., 132, N-14, N-15
Taylor, Robert W., N-39
Tedeschi, James T., 224, 248, N-9, N-26, N-30
Teevan, James J., N-21
Teilmann, K., N-10
Tennenbaum, Dainel J., 97, N-9
Tennyson, Ray, N-16
Terlouw, Gert-Jan, N-54
Terrill, Richard J., N-53
Tesoriero, James M., N-17, N-36

NAME INDEX

Thomas, Charles W., N-22
Thomas, Evan, 43
Thomas, George, N-46
Thomas, Jim, N-24
Thomas, William I., 129, 130, 191, N-14, N-22
Thompson, Carol Y., N-3
Thompson, Dick, N-10
Thompson, Kevin, 122, N-12
Thompson, M., N-16
Thornberry, Terence P., 122, 180, 181, N-3, N-12, N-16, N-17, N-19, N-20, N-31, N-36
Thornton, Joe, 96
Thrasher, Frederick M., N-14
Thrower, Ethan, 257
Thurman, Tracey, 250
Tittle, Charles R., 53, 122, N-5, N-12, N-15, N-21, N-22
Titus, Richard M., N-27, N-41
Tobias, Andrew, N-42
Toby, Jackson, 169, 177, N-18, N-24
Toch, Hans, N-7
Tompkins, John S., N-42
Tonry, Michael, 216, 356, N-14, N-24–N-27, N-29, N-41, N-44
Tontodonato, Pamela, N-31
Topinard, Paul, 12, N-1
Toufexis, Anastasia, N-9
Tracy, Paul E., 44, 45, 49, 328, N-3, N-42
Travis, Gail, N-53
Treaster, Joseph B., N-17
Trebach, Arnold S., N-49
Tremblay, Pierre, N-38
Trickett, Alan, N-26
Triplett, Ruth A., N-5, N-22
Troc-Nhu Ho, N-56
Tromanhauser, Edward D., N-16
Tulloch, M. I., N-8
Tunis, Sandra L., N-48
Turk, Austin T., 200, N-23, N-24
Turner, Carlton Akee, Jr., 92
Turner, J. W. Cecil, N-37

Uchida, Craig, N-27
Ugljesa, Zvekic, N-53

Valachi, Joseph, 261, 263
Valenti, Jack, 95
Van Bemmelen, J. M., N-23
Van der Poel, Sari, N-50
Van Dijk, Jan J. M, N-53
Vaughn, Michael S., N-55
Vaz, E. W., N-18
Verhovek, Sam Howe, N-29, N-35, N-36
Verrett, Mary Neil, 273
Verri, Pietro, 62
Viano, Emilio, N-26
Victor, Hope R., N-47
Vieraitis, Lynne M., N-13
Villar, Roger, 298

Villemez, Wayne J., 53, N-5, N-12
Virginia, H., N-46
Virkkunen, Matti, 109, N-11
Visher, Christy A., N-3, N-47
Vistica, Gregory L., 276
Volavka, Jan, 110, N-11
Vold, George B., 200, N-6, N-23
Volkman, Ernest, N-34
Voltaire, 64
von Hentig, Hans, 242, N-26, N-28
Voss, Harwin L., 146, N-5, N-16
Voss, Natalie D., N-38, N-56

Waddell, J. O., N-49
Waksal, Samuel, 322
Waksler, Frances C., 13, 14, N-1
Wald, Matthew L., N-39
Walder, Patrice, N-37
Waldo, G. P., N-9
Waldorf, Dan, N-18, N-49
Walker, Lenore E., N-30
Walker, Samuel, N-35
Walker, William O., III, N-48
Waller, Douglas, 11
Waller, John B., Jr., N-36
Wallerstein, James S., 38, N-2
Wallis, Lynne, 118
Walmsley, Roy, N-53
Walsh, Anthony, N-22
Walston, James, N-34
Walt, Steven, N-42
Walton, Paul, 204, N-13, N-23, N-24
Ward, David, N-22
Ward, Geoffrey C., 155
Waring, Elin J., 350, N-27, N-40
Warner, John, N-48
Warr, Mark, 137, N-15, N-16
Warren, Carol, N-22
Warren, Earl, 190
Warren, Friedman, 43
Washburn, S. L., N-6
Wasilchick, John, 219–221, N-25
Watanavanich, Prathan, N-44
Waters, Harry F., 95
Watkins, Sherron, 348
Watson, Sylvia M., N-8
Weatherburn, Don, N-21
Weaver, Frances, N-37
Weekart, David P., N-14
Weeks, Susan L., N-40
Wegner, Norma, N-48
Weihofen, Henry, N-39
Weinberg, Richard, 106, N-11
Weiner, Neil Alan, N-17, N-20, N-30, N-31, N-48
Weis, Joseph G., 39, 180, 182, N-3, N-21, N-47
Weisburd, David L., 350, N-19, N-21, N-27, N-40, N-42, N-44
Weisel, Deborah, N-17
Wekesser, Carol, N-51
Weller, Christine L., N-46

Wellford, Charles F., 196, N-20, N-22
Wells, L. Edward, N-20
Wendell, S., N-51
Wernz, Gerald W., N-41
Wertham, Frederic, 222, N-26
Weston, William, N-41, N-55
Wetzels, Peter, N-52
Whatley, Mark, N-31
Wheeler, Stanton, N-40, N-44
White, Byron, 377
White, Dan, 108
White, Helene Raskin, N-13
White, Jacqueline W., N-32
Whittaker, David, N-15
Wiatrowski, Michael D., N-19
Widom, Cathy Spatz, N-7, N-31
Wiechman, Dennis, N-56
Wiegand, Bruce R., N-53
Wiegman, O., N-8
Wiersema, Brian, N-29, N-36
Wikström, Per-Olof H., N-27, N-55
Wilbanks, William, N-28
Wild, Jonathan, 311
Wilkins, Leslie T., 33, N-2, N-55
Will, George F., 65
Williams, Frank P., III, N-12, N-52
Williams, J. Sherwood, N-17
Williams, Nigel, 396
Williams, Phil, N-33, N-56
Williams, Terry, 356
Williams, Timothy L., N-41
Wilson, Colin, N-33
Wilson, Edward O., 102, N-10
Wilson, James Q., 48, 106, 111, 283, 341, 356, N-3, N-10, N-11, N-21, N-43
Wilson, Margo I., N-29, N-55
Wilson, Nanci Koser, N-4, N-28
Wilson, William Julius, 119, 241, N-12, N-28
Winerip, Michael, N-35
Winslow, Robert W., N-50
Winslow, Virginia, N-50
Winters, Ken C., N-46
Wise, Edward M., N-52, N-53, N-57
Wish, Eric, N-47
Wisniewski, N., N-32
Witkin, Herman A., N-10
Woessnar, Paul H., N-56
Wolf, Jim, N-1
Wolfe, Nancy T., N-4
Wolfgang, Bilsky, N-52
Wolfgang, Marvin E., 44, 45, 49, 106, 151, 152, 224, 241, 242, 341, 368, N-3, N-6, N-8, N-10, N-16, N-17, N-26, N-28, N-30, N-31, N-48
Woodall, Ruth, N-37
Woodbury, Richard, N-35
Wooden, Wayne S., N-18, N-39
Woodiwiss, Michael, N-56
Woodson, Ernest, 303
Wormith, J. Stephen, N-8
Wren, Christopher, S., N-45, N-48

Wright, Bradley R. Entner, N-12
Wright, James D., N-36
Wright, John Paul, N-13
Wright, Richard T., 221, N-25, N-26, N-39
Wyle, Clement J., 38, N-2
Wyness, Robert, N-6

Yakovlev, Alexander, N-21
Yates, Andrea, 110
Ybarra, Gilbert, 171

Yeager, Peter Cleary, 340, 341, N-39, N-43, N-44
Yeisley, Mark R., N-13
Yeudall, Lorne T., N-11
Yochelson, Samuel, 97, N-9
Young, Jock, 204, N-13, N-23, N-24
Young, Timothy R., N-44
Young, Vernetta D., N-4
Yü-Hsiu Hsü, N-55

Zahn, Margaret A., 242, N-28
Zawitz, Marianne W., N-36

Zellman, Goul, N-15
Ziglar, Edward, 125
Zillman, Dolf, N-51
Zimring, Franklin E., N-50, N-51
Zinberg, Norman E., N-47
Zineb, El Khazouni, N-30
Znaniecki, Florian, 129, 130, N-14
Zorza, Joan, N-31
Zuckerman, Laurence, N-56
Zvekic, Ugljesa, N-55

Subject Index

Abandoned vehicles, 301
Abolitionist theory, 209
Accommodate, 124
Act requirement, 24
Addict robber, 258
Adelphia Communications, 349
Admitting the Holocaust (Langer), 207
Adoption studies, 103–104
Advance-fee loan/credit schemes, 327
Age, 45–50
Aggravated assault, 247
Aggression, 94
Aging-out phenomenon, 48
AIC, 387
AIDS, 359
Aircraft hijacking, 400
Al Qaeda, 6, 7
Alcohol abuse, 358, 367–370
Alcoholic robber, 258
Allergic reactions, 106–107
Allied Chemical, 342, 343
"Altruistic Punishment in Humans" (Fehr/Gachter), 178
Amateur thief, 291
American Airlines, 317
American Me, 157
American Skinheads - The Criminology and Control of Hate Crime (Hamm), 384
Amish, 128
Anarchist theory, 209
Annual Report on School Safety, 279
Anomie, 77, 116–117
Anti-Drug Abuse Act, 357
Antitrust legislation, 339
Appeal to higher loyalties, 175
Arab Security Studies and Training Centre, 387
Argus, 163
Arms trafficking, 7, 400
Arson, 312–313
Art theft, 293–295, 399
Arthur Andersen, 348, 349
Asian gangs, 143, 164
Aspartame, 107
Assassination, 238–239
Assault, 247–248
Atavistic stigmata, 68
Attachment, 87, 170–171
Aun Shinrikyo, 133, 272
Auto insurance schemes, 295, 301–302
Auto theft, 228, 229, 295–297
Autolock, 296
Automatism, 100
Autonomy, 154
Aversive instigators, 94

Bait-and-switch advertising, 326
Balkanization, 406
Baltimore, anti-drug campaign, 365
Bank of Credit & Commerce International (BCCI), 405
Bankruptcy fraud, 322–323, 402
Battered child syndrome, 248
Battered wives, 249–251
Battery, 247
BCCI, 405
Beccaria, Cesare, 62–64
Beggar's Opera, 311
Begging, 198–199
Behavioral modeling, 90
Belief, 171–172
Biochemical factors, 106–109
Biocriminology, 101, 110–111
Biological determinism, 67–73, 78
Biology and criminality, 101–110
 biochemical factors, 106–109
 diet, 107–108
 food allergies, 106–107
 genetics and criminality, 102–105
 hormones, 109
 hypoglycemia, 108–109
 intelligence, 105–106
 modern biocriminality, 101–102
 neurophysiological factors, 109–110
Birth cohort, 48–50
BJS, 35
Black Thursday, 117
Bloods, 161
Blue channels, 372
Boat theft, 297–298
Body parts, trade in, 401–402
Bogle family, 91
Boiler rooms, 322
Boredom in class, 146
Born criminal, 68, 69
Boyz in the Hood, 157
Brady Bill, 283, 284
Brain lesions/tumors, 109
Branch Davidians, 133, 272
Breaking of laws, 15–19
Bribery, 329, 331, 402
Buck v. Bell, 65
Buddhas of Afghanistan, 8, 9
Bureau of Justice Statistics (BJS), 35
Burglary, 219–221, 228, 310–311
Business opportunity fraud, 327
Buy-back programs, 283

Car theft, 228, 229, 295–297
Carjacking, 295–296
Case study, 32
Causation requirement, 25–26
Caused accidents, 302
Causes of Delinquency (Hirschi), 169
CDA, 378
Challenge of Crime in a Free Society, 18
Cheaters, punishing, 178
Check forging, 300
Cheyenne culture, 394
Chicago Area Project (CAP), 134–135
Child abuse, 251–252
Child pornography, 305, 306, 308, 378
Child prostitution, 376
Childhood deprivation, 87–90
Chinese gangs, 164
Chinese Triads, 263
Choice structuring properties, 216
Cholesterol, 101
Chop shops, 295
Chromosomes, 102
Chronic 6 percent, 49
Churning, 322
Cigarette use, 358
Citizenworks, 345
Civil law system, 386, 388, 389
Class, State, and Crime (Quinney), 204
Classical criminology, 60–67, 78
Clayton Antitrust Act, 339
Cocaine, 362
Coconut Grove disaster, 239
Code of Hammurabi, 15
Cohort studies, 48–50
College boys, 145
College campus crime, 222
Colombian cartels, 263
Colombian gangs, 164
Colors, 157
Commitment, 171
Common law system, 388, 389
Communications Decency Act (CDA), 378
Communist Manifesto (Marx), 202
Comparative criminology, 382–407
 comparative research, 390–392
 defined, 384
 empirical research, 392–394
 ethnic fragmentation, 406
 goals, 386
 historical overview, 385–386
 periodical literature, 390
 practical goals, 395–406
 preparatory work, 386–390
 socioeconomic development perspective, 395
 teenage prostitution, 396
 theory testing, 394–395
 transnational crimes, 397–406
Comparative Criminology (Mannheim), 391
Comparative research, 390–392
Comprehensive Drug Abuse Prevention and Control Act, 357
Comprehensive Gang Model, 163
Computer crime, 6–7, 401. *See* High-tech crimes
Computer network break-ins, 305–306

I-13

Computer vandalism, 306
Concurrence requirement, 27
Condemnation of the condemner, 175
Condition of the Working Class in England, The (Engels), 202
Conditioning, 98
Confidence game, 299
Conflict model, 15
Conflict theory, 196–202
    consensus model, 197
    empirical evidence, 201–202
    overview (table), 196
Conformity, 120–121, 177
Consensus model, 14, 197
Consumer fraud, 326–327
Containment theory, 177–180
Controlled Substances Act, 357
Convenience stores, 229–230
Convention for the Suppression of Unlawful Acts against the Safety of Civil Aviation, 272
Convention for the Suppression of Unlawful Seizure of Aircraft, 272
Convention on Offense and Certain Other Acts Committed on Board Aircraft, 272
Convention on the Prevention and Punishment of Crimes against Internationally Protected Persons Including Diplomatic Agents, 272
Corner boys, 145
Corporate crime, 331. *See also* White-collar crime
    antitrust legislation, 339
    civil penalties, 338–339
    criminal liability, 339, 340
    frequency/problems of definition, 331–332
    future of, 347–350
    governmental control, 338–339
    high-profile cases, 349
    investigating, 339–341
    models of corporate culpability, 337–338
    penalties, 336, 338–339
    phases of corporate criminal law, 332–336
    Sarbanes-Oxley Act, 318, 344–345
    sentencing guidelines, 336
Corporate crime database, 347
Corporate ethos, 337, 338
Corporate policy (CP), 337, 338
Corruption, 329–330, 402
Cortical arousal, 98
Course in Positive Philosophy (Comte), 67
CP, 337, 338
CPTED, 226
Crank, 360
CRAVED, 221
Credit card fraud, 300–301, 308
Crime
    basic requirements, 24–27
    cost of, 323
    defined, 13
    geography of, 225
    measuring, 28–44. *See also* Measuring crime

    severity of, 44, 45
    typologies, 28
Crime and the American Dream (Messner/Rosenfeld), 124
Crime mapping, 215
Crime prevention through environmental design (CPTED), 226
Crime rate, 35, 42–43, 184
Crime surfing
    chat room, 17
    computer crime, 302
    corporate crime, 337
    cost of crime, 323
    crime data, 36
    criminal justice system, 18
    cyberporn, 377
    death penalty, 203
    Durkheim, 77
    firearms, 281
    gangs, 129, 157, 158
    ICC, 404
    ICPO-Interpol, 403
    insanity defense, 99
    international crime rate, 402
    international criminology, 391
    JRSA, 32
    material deprivation, 89
    money laundering, 12
    national drug control policy, 354
    online fraud, 309
    school violence, 279
    situational crime prevention, 227, 232
    social bonds, 171
    Sourcebook of Criminal Justice Statistics, 41
    Southern Poverty Law Center, 273
    UNCJIN, 45
    victimization levels/neighborhoods, 134
    Watch Your Car program, 297
Crimen innominatum, 371
Crimes against property, 34, 288–314
    arson, 312–313
    burglary, 310–311
    comparative crime rates, 313
    fencing, 311–312
    fraud, 298–302
    high-tech crime, 302–310
    larceny, 290–298. *See also* Larceny
Crimes against the person, 34
Criminal and His Victim, The (von Hentig), 222
Criminal careers, 48
Criminal justice, 18
Criminal justice specialists, 18
Criminal justice system, 18
Criminal Man, The (Lombroso), 68
Criminal Personality, The (Yochelson/Samenow), 97
Criminalists, 3
Criminality and Economic Conditions (Bonger), 203
Criminals, 44–55
    age, 45–50
    gender, 50–53
    race, 54–55
    social class, 53–54

Criminology, 10–13, 18
Criminoloids, 70
Crips, 150, 161
Critical criminology, 204
Cults, 133
Cultural deviance theories, 127–140
    culture conflict theory, 139–140
    differential association theory, 135–138
    social disorganization theory, 129–135
Cultural disorientation, 100
Cultural transmission, 132
Culture conflict theory, 139–140
Culture of poverty, 119
Cut throat, 176
Cyber Patrol, 378
Cyber spies, 306
Cyber vandals, 305
Cyberporn, 305, 306, 308, 374, 377–379
Cybersmut, 378

Dan White's defense, 108
Dangerous Ground: The World of Hazardous Waste Crime (Rebovich), 346
Data, 29
Data collection, 29–33
    available data, 32–33
    case studies, 32
    experiments, 30–31
    participant/nonparticipant observation, 31–32
    surveys, 30
Date rape, 254
Deceptive advertising, 326
Defense of infancy, 27–28
Defense of public duty, 28
Defenses, 27–28, 100
Delinquent boys, 145
Delinquent gangs, 161
Delusional instigators, 94
Denial of injury, 175
Denial of responsibility, 175
Denial of service attacks, 305
Denial of the victim, 175
Denying the Holocaust (Lipstadt), 207
Destruction of cultural property, 7–9
Developmental/life course theory, 180–182
Deviance, 13, 129
Deviate sexual intercourse, 371
Diet, 107–108
Differential association-reinforcement, 95
Differential association theory, 135–138
Differential opportunity theory, 147–151
Direct control, 179
Direct experience, 93–94
Dirty money (money laundering), 5–6
Disgorgement, 346
Disney World, 228, 229
Displacement, 232
Displacement effect, 285
Division of Social Labor (Durkheim), 77
Dizygotic (DZ) twins, 103
Domestic violence, 249–252
Drive-by shootings, 158
Drop in crime, 42–43

SUBJECT INDEX

Drug abuse, 354–367
    cocaine, 362
    crime-related activities, 360
    drug control, 364–367
    drug distribution business, 356
    education, 366
    extent of, 357
    heroin, 362–363
    historical overview, 354–357
    international drug economy, 360–361
    legalization, 367
    marijuana, 363
    money laundering, 363
    patterns of, 357–360
    political impact, 363–364
    treatment, 366
    world drug smuggling routes, 361
Drug distribution business, 356
Drug trafficking, 4, 402
Drunk and Drugged Awareness Week, 369
Drunk driving, 367, 369–370
Due process, 190
DZ twins, 103

Ecocide, 9
Ego, 85
Eighth Avenue Boys, 155
Elder abuse, 252–253
Electroencephalogram, 110–111
Embezzlement, 330
Employee-related thefts, 330–331
Enron, 317, 347–350
Environmental crimes, 341–344
Environmental criminology, 215
Environmental Protection Agency (EPA), 342
Environmental theory, 212–234
    displacement, 232
    environmental criminology, 215
    rational-choice perspective, 215–217
    routine activity approach, 217–219
    situational crime prevention, 227–232
    situational theories of crime, 215–222
    theories of victimization, 222–226. *See also* Theories of victimization
    theory informs policy, 232
EPA, 342
Equal protection, 190
Ethics, 33
Ethnic fragmentation, 406
Ethnic gangs, 143, 164
Eugenics, 72
Excitement, 154
Experiment, 30–31
Extroversion, 97
Exxon Valdez oil spill, 9, 331, 342
Eysenck's conditioning theory, 97–98

Failure to act, 24
False pretenses, obtaining property by, 299
Families First, 185
Family atmosphere, 89

Family-based crime prevention (ecological context), 90
Family ganging, 302
Family-related crimes, 248–253
Federal antigang budget, 165
Federal Witness Protection Program, 263
Felicific calculus, 66
Felonies, 27
Felony murder, 239
Female delinquent subcultures, 159–160
Female gangs, 158–160
Female Offender, The (Lombroso), 50
Fence, 311
Fence (Steffensmeier), 311
Fencing, 311–312
Field experiment, 31
Fingerprint-enabled handgun, 285
Firearm-related offenses, 279–280
Firearms. *See* Guns
Focal concerns, 153–156
Food additives/dyes, 108
Food allergies, 106–107
Foreign lottery schemes, 327
Forensic scientists, 3
Fraternal twins, 103
Fraud, 298–302. *See also* White-collar crime
Fraudulent bankruptcy, 402
Free will, 62–66, 78
Freemen of Montana, 275
Fulcher v. State, 100
Fundamental psycholegal error, 100
Funnel of deviance, 13, 14

Galley slavery, 203
Gang murder, 245–246
Gangs, 143, 156–162
    delinquent, 161
    demographic profile, 159
    drug use, 153
    ethnic, 143, 164
    female, 158–160
    getting out, 165
    guns, 157–158
    hate, 161, 162
    motorcycle, 128–129
    New York City, 155
    risk factors, 174
    satanic, 161
    websites, 129, 157, 158
Gate of Heaven, 133
Gays, 371
Gender, 50–53
General Electric, 343
General strain theory, 126
General theories, 182–183
Genetics and criminality, 102–105
Genocide, 207–208
Geography of crime, 225
Girls in the Gang, The (Campbell), 160
Global Crossing, 349
Global Report on Crime and Justice, 392
Global sexual slavery, 376
Globalization. *See* Comparative criminology
Gods Must Be Crazy, The, 289

Good Samaritan, 24
Government-related fraud, 324–326
Guilty mind requirement, 26–27
Gun-control debate, 284–285
Gun Free Schools Act, 278
Guns
    controlling handgun use, 281–284
    displacement effect, 285
    fingerprint-enabled handgun, 285
    firearm-related offenses, 279–280
    gangs, 157–158
    gun control debate, 284–285
    youth, 280–281

Hacking, 305
Hale Doctrine, 253
Harm requirement, 25
Harrison Act, 356
Hashish, 363
Hate Crime Prevention Act, 274
Hate Crime Statistics Act, 274
Hate crimes, 272–274
Hate gangs, 161, 162
Hate groups, 129
Hazardous waste crime, 346
Head start, 126–127
Hell's Angels, 128, 129
Heroin, 362–363
HEUNI, 387
High-tech crimes, 302–310
    child pornography, 305, 306, 308
    credit card fraud, 308
    criminal justice problem, 310
    degree of criminal complexity, 304
    detection, 304
    hacking, 305
    high-tech criminal, 309–310
    industrial espionage, 306
    international component, 304
    mail bombings, 308
    password sniffers, 308
    profits of crime, 304
    role of victims/type of property, 302–304
    software privacy, 306
    vandalism, 305, 306
Hijacking, 400, 401
Hirschi-Gottfredson self-control model, 182–183
Hirschi's social bonds, 170–172
Hirschi's social control theory, 169–173
Hmong gangs, 143
Holocaust, 208
Home-improvement fraud, 326
Homeboys, 159
Homebuilders, 185
Homicide, 238–247
    cross-national comparisons, 246–247
    defined, 238
    extent of, 240–241
    gang murder, 245–246
    manslaughter, 239–240
    mass/serial murders, 243–245
    murder, 238–239
    nature of, 241–246
    no apparent motive, 243
    relatives/acquaintances, 243

Homicide, 238–247
    stranger, 242
    victim precipitation, 242
    young/old perpetrators, 243
Homosexuality, 371
"Hoops That Help" celebrity basketball game, 139
Hormones, 109
Hot-check artists, 300
Hot products, 221
Hot spots of crime, 224–226
House of Umoja, 163
Human nature, 110–111
Hypoglycemia, 108–109
Hypothesis, 29

ICC, 403–404
ICPO-Interpol, 403
ICVS, 390
Id, 85
Identical twins, 103
Identity theft, 307
ILANUD, 387
Illegal Corporate Behavior (Clinard et al.), 334
Illicit arms trafficking, 7, 400
Illicit drug trafficking, 4, 402
Illicit drug use. *See* Drug abuse
Incentive instigators, 94
Index crimes, 34
Indicators of School Crime and Safety, 279
Indirect control, 179
Industrial espionage, 306
Infiltration of legal business, 402
Ingredients of crime, 24–27
Inherited criminality, 72–73
Inner containment, 177
Innovation, 121
Insane criminals, 70
Insanity defense, 27, 99
Insider-related fraud, 330–331
Insider trading, 322
Instigators of aggression, 94
Instructional instigators, 94
Insurance fraud
    auto insurance schemes, 295, 301–302
    international aspects, 401
    medical fraud, 302
    New Jersey, 303
    types of, 327–328
Integrated theory, 180, 182
Intellectual property, theft of, 399–400
Intelligence, 105–106
Intended accidents, 301
Internalized control, 179
International Centre for Criminal Law Reform and Criminal Justice Policy, 387
International Convention against the Taking of Hostages, 272
International crime, 403. *See also* Comparative criminology
International Crime Victim Survey (ICVS), 390
International criminal court (ICC), 403–404

International Self-Report Delinquency (ISRD) study, 39
Internationally induced local crime problems, 397
Internet cafes, 7
Internet crime. *See* High-tech crimes
Internet sites. *See* Crime surfing
Interpol, 403
Investment schemes, 327
Involuntary manslaughter, 239
Involvement, 171
IQ, 105–106
ISPAC, 387
ISRD study, 39
Italian school, 68–72

Jamaican gangs, 164
Japanese Yakuza, 263
Job Corps, 127
Jokers, 155
Joyriding, 295
JRSA, 32
Jump-in, jump-out, 159
Junk-food defense, 108
Justice Research and Statistics Association (JRSA), 32
Justifiable homicide, 238
Justitia, 25

Kent State killings, 193
Kickbacks, 329
Kidnapping, 257
KISS, 161
Kohlberg's theory of moral development, 86–87, 88

La Cosa Nostra, 261, 263
Labeling theorists, 190
Labeling theory, 190–196
    assumptions, 191–192
    empirical evidence, 193–195
    evaluation of, 195–196
    1960s, 192–193
    origins, 191
    overview (table), 190
    racial profiling, 194, 195
Land fraud, 326–327
Land hijacking, 401
Larceny, 290–298
    amateur v. professional thieves, 291–292
    art theft, 293–295
    boat theft, 297–298
    elements, 290
    extent of, 291
    motor vehicle theft, 295
    shoplifting, 292–293
Latin Kings, 136
Law, Order, and Power (Chambliss/Seidman), 204
Laws of imitation, 76
LEAP, 138
Learnfare, 185
Learning aggression and violence, 90–96
Left realism, 208–209
Legality requirement, 25
Lesbians, 371

Lettres de cachet, 62
Life course developmental theory, 180–182
Life-course perspective, 48
Life of Mr. Jonathan Wild the Great, The (Fielding), 311
Lifestyle theory of victimization, 223
Lindbergh Act, 257
Lo-Jack, 296
Loading, 327
Lockdown, 132
Long Day's Journey into Night (O'Neill), 155
Longitudinal studies, 48
Lord of the Flies (Golding), 167
Lower-class focal concerns, 154
Luck, 154

Macrosociological studies, 169
MADD, 369
Mafia, 261. *See also* Organized crime
Mail bombs, 308
Major Fraud Act, 326
Making of laws, 13–15
Male aggression, 109
Malice aforethought, 238
Manchild in the Promised Land (Brown), 154
Manie sans délire, 98
Manslaughter, 239
Mapping crimes, 215
Marijuana, 363
Marijuana Tax Act, 356–357
Marxist criminology. *See* Radical theory
Mass murder, 243–245
MasterCard, 300
Material deprivation, 89
Maternal deprivation/attachment theory, 87–90
Matza's drift paradigm, 175
MBD, 110
Measuring crime, 28–44
    crime trends, 40–41
    data collection, 29–33
    location/times of criminal acts, 41–44
    NCVS, 37–38
    self-report surveys, 38–39
    severity of crime, 44
    UCR, 34–37
    victimization surveys, 37–38
    world crime, 47
Medical fraud, 302
Medical Jurisprudence of Insanity, The (Ray), 74
Mens rea, 26
Mental disorders and crime, 74, 98–101
Merrill Lynch, 349
Merton's theory of anomie, 119–120
Mexican gang, 164
Michigan Militia Paramilitary Group, 275
Microsociological studies, 169
Middle-class delinquency, 161–162
Militia groups, 273, 275
Miller v. California, 377
Minimal brain dysfunction (MBD), 110

SUBJECT INDEX

Minneapolis Domestic Violence Experiment, 251
Misconceptions, 3
Misdemeanors, 27
Mistake of fact, 28
Mobilization for Youth (MOBY), 162–163
Modeling instigators, 94
Modern biocriminality, 101–102
Modes of deviant behavior, 122
Money laundering, 5–6, 12, 363, 398
Mongolian Boys Society, 143
Monosodium glutamate, 107
Monozygotic (MZ) twins, 103
Moral development, 86–88
Moral entrepreneurs, 193
Moral insanity, 74
Morphing, 306
Mothers Against Drunk Driving (MADD), 369
Motor vehicle theft, 228, 229, 295–297
Motorcycle gangs, 128–129
MOVE, 139–140
Multicultural macho advertisements, 147
Multiple personalities, 100
Murder, 238–239
Mustang Ranch, 373
MZ twins, 103

National Child Abuse and Neglect Data System (NCANDS), 251
National Conscription Act, 155
National Crime Victimization Survey (NCVS), 37–38
National Criminal Justice Reference Service, 391
National Deviancy Conference (NDC), 204
National Environmental Policy Act (NEPA), 342
National Football League (NFL), 176
National Institute of Justice (NIJ), 35
National integrity system (NIS), 324–325
National Stolen Art File, 294
National Television Violence Study, 91, 93
Natural urban areas, 131
NCANDS, 251
NCVS, 37–38
Negligent homicide, 239
Neoclassical period, 60
Neolithic crime, 61
NEPA, 342
Net Nanny, 378
Neurophysiological factors, 109–110
Neuroticism, 97
New-company scam, 323
New criminology, 204
New Criminology, The (Taylor et al.), 204
New York Central Railroad, 332
New York City, hot spots, 226
NFL, 176
NGO Alliances in Crime Prevention and Criminal Justice, 387
NGOs, 387

NIBRS classifications of white-collar offenses, 320
NIJ, 35, 387
Nonparticipant observation, 31–32
Nuisance, 343

Observation, 31–32
Observational learning, 90–91
Obtaining property by false pretenses, 299
Occupational crimes, 321
Oetzi, 61
Office of National Drug Control Policy, 357
Official statistics, 34
Offshore tax heavens, 347
OGs, 163
Old-company scam, 323
Omega Boys Club, 171
On Crimes and Punishment (Beccaria), 63
Operation Weed and Seed, 135
Opportunistic robber, 258
Opportunity theory, 147–151, 215
Organizational criminality, 316–351
  corporate crime, 331. *See also* Corporate crime
  environmental crimes, 341–344
  future of, 347–350
  proposed reforms, 346–347
  reducing, 344–347
  Sarbanes-Oxley Act, 318, 344–345
  white-collar crime, 318–331. *See also* White-collar crime
Organized crime, 259–267
  business of, 262
  ethnic diversity, 266–267
Organized crime, *cont'd*
  history, 260–261
  structure/impact, 261–266
Origin of Species (Darwin), 67
Outer containment, 177
Outsiders, 191
Overutilization, 302
Owner dumping, 301

Page-jacked, 306
Panhandling, 198–199
Parking facilities, 230–231
Parricide, 92
Parrot Middle School, 171
Part I offenses, 34
Part II crimes, 34
Participant observation, 31–32
Password sniffers, 308
PATHE, 183
PCF, 337, 338
Peacemaking criminology, 209
Peine forte et dure, 62
Penetration of economic norms, 125
Penny Stock Reform Act, 322
Penologists, 203
Perry Preschool Project, 127
Personal and social control model, 175–177
Personality, 96–98
Phenylethylamine, 107

Phrenology, 68
Physiognomy, 67
Pico Rivera gang, 160
Pimp, 372
Ping-Ponging, 302
Pioneer Academy of Electronics, 171
Piracy
  open seas, on, 298, 400–401
  software, 306
Pleas of the Crown (Hale), 255
PMS, 100, 109
Police gun-confiscation program, 282
Police statistics, 34–37
Policyholder fraud, 327
Polish Peasant in Europe and America, The (Thomas/Znaniecki), 129
Political fraud, 329–330
Pooper-scooper regulations, 26
Pope v. Illinois, 377
Population, 30
Pornography, 373–379
  child, 305, 306, 308, 378
  feminist view, 377
  gaps between behavior and law, 379
  Internet, 305, 306, 308, 374, 377–379
  problem of definition, 374–375
  violence, and, 375
Positivist criminology, 67, 78
Potrero Hill Posse (PHP), 159
Predatory rape, 254
Premenstrual syndrome (PMS), 100, 109
Preschool classes, 125
Primary conflict, 140
Primary data, 30
Primary deviations, 191
Principles of Criminology (Sutherland), 136
Private Securities Litigation Reform Act, 347
Prize promotion, 327
Pro-choice advocates, 201
Proactive corporate fault (PCF), 337, 338
Professional Fence (Klockar), 311
Professional robber, 258
Professional thief, 292
Professional Thief, The (Sutherland), 32
Project Exile, 282
Project Freedom, 165
Property, crimes against. *See* Crimes against property
Prostitution, 371–373, 376, 396
Psychoanalytic theory, 85–86
Psychological determinism, 73–75, 78
Psychological studies of criminals, 75
Psychology and criminality, 85–98
  differential reinforcement, 94–96
  direct experiences, 93–94
  learning aggression and violence, 90–96
  maternal deprivation/attachment theory, 87–90
  moral development, 86–87
  observational learning, 90–91
  personality, 96–98
  psychoanalytic theory, 85–86
  social learning theory, 90–96

Psychopathy, 98
Psychosis, 98
Psychoticism, 97
Public order crimes, 352–380
    alcohol abuse, 367–370
    drug abuse, 354–367. *See also* Drug abuse
    pornography, 373–379. *See also* Pornography
    prostitution, 371–373, 376
    sexual morality offenses, 370–379
Punishing cheaters, 178
Punishment and the Social Structure (Rusche/Kirchheimer), 203
Punishment requirement, 27
Pyromaniacs, 312

Race, 54–55, 123
Racial profiling, 194, 195
Racketeer Influenced and Corrupt Organizations (RICO) Act, 263
Radical criminology, 204
Radical feminist theory, 208
Radical idealists, 208
Radical theory, 202–209
    abolitionist/anarchist theory, 209
    Bonger, 203
    class interests vs. interest groups, 205–206
    collapse of economic order, 206
    Engels/Marx, 202–203
    evaluation of, 205–208
    feminist theory, 208
    left realism, 208–209
    overview (table), 190
    peacemaking criminology, 209
    Rusche/Kirchheimer, 203
Random sample, 30
Rape, 253–257
Rational-choice perspective, 215–217
RCF, 337, 338
Reaction formation, 145
Reactive corporate fault (RCF), 337, 338
Rebellion, 121
Recovery room schemes, 327
Reloading, 327
Remove Intoxicated Drivers (RID), 369
Repeat victimization, 224
Research informs policy. *See* Theory informs policy
Retreatism, 121
Retreatist gangs, 149
RICO, 263
RID, 369
Ritualism, 121
Robbery, 221, 257–258
Robinson v. California, 24
Rock houses, 159
Rohypnol, 254
Roman (civil) law, 386, 388, 389
Roofies, 254
Routine-activity approach, 217–219
Russia, terrorism in, 10
Russian-American mafia, 264
Russian gangs, 164
Russian Mafia, 263

Sabre Tech, Inc., 318
SADD, 369
Sale of confidential information, 331
Sarbanes-Oxley Act, 318, 344–345
Satanic gangs, 161
Saturday-night specials, 280
Scared Straight, 31
School violence, 230–231, 276–279
Scissors job, 295
Sea piracy, 298, 400–401
SEC, 322
Secondary conflict, 140
Secondary data, 30, 32
Secondary deviations, 191
Secondary elaboration, 192
Securities and Exchange Commission (SEC), 322
Securities-related crimes, 321–322
Self-report surveys, 38–39
Sentence-enhancement statutes, 282
September 11th terrorist attacks, 4, 8, 10, 268–269
Serial murder, 243–245
Seven basic requirements, 24–27
Severity of crime, 44, 45
Sex-in, sex-out, 159
Sexual assault (rape), 253–257
Sexual morality offenses, 370–379
Sheldon's somatotypes, 72
Sherman Antitrust Act, 319, 339
Shoplifting, 219, 292–293
Sicilian Cosa Nostra, 263
Silent Scorpion, 296
Similar-name scam, 323
Simple assault, 247
Single-parent households, 154
Situational crime prevention, 227–232
Situational theories of crime, 215–222
Skinheads, 161, 162, 383–384, 397
Slash, 176
Slave trade, 401
Sleepwalking, 100
Smartness, 154
Social bonds, 170–172
Social class, 53–54, 122–123
Social control programs, 185
Social control theory, 166–187
    containment theory, 177–180
    defined, 168
    developmental/life course theory, 180–183
    drift, 175
    general theories, 182–183
    Hirsch's theory, 169–173
    integrated theory, 180, 182
    life course/developmental theory, 180–182
    microsociological perspective, 169–174
    personal and social control, 175–177
    social bonds, 170–172
    theory informs policy, 183–186
Social disorganization theory, 129–135
    behavioral effects, 132, 134
    economic effects, 134
    evaluation of, 134

Park-Burgess model, 130, 131
    psychological/social effects, 132
    Shaw-McKay model, 130–132
    theory informs policy, 134–135
Social interactionists, 191
Social learning theory, 90–96
Social norms, 13
Social norms of deference, 200
Social norms of dominance, 200
Sociological determinism, 75–77, 78
Sociopaths, 245
Sodomy, 371
Software piracy, 306
Solar Temple, 133
Soldier's disease, 354
Somatotype school of criminology, 72
Sons of Samoa, 164
Sourcebook of Criminal Justice Statistics, 41
Southern Poverty Law Center, 273, 275
Spouse abuse, 249–251
St. Valentine's Day massacre, 259
Staged accidents, 301
Staged claims, 301
Statutory rape, 370
Stealing. *See* Larceny
Steering, 302
Stock manipulation, 322
Stock market crash (1929), 117
S.T.O.P., 366
Strain theory, 117–127
    general strain theory, 126
    institutional imbalance, 124–125
    Merton's theory of anomie, 119–120
    modes of adaptation, 120–121
    race, 123
    social class, 122–123
    theory informs policy, 126–127
Stranger homicide, 242
Stranger rape, 254
Street gangs. *See* Gangs
Strict liability, 27
Strip and run, 295
Structural explanation, 117
Structural-functionalist perspective, 116
Students Against Drunk Drivers (SADD), 369
Subculture, 142–165
    Cohen's theory, 144–147
    defined, 144
    female gangs, 158–160
    gangs. *See* Gangs
    middle-class delinquency, 161–162
    Miller's focal concerns, 153–156
    opportunity theory, 147–151
    theory informs policy, 162–163
    violence, of, 151–153
Subculture of violence, 151–153
Successful-business scam, 323
Suicide, 117
Superego, 85
Surf Watch, 378
Survey, 30
Sutherland's nine propositions, 136–137
S.W.E.A.T. Team, 185
Synnomie, 185

SUBJECT INDEX

Taliban, 8
Tallahassee Convenience Store Study, 229–230
Target hardening, 227, 230
Tatari Design, 6
Tatex Trading G.m.b.H., 6
Tax fraud, 328–329
Teenage prostitution, 396
Telefunding schemes, 327
Telemarketing fraud, 326, 327
Television intoxication, 100
Television violence, 93, 95
Terrorism, 4–10, 268–272, 398–399
Theft. *See* Larceny
Theft of intellectual property, 399
Theories of victimization, 222–226
   geography of crime, 225
   hot spots of crime, 224–225
   interrelatedness of theories, 225–226
   lifestyle theories, 223–224
   repeat victimization, 224
   victim-offender interaction, 224
Theory, 29
Theory informs policy, 19–20
   differential association theory, 138
   environmental theory, 232
   social control theory, 183–186
   social disorganization theory, 134–135
   strain theory, 126–127
"There's a Lot of Us Folks Grateful to the Lone Ranger" (Quinney), 204
Thief-taker, 311
Thurman v. Torrington, 250
Title 21, 357
Tongan Crips, 164
Torts, 27
Toughness, 154
Trade in human body parts, 401–402
Trade secrets, 331
Trafficking
   arms, 7, 400
   drugs, 4, 402
   persons, 7, 401
Transnational crime, 397
Transparency International, 324–325, 403
Transparency International bribe payers index, 329, 331
Transparency International corruption perceptions index, 330
Travel-related schemes, 327
Treatment/storage/disposal (TSD) facilities, 346
Triads, 164, 362
Tryptophan, 108
TSD facilities, 346

TV violence, 93, 95
Twin studies, 103
Twinkie defense, 100, 108
Typologies of crime, 28
Tyramine, 107

UCR, 34–37, 38
Umoja, 163
UN agencies, 387
UN Crime Prevention and Criminal Justice Branch (UNCJS), 47
UNAFEI, 387
UNAFRI, 387
Unbreakable Autolock, 296
UNCJIN, 45, 387
UNCJS, 47
Underground railroad, 165
UNICRI, 387
Uniform Controlled Substances Act, 357
Uniform Crime Reports (UCR), 34–37, 38
Union Carbide disaster, 343
United Nations Centre for International Drug Control, 387
United Nations Crime and Justice Information Network (UNCJIN), 45
United States v. Darling, 341–342
Unraveling Juvenile Delinquency (Glueck/Glueck), 395
Upgrading, 302
U.S. Census, 30
U.S. Cosa Nostra, 263
Utilitarianism, 65, 66

Valet theft, 295
Variables, 30
Vicarious liability, 337
Victim-offender interaction, 224
Victim precipitation, 242
Victimization surveys, 37
Victimless crimes, 199
Victimology, 222
Vietnamese gangs, 164
Violations, 27
Violence gene, 104
Violence-prevention programs (Boston), 186
Violent crimes, 236–287
   assault, 247–248
   child abuse, 251–252
   elder abuse, 252–253
   family-related crimes, 248–253
   guns, 279–285
   hate crimes, 272–274
   homicide, 238–247. *See also* Homicide

   kidnapping, 257
   militias, 273, 275
   organized crime, 259–267. *See also* Organized crime
   rape, 253–257
   robbery, 257–258
   school violence, 276–279
   spouse abuse, 249–251
   terrorism, 268–272
Vipers, 16
Visa, 300
Volkswagen Beetle, 218
Volstead Act, 368
Voluntary manslaughter, 239

Watch Your Car program, 297
Websites. *See* Crime surfing
Wedtech Corporation, 324–325
Wheel of terrorism, 5
Whistle-blower, 348
Whistle-blower protection, 346
White-collar crime, 318–331. *See also* Corporate crime
   bankruptcy fraud, 322–323
   bribery/corruption/political fraud, 329–330
   consumer fraud, 326–327
   defined, 319
   future of, 347–350
   government-related fraud, 324–326
   insider-related fraud, 330–331
   insurance fraud, 327–328
   NIBRS classifications, 320
   potential abuses, 321
   securities-related crimes, 321–322
   tax fraud, 328–329
   victims, 320
White Collar Crime (Sutherland), 340
Wife abuse, 249–251
Wilderness camp, 179
Witness for Peace, 206
Woodstock Music and Art Fair, 359
World crime, 47
WorldCom, 349
Worldwide drug smuggling routes, 361

Xanthines, 107
Xerox, 349
XYY syndrome, 100, 102–103

Yanomamö, 118
Youth gangs. *See* Gangs

Zamora v. State, 100